CLARENCE BYRD

Clarence Byrd Inc.

IDA CHEN

Clarence Byrd Inc.

With contributions by
GARY DONELL

Study Guide
to accompany
Byrd & Chen's
Canadian
Tax
Principles

2017–2018 EDITION

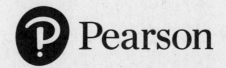 Pearson

ISBN 978-0-13-476019-3

Vice-President, Editorial: Anne Williams
Marketing Manager: Spencer Snell
Manager, Project Management: Avinash Chandra
Manager of Content Development: Suzanne Schaan
Developmental Editor: Suzanne Simpson Millar
Media Developer: Bogdan Kosenko
Production Editor: Leanne Rancourt
Permissions Project Manager: Joanne Tang
Cover Designer: Anthony Leung

Vice-President, Cross Media and Publishing Services: Gary Bennett

10 9 8 7 6 5 4 3 2 1

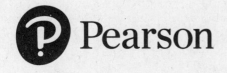

ISBN 978-0-13-476019-3

PREFACE

Complete Preface In Volume I

The complete preface to this three volume set of *Canadian Tax Principles* can be found in Volume I.

Companion Website

List Of 2017 Tax Rates And Credits For Your Use

A complete list of 2017 tax rates and credits to use when solving problems is available at the front of both Volumes 1 and 2. This information, as well as the Chapter 5 Appendix of common CCA rates, is available as a .PDF file on the companion website found at:

www.pearsoncanada.ca/byrdchen/ctp2018

Here you will also find:

- Updates and corrections to the textbook and Study Guide (please check periodically)
- Pearson eText of the complete set - 2 Volumes plus Study Guide
- Self Study Problems (The solutions are in this Study Guide)
- Supplementary Self Study Problems and Solutions
- Access to CPA Canada's Federal Income Tax Collection (FITAC)
- Access to Intuit Canada's ProFile tax return preparation software
- Practice Examinations and Solutions
- Power Point Presentations
- Glossary Flashcards
- 2017 tax rates, credits and common CCA Classes (PDF file)
- Tax Returns for examples and Self Study tax return problems
  In January, 2018, shortly after the first 2017 filing version of the ProFile tax program is available, updated sample tax returns and Tax Software Problems will also be available.

This Study Guide

Contents

Your two volume textbook is accompanied by this Study Guide. The chapters of this Study Guide correspond to the chapters of **Byrd & Chen's Canadian Tax Principles**. Each of these Study Guide chapters contains the following:

- Detailed guidance on how to work through the text and problems in the chapter.
- Detailed solutions to the Exercises in the textbook for the chapter and the and Self Study Problems available online.
- A list of learning objectives for the material in the chapter.

In addition, there are:

- Two sample personal tax returns and two Self Study Tax Software Problems in Chapters 4 and 11.
- A sample corporate tax return in Chapter 13.

Glossary

At the back of this Study Guide is a comprehensive Glossary that carefully defines more than 500 tax terms that are used throughout the text. Tied to this important resource, at the end of each chapter you will find a list of the Key Terms, without definitions, that were used in that chapter. This provides an additional resource for reviewing the text material in that, by reviewing this list, you can ensure that you are familiar with all of the concepts that are presented in the chapter.

To assist in this review, Glossary Flashcards for each Chapter are available online.

Using The Solutions

With respect to the problem solutions that are included in this book, the header at the top of each page identifies the solution on the page. The page numbers in this Study Guide have been numbered with the prefix "S-" to distinguish them from the page numbers of the textbook.

We encourage you to attempt to solve each Exercise or Self Study Problem prior to consulting these solutions. It is our opinion that one of the most unfortunate misconceptions that many students have is the belief that simply reading through a solution is a learning experience. It is not!

We welcome any corrections or suggestions for additions or improvements. These can be e-mailed to us at:

byrdinc@sympatico.ca

July, 2017   Clarence Byrd, Clarence Byrd Inc.
                                                Ida Chen, Clarence Byrd Inc.

CONTENTS

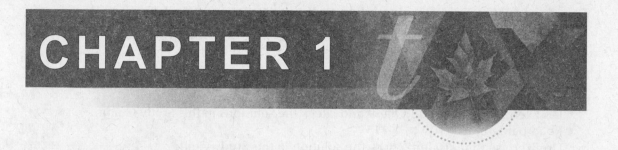

CHAPTER 1

How To Work Through Chapter 1

The Companion Website for this book can be found at:

www.pearsoncanada.ca/byrdchen/ctp2018

We suggest you access the website before using the text to familiarize yourself with the useful student resources available there. In particular, review the corrections and updates to the textbook and Study Guide that are posted there to save yourself unnecessary frustration.

We recommend the following approach in dealing with the material in this chapter:

The Canadian Tax System
- Read paragraph 1-1 to 1-12 (in the textbook).
- Do Exercises One-1 and One-2 (in the textbook) and check the solutions in this Study Guide. All solutions to Exercises and Self Study Problems can be found in this Study Guide and the page numbers all start with the prefix S-.
- Read paragraph 1-13 to 1-17.
- Do Exercise One-3 and check the solution in this Study Guide.
- Read paragraph 1-18 to 1-25.

Tax Policy Concepts And Qualitative Characteristics Of Tax Systems
- Read paragraph 1-26 to 1-28.
- Do Exercise One-4 and check the solution in this Study Guide.
- Do Self Study Problem One-1 which is available on the Companion Website and check the solution in this Study Guide.
- Read paragraph 1-29 to 1-34.
- Do Self Study Problem One-2 and check the solution in this Study Guide.
- Read paragraph 1-35 to 1-43.
- Do Self Study Problem One-3 and check the solution in this Study Guide.

Income Tax Reference Materials
- Read paragraph 1-44 to 1-75.
- Do Self Study Problem One-4 and check the solution in this Study Guide.

Liability For Income Tax
- Read paragraph 1-76 to 1-93.
- Do Exercise One-5 and check the solution in this Study Guide.

Residence Of Individuals, Including Part Year, Sojourner, And Deemed Residents
- Read paragraph 1-94 to 1-101.
- Do Exercise One-6 and check the solution in this Study Guide.
- Read paragraph 1-102 to 1-106.
- Do Exercise One-7 and check the solution in this Study Guide.
- Read paragraph 1-107 and 1-108.
- Do Exercises One-8 and One-9 and check the solutions in this Study Guide.
- Read paragraph 1-109 to 1-115.
- Do Exercise One-10 and check the solution in this Study Guide.

Individuals With Dual Residency
- Read paragraph 1-116 to 1-119.
- Do Exercise One-11 and check the solution in this Study Guide.
- Read paragraph 1-120 to 1-122.
- Do Self Study Problems One-5 to One-7 and check the solutions in this Study Guide.

Residence Of Corporations And Trusts
- Read paragraph 1-123 to 1-129.
- Do Exercises One-12 to One-14 and check the solutions in this Study Guide.
- Do Self Study Problems One-8 and One-9 and check the solutions in this Study Guide.
- Read paragraph 1-130 to 1-132.

Alternative Concepts Of Income
- Read paragraph 1-133 to 1-141.

Net Income For Tax Purposes
- Read paragraph 1-142 to 1-167.
- Do Exercises One-15 to One-17 and check the solutions in this Study Guide.
- Do Self Study Problems One-10 to One-12 and check the solutions in this Study Guide.

Net Income To Taxable Income
- Read paragraph 1-168 and 1-169.

Principles Of Tax Planning
- Read paragraph 1-170 to 1-188.
- Do Exercises One-18 and One-19 and check the solutions in this Study Guide.

Abbreviations To Be Used
- Read paragraph 1-189.

To Complete This Chapter
- If you would like more practice in problem solving, do the Supplementary Self Study Problems for the chapter. These problems and solutions are available on the Companion Website.
- Review the Key Terms Used In This Chapter in the textbook at the end of Chapter 1. Consult the Glossary for the meaning of any key terms you do not know.
- Test yourself with the Chapter 1 Glossary Flashcards available on the Companion Website.
- Ensure you have achieved the Chapter 1 Learning Objectives listed in this Study Guide.
- As a review, we recommend you view the PowerPoint presentation for Chapter 1 that is on the Companion Website.

Practice Examination
- Write the Practice Examination for Chapter 1 that is on the Companion Website. Mark your examination using the Practice Examination Solution that is on the Companion Website.

Solutions to Chapter One Exercises

Exercise One - 1 Solution

Max Jordan, the Jordan family trust, and Jordan Enterprises Ltd. could be required to file income tax returns. Jordan's Hardware, Jordan & Jordan and the Jordan Foundation are not taxable entities for income tax purposes.

Exercise One - 2 Solution

Under the GST legislation, all of the listed entities could be required to file a GST return. Where only individuals, corporations and trusts can be required to file an income tax return, the definition of a person (i.e., taxable entity) is much broader for GST purposes. As is explained in detail in Chapter 21, whether an entity is required to file a GST return is dependent on the level of commercial activity.

Exercise One - 3 Solution

Federal Tax Payable [(15%)($27,000)]	$4,050
Provincial Tax Payable [(7.5%)($27,000)]	2,025
Total Tax Payable [(15% + 7.5%)($27,000)]	$6,075

Exercise One - 4 Solution

Margie's HST paid totals $22,360 [(13%)($172,000)]. Based on her Taxable Income of $895,000, this would represent an effective rate of 2.5 percent ($22,360 ÷ $895,000).

Jane's HST paid totals $3,575 [(13%)($27,500)]. On her Taxable Income of $18,000, this would be an effective rate of 19.9 percent ($3,575 ÷ $18,000).

Exercise One - 5 Solution

She is not correct. Under ITA 2(3) she would be subject to Canadian taxes on employment income earned in Canada.

Exercise One - 6 Solution

While the situation is not completely clear, it is likely that the CRA would conclude that Simon is no longer a Canadian resident. By retaining his residence, he has maintained one of the primary residential ties. However, the fact that he was not able to sell the property, accompanied by the long-term lease to a third party would probably be sufficient evidence that this is not a significant residential tie. The retention of his membership in the Ontario Institute Of Chartered Public Accountants would be viewed as a secondary residential tie. However, S5-F1-C1 indicates that it would be unusual for a single secondary tie to be sufficient for an individual to be considered a Canadian resident.

Exercise One - 7 Solution

Jane did, in fact, sever most of her residential ties with Canada. This would suggest that she would not be considered a Canadian resident during the 26 months that she worked in Florida. However, the fact that she returned frequently to visit her boyfriend might lead the CRA to assess her on the basis of being a Canadian resident during this period, but it is not clear that such an assessment would be successful.

Exercise One - 8 Solution

Mark would be taxed on his worldwide income for the part of the year that he was resident in Canada. This would be the period January 1 through June 15, the date that his wife and children fly to the U.S. June 15 would be latest of the date that Mark leaves Canada (February 1), the date that Mark establishes U.S. residency (February 1), and the date that his wife and children depart Canada (June 15). It is unlikely that the fact that his house was not sold until a later date would influence his residence status.

Exercise One - 9 Solution

Mr. Kirsh will be a part year resident and liable for Canadian taxes on his worldwide income, including any income on the U.S. bank accounts, for the period September 1 through December 31 of the current year.

Exercise One - 10 Solution

While Ms. Blakey is the child of a Canadian High Commissioner, it appears that she is no longer a dependant of this individual. It would also appear that she has income in excess of the base for the basic personal tax credit for 2017 of $11,635. As a consequence, she would not be considered a deemed resident under ITA 250(1).

Exercise One - 11 Solution

Case 1 As it appears that Dizzy has a permanent home in Los Angeles, the tie-breaker rules would indicate that he is a resident of the United States. As he has been in Canada for more than 183 days in 2017, the sojourner rules might have made him a deemed Canadian resident. However, the tie-breaker rules in the international tax treaty would override this.

The boarding rooms and hotels would not be considered to be a permanent home given that Dizzy never intended to stay for a long period of time.

Case 2 As Donna was in Canada for more than 183 days in 2017, she is a deemed resident through the application of the sojourner rule, and therefore a dual resident. In applying the tie-breaker rules, the first factor that is considered is in which country the individual has a permanent home. With respect to this criteria, Donna would not be considered to have a permanent home in either country. She gave up her lease on the New York property and, given that she only planned to stay for a short period of time, the Toronto apartment would not be considered a permanent home. In the absence of a permanent home in either country, the next factor to consider would be the location of Donna's "centre of vital interests". This would appear to be the U.S. and, given this, the tie-breaker rules would make Donna a resident of the U.S. and a non-resident of Canada.

Exercise One - 12 Solution

Roswell Ltd. is a U.S. resident because it was incorporated in that country. It is also a Canadian resident under the mind and management test. In such dual residency cases, the tie-breaker rule in the Canada/U.S. tax treaty indicates that the taxes will be assessed in the country of incorporation. That means that Roswell Ltd. would be considered a resident of the U.S. and a non-resident of Canada.

Exercise One - 13 Solution

As the Company was incorporated in Canada after April 26, 1965, it would be deemed to be a Canadian resident under ITA 250(4). While the problem does not provide enough information to determine this, it is possible that the Company has dual residency with the country or countries where it does business. This could result in the application of one or more international tax treaties. Note that, in general, where a corporation does business is not relevant to the residency decision.

Exercise One - 14 Solution

Case 1 Taxco would be considered a deemed resident of Canada by ITA 250(4) since it was incorporated in Canada after April 26, 1965. Taxco would also be considered a factual resident of the U.S. since its mind and management are located there. Article IV(3) of the Canada/U.S. tax treaty however breaks the tie in favor of the place of incorporation. Taxco would therefore be considered a resident of Canada and a non-resident of the U.S.

Case 2 Junko would be considered a factual resident of Canada since its mind and management are situated in Canada. Junko would also be considered a resident of the U.S. since it was incorporated there. Article IV(3) of the Canada/U.S. tax treaty however breaks the tie in favor of the place of incorporation. Junko would therefore be considered a resident of the U.S. for treaty purposes and a non-resident of Canada.

Exercise One - 15 Solution

Mr. Blanton's Net Income For Tax Purposes is calculated as follows:

Income Under ITA 3(a):		
Net Employment Income		$42,000
Income Under ITA 3(b):		
Taxable Capital Gains	$24,000	
Allowable Capital Losses	Nil	24,000
Balance From ITA 3(a) And (b)		$66,000
Subdivision e Deductions		(13,000)
Balance Under ITA 3(c)		$53,000
Deduction Under ITA 3(d):		
Business Loss		(15,000)
Net Income For Tax Purposes (Division B Income)		**$38,000**

Exercise One - 16 Solution

Ms. Stodard's Net Income For Tax Purposes would be calculated as follows:

Income Under ITA 3(a):		
Interest Income		$33,240
Income Under ITA 3(b):		
Taxable Capital Gains	$24,750	
Allowable Capital Losses	(19,500)	5,250
Balance From ITA 3(a) And (b)		$38,490
Subdivision e Deductions		Nil
Balance Under ITA 3(c)		$38,490
Deduction Under ITA 3(d):		
Rental Loss		(48,970)
Net Income For Tax Purposes (Division B Income)		**Nil**

She would have a non-capital loss carry over of $10,480 ($38,490 - $48,970).

Exercise One - 17 Solution

Mrs. Bergeron's Net Income For Tax Purposes would be calculated as follows:

Income Under ITA 3(a):		
Net Employment Income		$42,680
Income Under ITA 3(b):		
Taxable Capital Gains	$27,400	
Allowable Capital Losses	(33,280)	Nil
Balance From ITA 3(a) And (b)		$42,680
Subdivision e Deductions		(8,460)
Balance Under ITA 3(c)		$34,220
Deduction Under ITA 3(d):		
Business Loss		(26,326)
Net Income For Tax Purposes (Division B Income)		**$ 7,894**

She would have an allowable capital loss carry over of $5,880 ($27,400 - $33,280).

Exercise One - 18 Solution

Mr. Chung is involved in income splitting, tax deferral, and possibly tax avoidance. He is getting the deduction from taxable income now and his wife will be taxed on the income in the future. All RRSP contributions normally create a tax deferral. The contribution will be deductible and the earnings on the contribution will accumulate on a tax free basis. However, all of these amounts will be taxable when they are withdrawn from the plan. There may also be tax avoidance. This will happen if his spouse is taxed at a lower rate than is currently applicable to Mr. Chung when the funds become taxable to her.

Exercise One - 19 Solution

As the dental plan is a benefit that can be received by Mr. Green without being taxed (private health care), tax avoidance is illustrated.

Self Study Solution One - 1

The HST is based on certain specified expenditures, not on the income level of the individual making the expenditure. In most cases, the proportion of an individual's income that is spent declines as the individual's level of income increases. This means that when a flat rate of tax is applied to a decreasing portion of the individual's income, the rate of taxation as a percentage of that income will decline.

For example, a 13 percent HST applied to $150,000 in expenditures made by a person with $250,000 in income would amount to only 7.8 percent of that person's income ($19,500 ÷ $250,000).

In contrast, that same 13 percent HST applied to $25,000 in expenditures made by a person with $20,000 in income would reflect a tax rate of 16.3 percent ($3,250 ÷ $20,000) of that person's income.

Self Study Solution One - 2

If tax simplification was the only objective, Mr. Right's proposal would be appropriate. However, such a system would be in conflict with other possible objectives of tax policy. For example, it would almost certainly be in conflict with the objective of fairness in that it would not provide for treating different types of income (capital gains vs. employment income) or people (the poor vs. the rich) in a suitable manner.

His system would also conflict with other objectives such as the goal of equity and after-tax income stability and the need for redistribution of income. In other words, in meeting the objective of simplicity, Mr. Right's system would ignore other possible objectives of a taxation system.

Self Study Solution One - 3

Note The descriptions of these tax measures are significantly simplified. The objective of this problem is to present the basic ideas so they can be understood without a detailed knowledge of tax, while still providing a basis for discussion. The following analysis is intended to be no more than suggestive of possible points that could be made. There are, of course, many alternative solutions.

Family Tax Cut
Possible comments here would be as follows:

Equity Or Fairness This provision was heavily criticized for providing most of its benefits to high income individuals. The tax cost of this provision was estimated to be $2.4 billion, very little of which was available to low income families and none to single parent families. Its repeal in 2016 was due in large part to its lack of fairness.

Simplicity   This was an extremely complex provision that few individuals, other than tax professionals, fully understood. Evidence of this: The government did not get the initial legislation right and was forced to issue revisions.

Increase In Lifetime Capital Gains Deduction

Possible comments here would be as follows:

Neutrality   The increase in the amount of the deduction for farmers and fishermen is not neutral. It favours farmers and fishermen with no benefits for any other group.

Simplicity   The determination of what properties are considered to be qualified for this deduction involves some very complex legislation.

Home Accessibility Tax Credit

Possible comments here would be as follows:

Neutrality   This provision is not neutral. Its benefits accrue exclusively to seniors, disabled individuals, and their families. Other individuals do not benefit from this provision.

Equity Or Fairness   Disabled seniors face accessibility challenges that are not present for most other individuals. Given this, it can be argued that helping this particular group involves fairer treatment of these individuals.

Reduction In Small Business Rate

Possible comments here would be as follows:

International Competitiveness   It is likely that this tax cut will make Canada a more attractive environment for small business.

Certainty   By announcing the decrease in advance, certainty of the future rate was provided.

Increase In Tax Free Savings Account Limits

Possible comments here would be as follows:

Equity Or Fairness   It was clear that this change would not benefit low income individuals. If an individual is making $20,000 per year, it is highly unlikely that this individual would have the first $5,500, much less an extra $4,500 to contribute. The reversal of the increase in 2016 was due in large part to its lack of fairness.

Simplicity   This change gets high marks for simplicity. Amounts earned on the assets in the account are not subject to tax, either while the assets are in the plan or when the earnings are removed from the plan.

Self Study Solution One - 4

The principal other sources of information can be described as follows:

1. **Draft Legislation**   This legislation often provides the only information available with respect to announced budget changes that require application in the current taxation year. Explanatory notes are included with released draft legislation but are always set out separately.

2. **Income Tax Regulations**   These Regulations provide detailed guidance with respect to the implementation and administrative enforcement of the provisions of the *Income Tax Act*.

3. **International Tax Treaties**   These are a group of bilateral tax treaties between Canada and other countries. They are designed to avoid double taxation of taxpayers who pay taxes in more than one jurisdiction and to prevent international tax evasion.

4. **Income Tax Folios**   Income Tax Folios are a new series of publications introduced in 2013 that deal with technical issues. The publications are organized into seven Series with each Series divided into Folios that contain Chapters on specific topics. As new Folios are introduced, the Interpretation Bulletins and Income Tax Technical Newsletters they are replacing are being cancelled.

5. **Interpretation Bulletins**   These IT-Bulletins give the CRA's interpretations of particular sections of the law which it administers and provide a vehicle for announcing significant changes in departmental interpretation. These Bulletins are being replaced over the next few years by the new series, Income Tax Folios (see item 6).

6. **Income Tax Application Rules, 1971 (ITARs)**   These are a set of transitional rules that were introduced when the *Income Tax Act* was heavily revised at the end of 1971. The rules were largely designed to ensure that the provisions of the new *Act* were not applied retroactively. Although they continue to be of some significance in a limited number of situations, their general importance has been greatly diminished over time.

7. **Income Tax Technical News**   These newsletters were an occasional publication of the CRA which provided detailed guidance on various current issues. Existing newsletters are being cancelled as new Income Tax Folios (see item 6) are gradually incorporating their content.

8. **Information Circulars**   These Circulars provide information with respect to procedural matters related to both the *Income Tax Act* and the Canada Pension Plan.

9. **CRA News Releases, Tax Tips and Fact Sheets** The CRA provides News Releases, tax tips and fact sheets on a variety of current subjects on its website.

10. **Guides And Pamphlets**   These non-technical publications provide guidance for the public on a variety of income tax issues (e.g., treatment of rental income).

11. **Advance Income Tax Rulings**   For a fee, the CRA will provide an Advance Income Tax Ruling on how it will tax a proposed transaction, subject to certain limitations and qualifications. These are rulings that are provided in response to requests from taxpayers.

12. **Technical Interpretations**   The CRA provides both written and telephone Technical Interpretations to the public free of charge. These Interpretations provide technical information on various current issues.

13. **Court Decisions**   Decisions by the Tax Court of Canada, the Federal Court and the Supreme Court on income tax cases serve to establish precedents for dealing with particular tax issues.

Self Study Solution One - 5

S5-F1-C1 indicates that, in general, the CRA will view an individual as becoming a non-resident on the latest of three dates:

- The date the individual leaves Canada.
- The date the individual's spouse or common-law partner and dependants leave Canada.
- The date the individual becomes a resident of another country.

As Paul's wife and daughter did not leave Canada, it would appear that the CRA would take the position that Paul did not stop being a resident of Canada.

As he purchased a house in the U.S., it is possible that he will also be viewed as a resident of that jurisdiction. If this is the case, the tie breaker rules that are contained in the tax treaty between Canada and the U.S. tax treaty must be applied. As Paul has a permanent home available in both locations, we need to apply the center of vital interests criterion. The personal ties appear to be stronger in Canada, so it is likely that the CRA would conclude that the center of vital interests is Canada. Given this, Paul would not be considered to be resident in the U.S.

Based on this conclusion, Paul should report his worldwide income in Canada, and claim a foreign tax credit for any U.S. tax paid on his employment income while he was living and working in the U.S.

Self Study Solution One - 6

Mr. Aiken And Mr. Baker
Assuming that their respective moves were permanent in nature, both Mr. Aiken and Mr. Baker would be treated as part year residents. This means that they would be considered residents of Canada only for that portion of the year that they were actually in Canada. As a result, they will be liable for Canadian taxes only for a part of the current year. The prorating of deductions and credits are determined in accordance with ITA 114 and ITA 118.91.

Mr. Chase
While Mr. Chase was in Canada for the same number of days as the other individuals, the fact that he was present only on a temporary basis makes him subject to the sojourning rule. Under this rule [see ITA 250(1)(a)], he will be considered a resident for the full year if he sojourns in Canada for 183 days or more during any calendar year. As Mr. Chase was present for 192 days, he would be viewed as a Canadian resident throughout the year.

However, as he appears to also be a resident of the U.S., his dual residency status would be resolved by the tie-breaker rules in the Canada/U.S. tax treaty. As he only has a permanent home in the U.S., the tie breaker rules would deem Mr. Chase not to be a resident of Canada. This means that he would be taxed in the U.S.

Self Study Solution One - 7

A. Jane Smith would be deemed a Canadian resident because she is a dependent child of a Canadian ambassador [ITA 250(1)(f)].

B. Marvin Black would not be considered a resident of Canada as he does not live in Canada. He would not be a deemed resident as S5-F1-C1 makes it clear that days spent commuting to Canada to earn employment income do not count as sojourning in Canada. However, he would likely be subject to Canadian taxation on the employment income earned in Canada [ITA 2(3)(a)].

C. John Leather would be considered a resident of Canada for the part of the year until September 12. As his presence in Canada during the first part of the year was not on a part time basis, he would not fall under the sojourning rules.

D. Members of the Canadian armed forces are deemed to be Canadian residents without regard to where they actually live. As Francine Donaire is exempt from French taxation due to her relationship to a deemed resident, she is a deemed resident of Canada [ITA 250(1)(g)].

E. More information would be required here. Depending on the nature of his stay in Canada, Robert could either be a part year resident of Canada or, alternatively, a non-resident earning employment income in Canada. If he established sufficient residential ties in Canada, it is possible that he would be viewed as a resident during his short stay. The importance of this is that, under this interpretation of the facts, he would be subject to Canadian income tax on his worldwide income during his stay. Alternatively, if he is not considered a resident during his stay in Canada, he is likely to be subject to Canadian tax on only his Canadian employment income.

F. The fact that Susan Allen is a Canadian citizen is irrelevant to the determination of residency. Since she appears to have no residential ties with Canada, she would not be considered a Canadian resident.

Self Study Solution One - 8

A. As AMT Ltd. was incorporated prior to April 27, 1965, it is not automatically considered to be a resident of Canada. However, under Canadian legislation the Company would be deemed a Canadian resident based on the fact that the mind and management was in Canada subsequent to that date. [ITA 250(4)(a) and (c)].

As the mind and management is now in the U.S., it would also be considered a U.S. resident. Given this dual residency, the tie-breaker rules in the Canada/U.S. Tax Treaty resolve the situation by making the Company a resident of its country of incorporation. This would result in AMT being considered a resident of Canada.

B. UIF Inc. was not incorporated in Canada and its mind and management are not currently within Canada. Therefore, UIF Inc. would not be considered a Canadian resident.

C. BDT Ltd. would be deemed a Canadian resident. This is because it was incorporated in Canada subsequent to April 26, 1965. [ITA 250(4)(a)]. However, as the mind and management is now in the U.S., it would also be considered a U.S. resident. Given this dual residency, the tie-breaker rules in the Canada/U.S. Tax Treaty resolve the situation by making the Company a resident of its country of incorporation. This would result in BDT being considered a resident of Canada.

D. While QRS Inc. was not incorporated in Canada, it would appear that its mind and management are located in Ontario. However, as it was incorporated in New York state, it will also be considered a resident of the U.S. As noted previously, in such cases, the tie-breaker rules in the Canada/U.S. Tax Treaty would make the Company a resident of the U.S. as that is the country of incorporation and not a Canadian resident.

Self Study Solution One - 9

A. Molly London would be considered a part year resident of Canada until October 31, the date of her departure and would be taxed on her worldwide income for this period. As her presence in Canada during the first part of the year was on a full time basis, she would not fall under the sojourning rules.

B. Daryl Bennett would not be considered a Canadian resident. As a result, none of his income would be subject to Canadian taxes. He sojourned in Canada for less than 183 days. He would therefore not be considered a deemed resident by the sojourner rule. As his residential ties appear to be in the U.S., he would be a U.S. resident. His Canadian citizenship would not affect his residency status.

C. Under the mind and management rule, Tweeks Inc. would be considered resident in Canada for the full year and would be taxed on its worldwide income for the year. While Tweeks Inc. was not incorporated in Canada, it would appear that its mind and management are located in Quebec. This would result in Tweeks Inc. being treated as a Canadian resident.

However, as Tweeks was incorporated in the U.S., it would also be considered a resident of that country. Given this dual residency, the tie-breaker rules in the Canada/U.S. Tax Treaty would resolve the situation by making the Company a resident of its country of incorporation. This would result in Tweeks being considered a resident of the U.S., and a non-resident of Canada. Its income would be taxed in the U.S.

D. Bordot Industries would be deemed a Canadian resident because it was incorporated in Canada subsequent to April 26, 1965 [ITA 250(4)(a)].

However, because the mind and management of the Company is in the U.S., it would also be considered a resident of that country. Given this dual residency, the tie-breaker rules in the Canada/U.S. Tax Treaty would resolve the situation by making the Company a resident of its country of incorporation. This would make Bardot Industries a resident of Canada, with its worldwide income taxed in Canada.

Self Study Solution One - 10

Case A

The Case A solution would be calculated as follows:

Income Under ITA 3(a):		
Employment Income	$50,000	
Interest Income	12,000	$62,000
Income Under ITA 3(b):		
Taxable Capital Gains	$95,000	
Allowable Capital Losses	(73,000)	22,000
Balance From ITA 3(a) And (b)		$84,000
Subdivision e Deductions		(8,000)
Balance From ITA 3(c)		$76,000
Deductions Under ITA 3(d):		
Business Loss		(23,000)
Net Rental Loss		(5,000)
Net Income For Tax Purposes (Division B Income)		$48,000

In this Case, Mr. Dorne has no carry overs available.

Case B

The Case B solution would be calculated as follows:

Income Under ITA 3(a):		
Employment Income	$45,000	
Net Rental Income	23,000	$68,000
Income Under ITA 3(b):		
Taxable Capital Gains	$25,000	
Allowable Capital Losses	(46,000)	Nil
Balance From ITA 3(a) And (b)		$68,000
Subdivision e Deductions		(10,500)
Balance From ITA 3(c)		$57,500
Deduction Under ITA 3(d):		
Business Loss		(51,000)
Net Income For Tax Purposes (Division B Income)		$ 6,500

In this Case, Mr. Dorne has a carry over of unused allowable capital losses in the amount of $21,000 ($46,000 - $25,000). The lottery prize is not considered to be income for tax purposes.

Self Study Solution One - 11

Case A

The Case A solution would be calculated as follows:

Income Under ITA 3(a):		
Employment Income	$73,300	
Rental Income	8,300	$81,600
Income Under ITA 3(b):		
Taxable Capital Gains	$42,400	
Allowable Capital Losses	(18,600)	23,800
Balance From ITA 3(a) And (b)		$105,400
Subdivision e Deductions		(6,200)
Balance From ITA 3(c)		$ 99,200
Deduction Under ITA 3(d):		
Business Loss		(14,700)
Net Income For Tax Purposes (Division B Income)		$ 84,500

In this Case, Mr. Marks has no loss carry overs at the end of the year.

Case B

The Case B solution would be calculated as follows:

Income Under ITA 3(a):		
Employment Income	$41,400	
Rental Income	5,900	$ 47,300
Income Under ITA 3(b):		
Taxable Capital Gains	$ 7,800	
Allowable Capital Losses	(11,600)	Nil
Balance From ITA 3(a) And (b)		$47,300
Subdivision e Deductions		(2,800)
Balance From ITA 3(c)		$44,500
Deduction Under ITA 3(d):		
Business Loss		(4,700)
Net Income For Tax Purposes (Division B Income)		$39,800

In this Case, Mr. Marks has an allowable capital loss carry over of $3,800 ($7,800 - $11,600).

Case C

The Case C solution would be calculated as follows:

Income Under ITA 3(a):		
Employment Income	$89,400	
Rental Income	5,300	$94,700
Income Under ITA 3(b):		
Taxable Capital Gains	$23,700	
Allowable Capital Losses	(21,200)	2,500
Balance From ITA 3(a) and (b)		$97,200
Subdivision e Deductions		(22,400)
Balance From ITA 3(c)		$74,800
Deduction Under ITA 3(d):		
Business Loss		(112,600)
Net Income For Tax Purposes (Division B Income)		Nil

In this Case, Mr. Marks would have a business loss carry over in the amount of $37,800 ($74,800 - $112,600).

Case D

The Case D solution would be calculated as follows:

Income Under ITA 3(a):		
Employment Income		$34,300
Income Under ITA 3(b):		
Taxable Capital Gains	$24,700	
Allowable Capital Losses	(26,300)	Nil
Balance From ITA 3(a) And (b)		$34,300
Subdivision e Deductions		(6,400)
Balance From ITA 3(c)		$27,900
Deduction Under ITA 3(d):		
Business Loss		(47,800)
Rental Loss		(20,100)
Net Income For Tax Purposes (Division B Income)		Nil

Mr. Marks would have a carry over of business and rental losses in the amount of $40,000 ($27,900 - $47,800 - $20,100) and of allowable capital losses in the amount of $1,600 ($24,700 - $26,300).

Self Study Solution One - 12

Case A

The Case A solution would be calculated as follows:

Income Under ITA 3(a):		
Employment Income	$45,000	
Income From Property	15,000	$60,000
Income Under ITA 3(b):		
Taxable Capital Gains	$25,000	
Allowable Capital Losses	(10,000)	15,000
Balance From ITA 3(a) And b)		$75,000
Subdivision e Deductions		(5,000)
Balance From ITA 3(c)		$70,000
Deduction Under ITA 3(d):		
Business Loss		(20,000)
Net Income For Tax Purposes (Division B Income)		$50,000

There are no carry overs from the current year.

Case B

The Case B solution would be calculated as follows:

Income Under ITA 3(a):		
Employment Income	$17,000	
Income From Property	12,000	$29,000
Income Under ITA 3(b):		
Taxable Capital Gains	$22,000	
Allowable Capital Losses	(8,000)	14,000
Balance From ITA 3(a) And (b)		$43,000
Subdivision e Deductions		(6,000)
Balance From ITA 3(c)		$37,000
Deduction Under ITA 3(d):		
Business Loss		(42,000)
Net Income For Tax Purposes (Division B Income)		Nil

Mr. Haynes' will have an unused business loss carry over from the current year of $5,000 ($42,000 - $37,000).

Case C

The Case C solution would be calculated as follows:

Income Under ITA 3(a):		
Employment Income	$24,000	
Income From Property	47,000	$71,000
Income Under ITA 3(b):		
Taxable Capital Gains	$22,000	
Allowable Capital Losses	(73,000)	Nil
Balance From ITA 3(a) And (b)		$71,000
Subdivision e Deductions		(4,000)
Balance From ITA 3(c)		$67,000
Deduction Under ITA 3(d):		
Business Loss		(48,000)
Net Income For Tax Purposes (Division B Income)		$19,000

Mr. Haynes will have a carry over from the current period of unused allowable capital losses in the amount of $51,000 ($73,000 - $22,000).

Case D

The Case D solution would be calculated as follows:

Income Under ITA 3(a):		
Employment Income	$18,000	
Income From Property	7,000	$25,000
Income Under ITA 3(b):		
Taxable Capital Gains	$13,000	
Allowable Capital Losses	(18,000)	Nil
Balance From ITA 3(a) And (b)		$25,000
Subdivision e Deductions		(12,000)
Balance From ITA 3(c)		$13,000
Deduction Under ITA 3(d):		
Business Loss		(20,000)
Net Income For Tax Purposes (Division B Income)		Nil

Mr. Haynes has a carry over from the current year of unused business losses in the amount of $7,000 ($20,000 - $13,000) and of unused allowable capital losses in the amount of $5,000 ($18,000 - $13,000).

Chapter 1 Learning Objectives

After completing Chapter 1, you should be able to:

1. List some of the different bases that can be used by the various levels of government to assess taxes (paragraph [P hereafter] 1-1 through 1-6).
2. List all of the types of entities that are subject to paying federal income taxes and GST (P 1-7 through 1-12).
3. Explain the relationship between the assessment of taxes at the federal level and the assessment of taxes at the provincial level (P 1-13 through 1-25).
4. List some of the ways that taxation is used to achieve economic objectives (P 1-26).
5. Describe the differences between progressive, regressive, and flat tax systems, including some of the advantages and disadvantages of each system (P 1-27 through 1-34).

6. Discuss the issue of who ultimately pays the cost of various types of taxes (P 1-35 and 1-36).
7. Explain the nature of tax expenditures (P 1-37 through 1-40).
8. Evaluate issues in tax policy on the basis of the qualitative characteristics of tax systems (P 1-41 through 1-43).
9. Describe the reference materials that are available on income tax databases (P 1-44 through 1-48).
10. Describe the general structure of the *Income Tax Act* (P 1-49 through 1-60).

11. List and explain the nature of other sources of income tax legislation (P 1-61 through 1-70).
12. Describe other sources of income tax information (P 1-71 through 1-75).
13. Describe the charging provisions of the *Income Tax Act* for residents and non-residents (P 1-76 through 1-93).
14. Determine the residence of an individual based on an evaluation of primary and secondary residential ties (P 1-94 through 1-101).
15. Evaluate the residency status of an individual who is temporarily absent from Canada or is only resident for part of the year (P 1-102 through 1-108).

16. Identify the types of individuals who will be deemed to be Canadian residents without regard to their actual physical location (P 1-109 through 1-122).
17. Determine the residence of corporations and trusts (P 1-123 through 1-132).
18. Describe, in general terms, the various views of income that are held by economists, accountants, and tax authorities (P 1-133 through 1-141).
19. Calculate Net Income For Tax Purposes by applying the rules found in Section 3 of the *Income Tax Act* (P 1-142 through 1-167).
20. Explain how Net Income For Tax Purposes is converted to Taxable Income (P 1-168 and 1-169).

21. Explain the principles of tax planning (P 1-170 through 1-173).
22. Explain and provide examples of tax avoidance or reduction, and tax deferral (P 1-174 through 1-181).
23. Explain and provide examples of income splitting (P 1-182 through 1-188).

How To Work Through Chapter 2

We recommend the following approach in dealing with the material in this chapter:

Administration Of The Department
- Read paragraph 2-1 to 2-7 (in the textbook).

Filing Requirements For Living And Deceased Individuals
- Read paragraph 2-8 to 2-16.
- Do Exercise Two-1 (in the textbook) and check the solution in this Study Guide.
- Read paragraph 2-17 to 2-19.
- Do Exercise Two-2 and check the solution in this Study Guide.

Withholdings For Income Tax
- Read paragraph 2-20 to 2-26.

Instalment Payments For Individuals
- Read paragraph 2-27 to 2-42.
- Do Exercises Two-3 to Two-5 and check the solutions in this Study Guide.
- Do Self Study Problem Two-1 which is available on the Companion Website and check the solution in this Study Guide.

Interest, Penalties And Balance Due Dates For Living And Deceased Individuals
- Read paragraph 2-43 to 2-54.
- Do Exercise Two-6 and check the solution in this Study Guide.
- Read paragraph 2-55 to 2-59.

Returns And Payments, Including Instalments, For Corporations
- Read paragraph 2-60 to 2-72.
- Do Exercises Two-7 and Two-8 and check the solutions in this Study Guide.

Balance Due Dates For Corporations
- Read paragraph 2-73 and 2-74.
- Do Exercise Two-9 and check the solution in this Study Guide.

Interest And Penalties For Corporations
- Read paragraph 2-75 to 2-78.
- Do Self Study Problems Two-2 to Two-4 and check the solutions in this Study Guide.

Returns And Payments For Trusts
- Read paragraph 2-79 to 2-86.
- Do Self Study Problem Two-5 and check the solution in this Study Guide.

General Administrative Issues, Including The "My Account" Service, Assessments, Refunds, And Adjustments To Returns
- Read paragraph 2-87 to 2-103.

Appeals And Notices Of Objection
- Read paragraph 2-104 to 2-118.
- Do Exercise Two-10 and check the solution in this Study Guide.
- Read paragraph 2-119 to 2-128.
- Do Self Study Problem Two-6 and check the solution in this Study Guide.

Tax Evasion, Avoidance, And Planning
- Read paragraph 2-129 to 2-138.

Collection And Enforcement
- Read paragraph 2-139 to 2-150.
- Do Self Study Problem Two-7 and check the solution in this Study Guide.

Taxpayer Relief Provisions
- Read paragraph 2-151 to 2-154.

To Complete This Chapter
- If you would like more practice in problem solving, do the Supplementary Self Study Problems for the chapter. These problems and solutions are available on the Companion Website.
- Review the Key Terms Used In This Chapter in the textbook at the end of Chapter 2. Consult the Glossary for the meaning of any key terms you do not know.
- Test yourself with the Chapter 2 Glossary Flashcards available on the Companion Website.
- Ensure you have achieved the Chapter 2 Learning Objectives listed in this Study Guide.
- As a review, we recommend you view the PowerPoint presentation for Chapter 2 that is on the Companion Website.

Practice Examination
- Write the Practice Examination for Chapter 2 that is on the Companion Website. Mark your examination using the Practice Examination Solution that is also on the Companion Website.

Solutions to Chapter Two Exercises

Exercise Two - 1 Solution
While Mr. Katarski's 2017 tax return does not have to be filed until June 15, 2018, his tax liability must be paid by April 30, 2018 in order to avoid the assessment of interest.

Exercise Two - 2 Solution
Sally Cheung's 2017 tax return must be filed by the later of six months after the date of her death and her normal filing date. As her husband has business income, her normal filing date is June 15, 2018. The later of the two dates would be August 15, 2018, six months after the date of her death. Her final return for 2018 would be due on June 15, 2019.

Exercise Two - 3 Solution
She is not required to make instalment payments as long as her current year (2017) net tax owing is less than $3,000.

Exercise Two - 4 Solution

As his net tax owing in the current year and one of the two preceding years is in excess of $3,000, he is required to make instalment payments. The minimum amount would be based on the preceding taxation year's net tax owing of $1,500, and would be $375 ($1,500 ÷ 4) per quarter. They are due on March 15, June 15, September 15, and December 15.

Exercise Two - 5 Solution

The net tax owing amounts can be calculated as follows:

2015 $1,000 ($53,000 - $52,000)
2016 $7,000 ($59,000 - $52,000)
2017 $4,000 ($64,000 - $60,000)

As the net tax owing exceeds $3,000 in the current year and the first preceding year, instalments are required. The three alternatives for calculating instalment payments are as follows:

- Based on the estimate for the current year, the instalments would be $1,000 ($4,000 ÷ 4).
- Based on the estimate for the preceding year, the instalments would be $1,750 ($7,000 ÷ 4).
- Based on the second preceding year, the first two instalments would each be $250 ($1,000 ÷ 4). The second two instalments would each be $3,250 {[1/2][$7,000 - ($250)(2)]}. The instalments would total $7,000, the same amount as under the preceding year alternative.

While the first two instalments are lower under the second preceding year alternative, the total for all the instalments under this alternative is $7,000, higher than the $4,000 total under the current year alternative. The current year alternative would be the best. They are due on March 15, June 15, September 15, and December 15. Note, however, that if the estimated taxes payable are below actual taxes payable for 2017, instalment interest may be charged.

Exercise Two - 6 Solution

Given the size of her net tax owing, ITA 163.1 will not be applicable and there will be no penalties for late instalments. The penalty for late filing will be based on the number of **complete** months of non-payment, which is two. It will be equal to 7 percent of taxes payable (5 percent, plus 1 percent per month). If, in one of the three preceding taxation years she has also late filed, the penalty could be 14 percent (10 percent, plus 2 percent per month) if the CRA has already sent a request for the return.

Interest will be assessed on the deficient instalments, calculated from the date on which the instalment was due. Interest will also be assessed on the balance owing on her filing date, along with the penalty for late filing. This interest will be assessed for the period May 1 through July 20, 2018. All of the interest will be calculated at the prescribed rate plus 4 percent.

Exercise Two - 7 Solution

Not Small CCPC   If we assume that Madco Ltd. is not a small CCPC, the first two instalments would be due on the last day of January and February, 2017. They would be based on the second preceding year and would be $2,667 each ($32,000 ÷ 12). The remaining 10 instalments would be based on the preceding year, less the $5,334 paid in the first two instalments. The amount would be $5,367 [($59,000 - $5,334) ÷ 10] and the instalments would be due on the last day of each month for March to December, 2017.

Small CCPC   If we assume that Madco Ltd. is a small CCPC, the first instalment would be due on March 31, 2017. The amount would be based on the second preceding year and would equal $8,000 ($32,000 ÷ 4). The remaining three instalments would be based on the preceding year, less the amount paid in the first instalment. These payments would be equal to $17,000 [($59,000 - $8,000) ÷ 3]. These payments would be due on the last days of June, September, and December, 2017.

Note that when the initial instalment(s) are based on the second preceding year, the total amount of instalments will be the same as when all of the instalments are based on the first preceding year. However, using the second preceding year is preferable in that it provides some deferral of taxes.

Exercise Two - 8 Solution

Not Small CCPC If we assume that Fadco is not a small CCPC, the minimum instalments would be based on the estimated taxes payable for the taxation year ending November 30, 2017. The amount would be $1,417 ($17,000 ÷ 12) and the instalments would be due on the last day of each month beginning in December, 2016 and continuing to November, 2017. Note that, if the estimate of tax payable for 2017 is too low, interest may be assessed on the deficiency.

Small CCPC If we assume that Fadco is a small CCPC, the instalments would be based on the estimated taxes payable for the taxation year ending November 30, 2017. The amount would be $4,250 ($17,000 ÷ 4). These amounts would be due on the last days of February, May, August, and November, 2017.

Exercise Two - 9 Solution

Radco Inc.'s tax return is due six months after the fiscal year end, on July 31, 2017. Unless Radco is able to claim the small business deduction, the final payment on their taxes is due two months after the year end, on March 31, 2017. If Radco is eligible for the small business deduction, the final payment can be deferred for an additional month, to April 30, 2017, provided the Taxable Income for the preceding taxation year did not exceed $500,000.

Exercise Two - 10 Solution

The notice of objection must be filed by the later of:

- 90 days after the date on the Notice of Reassessment (August 13, 2019); or
- one year after the due date for filing the return that is being reassessed (April 30, 2019).

The later of these two dates is August 13, 2019.

Self Study Solution Two - 1

Part A

Ms. Birch's net tax owing for the three relevant years can be calculated as follows:

2015 $1,500 ($23,000 - $21,500)
2016 $12,000 ($27,000 - $15,000)
2017 $3,200 ($21,200 - $18,000) Estimated

Ms. Birch would be required to make instalment payments during 2017, as her net tax owing for 2017 is estimated to be in excess of $3,000 and, in addition, her net tax owing in one of the two preceding years (2016) is in excess of $3,000.

Part B

Instalments will be due on March 15, June 15, September 15, and December 15 of 2017. The three alternative payment schedules can be described as follows:

One The instalments can be based on the 2017 estimates. This would give four equal instalments of $800 ($3,200 ÷ 4).

Two The instalments can be based on the 2016 figures. This would give four equal instalments of $3,000 ($12,000 ÷ 4). The instalments would total $12,000 under this alternative.

Three   The first two instalments could be based on the second preceding year. This amount would be $375 ($1,500 ÷ 4). The remaining two instalments would be based on the preceding year, less the amount of the first two instalments. This amount would be $5,625 {[$12,000 - (2)($375)] ÷ 2}. This is the calculation that would be used by the CRA for her instalment reminders and the instalments would total $12,000.

Alternative one is the best alternative, as the instalments will total $3,200. Under both alternatives two and three, the instalments will equal the prior year's net tax owing of $12,000 which results in a significant overpayment of taxes. No interest will be paid on this overpayment.

Part C

The answer here will depend on Ms. Birch's other debt obligations. If she fails to make the instalment payments she will be charged non-deductible interest at the prescribed rate plus 4 percent. However, if she has other debt with non-deductible interest, unpaid credit card balances for example, the rate on this debt may be higher than the rate charged on deficient instalments. This would mean that there would be an advantage in paying off this alternative debt, rather than making the instalment payments.

Self Study Solution Two - 2

Part A

There are three possible payment schedules that could be used by Amalmor Inc. in this situation. The amounts involved are calculated as follows:

Current Year Base   The payments could be 1/12th of the estimated taxes payable for the current year. This amount would be $7,917 ($95,000 ÷ 12).

Preceding Year Base   The payments could be 1/12th of the taxes that were paid in the immediately preceding year. This amount would be $6,667 ($80,000 ÷ 12).

Preceding And Second Preceding Years   A final alternative would be to base the first two payments on 1/12th of the taxes payable in the second preceding year, with the remaining ten payments based on 1/10th of the preceding year's total less the amounts paid in the first two instalments.

The first two instalments would be $5,208 ($62,500 ÷ 12), or a total of $10,416. In the remaining 10 months of the year, the 10 instalments would each be $6,958 [($80,000 - $10,416) ÷ 10].

The last alternative involves the same total as using the preceding year as a base. However, this alternative is preferable as it requires lower payments in the first two months which provides a small amount of tax deferral.

The instalments would be due on the last day of each month in 2017.

Part B

If we assume that Amalmor Inc. qualifies as a "small" CCPC, there would also be three alternative calculations:

Current Year Base   The payments could be 1/4 of the estimated taxes payable for the current year. This amount would be $23,750 ($95,000 ÷ 4).

Preceding Year Base   The payments could be 1/4 of the taxes that were paid in the immediately preceding year. This amount would be $20,000 ($80,000 ÷ 4).

Preceding And Second Preceding Years   A final alternative would be to base the first payment on 1/4 of the taxes paid in the second preceding year, with the remaining three payments based on the preceding year total, less the amounts paid in the first instalment. The first amount would be $15,625 ($62,500 ÷ 4). In the remaining 3 quarters of the year, the payments would be $21,458 [($80,000 - $15,625) ÷ 3].

The last alternative involves the same total as using the preceding year as a base. However, this alternative is preferable as it requires a lower first payment which provides a small amount of tax deferral.

These instalments would be due on the last days of March, June, September, and December, 2017.

Part C

If Amalcor is a public company, any remaining taxes payable must be paid within two months of the Company's year end. This is extended to three months for CCPCs that claim the small business deduction. Since in Part B, Amalcor is small CCPC, it would qualify for the extension.

Note that Amalcor would not have to qualify as a "small" CCPC to get the extension, it would just have to be able to claim the small business deduction which is available only to CCPCs. CCPCs and the small business deduction are covered in detail in Chapter 12.

Self Study Solution Two - 3

Case One

1. The individual's net tax owing in each of the three years is as follows:

    2015 = Nil ($72,300 - $73,700)
    2016 = $6,200 ($89,400 - $83,200)
    2017 = $3,300 ($78,300 - $75,000)

    As the net tax owing exceeds $3,000 in the current year and one of the two preceding years, instalments are required.

2. The three alternatives would be:

    *   Quarterly instalments of $825 ($3,300 ÷ 4) based on the current year estimate.
    *   Quarterly instalments of $1,550 ($6,200 ÷ 4) based on the first preceding year.
    *   Based on the second preceding year, the first two instalments would be nil. The remaining two instalments would be $3,100 each [($6,200 -
    *   Nil) ÷ 2] for a total of $6,200.

3. The best alternative to minimize instalments would be four quarterly instalments of $825, for a total of $3,300.

    The instalments are due on March 15, June, 15, September 15, and December 15.

Case Two

1. The individual's net tax owing in each of the three years is as follows:

    2015 = $7,200 ($72,300 - $65,100)
    2016 = Nil ($89,400 - $90,100)
    2017 = $6,400 ($78,300 - $71,900)

    As the net tax owing exceeds $3,000 in the current year and one of the two preceding years, instalments are required.

2. The three alternatives would be:

- Quarterly instalments of $1,600 ($6,400 ÷ 4) based on the current year estimate.
- Quarterly instalments of nil based on the first preceding year.
- Two quarterly instalments of $1,800 ($7,200 ÷ 4) based on the second preceding year. No further instalments would be required.

3. The best alternative would be quarterly instalments of nil based on the first preceding year.

Case Three

1. As the corporation's tax payable for both the current and the preceding year exceeds $3,000, instalments are required. As the corporation is a small CCPC, instalments will be quarterly.

2. The three acceptable alternatives would be as follows:

- Quarterly instalments of $19,575 ($78,300 ÷ 4) based on the current year estimate.
- Quarterly instalments of $22,350 ($89,400 ÷ 4) based on the first preceding year.
- One instalment of $18,075 ($72,300 ÷ 4) based on the second preceding year, followed by three instalments of $23,775 [($89,400 - $18,075) ÷ 3], a total of $89,400.

3. The best alternative would be four instalments of $19,575, for total payments of $78,300.

The instalments are due on March 31, June 30, September 30, and December 31.

Case Four

1. As the corporation's tax payable for both the current and the preceding year exceeds $3,000, instalments are required. As the corporation is not a CCPC so cannot be eligible for the small business deduction, monthly instalments are required.

2. The three acceptable alternatives would be as follows:

- Monthly instalments of $6,525 ($78,300 ÷ 12) based on the current year estimate.
- Monthly instalments of $6,208.33 ($74,500 ÷ 12) based on the first preceding year.
- Two monthly instalments of $6,025 ($72,300 ÷ 12) based on the second preceding year, followed by 10 monthly instalments of $6,245 {[($74,500 - (2)($6,025)] ÷ 10}, a total of $74,500.

3. In terms of minimizing instalment payments, both the second and third alternatives involve paying $74,500, which is less than the payment of $78,300 under the first alternative. While the problem does not ask you to take into consideration deferral, the third alternative would be the best in that the first two payments are lower.

The instalments would be due on the last day of each month, beginning in January.

Self Study Solution Two - 4

Case A

The individual's actual and estimated net tax owing is equal to the Tax Payable in each of the three years as follows:

2015 = $18,000
2016 = $14,400
2017 = $13,500 (Estimated)

As the estimated tax payable for the current year and the actual tax payable for the preceding year exceeds $3,000, instalments are required.

Using the estimated Tax Payable for the current year would result in the minimum instalment payments. Based on this year, the required quarterly instalments would be $3,375 ($13,500 ÷ 4).

They would be due on March 15, June 15, September 15, and December 15 and would total $13,500.

Since the actual federal and provincial taxes payable for 2017 of $16,000 is higher than the tax payable of $14,400 of the preceding year, the instalments should have been based on $14,400. The instalments should have been $3,600 ($14,400 ÷ 4) for each quarter.

Interest at the prescribed base rate plus 4 percent is charged on any portion of a required instalment payment that is not remitted on the required instalment due date. The interest is charged from the date the instalment is due until an offset occurs, or until the due date for the balance owing.

Case B

The individual's net tax owing in each of the three years is as follows:

2015 = $11,000 ($18,000 - $7,000)
2016 = Nil (Withholdings exceed tax payable. Note this is nil, not a negative amount.)
2017 = $4,500 ($13,500 - $9,000) (Estimated)

As the individual's net tax owing is expected to exceed $3,000 in 2017 and was more than $3,000 in 2015, the payment of instalments is required.

Using the 2016 net tax owing would result in minimum instalment payments. Based on this year, the required quarterly instalments would be nil.

The fact that the actual federal and provincial taxes payable for 2017 are higher than were estimated is not relevant in this Case.

Case C

The corporation's Tax Payable for the three years is as follows:

2015 = $18,000
2016 = $14,400
2017 = $13,500 (Estimated)

As the corporation's tax payable for both the current and the preceding year exceeds $3,000, instalments are required.

Using the estimated Tax Payable for the current year would result in the minimum instalment payments. As the corporation is a small CCPC, the required instalments would be quarterly. The amount would be $3,375 ($13,500 ÷ 4).

They would be due on the last days of March, June, September, and December, 2017.

Like Case A, since the actual federal and provincial taxes payable for 2017 of $16,000 is higher than the tax payable of $14,400 of the preceding year, the instalments should have been based on $14,400. The instalments should have been $3,600 ($14,400 ÷ 4) for each quarter.

Interest at the prescribed base rate plus 4 percent is charged on any portion of a required instalment payment that is not remitted on the required instalment due date. The interest is charged from the date the instalment is due until an offset occurs, or until the due date for the balance owing.

Case D

The corporation's Tax Payable for the three years is as follows:

2015 = $18,000
2016 = $14,400
2017 = $16,000 (Estimated and actual)

As the corporation's tax payable for both the current and the preceding year exceeds $3,000, instalments are required.

Using the estimated Tax Payable for 2016 would result in minimum instalment payments. As the corporation is not a CCPC so cannot be eligible for the small business deduction, the required instalments would be monthly. The amount would be $1,200 ($14,400 ÷ 12). They would be due on the last day of each month, beginning in January, 2017.

Self Study Solution Two - 5

The three taxable entities are individuals, corporations, and trusts. The required information for each is as follows:

Individuals   For individuals, the taxation year is the calendar year. For individuals without business income, the filing deadline is April 30 of the following year. Individuals with business income, and their spouse or common-law partner, have an extended filing deadline of June 15.

If an individual dies after October, the due date of the return for the year of death is extended to 6 months after the date of death. Instalment payments for all individuals, if required, are to be made quarterly on March 15, June 15, September 15, and December 15.

Corporations   Corporations can choose any fiscal year that does not exceed 53 weeks. The filing deadline is six months after the fiscal year end. In general, corporations must make instalments on the last day of each month.   However, if the corporation qualifies as a small CCPC, quarterly instalments are required on the last day of the last month of each 3 month period in the corporation's taxation year.

Trusts - Inter Vivos   Inter vivos trusts must use the calendar year as their taxation year. As the required tax return must be filed within 90 days of the taxation year end, returns for inter vivos trusts will be due March 31 (March 30 in leap years). Legislation requires that quarterly instalments be made on March 15, June 15, September 15, and December 15. Note, however, the CRA has generally not enforced this requirement.

Trusts - Testamentary The rules are the same for most testamentary trusts. However, the exception to this is a testamentary trust that has been designated a graduated rate estate (GRE). Such GREs can use a non-calendar fiscal year for up to three years subsequent to the death of the settlor. GRE returns are due 90 days after the date that has been selected as the taxation year end. Quarterly instalments are required, with the specific dates determined by the choice of taxation year end. It is likely that the CRA will not enforce the instalment requirement.

Self Study Solution Two - 6

Since Mr. Coffee has been your client for many years, there should be a signed Consent Form, T1013, filed with the CRA which authorizes you to represent him in his affairs. If you have not already been authorized to represent him online, it would be advantageous for you to request that Mr. Coffee take the steps needed to authorize you to access his file through the online Represent a Client service. This will enable you to deal with this dispute and any future disputes more quickly.

With respect to resolving this dispute, the first step would be a call to the CRA to discuss the matter. If there has been a misunderstanding of the facts, an error on your or the CRA's part, or missing information, this may be the only step required and the matter can be resolved.

However, if more formal steps are necessary they can be outlined as follows:

Notice of Objection   As the reassessment relates to the previous year's tax return, it is within the normal three year time limit for reassessment. This means that notice of objection can be filed within 90 days of the date on the Notice of Reassessment or (as Mr. Coffee is an individual) one year from the due date for the return under reassessment. This can be done through the mail by letter or using Form T400A, or online through the Represent A Client service. It should explain the facts and reasons why the reassessment is not justified.

Tax Court of Canada   If there is an adverse decision on the notice of objection, Mr. Coffee has up to 90 days after the mailing date of the response to the notice of objection to appeal to the Tax Court of Canada. Alternatively, if he does not receive a response to his notice of objection within 90 days, he will then be able to appeal to the Tax Court of Canada. As the amount involved is only $5,000, it would probably be advisable for Mr. Coffee to choose the informal procedures.

Federal Courts   If Mr. Coffee has elected the informal Tax Court of Canada procedures, no appeal of an adverse decision is possible. An appeal to the Federal Court - Appeals Division would, however, be possible if an adverse decision was rendered under the general procedures. In theory, an adverse decision by the Federal Court could be appealed to the Supreme Court of Canada. However, this can only happen if the Federal Court recommends it or the Supreme Court authorizes such action. This would be extremely unlikely given the amount involved.

Self Study Solution Two - 7

Part A

Based on these facts, Joan Bridge would be liable for a third party penalty. However, if she was able to determine that there was a reasonable basis upon which the Tax Court decision could be overturned by a higher court, the penalty would not apply.

Part B

Based on these facts, if Jack Hodge were to prepare and EFILE Barbra's return without obtaining the charitable donation receipt, Jack would be liable for a third party penalty. Given that the size of the donation is so disproportionate to Barbra's apparent income as to defy credibility, to EFILE the return without verifying the amount of the receipt would show an indifference as to whether the *Act* is complied with or would show a wilful, reckless, or wanton disregard of the law.

Part C

Marion Flexor is not liable for participating in an understatement of Jason March's taxes payable because she did not know that some of the expense receipts were personal in nature, and would not be reasonably expected to know that this was the case. This is because Marion relied in good faith on the information provided by Jason. Unlike the situation in Part B of this problem, since Jason's business had a significant profit, it would be reasonable to assume he had high travel costs.

Chapter 2 Learning Objectives

After completing Chapter 2, you should be able to:

1. Explain when an individual is required to file an income tax return (paragraph [P hereafter] P 2-8 to 2-13).
2. List the dates on which income tax returns must be filed by living and deceased individuals (P 2-14 to 2-19).
3. Explain the nature of, and need for, withholding for income tax (P 2-20 to 2-26).
4. Explain the circumstances which result in an individual having to make income tax instalment payments (P 2-27 to 2-31).
5. Calculate the amount of any income tax instalment payments required for individual taxpayers and determine their due date (P 2-32 to 2-42).

6. Explain how the prescribed interest rates are used to calculate interest on amounts owing to and from the CRA (P 2-43 to 2-49).
7. Calculate the penalties that will be assessed for the late filing of income tax returns and large late and deficient instalments (P 2-50 to 2-54).
8. Identify the dates on which balances owing by living and deceased individuals are due (P 2-55 and 2-59).
9. Identify the dates on which income tax returns must be filed by corporations and the filing alternatives that are available (P 2-60 to 2-66).
10. Calculate the amount of income tax instalment payments required for corporations, including small CCPCs (P 2-67 to 2-72).

11. Identify the dates on which balances owing by corporations are due (P 2-73 and 2-74).
12. Calculate the interest and penalties that will be assessed on late tax payments and for the late filing of corporate income tax returns (P 2-75 to 2-78).
13. Explain the general filing and payment requirements for testamentary and inter vivos trusts (P 2-79 to 2-86).
14. Explain the circumstances in which a taxpayer is required to file an information return (P 2-87).
15. Describe the record keeping requirements of the CRA (P 2-88 and 2-89).

16. Briefly describe the My Account and My Business Account services available on the CRA website (P 2-90).
17. Describe the Notice of Assessment, Notice of Reassessment and explain the reassessment period (P 2-91 to 2-93).
18. Explain when interest is paid on refunds and how it is calculated (P 2-94 to 2-99).
19. Explain how to make adjustments to previously filed tax returns (P 2-100 to 2-103).
20. Explain the initial procedures for disputing an assessment and the procedures for filing a notice of objection (P 2-104 to 2-118).

21. Describe further appeals procedures, including those made to the Tax Court of Canada, the Federal Court of Appeals, and the Supreme Court of Canada (P 2-119 to 2-128).
22. Explain the difference between tax evasion, avoidance and planning, including the concepts involved in the General Anti-Avoidance Rule (P 2-129 to 2-138).
23. Describe the collection and enforcement procedures available to the CRA (P 2-139 to 2-144).
24. Describe some of the penalties that can be assessed including those applicable to tax advisors and tax return preparers (P 2-145 to 2-150).
25. Briefly describe the taxpayer relief provisions (P 2-151 to 2-154).

CHAPTER 3

How To Work Through Chapter 3

We recommend the following approach in dealing with the material in this chapter:

Employment Income Defined
- Read paragraph 3-1 to 3-11 (in the textbook).
- Do Exercise Three-1 (in the textbook) and check the solution in this Study Guide.
- Do Self Study Problem Three-1 which is available on the Companion Website and check the solution in this Study Guide.
- Read paragraph 3-12 to 3-13.

Employee Versus Self-Employed
- Read paragraph 3-14 to 3-44.
- Do Self Study Problem Three-2 and check the solution in this Study Guide.

Salaries And Fringe Benefits
- Read paragraph 3-45 to 3-63.
- Do Exercises Three-2 and Three-3 and check the solution in this Study Guide.
- Read paragraph 3-64 to 3-76.
- Do Exercise Three-4 and check the solution in this Study Guide.

GST/HST/PST On Taxable Benefits
- Read paragraph 3-77 to 3-78.
- Do Exercise Three-5 and check the solution in this Study Guide.

Automobile Benefits (Standby Charge And Operating Cost Benefit)
- Read paragraph 3-79 to 3-116.
- Do Exercise Three-6 and check the solution in this Study Guide.
- Read paragraph 3-117 to 3-122.
- Do Exercise Three-7 and check the solution in this Study Guide.
- Read paragraph 3-123 and 3-124.
- Do Self Study Problems Three-3 to Three-5 and check the solutions in this Study Guide.

Allowances
- Read paragraph 3-125 to 3-137.
- Do Exercises Three-8 and Three-9 and check the solutions in this Study Guide.
- Read paragraph 3-138 to 3-142.
- Do Exercise Three-10 and check the solution in this Study Guide.

Employee Insurance Benefits
- Read paragraph 3-143 to 3-148.
- Do Exercise Three-11 and check the solution in this Study Guide.

Loans To Employees

- Read paragraph 3-149 to 3-154.
- Do Exercise Three-12 and check the solution in this Study Guide.
- Read paragraph 3-155 to 3-159.
- Do Exercise Three-13 and check the solution in this Study Guide.
- Do Self Study Problem Three-6 and check the solution in this Study Guide.

Stock Option Benefits

- Read paragraph 3-160 to 3-174.
- Do Exercise Three-14 and check the solution in this Study Guide.
- Read paragraph 3-175 to 3-179.
- Do Exercise Three-15 and check the solution in this Study Guide.
- Do Self Study Problems Three-7 to Three-9 and check the solution in this Study Guide.

Other Inclusions

- Read paragraph 3-180 to 3-188.

Specific Deductions Including Salesperson's Expenses And Work Space In The Home Costs

- Read paragraph 3-189 to 3-205.
- Do Exercise Three-16 and check the solution in this Study Guide.
- Read paragraph 3-206 to 3-215.
- Do Self Study Problems Three-10 to Three-14 and check the solutions in this Study Guide.

To Complete This Chapter

- If you would like more practice in problem solving, do the Supplementary Self Study Problems for the chapter. These problems and solutions are available on the Companion Website.
- Review the Key Terms Used In This Chapter in the textbook at the end of Chapter 3. Consult the Glossary for the meaning of any key terms you do not know.
- Test yourself with the Chapter 3 Glossary Flashcards available on the Companion Website.
- Ensure you have achieved the Chapter 3 Learning Objectives listed in this Study Guide.
- As a review, we recommend you view the PowerPoint presentation for Chapter 3 that is on the Companion Website.

Practice Examination

- Write the Practice Examination for Chapter 3 that is on the Companion Website. Mark your examination using the Practice Examination Solution that is also on the Companion Website.

Solutions to Chapter Three Exercises

Exercise Three - 1 Solution

The bonus will be taxed in Mr. Neelson's hands in the year of receipt. This means that it will be included in his 2018 tax return. With respect to Neelson Inc., the bonus is not payable until more than 180 days after the September 30 fiscal year end. Note that the limit is 180 days from the fiscal year end, not the date on which the bonus was declared.

As a consequence, the Company will not be able to deduct the bonus in the year ending September 30, 2017, the year of declaration. It will be deducted in the year ending September 30, 2018, the year of payment.

Exercise Three - 2 Solution

The tax consequences associated with each of the listed items are as follows:

Gift	Tax Consequence
$15 T-Shirt	No consequences as value is immaterial
$75 Birthday Gift	Taxable as it is a near cash gift
$400 Performance Reward	Taxable as it is performance related
$275 10-Year Award	Non-taxable as it is under $500
$300 Wedding Gift	These remaining three gifts qualify as non-taxable. However, their total value is $700 ($300 + $250 + $150).
$250 Weight Loss Award	
$150 Holiday Season Gift	The $200 excess over $500 will be taxable.

Exercise Three - 3 Solution

The tax consequences of the various items would be as follows:

- Discounts on merchandise do not create a taxable benefit provided they are available to all employees and do not reduce the price below the employer's cost.

- It could be argued that these tuition fees are related to business activity. If the argument is successful, the payment would not be taxable to John. If unsuccessful, the $2,000 would be a taxable benefit.

- Special clothing is not a taxable benefit if it is distinctive and the employee is required to wear it at work, or if it is required to protect the employee from some type of employment related hazard. It is unlikely that business clothing would fall into this category as it could be used for personal purposes. The $8,500 should be included in John's income as a taxable benefit.

- The $450 gift would not be taxable to John.

- Employer paid premiums for private health care plans are not a taxable benefit.

Exercise Three - 4 Solution

From Jill's point of view, the best alternative is probably the dental plan. Its value is significantly enhanced by the fact that it can be received without tax consequences. The annual vacation trip is clearly a taxable benefit. With respect to the $4,000 birthday gift, the $3,500 excess over the limit of $500 will be taxable. Note that the desirability of the dental plan would be affected by whether her spouse has a dental plan.

Exercise Three - 5 Solution

Ms. Correli's taxable benefit would be $4,725, the $4,500 cost of the trip, plus the additional $225 in GST.

Exercise Three - 6 Solution

As Mrs. Lee's employment related use is more than 50 percent of the total (16,000 out of 28,000), she is eligible for a reduction in the full standby charge. She is also eligible for the alternative one-half of the standby charge calculation of the operating cost benefit. Given these factors, the taxable benefit would be calculated as follows:

Standby Charge	
[(2%)(12)($25,000 + $1,250 + $2,000)(12,000 ÷ 20,004*)]	$4,067
Operating Cost Benefit - Lesser Of:	
• [($0.25)(12,000)] = $3,000	
• [(1/2)($4,067)] = $2,034	2,034
Total Benefit	$6,101

*[(12 Months)(1,667)]

Exercise Three - 7 Solution

The actual operating costs paid by the employer do not affect these calculations. Rounded to the nearest whole number, 325 days results in 11 months of availability. As Mr. Forthwith's employment related use is more than 50 percent, he is eligible for a reduction in the full standby charge. He is also eligible for the alternative one-half of the standby charge calculation of the operating cost benefit. Given these factors, the taxable benefit would be calculated as follows:

Standby Charge [(2/3)($525 + $68)(11)(3,000 ÷ 18,337*)]	$ 711
Operating Cost Benefit - Lesser Of:	
• [($0.25)(3,000)] = $750	
• [(1/2)($711)] = $356	356
Total Benefit	$1,067

*[(11)(1,667)]

Exercise Three - 8 Solution

Because the allowance is not based on kilometers driven, she will have to include the $3,600 allowance in her income. Because the allowance has been included in income, she can deduct the employment related portion of her actual automobile costs against this amount. This would be $1,936 [($7,150)(6,500 ÷ 24,000)]. The net inclusion would be $1,664 ($3,600 - $1,936).

Exercise Three - 9 Solution

As the milage allowance paid by the employer was based on the number of employment related kilometers driven, the $3,500 [(35,000 Km.)($0.10)] will not be included on his T4 Information Return and, as a consequence, it does not have to be included in his employment income. However, he will not be able to deduct his actual costs of owning and operating the automobile.

Mr. Lorenz's actual deductible costs total $11,900 [($5,400 + $15,000)(35,000/60,000)], well in excess of the allowance of $3,500. While Mr. Lorenz could attempt to include the allowance in income and deduct the actual costs, this approach could be disallowed by the CRA.

Exercise Three - 10 Solution

The hotel allowance would appear to be reasonable and would not be included in Ms. Ohm's T4. Given this, it will not be included in her net employment income. Even though her actual costs of $18,300 are in excess of the $16,400 allowance, it would be difficult for Ms. Ohm to argue that the $200 figure is not reasonable. Given this, she does not have the choice of including the $16,400 in income and deducting the actual amount of $18,300.

As the milage charge is based on kilometers, it will not be included in her T4. In addition, since the amount appears to be reasonable in terms of actual costs, she does not have the choice of including it in income and deducting the actual costs. In fact, it would not be to Ms. Ohm's advantage to do so as her actual costs would be $2,880 [($7,200)(9,400/23,500)], which is less than the $3,854 payment she received.

No amounts would be included in Ms. Ohm's net employment income and no amounts would be deductible.

Exercise Three - 11 Solution

As his employer contributes to the plan and the contributions do not create a taxable benefit, the $5,250 in benefits received during the year will be included in his employment income. This will be reduced by the $525 ($300 + $225) in non-deductible contributions that he made during 2016 and 2017, leaving a net inclusion of $4,725 ($5,250 - $525).

Exercise Three - 12 Solution

Whether or not the loan qualifies as a home relocation loan would make no difference in the calculation of Mrs. Caldwell's taxable benefit. The only difference would be the availability of a deduction from Taxable Income in the case of the home relocation loan.

The ITA 80.4(1) benefit is calculated as follows:

The Lesser Of:
- [($100,000)(2%)(1/4) + ($100,000)(3%)(1/4) + ($100,000)(1%)(2/4)] = $1,750
- [($100,000)(2%)] = $2,000 $1,750

Less Interest Payment [($100,000)(1%)]   (1,000)

Net Benefit $ 750

As this is a home purchase loan, the annual benefit cannot exceed the benefit that would result from applying the 2 percent rate that was in effect when the loan was made. Note that the 2 percent rate is not compared to the prescribed rate on a quarter-by-quarter basis, but on an annual basis. The lower figure of $1,750 would then be reduced by the $1,000 in interest paid.

Exercise Three - 13 Solution

In the absence of the interest free loan, the employee would borrow $125,000 at 5 percent, requiring an annual interest payment of $6,250. The after tax cash outflow associated with the employer providing sufficient additional salary to carry this loan would be calculated as follows:

Required Salary [$6,250 ÷ (1 - 0.42)]	$10,776
Corporate Tax Savings From Deducting Salary [($10,776)(26%)]	(2,802)
Employer's After Tax Cash Flow - Additional Salary	$ 7,974

Alternatively, if the loan is provided, the employee will have a taxable benefit of $2,500 [(2%)($125,000)], resulting in taxes payable of $1,050 [(42%)($2,500)]. To make this situation comparable to the straight salary alternative, the employer will have to provide the employee with both the loan amount and sufficient additional salary to pay the taxes on the imputed interest benefit. The amount of this additional salary would be $1,810 [$1,050 ÷ (1 - 0.42)]. The employer's after tax cash flow associated with providing the additional salary and the loan amount would be calculated as follows:

Required Salary [$1,050 ÷ (1 - 0.42)]	$1,810
Corporate Tax Savings From Deducting Salary [($1,810)(26%)]	(471)
After Tax Cost Of Salary To Cover Taxes On Benefit	$1,339
Employer's Lost Earnings [(7%)(1 - 0.26)($125,000)]	6,475
Employer's After Tax Cash Flow - Loan	$7,814

Given these results, providing the loan appears to be the better alternative.

Exercise Three - 14 Solution

At time of exercise, Mr. Guise will have an employment income benefit of $21,250 [($31.50 - $23.00)(2,500 Shares)]. As the option price at issue exceeded the fair market value at issue, Mr. Guise will be able to deduct $10,625 [(1/2)($21,250)] in the determination of Taxable Income. These results are summarized in the following table:

Fair Market Value Of Shares Acquired [(2,500)($31.50)]	$78,750
Cost Of Shares [(2,500)($23)]	(57,500)
ITA 7(1)(a) Employment Income Inclusion =	
Increase In Net Income For Tax Purposes	**$21,250**
ITA 110(1)(d) Deduction [(1/2)($21,250)]	(10,625)
Increase In Taxable Income	**$10,625**

When the shares are sold, there will be an allowable capital loss, calculated as follows:

Proceeds Of Disposition [($28.00)(2,500)]	$70,000
Adjusted Cost Base [($31.50)(2,500)]	(78,750)
Capital Loss	($ 8,750)
Inclusion Rate	1/2
Allowable Capital Loss	($ 4,375)

Mr. Guise will only be able to deduct this loss in 2017 to the extent that he has taxable capital gains on other dispositions. It cannot be deducted against the employment income inclusion.

Exercise Three - 15 Solution

There will be no tax consequences in either 2015 when the options are received, or in 2016, when the options are exercised. This latter result reflects the fact that the acquired shares are those of a Canadian controlled private corporation.

At the time the shares are sold in 2017, there will be an employment income benefit of $58,500 [($75.00 - $42.50)(1,800 Shares)]. As the option price of $42.50 was below the fair market value of $45 at the time the options were issued, there is no deduction under ITA 110(1)(d). Although she could have been eligible for the deduction under ITA 110(1)(d.1), she did not hold the shares for the required two years. These results are summarized in the following table:

Deferred Employment Income:

Fair Market Value Of Shares Acquired [(1,800)($75)]		$135,000
Cost Of Shares [(1,800)($42.50)]		(76,500)

ITA 7(1)(a) Employment Income Inclusion =	
Increase In **Net Income For Tax Purposes**	**$ 58,500**
ITA 110(1)(d) Deduction (Option Price < FMV)	N/A
ITA 110(1)(d.1) Deduction (Held Less Than 2 Years)	N/A
Increase In **Taxable Income**	**$ 58,500**

When she sells the shares in 2017, Ms. Van will have an allowable capital loss calculated as follows:

Proceeds Of Disposition [($49)(1,800)]	$ 88,200
Adjusted Cost Base [($75)(1,800)]	(135,000)
Capital Loss	($ 46,800)
Inclusion Rate	1/2
Allowable Capital Loss	($ 23,400)

Ms. Van will only be able to deduct this loss in 2017 to the extent that she has taxable capital gains on other dispositions. It cannot be deducted against the employment income inclusion.

Exercise Three - 16 Solution

The potential deduction is $27,100 [$8,000 + (1/2)($12,000) + $13,100]. However, this total exceeds his commissions and, if these amounts are deducted under ITA 8(1)(f), his deduction will be limited to the commissions of $12,200.

Alternatively, if he uses ITA 8(1)(h), he cannot deduct the advertising or the entertainment, limiting the amount of this deduction to $13,100.

As the two provisions cannot be used simultaneously, Morton would use the larger figure of $13,100 that is available under ITA 8(1)(h).

Self Study Solution Three - 1

The required information for the four Cases included in this problem is as shown in the following table:

	Deduction - Empire Inc. Year Ending October 31	Inclusion-Ms. Betz Calendar Year
Case A	2017	2017
Case B	2017	2018
Case C	2018	2018
Case D	2017	2017

In Case A, the bonus is deducted when accrued because it is paid within 180 days of Empire's 2017 year end. It is taxed when received.

In Case B, the bonus is deducted when accrued because it is paid within 180 days of Empire's 2017 year end. It is taxed when received.

In Case C, the bonus is not paid within 180 days of Empire's year end. As a consequence, it cannot be deducted until the year ending October 31, 2018. However, as it is paid within 3 years of Empire's 2017 year end it is not a salary deferral arrangement. This means it does not have to be included in Ms. Betz's Taxable Income until 2018.

In Case D, the bonus is not paid until more than 3 years after the end of the calendar year in which Ms. Betz rendered the services. This makes it a salary deferral arrangement, resulting in Ms. Betz having to include it in her 2017 Taxable Income. Empire will deduct the bonus in the fiscal year ending October 31, 2017.

Self Study Solution Three - 2

Quantitative Considerations

If the individual's services are acquired as an employee, the 2017 costs would be as follows:

Basic Salary	$250,000
Company Benefits [($250,000)(8%)]	20,000
CPP (Maximum)	2,564
Employer's Share Of EI [(1.4)(1.63%)($51,300)]	1,171
Payroll Tax [(2%)($250,000)]	5,000
Total Cost	$278,735

This is very close to the $280,000 that would have to be paid to the individual if he is classified as an independent contractor.

Other Considerations

While the quantitative factors slightly favour employee classification, this is probably not the best choice. Other factors that should be considered:

- self-employed status relieves the company from any ongoing commitment beyond the period specified in the contract,
- Farnham Ltd. would not be legally responsible for any errors in the work of the engineer if he is self-employed,
- the fact that employment contracts usually require that salary and related benefits grow over time, and
- the added administrative costs of withholding amounts from his salary if he is an employee.

It would appear to be more advantageous to structure the arrangement so that this individual qualifies as an independent contractor.

Self Study Solution Three - 3

Acura TLX

With employment related usage at more than 50 percent of the total, Ms. Vines can reduce the standby charge on the basis of actual personal usage and Ms. Vines can calculate the operating cost benefit as one-half of the standby charge which results in a lower benefit. The taxable benefit on this vehicle would be calculated as follows:

Standby Charge [(2%)($39,000 + $1,950 + $1,950)(5)(3,400 ÷ 8,335*)]	$1,750
Operating Cost Benefit - Lesser Of:	
• [(3,400)($0.25)] = $850	
• [(1/2)($1,750)] = $875	875
Total Benefit On Acura TLX	$2,625

*[(5)(1,667)]

Ford Taurus

The $100 insurance included in the monthly lease payment is removed from the standby charge calculation as it is an operating cost.

As the car was driven more than 50 percent for employment related purposes, a reduction in the standby charge is available (but is nil in this case) and Ms. Vines can calculate the operating cost benefit as one-half of the standby charge which results in a lower benefit. The taxable benefit on this vehicle is calculated as follows:

Standby Charge [(2/3)(6)($699 - $100)(10,002* ÷ 10,002*)]	$2,396
Operating Cost Benefit - Lesser Of:	
• [(14,600)($0.25)] = $3,650	
• [(1/2)($2,396)] = $1,198	1,198
Total Benefit On Ford Taurus	$3,594

*[(6)(1,667)] - since the numerator (personal kilometers of 14,600) cannot exceed the denominator, the effect of applying the reduction fraction is nil (10,002 ÷ 10,002).

Total Benefit

The total taxable benefit would be calculated as follows:

Total Benefit - Acura	$2,625
Total Benefit - Ford	3,594
Reimbursement To Company [($0.10)(3,400 Km + 14,600 Km)]	(1,800)
Total Taxable Benefit	$4,419

Notes:

• The taxable benefit calculation is not influenced by restrictions on the amount that the Company can deduct with respect to the Acura.

• Calculation of the operating cost benefits is not influenced by the employer's actual operating costs.

Self Study Solution Three - 4

Mr. Sam Stern

The taxable benefit for the president of the Company would be calculated as follows:

Standby Charge [(2%)($78,000)(8)]	$12,480
Operating Cost Benefit [(32,000)($0.25)]	8,000
Taxable Benefit	$20,480

As Mr. Stern did not drive the car more than 50 percent for employment related purposes, no reduction in the standby charge is available. Since his employment related use was not more than 50 percent, he cannot use the alternative calculation of the operating cost benefit.

Ms. Sarah Blue

The taxable benefit for the marketing vice president would be calculated as follows:

Standby Charge [(2/3)(12)($900)(5,000/20,004)]	$1,800
Operating Cost Benefit - Lesser Of:	
• [(5,000)($0.25)] = $1,250	
• [(1/2)($1,800)] = $900	900
Taxable Benefit	$2,700

As employment related driving was more than 50 percent of the total, Ms. Blue can reduce the standby charge on the basis of actual personal usage. As the car was driven more than 50 percent for employment related purposes, Ms. Blue can calculate the operating cost benefit as one-half of the standby charge which results in a lower benefit.

Mr. John Stack

The taxable benefit for the finance vice president would be calculated as follows:

Standby Charge [(2%)($48,000)(12)(10,000/20,004]	$5,759
Operating Cost Benefit - Lesser Of:	
• [(10,000)($0.25)] = $2,500	
•](1/2)($5,759)] = $2,880	2,500
Payment For Use Of Company Car	(7,000)
Taxable Benefit	$1,259

Mr. Stack's employment related driving was more than 50 percent of the total and, as a consequence, he can reduce his standby charge on the basis of actual personal milage. Mr. Stack could have calculated the operating cost benefit as one-half of the standby charge, but this would have resulted in a higher benefit.

Mr. Alex Decker

The taxable benefit for the industrial relations vice president would be calculated as follows:

Standby Charge [(2/3)(10)($500)(8,500/16,670)]	$1,700
Operating Cost Benefit - Lesser Of:	
• [(8,500)($0.25)] = $2,125	
• [(1/2)($1,700)] = $850	850
Taxable Benefit	$2,550

As Mr. Decker's employment related driving is more than 50 percent of the total, he can reduce his standby charge on the basis of actual personal milage. While the $10,000 deposit will affect the deductibility of the lease payments by the employer, it does not influence the calculation of the taxable benefit to Mr. Decker. As the car was driven more than 50 percent for employment related purposes, Mr. Decker can calculate the operating cost benefit as one-half of the standby charge which results in a lower benefit.

Tax Planning

With respect to the tax planning of management compensation, two points can be made. First, the question of providing company cars as a method of compensation should be examined on a case-by-case basis.

In situations where a car is owned by the Company and provided to an executive for a fairly long period of time, the taxable benefit assessed may exceed the value of the benefit. For example, over five years, the taxable benefit without regard for operating costs on Mr. Stern's Mercedes could total $93,600 [(2%)(60)($78,000)]. This is more than $15,000 in excess of the cost of the car.

With the limitations on the deductibility of CCA and leasing costs on cars, the after tax cost to the Company of owning and leasing luxury cars can be very high. While a complete analysis of this issue will depend on a number of variables, it is possible that some of these executives would be better off receiving additional amounts of salary and billing the Company for employment related mileage driven in their own cars.

The second point to be made here is that, except in situations where the car is kept for very short periods of time, the employee will be allocated a smaller taxable benefit if the Company were to lease the car rather than buy it. In general, monthly lease payments on a three year lease will tend to be between 2 percent and 2.5 percent of the capital cost of the cars.

As the leasing standby charge is based on two-thirds of the monthly lease payment, it is clear that the standby charge under this type of arrangement will be less than the 2 percent per month that is assessed when the Company owns the car. However, for shorter lease terms, the lease payment will be a greater percentage of the capital cost and this relationship may reverse.

Other tax planning techniques would involve any procedure that would reduce the capital cost of purchased cars or the lease payments on leased cars. Such procedures would include high residual values on leasing arrangements and low trade in values assigned to old cars when new ones are purchased. In addition, it might be possible to reduce a taxable benefit, such as the one being allocated to Mr. Stern, by selling his car to a leasing company with an immediate leaseback arrangement. Although large refundable deposits on leasing arrangements would reduce the lease payment and therefore the standby charge, there would be a tax cost to the employer (see Chapter 6).

Self Study Solution Three - 5

Employer Continues To Provide Automobile

If the employer continues to provide the car, John's only cash outflow will be the taxes assessed on the taxable benefit that results from his having the car available. This outflow under the two Cases would be calculated as follows:

	Case A $35,000 Cost	Case B $70,000 Cost
Standby Charge		
[(2%)($35,000)(12)]	$ 8,400	
[(2%)($70,000)(12)]		$ 16,800
Operating Cost Benefit [(40,000 Kilometers)($0.25)]	10,000	10,000
Total Annual Benefit	$18,400	$26,800
Number Of Years	2	2
Total Benefit	$36,800	$53,600
John's Marginal Tax Rate	48%	48%
Total Taxes On Taxable Benefit	$17,664	$25,728

Note that, because John's use of the car is not primarily (more than 50 percent) for employment purposes, he cannot use the alternative one-half of standby charge calculation of the operating cost benefit.

John Purchases The Automobile

If John purchases the car and pays his own operating costs, the total cash outflow in both Cases would be calculated as follows:

Purchase Price	$20,000
Estimated Resale Value	(12,000)
Operating Costs [(2)(40,000 Kilometers)($0.20)]	16,000
Total Cash Outflow	$24,000

Conclusion - Case A ($35,000)

On the basis of undiscounted cash flows, the best alternative would be to have John's employer continue to provide him with the car. If the cash flows were discounted, the results would be even more favourable for this alternative.

Conclusion - Case B ($70,000)

Since the original cost of the car was $70,000, on the basis of undiscounted cash flows, the best alternative would be to have John purchase the car since the taxable benefit is so high.

Although the requirements of the problem ask that only the cash flows be considered, we would note that the alternative of purchasing the car carries more uncertainty. Both the resale value and the actual operating costs are estimates. If there was a large variation from the estimate for either or both of these amounts, it could substantially affect the total cash outflow of the purchase alternative.

Self Study Solution Three - 6

Approach

The appropriate comparison in evaluating the interest free loan arrangement would be to determine the cost to the Company of providing the loan and then compare this amount with the cost of providing an equivalent benefit in the form of straight salary. The following analysis calculates the Company's lowest cost route to providing Mr. Malone with the financing required, assuming he is not a shareholder.

Cost Of Providing For Interest Payments On Commercial Loan

As the problem indicates, Mr. Malone can borrow on a loan at a rate of interest of 5 percent. This means that the annual interest payments on $200,000 would amount to $10,000. If the interest is deductible, the after tax cost of this interest would be reduced to $4,900 [($10,000)(1 - .51)].

Mr. Malone is in the 51 percent tax bracket and, if the interest is not deductible, $20,408 [$10,000 ÷ (1 - .51)] of before tax salary would be required to provide the necessary $10,000 in after tax funds. If the interest is deductible, the Company will only have to provide for the $4,900 after tax cost of the loan to Mr. Malone, an amount of $10,000 [$4,900 ÷ (1 - .51)]. The annual cost to the Company of providing for this alternative under both assumptions would be as follows:

	Not Deductible	Deductible
Gross Salary Increase [$10,000 ÷ (1 - .51)]	$20,408	
Gross Salary Increase [$4,900 ÷ (1 - .51)]		$10,000
Reduction In Corporate Taxes		
[(25%)($20,408)]	(5,102)	
[(25%)($10,000)]		(2,500)
Net Cost To Company - Additional Salary	$15,306	$ 7,500

Cost Of Providing Interest Free Loan

Mr. Malone would be assessed a taxable benefit on the loan in the amount of imputed interest at the Regulation 4301 rate. The benefit would amount to $4,000 [(2%)($200,000)] for one year. In order to make the two alternatives comparable, if the interest is not deductible, it is necessary to recognize that Mr. Malone would pay an additional $2,040 [(51%)($4,000)] in taxes on this benefit and, as a consequence, the Company would have to pay him an additional $4,163 [$2,040 ÷ (1 - .51)] in salary to provide for this outflow of funds.

If the interest is deductible, the imputed interest would be deemed interest paid. As he is using all of the funds provided to produce investment income, the full amount would be deductible, resulting in no net change in taxes. If this is the case, this alternative only requires looking at the cost of the loan to the company.

The annual cost to the Company of the loan alternative under both assumptions can be calculated as follows:

	Not Deductible	Deductible
Gross Salary Increase [$2,040 ÷ (1 - .51)]	$ 4,163	N/A
Reduction In Corporate Taxes [(25%)($4,163)]	(1,041)	N/A
Lost Earnings On Funds Loaned [(18%)($200,000)]	36,000	$36,000
Corporate Taxes On Imputed Earnings [(25%)($36,000)]	(9,000)	(9,000)
Net Cost To Company - Loan	$30,122	$27,000

Conclusion

On the basis of the preceding analysis, it can be concluded that the Company should provide additional salary rather than providing Mr. Malone with an interest free loan of $200,000 whether or not his interest is deductible. This alternative results in a net annual cost to the Company which is either $14,816 ($30,122- $15,306) or $19,500 ($27,000 - $7,500) lower. Given the very high earnings rate on funds used by Technocratic, this result is not unexpected.

Self Study Solution Three - 7

Case A

2015 In 2015, the year in which the options are issued, there would be no tax consequences for Ms. Wu.

2016 The tax consequences in 2016 would be as follows:

Fair Market Value At Exercise [(12,000)($31)]	$372,000
Cost Of Shares [(12,000)($22)]	(264,000)
Employment Income Inclusion = Increase In **Net Income For Tax Purposes**	$108,000
Deduction Under ITA 110(1)(d) [(1/2)($108,000)]	(54,000)
Increase In **Taxable Income**	$ 54,000

2017 When the shares are sold in 2017, the tax consequences would be as follows:

Proceeds Of Disposition [(12,000)($28)]	$336,000
Adjusted Cost Base [(12,000)($31)]	(372,000)
Capital Loss	($ 36,000)
Inclusion Rate	1/2
Allowable Capital Loss	($ 18,000)

Ms. Wu will only be able to deduct this loss in 2017 to the extent that she has taxable capital gains on other dispositions.

Case B

2015 There are no tax consequences in 2015.
2016 There are no tax consequences in 2016.
2017 In 2017, the employment income inclusion would be as follows:

Fair Market Value At Exercise [(12,000)($31)]	$372,000
Cost Of Shares [(12,000)($22)]	(264,000)
Employment Income Inclusion = Increase In **Net Income For Tax Purposes**	$108,000
Deduction Under ITA 110(1)(d) [(1/2($108,000)]	(54,000)
Increase In **Taxable Income**	$ 54,000

In addition, there would be an allowable capital loss calculated as follows:

Proceeds Of Disposition [(12,000)($28)]	$336,000
Adjusted Cost Base [(12,000)($31)]	(372,000)
Capital Loss	($ 36,000)
Inclusion Rate	1/2
Allowable Capital Loss	($ 18,000)

Ms. Wu will only be able to deduct this loss in 2017 to the extent that she has taxable capital gains on other dispositions.

Self Study Solution Three - 8

Case A - Canadian Controlled Private Corporation

- Year of granting - No tax effect.
- Year of exercise - No tax effect.
- Year of sale - The tax effects would be as follows:

Fair Market Value Of Shares Acquired [($8.30)(2,500)]	$20,750.00
Cost Of Shares [($8.00)(2,500)]	(20,000.00)
Employment Income	$ 750.00
Taxable Capital Gain [(2,500)($8.55 - $8.30)(1/2)]	312.50
Increase In **Net Income For Tax Purposes**	$1,062.50
Deduction Under ITA 110(1)(d) [(1/2)($750)]	(375.00)
Increase In **Taxable Income**	$ 687.50

Case B - Canadian Public Company

- Year of granting - No tax effect.
- Year of exercise - As the option price was greater than the fair market value of the shares at the time the options were issued, the ITA 110(1)(d) deduction can be taken. The results for this year would be as follows:

Fair Market Value Of Shares Acquired [($8.30)(2,500)]	$20,750.00
Cost Of Shares [($8.00)(2,500)]	(20,000.00)
Employment Income = Increase In **Net Income For Tax Purposes**	$ 750.00
Deduction Under ITA 110(1)(d) [(1/2)($750)]	(375.00)
Increase In **Taxable Income**	$ 375.00

- Year of sale - The taxable capital gain would be both the increase in **Net Income For Tax Purposes** and the increase in **Taxable Income** for the year. The taxable capital gain would be calculated as follows:

Taxable Capital Gain [(2,500)($8.55 - $8.30)(1/2)]	$312.50

Case C - Canadian Public Company

- Year of granting - No tax effect.
- Year of exercise - As the option price was less than the fair market value of the shares at the time the options were issued, the ITA 110(1)(d) deduction from Taxable Income is not available. The tax effects would be as follows:

Fair Market Value Of Shares Acquired [($8.30)(2,500)]	$20,750.00
Cost Of Shares [($8.00)(2,500)]	(20,000.00)
Employment Income = Increase In **Net Income For Tax Purposes**	$ 750.00
Deduction Under ITA 110(1)(d)	Nil
Increase In Net Income And **Taxable Income**	$ 750.00

• Year of sale - The taxable capital gain would be both the increase in **Net Income For Tax Purposes** and the increase in **Taxable Income** for the year. The taxable capital gain would be calculated as follows:

Taxable Capital Gain [(2,500)($8.55 - $8.30)(1/2)]	$312.50

Case D - Canadian Controlled Private Corporation

The required information under the assumption that Borden Ltd. is a Canadian controlled private corporation is as follows:

• Year of granting and exercise - No tax effect.
• Year of sale - As the option price was less than the fair market value of the shares at the time the options were granted, no deduction is available under ITA 110(1)(d). However, Ms. Balzac held the shares for two years after their acquisition and, as a consequence, she can claim a deduction against employment income under ITA 110(1)(d.1). The tax effects would be as follows:

Fair Market Value Of Shares Acquired [($8.30)(2,500)]	$20,750.00
Cost Of Shares [($8.00)(2,500)]	(20,000.00)
Employment Income	$ 750.00
Taxable Capital Gain [(2,500)($8.55 - $8.30)(1/2)]	312.50
Increase In **Net Income For Tax Purposes**	$ 1,062.50
Deduction Under ITA 110(1)(d)	N/A
Deduction Under ITA 110(1)(d.1) [(1/2)($750)]	(375.00)
Increase In **Taxable Income**	$ 687.50

Self Study Solution Three - 9

Salary From Maritime Trust [(6/12)($105,000)]		$ 52,500
Salary From Bolten [(6/12)($90,000)]		45,000
Total Salaries		$ 97,500
Maritime Trust Stock Options (Note 1):		
Market Price Of Shares [(5,000)($16)]	$80,000	
Option Price [(5,000)($15)]	(75,000)	5,000
Bolten Financial Services Stock Options (Note 1)		Nil
Automobile Benefit (Note 2):		
Standby Charge [(2%)($40,000)(4)(6,668/6,668)]	$3,200	
Operating Cost Benefit - Lesser Of:		
• [(10,000)($0.25)] = $2,500		
• [(1/2)($3,200)] = $1,600	1,600	4,800
Loan Benefit (Note 3)		2,000
Net Employment Income		$109,300

Notes:

1. As Bolten Financial Services is a Canadian controlled private corporation, the exercise of the option to purchase its common stock does not result in a taxable benefit at the time of exercise. Since Maritime Trust Inc. is a public company, the exercise of the option to purchase its common stock does result in a taxable benefit at the time of exercise. Mr. Jurgens has a stock option deduction equal to $2,500 [(1/2)($5,000)] under ITA 110(1)(d) created by the exercise of the Maritime Trust stock option. However, the stock option deduction would reduce Taxable Income and would not affect net employment income. The Bolten stock option income inclusion of $2,000 [(1,000)($22 - $20)] and deduction of $1,000 [(1/2)($2,000)] are both deferred until the shares are sold.

2. As Mr. Jurgens' employment related milage is more than 50 percent of the total milage, he can make use of the reduced standby charge formula. In this case, however, his personal usage exceeded the 6,668 [(4)(1,667)] kilometer maximum usage allowed by the reduction, so the reduction is nil. His employment related milage is more than 50 percent of the total and, as a consequence, he can elect to calculate the operating cost benefit as one-half of the standby charge. Since this is less than the amount determined through the usual calculation, it would be the operating cost benefit.

3. The imputed interest on the interest free loan must be included in employment income under the requirements of ITA 6(9), a benefit which is defined in ITA 80.4(1). The amount of the benefit is $2,000 [(2%)($200,000)(6/12)]. Note that there is a deduction under ITA 110(1)(j) for the amount of this benefit which relates to an interest free home relocation loan of $25,000. However, this is a deduction in the calculation of Taxable Income and will not affect the amount of net employment income.

4. The interest and dividend income is not included in the calculation of net employment income.

Self Study Solution Three - 10

Ms. Kline's net employment income for the year would be calculated as follows:

Gross Salary	$73,500
Registered Pension Plan Contributions	(2,400)
Automobile Benefit (Note One)	270
Contributions To Group Disability Plan (Note Two)	Nil
Disability Insurance Benefit (Note Two)	1,400
Professional Dues	(1,650)
Stock Option Benefit [(200)($70 - $50)] (Note Three)	4,000
Net Employment Income	$75,120

Note One Based on the fact that Ms. Kline's employment related usage is more than 50 percent of total usage, the automobile benefit is calculated as follows:

Standby Charge [(2/3)(11)($700 - $50)(3,000/18,337*)]	$ 780
Operating Cost Benefit - Lesser Of:	
• [(3,000)($0.25)] = $750	
• [(1/2)($780)] = $390	390
Total Before Payments	$1,170
Payments For Personal Use [(3,000)($0.30)]	(900)
Taxable Benefit	$ 270

*[(11)(1,667)]

As Ms. Kline's employment related usage is more than 50 percent, she can elect to use one-half the standby charge as the operating cost benefit.

Note Two   The contributions to the group disability plan are not deductible, but can be applied against the $1,800 received under the plan during the year. Since the employer's contributions to this plan are not a taxable benefit, the $1,800 in benefits received must be included in employment income. However, this benefit can be reduced by the $400 ($225 + $175) in total contributions that she has made in 2016 and 2017.

Note Three   Although Ms. Kline would qualify for the deduction of one-half of the stock option benefit under ITA 110(1)(d), it is a deduction from Taxable Income and would not affect the calculation of the required figure in this problem, net employment income.

Self Study Solution Three - 11

As Ms. Firth paid all of her own operating expenses, there is no taxable benefit for vehicle operating costs. However, she has to include the $7,200 car allowance in income. Given this, she can deduct a pro rata share of her actual expenses. The deduction would be $5,728 [($6,200)(85,000 km ÷ 92,000 km)].

Ms. Firth's total entertainment, meal, and travel expenses that would be deductible under ITA 8(1)(f) are as follows:

Entertainment Expenses [(1/2)($6,500)]	$3,250
Travel Meals [(1/2)($1,300)]	650
Lodging	3,500
Automobile Operating Costs [($6,200)(85,000 ÷92,000)]	5,728
Total Salesperson Expenses	$13,128

As this total is less than her commission income of $14,000, they can all be deducted under ITA 8(1)(f).

Ms. Firth's net employment income for the year would be calculated as follows:

Gross Salary		$72,000
Commission Income		14,000
Additions:		
Disability Insurance Receipts,		
Less Employee's Premium ($2,000 - $250)	$ 1,750	
Car Allowance	7,200	
Automobile Benefit (Note 1)	2,471	
Term Life Insurance Benefit [($1,350)(2/3)]	900	
Low Interest Loan Benefit [($400,000)(2%) - $3,000]	5,000	
Gift (Note 2)	Nil	
Stock Option Benefit [(1,000)($7 - $5)] (Note 3)	2,000	
Tennis Club Membership (Note 4)	Nil	
Travel Allowance	3,600	22,921
Deductions:		
Registered Pension Plan Contributions (Note 5)	($ 3,200)	
Salesperson Expenses (Preceding Calculation)	(13,128)	(16,328)
Net Employment Income		$92,593

Note 1 The personal benefit on the company car would be calculated as follows:

Reduced Standby Charge [(2%)($58,000)(11)(7,000/18,337*)]	$4,871
Operating Costs Benefit	Nil
Total Benefit	$4,871
Less: Payments Withheld By Employer	(2,400)
Taxable Benefit	$2,471

* [(1,667)(11)]

Note 2 Employers can provide their employees with a non-cash gift with a value of less than $500 without creating a taxable benefit. The mini iPad costs less than $500.

Note 3 Although Ms. Firth would qualify for the deduction of one-half of the stock option benefit under ITA 110(1)(d), it is a deduction from Taxable Income and would not affect the calculation of net employment income.

Note 4 The $2,500 membership to the Mountain Tennis Club paid by the Company for Ms. Firth is not a taxable benefit since the primary beneficiary appears to be the Company.

Note 5 Contributions made to a registered pension plan under the terms of the plan are deductible. The matching contributions made by the employer are not a taxable benefit.

Other Excluded Items Other items not included and the reason for their exclusion:

- Federal and provincial income taxes withheld are not deductible.

- The purchase of Canada Savings Bonds is a non-deductible capital expenditure. Any interest charged on the payroll deduction purchase is deductible from Net Income For Tax Purposes, but does not affect employment income.

Self Study Solution Three - 12

Mr. Jones' net employment income would be calculated as follows:

Salary			$25,800
Taxable Benefit From Fishing Trip			2,450
Commission Income			
Sales Commissions		$47,700	
Deductions:			
Airline Tickets	($2,350)		
Office Supplies	(415)		
Client Entertainment			
[(50%)($1,750)]	(875)		
CCA (Note 1)	(2,520)		
Operating Costs (Note 2)	(5,040)	(11,200)	36,500
Net Employment Income			$64,750

Note 1 The deductible capital cost allowance on the car would be calculated as follows:

Full Capital Cost Allowance*	$ 3,600
Employment Related Usage Proportion (35,000/50,000)	70%
Deductible Amount	$ 2,520

*While this subject is not covered until Chapter 5, the maximum capital cost allowance would be calculated as follows:

$$\$3,600 = [(\$24,000)(30\%)(1/2)]$$

Note 2   As the car was used 30 percent on personal matters, only $5,040 [(70%)($7,200)] in operating costs would be deductible.

Other Notes

- The laptop computer is a capital expenditure and is not deductible as an expense. Since an employee cannot deduct CCA except for an automobile, musical instrument, or aircraft, the purchase of the laptop computer would not have any effect on either employment income or taxes payable.

- The payment for Blue Cross would be eligible for the medical expenses tax credit, but would not be deductible in the calculation of net employment income. The life insurance premiums would not have any effect on either employment income or taxes payable.

- Discounts for employees on merchandise normally sold by an employer are not generally considered to be a taxable benefit.

Self Study Solution Three - 13

Part A

As Mr. Worthy's income includes commissions, he has a choice of deducting his expenses under a combination of ITA 8(1)(f), (i), and (j) or, alternatively under a combination of ITA 8(1)(h), (h.1), (i), and (j).

Deductions under ITA 8(1)(f) are limited to the amount of commissions earned. Alternatively, traveling costs and motor vehicle costs other than capital costs can be deducted under ITA 8(1)(h) and ITA 8(1)(h.1). Deductions under these provisions are not limited to commission income. As discussed in the text, he cannot use both ITA 8(1)(f) and the combination of ITA 8(1)(h) and (h.1).

As the deduction under ITA 8(1)(f) is limited by commission income, alternative calculations are required to determine the maximum deduction. In the calculations which follow, we have minimized the effect of the commission income limit by listing any item that can be deducted under either ITA 8(1)(f) or ITA 8(1)(i) or (j) under the ITA 8(1)(i) and (j) column.

For example, house utilities and maintenance could be deducted under either ITA 8(1)(f) or 8(1)(i). We have included them under ITA 8(1)(i) in order to minimize the deductions that are limited by commission income.

The required calculations are as follows:

	ITA 8(1)(f) (Limited To $11,000)	ITA 8(1) (h) and (h.1)	ITA 8(1) (i) and (j)
Work Space In The Home Costs			
Monthly Charge For Residential Line	-	-	-
Long Distance Telephone Charges	-	-	$ 400
Cellular Phone Airtime	-	-	800
Office Supplies	-	-	295
House Utilities	-	-	485
House Maintenance	-	-	255
House Insurance	$ 70	-	-
Property Taxes	265	-	-
Capital Cost Allowance - House	-	-	-
Mortgage Interest	-	-	-
Automobile Costs:			
Operating Costs [(80%)($2,700)]	2,160	2,160	-
Car Interest [(80%)($2,300)]	-	-	1,840
Car CCA [(80%)($2,450)]	-	-	1,960
Entertainment			
Deductible Portion [(50%)($2,550)]	1,275	-	-
Travel Costs			
Hotels	2,850	$2,850	-
Deductible Portion Of Meals			
[(50%)($900)]	450	450	-
Office Furniture			
Interest	-	-	-
Capital Cost Allowance	-	-	-
Total	$7,070	$5,460	$6,035

Using the preceding calculations, Mr. Worthy's minimum net employment income can be calculated as follows:

Salary		$65,000
Commissions	$11,000	
Expenses Under ITA 8(1)(f) - Limited To Commissions	(7,070)	3,930
Total		$68,930
Expenses Under ITA 8(1)(i) and (j)		(6,035)
Net Employment Income		$62,895

Expenses in excess of commission income cannot be deducted under ITA 8(1)(f). Since the total of the expenses is less than the commissions of $11,000, they can all be deducted. The deduction of automobile capital costs (CCA and financing costs) under ITA 8(1)(j) is permitted without regard to other provisions used.

Notes:

1. The monthly telephone charge is not deductible. The long distance charges and cellular telephone airtime to clients can be deducted. The deduction for supplies can be deducted under ITA 8(1)(f) or (i). They have been deducted under ITA 8(1)(i), which is not limited by the commission income.

2. Only 50 percent of entertainment and meals when traveling are deductible.

3. ITA 8(1)(f) prohibits the deduction of amounts associated with capital assets except as they are permitted under ITA 8(1)(j) and ITA 8(1)(p). These latter Paragraphs only permit interest or capital cost allowance to be deducted when it is related to an automobile, aircraft, or musical instrument. Therefore, the interest and the capital cost allowance on the house and the office furniture would not be deductible against employment income. This is a good illustration of the importance of distinguishing between employment income and business income. While these amounts cannot be deducted against employment income, they would likely be deductible against business income.

4. As the car is used 20 percent for personal purposes, this proportion of the operating costs, capital cost allowance, and interest costs will not be deductible.

5. The deduction for work space in the home costs has been split between ITA 8(1)(i) and (f). Since the maintenance portion can be deducted under ITA 8(1)(i) by any employee, it is not limited by the commission income. The insurance and property tax components are limited as they can only be deducted under ITA 8(1)(f). A limitation, which is not illustrated in this problem, prevents the deduction of work space in the home costs from creating an employment loss. If any of these costs had not been deductible during the current year, they could be deducted against employment income in any subsequent year as long as a loss is not created or increased by their deduction.

6. Mr. Worthy's employer must sign Form T2200 certifying that Mr. Worthy is required to incur travel expenses and maintain his own work space. Mr. Worthy must retain this signed form with his records in order to deduct car and home office expenses.

Part B

If Mr. Worthy deducted the ITA 8(1)(f) expenses, they would be limited to his commission income of $4,000. Alternatively, he can use the combination of ITA 8(1)(h) and (h.1). His minimum net employment income under both alternatives can be calculated as follows:

	ITA 8(1)(f)	ITA 8(1)(h)(h.1)
Salary	$65,000	$65,000
Commissions	4,000	4,000
Expenses Under ITA 8(1)(f) - Limited To Commissions	(4,000)	Nil
Subtotal	$65,000	$69,000
Expenses Under ITA 8(1)(h) and (h.1)	Nil	(5,460)
Expenses Under ITA 8(1)(i) and (j)	(6,035)	(6,035)
Net Employment Income	$58,965	$57,505

Using the combination of ITA 8(1)(h), (h.1), (i), and (j) produces a lower net employment income figure. Note that when this approach is used, work space in the home costs are limited to utilities and maintenance. Further, there is no deduction for entertainment costs. However, this approach results in deductions totalling $1,460 ($5,460 - $4,000) more than the amount available using ITA 8(1)(f), (i), and (j) due to the effect of the commission income limit.

Self Study Solution Three - 14

Mitch Lesner's net employment income would be calculated as follows;

Item 1 - Signing Bonus (Note 1)	$10,000
Item 1 - Salary Received (Note 1)	62,550
Item 1 - RPP Contributions Withheld	(1,200)
Item 1 - Other Items (Note 1)	Nil
Item 2 - Bonus Received (Note 2)	2,000
Item 3 - Counseling Services (Note 3)	Nil
Item 4 - Group Medical Coverage (Note 4)	Nil
Item 5 - Employer Contribution To RPP (Note 5)	Nil
Item 6 - Professional Dues Paid (Note 6)	(785)
Item 6 - Employer Reimbursement Of Professional Dues (Note 6)	628
Item 7 - Wedding Gifts (Note 7)	Nil
Item 8 - Squash Club Membership (Note 8)	Nil
Item 9 - Housing Loss Reimbursement (Note 9)	1,300
Item 10 - Imputed Interest On Housing Loan (Note 10)	170
Item 11 - Stock Option Benefit (Note 11)	1,280
Item 12 - Automobile Benefit (Note 12)	741
Item 13 - Stationery And Supplies	(129)
Item 13 - Long Distance Calls	(74)
Item 13 - Home Office (Note 13)	(563)
Item 14 - Home Office Allowance (Note 14)	1,500
Net Employment Income	$77,418

Note 1 Amounts received prior to, during or after employment are required to be included in employment income when received.

Salary and other forms of remuneration such as bonuses are included in income when received regardless of when earned.

Income taxes, CPP and EI withheld are not deductible. Note, however, that the CPP and EI are eligible for a non-refundable tax credit that will reduce Tax Payable.

Note 2 Only the $2,000 amount of the bonus that was received in 2017 will be included in that year's Net Income For Tax Purposes. The remaining $5,450 will not be included in Net Income For Tax Purposes until it is received in 2018.

Note 3 Employer provided mental health counseling services are not considered to be a taxable benefit.

Note 4 Group medical plans are generally referred to as Private Health Insurance Plans. Employer paid premiums for such plans are not considered to be a taxable benefit.

Note 5 Employer contributions to RPPs are not considered to be a taxable benefit.

Note 6 The reimbursement of employee professional dues is considered a taxable benefit, but the employee is generally entitled to an employment expense deduction for annual professional membership dues under ITA 8(1)(i).

Note 7 Non-cash gifts from employers that total less than $500 per year are not considered taxable benefits. The employer's share of the wedding gifts was $425.

Note 8 Fees for club memberships where the primary advantage is to the employer are not considered to be a taxable benefit.

Note 9 Employer-reimbursed housing losses fall into two categories – regular housing losses and eligible housing losses. Eligible housing losses occur when there is an eligible relocation which generally means a relocation or move the expenses of which would qualify for a moving expense deduction had they been paid by the employee. In this case the move is an eligible relocation meaning that the reimbursement qualifies as an eligible housing loss. The employer reimbursed $17,600 [(80%)($22,000)]. The taxable portion of the loss reimbursement is $1,300 [(1/2)($17,600 - $15,000)]. The remaining tax free amount of $16,300 can be calculated as ($17,600 - $1,300) or [$15,000 + (1/2)($17,600 - $15,000)].

Note 10   When an employee receives an interest-free or low interest loan an imputed interest benefit is calculated. The interest benefit is $170 [(1%)($200,000)(31/365)]. Note that the alternative calculation, based on months outstanding, would result in a value of $167 [(1%)($200,000) ÷ 12]. It appears that this value would be accepted by the CRA.

There is no reduction in that amount since Mitch is not required to repay any of the interest. As this loan would qualify as a home relocation loan, Mitch will claim a home relocation loan deduction in the calculation of Taxable Income. However, this would have no effect on the required net employment income calculation.

Note 11   Despite the fact that the option price was 20 percent below fair market value, the issuance of the stock options does not create employment income. However, when he exercises the option by purchasing shares, there is a benefit as follows:

Market Value At Exercise Date ($12,800 ÷ 80%)	$16,000
Option Price	(12,800)
Value of Benefit (200 Shares)	$ 3,200
Per Share Benefit ($3,200 ÷ 200)	$16 Per Share

As Oxford Associates is a CCPC, this benefit can be deferred until the shares are sold. As 80 shares are sold, there will be a 2017 net employment income inclusion of $1,280 [(80)($16)]. Note that, while this is not relevant to the determination of net employment income, no deduction would be available under either ITA 110(1)(d) or 110(1)(d.1) as the option price will always be less than the fair market value at the time the option was granted.

In addition to the employment income inclusion, there is a taxable capital gain of $1,280 {[1/2][$8,960 - (80/200)($16,000)]}. However, capital gains are not a component of net employment income.

Note 12   The kilometers driven in the year total 19,252 (19,414 − 162), of which 5,198 are personal and 14,054 (19,252 - 5,198) are employment related. Since the employment related driving accounts for more than 50 percent (14,054 ÷ 19,252 = 73%), a reduced standby charge is available. The automobile benefit would be calculated as follows:

Standby Charge [(2/3)(8)($430)(5,198 ÷ 13,336*)]	$ 894
Operating Cost Benefit - Lesser Of:	
• [($0.25)(5,198)] = $1,300	
• [(1/2)($894) = $447	447
Total Benefit	$1,341
Reimbursement To Employer [(8)($75)]	(600)
Net Benefit	$ 741

*[(8)(1,667)]

Note 13 Based on floor space, the home office occupies 8.5 percent of the apartment [100 ÷ 1,176]. The work space in the home expenses that may be claimed for the period June 1 to November 30 are the following:

Rent Paid [(6)($960)]	$5,760
Electricity Paid [($870)(6 ÷ 8.5 Months)]	614
Paint	253
Total Eligible Expenses	$6,627
Home Office Use	8.5%
Deductible Expense	$ 563

Note 14 Allowances received are included in employment income unless the allowance is specifically excluded by ITA 6(1)(b). There is no exclusion for this allowance. The amount is $1,500 [(6)($250)].

Chapter 3 Learning Objectives

After completing Chapter 3, you should be able to:

1. Explain the basic concept of employment income (paragraph [P hereafter] 3-1 to 3-6).
2. Explain the reasons for using, and rules associated with, bonus arrangements for employees (P 3-7 to 3-13).
3. Distinguish between an employee and a self-employed individual earning business income and list the advantages and disadvantages of both classifications (P 3-14 to 3-44).
4. Explain how salaries and fringe benefits in general are taxed (P 3-45 to 3-55).
5. List the benefits that can be excluded from employment income under ITA 6(1)(a) and the benefits that must be included in income under the other Paragraphs in ITA 6(1) (P 3-56 to 3-59).

6. Apply the content of IT-470R with respect to the tax status of the various employee benefits described in the Bulletin (P 3-60 to 3-63).
7. Explain the basic elements of tax planning for employee benefits (P 3-64 to 3-76).
8. Describe the effects of GST/HST/PST on taxable benefits (P 3-77 and 3-78).
9. Calculate the standby charge and operating cost benefits that apply to employees who are provided with an automobile that is leased or owned by their employer (P 3-79 to 3-122).

10. Explain basic tax planning for company cars (P 3-123 and 3-124).
11. Explain the tax treatment of allowances that are provided by employers to their employees for travel costs (P 3-125 to 3-142).
12. Describe the tax status of various types of insurance benefits that are provided by employers to their employees (P 3-143 to 3-154).
13. Calculate the tax consequences of low-rate or interest free loans to employees (P 3-155 to 3-159).
14. Calculate the tax consequences that result from employees receiving and exercising stock options, and from the subsequent sale of the acquired shares (P 3-160 to 3-179).

15. List and describe other inclusions in employment income (P 3-180 to 3-188).
16. List and describe specific deductions against employment income that are listed in ITA 8 (P 3-189 to 3-209).
17. Explain how deductible work space in the home costs for employees are calculated (P 3-210 to 3-215).

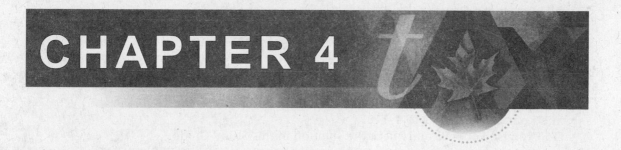

How To Work Through Chapter 4

We recommend the following approach in dealing with the material in this chapter:

Note On Changes For 2017
- Read the Note explaining important changes effective for 2017.

Taxable Income Of Individuals
- Read the beginning of the Chapter to paragraph 4-12 (in the textbook).
- Do Exercise Four-1 (in the textbook) and check the solution in this Study Guide.
- Read paragraph 4-13.

Federal And Provincial Tax Payable Before Credits
- Read paragraph 4-14 to 4-26.
- Do Exercise Four-2 and check the solution in this Study Guide.
- Read paragraph 4-27 to 4-31.

Credits Against Tax Payable - Calculating The Amount
- Read paragraph 4-32 to 4-36.

Spousal, Eligible Dependant And Canada Caregiver For Child Tax Credits
- Read paragraph 4-37 to 4-42.
- Do Exercise Four-3 and check the solution in this Study Guide.
- Do Self Study Problem Four-1 which is available on the Companion Website and check the solution in this Study Guide.
- Read paragraph 4-43 to 4-52.

Basic Personal And Caregiver Tax Credits
- Read paragraph 4-53 to 4-63.
- Do Exercises Four-4 to Four-6 and check the solution in this Study Guide.
- Read paragraph 4-64 and 4-65.
- Do Exercise Four-7 and check the solution in this Study Guide.

Age, Pension, Canada Employment And Adoption Expenses Tax Credits
- Read paragraph 4-66 and 4-67.
- Do Exercise Four-8 and check the solution in this Study Guide.
- Read paragraph 4-68 to 4-80.
- Do Exercise Four-9 and check the solution in this Study Guide.

Public Transit Passes And Home Accessibility Tax Credits
- Read paragraph 4-81 to 4-96.
- Do Exercise Four-10 and check the solution in this Study Guide.

First Time Home Buyer's And
Volunteer Firefighters And Search And Rescue Workers Tax Credits
- Read paragraph 4-97 to 4-103.

Charitable Donations Credit
- Read paragraph 4-104 to 4-111.
- Do Exercise Four-11 and check the solution in this Study Guide.
- Read paragraph 4-112 to 4-118.
- Do Exercise Four-12 and check the solution in this Study Guide.

Medical Expense Credit
- Read paragraph 4-119 to 4-129.
- Do Exercise Four-13 and check the solution in this Study Guide.

Disability Credit
- Read paragraph 4-130 to 4-137.
- Do Exercise Four-14 and check the solution in this Study Guide.
- Read paragraph 4-138 to 4-140.

Education Related Credits Including Carry Forwards And Transfers
- Read paragraph 4-141 to 4-148.
- Do Exercise Four-15 and check the solution in this Study Guide.
- Read paragraph 4-149 to 4-158.
- Do Exercise Four-16 and check the solutions in this Study Guide.

Employment Insurance And Canada Pension Plan Tax Credits
- Read paragraph 4-159 to 4-165.

Credit Transfers To A Spouse Or Common-Law Partner
- Read paragraph 4-166 to 4-168.
- Do Exercise Four-17 and check the solution in this Study Guide.
- Do Self Study Problems Four-2 and Four-3 and check the solutions in this Study Guide.

Political Contributions Credit
- Read paragraph 4-169 to 4-172.
- Do Exercise Four-18 and check the solution in this Study Guide.

Labour Sponsored Venture Capital Corporation (LSVCC) Credit
- Read paragraph 4-173 to 4-177.
- Do Self Study Problems Four-4 and Four-5 and check the solutions in this Study Guide.

Refundable Credits - GST And Refundable Medical Expense Supplement
- Read paragraph 4-178 to 4-189.
- Do Exercise Four-19 and check the solution in this Study Guide.

Refundable Credits - Working Income Tax Benefit And Teacher School Supply
- Read paragraph 4-190 to 4-196.

EI And OAS Repayment (Clawback)
- Read paragraph 4-197 to 4-207.
- Do Exercise Four-20 and check the solution in this Study Guide.

Comprehensive Example
- Read paragraph 4-208.
- Do Self Study Problems Four-6 to Four-8 and check the solutions in this Study Guide.

Sample Personal Tax Return For Chapter 4
- Read the Sample Personal Tax Return For Chapter 4 found in this Chapter of this Study Guide. The complete tax returns are available on the Companion Website in two formats, a T1 ProFile return file and a .PDF file.

Tax Software Self Study Problem
- Read the Suggestions For Working With ProFile Software found in this Chapter of this Study Guide.
- Do Tax Software Self Study Problem - Chapter 4 using the ProFile T1 Software. The Self Study Problem is found in this Chapter of this Study Guide. The complete tax return is available on the Companion Website.

To Complete This Chapter
- If you would like more practice in problem solving, do the Supplementary Self Study Problems for the chapter. These problems and solutions are available on the Companion Website.
- Review the Key Terms Used In This Chapter in the textbook at the end of Chapter 4. Consult the Glossary for the meaning of any key terms you do not know.
- Test yourself with the Chapter 4 Glossary Flashcards available on the Companion Website.
- Ensure you have achieved the Chapter 4 Learning Objectives listed in this Study Guide.
- As a review, we recommend you view the PowerPoint presentation for Chapter 4 that is on the Companion Website.

Practice Examination
- Write the Practice Examination for Chapter 4 that is on the Companion Website. Mark your examination using the Practice Examination Solution that is also on the Companion Website.

Sample Personal Tax Return For Chapter 4

The following example contains a T1 individual income tax returns completed using the ProFile T1 Personal Income Tax Program for 2016 tax returns from Intuit Canada. As software for 2017 is not yet available, this example contains 2016 rates and credits.

The updated 2017 filing version of the ProFile software will be available in January, 2018. Non-filing versions will be available prior to that date, but include a number of 2017 draft forms that have not yet been updated. On installation, the program defaults to check for updates, so non-filing versions may be installed automatically. In January, 2018, after the first 2017 filing version is released, the updated 2017 version of this sample return will be available on the Companion website at:

www.pearsoncanada.ca/byrdchen/ctp2018

This example is expanded in Chapter 11 to contain other components of Taxable Income and Tax Payable. In the following example, the relevant T1 schedule or ProFile form name is provided in square brackets to make it easier for users to find where the information is input.

Sample Files On Companion Website

To View The Tax Return Files

The complete sample tax returns are available on the Companion Website in two versions, a T1 ProFile return file and a .PDF file.

To view the ProFile return files (files with a .16T extension), you must have the ProFile program installed. For information on how to obtain the program for free, see the Companion Website.

To view the .PDF files, you must have the Adobe Reader program installed. This program can be installed for free from the Adobe website (www.adobe.com).

Tips To Increase The Benefits From Viewing The ProFile Files

When viewing the sample return ProFile file, we suggest the following:

- Press <F1> on any ProFile form or field to display related information in the help system. In ProFile dialog boxes, click the [?] symbol in the top right corner, then click any element for help on that item.

- By pressing <F4> you will open the Form Explorer. In the categories of forms appearing in the shaded box on the left, if you choose "A. Used" near the bottom of the column, all the forms that have calculations for the return will be shown. You can then double click on the form itself to view it.

- Right clicking on a number in a field shows a variety of options, including the form or schedule where the amount originated from.

- Clicking on "Show Auditor" under the "Audit" list will display any warnings or potential errors.

For students who would like more assistance in using the software, we have provided "Suggestions For Working With ProFile Software" in this Study Guide following this example.

Sample Problem Data

DISCLAIMER: All characters appearing in this example are fictitious. Any resemblance to real persons, living or dead, is purely coincidental.

George Pilot (SIN 527-000-145) is a married, semi-retired air force pilot living in Banff, Alberta. His wife, Deborah (SIN 130-692-544) was mauled by a grizzly bear while hiking 3 years ago. The attack left her blind and limited her mobility.

They have been your clients for many years. George was born on February 24, 1965 and Deborah was born on April 10, 1969. They are both Canadian citizens.

After some discussion with George and Deborah, you confirm that they have never owned any foreign property. They both authorize the CRA to provide information to Elections Canada and authorize you to e-file their returns. They are currently living at 69 BBB Street in Banff, Alberta T9Z 0C0. Their home phone number is (403) 111-1111.

George and Deborah have three children:

- Bryan (SIN 527-000-947) was born on March 12, 2009 and had no income during the year.

- Janice (SIN 527-000-269) was born on June 6, 2003 and is in high school. She had income from babysitting totalling $400 during 2016.

- Willa (SIN 527-000-228) was born on January 22, 1997 and is attending university in Edmonton. Willa had Net Income of $3,300 during 2016.

George loves flying and was hired in February to fly fire bombers June 1 to September 30 for the provincial forest service fire control squad located in Banff.

George informs you that on February 12, 2016, he received $2 million from his mother's estate. Using some of these funds, George bought a house in Banff. The remainder of the funds were invested with his stockbroker, $$$$ Inc. In this Chapter 4 version of the example, assume there is no investment income from these funds.

Deborah had no income other than the Universal Child Care Benefit of $720 during the year. [RC62 on George's return]

George brings you the following receipts and documents:

1. A T4 (included in this example).

2. A T2202A "Tuition And Education Amounts Certificate" for himself from Athabasca University. It showed he was a part time student for 6 months and paid $591 in tuition for 2016. [T2202]

3. Two charitable donation receipts. One in George's name for $1,000 from the Canadian Wildlife Federation dated April 10, 2016. He has donated regularly to this registered charity. A second receipt in Deborah's name for $100 from the Canadian National Institute for the Blind (CNIB) dated December 3, 2016. This is her second donation to this registered charity. [Donations]

4. A statement from the Banff Dental Clinic that George paid a total of $1,650 during 2016. This consisted of $850 for himself on November 24, and $200 each for Deborah, Bryan, Willa and Janice on December 15. [Medical]

5. An invoice from the CNIB in Deborah's name for $375 dated December 26, 2016 for computer peripherals designed exclusively for a person who is blind to use a computer. She had obtained a prescription from her doctor specifying her need for this equipment. [Medical]

6. Twelve monthly bus passes that were purchased during 2016 by Janice for $30 per month. [OtherCredits]

7. An agreement of purchase and sale for a house at 69 BBB St. in Banff. The purchase price was $800,000 and the invoice for legal fees totalled $1,200. The deal closed March 31, 2016 and George paid the purchase price of the house in cash. George and his family had been living in a rented townhouse for the last 5 years. Prior to that George had owned a house, but it went to his ex-wife in the divorce settlement. Deborah has never owned a principal residence. [OtherCredits for the Home Buyers' Credit.]

8. George spent $14,700 during 2016 on various permanent modifications to the house. His goal for these changes was to allow Deborah to be more mobile inside and outside the house (ex., outside ramps and railings in the halls and stairways) and to reduce the risk of harm to her (a walk-in bathtub). George has detailed invoices for the renovations. Since Deborah's mobility impairment is not severe, these expenditures do not qualify as allowable medical expenses. [Schedule 12]

9. An instalment statement for 2016 that showed that George had paid the CRA instalments of $1,500 on September 14 and December 14 ($3,000 in total). These were the instalments requested by the CRA for the year due to his self-employed income in the previous year. [OtherCredits]

General Notes

- You must open Deborah's return (F5) to claim her disability tax credit on the info page even if she is not filing. If you don't, Deborah's disability tax credit can't be transferred to George.
- When the Universal Child Care Benefits are input on George's Form RC62, the amounts

will be transferred to show on S2 as Deborah's income.

- Inheritances are not taxable.
- Due to his low Net Income For Tax Purposes, George is eligible for the refundable medical expense supplement and the working income tax benefit.
- Although George could consider carrying forward his medical expenses because his non-refundable tax credits are greater than his tax payable, if he did so, he would not receive the refundable medical expense supplement.
- Since Willa is over 17 years of age, her medical expenses are reduced by 3 percent of her Net Income For Tax Purposes.
- Due to his nil Tax Payable, George's charitable donations and his education related credits are all carried forward.

Item Specific Notes

- (Item 3) Since George has donated regularly to a charity and Deborah has previously donated to the CNIB, he will not be eligible for the first-time donor's super credit on Schedule 9. For couples, the CRA's administrative practices permit either spouse to claim some or all of the donations made by the couple. This is not relevant in this version as the donations are carried forward.

- (Item 5) Both ITA 118.2 and Income Tax Folio S1-F1-C1 clearly state that medical expenses can only be deducted by the individual who paid for them. However, in the T1 Guide, this rule is contradicted for couples. According to this Guide, either spouse can claim the medical expense credit, without regard to who actually paid for the expenses. This administrative position is used in practice. As a result, George is claiming the amount Deborah paid for the computer peripherals.

- (Item 7) The Home Buyers' Tax Credit of $750 [(15%)($5,000)] is available since George had been living in a rented town house for five years and neither he nor Deborah had another principal residence. However, since George's non-refundable tax credits already exceed his Tax Payable, he cannot take advantage of this credit and it cannot be carried forward.

- (Item 8) George's receipts for the expenses eligible for the Home Accessibility Credit total more than the $10,000 maximum for the year on Schedule 12. As a result the maximum credit of $1,500 [(15%)($10,000)] is available. However, since George's non-refundable tax credits already exceed his Tax Payable, he cannot take advantage of this credit either and it cannot be carried forward.

Tax Planning Points

- Willa should file a return in order to receive the GST credit and to help her keep track of her tuition credit carry forward.

- (Item 9) George has paid installments based on the CRA's Instalment Reminders. Given the amount of his refund, they were unnecessary. George should review his estimated net tax owing periodically in the future to determine whether instalments should be paid.

Completed Tax Returns

The complete sample tax returns are available on the Companion Website in two versions, a T1 ProFile return file and a .PDF file.

Suggestions For Working With ProFile Software

Before You Start

To get the maximum benefit from using the ProFile tax software program, we strongly advise that you do the tutorial "Getting Started" included within the program under the Training tab. The data in the sample tax returns can be used in the tutorial. Also on the Training tab is access to "Other Training Options" which include online training and many how-to videos.

Creating A New T1 Return

To provide some guidance on how to use ProFile to create a simple new personal tax return, we suggest the following approach.

1. Start the ProFile software. Open a new file. Ensure that you have chosen the new file in the correct software (T1) and year (2016 or 2017 if the updated data is available).

2. By default, ProFile will open on the form "Info". Fill in the highlighted cells and answer all questions that are applicable. If you do not fill in the highlighted areas, ProFile will generate an audit message. At a minimum, you will need the following information:

   - Taxpayer's Social Insurance Number (SIN)
   - Taxpayer's first and last name
   - Address, city, province, and postal code
   - Telephone number
   - Taxpayer's birth date

   If applicable, you will also need to enter any relevant information for the spouse on the "Info" form. At a minimum, the following information will be necessary:

   - Spouse's Social Insurance Number (SIN)
   - Spouse's first and last name
   - Address, city, province, and postal code
   - Telephone number
   - Spouse's birth date

3. Using the Form Explorer (F4), go to the Dependant form and enter all relevant information about any dependants. At a minimum, the following information will be necessary:

   - Dependant's Social Insurance Number (SIN) if there is one
   - Dependant's first and last name
   - Dependant's relationship to the taxpayer
   - Dependant's birth date
   - Dependant's Net Income
   - Address, city, province, and postal code

   Note that if there are child care expenses, the information will flow here from T778. If the Dependant has tuition amounts and is not filing a tax return, the education related information should be entered on the Dependant form.

4. Using the Form Explorer (F4), open the relevant information slip form. Enter all relevant information in the appropriate forms. Some common information slip forms are:

   - T3 - Statement of Trust Income
   - T4 - Statement of Remuneration Paid
   - T5 - Statement of Investment Income
   - T2202 - Tuition and Education Amounts
   - T4AOAS - Statement of Old Age Security

5. Enter any other relevant income information on the appropriate forms. These forms may include the following:

- S3Details - Capital Gains Entry
  (this form, not Schedule 3, must be used to input details on capital dispositions)
- T2125 - Statement of Business Or Professional Activities
- T2125Asset - T2125 Asset Details
- T2125CCA - T2125 CCA Details
- T776 - Statement of Real Estate Rentals
- T776Asset - T776 Asset Details
- T776CCA - T776 CCA Details

6. Enter any relevant deduction information on the appropriate forms. These forms may include the following:

- RRSP - RRSP Deduction
- T777 - Statement of Employment Expenses (Use the jump link to T777Details in upper right hand corner of form if applicable)
- T778 - Child Care Expense Deduction
- Support - Support Payments
- Auto - Motor Vehicle Expenses
- S4 - Statement of Investment Income
  (much of the information for this schedule will be carried forward from the T3, T5, and other information slips, but a few items such as carrying charges are entered directly on Schedule 4)
- LossNetCap - Net Capital Losses (carry forward information)
- LossNonCap - Non-Capital Losses (carry forward information)

7. Enter any relevant tax credit information on the appropriate forms. These forms may include the following:

- Donations - Charitable Donations
- Medical - Medical Expenses

8. Enter any remaining relevant information in the appropriate schedule. These schedules may include the following:

- S2 - Federal Amounts Transferred From Your Spouse or Common-Law Partner (primarily used if spouse or common-law partner is not filing a tax return)
- T1032 - Joint Election To Split Pension Income

9. Use the function "Show Auditor" under the "Audit" list to check for warnings or potential errors.

Tips For Using ProFile Software

- Press the F5 key or choose Spouse from the Form menu to display the return of the spouse.

- If you cannot determine where a specific slip or other information should be input, one way to search for the correct form is to open the Form Explorer (F4) and choose the "Key" mode icon in the top right corner of the menu. If you type a key word into the line above the listing of key words, the appropriate form may be found.

- Press the F4 key to view the Form Explorer. Choose the form "Summary" to see the tax data of both spouses on the same one page summary. (Second column will be blank for a single taxpayer.)

- If you want to print only the form you have on the screen, use the print icon identified with 1 in the tool bar. The other print icon opens the print selection screen for printing complete returns. If you want to print just one copy of the return, deselect the print sets you don't want on the print selection screen. Before you print the return, review the forms that have been selected in the print set to ensure that you will not be printing forms you do not require. If it is a coupled return, the print settings for the spouse should be reviewed before clicking on Print as both returns will be printed.

- Review marks can be used to flag information that should be reviewed. The cell with the review mark will be listed when the Show Auditor feature is turned on.

- A memo and/or a tape can be attached to a cell to provide backup information.

- If you are having problems with a specific issue, go to the Training tab, "Other Training Options", to access the online how-to videos which may help solve your problems.

Tax Software Self Study Problem - Chapter 4

Note   The following problem contains 2016 (not 2017) information as software for 2017 is not yet available. If you have an updated 2017 version of ProFile installed on your computer, ensure that when you begin, you open a file for 2016, not 2017 as this data is for 2016. Shortly after the first filing version of the 2017 Intuit ProFile software is available in January, 2018, the updated 2017 version of this problem will be available on the textbook web site at:

www.pearsoncanada.ca/byrdchen/ctp2018

This Tax Software Self Study Problem is expanded in Chapter 11 to contain other components of Taxable Income and Tax Payable.

DISCLAIMER: All characters appearing in this problem are fictitious. Any resemblance to real persons, living or dead, is purely coincidental.

Ms. Eleanor Victoria's husband died two years ago. After her husband died, she moved from her house in Prince George, B.C., to a rented house in Victoria, B.C.

Ms. Victoria's widowed mother, Marjorie Vancouver lives with Ms. Victoria and takes care of the house, Ms. Victoria's younger daughter, Amy, and all of the household cooking. In addition to OAS benefits, Marjorie has a very small income from her deceased husband's life insurance policy. She has never filed a tax return and she is not infirm.

Diane Victoria, Eleanor's older daughter, is studying psychology at McGill University in Montreal. Her field is addiction research with a special emphasis on gambling. She does volunteer work at a gambling addiction treatment centre in Montreal in the summers. As Eleanor has paid for her tuition and living costs, Diane has agreed that the maximum education related amount should be transferred to her mother.

Diane has decided not to file a tax return this year as she knows she does not owe any taxes. Her income was earned driving for a client of the addiction treatment centre who had lost his licence after being charged with impaired driving.

Information concerning Ms. Victoria for 2016 is given on the following pages.

Required: With the objective of minimizing Ms. Victoria's Tax Payable, prepare the 2016 income tax return of Eleanor Victoria using the ProFile tax software program. List any assumptions you have made, and any notes and tax planning issues you feel should be discussed with Ms. Victoria. Ignore HST implications in your solution by assuming that Ms. Victoria does not qualify for the GST/HST rebate.

Personal Information

Title	Ms.
First Name	Eleanor
Last Name	Victoria
SIN	527-000-087
Date of birth (Y/M/D)	1969-05-15
Marital Status	Widowed
Canadian citizen?	Yes
Provide information to Elections Canada?	Yes
Own foreign property of more than $100,000 Canadian?	No

Taxpayer's Address

111 VVV Street Victoria, B.C. V4H 3W4

Phone number (250) 111-1111

Dependants

Dependants	Child 1	Child 2	Mother
First Name	Diane	Amy	Marjorie
Last Name	Victoria	Victoria	Vancouver
SIN	527-000-293	None	527-000-483
Date of birth (Y/M/D)	1996-05-14	2004-10-11	1944-05-21
Net income	$2,300	$360	$8,000
UCCB received (RC62)	N/A	$360	N/A

T4

T4	Box	Amount
Issuer - 1750 Canada Inc.		
Employment income	14	60,201.80
Employee's CPP contributions	16	2,544.30
Employee's EI premiums	18	955.04
RPP contributions	20	2,406.16
Pension adjustment	52	7,829.00
Income tax deducted	22	6,408.00
Employment commissions	42	0
Union dues	44	748.59
Charitable donations	46	175.00

Eleanor has a signed T2200 from her employer specifying her work requires her to have an office in the home. She meets the conditions required to deduct work space in the home expenses. Of the 1,800 square feet in the house, her office, waiting area and storage space totals 310 square feet.

During 2016 she paid the following:

Rent for the year (No GST charged)	$30,000
Utilities (hydro and gas) for the year	2,500
Cleaning services (No GST charged)	1,200
Insurance for household effects (No GST charged)	400
Car insurance (No GST charged)	700

T2202A - (Diane)	Box	Amount
Tuition fees - for Diane Victoria (daughter)	A	7,000
Number of months in school - part-time	B	2
Number of months in school - full-time	C	8

Eleanor and her family had the following medical expenses, all of which Eleanor paid for:

Patient	(Y/M/D)	Medical Expenses	Description	Am't
Eleanor	2016-08-15	Grace Hospital	Ambulance charge	392
Eleanor	2016-08-18	Paramed Home Health	Nursing care	1,350
Marjorie	2016-05-20	Dr. Zhang (Optometrist)	Contact lenses	110
Marjorie	2016-07-06	Pharmacy	Prescription	75
Diane	2016-09-01	Dr. Glassman	Physiotherapist	100
Amy	2016-05-11	Walk Right Foot Clinic	Orthotics	450
Amy	2016-01-23	Dr. Tamo	Dental Fees	1,120

Because of donations in previous years, neither Diane nor Eleanor qualify for the first-time donor super credit.

Donor	Charitable Donation Receipts	Am't
Eleanor	Heart and Stroke	375
Eleanor	Terry Fox Foundation	50
Diane	Addiction Research Council of Canada	100

Solutions to Chapter Four Exercises

Exercise Four - 1 Solution

The net effect of this home relocation loan on Taxable Income would be as follows:

Taxable Benefit Under ITA 80.4(1)(a) - Lesser Of:
- [(4%)(2/4)($82,000) + (5%)(2/4)($82,000)] = $3,690
- [(4%)(4/4)($82,000)] = $3,280

Taxable Benefit Under ITA 80.4(1)(a)	$3,280
Reduction For Payments Under ITA 80.4(1)(c) - [(2%)($82,000)]	(1,640)
Total ITA 80.4(1) Benefit	$1,640

ITA 110(1)(j) Deduction - Lesser Of:
- ITA 80.4(1) Benefit = $1,640
- [(4%)($25,000)(4/4)] = $1,000

ITA 110(1)(j) Deduction	(1,000)
Net Addition To Taxable Income	$ 640

Despite the fact that the prescribed rate has increased, the taxpayer can continue to use the rate in effect at the time the loan was made to calculate the taxable benefit. This can continue for a period of five years. Note that the ITA 110(1)(j) deduction is calculated as if the loan had been for $25,000 rather than $82,000. The ITA 110(1)(j) deduction is not available after 2017.

Exercise Four - 2 Solution

The required Tax Payable would be calculated as follows:

Tax Payable On First $45,916 At 20.05 Percent (15.00% + 5.05%)	$ 9,206
Tax Payable On Next $10,784 ($56,700 - $45,916)	
At 29.65 Percent (20.5% + 9.15%)	3,197
Total Tax Payable Before Credits	$12,403

Her average rate of tax is 21.9 percent ($12,403 ÷ $56,700).

Exercise Four - 3 Solution

Assuming Johan's wife does not have a mental or physical infirmity, the required amount would be calculated as follows:

Basic Personal Amount (Johan)	$ 11,635
Spousal Amount ($11,635 - $2,600)	9,035
Credit Base	$20,670
Rate	15%
Personal Tax Credits - No Infirmity	$ 3,101

If there was a mental or physical infirmity, the amount would be calculated as follows:

Basic Personal Amount (Johan)	$ 11,635
Spousal Amount ($11,635 + $2,150 - $2,600)	11,185
Credit Base	$22,820
Rate	15%
Personal Tax Credits - With Infirmity	$ 3,423

Exercise Four - 4 Solution

As her father is not infirm, Joan would not be entitled to a Canada caregiver credit for him. She is entitled to a Canada caregiver credit for her mother who is infirm. The credit would be:

$$[15\%][\$6,883 - (\$21,400 - \$16,163)] = \$247$$

Exercise Four - 5 Solution

Marcia will be entitled to the spousal tax credit, including the additional amount for an infirm spouse. In addition, she can claim the Canada caregiver credit for her infirm adult son. The total credits would be calculated as follows:

Spousal Including Infirm Amount	
($11,635 + $2,150 - $5,600)	$ 8,185
Canada Caregiver ($6,883 - Nil)	6,883
Total Base	$15,068
Rate	15%
Marcia's Tax Credits Related To Spouse And Son	$ 2,260

Exercise Four - 6 Solution

Darcy would claim the eligible dependant credit for Janice, including the additional amount for an infirm eligible dependant. Because of this, no additional claim for the Canada caregiver amount for a child can be made under ITA 118(1)(b.1). His credit would be as follows:

$$[(15\%)(\$11,635 + \$2,150)] = \$2,068$$

Exercise Four - 7 Solution

The base for Sandy's eligible dependant credit for her mother would be nil ($11,635 + $2,150 - $18,000), resulting in an eligible dependant tax credit of nil. Her calculation of the regular Canada caregiver amount would result in a base of $5,046 [$6,883 - ($18,000 - $16,163)]. As the eligible dependant tax credit was nil, the additional amount is $5,046 ($5,046 - Nil), resulting in a credit of $757 [(15%)($5,046)].

Exercise Four - 8 Solution

Mr. Smythe's age credit would be $745 {[15%][$7,225 - (15%)($51,500 - $36,430)]}.

Exercise Four - 9 Solution

The adoption expenses tax credit would be calculated as follows:

Cost Of First China Trip (See Note)	$ 4,250
Cost Of Second China Trip	6,420
Chinese Orphanage Fee	1,600
Canadian Adoption Agency Fee	3,200
Legal Fees	2,700
Medical Costs (Qualify For Medical Expense Credit)	Nil
Total Eligible Expenses	$18,170

Since the $5,000 employer reimbursement is a taxable benefit and included in employment income, it does not reduce the total eligible adoption expenses.

The adoption period begins at the time that an application is made for registration with an adoption agency licensed by a provincial government. This means that all of the expenses listed in the preceding table would be eligible expenses made during the adoption period. However, for 2017, there is an overall limit of $15,670 and the maximum credit that can be claimed is $2,351 [(15%)($15,670)].

Exercise Four - 10 Solution

The snow removal contract would not be a qualifying expenditure. The base for the home accessibility tax credit would be limited to the lesser of $10,000 and the qualifying expenditures of $8,500. This will result in a credit of $1,275 [(15%)($8,500)].

Either spouse can claim the credit and it will be worth the same amount to either spouse. Since it is non-refundable, whoever claims the credit should have at least $1,275 in federal Tax Payable. Alternatively, the $8,500 base amount can be split between the two spouses.

Exercise Four - 11 Solution

With Net Income For Tax Purposes of $350,000, the maximum base for Mr. Hoffman's credit is $262,500 [(75%)($350,000)]. As his eligible charitable gifts are less than this, he can use the full amount as the base for his credit. Given this, the calculation of the credit is as follows:

$$[(15\%)(A)] + [(33\%)(B)] + [(29\%)(C)], \text{ where}$$

A = $200
B = The Lesser Of:
   • $225,000 - $200 = $224,800
   • $325,000 - $202,800 = $122,200 (Note Taxable Income is used here)
C = $102,600 [$225,000 - ($200 + $122,200)]

The charitable donation credit would be equal to $70,110, calculated as [(15%)($200)] + [(33%)($122,200)] + [(29%)($102,600)].

Exercise Four - 12 Solution

With Net Income For Tax Purposes of $350,000, the maximum base for Mr. Hoffman's credit is $262,500 [(75%)($350,000)]. As his eligible gifts are less than this, he can use the full amount as the base for his credit. Given this, the calculation of the credit without the FDSC is as follows:

$$[(15\%)(A)] + [(33\%)(B)] + [(29\%)(C)], \text{ where}$$

A = $200
B = The Lesser Of:
- $225,000 - $200 = $224,800
- $250,000 - $202,800 = $47,200 (Note Taxable Income is used here)
C = $177,600 [$225,000 - ($200 + $47,200)]

The first-time super donor credit is the maximum allowable and is equal to $250 [(25%)($1,000)].

The charitable donation credit would be equal to $67,360, calculated as [(15%)($200)] + [(33%)($47,200)] + [(29%)($177,600)] + $250.

Exercise Four - 13 Solution

Amount B Qualifying Expenses ($4,330 + $4,600)		$ 8,930
Amount C - Lesser Of:		
• [(3%)($150,000)] = $4,500		
• 2017 Threshold Amount = $2,268		(2,268)
Subtotal		$ 6,662
Amount D		
Max's Medical Expenses	$8,425	
Reduced By The Lesser Of:		
• $2,268		
• [(3%)($8,250)] = $248	(248)	8,177
Matt's Medical Expenses	$ 120	
Reduced By The Lesser Of:		
• $2,268		
• [(3%)($6,000)] = $180	(180)	Nil*
Allowable Amount Of Medical Expenses		$14,839
Amount A The Appropriate Rate (Minimum Rate)		15%
Medical Expense Tax Credit		$ 2,226

* As medical expenses can only be reduced to nil, the net result cannot be negative in this calculation.

Exercise Four - 14 Solution

As Keith has no income, his disability credit can be transferred to John. As Keith is over 17, the disability child supplement is not available. In addition to the disability credit, John will be able to take the caregiver credit, the base for which would include the family caregiver amount, as well as a credit for Keith's medical expenses. Since the caregiver credit is claimed, the infirm dependant over 17 credit is not available.

The total credits related to Keith would be as follows:

Transfer Of Keith's Disability Amount		$ 8,113
Caregiver, Including FCA ($4,732 + $2,150))		6,882
Keith's Medical Expenses	$16,240	
Reduced By The Lesser Of:		
• $2,268		
• [(3%)(Nil)] = Nil	Nil	16,240
Total Credit Base		$31,235
Rate		15%
Total Credits Related To Keith		$ 4,685

Exercise Four - 15 Solution

Ms. Bright's education related tax credits would be calculated as follows:

Tuition Amount:		
Total (Including $1,000 Prepayment)	$3,200	
Ineligible Ancillary Fees ($400 - $250)	(150)	$3,050
Interest On Student Loan		325
Total Credit Base		$3,375
Rate		15%
Total Available Credits		$ 506

Exercise Four - 16 Solution

The available tuition credit would be calculated as follows:

Tuition Amount (Maximum Transfer = $5,000)	$23,500
Rate	15%
Tuition Credit (Maximum Transfer = $750)	$ 3,525

Note that the transfer and carry forward amounts calculated in the following alternative approaches ignore his medical expense credit.

Income Tax Act Approach The $750 maximum transfer of the tuition credit must be reduced by Jerry's Tax Payable, before deducting his medical expense credit, of $92 [(15%)($12,250 - $11,635)]. This will leave a maximum transfer of $658 ($750 - $92) and a carry forward credit of $2,775 ($3,525 - $92 - $658).

Tax Return Approach The $5,000 maximum transfer of the tuition credit must be reduced by $615 ($12,250 - $11,635)], the excess of Jerry's Taxable Income over his basic personal amount. This results in a maximum transfer of $4,385 ($5,000 - $615) and a carry forward amount of $18,500 ($23,500 - $615 - $4,385). Multiplying this by 15 percent gives the same $2,775 that we calculated under the alternative approach.

Exercise Four - 17 Solution

His tax credits would be calculated as follows:

Basic Personal Amount	$ 11,635
Spousal Amount Including FCA ($11,635 + $2,150 - Nil)	13,785
Age [$7,225 - (15%)($42,000 - $36,430)]	6,390
Pension Income*	2,000
Transfer Of Spouse's Age	7,225
Transfer Of Spouse's Disability	8,113
Transfer Of Spouse's Tuition - Lesser Of:	
• Actual Tuition = $2,200	
• Maximum Transfer = $5,000	2,200
Credit Base	$51,348
Rate	15%
Total Credits	$ 7,702

* A payment from a life annuity purchased with funds in an RRSP is eligible pension income.

Exercise Four - 18 Solution

Ms. Unger's $487 credit would be calculated as follows:

	Contributions	Credit Rate	Tax Credit
First	$400	3/4	$300
Next	350	1/2	175
Remaining	35	1/3	12
Maximum Credit	$785		$487

Exercise Four - 19 Solution

The regular medical expense credit would be calculated as follows:

Medical Expenses	$6,250
Lesser Of:	
• [(3%)($27,400)] = $822	
• 2017 Threshold Amount = $2,268	(822)
Allowable Amount Of Medical Expenses	$5,428

The refundable supplement would be calculated as follows:

Lesser Of:	
• $1,203 (2017 Maximum)	
• [(25%)($5,428)] = $1,357	$1,203
Reduction [(5%)($27,400 - $26,644)]	(38)
Refundable Medical Expense Supplement	$1,165

Ms. Brunt's total Tax Payable (Refund) would be calculated as follows:

Tax Payable Before Credits [(15%)($27,400)]		$4,110
Non-Refundable Credits:		
Basic	$ 11,635	
Common-Law Partner	11,635	
Allowable Medical Expenses	5,428	
Total	$28,698	
Rate	15%	(4,305)
Tax Before Refundable Supplement		$ Nil*
Refundable Medical Expense Supplement		(1,165)
Tax Payable (Refund)		($1,165)

* As Tax Before Refundable Supplement can only be reduced to nil, the net result cannot be negative for this subtotal.

Exercise Four - 20 Solution

Ms. Jacobi's income before deducting either the EI or OAS repayments would be as follows:

Net Employment Income	$65,000
EI Benefits	10,000
OAS Benefits	7,000
Income Before Deductions	$82,000

Dealing first with the EI repayment, Ms. Jacobi would have to repay $3,000, the lesser of:

- $3,000 [(30%)($10,000)]
- $5,363 [(30%)($82,000 - $64,125)]

Using this deduction, the clawback of her OAS payments would be the lesser of:

- $7,000, the OAS payments included in income, and
- $632 [(15%)($82,000 - $3,000 - $74,788)].

As a result, her Net Income For Tax Purposes would be as follows:

Income Before Deductions	$82,000
ITA 60(v.1) Deduction (EI)	(3,000)
ITA 60(w) Deduction (OAS)	(632)
Net Income For Tax Purposes	$78,368

Self Study Solution Four - 1

Case One

In this Case One, the combined Tax Payable would be calculated as follows:

Barbra's Tax Payable		
Federal Tax Before Credits [(15%)($42,000)]	$ 6,300	
Basic Personal Credit [($11,635)(15%)]	(1,745)	$ 4,555
Sally's Tax Payable		
Tax On First $142,353	$29,436	
Tax On Next $37,647 ($180,000 - $142,353) At 29%	10,918	
Federal Tax Before Credits	$40,354	
Basic Personal Credit [($11,635)(15%)]	(1,745)	38,609
Combined Tax Payable		$43,164

Case Two

In this Case Two, the Tax Payable for each individual would be the same and the combined Tax Payable would be calculated as follows:

Barbra's Tax Payable		
Tax On First $91,831	$16,300	
Tax On Next $19,169 ($111,000 - $91,831) At 26%	4,984	
Federal Tax Before Credits	$21,284	
Basic Personal Credit [($11,635)(15%)]	(1,745)	$19,539
Sally's Tax Payable		
Tax On First $91,831	$16,300	
Tax On Next $19,169 ($111,000 - $91,831) At 26%	4,984	
Federal Tax Before Credits	$21,284	
Basic Personal Credit [($11,635)(15%)]	(1,745)	19,539
Combined Tax Payable		$39,078

Case Three

In this Case Three, only Barbra would have Tax Payable which would be calculated as follows:

Tax On First $202,800	$46,966
Tax On Next $19,200 ($222,000 - $202,800) At 33%	6,336
Federal Tax Before Credits	$53,302
Basic Personal Credit [($11,635)(15%)]	(1,745)
Common-Law Partner Credit [($11,635)(15%)]	(1,745)
Barbra's Tax Payable	$49,812

Self Study Solution Four - 2

Case 1

Leonard Wilkins will qualify for the following credits:

Basic Personal Amount	$11,635
Spousal ($11,635 - $8,720)	2,915
Canada Caregiver	6,883
Total Credit Base	$21,433
Rate	15%
Total Credits	$ 3,215

Case 2

Pete Webb will qualify for the following credits:

Basic Personal Amount	$11,635
Spousal ($11,635 - $3,920)	7,715
EI (Maximum)	836
CPP (Maximum)	2,564
Canada Employment	1,178
Total Credit Base	$23,928
Rate	15%
Total Credits	$ 3,589

Case 3

Candace Hall will qualify for the following tax credits:

Basic Personal Amount	$11,635
Spousal ($11,635 - $5,130)	6,505
Age [$7,225 - (15%)($69,420 - $36,430)]	2,277
Pension Income	2,000
Total Credit Base	**$22,417**
Rate	15%
Total Credits	**$ 3,363**

Note that, because her income is below the $74,788 income threshold, there will be no clawback of Ms. Hall's OAS receipts.

Case 4

Gladys Crawford will qualify for the following tax credits:

Basic Personal Amount	$11,635
Spousal ($11,635 - $2,600)	9,035
Medical Expenses (See Note)	20,948
Total Credit Base	**$41,618**
Rate	15%
Total Credits	**$ 6,243**

Note The claim for medical expenses is determined as follows:

Expenses For Gladys, Her Spouse, And Under 18 Children ($5,150 + $4,240 + $2,040 + $3,220)		$14,650
Reduced By The Lesser Of:		
• [(3%)($126,470)] = $3,794		
• 2017 Threshold Amount = $2,268		(2,268)
20 Year Old's Medical Expenses	$8,840	
Reduced By The Lesser Of:		
• [(3%)($9,130)] = $274		
• $2,268	(274)	8,566
Allowable Medical Expenses		**$20,948**

Case 5

Austin Schneider will qualify for the following credits:

Basic Personal Amount	$11,635
Eligible Dependant (See Note)	11,635
Total Credit Base	**$23,270**
Rate	15%
Total Credits	**$ 3,491**

Note The eligible dependant credit can be taken for any child. It should not be claimed for the 14 year old as the amount of the credit would be reduced due to his income.

Self Study Solution Four - 3

Federal Tax Before Credits

For all of the following Cases, the Federal Tax Before Credits would be calculated as follows:

Tax On First $45,916	$ 6,887
Tax On Next $32,084 ($78,000 - $45,916) At 20.5 Percent	6,577
Federal Tax Before Credits	$13,464

Case A

The solution to this Case can be completed as follows:

Federal Tax Before Credits (As Previously Calculated)		$13,464
Basic Personal Amount	($11,635)	
Eligible Dependant	(11,635)	
Tuition	(5,640)	
Credit Base	($28,910)	
Rate	15%	(4,337)
Federal Tax Payable		$ 9,127

Case B

The solution to this Case can be completed as follows:

Federal Tax Before Credits (As Previously Calculated)		$13,464
Basic Personal Amount	($11,635)	
EI	(836)	
CPP	(2,564)	
Canada Employment	(1,178)	
Credit Base	($16,213)	
Rate	15%	(2,432)
Charitable Donations (See Note)		
[(15%)($200) + (29%)($35,000 - $200)]		(10,122)
Federal Tax Payable		$ 910

Note With a Net Income For Tax Purposes of $78,000, Ms. Sykes' maximum claim for charitable donations is $58,500 [(75%)($78,000)]. However, if this amount was claimed, the resulting credit would exceed her Tax Payable. By claiming $35,000, the unused donation of $115,000 ($150,000 - $35,000) can be carried forward for up to 5 years. As none of her income is taxed at 33 percent, this rate will not be applicable to the calculation of the charitable donations tax credit.

The $2,000,000 that she won in the lottery is not included in her Net Income For Tax Purposes.

Case C

The solution to this Case can be completed as follows:

Federal Tax Before Credits (As Previously Calculated)		$13,464
Basic Personal Amount	($11,635)	
Spousal ($11,635 - $7,600)	(4,035)	
Caregiver Amount For A Child - Martin	(2,150)	
Transfer Of Martin's Disability	(8,113)	
Disability Supplement (No Child Care Costs)	(4,773)	
Credit Base	($30,706)	
Rate	15%	(4,606)
Federal Tax Payable		$ 8,858

As Harry is not mentally or physically infirm, no Canada caregiver amount is available for him.

Case D

The solution to this Case can be completed as follows:

Federal Tax Before Credits (As Previously Calculated)		$13,464
Basic Personal Amount	($11,635)	
Spousal ($11,635 - $2,540)	(9,095)	
EI	(836)	
CPP	(2,564)	
Canada Employment	(1,178)	
Medical Expenses (See Note)	(8,283)	
Credit Base	($33,591)	
Rate	15%	(5,039)
Federal Tax Payable		$ 8,425

Note The claim for medical expenses is determined as follows:

Wanda, Buff, And Janice ($2,100 + $360 + $3,645)		$6,105
Reduced By The Lesser Of:		
• [(3%)($78,000)] = $2,340		
• 2017 Threshold Amount = $2,268		(2,268)
Mark's Medical Expenses	$4,520	
Reduced By The Lesser Of:		
• [(3%)($2,460)] = $74		
• $2,268	(74)	4,446
Total Medical Expense Claim		$8,283

Case E

The solution to this Case can be completed as follows:

Federal Tax Before Credits (As Previously Calculated)		$13,464
Basic Personal Amount	($11,635)	
Spousal Including Infirm Amount		
($11,635 + $2,150 - $9,600)	(4,185)	
EI	(836)	
CPP	(2,564)	
Canada Employment	(1,178)	
Transfer Of Buff's Disability Amount	(8,113)	
Transfer Of Buff's Age Amount	(7,225)	
Transfer Of Buff's Pension Amount	(2,000)	
Transfer Of Tuition Amounts (See Note)	(5,000)	
Credit Base	($42,736)	
Rate	15%	(6,410)
Federal Tax Payable		$ 7,054

Note   While the base for Buff's tuition credit is $8,450, the transfer is limited to $5,000. The unused amount of $3,450 ($8,450 - $5,000) can be carried forward indefinitely, but can only be claimed by Buff.

Self Study Solution Four - 4

Mr. Lane's federal tax payable (refund) would be calculated as follows:

Net Income For Tax Purposes And Taxable Income		$70,000
Tax On First $45,916		$ 6,887
Tax On Next $24,084 ($70,000 - $45,916) At 20.5 Percent		4,937
Federal Tax Before Credits		$11,824
Basic Personal Amount	($11,635)	
Eligible Dependant (Note 1)	(11,635)	
EI	(836)	
CPP (maximum)	(2,564	
Canada Employment	(1,178)	
Medical Expenses (Note 2)	(2,300)	
Credit Base	($30,148)	
Rate	15%	(4,522)
Federal Political Tax Credit [(3/4)($400) + (1/2)($50)]		(325)
Federal Tax Payable		$ 6,977
CPP Overpayment ($2,599 - $2,564)		(35)
Federal Tax Withheld (Given)		(10,100)
Federal Tax Payable (Refund)		($ 3,158)

Note 1   The eligible dependant amount can be claimed for either his 10 or 12 year old child. His 15 year old son would not be selected as he has Net Income For Tax Purposes of $8,200.

Note 2   Allowable medical expenses are as follows:

Minor Child's Medical Expenses	$4,400
Reduced By The Lesser Of:	
• [(3%)($70,000)] = $2,100	
• 2017 Threshold Amount = $2,268	(2,100)
Allowable Medical Expenses	**$2,300**

Since his 15 year old son is under 18 years of age, his allowable medical expenses are not affected by his Net Income For Tax Purposes. If he was 18 or older, they would be.

Self Study Solution Four - 5

Part A
The Tax Payable calculation for Marg is as follows:

Taxable Income	$15,300
Basic Personal Amount	(11,635)
EI	(249)
CPP	(584)
Canada Employment	(1,178)
Subtotal	$ 1,654
Tuition Amount Claimed (Note 1)	(1,654)
Subtotal	Nil
Rate	15%
Federal Tax Payable (Refund)	Nil

Note 1   Marg has a tuition amount available of $6,300. Of this total, she will use $1,654 to reduce her current Tax Payable to nil. This leaves an unused amount of $4,646 ($6,300 - $1,654). Of this amount, $3,346 ($5,000 - $1,654) can be transferred to her father. This will leave her with a carry forward amount of $1,300 ($6,300 - $1,654 - $3,346). Since Marg's medical expenses were paid for by her father, she cannot claim them herself and they must be claimed by her father. Even if she had paid for them herself and claimed them, she would not increase the transfer to her father as the medical expense tax credit is not taken into consideration in determining the tuition amount that can be transferred.

Part B
Mr. Barth's minimum Net Income For Tax Purposes for the year would be calculated as follows:

Gross Salary	$ 82,500
Additions:	
Bonus (Note 2)	20,000
Automobile Benefit (Note 3)	7,400
Counseling Benefit (Note 4)	1,500
Imputed Interest Benefit (Note 5)	375
Stock Option Benefit [($18 - $15)(1,000)] (Note 6)	3,000
Deductions:	
Registered Pension Plan Contributions	(3,200)
Professional Dues	(1,800)
Net Income For Tax Purposes	**$109,775**

Note 2   As the bonus is not payable until more than 3 years after the end of the employer's taxation year, it is a salary deferral arrangement and must be included in income under ITA 6(11).

Note 3   Since Mr. Barth's employment related usage is not more than 50 percent, there is no reduction of the full standby charge. In addition, he cannot use the alternative calculation of the operating cost benefit. Given this, the automobile benefit is calculated as follows:

Standby Charge [(2%)($47,500)(10)]	$9,500
Operating Cost Benefit [(6,000)($0.25)]	1,500
Payments Withheld	(3,600)
Taxable Benefit	$7,400

Note 4   Counseling services, with the exception of those items specified under ITA 6(1), are considered taxable benefits. The items specified under ITA 6(1)(a)(iv) are counseling with respect to mental or physical health or with respect to re-employment or retirement. As a consequence, the counseling on personal finances is a taxable benefit.

Note 5   The imputed interest benefit is calculated as follows:

Taxable Benefit [($150,000)(2%)(3/12)]	$750
Reduction For Interest Paid	(375)
Net Addition To Employment Income	$375

Note 6   As the option price was greater than the market price at the time the options were issued, one-half of this amount can be deducted in the determination of Taxable Income. The adjusted cost base of the stock option shares is equal to their fair market value at the exercise date ($18 per share). Since they were sold for $18 per share, there is no capital gain or loss.

Taxable Income

The loan to purchase a ski chalet would not be a home relocation loan and there would be no deduction from Taxable Income related to the interest benefit. Mr. Barth's Taxable Income would be calculated as follows:

Net Income For Tax Purposes = Net Employment Income	$109,775
Stock Option Deduction [(1/2)($3,000)] (Note 6)	(1,500)
Taxable Income	$108,275

Tax Payable

Mr. Barth's Tax Payable would be calculated as follows:

Tax On First $91,831		$16,300
Tax On Next $16,444 ($108,275 - $91,831) At 26 Percent		4,275
Federal Tax Before Credits		$20,575
Basic Personal Amount	($11,635)	
Spousal Including Infirm Amount		
($11,635 + $2,150 - $1,250)	(12,535)	
Spouse's Disability	(8,113)	
EI	(836)	
CPP	(2,564)	
Canada Employment	(1,178)	
Medical Expenses (Note 7)	(1,743)	
Marg's Tuition Transfer (See Part A)	(3,346)	
Credit Base	($41,950)	
Rate	15%	(6,293)
Charitable Donations (Note 8)		
[(15%)($200) + (29%)($2,000 - $200)]		(552)
Net Federal Tax		$13,730
Federal Income Tax Withheld During Year		(16,000)
Federal Tax Payable (Refund)		($ 2,270)

Note 7 Allowable medical expenses are as follows:

John And Spouse Medical Expenses ($200 + $3,550)		$3,750
Reduced By The Lesser Of:		
• [(3%)($109,775)] = $3,293		
• 2017 Threshold Amount = $2,268		(2,268)
Marg's Medical Expenses	$720	
Reduced By The Lesser Of:		
• [(3%)($15,300)] = $459		
• $2,268	(459)	261
Allowable Medical Expenses		$1,743

Note 8 As none of his income is taxed at 33 percent, this rate will not be applicable to the calculation of the charitable donations tax credit.

Self Study Solution Four - 6

Mr. Kern's minimum Net Income For Tax Purposes for the year would be calculated as follows:

Gross Salary	$67,600
Additions:	
Automobile Benefit (Note 1)	857
Disability Insurance Benefit (Note 2)	1,300
Stock Option Benefit [($83 - $75)(200)]	1,600
Deductions:	
Registered Pension Plan Contributions	(1,800)
Contributions To Group Disability Plan	Nil
Professional Dues	(1,233)
Net Income For Tax Purposes	$68,324

Note 1 Based on the fact that Mr. Kern's employment related usage is more than 50 percent of total usage, the automobile benefit is calculated as follows:

Standby Charge [(2/3)(9)($815 - $89)(3,000/15,003*)]	$ 871
Operating Cost Benefit - Lesser Of:	
• [(3,000)($0.25)] = $750	
• [(1/2)($871)] = $436	436
Total Before Payments	$1,307
Payments For Personal Use [($50)(9)]	(450)
Taxable Benefit	$ 857

*[(9)(1,667)]

As Mr. Kern's employment related usage is more than 50 percent, he can elect to use one-half the standby charge as the operating cost benefit.

Note 2 As his employer contributed to the plan and the contributions did not create a taxable benefit, the $1,650 in benefits received during the year must be included in employment income. However, this benefit is reduced by the $350 ($200 + $150) in total contributions that he has made in 2016 and 2017.

Taxable Income

Taxable Income would be calculated as follows:

Net Income For Tax Purposes	$68,324
Stock Option Deduction [(1/2)($1,600)]	(800)
Taxable Income	$67,524

Tax Payable

Tax Payable would be calculated as follows:

Tax On First $45,916		$ 6,887
Tax On Next $21,608 ($67,524 - $45,916) At 20.5 Percent		4,430
Federal Tax Before Credits		$11,317
Basic Personal Amount	($11,635)	
Spousal ($11,635 - $3,660)	(7,975)	
EI	(836)	
CPP	(2,564)	
Canada Employment	(1,178)	
Medical Expenses (Note 3)	(3,907)	
David's Transfer Of Tuition (Note 4)	(5,000)	
Credit Base	($33,095)	
Rate	15%	(4,964)
Charitable Donations Carried Forward (Note 5)		
[(15%)($200) + (29%)($500 - $200)]		(117)
Net Federal Tax		$ 6,236
Federal Amounts Withheld During Year (Given)		(7,200)
Federal Tax Payable (Refund)		($ 964)

Note 3 The allowable medical expenses would be calculated as follows:

Samuel And Spouse Medical Expenses ($2,100 + $770) $2,870
Reduced By The Lesser Of:
* [(3%)($68,324)] = $2,050
* 2017 Threshold Amount = $2,268   (2,050)

David's Medical Expenses $3,260
Reduced By The Lesser Of:
* $2,268
* [(3%)($5,780)] = $173   (173)   3,087

Allowable Medical Expenses $3,907

Note 4 The transfer from David is as follows:

Tuition Fees $ 6,700
Maximum Transfer   (5,000)

Carry Forward (For David's Use Only) $ 1,700

David's Tax Payable is completely eliminated by his basic personal credit. He can transfer a maximum of $5,000 of his tuition amount to his father. The remaining $1,700 can be carried forward indefinitely, but must be used by David.

Note 5 As none of his income is taxed at 33 percent, this rate will not be applicable to the calculation of the charitable donations tax credit.

Self Study Solution Four - 7

Part A

Mr. Strong's minimum Net Income For Tax Purposes would be calculated as follows:

Salary $72,000
Additions:
   Employer's Disability Contribution
     (Not A Taxable Benefit)   Nil
   Automobile Benefit (Note 1)   7,750
   Tuition For Chants Course (Note 2)   600
   Travel Costs (Note 3)   Nil
   Home Relocation Loan Benefit (Note 4)   1,500
Deductions:
   RPP Contributions   (4,200)
   Cost Of Tools - Maximum (Note 5)   (500)

Net Income For Tax Purposes $77,150

Note 1 The automobile benefit would be calculated as follows:

Standby Charge [(2/3)(10)($565 - $40)] $3,500
Operating Cost Benefit [($0.25)(17,000)]   4,250

Total Benefits $7,750

As Mr. Strong's employment related use was less than 50 percent, there is no reduction in the standby charge and he cannot use the alternative calculation of the operating cost benefit.

Note 2 Employer paid tuition is a taxable benefit unless it is for the benefit of that employer. While the spoken French course appears to be for the benefit of the employer, it would be difficult to argue that the employer would benefit from a course in 16th century liturgical chants.

Note 3 As the travel costs were reimbursed, there is no deduction. As long as the costs were reasonable, there would be no benefit from the reimbursement.

Note 4 The ITA 80.4(1) loan benefit would be $1,500, the lesser of:

- [($150,000)(2% - Nil)(1/4) + ($150,000)(1% - Nil)(2/4)] $1,500
- [($150,000)(2% - Nil)(3/4)] $2,250

Note 5 Mr. Strong can deduct the cost of tradesperson's tools that cost more than $1,178. However, the overall limit for this deduction is $500 per year.

Part B

Mr. Strong's minimum Taxable Income would be calculated as follows:

Net Income For Tax Purposes	$77,150
Home Relocation Loan Deduction (Note 6)	(250)
Taxable Income	$76,900

Note 6 The deduction would be $250, the lesser of:

- ITA 80.4(1) Benefit $1,500
- [($25,000)(2% - Nil)(1/4) + ($25,000)(1% - Nil)(2/4)] $ 250

Part C

Based on the Taxable Income calculated in Part B, Mr. Strong's Tax Payable would be calculated as follows:

Tax On First $45,916		$ 6,887
Tax On Next $30,984 ($76,900 - $45,916) At 20.5 Percent		6,352
Tax Before Credits		$13,239
Credits:		
Basic Personal Amount	($11,635)	
Spousal ($11,635 - $5,600)	(6,035)	
Caregiver (Note 7)	Nil	
EI Premiums	(836)	
CPP Contributions	(2,564)	
Canada Employment	(1,178)	
Monthly Transit Passes [($60)(2)(10)]	(1,200)	
Tuition (Note 8)	(600)	
Medical Expenses (Note 9)	(3,837)	
Credit Base	($27,885)	
Rate	15%	(4,183)
Charitable Donations (Note 10)		
[(15%)($200) + (29%)($1,200 - $200)]		(320)
Federal Tax Payable		$ 8,736

Note 7 Because his mother is not mentally or physically infirm, Lance cannot claim the Canada caregiver credit.

Note 8 When an employer reimburses tuition costs, the tuition credit can be claimed if the reimbursement is included in the employee's income.

Note 9 The base for Mr. Strong's medical expense credit can be calculated as follows:

Mr. Strong, His Spouse, And Minor Children		
($1,250 + $2,300 + $850)		$4,400
Reduced By The Lesser Of:		
• [(3%)($77,150)] = $2,315		
• 2017 Threshold Amount = $2,268		(2,268)
Mother's Medical Expenses	$1,960	
Reduced By The Lesser Of:		
• $2,268		
• [(3%)($8,500)] = $255	(255)	1,705
Allowable Medical Costs		$3,837

Note 10 Mr. Strong cannot claim a credit for the $1,500 of donated services. As none of his income is taxed at 33 percent, this rate will not be applicable to the calculation of the charitable donations tax credit.

Note 11 Mr. Strong cannot claim the First-Time Home Buyers' Credit as he owned a house within 4 years of purchasing the heritage home.

Self Study Solution Four - 8

Part A

Mr. Bosworth's minimum Net Income For Tax Purposes would be calculated as follows:

Salary	$180,000
Additions:	
Commissions	11,500
Bonus (Note 1)	Nil
Life Insurance Premiums (Employer's Contribution)	460
Automobile Benefit (Note 2)	6,800
Stock Option Benefit (Note 3)	13,000
Gift ($2,500, Less $500 Limit On Gifts)	2,000
Deductions:	
RPP Contributions	(5,200)
Employment Expenses (Note 4)	(20,371)
Net Income For Tax Purposes	$188,189

Note 1 As none of the bonus was paid during the year, none of it will be included in Net Income For Tax Purposes.

Note 2 The standby charge would be calculated as follows:

$$[(2/3)(12)(\$925 - \$75)(20,004 \div 20,004)] = \$6,800$$

As Mr. Bosworth's personal milage exceeds 20,004 kilometers, there is no reduction in the standby charge. There would be no operating cost benefit as Mr. Bosworth paid for all of the operating costs.

Note 3 The total employment income inclusion would be $13,000 [(5,000)($12.35 - $9.75)]. As the option price was equal to the market price at the time the options were issued, $6,500 [(1/2)($13,000)] can be deducted in the determination of Taxable Income.

Note 4   Potentially deductible expenses are as follows:

Car Operating Costs [(41,000 ÷ 62,000)($10,300)]	$ 6,811
Meals [(50%)($6,420)]	3,210
Hotels	10,350
Subtotal for ITA 8(1)(h) and (h.1)	**$20,371**
Advertising	12,400
Entertainment [(50%)($6,500)]	3,250
Total for ITA 8(1)(f) - Limited To Commissions	**$36,021**

All of these costs can be deducted under ITA 8(1)(f). However, the total deduction is limited to commission income which is only $11,500. Alternatively, the car operating costs, meals, and hotels, can be deducted under ITA 8(1)(h) and (h.1). As shown in the preceding table, this total would be $20,371. As Mr. Bosworth cannot simultaneously use ITA 8(1)(f) and the combination of ITA 8(1)(h) and (h.1), he will minimize his Net Income For Tax Purposes by deducting under the latter provisions.

Part B

Mr. Bosworth's minimum Taxable Income would be calculated as follows:

Net Income For Tax Purposes	$188,189
Stock Option Deduction [(1/2)($13,000)]	(6,500)
Taxable Income	$181,689

Part C

Based on the Taxable Income calculated in Part B, Mr. Bosworth's federal Tax Payable would be calculated as follows:

Tax On First $142,353		$29,436
Tax On Next $39,336 ($181,689 - $142,353) At 29 Percent		11,407
Tax Before Credits		$40,843
Credits:		
Basic Personal Amount	($11,635)	
Spouse ($11,635 - $6,450)	(5,185)	
Canada Caregiver Amount For Child	(2,150)	
Transfer Of Daughter's Disability	(8,113)	
Disability Supplement (Note 5)	Nil	
EI Premiums	(836)	
CPP Contributions	(2,564)	
Canada Employment	(1,178)	
Tuition - Andrew	(1,670)	
Transfer Of Son's Tuition (Note 6)	(4,185)	
Medical Expenses (Note 7)	(14,398)	
Credit Base	($51,914)	
Rate	15%	(7,787)
Charitable Donations (Note 8)		
[(15%)($200) + (29%)($2,400 - $200)]		(668)
Federal Tax Payable		$32,388

Note 5   Since the daughter's $9,000 attendant care costs that are included in the medical expenses total more than $7,504 ($4,732 + $2,772), the disability supplement is reduced to nil.

Note 6   As the son has Net Income For Tax Purposes of $12,450, he must use $815 ($12,450 - $11,635) of this total. This means that the maximum transfer to his father will be $4,185 ($5,000 - $815). This will leave the son with the following carry forward:

Tuition Amount Including Ancillary Fees ($7,650 + $560)	$8,210
Used By Son In 2017	(815)
Transferred To His Father	(4,185)
Carry Forward (For Son's Use Only)	$3,210

The carry forward amount $3,210 can be carried forward indefinitely, but must be used by the son.

Note 7   The base for Mr. Bosworth's medical expense credit can be calculated as follows:

Eligible Medical Expenses		
Andrew, His Spouse And Minor Child		
($1,200 + $2,250 + $11,250)		$14,700
Reduced By The Lesser Of:		
• [(3%)($188,189)] = $5,646		
• 2017 Threshold Amount = $2,268		(2,268)
Son's Medical Expenses	$2,340	
Reduced By The Lesser Of:		
• $2,268		
• [(3%)($12,450)] = $374	(374)	1,966
Allowable Medical Expenses		$14,398

Note 8   As none of his income is taxed at 33 percent, this rate will not be applicable to the calculation of the charitable donations tax credit.

Solution to Tax Software Self Study Problem - Chapter 4

The complete tax return is available on the Companion Website in two versions, a T1 ProFile return file and a .PDF file.. Note that prior to late January, 2018, the returns will be for 2016, not 2017 as the 2017 filing version will not yet be available.

For more information on how to use the ProFile tax program, refer to the Chapter 4 sample tax return in this Study Guide.

Notes To Tax Return

- Diane transfers the $5,000 maximum education related credits to Eleanor and carries forward the remaining $6,000 [$7,000 + (8)($400) + (8)($65) + (2)($120) + (2)($20) - $5,000]. The carry forward can only be used by Diane.

- Eleanor cannot claim the charitable donation made by Diane, but Diane can carry it forward for up to five years.

- Since Amy is under 18 and wholly dependent, Eleanor claimed the eligible dependant credit for Amy.

- Eleanor elected to include the UCCB in Amy's income as this will reduce Eleanor's tax liability.

- Eleanor claimed the full caregiver credit for Marjorie as her income is well below the income threshold. Note that, because Marjorie is not infirm, the family caregiver amount is not added to this credit.

- Since Diane and Marjorie are over 17 years of age, their medical expenses are reduced by 3 percent of their Net Income For Tax Purposes. This means that none of Marjorie's medical expenses can be claimed by Eleanor.

- In calculating work space in the home costs, the household insurance is not deductible as the T4 information shows she has no commission income. The car insurance is not relevant as there is no information that Eleanor uses her car for employment related purposes.

Tax Planning Points

- Although she is not required to file, Marjorie should file a tax return, otherwise she will not be eligible for the GST credit.

- Although she is not required to file, Diane should file a tax return, otherwise she will not be eligible for the GST credit and she will not benefit from the RRSP deduction room created during the year. Filing a tax return will also make her education related tax credits and charitable donation tax credit easier to keep track of for carry forward purposes.

Chapter 4 Learning Objectives

Note Regarding Rates And Credits

A schedule of rates, brackets, credit amounts and other data is available at the beginning of both Volumes of this textbook, (but not this Study Guide) and on the Companion Website. We expect you to refer to this information when calculating the credits covered in this chapter (i.e., you are not expected to memorize the rates, brackets and credit bases).

After completing Chapter 4, you should be able to:

1. Calculate Taxable Income when an individual has basic deductions against Net Income For Tax Purposes. (paragraph [P hereafter] 4-1 to 4-13).
2. Calculate federal and provincial Tax Payable before the consideration of any tax credits (P 4-14 to 4-31).
3. Calculate the personal tax credits described in ITA 118(1) which include the:
    *   spousal,
    *   eligible dependant,
    *   Canada caregiver for a child,
    *   basic,
    *   Canada caregiver (P 4-32 to 4-65).
4. Calculate the age tax credit (P 4-66 and 4-67).
5. Calculate the pension income tax credit (P 4-68 to 4-72).

6. Calculate the Canada employment tax credit (P 4-73 to 4-75).
7. Calculate the adoption expenses tax credit (P 4-76 to 4-80).
8. Calculate the public transit passes tax credit (P 4-81 to 4-85).
9. Calculate the home accessibility tax credit (P 4-86 to 4-96).

10. Calculate the first time home buyer's tax credit (P 4-97 to 4-99).
11. Calculate the volunteer firefighters and search and rescue workers tax credit (P 4-100 to 4-103).
12. Calculate the charitable donations tax credit, including the first-time donor's super tax credit, when the donation is in the form of cash (P 4-104 to 4-118).
13. Calculate the medical expense tax credit (P 4-119 to 4-129).
14. Calculate the disability tax credit (P 4-130 to 4-140).

15. Calculate the tax credits related to tuition fees, examination fees, ancillary fees, and student loan interest. (P 4-141 to 4-148).
16. Calculate the amount of education related tax credits that can be carried forward or transferred to another individual (P 4-149 to 4-158).
17. Calculate the Employment Insurance and Canada Pension Plan credits (P 4-159 to 4-165).
18. List the types and amounts of tax credits that can be transferred to a spouse or common-law partner (P 4-166 to 4-168).
19. Calculate the political contributions tax credit (P 4-169 to 4-172).

20. Calculate the labour sponsored venture capital corporation tax credit (P 4-173 to 4-177).
21. Explain the basic provisions of the refundable GST credit (P 4-178 to 4-185).
22. Calculate the refundable medical expense supplement (P 4-186 to 4-189).
23. Calculate the working income tax benefit and WITB disability supplement (P 4-190 to 4-193).
24. Calculate the refundable teacher and early childhood educator school supply tax credit (P 4-194 to 4-196).
25. Calculate the OAS and EI clawbacks (P 4-197 to 4-207).
26. Complete a simple personal tax return using the ProFile T1 tax preparation software program.

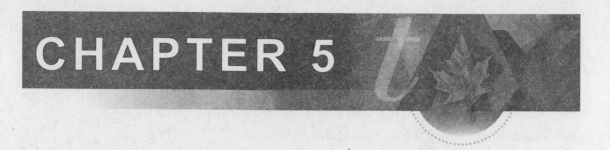

How To Work Through Chapter 5

We recommend the following approach in dealing with the material in this chapter:

Tax And Accounting Procedures Compared
- Read the beginning of the chapter to 5-11 (in the textbook).

Additions To Capital Cost, Including Available For Use Rules
- Read paragraph 5-12 to 5-33.

Capital Cost Allowances - General Overview and Rates For Common Classes
- Read paragraph 5-34 to 5-37.
- Do Exercise Five-1 (in the textbook) and check the solution in this Study Guide.

Half-Year (a.k.a. First Year) Rules
- Read paragraph 5-38 to 5-42.
- Do Exercises Five-2 to Five-5 and check the solutions in this Study Guide.

Short Fiscal Periods
- Read paragraph 5-43 to 5-47.
- Do Exercise Five-6 and check the solution in this Study Guide.

Class 14.1 (Including Goodwill) And The Repeal Of The CEC Regime
- Read paragraph 5-48 to 5-62.

Tax Planning Considerations For CCA
- Read paragraph 5-63 to 5-67.
- Do Exercise Five-7 and check the solution in this Study Guide.

Dispositions Of Depreciable Assets
- Read paragraph 5-68 to 5-76.
- Do Exercise Five-8 and check the solution in this Study Guide.

Recapture of Capital Cost Allowance
- Read paragraph 5-77 to 5-80.
- Do Exercise Five-9 and check the solution in this Study Guide.

Terminal Losses
- Read paragraph 5-81 to 5-85.
- Do Exercises Five-10 and Five-11 and check the solutions in this Study Guide.

Dispositions Of Class 14.1 - Differences From Other Classes
- Read paragraph 5-86 to 5-92.
- Do Exercise Five-12 and check the solution in this Study Guide.
- Read paragraph 5-93 to 5-95.

Summary Of Tax Consequences
- Read paragraph 5-96.

CCA Schedule - Example
- Read paragraph 5-97 to 5-98.
- Do Self Study Problems Five-1 to Five-5 which are available on the Companion Website and check the solutions in this Study Guide.

Separate Class Election
- Read paragraph 5-99 to 5-106.
- Do Exercise Five-13 and check the solution in this Study Guide.
- Read paragraph 5-107 to 5-108.

Change In Use For Automobiles And Other Special Situations
- Read paragraph 5-109 to 5-114.

CEC To Class 14.1 - Transitional Rules
- Read paragraph 5-115 to 5-125.
- Do Exercise Five-14 and check the solution in this Study Guide.
- Read paragraph 5-126 to 5-130.
- Do Exercise Five-15 and check the solution in this Study Guide.
- Read paragraph 5-131 to 5-135.
- Do Exercise Five-16 and check the solution in this Study Guide.
- Read paragraph 5-136 to 5-144.
- Do Self Study Problems Five-6 to Five-8 and check the solutions in this Study Guide.
- Read paragraph 5-145 to 5-149.

To Complete This Chapter
- If you would like more practice in problem solving, do the Supplementary Self Study Problems for the chapter. These problems and solutions are available on the Companion Website.
- Review the Key Terms Used In This Chapter in the textbook at the end of Chapter 5. Consult the Glossary for the meaning of any key terms you do not know.
- Test yourself with the Chapter 5 Glossary Flashcards available on the Companion Website.
- Ensure you have achieved the Chapter 5 Learning Objectives listed in this Study Guide.
- As a review, we recommend you view the PowerPoint presentation for Chapter 5 that is on the Companion Website.

Practice Examination
- Write the Practice Examination for Chapter 5 that is on the Companion Website. Mark your examination using the Practice Examination Solution that is also on the Companion Website.

Solutions to Chapter Five Exercises

Exercise Five - 1 Solution

The correct classes for each of the assets would be as follows:

Asset	Class
Taxicab	16
Manufacturing and processing equipment	53
Franchise with a limited life	14
Passenger vehicle with a cost of $120,000*	10.1
Government licence with an unlimited life	14.1
Water storage tank	6
Photocopy machine (office equipment not specifically listed elsewhere)	8
Leasehold improvements	13
Rental building (not including the land)*	1

*These two assets would have to be allocated to separate classes. In addition, as covered later in the Chapter, the taxpayer could elect to include the photocopy machine in a separate class if its capital cost is $1,000 or more.

Exercise Five - 2 Solution

The impact would be calculated as follows:

Correct CCA [($326,000)(1/2)(30%)]	$48,900
CCA Recorded In 2017 [($326,000)(1/2)(4%)]	(6,520)
Understatement Of 2017 CCA	$42,380

Exercise Five - 3 Solution

The required CCA calculations would be as follows:

On 2012 Improvements ($52,000 ÷ 15)	$3,467
On 2017 Improvements [($31,000 ÷ 10)(1/2)]	1,550
2017 Capital Cost Allowance	$5,017

Exercise Five - 4 Solution

The required information would be calculated as follows:

January 1, 2017 UCC Balance		$212,000
Add: Additions	$37,400	
Deduct: Dispositions (Amount Of Deduction Given)	(18,300)	19,100
Deduct: One-Half Net Additions [(1/2)($19,100)]		(9,550)
CCA Base		$221,550
CCA [(20%)($221,550)]		(44,310)
Add: One-Half Net Additions		9,550
January 1, 2018 UCC Balance		$186,790

The maximum 2017 CCA is $44,310 and the January 1, 2018 UCC balance is $186,790.

Exercise Five - 5 Solution

The required calculations are as follows:

Acquisition Amount	$375,000
CCA For 2017 [($375,000 ÷ 10)(275/365)]	(28,253)
January 1, 2018 UCC Balance	$346,747

Note that the half year rule is not applicable to Class 14 assets. However, the amount of CCA must be pro rated for the year, based on the number of days that the asset is owned.

Exercise Five - 6 Solution
The maximum CCA for the year is $4,821 [(1/2)(20%)($115,000)(153/365)].

Exercise Five - 7 Solution
Following the general rule that, when less than the maximum CCA is to be deducted, the amounts deducted should be taken from the class(es) with the lowest rates, the required calculations would be as follows:

Required Total		$45,000
Maximum CCA - Class 1 [(4%)($426,000)]	($17,040)	
Maximum CCA - Class 8 [(20%)($126,000)]	(25,200)	(42,240)
Required Balance		$ 2,760

As they are both 30 percent declining balance classes, the remaining $2,760 could be taken from either Class 10 or Class 10.1. It would be advisable to use Class 10.1, as recapture is not recorded for this class. In addition, if the Class 10.1 vehicle is going to be disposed of in the near future, it could be better tax planning to take the maximum CCA for Class 10.1 of $6,300 [(30%)($21,000)] and reduce the Class 8 CCA to $21,660 ($45,000 - $6,300 - $17,040). Since there is no recapture for Class 10.1, this could increase aggregate future deductions of the other classes. Whether this would be advantageous depends on the anticipated proceeds of disposition.

Exercise Five - 8 Solution
The only tax consequence would be a taxable capital gain of $2,500 [(1/2)($23,000 - $18,000)].

Following the basic rule for dispositions, we would subtract from the Class 8 UCC the lesser of the proceeds of disposition ($23,000) and the capital cost of the individual asset ($18,000). Subtracting the lesser figure of $18,000 would leave a large positive balance in Class 8. As there are no other dispositions during the year, we can conclude that the balance will be positive at the end of the year. This fact, combined with the presence of many other assets in Class 8 means that there will be no recapture and no terminal loss.

Exercise Five - 9 Solution
The required information would be calculated as follows:

UCC Of The Class At The Beginning Of The Year	$24,883
Add: Acquisitions During The Year	Nil
Deduct: Dispositions During The Year - Lesser Of:	
• Capital Cost = $27,000	
• Proceeds Of Disposition = $28,500	(27,000)
Deduct: One-Half Net Additions	N/A*
Negative Ending Balance	($ 2,117)
Recapture Of CCA	2,117
January 1, 2018 UCC Balance	Nil

*This adjustment for one-half of the excess of additions over disposal deductions is only made when the net amount is positive.

The effect would be an addition to business income of $2,117 in recaptured CCA. Note that, unlike terminal losses (See Exercise Five-10), the fact that there is still an asset in the class is irrelevant.

While there would also be a taxable capital gain of $750 [(1/2)($28,500 - $27,000)], this would not be included in business income.

Exercise Five - 10 Solution

The required information would be calculated as follows:

UCC Of The Class At The Beginning Of The Year	$24,883
Add: Acquisitions During The Year	Nil
Deduct: Dispositions During The Year - Lesser Of:	
• Capital Cost = $54,000	
• Proceeds Of Disposition = $18,000	(18,000)
Ending Balance With No Remaining Assets	$ 6,883
Terminal Loss	(6,883)
January 1, 2018 UCC Balance	Nil

As there is a positive balance in Class 8 at the end of the year, but no remaining assets, there would be a terminal loss of $6,883. This loss is deducted in the calculation of net business income.

Exercise Five - 11 Solution

The accounting results would be calculated as follows:

Proceeds Of Disposition	$126,000
Net Book Value	(43,500)
Accounting Gain	$ 82,500

For tax purposes, there would be a taxable capital gain calculated as follows:

Proceeds Of Disposition	$126,000
Capital Cost	(97,000)
Capital Gain	$ 29,000
Inclusion Rate	1/2
Taxable Capital Gain	$ 14,500

The capital cost of $97,000 would be subtracted from the UCC, leaving a balance of $2,365,000 ($2,462,000 - $97,000).

While this disposition would reduce the maximum CCA for the current and subsequent years, there would be no recapture (the balance in Class 8 is still positive) or terminal loss (there are still assets in Class 8).

Exercise Five - 12 Solution

CCA on Class 14.1 for 2017 would be calculated as follows:

January 1, 2017 Balance	Nil
2017 Additions ($85,000 + $105,000)	$190,000
One-Half Net Additions [(1/2)($190,000)]	(95,000)
CCA Base	$ 95,000
2017 CCA [(5%)($95,000)]	(4,750)
One-Half Net Additions	95,000
January 1, 2018 UCC	$185,250
Deduct: Dispositions During The Year - Lesser Of:	
Capital Cost = $190,000 (See Note)	
Proceeds Of Disposition = $180,000	(180,000)
UCC Subsequent to The Sales	$ 5,250

Note The capital cost of the single goodwill asset is $190,000, the total of the purchased goodwill.

There would be no immediate tax consequences resulting from the dispositions. Subsequent to the sales, Dextrin Inc. has a Class 14.1 UCC of $5,250 consisting of goodwill with a capital cost of $10,000 ($190,000 - $180,000).

Exercise Five - 13 Solution

Photocopiers would be included in Class 8, a 20 percent declining balance class. The following table compares the CCA if no election is made with the results if the separate class election is made.

	No Election 10 Copiers	With Election 2 Copiers	With Election 8 Copiers
January Acquisitions @ $20,000	$200,000	$40,000	$160,000
Dispositions	(6,000)	(6,000)	N/A
Terminal Loss		$34,000	
December Acquisitions @ $22,000	44,000	$44,000	
One-Half Net Additions	(119,000)	(22,000)	(80,000)
Base Amount For CCA Claim	$119,000	$22,000	$ 80,000
Class 8 CCA Rate	20%	20%	20%
CCA	$ 23,800	$ 4,400	$ 16,000

If no election is made, there will be a deduction for CCA of $23,800. Alternatively, if each machine is allocated to a separate class, there will be a deduction for CCA of $20,400 ($4,400 + $16,000). In addition, there will be a terminal loss of $34,000. The use of the election increases the total deductible amount by $30,600 [($4,400 + $16,000) + $34,000 - $23,800].

Exercise Five - 14 Solution

The maximum Class 14.1 CCA for 2017 would be calculated as follows:

	Pre-2017 CEC	Post-2016 Assets
Opening UCC	$149,610	Nil
Add: Acquisitions During The Year	N/A	$89,000
Deduct: One-Half Net Additions	N/A	(44,500)
CCA Base	$149,610	$44,500
CCA Rate	7%	5%
Maximum 2017 CCA	$ 10,473	$ 2,225

The total CCA for Class 14.1 is equal to $12,698 ($10,473 + $2,225).

Exercise Five - 15 Solution

The amount that would have been added to the CEC account in 2014 totalled $150,000 [(3/4)($120,000 + $80,000)]. Using this information, the capital cost of the two unlimited life franchises would be calculated as follows:

[(4/3)($120,654)]	$160,872
[(4/3)($150,000 - $120,654)]	39,128
Capital Cost - Unlimited Life Franchises	$200,000

Note that the capital cost is equal to the amount paid since there have been no dispositions.

Exercise Five - 16 Solution

The relevant calculations here are as follows:

CEC Additions [(3/4)(($126,000 + $185,000 + $94,000)]	$303,750
Dispositions [(3/4)($142,000 + $220,000)]	(271,500)
CEC Balance	$ 32,250
2016 CEC Deduction [(7%)($32,250)]	(2,258)
December 31, 2016 CEC	$ 29,992

The total capital cost for the remaining asset is calculated as follows:

[(4/3)($29,992)]	$39,989
[(4/3)($2,258)]	3,011
Capital Cost	$43,000

There was a gain of $16,000 ($142,000 - $126,000) on the sale of the first franchise and a gain of $35,000 ($220,000 - $185,000) on the second franchise. The amount allocated to the third franchise reflects its $94,000 cost reduced by the gains on the other two franchises. This leaves a capital cost of $43,000 ($94,000 - $16,000 - $35,000).

Self Study Solution Five - 1

The required calculation of the maximum CCA is as follows:

	Class 1	Class 8	Class 10
Opening Balance	$2,597,000	$718,000	$524,000
Additions	Nil	Nil	374,000
Proceeds Of Disposition	Nil	Nil	(234,000)
One-Half Net Additions	Nil	Nil	(70,000)
CCA Base	$2,597,000	$718,000	$594,000
CCA Rate	4%	20%	30%
Maximum CCA	$ 103,880	$143,600	$178,200

This gives a maximum amount for CCA of $425,680 for the taxation year ($103,880 + $143,600 + $178,200).

Part B

Since the Company only has Net and Taxable Income before CCA of $328,000 and the problem states that loss carry overs should not be considered, maximum CCA would not be deducted as this would produce a loss. Only $328,000 in CCA should be taken in order to reduce the Taxable Income to nil.

Given that the CCA deduction is limited to $328,000, it would normally be deducted in the class or classes with the lowest rates. This would leave the unused amounts in classes with higher rates which, in turn, would maximize the amount that could be deducted in the first profitable years. Taking this approach, the $328,000 would be deducted as follows:

Class 1 (Maximum Available)	$103,880
Class 8 (Maximum Available)	143,600
Class 10 (Required Balance)	80,520
Total CCA	$328,000

This CCA deduction would reduce Taxable Income to nil.

Note that if there were immediate plans to sell the building for more than its opening UCC, this could affect the choice of Classes to deduct CCA from as any additional CCA taken on Class 1 would have to be added to income as recaptured CCA when the building is sold.

Self Study Solution Five - 2

Class 1

The required information is calculated as follows:

Opening Balance	$115,000
Additions	Nil
Dispositions - Lesser Of:	
• Cost = $190,000	
• Proceeds Of Disposition = $110,000	(110,000)
Ending Balance With No Remaining Assets In Class	$ 5,000
Terminal Loss	(5,000)
January 1, 2018 UCC Balance	Nil

Since the building sold is the last asset in the class, there is a terminal loss of $5,000 which is deducted in the determination of business income. The proceeds of disposition for the building total $110,000 ($260,000 - $150,000). As the adjusted cost base of the land is equal to the proceeds of disposition, there is no gain on the disposition of the land.

Class 8

The required information is calculated as follows:

Opening Balance		$ 96,000
Additions	$52,000	
Dispositions - Lesser Of:		
• Cost = $75,000		
• Proceeds Of Disposition = $35,000	(35,000)	17,000
One-Half Net Additions [(1/2)($17,000)]		(8,500)
CCA Base		$104,500
CCA At 20 Percent		(20,900)
One-Half Net Additions		8,500
January 1, 2018 UCC Balance		$ 92,100

Class 10

The required information is calculated as follows:

Opening Balance		$ 6,700
Additions	$ 8,000	
Dispositions - Lesser Of:		
• Cost = $20,000		
• Proceeds = $25,000	(20,000)	(12,000)
One-Half Net Additions (Only If Positive)		N/A
Negative Ending Balance		($ 5,300)
Recaptured CCA (i.e. Recapture)		5,300
January 1, 2018 UCC Balance		Nil

As the cost of the used car is less than $30,000, its cost is added to Class 10. With respect to the retirement, only the capital cost of the truck sold is deducted from Class 10. The excess of the $25,000 proceeds over the capital cost of $20,000 is a $5,000 capital gain, one-half of which would be taxable. The $12,000 net deduction creates a negative balance in the class and, as a consequence, no CCA will be taken for 2017. However, the negative balance of $5,300 will have to be taken into income as recapture.

Class 53

The required information is as follows:

Opening Balance	$75,000
CCA At 50 Percent	(37,500)
January 1, 2018 UCC Balance	$37,500

Summary Of Results (Required)

The preceding results can be summarized as follows:

Terminal Loss - Class 1	($ 5,000)
CCA - Class 8	(20,900)
Recapture - Class 10	5,300
CCA - Class 53	(37,500)
Decrease In Net Business Income	($58,100)
Taxable Capital Gain - Class 10 [(1/2)($25,000 - $20,000)]	2,500
Decrease In Net Income For Tax Purposes	($55,600)

Note that detailed coverage of capital gains is available in Chapter 8 of the text.

Self Study Solution Five - 3

2012 Solution

The required calculations are as follows:

Additions To Class [(20 Cars)($12,000)]	$240,000
One-Half Net Additions [(1/2)($240,000)]	(120,000)
CCA Base	$120,000
CCA [(30%)($120,000)(122/365)]	(12,033)
One-Half Net Additions	120,000
January 1, 2013 UCC Balance	$227,967

Note that one-half of the net additions for the year is deducted to provide the basis for calculating the 2012 CCA, and then added back to establish the opening UCC base for the next period. The other point that is illustrated in this first year is application of the short fiscal period rules. As the business was established on September 1, 2012, its operations were carried out for only 122 of the 365 days in that year. This means that only a proportionate share of the annual CCA charge may be taken. Note that it is the length of the taxation year, not the period of ownership of the assets, which establishes the fraction of the year for which CCA is to be recorded.

2013 Solution

The required calculations are as follows:

Opening Balance For The Class	$227,967
Additions [(5 Cars)($12,500)]	62,500
Dispositions - Lesser Of:	
• Capital Cost = 3 @ $12,000 = $36,000	
• Proceeds Of Disposition = $27,500	(27,500)
One-Half Net Additions [(1/2)($62,500 - $27,500)]	(17,500)
CCA Base	$245,467
CCA [(30%)($245,467)]	(73,640)
One-Half Net Additions	17,500
January 1, 2014 UCC Balance	$189,327

Here again, one-half of the net additions for the year are deducted in establishing the base for calculating CCA, with the same amount being added back to determine the opening UCC for the next period.

2014 Solution

The required calculations are as follows:

Opening Balance For The Class	$189,327
Dispositions - Lesser Of:	
• Capital Cost = 4 @ $12,000 = $48,000	
• Proceeds Of Disposition = $38,000	(38,000)
One-Half Net Additions	N/A
CCA Base	$151,327
CCA [(30%)($151,327)]	(45,398)
January 1, 2015 UCC Balance	$105,929

The calculations are simplified by the absence of additions to the delivery car fleet. To establish the CCA base, it is only necessary to deduct the proceeds of the dispositions. The new UCC is the CCA base, less the CCA for the period.

2015 Solution

The required calculations are as follows:

Opening Balance For The Class	$105,929
Dispositions - Lesser Of:	
• Capital Cost = 13 @ $12,000	
+ 3 @ $12,500 = $193,500	
• Proceeds Of Disposition = $128,000	(128,000)
Negative Ending Balance	($ 22,071)
Recaptured CCA (i.e. Recapture)	22,071
January 1, 2016 UCC Balance	Nil

The inability to replace the fleet cars in a timely fashion was a costly mistake in that the $22,071 in recapture will be included in the 2015 Net Income. In a more realistic situation, it is likely that actions would have been taken to delay the retirement of the older cars and, thereby, avoid the tax implications of recapture. Note also that when recapture occurs, the balance in the class for the next period is reduced to zero.

2016 Solution

The required calculations are as follows:

Opening Balance For The Class	Nil
Acquisitions [(25 Cars)($16,000)]	$400,000
One-Half Net Additions [(1/2)($400,000)]	(200,000)
CCA Base	$200,000
CCA [(30%)($200,000)]	(60,000)
One-Half Net Additions	200,000
January 1, 2017 UCC Balance	$340,000

As was the case in 2012 and 2013, one-half of the net additions must be deducted in establishing the base for CCA and then added back to determine the opening UCC balance for the next period.

2017 Solution

The required calculations are as follows:

Opening Balance For The Class	$340,000
Dispositions - Lesser Of:	
• Capital Cost = 2 @ $12,500	
+ 25 @ $16,000 = $425,000	
• Proceeds Of Disposition = $268,000	(268,000)
Ending Balance With No Remaining Assets In Class	$ 72,000
Terminal Loss	(72,000)
January 1, 2018 UCC Balance	Nil

After all of the assets in Class 10 have been retired there is still a $72,000 UCC balance. This results in a terminal loss that will be deducted in full from the Net Income of Golden Dragon Ltd. The terminal loss will also be deducted from the UCC balance leaving a January 1, 2018 balance of nil.

Self Study Solution Five - 4

Class 1 and Class 3 - Buildings

As the new non-residential building has been allocated to a separate Class 1 and is used 100 percent for non-residential purposes, it is eligible for an enhanced CCA rate. As no manufacturing and processing is involved, the enhanced rate will be 6 percent. Based on this, the maximum 2017 CCA amounts and January 1, 2018 UCC balances are as follows:

	Separate Class 1	Class 3
Addition	$258,000	N/A
One-Half Net Additions	(129,000)	
CCA Base/Opening UCC	$129,000	$1,562,000
Maximum CCA:		
[(6%)($129,000)]	(7,740)	
[(5%)($1,562,000)]		(78,100)
Add: One-Half Net Additions	129,000	N/A
January 1, 2018 UCC	$250,260	$1,483,900

Class 8 - Office Furniture And Equipment

The required calculations for this class would be as follows:

Opening Balance		$278,000
Additions	$72,000	
Disposition of Furniture - Lesser Of:		
• Capital Cost = $38,000		
• Proceeds Of Disposition = $42,000	(38,000)	
Disposition Due To Fire - Lesser Of:		
• Capital Cost = $18,000		
• Proceeds Of Disposition = $11,000	(11,000)	23,000
One-Half Net Additions [(50%)($23,000)]		(11,500)
CCA Base		$289,500
2017 CCA [(20%)($289,500)]		(57,900)
One-Half Net Additions		11,500
January 1, 2018 UCC Balance		$243,100

There would also be taxable capital gain on the furniture disposition, calculated as follows:

Proceeds Of Disposition	$42,000
Capital Cost	(38,000)
Capital Gain	$ 4,000
Inclusion Rate	1/2
Taxable Capital Gain	$ 2,000

Class 10 - Vehicles

The required calculations for this class would be as follows:

Opening Balance		$204,000
Additions	$63,000	
Disposition of Truck - Lesser Of:		
• Capital Cost = $37,000		
• Proceeds Of Disposition = $12,000	(12,000)	51,000
One-Half Net Additions [(1/2)($51,000)]		(25,500)
CCA Base		$229,500
2017 CCA [(30%)($229,500)]		(68,850)
One-Half Net Additions		25,500
January 1, 2018 UCC Balance		$186,150

Class 13 - Leasehold Improvements

In general, leasehold improvements will be written off over the term of the lease on a straight line basis. For purposes of applying this calculation, the term of the lease includes the first renewal option beginning in a period after the improvements were made. In the case of the original improvements, the period to be used is 10 years. With respect to the improvements during the current period, the write-off period will be 8 years. Also note that Class 13 assets are subject to the first year rules on net additions. The required calculation is as follows:

Opening Balance	$106,250
Additions	58,000
CCA Base	$164,250
2017 CCA:	
• First Improvements ($125,000 ÷ 10)	(12,500)
• Current Improvements [($58,000 ÷ 8)(1/2)]	(3,625)
January 1, 2018 UCC Balance	$148,125

Class 50 - Computers

The required calculations are as follows:

Opening Balance	$11,000
Additions	17,000
One-Half Net Additions [(1/2)($17,000)]	(8,500)
CCA Base	$19,500
2017 CCA [(55%)($19,500)]	(10,725)
One-Half Net Additions	8,500
January 1, 2018 UCC	$ 17,275

Class 53 - Manufacturing Equipment

The required calculations are as follows:

Opening Balance	$126,000
Disposition - Lesser Of:	
• Capital Cost = $168,000	
• Proceeds Of Disposition = $89,000	(89,000)
Ending Balance With No Remaining Assets In Class	$ 37,000
Terminal Loss	(37,000)
January 1, 2018 UCC Balance	Nil

After all of the assets in Class 53 have been retired there is still a $37,000 UCC balance. This results in a terminal loss that will be deducted in full from the Net Income of Burton Steel Ltd. The terminal loss will also be deducted from the UCC balance.

Summary Of The Results (Not Required)

The maximum CCA for the year ending December 31, 2017 and the January 1, 2018 UCC balances can be summarized as follows:

	Maximum CCA	UCC
Class 1	$ 7,740	$ 250,260
Class 3	78,100	1,483,900
Class 8	57,900	243,100
Class 10	68,850	186,150
Class 13	16,125	148,125
Class 50	10,725	17,275
Class 53	Nil	Nil

In addition, the following income effects resulted from the information provided in the problem:

Taxable Capital Gain On Class 8 Assets [(1/2)($4,000)]	$ 2,000
Terminal Loss On Class 53 Assets	(37,000)
Total Deduction	($35,000)

Self Study Solution Five - 5

Case One

For the year ending December 31, 2017, the maximum CCA, as well as the UCC balance for January 1, 2018 for Traxit's Class 14.1 would be as calculated as follows:

January 1, 2017 Balance	Nil
2017 Additions ($56,000 + $124,000)	$180,000
One-Half Net Additions [(1/2)($180,000)]	(90,000)
CCA Base	$ 90,000
2017 CCA [(5%)($90,000)]	(4,500)
One-Half Net Additions	90,000
January 1, 2018 UCC	$ 175,500

The results for 2018, including maximum CCA of $3,925, would be calculated as follows:

January 1, 2018 UCC	$175,500
Disposition - Lesser Of:	
Capital Cost = $180,000	
Proceeds Of Disposition = $97,000	(97,000)
CCA Base	$ 78,500
2018 CCA [(5%)($78,500)]	(3,925)
January 1, 2019 UCC	$ 74,575

There would be no immediate tax consequences resulting from the sale of goodwill, other than a reduction in the UCC. Note that the capital cost in the calculation is of the single goodwill property.

Case Two

For the year ending December 31, 2017, the maximum CCA, as well as the UCC balance for January 1, 2018 for Traxit's Class 14.1 would be as calculated as follows:

January 1, 2017 Balance	Nil
2017 Additions ($34,000 + $47,000)	$81,000
One-Half Net Additions [(1/2)($81,000)]	(40,500)
CCA Base	$ 40,500
2017 CCA [(5%)($40,500)]	(2,025)
One-Half Net Additions	40,500
January 1, 2018 UCC	$78,975

The results for 2018 would be as follows:

January 1, 2018 UCC	$78,975
Disposition - Lesser Of:	
Capital Cost = $81,000	
Proceeds Of Disposition = $85,000	(81,000)
Negative Ending Balance	($ 2,025)
Recapture Of CCA	2,025
January 1, 2019 UCC	Nil

Proceeds Of Disposition	$85,000
Capital Cost	(81,000)
Capital Gain	$ 4,000
Inclusion Rate	1/2
Taxable Capital Gain	$ 2,000

There would be an increase in Net Income For Tax Purposes of $4,025 ($2,025 + $2,000).

Self Study Solution Five - 6

Part A

The required calculation of the maximum CCA and CEC is as follows:

Class 8 [(20%)($163,000)]	$ 32,600
Class 10 (Note 1)	37,050
Class 12 (Note 2)	42,000
Class 13 (Note 3)	24,000
Class 14.1 [(7%)($153.000)] (Note 4)	10,710
Maximum Total	$146,360

Note 1   The Class 10 CCA would be calculated as follows:

Opening Balance	$112,000
Additions	52,000
Proceeds Of Disposition (Less Than Cost)	(29,000)
One-Half Net Additions [(1/2)($52,000 - $29,000)]	(11,500)
CCA Base	$123,500
CCA Rate	30%
Maximum CCA	$ 37,050

Note 2   The rate for Class 12 is 100 percent. However, some additions to this Class are subject to the half-year rules. The presence of an opening balance of $42,000 and the statement that maximum CCA has always been taken, indicates that there must have been $84,000 of costs in 2016 that were subject to this rule. Given this, the entire balance can be deducted in 2017.

Note 3   The $204,000 balance in Class 13 is equal to 85 percent of $240,000. This means that during the two years 2015 and 2016, 15 percent of their cost was deducted as CCA. As the half-year rules are applicable to this Class, this represents a half year for 2015 and a full year for 2016. Since Class 13 is a straight-line Class, this indicates that the CCA rate is 10 percent (15% ÷ 1.5). Based on this analysis, maximum CCA for 2017 would be $24,000 [(10%)($240,000)].

Note 4 While the basic rate for Class 14.1 is 5 percent, the transitional rules allow continued use of the old CEC rate of 7 percent on balances carried forward from 2016. The use of this rate is available through 2026.

Part B
Since the Company only has Net and Taxable Income before CCA of $43,000 and the problem states that loss carry overs should not be considered, maximum CCA would not be deducted. Only $43,000 in CCA should be taken in order to reduce the Taxable Income to nil.

As to which CCA Classes should be reduced, the usual procedure is to deduct the required amount from the balances with the lowest rates. By leaving the balances with higher rates untouched, larger amounts of CCA can be deducted in later periods as required.

Taking this approach, the recommended CCA would be as follows:

Class 14.1 (Maximum Available)	$10,710
Class 13 (Maximum Available)	24,000
Class 8 ($43,000 - $10,710 - $24,000)	8,290
Total CCA	$43,000

The deduction of this amount of CCA would serve to reduce Taxable Income to nil.

Self Study Solution Five - 7

Part A

Class 1 - Buildings (Existing And Separate Class)
As the new building has been allocated to a separate Class 1, two calculations are required here. The CCA on the existing Class 1 would be as follows:

Opening UCC Balance		$590,000
Disposition - Lesser Of:		
Proceeds = $290,000 ($440,000 - $150,000)		
Capital Cost = $300,000 ($475,000 - $175,000)	(290,000)	
CCA Base		$300,000
Rate		4%
Maximum CCA		$ 12,000

Since the replacement building is new, used 100 percent for non-residential purposes and allocated to a separate Class 1, it qualifies for an enhanced CCA rate. As it is not used for manufacturing and processing, the enhanced rate is 6 percent. Using this rate, the CCA on the new building would be as follows:

Opening UCC Balance	Nil
Additions ($500,000 - $125,000)	$375,000
One-Half Net Additions	(187,500)
CCA Base	$187,500
Rate	6%
Maximum CCA	$ 11,250

Class 8 - Furniture

The required calculation here would be as follows:

Opening UCC Balance	$570,000
Additions	14,000
One-Half Net Additions	(7,000)
CCA Base	$577,000
Rate	20%
Maximum CCA	$115,400

Class 10 - Vehicles

The required calculations here would be as follows:

Opening UCC Balance	$61,000
Additions	22,000
One-Half Net Additions*	Nil
CCA Base	$83,000
Rate	30%
Maximum CCA	$24,900

*As the acquired truck was a depreciable property (it had a UCC balance) transferred from a non-arm's length person, the half-year rules do not apply to this acquisition. The shareholder's UCC does not affect the CCA calculations for Bartel Ltd.

Class 14 - Limited Life Franchise

The franchise would be allocated to Class 14 and amortized on a straight line basis over its legal life. The maximum CCA would be $20,000 ($120,000 ÷ 6). Note that the half-year rule is not applicable to Class 14.

Class 14.1 - Goodwill And Unlimited Life Franchise

Class 14.1 is, as of 2017, a Class that includes business assets that were in Cumulative Eligible Capital (CEC) prior to January 1, 2017. In order to calculate the January 1, 2017 balance in this account, it is necessary to determine the CEC balance as of December 31, 2016. The required calculations are as follows:

	CEC Balance	CEC Deductions
Goodwill Purchased [(3/4)($92,000)]	$69,000	
Unlimited Life Franchise [(3/4)($28,000)]	21,000	
2015 Base	$90,000	
CEC Amount At 7 Percent	(6,300)	$6,300
January 1, 2016 Balance	$83,700	
2016 Disposition [(3/4)($59,000)]	(44,250)	
2016 Base	$39,450	
CEC Amount At 7 Percent	(2,762)	2,762
CEC Balance - December 31, 2016 And Total CEC Deduction	$36,688	$9,062

In this situation, this December 31, 2016 CEC balance will become the January 1, 2017 UCC balance for Class 14.1. While the basic rate for Class 14.1 is 5 percent, transitional legislation allows a taxpayer to use the old CEC rate of 7 percent on carry forward balances. This rate is available through 2026. Given this, maximum CCA on Class 14.1 is calculated as follows:

January 1, 2017 UCC	$36,688
2017 CCA [(7%)($36,688)]	(2,568)
January 1, 2018 UCC	$34,120

Summary (Not Required)

The maximum CCA is as follows:

Class 1	$ 12,000
Class 1	11,250
Class 8	115,400
Class 10	24,900
Class 14	20,000
Class 14.1	2,568
Maximum CCA	$186,118

Part B

The capital cost of the goodwill is equal to 4/3 of the December 31, 2016 CEC balance, plus 4/3 of any CEC deductions that have not been recaptured. The required calculation is as follows:

[(4/3)($36,688)]	$48,917
[(4/3)($6,300 + $2,762)]	12,083
Capital Cost Of Goodwill	$61,000

To understand the economics of this result, you need to note that when the unlimited life franchise was sold, there was an economic gain of $31,000 ($59,000 - $28,000). However, under the old CEC procedures, this was not recognized as a gain. Rather, this amount was deducted from the CEC balance, in effect reducing the amount that was still available to be written off for the goodwill. This explains why, despite the fact that the goodwill had cost $92,000, the remaining capital cost is only $61,000 ($92,000 - $31,000).

Self Study Solution Five - 8

Class 1 - Building

There were no additions or dispositions in this class. As a consequence, the maximum 2017 CCA would be $25,000 [(4%)($625,000)]. The January 1, 2018 UCC of Class 1 would be $600,000 ($625,000 - $25,000).

Class 8 - Office Furniture And Equipment

The required calculations for this class would be as follows:

Opening UCC Balance		$155,000
Additions	$27,000	
Dispositions - Lesser Of:		
• Capital Cost = $22,000		
• Proceeds Of Disposition = $35,000	(22,000)	5,000
One-Half Net Additions [(1/2)($5,000)]		(2,500)
CCA Base		$157,500
2017 CCA [(20%)($157,500)]		(31,500)
One-Half Net Additions		2,500
January 1, 2018 UCC Balance		$128,500

The sale of the furniture and equipment would result in a taxable capital gain that would be calculated as follows:

Proceeds Of Disposition	$35,000
Capital Cost	(22,000)
Capital Gain	$13,000
Inclusion Rate	1/2
Taxable Capital Gain	$ 6,500

Class 10 - Vehicles

The required calculations for this class would be as follows:

Opening UCC Balance			$118,000
Additions		$33,000	
Disposition of Truck - Lesser Of:			
• Capital Cost = $23,000			
• Proceeds Of Disposition = $8,500		(8,500)	
Disposition of Car - Lesser Of:			
• Capital Cost = $17,000			
• Proceeds Of Disposition = $8,000		(8,000)	16,500
One-Half Net Additions [(1/2)($16,500)]			(8,250)
CCA Base			$126,250
2017 CCA [(30%)($126,250)]			(37,875)
One-Half Net Additions			8,250
January 1, 2018 UCC Balance			$ 96,625

Note that the amount received from the insurance company on the destroyed vehicle is treated as proceeds from a disposition.

Class 12 - Tools

Tools that cost $500 or less are allocated to Class 12 where they are not subject to the half-year rule. This means that they are eligible for a write-off rate of 100 percent in the year of acquisition. As a consequence, the entire $34,000 can be deducted as CCA for 2017, leaving a nil January 1, 2018 UCC balance.

Class 13 - Leasehold Improvements

In general, leasehold improvements will be written off over the term of the lease on a straight line basis. For purposes of applying this calculation, the term of the lease would include the first renewal option, beginning in a period after the improvements were made. In the case of the original improvements, the period to be used is 12 years. With respect to the improvements during the current year, the write-off period will be 9 years. Also note that Class 13 assets are subject to the half-year rules on net additions. The required calculations are as follows:

Opening UCC Balance		$ 61,750
Additions		45,000
CCA Base		$106,750
CCA:		
• 2013 Improvements ($78,000 ÷ 12)	($6,500)	
• 2017 Improvements [($45,000 ÷ 9)(1/2)]	(2,500)	(9,000)
January 1, 2018 UCC Balance		$ 97,750

Class 14.1 - Intangible Assets

As there was no balance in the Company's Cumulative Eligible Capital Account on December 31, 2016, the opening balance for the new Class 14.1 would be nil. Given this, the required calculations for this Class are as follows:

January 1, 2017 UCC	Nil
Disposition - Lesser Of:	
Capital Cost = Nil	
Proceeds Of Disposition = $87,000	Nil
January 1, 2018 UCC Balance	Nil
Proceeds Of Disposition	$87,000
Capital Cost	Nil
Capital Gain	$87,000
Inclusion Rate	1/2
Taxable Capital Gain	$43,500

Class 50 - Computer Hardware

The required calculations are as follows:

Opening UCC Balance	$ Nil
Additions	28,000
One-Half Net Additions	(14,000)
CCA Base	$14,000
2017 CCA [(55%)($14,000)]	(7,700)
One-Half Net Additions	14,000
January 1, 2018 UCC Balance	$20,300

Class 53 - Manufacturing Equipment

The required calculations are as follows:

Opening UCC Balance	$217,000
Dispositions - Lesser Of:	
• Capital Cost = $752,000	
• Proceeds Of Disposition = $188,000	(188,000)
Ending Balance With No Remaining Assets In Class	$ 29,000
Terminal Loss	(29,000)
January 1, 2018 UCC Balance	Nil

After all of the assets in Class 53 have been retired there is still a $29,000 UCC balance. This results in a terminal loss that will be deducted in full from the Net Income of Atlantic Manufacturing Company.

Other Income Effects

In addition, the following income effects resulted from the information provided in the problem:

Taxable Capital Gain On Class 8 Assets	$ 6,500
Taxable Capital Gain On Class 14.1 Assets	43,500
Terminal Loss On Class 53 Assets	(29,000)
Total Inclusion	$21,000

Summary Of CCA And UCC Results (Not Required)

The maximum 2017 CCA and the January 1, 2018 UCC balances can be summarized as follows:

	Maximum CCA	UCC
Class 1	$ 25,000	$600,000
Class 8	31,500	128,500
Class 10	37,875	96,625
Class 12	34,000	Nil
Class 13	9,000	97,750
Class 14.1	Nil	Nil
Class 50	7,700	20,300
Class 53	Nil	Nil

Chapter 5 Learning Objectives

After completing Chapter 5, you should be able to:

1. Describe the differences between the accounting procedures used for depreciable assets and the tax procedures used for these assets (paragraph [P hereafter] 5-1 to 5-11).
2. Determine the types of costs that are included in the amounts that are added to depreciable asset classes (P 5-12 to 5-26).
3. Recall the basic available for use rules (P 5-27 to 5-29).
4. Recall the general rules for segregating depreciable assets into classes (P 5-30 to 5-32).
5. Recall the types of assets that must be allocated to separate classes (P 5-33).

6. Explain the basic elements of the CCA system (P 5-34 and 5-36).
7. Apply the rates and methods that are applicable to common CCA classes in order to determine the maximum CCA for the period (P 5-37).
8. Apply the half-year (first year) rules in the determination of maximum CCA for the period (P 5-38 to 5-42).
9. Apply the short fiscal period rules in the determination of maximum CCA for the period (P 5-43 to 5-47).
10. Describe the additions to Class 14.1 and the special treatment for goodwill and the December 31, 2016 CEC balance. (P 5-48 to 5-62).

11. Explain the tax planning considerations that are involved when a business takes less than maximum CCA (P 5-63 to 5-67).
12. Determine the tax consequences associated with dispositions of depreciable assets, including recapture, terminal losses, and capital gains (P 5-68 to 5-85).
13. Explain how the treatment of dispositions in Class 14.1 differs from that for other CCA Classes (P 5-86 to 5-95).
14. Create the commonly used CCA schedule for a situation with depreciable assets (P 5-96 to 5-98).
15. Apply the provisions relating to separate class elections (P 5-99 to 5-108).

16. Apply the provisions relating to the change in use of automobiles. (P 5-109 to 5-114).
17. Apply the CEC To Class 14.1 transitional rules (P 5-115 to 5-149).

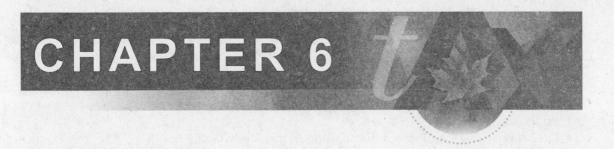

CHAPTER 6

How To Work Through Chapter 6

We recommend the following approach in dealing with the material in this chapter:

Overview And Classification Of Business Income
- Read paragraph 6-1 to 6-16 (in the textbook).

Business Income Vs. Property Income
- Read paragraph 6-17 to 6-27.
- Do Exercise Six-1 (in the textbook) and check the solution in this Study Guide.

Business Income Vs. Capital Gains
- Read paragraph 6-28 to 6-42.
- Do Exercise Six-2 and check the solution in this Study Guide.

Business Income And GAAP
- Read paragraph 6-43 to 6-45.

Inclusions - Amounts Received And Receivable
- Read paragraph 6-46 to 6-53.

Reserves For Doubtful Debts, Undelivered Goods And Unpaid Amounts
- Read paragraph 6-54 to 6-61.
- Do Exercise Six-3 and check the solution in this Study Guide.
- Read paragraph 6-62.
- Do Exercise Six-4 and check the solution in this Study Guide.
- Read paragraph 6-63.
- Do Exercise Six-5 and check the solution in this Study Guide.
- Do Self Study Problems Six-1 and Six-2 which are available on the Companion Website and check the solutions in this Study Guide.

Other Inclusions
- Read paragraph 6-64 to 6-65.

Limitations On Deductions From Business And Property Income, Including Work Space In The Home Costs
- Read paragraph 6-66 to 6-93.
- Do Exercise Six-6 and check the solution in this Study Guide.
- Read paragraph 6-94 to 6-100.
- Do Exercise Six-7 and check the solution in this Study Guide.
- Do Self Study Problem Six-3 and check the solution in this Study Guide.
- Read paragraph 6-101 to 6-103.

Limitations On Deductions From Business, Property, And Employment Income, Including Reasonableness, Meals And Entertainment

- Read paragraph 6-104 to 6-112.

Restrictions On Automobile Costs

- Read paragraph 6-113 to 6-118
- Do Exercise Six-8 and check the solution in this Study Guide.
- Read paragraph 6-119 to 6-126.
- Do Exercise Six-9 and check the solution in this Study Guide.
- Do Self Study Problems Six-4 to Six-6 and check the solutions in this Study Guide.

Leasing Property

- Read paragraph 6-127 to 6-129.
- Do Exercise Six-10 and check the solution in this Study Guide.

Illegal Payments, Fines And Penalties

- Read paragraph 6-130 and 6-132.

Specific Deductions From Business Income, Including Cost Of Sales

- Read paragraph 6-133 to 6-141.
- Do Exercise Six-11 and check the solution in this Study Guide.
- Do Self Study Problem Six-7 and check the solution in this Study Guide.
- Read paragraph 6-142 to 6-143.

Reconciliation Of Accounting Net Income And Net Income For Tax Purposes

- Read paragraph 6-144 to 6-149.
- Do Self Study Problems Six-8 to Six-10 and check the solutions in this Study Guide.

Taxation Year And Additional Business Income

- Read paragraph 6-150 to 6-157.
- Do Exercise Six-12 and check the solution in this Study Guide.
- Do Self Study Problem Six-11 and check the solution in this Study Guide.

Farming Income And Losses, Including Restricted Farm Losses

- Read paragraph 6-158 to 6-164.
- Do Exercise Six-13 and check the solution in this Study Guide.
- Read paragraph 6-165 to 6-169.

Professional Income (Billed Basis Of Recognition)

- Read paragraph 6-170 to 6-172.
- Do Exercise Six-14 and check the solution in this Study Guide.
- Do Self Study Problems Six-12 and Six-13 and check the solutions in this Study Guide.

Sale Of A Business, Including ITA 22 Election On Accounts Receivable

- Read paragraph 6-173 to 6-178.
- Do Exercise Six-15 and check the solution in this Study Guide.
- Do Self Study Problem Six-14 to Six-16 and check the solutions in this Study Guide.

To Complete This Chapter

- If you would like more practice in problem solving, do the Supplementary Self Study Problems for the chapter. These problems and solutions are available on the Companion Website.
- Review the Key Terms Used In This Chapter in the textbook at the end of Chapter 6. Consult the Glossary for the meaning of any key terms you do not know.
- Test yourself with the Chapter 6 Glossary Flashcards available on the Companion Website.
- Ensure you have achieved the Chapter 6 Learning Objectives listed in this Study Guide.

- As a review, we recommend you view the PowerPoint presentation for Chapter 6 that is on the Companion Website.

Practice Examination
- Write the Practice Examination for Chapter 6 that is on the Companion Website. Mark your examination using the Practice Examination Solution that is also on the Companion Website.

Solutions to Chapter Six Exercises

Exercise Six - 1 Solution
With a single transaction, Joan's activity clearly does not fall within the general definition of operating a business. However, the real question is whether this transaction would be considered an adventure or concern in the nature of trade. As she is not behaving like a dealer and does not appear to have an intent to sell the song rights, it is unlikely that this transaction would be viewed as an adventure or concern in the nature of trade. This means that the royalties would be treated as property income, rather than business income. While this classification would not be important as long as she holds the rights, if there is a disposition of these rights, any gain would be treated as a capital gain, rather than as a fully taxable business gain.

Exercise Six - 2 Solution
Provided that she can demonstrate that her intent was to operate the building as a rental property, the gain should qualify as a capital gain. The fact that the offer was unsolicited would support this conclusion.

Exercise Six - 3 Solution
The Bad Debt Expense would be as follows:

2017 Estimate Of Future Bad Debts (Credit Allowance)	($18,400)
Increase In Expense To Eliminate Debit Balance In Allowance	
($17,200 Actual Write-Offs - $16,000 Allowance)	(1,200)
2017 Bad Debt Expense For Accounting Purposes	($19,600)

For tax purposes, the net decrease for the year will be the same $19,600 calculated as follows:

Add: 2016 Reserve For Tax Purposes		$ 16,000
Deduct:		
2017 Actual Write-Offs	($17,200)	
2017 Reserve For Tax Purposes	(18,400)	(35,600)
2017 Net Deduction For Tax Purposes		($19,600)

Exercise Six - 4 Solution
The amount to be included in net business income would be calculated as follows:

Cash Sales	$53,400
Accounts Receivable	26,300
Reserve For Undelivered Services	(5,600)
Reserve For Doubtful Accounts	(425)
Total Increase	$73,675

Exercise Six - 5 Solution
As some of the proceeds are not receivable for more than two years after the date of sale, a reserve can be deducted under ITA 20(1)(n) for the years 2017, 2018, and 2019. As

December 31, 2020 is more than 36 months after the sale was made, no reserve can be deducted for 2020 or 2021. Note that the previous year's reserve is added to income before deducting the new reserve. The maximum reserve is based on the gross profit of $65,000. None of this profit will be recognized in 2017 as no proceeds are received. In 2018 and 2019, 25 percent of the profit will be recognized, with the remainder being in 2020 when no reserve can be deducted.

The maximum reserve that can be deducted in each year, as well as the minimum income to be recognized in each year, is shown in the following schedule:

	Income	Proceeds Rec'd
2017 Reserve = [(100%)($65,000)] = $65,000	Nil	Nil
2018 Reserve = [(75%)($65,000)] = $48,750	$16,250	$ 30,000
2019 Reserve = [(50%)($65,000)] = $32,500	16,250	30,000
2020 Reserve = Nil (>36 Months From Sale)	32,500	30,000
2021 Reserve = Nil (All Proceeds Received)	Nil	30,000
Totals	$65,000	$120,000

Note that the technically correct calculation of income involves adding back the previous year's reserve and deducting the new reserve. For example, the calculation for 2019 involves adding back the 2018 reserve of $48,750 and deducting the new reserve of $32,500 to calculate the income of $16,250 ($48,750 - $32,500).

Exercise Six - 6 Solution

As Ms. Johnson owns 30 percent of the common shares, she is clearly a specified shareholder under ITA 18(5). Her relevant equity balance would be $1,620,000 [(30%)($2,400,000) + (100%)($900,000)]. Given this, the disallowed interest would be calculated as follows:

Total Interest Paid To Ms. Johnson [(9%)($4,500,000)]	$405,000
Maximum Deductible Interest [(9%)(1.5)($1,620,000)]	(218,700)
Disallowed Interest	$186,300

Exercise Six - 7 Solution

The following work space in the home costs would be deductible in each of the three scenarios:

	Part A	Part B	Part C
Utilities	$2,400	$ 2,400	$ 2,400
Maintenance And Repairs	4,600	4,600	4,600
Property Taxes	Nil	5,200	5,200
House Insurance	Nil	2,300	2,300
Interest On Mortgage	Nil	Nil	7,800
House CCA	Nil	Nil	12,000
Subtotal	$7,000	$14,500	$34,300
Percentage	25%	25%	25%
Subtotal	$1,750	$ 3,625	$ 8,575
Repainting And Rewiring (100%)	1,000	1,000	1,000
Internet Service Fees [(95%)($960)]	Nil	Nil	912
Monthly Phone [(95%)($600)]	Nil	Nil	570
Long Distance Charges (100%)	390	390	390
Maximum Deduction	$3,140	$ 5,015	$ 11,447

Exercise Six - 8 Solution

With respect to the amount of CCA, since the business commenced operations on September 15, 2017, the CCA is limited to the proportion of the year the business was in operation (108/365) and the first year rules would apply. The fact that the car was purchased on October 1 does not affect the short fiscal year calculation.

The base amount for the CCA calculation is limited to the Class 10.1 maximum of $30,000. With respect to the interest, the car was financed for a total of 92 days with a limit of $10 per day. As a result, the amounts that can be deducted are as follows:

CCA [(1/2)(108/365)(30%)($30,000)]		$1,332
Interest Costs - Lesser Of:		
• Amount Paid = $1,200		
• [($10)(92 Days)] = $920		920
Total Deduction		**$2,252**

Exercise Six - 9 Solution

The amount he can deduct is limited to $2,229, the least of:

- $4,925 [($985)(5)];
- $4,080 [($800)(153/30)]; and
- $2,229 {[$4,925][$30,000 ÷ (85%)($78,000)]}.

Exercise Six - 10 Solution

For tax purposes, the lease would be treated as an operating lease, with the deduction being based only on the lease payments. Under GAAP, the lease would have to be treated as a purchase and capitalized. This is because during the lease term the lease transfers "substantially all of the benefits and risks of ownership related to the leased property from the lessor to the lessee". This means that the accounting deductions would be for amortization on the capitalized asset and interest costs on the associated liability.

Exercise Six - 11 Solution

The average per unit cost of $2.87 ($663,850 ÷ 231,000) is calculated as follows:

Price	Units	Total
$2.50	50,000	$125,000
$2.85	35,000	99,750
$2.95	62,000	182,900
$3.05	84,000	256,200
Totals	231,000	$663,850

The following calculations will be used in this solution.

Fair Market Value (Using Replacement Cost) [($3.10)(102,000)]	$316,200
Fair Market Value (Using Net Realizable Value) [(90%)($4.50)(102,000)]	413,100
FIFO Cost [(84,000)($3.05) + (102,000 - 84,000)($2.95)]	309,300
Average Cost [($2.87)(102,000)]	292,740

For tax purposes, the inventory value can be determined by any of the following methods.

Fair Market Value = Replacement Cost	$316,200
Fair Market Value = Net Realizable Value	413,100
Lower of FIFO Cost ($309,300) or Replacement Cost ($316,200)	309,300
Lower of FIFO Cost ($309,300) or Net Realizable Value ($413,100)	309,300
Lower of Average Cost ($292,740) or Replacement Cost ($316,200)	292,740
Lower of Average Cost ($292,740) or Net Realizable Value ($413,100)	292,740

Exercise Six - 12 Solution

Mr. Gelato's additional business income for 2017 will be $18,551 [($12,300)(184 Days ÷ 122 Days)]. The 184 days is for the period July 1 through December 31, while the 122 days is for the period March 1 through June 30. The total business income that Mr. Gelato will have to report for 2017 is $30,851 ($12,300 + $18,551).

Exercise Six - 13 Solution

For Ms. Morph, farming is clearly a secondary source of income. Given this, her farm losses will be restricted. The amount she can deduct for 2017 will be limited to $10,600 [$2,500 + (1/2)($18,700 - $2,500)]. The remaining $8,100 ($18,700 - $10,600) restricted farm loss is available for carry over.

Exercise Six - 14 Solution

Mr. Winters' income for the current year under the three alternatives would be as follows:

Cash Basis   Income would be $252,000 ($35,000 + $57,000 + $160,000).

Billed Basis   Income would be $220,000 ($35,000 + $185,000).

Accrual Basis   Income would be $245,000.

Exercise Six - 15 Solution

Mr. Nero would include in his business income the 2016 reserve of $3,800. He could then deduct the $5,250 ($53,450 - $48,200) loss on the receivables. The net tax effect for Mr. Nero would be a deduction in the determination of business income of $1,450 ($5,250 - $3,800).

Mr. Labelle would have to include the $5,250 difference between the face value and the price paid in income. Subsequent to the sale, 100 percent of any difference between the $53,450 face value of the receivables and amounts actually collected will be deductible when calculating Mr. Labelle's net business income.

Mr. Labelle could establish a new reserve for doubtful debts related to any uncollected receivables that are outstanding at the end of the year.

Self Study Solution Six - 1

The net deduction for bad debts in the calculation of 2017 business income would be calculated as follows:

Add:	
2016 Reserve For Doubtful Debts	$11,500
Recoveries Of 2016 Bad Debts During 2017	1,500
Deduct:	
Actual Bad Debt Write-Offs During 2017 ($8,800 - $700)	(8,100)
2017 Reserve For Doubtful Debts ($15,900 + $700)	(16,600)
2017 Net Deduction From Business Income	($11,700)

Note that the $700 that was due from Dr. Allworth's personal friend has been treated as part of the reserve for doubtful debts, rather than as part of the write-offs for the period. The $190 recovery in 2016 would have been included in income in 2016 and would not affect 2017 income.

Self Study Solution Six - 2

The results for the 2 years would be as follows:

	2017	2018
Cash Sales ($185,000 - $65,000)	$120,000	
Cash Sales ($240,000 - $50,000)		$190,000
Sales On Account	65,000	50,000
Reserve For Doubtful Debts:		
Add Prior Year Reserve	Nil	5,000
Deduct Current Year Reserve	(5,000)	(3,500)
Deduct Actual Write-Offs	Nil	(5,500)
Advances From Customers	23,000	13,400
Reserve For Undelivered Merchandise:		
Add Prior Year Reserve	Nil	23,000
Deduct Current Year Reserve	(23,000)	(13,400)
Gross Profit On Unused Materials Sale	10,000	Nil
Reserve For Unpaid Amounts:		
Add Prior Year Reserve		4,000
Deduct Current Year Reserve*		
{[$10,000][($50,000 - $30,000) ÷ $50,000]}	(4,000)	
{[$10,000][($50,000 - $40,000) ÷ $50,000]}		(2,000)
Net Effect	$186,000	$261,000

*As some of the proceeds on the sale of unused landscaping materials are not due until two years after the date of the sale, a reserve for unpaid amounts can be deducted. The three year time limit is not relevant as the balance is completely paid off within that time period.

Self Study Solution Six - 3

Part A

Under ITA 18(12), the following conditions must be satisfied in order for expenses related to work space in a self-contained domestic establishment to be deductible:

- the work space is either the individual's principal place of business; or

- the work space is used exclusively for the purpose of earning income from business and is used on a regular and continuous basis for meeting clients, customers, or patients of the individual in respect of the business.

With respect to Ms. Hart's mail order business, the allocated space in her home would appear to be her principal place of business. This means that she would be able to deduct work space in home costs in determining her net business income.

Part B

The calculation of the minimum net business income to be reported in Veronica's personal tax return is as follows:

Revenues		$89,000
Less: Expenses Other Than Home Work Space Costs:		
Cost Of Merchandise Sold	($46,000)	
Packaging Materials	(1,547)	
Shipping Costs	(3,216)	
Miscellaneous Office Supplies	(825)	
Telephone	(210)	
Advertising Brochures	(156)	
CCA (Note 1)	(2,056)	(54,010)
Income Before Home Work Space Costs		$34,990
Less: Home Work Space Costs (Note 2)		(2,174)
Net Business Income		$32,816

Note 1 Maximum CCA amounts on the assets of the business (not including CCA on the house) for the short fiscal year would be calculated as follows (alternative calculations shown in the two columns):

	100%	Short Fiscal Year (346/365)
Class 8 [($14,000)(1/2)(20%)]	$1,400	$1,327
Class 50 [($1,350)(1/2)(55%)]	371	352
Class 12 [($795)(1/2)(100%)]	398	377
Total	$2,169	
Short Fiscal Year Factor	346/365	
Maximum CCA	$2,056	$2,056

Note 2 The home work space costs would be calculated as follows:

Utilities For Home (Heat, Light, And Water)	$ 2,850
Mortgage Interest Paid	4,183
House Insurance	400
Property Taxes	1,230
Repairs And Maintenance For Home	1,125
Total Out-Of-Pocket Costs	$ 9,788
Class 1 CCA [($355,000 - $80,000)(1/2)(4%)]	5,500
Total Costs For The Home	$15,288
Percentage Of Floor Space	15%
Subtotal	$ 2,293
Short Fiscal Year Factor	346/365
Deductible Home Work Space Costs	$ 2,174

Part C

There are two issues that should be discussed with Veronica.

- As this problem asks for "minimum" net business income, CCA must be deducted on Ms. Hart's home. The problem with this is that, if she takes CCA, it could jeopardize the principal residence exemption on this property, resulting in the payment of taxes on a portion of the taxable capital gain that might arise on any future sale of the property, assuming real estate prices are increasing. This is discussed in more detail in Chapter 8.

- Although it is not relevant for this year, Ms. Hart should be aware that the deduction of work space in home costs cannot be used to create a loss in the future. However, any amount not deductible because it is greater than her income can be deducted in any subsequent year provided there is sufficient income from the same business in that year. This provides for an unlimited carry forward of unused work space in home costs (see IT-514, *Work Space in Home Expenses*).

Self Study Solution Six - 4

Part A

In Part A(i), Ms. Wise is an employee and, because her income includes commissions, she can deduct expenses related to the production of employment income under ITA 8(1)(f), provided no deduction is made under ITA 8(1)(h) or ITA 8(1)(h.1).

Deductions under ITA 8(1)(f) are limited to the amount of commissions earned. Alternatively, traveling costs and motor vehicle costs other than capital costs can be deducted under ITA 8(1)(h) and ITA 8(1)(h.1). Deductions under these provisions are not limited to commission income.

The deduction of dues and other expenses under ITA 8(1)(i) and automobile capital costs (CCA and financing costs) under ITA 8(1)(j) is permitted without regard to other provisions used.

	ITA 8(1)(f) (Limited To $15,000)	ITA 8(1) (h) and (h.1)	ITA 8(1) (i) and (j)	Part A(ii)
Professional Dues	-	-	$ 600	$ 600
Automobile Costs:				
Operating Costs [(35,000/50,000)($6,000)]	$ 4,200	$ 4,200	-	4,200
Financing Costs [(35,000/50,000)($2,500)]	-	-	1,750	1,750
CCA (See Note)	-	-	5,355	5,355
Home Office Costs:				
Utilities [(40%)($3,550)]	-	-	1,420	1,420
Maintenance [(40%)($1,500)]	-	-	600	600
Insurance [(40%)($950)]	380	-	-	380
Property Taxes [(40%)($4,700)]	1,880	-	-	1,880
Interest [(40%)($13,500)]	-	-	-	5,400
CCA [($140,000)(4%)]	-	-	-	5,600
Travel Costs	23,000	23,000	-	23,000
Non-Deductible Meals [(50%)($8,000)]	(4,000)	(4,000)	-	(4,000)
Country Club Charges	12,000	-	-	12,000
Non-Deductible Membership Fees	(2,500)	-	-	(2,500)
Non-Deductible Meals [(50%)($9,500)]	(4,750)	-	-	(4,750)
Total	$30,210	$23,200	$9,725	$50,935

Note The car will be allocated to Class 10.1 at a value of $30,000, the 2016 limit. The excess of $23,000 will not be deductible. Maximum CCA for 2016 would have been $4,500 [(30%)(1/2)($30,000)]. The deductible amount for 2016 would have been this amount, multiplied by the portion of her total usage that was related to income producing activity.

The January 1, 2017 UCC would be $25,500 ($30,000 - $4,500) and maximum CCA for 2017 would have been $7,650 [(30%)($25,500)]. Note that, in determining the relevant UCC value, the full amount of maximum 2016 CCA was deducted, not just the portion that was actually deducted in that year. The deductible amount for 2017 equals $5,355 [(35,000/50,000)($7,650)].

The deduction for home office costs has been split between ITA 8(1)(i) and (f). Since the utilities and maintenance portion can be deducted under ITA 8(1)(i), it is not limited by the commission income. The insurance and property tax components are limited as they are deducted under ITA 8(1)(f). A limitation, which is not illustrated in this problem, prevents the deduction of home office costs from creating an employment loss.

As the ITA 8(1)(f) amount is limited to the $15,000 in commission income, the total deduction using ITA 8(1)(f), (i) and (j), is $24,725 ($15,000 + $9,725).

The total deduction using ITA 8(1)(h), (h.1), (i) and (j), is $32,925 ($23,200 + $9,725). Note that when this approach is used, home office costs are limited to utilities and maintenance. Further, there is no deduction for entertainment costs. However, this approach results in deductions totaling $8,200 ($32,925 - $24,725) more than the amount available using ITA 8(1)(f), (i), and (j) due to the effect of the commission income limit.

Comparing Parts A (i) and A (ii), there is a difference of $18,010 ($50,935 - $32,925) between the maximum employee and self-employed calculations, illustrating the importance of the difference between being an employee and being self-employed. This problem is, of course, somewhat unrealistic in that, if Ms. Wise was an employee, it is likely that she would be compensated or reimbursed for at least part of her employment related expenses.

Part B

As will be discussed in Chapter 8, capital gains on an individual's principal residence are, in general, not subject to income taxes. While a strict application of the relevant rules would remove from principal residence status the portion of Ms. Wise's home that was used for income producing activities, the administrative procedures of the CRA do not follow this approach. It appears that, as long as no CCA is taken on the work space portion of the home, 100 percent of the property will qualify as a principal residence. Given this, and the assumption that real estate prices are increasing, it would not be wise for Ms. Wise to take CCA on her office space.

Self Study Solution Six - 5

Part A

As the lease was entered into in 2016, the 2016 limits on deductibility apply for the life of the lease. The maximum deduction for automobile lease payments for 2016 would be the least of:

- $1,800

- $\left[\$800 \times \dfrac{31}{30}\right] - \text{Nil} - \left[(\$10,000 - \$1,000) \times 2\% \times \dfrac{31}{365}\right] - \$500 = \$311$

- $\left[\$1,800 \times \dfrac{\$30,000}{(85\%)(\$85,000)}\right] - \left[(\$10,000 - \$1,000) \times 2\% \times \dfrac{31}{365}\right] - \$500 = \$232$

The least of the three figures is $232 and this will be the maximum 2016 deduction for Borris Industries.

The maximum deduction for automobile lease payments for 2017 would be the least of:

- $[(\$1,800)(12)] = \$21,600$

- $\left[\$800 \times \dfrac{396}{30}\right] - \$232 - \left[(\$10,000 - \$1,000) \times 2\% \times \dfrac{396}{365}\right] - \$6,500 = \$3,633$

- $\left[\$21,600 \times \dfrac{\$30,000}{(85\%)(\$85,000)}\right] - \left[(\$10,000 - \$1,000) \times 2\% \times \dfrac{365}{365}\right] - \$6,000 = \$2,789$

The least of the three figures is \$2,789 and this will be the maximum 2017 deduction for Borris Industries.

Part B

In 2016, the Mercedes was used solely for personal purposes. In 2017, it was used primarily (more than 50 percent) for employment purposes, so he is eligible for the reduced standby charge and the alternative operating cost benefit calculation. However, since Mr. Borris' personal usage exceeds 20,004 kilometers during the year, the multiplier of the reduction formula is equal to 1 (20,004 ÷ 20,004). Given this, there is no reduction of the standby charge.

The taxable benefit that will be included in the Net Income For Tax Purposes of Mr. Borris for the two years (note the 2016 rate is different from 2017) is calculated as follows:

Standby Charge - No Reduction [(2/3)(1)(\$1,800)]	\$1,200
Operating Cost Benefit - No Alternative [(\$0.26)(2,500)]	650
Repayment	(500)
2016 Total Benefit	\$1,350

Standby Charge - No Reduction [(2/3)(12)(\$1,800)]	\$14,400
Operating Cost Benefit - Lesser Of:	
• [(1/2)(\$14,400) = \$7,200	
• [(\$0.25)(22,000)] = \$5,500	5,500
Repayment [(\$500)(12)]	(6,000)
2017 Total Benefit	\$13,900

Self Study Solution Six - 6

Analysis

The choice between the two alternatives will be based on the comparative cash flows of the two alternatives. The relevant calculations are provided in the sections which follow.

Employer Provides Automobile

If Jerry elects to have the employer provide the Lexus, he will have a taxable benefit in each year. Since his employment related milage is greater than 50 percent, he is eligible for the reduced standby charge and the alternative operating cost benefit calculation. The after tax consequence of this choice would be as follows:

Standby Charge (Reduced)	
[(2%)(12)(\$48,000)(15,000 ÷ 20,004)]	\$8,638
Operating Cost Benefit - Lesser Of:	
• [(1/2)(\$8,638)] = \$4,319	
• [(\$0.25)(15,000)] = \$3,750	3,750
Total Automobile Benefit	\$12,388
Marginal Tax Rate	51%
Annual Increase In Tax	\$ 6,318

Jerry Buys the Automobile

The pre-tax cash inflows (outflows) associated with this alternative are as follows:

	2017	2018	2019
Margin Loan Proceeds	$48,000	N/A	N/A
Lexus Purchase	(48,000)	N/A	N/A
Allowance Received	18,000	$18,000	$18,000
Loan Repayment	(16,000)	(16,000)	(16,000)
Proceeds From Sale Of Car	N/A	N/A	20,000
Operating Costs [($0.24)(55,000)]	(13,200)	(13,200)	(13,200)
Financing Cost			
[(5%)($48,000)]	(2,400)		
[(5%)($32,000)]		(1,600)	
[(5%)($16,000)]			(800)
Pre-Tax Cash Inflows (Outflows)	($13,600)	($12,800)	$ 8,000

The tax savings (costs) associated with this alternative are as follows:

	2017	2018	2019
Operating Costs [($0.24)(55,000)]	($13,200)	($13,200)	($13,200)
Financing Costs (Less Than $10/Day)	(2,400)	(1,600)	(800)
CCA (See Note)			
[(1/2)(30%)($30,000)]	(4,500)		
[(30%)($25,500)]		(7,650)	
[(1/2)(30%)($17,850)]			(2,678)
Total Automobile Costs	($20,100)	($22,450)	($16,678)
Employment Usage (40,000 ÷ 55,000)	72.7%	72.7%	72.7%
Deductible Amount	($14,613)	($16,321)	($12,125)
Allowance	18,000	18,000	18,000
Inclusion In Taxable Income	$ 3,387	$ 1,679	$ 5,875
Marginal Tax Rate	51%	51%	51%
Increase In Tax	$ 1,727	$ 856	$ 2,996

Note As a Class 10.1 asset is involved, the CCA base is limited to $30,000. When the asset is sold, no recapture or terminal loss can be recognized on Class 10.1. However, one-half year CCA can be deducted in the year of disposal.

The net after tax cash outflow would be calculated as follows:

	2017	2018	2019
Pre-Tax Cash Inflow (Outflow)	($13,600)	($12,800)	$8,000
Tax Inflow (Outflow)	(1,727)	(856)	(2,996)
Net Cash Inflow (Outflow)	($15,327)	($13,656)	$5,004

Best Alternative

A comparison of the two alternatives is as follows:

Net Cash Inflows (Outflows)	2017	2018	2019	Total
Employer Provided	($ 6,318)	($ 6,318)	($6,318)	($18,954)
Employee Purchase	(15,327)	(13,656)	5,004	(23,979)

Without consideration of the time value of money, the employer provided alternative appears preferable. The total cash outflow under this approach is $18,954 as compared to $23,979 under the employee purchase alternative. Without becoming involved in the calculations, you would find that, even if recognition is given to the time value of money, the employer provided alternative would continue to be the best alternative.

Other Considerations

There are a number of other considerations that could affect the choice of the best alternative, such as if the actual number of kilometers driven, or personal kilometers driven was to be different from the estimated, or if the resale value of the Lexus was not actually $20,000, but dealing with these factors is beyond the scope of this problem.

Self Study Solution Six - 7

Market Determination - Two Possible Values

For tax purposes, the Company can measure market using either replacement cost or net realizable value. These values would be as follows:

Replacement Cost [($51)(6,000)]	$306,000

Net Realizable Value [($58)(6,000)]	$348,000

While it is not an acceptable practice under GAAP, the CRA will accept the use of market values, without regard to their relationship to cost.

Cost Determination - Two Possible Values

In the determination of cost, taxpayers are permitted to use specific identification (this would not appear to be practical here), a First In, First Out (FIFO) assumption, or Average Cost.

Using the First In, First Out method, the appropriate value for the ending inventory would be determined as follows:

3,000 Units At $52.00	$156,000
2,000 Units At $48.00	96,000
1,000 Units At $43.00	43,000
6,000 Units At FIFO Cost	$295,000

Based on average cost, the ending inventory value would be calculated as follows:

Number Of Units	6,000
Average Cost [($1,256,000 ÷ 28,000)]	44.86
6,000 Units At Average Cost	$269,160

Lower Of Cost And Market - Four Possible Values

For tax purposes, the possible values here would be as follows:

Lower Of Replacement Cost And FIFO Cost	$295,000
Lower Of Replacement Cost And Average Cost	269,160
Lower Of Net Realizable Value And FIFO Cost	295,000
Lower Of Net Realizable Value And Average Cost	269,160

For accounting purposes, only the last two values would be acceptable.

Self Study Solution Six - 8

The minimum net business income of Yossarian Tools would be calculated as follows:

Accounting Net Income	$298,000
Additions:	
Item 1 - Increase In Warranty Reserve	14,500
Item 2 - Parking Tickets	980
Item 4 - Amortization Expense	53,750
Item 6 - Contributions To Registered Charity (Note 1)	4,300
Item 9 - Golf Club Membership	1,400
Item 9 - 50% Of Business Meals (50% of $3,400)	1,700
Item 10 - Appraisal Costs (Note 2)	7,400
Item 11 - Fee Paid To Son (Note 3)	12,000
Subtotal	$394,030
Deduction:	
Item 4 - CCA	(62,000)
Net Business Income	$332,030

Note 1 Donations to charities cannot be deducted in the calculation of net business income. They will be the basis for a tax credit in the calculation of Tax Payable for Mr. Yossarian.

Note 2 The fees paid to appraise certain Company assets for sale would be added to the adjusted cost base of these assets.

Note 3 As it is extremely unlikely that 6 year olds will be buying power tools, it does not appear that the fee paid to Mr. Yossarian's son is reasonable. As a result, it would not be deductible.

Other Items Further explanation related to the items not included in the preceding calculation of Net Business Income are as follows:

Item 3 As the landscaping costs have already been deducted in accounting Net Income, they do not require adjustment for tax purposes.

Item 5 While interest on late income tax instalments is clearly not deductible, there does not appear to be a similar prohibition against interest on late property taxes. We would note here that all fines and penalties are not deductible. This would not appear to include interest for late payment of municipal taxes.

Item 7 The tax treatment of such payments would be the same as the accounting treatment.

Item 8 The tax treatment of volume discounts would be the same as the accounting treatment.

Item 12 As the profits from the illegal business have already been included in accounting Net Income, they do not require adjustment for tax purposes.

Item 13 The tax treatment of the car lease and operating costs would be the same as the accounting treatment. As the monthly lease payment is less than the prescribed amounts for the deduction of automobile costs and the car is used 100 percent for business purposes, no adjustment for tax purposes is required.

Self Study Solution Six - 9

The Net Income For Tax Purposes would be calculated as follows:

Accounting Income After Taxes	$340,000
Additions:	
Item 1 - Income Tax Expense	86,000
Item 2 - Donations To Charities (Note 1)	3,500
Item 3 - Amortization Expense	241,000
Item 5 - Amount Paid To Cousin (Note 2)	10,000
Item 6 - Foreign Advertising (Note 3)	Nil
Item 7 - Warranty Reserve (Note 4)	9,000
Item 8 - Bad Debts (Note 5)	Nil
Item 11 - Non-Deductible Meals And Entertainment (50% Of $13,500)	6,750
Item 12 - Amortization Of Bond Discount	1,800
Item 13 - Non-Deductible Lease Payments (Note 6)	13,037
Subtotal	$711,087
Deductions:	
Item 4 - Capital Cost Allowance	(389,000)
Item 9 - Issue Costs (Note 7)	(1,600)
Item 10 - Landscaping Costs	(11,000)
Net Income For Tax Purposes	$309,487

Note 1 The donations to registered charities will be deductible in the computation of Taxable Income, but not in the computation of Net Income For Tax Purposes. Charitable donations are a deduction for corporations, although they are the basis for a tax credit for individuals.

Note 2 Under ITA 67, this amount would be disallowed as not being reasonable in the circumstances.

Note 3 As the advertising was not directed at the Canadian market, it can be deducted for tax purposes and no adjustment is required.

Note 4 For tax purposes, warranty costs can only be deducted as incurred. Therefore, the $9,000 ($27,000 - $18,000) increase in the warranty reserve must be added back to accounting income.

Note 5 As the same bad debt estimates were used for tax purposes and accounting purposes, no adjustment is required with respect to bad debts.

Note 6 Under ITA 67.3, the deductible amount of the lease payments is limited to the least of:

- $18,000
- [($800)(365/30)] = $9,733
- {[$18,000][$30,000 ÷ (85%)($128,000)]} = $4,963

The non-deductible portion of the lease payments is $13,037 ($18,000 - $4,963). The non-employment related kilometers will affect Mike's taxable benefit, but does not affect the deductibility of the operating costs to the Company or decrease the deductible portion of the lease payments.

Note 7 Under ITA 20(1)(e), issue costs must be amortized at the rate of 20 percent per year. As the full amount was treated as an asset in the accounting records, the required adjustment is a deduction of $1,600 [(20%)($8,000)].

Self Study Solution Six - 10

The Net Income For Tax Purposes of Darlington Inc. would be calculated as follows:

Accounting Income	$ 596,000
Additions:	
Item 1 - Income Tax Expense	55,000
Item 3 - Foreign Advertising (Note 1)	Nil
Item 4 - Amortization Expense	623,000
Item 4 - Taxable Capital Gain On Class 8 Disposition	
[($550,000 - $400,000)(1/2)]	75,000
Item 5 - Non-Deductible Meals And Entertainment	
[(50%)($41,400)]	20,700
Item 6 - Club Fees	2,500
Item 7 - Property Taxes On Vacant Land (Note 4)	15,000
Subtotal	$1,387,200
Deductions:	
Item 2 - Landscaping Costs (Note 2)	(95,000)
Item 4 - Accounting Gain On Class 8 Disposition	(225,000)
Item 4 - CCA (Note 3)	(925,750)
Terminal Loss (See Class 10 CCA Calculation)	(113,000)
Net Income For Tax Purposes	$ 28,450

Note 1 ITA 19.01 provides for the full deduction of advertising costs in foreign periodicals directed at the Canadian market, provided 80 percent or more of their non-advertising content is original editorial content. If the original editorial content is less than 80 percent, the deduction is equal to 50 percent of the costs. Note that this applies only to periodicals and not other print or broadcast media.

Note 2 Landscaping costs are fully deductible.

Note 3 The calculations for determining CCA are as follows:

Class 1 - Buildings The required calculations for this class would be as follows:

Headquarters Building

January 1, 2017 UCC Balance	$1,000,000
CCA At 4 Percent	(40,000)
January 1, 2018 UCC Balance	$ 960,000

New Building (Separate Class)

Addition ($650,000 - $125,000)	$525,000
One-Half Net Additions	(262,500)
CCA Base	$262,500
CCA At 6 Percent	(15,750)
One-Half Net Additions	262,500
January 1, 2018 UCC Balance	$509,250

Class 8 - Office Furniture And Equipment The required calculations for this class would be as follows:

January 1, 2017 UCC Balance		$4,200,000
Additions	$700,000	
Dispositions - Lesser Of:		
• Proceeds = $550,000		
• Cost = $400,000	(400,000)	300,000
One-Half Net Additions		(150,000)
CCA Base		$4,350,000
CCA At 20 Percent		(870,000)
One-Half Net Additions		150,000
January 1, 2018 UCC Balance		$3,630,000

With respect to the sale that occurred during the year, there would be a capital gain of $150,000 ($550,000 - $400,000). One-half, or $75,000, is included in the Company's Net Income For Tax Purposes, and the accounting gain of $225,000 is deducted.

Class 10 - Vehicles   The calculations for this Class are as follows:

January 1, 2017 UCC Balance	$800,000
Disposition - Lesser Of:	
Capital Cost = $1,200,000	
Proceeds Of Disposition = $687,000	(687,000)
Ending Balance With No Remaining Assets In Class	$113,000
Terminal Loss	(113,000)
January 1, 2018 UCC	Nil

Note 4   The property taxes on the vacant land are not deductible. They can be added to the cost of the land if the land was acquired for the purpose of earning either business or property income and may be deducted to the extent of any net income earned on the land.

Summary Of The Results (Not Required)

The maximum 2017 CCA and January 1, 2018 UCC balances can be summarized as follows:

Class	Maximum CCA	UCC
Class 1 - Main Class	$ 40,000	$ 960,000
Class 1 - Separate Class	15,750	509,250
Class 8	870,000	3,630,000
Class 10	Nil	Nil
Total	$925,750	

In addition, there was a taxable capital gain on the sale of the Class 8 assets of $75,000 and a terminal loss in Class 10 of $113,000.

Self Study Solution Six - 11

Part I

A. As covered in this Chapter 6, ITA 12(1)(l) requires inclusion of business income from a partnership. As explained in more detail in Chapter 18, Partnerships, each partner's share of partnership profits is considered personal income of each partner. The profit is calculated as though the partnership was an individual resident of Canada. Once determined, it is allocated as per the partnership agreement, with the allocated amount being included in the individual tax returns of each partner.

B. The basic rules of ITA 249.1(1) require that, in general, a partnership with members who are individuals use a December 31 fiscal year end. While ITA 249.1(4) allows a partnership to elect a fiscal year end other than December 31, this election requires complex adjustments for Additional Business Income that may or may not be worthwhile.

C. This question requires an analysis of whether the arrangement with the seamstresses is one of employment. This material is discussed in Chapter 3 which covers employment income. Detailed guidance can be found in the CRA Guide titled "Employee Or Self-Employed?" (RC4110).

The general approach to the employee vs. self-employed question is to determine the intent of the parties to the arrangement. While not conclusive, the first question that will be examined in making this determination is whether the business and the workers intended to have an employee/employer relationship or, alternatively, have the work done by the individuals as self-employed contractors. While there is not sufficient information to make this determination given the information in the problem, the partners should be advised that intent should be determined and supported by the appropriate actions (e.g., have the workers register for GST if they wish to treat them as self-employed contractors).

In the absence of information on intent, other factors can be considered as follows:

Control   It appears that Montpetit does not exercise a large degree of control over the seamstresses. They are free to work when they choose and may provide their services to different payers at the same time. The seamstresses can choose to accept or refuse work from Montpetit.

Ownership Of Tools And Equipment   The seamstresses provide the tools and equipment required for the work and the work is done in their homes, not in space provided by Montpetit.

Ability To Subcontract Or Hire Assistants   It appears that Montpetit does not exercise control over who does the work as long as the quality is satisfactory.

Financial Risk   Since the work is done for a set fee and the fabric and accessories are provided, there is no financial risk for seamstresses.

Responsibility For Investment And Management   There is not enough information for this factor to be considered.

Opportunity For Profit   Since the work is done for a set fee, a seamstress cannot increase her proceeds and hence the profit from a gown. Since the fabric and accessories are supplied and there would appear to be no other material expenditures needed for a gown, there is no opportunity to decrease expenses and increase profit on a gown. As a result, it does not appear that a profit could arise.

In addition to these factors, the work is for a specific gown, not general sewing as part of an ongoing relationship.

On balance, the seamstress contracts for the creation of designer gowns are likely contracts for service (self-employment contracts). Given this, source deductions would not be required.

Part II

A. The $2,400 legal fees would be allocated to Class 14.1. The rate for this Class is 5 percent and it is subject to the half-year rule. For the current year, partnership could deduct CCA of $60 [(5%)(1/2)($2,400)].

B. The sewing machines are capital expenditures and cannot be deducted in the current year. However, a deduction will be available for CCA on these amounts. The sewing accessories can be deducted in the first year as they will be used and replaced in the same year.

C. While this point is not covered in the Business Income Chapter, because of its non-arm's length nature, interest paid to partners cannot be deducted in the determination of partnership income (see Chapter 18 on partnerships). Rather it will be treated as a drawing by the partners.

The $10,000 contributions are of a capital nature and are not deductible in the calculation of personal Taxable Income.

D. The designer clothes held on consignment at year end are inventory of the partnership and are not deductible as cost of sales. The inventory will be valued either at lower of cost and market or, alternatively, market. The cost is given as $95,000 ($50,000 + $45,000) and the retail price is given as $260,000. It is likely that the net realizable value will be less than the full retail value, but the value cannot be determined with the information given.

E. The $15,000 payment for a limited term distribution right is a capital cost that cannot be currently deducted. However, it would be allocated to Class 14 (limited life intangibles) where it will be available for the deduction of CCA.

F. The payment of the annual membership is not deductible. The Crepe Suzette Diner expenses for entertainment of clients would be deductible, but they are subject to a 50 percent limitation, which means $750 [(50%)($1,500)] of these costs would be allowed as a business expense. The personal usage is not deductible.

Self Study Solution Six - 12

Christine's minimum net business income can be calculated as follows:

Design Power
Statement of Income and Expenses
For The Seven Month Period Ended December 31, 2017

Revenues		
Revenue collected	$22,000	
Revenue billed	4,000	
Work-In-Progress (Note 1)	1,500	$27,500
Expenses		
Capital cost allowance (Note 2)	($2,383)	
Work space in home expenses		
[(20%)($6,400)]	(1,280)	
Legal and business license fees	(1,000)	
Meals and entertainment [(50%)($500)]	(250)	
Automobile expenses (Note 3)	(1,960)	
Office and computer supplies	(650)	
Printing sub-contract fees	(1,800)	(9,323)
Net Business Income		$18,177

Note 1 Visual designers are not eligible for the special rule under ITA 34 which allows some professionals to recognize revenues on a billed basis.

Note 2 CCA amounts are calculated as follows:

	Class 8 Furniture	Class 10 Car	Class 50 Computer	Class 12 Software
Additions	$2,000	$18,000	$5,000	$1,200
One-Half Net Additions	(1,000)	(9,000)	(2,500)	(600)
CCA Base	$1,000	$ 9,000	$2,500	$ 600
CCA Rate	20%	30%	55%	100%
CCA For Full Year	$ 200	$ 2,700	$1,375	$ 600
Non-Business Car Usage (30%)	N/A	(810)	N/A	N/A
Balance	$ 200	$ 1,890	$1,375	$ 600
Short Fiscal Period Factor	214/365	214/365	214/365	214/365
Deductible Amount	$ 117	$ 1,108	$ 806	$ 352

The non-business usage of the car is 30 percent. CCA is also restricted by the fact that Christine's taxation year only contains 214 days. Given these factors, the total maximum CCA is $2,383 ($117 + $1,108 + $806 + $352). Note that the CCA calculation is based on the portion of the year since the inception of the business, not the portion of the year since the assets were acquired.

Note 3 As the interest amount is well below the prescribed limit, the amount is eligible for deduction, limited only by the amount of business usage. Also note that no portion of the down payment is deductible.

Given these considerations, the deduction for automobile costs can be calculated as follows:

Gasoline And Oil	1,100
Licence And Registration	200
Insurance	800
Interest On Car Loan	700
Potential Automobile Cost Deduction	$2,800
Business Usage	70%
Deductible Amount	$1,960

Self Study Solution Six - 13

Carla's minimum net business income can be calculated as follows:

Carla Jensen
Statement Of Business Income
For The Year Ending December 31, 2017

Revenues		
Revenue Collected		$105,000
Billed Receivables (Note 1)		
Add Closing Balance	$42,000	
Deduct Opening Balance	(37,000)	5,000
Total Revenues		$110,000
Expenses		
Building Operating Costs	($24,500)	
Vehicle Operating Costs	(7,200)	
Payments To Assistants	(13,500)	
Miscellaneous Office Costs	(3,750)	
Business Meals [(50%)($4,200)]	(2,100)	
CCA (Note 2)	(27,693)	
Terminal Loss For Class 10 (Note 3)	(4,955)	(83,698)
Net Business Income		$ 26,302

Note 1 As Carla is a professional accountant she is eligible for the special rule under ITA 34 which allows her to recognize revenue on a billed basis. This means that she does not have to include her unbilled work-in-progress in her net business income.

Note 2 The total CCA deductible would be as follows:

Class 1 (Calculation Follows)	$13,560
Class 8 (Calculation Follows)	12,100
Class 50 (Calculation Follows)	495
Class 12 (Calculation Follows)	363
Class 14.1 (Calculation Follow)	1,175
Total CCA	$27,692

Class 1 As the building is used 100 percent for non-residential purposes, it is eligible for the enhanced rate of 6 percent. This means that the maximum CCA would be:

Class 1 [($226,000)(6%)]	$13,560

Class 8 The required calculations are as follows:

Opening Balance		$46,500
Additions	$34,000	
Disposal - Lesser Of:		
• Proceeds = $6,000		
• Cost = $18,000	(6,000)	28,000
One-Half Net Additions		(14,000)
CCA Base		$60,500
Rate		20%
Class 8 CCA		$12,100

Class 50   The CCA on the new computer would be calculated as follows:

Class 50 [(1/2)($1,800)(55%)]	$495

Class 12   The CCA on the applications software would be calculated as follows:

Class 12 [(1/2)($725)(100%)]	$363

Class 14.1   The CCA on the client list would be calculated as follows:

Class 14.1 [(5%)(1/2)($47,000)]	$1,175

Note 3   As the only vehicle used by the business was disposed of during the year, there is no CCA for Class 10. However, as there is a balance left in the Class, there would be a terminal loss calculated as follows:

UCC Of The Class At The Beginning Of The Year	$17,255
Deduct: Dispositions During The Year - Lesser Of:	
• Capital Cost = $20,300	
• Proceeds Of Disposition = $12,300	(12,300)
Ending Balance With No Remaining Assets = Terminal Loss	$ 4,955

Note 4   The car leasing costs would be wholly deductible as the monthly lease charge and the manufacturer's list price are within the prescribed limits.

Self Study Solution Six - 14

Part A - No Election

If the ITA 22 election is not made, the tax consequences for George Pentel would be as follows:

Add: 2016 Reserve For Doubtful Debts	$12,000
2017 Income Inclusion	$12,000

While George has a capital loss of $8,500 [(1/2)($352,000 - $335,000)], he will not be able to deduct this amount as he has had no capital gains in the previous three years and does not expect to have any in the current or subsequent years.

If the ITA 22 election is not made, the tax consequences to Molly Stone would be as follows:

Proceeds Of Disposition (Amount Collected)	$337,000
Adjusted Cost Base	(335,000)
Capital Gain	$ 2,000
Non-Taxable One-Half	(1,000)
2017 Income Inclusion	$ 1,000

Part A - Election

If the ITA 22 election is made, the tax consequences for George would be as follows:

Add: 2016 Reserve For Doubtful Debts	$12,000
Deduct: Business Loss ($352,000 - $335,000)	(17,000)
2017 Deduction From Income	($ 5,000)

If the ITA 22 election is made, the tax consequences to Molly Stone would be as follows:

Add: Face Value - Price Paid ($352,000 - $335,000)	$17,000
Deduct: Actual Write-Offs ($352,000 - $337,000)	(15,000)
2017 Income Inclusion	$ 2,000

Part B

For George Pentel, the ITA 22 election is clearly desirable, converting a $12,000 income inclusion into a $5,000 deduction.

For Molly Stone, the fact that actual collections ($337,000) exceed the estimated value of the Accounts Receivable on the date of the sale ($335,000), means that the ITA 22 election would not be desirable. It would double her income inclusion from $1,000 to $2,000.

Self Study Solution Six - 15

Net Employment Income

The Net Employment Income component of Net Income For Tax Purposes would be calculated as follows:

Salary	$68,000
Commissions	13,500
RPP Contributions	(2,800)
Professional Association Dues	(250)
Automobile Benefit (Note 1)	792
Home Office Costs (Note 2)	(596)
Meals And Entertainment [(1/2)($4,350)]	(2,175)
Net Employment Income	$76,471

Note 1 The automobile benefit would be calculated as follows:

Standby Charge [(2%)($32,000)(11)(4,500 ÷ 18,337)]	$1,728
Operating Cost Benefit - Lesser Of:	
• [($0.25)(4,500)] = $1,125	
• ($1,728 ÷ 2) = $864	864
Total Benefit Before Repayment	$2,592
Repayment	(1,800)
Taxable Benefit	$ 792

Note 2 As an employee, Ms. Compton cannot deduct any part of the mortgage interest or take CCA on the cost of the property. Any employee can deduct utilities and maintenance and, because Ms. Compton's employment income includes commissions, she can also deduct the property tax and insurance costs. The total available deduction is $596 [(15%)($2,450 + $1,100 + $425)].

Net Business Income

The Net Business Income component of Net Income For Tax Purposes would be calculated as follows:

Accounting Net Income		$53,500
Add:		
Amortization Expense	$12,800	
Non-Deductible Meals and		
Entertainment [(1/2)($6,000)]	3,000	15,800
Subtotal		$69,300
Deduct:		
CCA (Note 3)	($26,200)	
Landscaping Costs	(8,600)	(34,800)
Net Business Income		$34,500

Note 3 Maximum CCA would be calculated as follows:

Class 1 [(4%)($233,000)]			$ 9,320
Class 8			
Opening Balance		$41,500	
Additions	$13,400		
Disposals - Lesser Of:			
Cost = $12,000			
Proceeds = $8,600	(8,600)		
Net Additions	$ 4,800		
Portion Added To CCA Base	1/2	2,400	
CCA Base		$43,900	
Rate		20%	8,780
Class 10 [(30%)($27,000)]			8,100
Total			$26,200

Net Income For Tax Purposes And Taxable Income

Ms. Compton has no deductions in the calculation of Taxable income. Given this, her Net Income For Tax Purposes and Taxable Income are as follows:

Net Employment Income	$76,471
Net Business Income	34,500
Net Income For Tax Purposes And Taxable Income	$110,971

Federal Tax Payable

The required calculations are as follows:

Tax On First $91,831		$16,300
Tax On Next $19,140 ($110,971 - $91,831) At 26 Percent		4,976
Tax Before Credits		$21,276
Tax Credits:		
Basic Personal Amount	($11,635)	
Eligible Dependent - Allison	(11,635)	
Canada Caregiver - John (Note 4)	(6,883)	
Transfer Of John's Disability	(8,113)	
EI Premiums	(836)	
CPP Contributions	(2,564)	
Canada Employment	(1,178)	
Transfer Of Tuition Credit - Lesser Of:		
• $5,000		
• $2,850	(2,850)	
Medical Expenses (Note 5)	(15,632)	
Total Credit Base	($61,326)	
Rate	15%	(9,199)
Charitable Donations (Note 6)		
[(15%)($200) + (29%)($1,250 - $200)]		(335)
Political Contributions [(3/4)($350)]		(263)
Federal Tax Payable		$11,479

Note 4 While the eligible dependant credit could be claimed for either Allison or John, the better choice is Allison. This will allow the full Canada caregiver credit to be claimed for John because he is physically disabled.

Note 5 The claim for medical expenses is determined as follows:

Medical Expenses For Ms. Compton And Allison ($4,220 + $2,180)		$ 6,400
Lesser Of:		
• [(3%)($110,971)] = $3,329		
• 2017 Threshold Amount = $2,268		(2,268)
Balance Before Dependants 18 And Over		$ 4,132
John's Medical Expenses	$11,500	
Reduced By The Lesser Of:		
• $2,268		
• [(3%)(Nil)] = Nil	Nil	11,500
Total Medical Expense Claim		$15,632

Note 6 As none of her income is taxed at 33 percent, this rate will not be applicable to the calculation of the charitable donations tax credit.

Self Study Solution Six - 16

Net Employment Income
The required calculations here are as follows:

Salary		$ 84,000
Additions		
Commissions		39,000
Hotel And Meal Allowance		Nil
Car Allowance [($600)(12)]		7,200
Stock Option Benefit [($9.50 - $4.25)(2,200)]		11,550
Deductions		
RPP Contributions	(	5,600)
Car Operating Costs [($6,800)(32,500 ÷ 38,000)]	(	5,816)
Car CCA [($30,000)(30%)(1/2)(32,500 ÷ 38,000)]	(	3,849)
Net Employment Income		$126,485

Ms. Arden received an allowance $13,200 [(12)($1,100)] to cover the costs of hotels and meals. As her actual costs are $13,900 ($7,700 + $6,200), this allowance appears to be reasonable. Given this, it does not have to be included in income. As the allowance is not included in Ms. Arden's income, she cannot deduct her actual costs.

As it is not deductible for tax purposes, the amount withheld for parking has no effect on Ms. Arden's employment income.

Net Business Income

The required calculations here are as follows:

Cash Basis Income (Given)		$56,500
December 31 Receivables		5,200
December 31 Inventories		18,700
December 31 Payables	(	8,240)
CCA On Building [($272,000 - $78,000)(6%)(1/2)]*	(	5,820)
CCA On Furniture And Fixtures [($48,000)(20%)(1/2)]	(	4,800)
Net Business Income		$61,540

*It would appear that the new building will be used exclusively for non-residential purposes. Given this it will be eligible for the 6 percent CCA rate, provided that it is kept in a separate Class 1.

Net Income For Tax Purposes

Net Income For Tax Purposes would be calculated as follows:

Net Employment Income	$126,485
Net Business Income	61,540
Net Income For Tax Purposes	$188,025

Taxable Income

The required calculation is as follows:

Net Income For Tax Purposes		$188,025
Stock Option Deduction [($11,550)(1/2)]	(	5,775)
Taxable Income		$182,250

Tax Payable

The required calculations are as follows:

Tax On First $142,353		$29,436
Tax On Next $39,897 ($182,250 - $142,353) At 29 Percent		11,570
Tax Before Credits		$41,006
Tax Credits:		
Basic Personal Amount (Ms. Arden)	($11,635)	
Common-Law Partner ($11,635 - $9,800)	(1,835)	
Canada Caregiver - Helen	(6,883)	
EI	(836)	
CPP	(2,564)	
Canada Employment	(1,178)	
Transfer Of Tuition Credit - Lesser Of:		
• $5,000		
• $7,200	(5,000)	
Medical Expenses (See Note 1)	(12,224)	
Total Credit Base	($42,155)	
Rate	15%	(6,323)
Charitable Contributions (Note 2)		
[(15%)($200) + (29%)($1,200 - $200)]		(320)
Federal Tax Payable		$34,363

Note 1 The medical expense credit base would be calculated as follows:

Medical Expenses For Ms. Arden And Maria		
($3,940 + $2,450)		$ 6,390
Reduced By The Lesser Of:		
• [[(3%)($188,025)] = $5,641		
• 2017 Threshold Amount = $2,268		(2,268)
Balance Before Dependants 18 And Over		$ 4,122
Helen's Medical Expenses	$7,250	
Reduced By The Lesser Of:		
• $2,268		
• [(3%)($7,200)] = $216	(216)	7,034
Jeff's Medical Expenses	$1,260	
Reduced By The Lesser Of:		
• $2,268		
• [(3%)($6,400)] = $192	(192)	1,068
Total Medical Expense Claim		$12,224

Note 2 As none of her income is taxed at 33 percent, this rate will not be applicable to the calculation of the charitable donations tax credit.

Chapter 6 Learning Objectives

After completing Chapter 6, you should be able to:

1. Classify property based on its use and determine what type of income will be produced while the asset is being held and when it is disposed of (paragraph [P hereafter] 6-1 to 6-16).
2. Describe the tax factors that can be affected by the classification of income as business or property (P 6-17 to 6-27).
3. Distinguish between business income and capital gains, including the criteria used by the courts in making this distinction (P 6-28 to 6-42).
4. Describe the major differences between net business income and Net Income as determined under GAAP (P 6-43 to 6-45).
5. Recall the various items that are included in net business income (P 6-46 to 6-53 and P 6-64 to 6-65).

6. Apply the system of reserves that can be used in determining net business income (P 6-54 to 6-63).
7. Apply the limitations on deductions that apply to business and property income, including those on home office costs (P 6-66 to 6-103).
8. Apply the limitations on deductions that apply to business, property and employment income, including those related to meals and entertainment and automobile costs (P 6-104 to 6-132).
9. Apply the inventory valuation procedures that are used for determining net business income (P 6-133 to 6-141).
10. Recall the deductions that are specified in the *Income Tax Act* for calculating net business income (P 6-142 to 6-143).

11. Reconcile accounting Net Income with net business income (P 6-144 to 6-149).
12. Recall the rules for determining taxation years and calculate additional business income for non-calendar fiscal years (P 6-150 to 6-157).
13. Apply the special provisions related to farm activities and farm losses (P 6-158 to 6-169).
14. Apply the special rule for unbilled work in process applicable to the income of some professionals (P 6-170 to 6-172).
15. Apply the provisions related to the disposition of inventories and accounts receivable in situations where a business is being sold (P 6-173 to 6-178).

CHAPTER 7

How To Work Through Chapter 7

We recommend the following approach in dealing with the material in this chapter:

Property Income - General Concept
- Read paragraph 7-1 to 7-5 (in the textbook).

Interest As A Deduction, Including IT Folio S3-F6-C1
- Read paragraph 7-6 to 7-28.
- Do Self Study Problem Seven-1 which is available on the Companion Website and check the solution in this Study Guide.

Discount And Premium On Long-Term Issued Debt
- Read paragraph 7-29 to 7-35.
- Do Exercise Seven-1 (in the textbook) and check the solution in this Study Guide.
- Read paragraph 7-36 to 7-37.
- Do Exercise Seven-2 and check the solution in this Study Guide.

Interest Income - General Provisions
- Read paragraph 7-38 to 7-45.
- Do Exercise Seven-3 and check the solution in this Study Guide.

Discount And Premium On Long-Term Debt Holdings
- Read paragraph 7-46 to 7-47.

Accrued Interest At Transfer
- Read paragraph 7-48 to 7-50.
- Do Exercise Seven-4 and check the solution in this Study Guide.

Payments Based On Production Or Use (Royalties)
- Read paragraph 7-51 to 7-53.

Rental Income
- Read paragraph 7-54 to 7-65.
- Do Exercise Seven-5 and check the solution in this Study Guide.
- Do Self Study Problem Seven-2 and check the solution in this Study Guide.

Eligible And Non-Eligible Cash Dividends Received
- Read paragraph 7-66 to 7-85.
- Do Exercise Seven-6 and check the solution in this Study Guide.
- Read paragraph 7-86 to 7-93.
- Do Exercise Seven-7 and check the solution in this Study Guide.

Comparison Of Investment Returns
- Read paragraph 7-94 to 7-95.
- Do Self Study Problems Seven-3 to Seven-6 and check the solutions in this Study Guide.

Income Trusts
- Read paragraph 7-96 to 7-109.
- Do Exercise Seven-8 and check the solution in this Study Guide.

Mutual Funds
- Read paragraph 7-110 to 7-120.
- Do Exercise Seven-9 and check the solution in this Study Guide.
- Do Self Study Problem Seven-7 and check the solution in this Study Guide.

Stock Dividends And Capital Dividends
- Read paragraph 7-121 to 7-126.
- Do Exercise Seven-10 and check the solution in this Study Guide.

Foreign Source Income
- Read paragraph 7-127 to 7-130.
- Do Exercise Seven-11 and check the solution in this Study Guide.

Shareholder Benefits
- Read paragraph 7-131 to 7-133.

Tax Credits Revisited - Dividend And Foreign Tax Credits
- Read paragraph 7-134 to 7-137.
- Do Self Study Problems Seven-8 and Seven- 9 and check the solutions in this Study Guide.

To Complete This Chapter
- If you would like more practice in problem solving, do the Supplementary Self Study Problems for the chapter. These problems and solutions are available on the Companion Website.
- Review the Key Terms Used In This Chapter in the textbook at the end of Chapter 7. Consult the Glossary for the meaning of any key terms you do not know.
- Test yourself with the Chapter 7 Glossary Flashcards available on the Companion Website.
- Ensure you have achieved the Chapter 7 Learning Objectives listed in this Study Guide.
- As a review, we recommend you view the PowerPoint presentation for Chapter 7 that is on the Companion Website.

Practice Examination
- Write the Practice Examination for Chapter 7 that is on the Companion Website. Mark your examination using the Practice Examination Solution that is also on the Companion Website.

Solutions to Chapter Seven Exercises

Exercise Seven - 1 Solution

Tax Consequences   The tax consequences would be as follows:

Annual Deduction - 2017 Through 2019 [($1,000,000)(4%)]	$40,000

Maturity Amount	$1,000,000
Proceeds Of Sale	(985,000)
2019 Loss	$ 15,000

The bonds are sold for more than 97 percent of their maturity amount. In addition, the four-thirds test is met since the effective interest rate of 4.6 percent is less than four-thirds of the coupon rate [(4%)(4/3) = 5.3%]. As a result, this loss would be fully deductible. This gives a total deduction of $135,000 over the 3 year period [(3)($40,000) + $15,000].

Accounting Consequences   The accounting consequences would be as follows:

Annual Interest Payment [($1,000,000)(4%)]	$40,000
Discount Amortization [($1,000,000 - $985,000) ÷ 3]	5,000
Annual Interest Expense - 2017 Through 2019	$45,000

Payment of the maturity amount in 2019 would have no tax consequences. Note that the total for the 3 year period would be the same $135,000 [(3)($45,000)] that was deducted for tax purposes.

Exercise Seven - 2 Solution

The tax consequences under each of the three assumptions would be as follows:

Money Lender   In this case, there would be an income inclusion of $400,000 ($1,400,000 - $1,000,000) in the current year. The interest deduction for the year would be $180,000 [(18%)($1,000,000)].

No Deliberate Premium   In this case, the premium would have no immediate tax consequences and there would be no tax consequences when the bonds mature. The interest deduction for the year would be $180,000 [(18%)($1,000,000)]. Given that the bonds are paid off for less than the proceeds from their issuance, this result provides the issuer of the bonds with a tax free capital receipt of $400,000.

Deliberate Premium   In this case, the premium would be amortized at the rate of $40,000 per year ($400,000 ÷ 10). This means the interest deduction for the year would be $140,000 ($180,000 - $40,000).

Exercise Seven - 3 Solution

The total interest to be recorded on the instrument is $28,800 [($60,000)(8%)(6 years)]. It will be allocated as follows:

Year	Interest Paid	Interest Reported
2017	Nil	Nil
2018	Nil	$ 4,800
2019	Nil	4,800
2020	$15,600	6,000
2021	Nil	3,600
2022	Nil	4,800
2023	13,200	4,800
Total	$28,800	$28,800

2017 As no anniversary date occurred and no interest was received during 2017, no interest will have to be included in Ms. Dumont's 2017 tax return.

2018 The first anniversary date occurs on September 30 and this requires the recognition of $4,800 [(8%)($60,000)] of interest.

2019 The second anniversary date occurs and this requires the recognition of an additional $4,800 of interest.

2020 An additional $4,800 will have to be recognized because of the third anniversary date. Also during this year, a payment of $15,600 [($4,800)(3.25)] is received. Of this total, $14,400 [(3)($4,800)] has been recognized because of the three anniversary dates. This will require the recognition of an additional $1,200 ($15,600 - $14,400) in 2020, bringing the total for the year to $6,000 ($4,800 + $1,200).

2021 The anniversary date will require recognition of $4,800. However, only $3,600 of this amount will be included as $1,200 was received and recognized in 2020.

2022 $4,800 will be recognized on the anniversary date.

2023 A payment of $13,200 [(2.75)($4,800)] will be received. As $8,400 ($3,600 + $4,800) of the amount received has been recorded on the two anniversary dates, the total for 2023 will be $4,800 ($13,200 - $8,400).

Exercise Seven - 4 Solution

Mr. Lay will include the full $6,000 received in income. However, he can deduct the interest that was accrued on the bonds at the time of purchase of $1,989 [($3,000)(120/181)]. The net amount that will be included in his tax return is $4,011 ($6,000 - $1,989).

Exercise Seven - 5 Solution

The maximum CCA for Class 1 would be calculated as follows:

Capital Cost ($185,000 - $42,000)	$143,000
Improvements	35,000
Total Additions	$178,000
One-Half Net Additions	(89,000)
CCA Base	$ 89,000
Rate	4%
Maximum CCA	$ 3,560

The required rental income calculation would be as follows:

Rental Revenues	$7,200
Rental Expenses Other Than CCA	(5,100)
Rental Income Before CCA	$2,100
CCA (Maximum)	(2,100)
Net Rental Income	Nil

As CCA cannot be used to create a net rental loss, the actual deduction is limited to $2,100, the rental income before CCA. Also note that the maximum available CCA is not limited by the fact the property was purchased in September as the calendar year is considered the fiscal year for property income purposes for individuals.

Exercise Seven - 6 Solution

The Tax Payable by Ms. Holt would be calculated as follows:

Eligible Dividends Received	$15,000
Gross Up At 38 Percent	5,700
Taxable Dividends	$20,700
Combined Federal/Provincial Tax Rate (29% + 14.5%)	43.5%
Tax Before Dividend Tax Credit	$ 9,005
Dividend Tax Credit [(6/11 + 30%)($5,700)]	(4,819)
Federal And Provincial Tax Payable	$ 4,186

The after tax retention is $10,814 ($15,000 - $4,186). Note that to calculate this amount, the taxes are deducted from the dividends received and not the grossed up taxable dividends.

Exercise Seven - 7 Solution

The Tax Payable by Mr. Johns would be calculated as follows:

Non-Eligible Dividends Received	$17,000
Gross Up At 17 Percent	2,890
Taxable Dividends	$19,890
Combined Federal/Provincial Tax Rate (29% + 12%)	41%
Tax Before Dividend Tax Credit	$8,155
Dividend Tax Credit [(21/29 + 30%)($2,890)]	(2,960)
Federal And Provincial Tax Payable	$ 5,195

The after tax retention is $11,805 ($17,000 - $5,195). Note that to calculate this amount, the taxes are deducted from the dividends received and not the grossed up taxable dividends.

Exercise Seven - 8 Solution

John will include an additional $7,000 [(2,000)($5.00 - $1.50)] in his Net Income For Tax Purposes. His adjusted cost base will be increased by the $10,000 [(2,000)($5.00)] reinvestment of the distribution and reduced by the $3,000 [(2,000)($1.50)] return of capital.

The reinvestment of the $10,000 distribution will result in the acquisition of an additional 175.44 ($10,000 ÷ $57) units. The adjusted cost base calculations are as follows:

	Amount	Number Of Units
Original Investment	$110,000	2,000.00
Reinvestment Of Distribution	10,000	175.44
Tax Free Return Of Capital	(3,000)	N/A
Adjusted Cost Base/Number Of Units	$117,000	2,175.44

This will result in an average cost of $53.78 ($117,000 ÷ 2,175.44) per unit.

Exercise Seven - 9 Solution

Given the purchase price per unit is $13, the reinvestment will result in Ms. Tiompkins receiving 80.77 ($1,050 ÷ $13) additional units. This will leave her holding 3,580.77 units with an adjusted cost base of $40,425 ($39,375 + $1,050). Her adjusted cost base per unit after the reinvestment is $11.29 ($40,425 ÷ 3,580.77).

Exercise Seven - 10 Solution

The required calculations would be as follows:

Original Shares Held	200,000
Stock Dividend Percentage	10%
New Shares Acquired	20,000
Per Share Addition To Paid Up Capital	$15
Eligible Stock Dividend Received	$300,000
Gross Up At 38 Percent	114,000
Taxable Eligible Dividend	$414,000

There would be a federal dividend tax credit of $62,182 [(6/11)($114,000)]. The $300,000 stock dividend would be added to the $2,400,000 [($12)(10%)(2,000,000)] original cost of his shares and the adjusted cost base per share would be calculated as follows:

$$[(\$2,400,000 + \$300,000) \div (200,000 + 20,000)] = \$12.27$$

Note that his percentage of ownership remains at 10 percent (220,000 ÷ 2,200,000).

Exercise Seven - 11 Solution

The federal Tax Payable on the amount received assuming it is foreign non-business income or business income would be calculated as follows:

	Non-Business Income	Business Income
Amount Received	$22,500	$22,500
Foreign Tax Withheld	7,500	7,500
Inclusion For Foreign Income	$30,000	$30,000
Deduction Of Excess Withholding		
[$7,500 - (15%)($30,000)]	(3,000)	N/A
Increase In Taxable Income	$27,000	$30,000
Rate	29%	29%
Tax Payable Before Credit	$ 7,830	$ 8,700
Foreign Tax Credit [(15%)($30,000)]	(4,500)	
Foreign Tax Credit (Amount Withheld)		(7,500)
Federal Tax Payable	$ 3,330	$ 1,200

Note that the total tax cost if the foreign income is business income is $8,700 ($7,500 +

$1,200). This is the same amount that would have been paid by Norah on the receipt of $30,000 of Canadian source business income [(29%)($30,000) = $8,700]. This compares to a tax cost of $10,830 ($7,500 + $3,330) in the non-business income case. This reflects the fact that the $3,000 deduction of the excess foreign tax withholding is not as valuable as the $3,000 credit against Tax Payable that was received in the business income case.

Self Study Solution Seven - 1

Case A
The interest would be deductible as the direct use of the borrowed funds was to acquire the Bee Ltd. shares.

Case B
Since the proceeds exceed the borrowings, Ms. Burns has complete flexibility with respect to linking. She could allocate all of the $225,000 to property B or alternatively, $50,000 to property A, with the other $175,000 going to property B. Any other allocation totaling $225,000 would be acceptable.

Case C
When the value of the replacement property is less than the amount borrowed, the taxpayer must use a pro-rata allocation of the borrowed money. In this case, the result would be an allocation of $71,053 [($60,000 ÷ $190,000)($225,000)] to property A and an allocation of $153,947 [($130,000 ÷ $190,000)($225,000)] to property B.

Case D
Under ITA 20.1 (the disappearing source rules), the $145,000 balance will be deemed to be used to produce income. Therefore, he can continue to deduct the interest.

Self Study Solution Seven - 2

2016
The maximum CCA for 2016 would be calculated as follows:

	Class 1	Class 8
Addition	$575,000	$18,500
One-Half Net Additions	(287,500)	(9,250)
CCA Base	$287,500	$ 9,250
Maximum CCA:		
[(4%)($287,500)]	(11,500)	
[(20%)($9,250)]		(1,850)
Add: One-Half Net Additions	287,500	9,250
January 1, 2017 UCC	$563,500	$16,650

Net rental income for 2016 would be calculated as follows:

Rental Revenue	$43,500
Expenses Other Than CCA	(28,000)
Income Before CCA	$15,500
Class 1 CCA	(11,500)
Class 8 CCA	(1,850)
Net Rental Income	$ 2,150

Note that when an individual uses assets to produce property income (e.g., rental income), the full calendar year is considered to be the taxation year of the individual. This means that the short fiscal period rules are not applicable to Ms. Fox.

2017

The terminal loss for Class 8 would be calculated as follows:

January 1, 2017 UCC	$16,650
Disposition - Lesser Of:	
• Proceeds Of Disposition = $14,000	
• Cost = $18,500	(14,000)
Balance Before Terminal Loss	$ 2,650
Terminal Loss	(2,650)
January 1, 2018 UCC - Class 8	Nil

The terminal loss will be deducted from the Class 8 UCC leaving a January 1, 2018 balance of nil.

The maximum CCA for 2017 would be $22,540 [(4%)($563,500)]. However, as the deduction of CCA cannot be used to create a loss, the actual amount for the year would be limited to $10,350 as shown in the calculation of Net Rental Income:

Rental Revenue	$45,000
Expenses Other Than CCA And Terminal Loss	(32,000)
Terminal Loss On Class 8 Assets	(2,650)
Income Before CCA	$10,350
CCA (Limited To Income Before CCA)	(10,350)
Net Rental Income	Nil

The January 1, 2018 UCC for the Class 1 building would be calculated as follows:

January 1, 2017 UCC	$563,500
CCA Deducted	(10,350)
January 1, 2018 UCC - Class 1	$553,150

Self Study Solution Seven - 3

Common Stock Investment

Dividends [($2.25)(12,000)]	$27,000
Gross Up Of 38 Percent	10,260
Taxable Capital Gain [($49.50 - $48.50)(12,000)(1/2)]	6,000
Taxable Income	$43,260
Combined Federal/Provincial Tax Rate (29% + 13%)	42%
Tax Before Dividend Tax Credit	$18,169
Dividend Tax Credit [(6/11 + 28%)($10,260)]	(8,469)
Tax Payable	$ 9,700

Dividend	$27,000
Capital Gain (100%)	12,000
Tax Payable	(9,700)
After Tax Return	$29,300

Guaranteed Investment Certificate

Interest [($582,000)(3%)]	$17,460
Combined Federal/Provincial Tax Rate (29% + 13%)	42%
Tax Payable	$ 7,333

Interest Received	$17,460
Tax Payable	(7,333)
After Tax Return	$10,127

Discount Bond

Interest [($600,000)(4%)]	$24,000
Taxable Capital Gain [($600,000 - $582,000)(1/2)]	9,000
Taxable Income	$33,000
Combined Federal/Provincial Tax Rate (29% + 13%)	42%
Tax Payable	$13,860

Interest Received	$24,000
Capital Gain (100%)	18,000
Tax Payable	(13,860)
After Tax Return	$28,140

Self Study Solution Seven - 4

In the following solution, note that the after tax return amount does not include the original investment. Some students add $600,000 to the after tax return which is not correct.

Guaranteed Investment Certificate
The required calculations for this investment are as follows:

Interest Received [($600,000)(4.5%)]	$27,000
Combined Federal/Provincial Tax Rate (29% + 12%)	41%
Tax Payable	$11,070

Interest Received	$27,000
Tax Payable	(11,070)
After Tax Return - Guaranteed Investment Certificate	$15,930

Preferred Shares
The required calculations for this investment are as follows:

Dividends Received [($600,000)(5.25%)]	$31,500
Gross Up of 38 Percent	11,970
Taxable Income	$43,470
Combined Federal/Provincial Tax Rate (29% + 12%)	41%
Tax Payable Before Dividend Tax Credit	$17,823
Federal/Provincial Dividend Tax Credit [($11,970)(6/11 + 28%)]	(9,881)
Total Tax Payable	$ 7,942

Dividends Received (Before Gross Up)	$31,500
Tax Payable	(7,942)
After Tax Return - Preferred Shares	$23,558

High Tech Shares

The required calculations for this investment are as follows:

Proceeds Of Disposition	$675,000
Adjusted Cost Base	(600,000)
Capital Gain	$ 75,000
Inclusion Rate	1/2
Taxable Capital Gain	$37,500
Combined Federal/Provincial Tax Rate (29% + 12%)	41%
Tax Payable	$15,375

Capital Gain Realized (100%)	$75,000
Tax Payable	(15,375)
After Tax Return - High Tech Shares	$59,625

Self Study Solution Seven - 5

The major considerations in deciding between the three alternative investment strategies are the after tax return and the certainty of the related cash flows.

Guaranteed Investment Certificate   As long as the certificate is purchased from a financial institution that is guaranteed by the federal government, there is virtually no risk that the principal or interest could be lost. Your combined federal and provincial tax rate for interest is 44 percent (29% + 15%). This means that the $100,000 investment would provide an after-tax amount calculated as follows:

Interest [($100,000)(5.5%)]	$5,500
Federal/Provincial Tax Payable [($5,500)(33% + 18%)]	(2,805)
After Tax Cash Flow - Guaranteed Investment Certificate	$2,695

Common Stock Purchase   If you invest the $100,000 in common stock, you will be exposing yourself to a greater risk and uncertainty of cash flows than the guaranteed investment certificate alternative. There is no guarantee that the stock will pay a dividend of $5,000 during the year. There is the possibility that more or less than $5,000 will be paid. In addition, the estimated market price of at least $106,000 on December 31, 2017 is not certain. The price on that date could be higher or lower.

Assuming that the stock does pay $5,000 in dividends and you sell the shares for $106,000 on December 31, 2017, your after tax return on the investment is as follows:

Dividends Received	$5,000
Gross Up [(38%)($5,000)]	1,900
Taxable Dividends	$6,900
Taxable Capital Gain [(1/2)($106,000 - $100,000)]	3,000
Taxable Income	$9,900
Combined Tax Rate (33% + 18%)	51%
Tax Payable Before Dividend Tax Credit	$5,049
Dividend Tax Credit [($1,900)(6/11 + 27%)]	(1,549)
Tax Payable	$3,500

Dividends Received	$5,000
Capital Gain (100%)	6,000
Tax Payable	(3,500)
After Tax Cash Flow - Common Stock Purchase	$7,500

Rental Property   If you invest the $100,000 in real estate, you will be choosing the highest risk alternative. Rental properties can require significant personal involvement if there are problems with the tenant or repairs become necessary.   The transaction costs (e.g., real estate commissions and legal fees), would be much higher on this investment than on either of the other two.   In addition, the real estate investment is the least liquid of the three alternatives and you might encounter difficulties in the disposition of this investment. The estimated net proceeds of $175,000 on December 31, 2017 is not certain. The net proceeds could be higher or lower.

Assuming that the property has the anticipated revenues and expenses and you net $175,000 when you sell the property on December 31, 2017, your after tax return on the investment is as follows:

Gross Rents	$13,200
Expenses	(9,600)
CCA (Property Sold Prior To Year End)	Nil
Net Rental Income	$ 3,600

In addition to this net rental income, you anticipate a capital gain of $10,000 ($175,000 - $165,000), of which one-half, or $5,000, would be included in your income. Based on these figures, the Tax Payable would be calculated as follows:

Net Rental Income	$3,600
Taxable Capital Gain	5,000
Taxable Income	$8,600
Tax Rate (33% + 18%)	51%
Tax Payable	$4,386

The total after tax cash flow would be as follows:

Net Rental Income	$ 3,600
Capital Gain (Cash Flow is 100% Of Gain)	10,000
Tax Payable	(4,386)
After Tax Cash Flow - Rental Property	$ 9,214

Conclusion   Based purely on after tax returns, it would appear that you should acquire the rental property. However, as previously indicated, this alternative involves the most risk and uncertainty.

In choosing between the guaranteed investment certificate and the shares of Norton Ltd., the after tax cash flows from the shares are considerably higher. However, the return on the shares is made up of dividends and a potential capital gain, both of which are more uncertain than the interest on the guaranteed investment certificate. Given this, the possibility of greater than anticipated dividends and/or capital gains must be weighed against the additional risk of lower than anticipated returns.

Other factors which may influence your decision are as follows:

- The funds are locked into the investment certificate and can only be withdrawn prior to maturity at a severe interest penalty, if at all.

- The investment in common stock would give you more flexibility if you should require some of the funds before the end of the year. All or some portion of the stockholding could be sold during the year.

- Any dividends or rent that is paid will be available for your use as at the payment date. The interest will not be available to you until maturity.

Self Study Solution Seven - 6

Mrs. Norton's minimum Net Income For Tax Purposes would be calculated as follows:

Income From A Business Or Profession:		
Professional Revenues	$169,500	
Operating Business Expenses	(42,800)	
Convention Expenses (Note 1)	(1,500)	$125,200
Investment Income:		
Dividends Received	$ 1,000	
Gross Up Of 38 Percent	380	
Interest Income	1,250	2,630
Rental Income:		
Rents Received	$12,000	
Cash Expenses	(8,000)	
CCA (Note 2)	(4,000)	Nil
Net Income For Tax Purposes		$127,830

Notes:

1. Unless the scope of Mrs. Norton's business is likely to extend to Asia, the costs of the Singapore convention cannot be deducted.

2. CCA cannot be used to create a net rental loss. Consequently, even though the calculated maximum CCA is $12,000 [(4%)($300,000)], the maximum amount that can be deducted is $4,000.

Self Study Solution Seven - 7

Taxable Income And Tax Payable

The amount of taxable income and tax payable resulting from the two investments would be calculated as follows:

Real Property Distribution [($4.50)(5,000)]	$22,500	
Return Of Capital [($1.25)(5,000)]	(6,250)	$16,250
Infidelity Capital Gain [($2.00)(10,000)]	$20,000	
Non-Taxable One-Half	(10,000)	10,000
Infidelity Eligible Dividends [($2.75)(10,000)]	$27,500	
Dividend Gross Up [(38%)($27,500)]	10,450	37,950
Infidelity Interest [($2.25)(10,000)]		22,500
Taxable Income		$86,700
Tax Rate (29% + 11%)		40%
Tax Before Dividend Tax Credit		$34,680
Dividend Tax Credit [($10,450)(6/11 + 28%)]		(8,626)
Tax Payable		$26,054

Adjusted Cost Base - Real Property

The reinvestment of the $22,500 distribution at $52.00 per unit would acquire an additional 432.69 units. After recognizing these changes, the adjusted cost base per unit would be as follows:

$$\$49.01 \; [(\$250,000 + \$22,500 - \$6,250) \div (5,000 + 432.69)]$$

Adjusted Cost Base - Infidelity

The reinvestment of the $70,000 [($7.00)(10,000)] distribution at $83.00 per unit would acquire an additional 843.37 units. After recognizing these changes, the adjusted cost base per unit would be as follows:

$$\$84.84 \; [(\$850,000 + \$70,000) \div (10,000 + 843.37)]$$

Self Study Solution Seven - 8

The required calculations are as follows:

Net Employment Income   Ms. Spring's 2017 Net Employment Income would be calculated as follows:

Salary	$64,000
RPP Contributions	(2,960)
Disability Benefits (Note 1)	4,945
Work Space In Home Allowance [(12)($400)]	4,800
Work Space In Home Expenses (Note 2)	(471)
Net Employment Income	$70,314

Note 1 As the employer contributes to the plan and the contributions do not create a taxable benefit, the benefits received during the year will be included in employment income. Although the disability insurance premiums that Ms. Spring pays are not deductible, they would reduce the taxable portion of any amounts subsequently received under the plan. As a result, the amount to be included in employment income is $4,945 ($5,600 - $200 - $250 - $205).

Note 2 As Ms. Spring has no commission income, she can only deduct costs associated with electricity, water, maintenance, and repairs. The deductible amount is $471 [(15%)($1,340 + $1,800)].

Property Income   Ms. Spring's 2017 property income would be calculated as follows:

Gross Rents	$42,000
Expenses Other Than CCA	(32,500)
Recapture of CCA (Note 3)	5,000
Rental Income Before CCA	$14,500
CCA (Note 3)	(14,500)
Net Rental Income	$ Nil
Canadian Dividends Received	9,300
Gross Up On Canadian Dividends (38%)	3,534
Foreign Dividends - No Gross Up	
(Amount Before 15% Withholding)	5,600
Property Income	$18,434

Note 3 The recapture and maximum available CCA for 2017 would be calculated as follows:

January 1, 2017 UCC of Property A	$156,000
Disposals - Lesser Of:	
• Capital Cost ($245,000 - $40,000) = $205,000	
• Proceeds Of Disposition	
($201,000 - $40,000) = $161,000	(161,000)
Negative Ending Balance = Recapture Of CCA	($ 5,000)

Property A (Sold)	$ Nil
Property B [(4%)($276,000)]	11,040
New Property [(4%)(1/2)($322,000 - $75,000)]	4,940
Maximum CCA Available	$15,980

While there is $15,980 in CCA available, this deduction cannot be used to create a rental loss. This means that the maximum deduction is equal to $14,500, the amount of rental income before the deduction of CCA. Note that the recaptured CCA is included in Rental Income Before CCA.

Net Income For Tax Purposes And Taxable Income

There are no Taxable Income deductions available. As a consequence, Taxable Income is equal to Net Income For Tax Purposes.

Net Employment Income	$70,314
Property Income	18,434
Net Income For Tax Purposes And Taxable Income	$88,748

Tax Payable

Tax Payable would be calculated as follows:

Tax On First $45,916			$ 6,887
Tax On Next $42,832 ($88,748 - $45,916) At 20.5 Percent			8,781
Tax Before Credits			$15,668
Basic Personal Amount - Ms. Spring	($11,635)		
Eligible Dependant Including Infirm Amount - Mark			
($11,635 + $2,150)(Note 4)	(13,785)		
EI Premiums	(836)		
CPP Contributions	(2,564)		
Canada Employment	(1,178)		
Transfer Of Amy's Education Credits (Note 5)	(5,000)		
Medical Expenses (Note 6)	(10,831)		
Credit Base	($45,829)		
Rate		15%	(6,874)
Subtotal			$ 8,794
Dividend Tax Credit [(6/11)($3,534)]			(1,928)
Foreign Tax Credit (Amount Withheld = 15%)			(840)
Federal Tax Payable			$ 6,026

Note 4 Amy does not qualify for the eligible dependant credit as she is not disabled and not under 18 years of age at any time during the taxation year. Although Mark is not under 18 years of age, he is dependent because of a physical disability. This means that Mark is eligible for the eligible dependant credit. Because the eligible dependant credit will be taken for Mark, the regular Canada caregiver credit cannot be claimed for him.

Note 5 As Amy's income is below the basic personal amount, she cannot use any of her tuition credit. Given this, the maximum transfer of Amy's tuition credit is equal to the lesser of:

- The actual tuition of $8,200.
- The absolute maximum of $5,000.

Note 6 The medical expense credit base would be calculated as follows:

Medical Expenses Of Ms. Spring		$ 962	
Lesser Of:			
• [(3%)($88,748)] = $2,662			
• 2017 Threshold Amount = $2,268		(2,268)	
Balance Before Dependants 18 And Over		Nil	
Amy's Medical Expenses	$2,450		
Reduced By The Lesser Of:			
• $2,268			
• [(3%)($7,300)] = $219	(219)	2,231	
Mark's Medical Expenses	$8,600		
Reduced By The Lesser Of:			
• $2,268			
• [(3%)(Nil)] = Nil	Nil	8,600	
Medical Expense Tax Credit Base		$10,831	

Self Study Solution Seven - 9

Net Business Income

Derek's Net Business Income is calculated as follows:

Accounting Net Income		$211,000
Additions:		
Amortization Expense	$18,000	
Meals And Entertainment (Note 1)	5,750	
Automobile Operating Costs - Personal (Note 2)	1,350	25,100
		$236,100
Deductions:		
Capital Cost Allowance		
Automobile (Note 3)	($ 3,234)	
Furniture And Fixtures (Note 4)	(9,300)	
Building [(6%)($450,000)] (Note 5)	(27,000)	(39,534)
Net Business Income For Tax Purposes		$196,566

Note 1   As the business deducted 100 percent of the meals and entertainment costs, the non-deductible one-half of this amount needs to be added back to arrive at Net Business Income For Tax Purposes.

Note 2   As the business deducted 100 percent of the automobile operating costs, the portion related to Derek's personal use must be added back. This amount would be $1,350 [($4,800)(9,000 ÷ 32,000)].

Note 3   The addition to UCC for the car would be limited to $30,000 and it would be allocated to a separate Class 10.1. Maximum CCA for 2017 would be $4,500 [(1/2)(30%)($30,000)]. However, the business can only deduct $3,234 [($4,500)(23,000 ÷ 32,000)].

Note 4   CCA for Class 8 would be calculated as follows:

UCC January 1, 2017		$42,000
Additions		12,000
Disposals - Lesser Of:		
Proceeds Of Disposition = $3,000		
Capital Cost = $10,000		(3,000)
One-Half Net Additions [(1/2)($12,000 - $3,000)]		(4,500)
Base For CCA		$46,500
Rate		20%
Class 8 CCA		$ 9,300

Note 5   As the building was acquired new and was used 100 percent for non-residential purposes, it is eligible for the 6 percent CCA rate. The fact that it was the only building owned by the business would result in it automatically being allocated to a separate class, but it must remain in a separate Class 1 to continue to qualify for the 6 percent rate.

Property Income

Derek's property income is calculated as follows:

Eligible Dividends On Breax	$ 8,000
Gross Up On Eligible Dividends [(38%)($8,000)]	3,040
Realco Income Trust Units [(5,000)($1.50)]	7,500
Debt Securities (Note 6)	12,000
Foreign Term Deposit (Note 7)	15,000
Total Property Income	$45,540

Note 6   Derek would have to recognize $8,000 [(8%)($100,000)] in interest on the July 1, 2017 anniversary of the debt security. In addition, because a $12,000 payment is received on December 31, 2017, he would have to recognize an additional $4,000 ($12,000, less the $8,000 recognized on the anniversary date).

Note 7   As non-business income is involved, the tax credit will be limited to $3,000 [(15%)($20,000)]. The remaining $5,000 ($8,000 - $3,000) can be deducted against the interest. This leaves an inclusion of $15,000 ($20,000 - $5,000).

Capital Gain

The adjusted cost base of the Breax shares that were sold was $52 ($130,000 ÷ 2,500). Given this, the capital gain on the Breax common shares would be calculated as follows:

Proceeds [($65)(1,000)]	$65,000
Adjusted Cost Base [($52)(1,000)]	(52,000)
Capital Gain	$13,000
Inclusion Rate	1/2
Taxable Capital Gain	$ 6,500

Net Income For Tax Purposes And Taxable Income

There are no Taxable Income deductions available. As a consequence, Taxable Income is equal to Net Income For Tax Purposes.

Net Business Income	$196,566
Total Property Income	45,540
Taxable Capital Gain	6,500
Net Income For Tax Purposes And Taxable Income	$248,606

Tax Payable

Tax Payable would be calculated as follows:

Tax On First $202,800		$46,966
Tax On Next $45,806 ($248,606 - $202,800) At 33 Percent		15,116
Tax Before Credits		$62,082
Tax Credits:		
Basic Personal Amount (Derek)	($11,635)	
Spouse ($11,635 - $9,500)	(2,135)	
Canada Caregiver For A Child	(2,150)	
Disability Transferred From Brad	(8,113)	
Disability Supplement For Brad (Note 8)	Nil	
First Time Home Buyers	(5,000)	
Transfer Of Bill's Tuition Credit (Note 9)	(5,000)	
Medical Expenses (Note 10)	(18,732)	
Total Credit Base	($52,765)	
Rate	15%	(7,915)
Dividend Tax Credit On Eligible Dividends		
[(6/11)($3,040)]		(1,658)
Foreign Tax Credit [(15%)($20,000)]		(3,000)
Federal Tax Payable		$49,509

Note 8   Since Brad's medical expenses claimed for the medical expense tax credit total more than $7,505 ($4,733 + $2,772), Derek cannot claim the disability supplement for him.

Note 9   As Bill's income is below the basic credit amount of $11,635, he cannot use any of his available tuition credit. Given this, the maximum transfer is the lesser of:

- The actual tuition of $8,500.
- The absolute maximum of $5,000.

Note 10   The base for the medical expense tax credit is calculated as follows:

Medical Expenses Of Derek, Emily, Brad And Barbara		
($1,400 + $1,600 + $11,400 + $2,300)		$ 16,700
Lesser Of:		
• [(3%)($248,606)] = $7,458		
• 2017 Threshold Amount = $2,268		(2,268)
Balance Before Dependants 18 And Over		$ 14,432
Bill's Medical Expenses	$4,600	
Reduced By The Lesser Of:		
• $2,268		
• [(3%)($10,000)] = $300	(300)	4,300
Medical Expense Tax Credit Base		$18,732

Chapter 7 Learning Objectives

After completing Chapter 7, you should be able to:

1. Explain the nature of property income (paragraph [P hereafter] 7-1 to 7-5).
2. Describe the rules applicable to the deductibility of interest payments and be able to apply these rules to various types of borrowing (P 7-6 to 7-28).
3. Apply the provisions relating to the treatment of discount and premium on long-term issued debt (P 7-29 to 7-37).
4. Calculate the taxable amount of interest income for both individuals and corporations (P 7-38 to 7-45).
5. Explain the tax treatment of discounts and premiums on long-term debt holdings (P 7-46 and 7-47).

6. Apply the provisions related to accrued interest at the time of transfer of debt obligations (P 7-48 to 7-50).
7. Describe tax procedures for royalties and payments based on production or use (P 7-51 to 7-53).
8. Calculate net rental income (P 7-54 to 7-65).
9. Apply the gross up and tax credit procedures to determine the tax consequences of receiving eligible and non-eligible dividend income (P 7-66 to 7-93).
10. Compare the after-tax returns from various types of investments (P 7-94 to 7-95).

11. Discuss the provisions relating to investments in income trusts (P 7-96 to 7-109).
12. Discuss the provisions relating to investments in mutual funds (P 7-110 to 7-120).
13. Explain the general treatment of stock dividends and capital dividends (P 7-121 to 7-126).
14. Explain the general tax treatment of withholdings on foreign source business and non-business income (P 7-127 to 7-130).
15. Explain the general treatment of shareholder benefits (P 7-131 to 7-133).

CHAPTER 8

How To Work Through Chapter 8

We recommend the following approach in dealing with the material in this chapter:

Economic Background And General Rules For Capital Gains Taxation
- Read paragraph 8-1 to 8-30 (in the textbook).
- Do Exercises Eight-1 and Eight-2 (in the textbook) and check the solutions in this Study Guide.
- Read paragraph 8-31 to 8-36.

Identical Properties
- Read paragraph 8-37 to 8-38.
- Do Exercise Eight-3 and check the solution in this Study Guide.
- Do Self Study Problem Eight-1 which is available on the Companion Website and check the solution in this Study Guide.

Partial Dispositions And Warranties On Capital Assets
- Read paragraph 8-39 to 8-41.
- Do Exercise Eight-4 and check the solution in this Study Guide.
- Do Self Study Problem Eight-2 and check the solution in this Study Guide.

Capital Gains Reserves
- Read paragraph 8-42 to 8-61.
- Do Exercise Eight-5 and check the solution in this Study Guide.
- Do Self Study Problems Eight-3 and Eight-4 and check the solutions in this Study Guide.

Bad Debts On Sales Of Capital Property
- Read paragraph 8-62 to 8-63.
- Do Exercise Eight-6 and check the solution in this Study Guide.
- Do Self Study Problems Eight-5 and Eight-6 and check the solutions in this Study Guide.

Special Rule For Sales Of Real Property
- Read paragraph 8-64 to 8-71.
- Do Exercise Eight-7 and check the solution in this Study Guide.

Principal Residence
- Read paragraph 8-72 to 8-81.
- Do Exercises Eight-8 and Eight-9 and check the solutions in this Study Guide.
- Do Self Study Problem Eight-7 and check the solution in this Study Guide.
- Read paragraph 8-82 to 8-86.

Personal Use And Listed Personal Property
- Read paragraph 8-87 to 8-94.
- Do Exercise Eight-10 and check the solution in this Study Guide.

- Do Self Study Problem Eight-8 and check the solution in this Study Guide.

Gains And Losses On Foreign Currency
- Read paragraph 8-95 to 8-106.
- Do Exercise Eight-11 and check the solution in this Study Guide.
- Do Self Study Problem Eight-9 and check the solution in this Study Guide.

Options
- Read paragraph 8-107 to 8-112.

Deemed Dispositions - Change In Use Including Principal Residences
- Read paragraph 8-113 to 8-121.
- Do Exercise Eight-12 and check the solution in this Study Guide.
- Read paragraph 8-122 to 8-128.
- Do Exercise Eight-13 and check the solution in this Study Guide.
- Read paragraph 8-129 to 8-130.
- Do Exercise Eight-14 and check the solution in this Study Guide.
- Do Self Study Problems Eight-10 and Eight-11 and check the solutions in this Study Guide.
- Read paragraph 8-131.

Deemed Dispositions - Departures From Canada
- Read paragraph 8-132 to 8-133.
- Do Exercises Eight-15 and Eight-16 and check the solutions in this Study Guide.
- Do Self Study Problem Eight-12 and check the solution in this Study Guide.

Deferral Provisions On Small Business Investments
- Read paragraph 8-134 to 8-136.
- Do Exercise Eight-17 and check the solution in this Study Guide.
- Do Self Study Problem Eight-13 and check the solution in this Study Guide.

Deferral Provisions On Replacement Property For Capital Gains And CCA
- Read paragraph 8-137 to 8-153.
- Do Exercise Eight-18 and check the solution in this Study Guide.

Replacement Property - Combined Use Of Deferral Elections
- Read paragraph 8-154 to 8-165.
- Do Exercise Eight-19 and check the solution in this Study Guide.

Capital Gains And Tax Planning
- Read paragraph 8-166 to 8-168.
- Do Self Study Problems Eight-14 to Eight-18 and check the solutions in this Study Guide.

To Complete This Chapter
- If you would like more practice in problem solving, do the Supplementary Self Study Problems for the chapter. These problems and solutions are available on the Companion Website.
- Review the Key Terms Used In This Chapter in the textbook at the end of Chapter 8. Consult the Glossary for the meaning of any key terms you do not know.
- Test yourself with the Chapter 8 Glossary Flashcards available on the Companion Website.
- Ensure you have achieved the Chapter 8 Learning Objectives listed in this Study Guide.
- As a review, we recommend you view the PowerPoint presentation for Chapter 8 that is on the Companion Website.

Practice Examination
Write the Practice Examination for Chapter 8 that is on the Companion Website. Mark your examination using the Practice Examination Solution that is also on the Companion Website.

Solutions to Chapter Eight Exercises

Exercise Eight - 1 Solution

The capital cost of this Class 1 asset would be $3,500,000 ($5,600,000 - $600,000 - $1,500,000). As it is used 100 percent for non-residential purposes and is in a separate Class 1, the maximum CCA in this first year would be $105,000 [(1/2)($3,500,000)(6%)].

Exercise Eight - 2 Solution

Proceeds Of Disposition [(1,000)($14.50)]	$14,500
Adjusted Cost Base [(1,000)($23.00)]	(23,000)
Total Capital Loss	($ 8,500)
Disallowed Portion [(600)($23 - $14.50)]	5,100
Adjusted Capital Loss	($ 3,400)
Inclusion Rate	1/2
Allowable Capital Loss	($ 1,700)

The adjusted cost base of the acquired shares would be calculated as follows:

Purchase Price [(600)($13.75)]	$8,250
Disallowed Loss [(600)($23 - $14.50)]	5,100
Adjusted Cost Base	$13,350

Exercise Eight - 3 Solution

The relevant average cost calculations are as follows:

Acquisition Date Or Sale Date	Shares Purchased (Sold)	Cost Per Share	Total Cost	Average Cost/Share
January 15, 2016	650	$23.50	$15,275	
March 12, 2016	345	24.25	8,366	
Subtotal	995		$23,641	$23.76
September 15, 2016	(210)	$23.76	(4,990)	
Subtotal	785		$18,651	
February 14, 2017	875	$26.75	23,406	
Subtotal	1,660		$42,057	$25.34
October 1, 2017	(340)	$25.34	(8,616)	
End Of Year Balances	1,320		$33,441	

Ms. Montrose's taxable capital gain for 2016 is calculated as follows:

Proceeds Of Disposition [($25.50)(210)]	$5,355
Adjusted Cost Base [($23.76)(210)]	(4,990)
Capital Gain	$ 365
Inclusion Rate	1/2
Taxable Capital Gain	$ 183

Ms. Montrose's taxable capital gain for 2017 is calculated as follows:

Proceeds Of Disposition [($29.50)(340)]	$10,030
Adjusted Cost Base [($25.34)(340)]	(8,616)
Capital Gain	$ 1,414
Inclusion Rate	1/2
Taxable Capital Gain	$ 707

Exercise Eight - 4 Solution

For 2016, there will be a taxable capital gain of $27,500 [(1/2)($292,000 - $237,000)]. For 2017, there will be an allowable capital loss of $2,400 [(1/2)($4,800)]. This allowable capital loss will only be deductible in the determination of 2017 Net Income For Tax Purposes, to the extent that there are 2017 taxable capital gains. Any undeducted loss is subject to the carry over provisions described in Chapter 11. This would include carrying the loss back to apply against the 2016 taxable capital gain.

Exercise Eight - 5 Solution

Mr. Goodson's capital gain on this transaction is $71,800 ($382,000 - $293,000 - $17,200) and the uncollected proceeds are $300,000 ($382,000 - $82,000). Given this, the maximum reserve for 2016 is $56,387, the lesser of:

• [($71,800)($300,000 ÷ $382,000)]	$56,387 (Reserve)
• [($71,800)(20%)(4 - 0)]	$57,440 (Reserve)

His taxable capital gain for 2016 is $7,707 [(1/2)($71,800 - $56,387)].

At the end of 2017, the uncollected proceeds are $240,000 ($300,000 - $60,000). Based on this, the capital gain to be recognized for 2017 would be as follows:

2016 Reserve Added To Income	$56,387
2017 Reserve - Lesser Of:	
• [($71,800)($240,000 ÷ $382,000)] = $45,110	
• [($71,800)(20%)(4 - 1)] = $43,080	(43,080)
2017 Capital Gain	$13,307

His taxable capital gain for 2017 is $6,654 [(1/2)($13,307)].

Exercise Eight - 6 Solution

For 2016, there will be an allowable capital loss of $7,500 [(1/2)($110,000 - $125,000)]. For 2017, there will be an allowable capital loss of $17,500 [(1/2)(Nil - $35,000)]. The total allowable capital loss of $25,000 ($7,500 + $17,500) over the two years is equivalent to the allowable capital loss that would have resulted if the property had been sold for cash of $75,000. The capital loss would equal $50,000 ($125,000 - $75,000) and the allowable capital loss would be $25,000 [(1/2)($50,000)].

These allowable capital losses will only be deductible against taxable capital gains. However, they can be carried over to other years in which the taxpayer has taxable capital gains and deducted in the determination of Taxable Income. (See Chapter 11.)

Exercise Eight - 7 Solution

A comparison of the tax effects for Part 1 and Part 2 is as follows:

(See Following Explanations)	Part 1	Part 2
Building - Fair Market Value	$500,000	
Building - Deemed Proceeds		$615,000
UCC	(615,000)	(615,000)
Terminal Loss	($115,000)	Nil

(See Following Explanations)	Part 1	Part 2
Land - Fair Market Value	$750,000	
Land - Deemed Proceeds ($1,250,000 - $615,000)		$635,000
Adjusted Cost Base	(425,000)	(425,000)
Capital Gain	$325,000	$210,000
Inclusion Rate	1/2	1/2
Taxable Capital Gain	$162,500	$105,000
Terminal Loss	(115,000)	Nil
Net Income Inclusion	$ 47,500	$105,000

Part 1 Explanation   In the absence of the special rule, there would be a taxable capital gain of $162,500 on the land. This would be reduced by the $115,000 ($615,000 - $500,000) terminal loss on the building, resulting in a net income inclusion of $47,500.

Part 2 Explanation   ITA 13(21.1)(a) modifies the results in such situations by deeming the proceeds of disposition for the building to be:

The Lesser Of:

- The FMV of the land and building $1,250,000
  Reduced By The Lesser Of:
  - The ACB of the land = $425,000
  - The FMV of the land = $750,000   (425,000) $825,000

- The Greater Of:
  - The FMV of the building = $500,000
  - The Lesser Of:
     The cost of the building = $930,000
     The UCC of the building = $615,000 $615,000

With the building proceeds at $615,000, the terminal loss is eliminated. The $635,000 deemed proceeds for the land result in a capital gain of $210,000. In effect, this eliminates the terminal loss of $115,000 by reducing the capital gain by the same amount (from $325,000 to $210,000) and increases the net income inclusion by one-half of this amount or $57,500 ($105,000 - $47,500).

Exercise Eight - 8 Solution

There would be no tax consequences due to the sales. There would be a capital gain on the first sale of $20,500 ($109,500 - $89,000). This gain could be eliminated by designating the first property as his principal residence for the six years 2008 through 2013. The gain reduction would be calculated as follows:

$$\left(\$20,500 \times \frac{(6+0)\ *}{6} \right) = \$20,500 \quad (\textbf{Reduction}, \text{Not Gain})$$

* Although the gain reduction formula includes a +1 in the numerator, the numerator cannot exceed the denominator as the gain reduction cannot be larger than the total capital gain.

The $26,000 ($178,000 - $152,000) capital gain on the second home could be eliminated by designating the second property as his principal residence for the years 2014 through 2017 and adding the plus one in the numerator. The gain reduction would be calculated as follows:

$$\left(\$26{,}000 \times \frac{(4+1)}{5} \right) = \$26{,}000 \quad \textbf{(Reduction}, \text{Not Gain)}$$

Exercise Eight - 9 Solution
The total gain on the two properties can be calculated as follows:

	City Home (12 Years)	Cottage (9 Years)
Sales Price	$198,000	$143,500
Adjusted Cost Base	(126,000)	(85,000)
Total Capital Gain	$ 72,000	$ 58,500

In this example, the years 2009 through 2017 could be allocated to either property. This raises the question of which property should be the designated the principal residence during these years. If both properties had been owned for the same length of time, you would simply allocate the number of years owned, less 1 year, to the property with the larger gain. However, that is not the case here. Given the different ownership periods, the optimum solution requires the calculation of annual increases in value for each property.

The annual calculations are as follows:

Annual Gain - City Home ($72,000 ÷ 12)	$6,000
Annual Gain - Cottage ($58,500 ÷ 9)	$6,500

Given these values, the years 2010 through 2017 (1 year less than owned) should be allocated to the cottage. When these 8 years are combined with the plus 1 in the numerator of the reduction formula, the $58,500 gain on the cottage will be completely eliminated. This leaves the years 2006 through 2009 for the Ottawa house, resulting in the following gain reduction:

$$\left(\$72{,}000 \times \frac{(4+1)}{12} \right) = \$30{,}000 \quad \textbf{(Reduction}, \text{Not Gain)}$$

This will leave a total capital gain on the sale of the two properties of $42,000 ($58,500 - $58,500 + $72,000 - $30,000).

Exercise Eight - 10 Solution
The results would be as follows:

	Personal Use Property	Listed Personal Property
Gain On Sailboat ($68,000 - $43,000)	$25,000	
Gain On Oil Painting ($25,000 - $1,000)		$24,000
Loss On Personal Automobile	Nil	
Loss On Necklace ($18,000 - $46,000)		(28,000)
Capital Gain	$25,000	Nil
Inclusion Rate	1/2	N/A
Net Taxable Capital Gain	$12,500	Nil

The only tax consequence of these dispositions is a taxable capital gain of $12,500 [(1/2)($25,000)]. The gain on the oil painting is completely eliminated by the loss on the necklace. As this loss on the necklace is greater than the gain on the painting, there is a listed personal property loss carry over of $2,000 [(1/2)($28,000 - $24,000)].

Exercise Eight - 11 Solution

In 2016, as a result of his share purchase, Mr. Pratt will have an exchange gain of $612 [(450)(TT$68)(C$0.23 - C$0.21)]. As this qualifies as an ITA 39(2) foreign currency capital gain, he will only include $206 [(1/2)($612 - $200)] of this in his Net Income For Tax Purposes.

In 2017, there will be a capital gain on the sale of $1,170 {[(450)(TT$96)(C$0.19)] - [(450)(TT$68)(C$0.23)]}. None of this gain qualifies under ITA 39(2), so there would be no $200 exclusion. Mr. Pratt's 2017 Net Income For Tax Purposes will include $585 [(1/2)($1,170)] of this gain.

Exercise Eight - 12 Solution

The change in use will trigger capital gains on the land and building as follows:

	Land	Building
Proceeds Of Disposition	$120,000	$111,000
Adjusted Cost Base	(20,000)	(23,000)
Capital Gain	$100,000	$ 88,000
Inclusion Rate	1/2	1/2
Taxable Capital Gain	$ 50,000	$ 44,000

For capital gains purposes, the new capital cost will be $111,000 for the building and $120,000 for the land.

As the change is from personal to business use and the fair market value is greater than the cost, the new UCC for the building will be its cost, plus one-half of the difference between the fair market value and the cost. The relevant CCA calculation is as follows:

Original Cost	$23,000
Bump Up [(1/2)($111,000 - $23,000)]	44,000
Cost For CCA Purposes = UCC	$67,000
One-Half Net Additions	(33,500)
CCA Base	$33,500
Rate	4%
2017 CCA	$ 1,340

Note that for individuals, the calendar year is considered the fiscal year for property income purposes. As a consequence, there is no adjustment for a short fiscal period in the year of acquisition. Also note that, while the half-year rules are generally not applicable to non-arm's length transfers, this exemption is only available when the property was used to produce business or property income prior to the transfer which is not the case here.

Exercise Eight - 13 Solution

No ITA 45(2) Election The 2016 change in use would be treated as a deemed disposition/re-acquisition at the fair market value of $210,000. As the home was personal use property, the $10,000 loss ($210,000 - $220,000) would not be deductible.

The maximum CCA for 2016 would be $4,200 [($210,000)(4%)(1/2)]. This would result in a net rental income for 2016 of $4,800 ($21,600 - $12,600 - $4,200).

When the property is sold in 2017, she would have a taxable capital gain of $67,500 [($345,000 - $210,000)(1/2)]. In addition, there would be recapture of CCA of $4,200, the amount of CCA taken in 2016 for a total income inclusion of $71,700 ($67,500 + $4,200).

ITA 45(2) Election   If she did not take CCA in 2016, her net rental income would be $9,000 ($21,600 - $12,600), $4,200 higher than when no ITA 45(2) election is made. However, she could then elect under ITA 45(2) and this means that the property could continue to be designated as her principal residence in 2017. Given this, the capital gain could be eliminated by the principal residence deduction. This is clearly a better alternative as shown in the following table:

	No Election	ITA 45(2) Election
2016 Income	$ 4,800	$9,000
2017 Income	71,700	Nil
Total	$76,500	$9,000

Exercise Eight - 14 Solution

No ITA 45(3) Election   The maximum CCA for 2016 would be $7,500 [($375,000)(4%)(1/2)]. Deducting this amount would result in a 2016 net rental income of $2,300 ($9,800 - $7,500).

Because he has deducted CCA for this year, he cannot treat the property as his principal residence and, when he moves in on January 1, 2017, the change in use will create a deemed disposition/re-acquisition at the fair market value of $450,000. This will result in a taxable capital gain of $37,500 [($450,000 - $375,000)(1/2)]. There would also be recapture of the $7,500 of CCA taken in 2016.

When he sells the property at the end of the year for $510,000, there will be an additional taxable capital gain of $30,000 [($510,000 - $450,000)(1/2)]. However, as he lived in the condominium during 2017, this gain would be eliminated through the use of the principal residence exemption. This would leave a 2017 income inclusion of $45,000 ($37,500 + $7,500 + $30,000 - $30,000).

ITA 45(3) Election   If he does not take CCA in 2016, his net rental income will be $9,800. However, if he makes the ITA 45(3) election, the unit can be designated as his principal residence for both 2016 and 2017. This means that there will be no additional income in 2017. This is clearly a better alternative as shown in the following table:

	No Election	ITA 45(3) Election
2016 Income	$ 2,300	$9,800
2017 Income	45,000	Nil
Total	$47,300	$9,800

Exercise Eight - 15 Solution

There would be a deemed disposition on his departure, leaving him liable for the taxes on a $55,000 [(1/2)($1,030,000 - $920,000)] taxable capital gain.

Exercise Eight - 16 Solution

As real property is exempt from the deemed disposition provision contained in ITA 128.1(4)(b), there would be no tax consequences with respect to the rental property at the time of Ms. Twain's departure. However, real property is Taxable Canadian Property and, as a consequence, as explained in Chapter 1, she would be liable for Canadian taxes on both recapture and capital gains resulting from a subsequent sale of the property, even after she becomes a non-resident.

Exercise Eight - 17 Solution

The capital gain would be calculated as follows:

Proceeds Of Disposition	$1,350,000
Adjusted Cost Base	(750,000)
Capital Gain	$ 600,000

As the lesser of the proceeds of disposition and the cost of the replacement shares is the $1,200,000 cost of the replacement shares, the maximum deferral would be $533,333 [($600,000)($1,200,000 ÷ $1,350,000)].

The adjusted cost base of the new shares would be calculated as follows:

Initial Cost	$1,200,000
Deferred Capital Gain	(533,333)
Adjusted Cost Base	$ 666,667

Exercise Eight - 18 Solution

The Company would have to record recapture of $750,000 ($650,000 - $1,400,000) for 2016. This is reversed during 2017 by electing under ITA 13(4). Since the replacement cost of the new building exceeds the normal recapture of CCA, the amended recapture of CCA is nil. Using the ITA 13(4) formula, the amended 2016 recapture of CCA would be calculated as follows:

UCC Balance			$650,000
Deduction:			
Lesser Of:			
• Proceeds Of Disposition = $1,400,000			
• Capital Cost = $1,500,000		$1,400,000	
Reduced By The Lesser Of:			
• Normal Recapture = $750,000			
• Replacement Cost = $2,350,000	(750,000)		(650,000)
Recapture Of CCA (Amended)			Nil

The result is that the UCC of the replacement building would be limited to $1,600,000 ($2,350,000 - $750,000). This also reflects the economic substance of the replacement transaction ($650,000 + $2,350,000 - $1,400,000 = $1,600,000).

Exercise Eight - 19 Solution

As the replacement did not occur until 2017, Hadfeld's 2016 tax return will include a capital gain of $225,000 ($950,000 - $725,000), of which one-half or $112,500 is taxable, and recapture of $101,850 ($725,000 - $623,150).

Since the cost of the replacement property exceeded the proceeds of disposition for the old property, these amounts can be reversed in 2017 through a 2016 amended return. The deemed capital cost and UCC of the new building are as follows:

Actual Capital Cost	$980,000
Capital Gain Deferred By Election ($950,000 - $725,000)	(225,000)
Deemed Capital Cost	$755,000
Recapture Deferred By Election ($725,000 - $623,150)	(101,850)
2017 UCC	$653,150

Each of these amounts are $30,000 more than the old capital cost and UCC. This reflects the $30,000 ($980,000 - $950,000) over and above the insurance proceeds that the Company spent on replacing the building.

Self Study Solution Eight - 1

Acquisition Or Sale Date	Shares Purchased (Sold)	Cost Per Share	Total Cost	Average Cost/Share
October 15, 2011	5,500	$40.00	$220,000	
November 8, 2011	(1,500)	(40.00)	(60,000)	
December 12, 2013	3,200	79.00	252,800	
Subtotal	7,200		$412,800	$ 57.33
February 3, 2014	(2,600)	(57.33)	(149,058)	
Subtotal	4,600		$263,742	
January 15, 2015 Stock Dividend	460	99.00	45,540	
June 15, 2015	3,800	104.00	395,200	
Subtotal	8,860		$704,482	
December 23, 2016 Stock Dividend	886	125.00	110,750	
March 15, 2017 Balances	9,746		$815,232	

The taxable capital gain resulting from the November 8, 2011 sale of shares would be calculated as follows:

Proceeds Of Disposition [(1,500)($52)]	$78,000
Adjusted Cost Base [(1,500)($40)]	(60,000)
Capital Gain	$18,000
Inclusion Rate	1/2
Taxable Capital Gain	$ 9,000

The taxable capital gain resulting from the February 3, 2014 sale of shares would be calculated as follows:

Proceeds Of Disposition [(2,600)($94)]	$244,400
Adjusted Cost Base [(2,600)($57.33)]	
(See preceding table for per share adjusted cost base)	(149,058)
Capital Gain	$ 95,342
Inclusion Rate	1/2
Taxable Capital Gain	$ 47,671

The taxable capital gain resulting from the March 15, 2017 sale of shares would be calculated as follows:

Proceeds Of Disposition [(9,746)($174)]	$1,695,804
Adjusted Cost Base (Remainder)	(815,232)
Capital Gain	$ 880,572
Inclusion Rate	1/2
Taxable Capital Gain	$ 440,286

Self Study Solution Eight - 2

No recognition can be given to the warranty at the time the land is sold. This means that a taxable capital gain of $600,000 [(1/2)($2,600,000 - $1,400,000)] will result from this sale. However, since no reduction in the capital gain can be made to reflect potential outlays under the warranty, the subsequent outlays that are required under the warranty agreement will be treated as a capital loss. Thus, the $1,040,000 payment that is required in 2017 will result in a $520,000 [(1/2)($1,040,000)] allowable capital loss.

This allowable capital loss must first be deducted against taxable capital gains that occur in 2017. If such gains are not sufficient to absorb the loss, some or all of the $520,000 can be carried back to 2016 to be applied against the gain that was recognized when the sale occurred.

Any loss that is not carried back can be carried forward indefinitely and applied against future capital gains. (Loss carry overs are covered in Chapter 11.)

Self Study Solution Eight - 3

Capital Gain And Reserve Limits
The total amount of the taxable capital gain can be calculated as follows:

Proceeds Of Disposition	$1,730,000
Adjusted Cost Base	(430,000)
Total Capital Gain	$1,300,000
Inclusion Rate	1/2
Total Taxable Capital Gain	$ 650,000

Under ITA 40(1)(a)(iii), the amount that can be deducted as a capital gains reserve is equal to the lesser of:

- [(Capital Gain)(Proceeds Not Yet Due ÷ Total Proceeds)]
- [(Capital Gain)(20%)(4 - Number Of Preceding Years Ending After Disposition)]

The first of the limiting factors is based, as would be expected, on the pattern of collections. In contrast, the second factor serves to require that at least 20 percent of any gain be recognized in the year of disposition and each subsequent year, regardless of the pattern of cash collections.

The payment schedule for the sale required a 30 percent down payment ($519,000/$1,730,000), followed by annual payments of 5 percent ($86,500/$1,730,000) in the following years. Given this, the reserve percentages under the two components of the ITA 40(1)(a)(iii) schedule are as follows:

Year	Proceeds Not Yet Due	20 Percent Formula
2017	70%	80%
2018	65%	60%
2019	60%	40%
2020	55%	20%
2021	50%	Nil

2017
The maximum reserve for 2017 would be the lesser of:

- [($1,300,000)($1,211,000 ÷ $1,730,000)] = $910,000
- [($1,300,000)(20%)(4 - 0)] = $1,040,000

The lesser figure is $910,000, reflecting the fact that the down payment was greater than 20 percent. Given this, the taxable capital gain for 2017 would be calculated as follows:

Total Capital Gain	$1,300,000
Reserve	(910,000)
Capital Gain	$ 390,000
Inclusion Rate	1/2
Taxable Capital Gain For 2017	$ 195,000

2018

The maximum reserve for 2018 would be the lesser of:

- [($1,300,000)($1,124,500 ÷ $1,730,000)] = $845,000
- [($1,300,000)(20%)(4 - 1)] = $780,000

The lesser figure is $780,000. This reflects the fact that the required recognition of 40 percent exceeds the percentage of the proceeds collected (35%). Given this, the taxable capital gain for 2018 would be calculated as follows:

Previous Year's Reserve	$910,000
New Reserve	(780,000)
Capital Gain	$130,000
Inclusion Rate	1/2
Taxable Capital Gain For 2018	$ 65,000

2019, 2020 And 2021

In these years, the 20 percent formula continues to provide the lower figure and the reserve would decline as follows:

- 2019 [($1,300,000)(20%)(4 Years - 2 Years)] = $520,000
- 2020 [($1,300,000)(20%)(4 Years - 3 Years)] = $260,000
- 2021 [($1,300,000)(20%)(4 Years - 4 Years)] = Nil

Based on this, the taxable capital gain for these three years will be calculated as follows:

	2019	2020	2021
Previous Year's Reserve	$780,000	$520,000	$260,000
New Reserve	(520,000)	(260,000)	Nil
Capital Gain	$260,000	$260,000	$260,000
Inclusion Rate	1/2	1/2	1/2
Taxable Capital Gain	$130,000	$130,000	$130,000

At the end of 2021, the entire taxable capital gain of $650,000 will have been recognized:

2017	$195,000
2018	65,000
2019	130,000
2020	130,000
2021	130,000
Total	$650,000

Self Study Solution Eight - 4

Capital Gain

Without regard to the assumptions about the down payment, the total capital gain for Ms. Gerhardt is $750,000 ($1,350,000 - $600,000). The taxable capital gain is $375,000 [(1/2)($750,000)].

Reserve Limits

Under ITA 40(1)(a)(iii), the amount that can be deducted as a capital gains reserve is equal to the lesser of:

- [(Capital Gain)(Proceeds Not Yet Due ÷ Total Proceeds)]
- [(Capital Gain)(20%)(4 - Number Of Preceding Years Ending After Disposition)]

The second part of this formula serves to require that at least 20 percent of the gain be recognized in the year of disposition and each subsequent year, without regard to the pattern of cash collected.

Part A

The reserve percentage under the two components of ITA 40(1)(a)(iii) would be as follows:

Year	Proceeds Not Yet Due	20 Percent Formula
2017	55%	80%
2018	50%	60%
2019	45%	40%
2020	40%	20%
2021	35%	Nil

For the years 2017 and 2018, the proceeds not yet due calculation provides the lower figure. Based on this, the gains to be recognized in these two years would be calculated as follows:

2017 Capital Gain	$750,000
2017 Reserve [($750,000)(55%)]	(412,500)
Capital Gain	$337,500
Inclusion Rate	1/2
Taxable Capital Gain For 2017	$168,750

2017 Reserve Added To Income	$412,500
2018 Reserve [($750,000)(50%)]	(375,000)
Capital Gain	$ 37,500
Inclusion Rate	1/2
Taxable Capital Gain For 2018	$ 18,750

In the years 2019 through 2021, the 20 percent formula provides the lower reserve. As a result, the reserves for these three years are as follows:

- 2019 [($750,000)(20%)(4 Years - 2 Years)] = $300,000
- 2020 [($750,000)(20%)(4 Years - 3 Years)] = $150,000
- 2021 [($750,000)(20%)(4 Years - 4 Years)] = Nil

Based on this, the taxable capital gain for these three years will be calculated as follows:

	2019	2020	2021
Previous Year's Reserve	$375,000	$300,000	$150,000
New Reserve	(300,000)	(150,000)	Nil
Capital Gain	$ 75,000	$150,000	$150,000
Inclusion Rate	1/2	1/2	1/2
Taxable Capital Gain	$ 37,500	$ 75,000	$75,000

Part B

In this case, the reserve percentage components would be as follows:

Year	Proceeds Not Yet Due	20 Percent Formula
2017	85%	80%
2018	80%	60%
2019	75%	40%
2020	70%	20%
2021	65%	Nil

In this case, the 20 percent formula calculation provides the lower figure for the reserve in each of the 5 years. Using this as the basis for the reserve will result in the recognition of $150,000 [(20%)($750,000)] of the gain in each of the five years. The taxable amount in each year will be $75,000 [(1/2)($150,000)], for a total of $375,000 over the five years 2017 through 2021.

Summary

As shown in the following table, the entire $375,000 taxable capital gain has been recognized in both Cases over the first 5 years, regardless of when the total proceeds will be completely collected.

Year	Part A	Part B
2017	$168,750	$ 75,000
2018	18,750	75,000
2019	37,500	75,000
2020	75,000	75,000
2021	75,000	75,000
Gain Recognized	$375,000	$375,000

Self Study Solution Eight - 5

For 2016, Mrs. Simpkins would have a capital gain of $10,000 ($25,000 - $15,000), of which one-half is taxable, resulting in a taxable capital gain of $5,000. While this could have been reduced through the use of reserves, Mrs. Simpkins chose not to do so.

In 2017, the inability to collect the note payment would result in a capital loss of $10,000 (Nil - $10,000). The $5,000 allowable amount of this loss must first be applied against any taxable capital gains that are realized in 2017. If such gains are not sufficient to absorb the loss, all or part of the $5,000 can be carried back and applied against the taxable capital gain that was recognized in 2016 (assuming there were no 2016 allowable capital losses net against it).

Any loss that is not carried back can be carried forward indefinitely and applied against future capital gains. (Loss carry overs are covered in Chapter 11.)

Self Study Solution Eight - 6

Capital Gains Reserve

With respect to the capital gains, under ITA 40(1)(a)(iii), the amount that can be deducted as a capital gains reserve is equal to the lesser of:

- [(Capital Gain)(Proceeds Not Yet Due ÷ Total Proceeds)]
- [(Capital Gain)(20%)(4 - Number Of Preceding Years Ending After Disposition)]

2017 Results

The only tax consequence in this year is the capital gain that occurs on the sale. The gain, along with the maximum deductible reserve, would be calculated as follows:

Proceeds Of Disposition	$6,680,000
Adjusted Cost Base	(2,160,000)
Capital Gain	$4,520,000
Reserve - Lesser Of:	
• [($4,520,000)($4,500,000 ÷ $6,680,000)] = $3,044,910	
• [($4,520,000)(20%)(4 - 0)] = $3,616,000	(3,044,910)
Capital Gain	$1,475,090
Inclusion Rate	1/2
Taxable Capital Gain	$ 737,545

As no provision can be made for the estimated cost of the warranty, the total Net Income For Tax Purposes inclusion for 2017 would be $737,545.

2018 Results

For this year, the reserve would be the lesser of:

- [($4,520,000)($3,000,000 ÷ $6,680,000)] = $2,029,940
- [($4,520,000)(20%)(4 - 1)] = $2,712,000

Based on this, the total inclusion in Net Income For Tax Purposes for 2018 would be as follows:

2017 Reserve Added To Income	$3,044,910
2018 Reserve	(2,029,940)
Capital Gain	$1,014,970
Inclusion Rate	1/2
Taxable Capital Gain	$ 507,485
Interest [(4%)($4,500,000)]	180,000
Total	$ 687,485

2019 Results

For this year, the reserve would be the lesser of:

- [($4,520,000)($1,500,000 ÷ $6,680,000)] = $1,014,970
- [($4,520,000)(20%)(4 - 2)] = $1,808,000

He will have a capital gain consisting of the addition of the 2018 reserve in income and the deduction of a new reserve for 2019. He will also have a capital loss due to the $1,000,000 payment to the developer. As this payment is required by a warranty on a capital asset, it is a capital loss.

Based on this, the total inclusion in Net Income For Tax Purposes for 2019 would be as follows:

2018 Reserve Added To Income	$2,029,940
2019 Reserve	(1,014,970)
Capital Gain	$1,014,970
Capital Loss On Warranty Payment On Capital Asset	(1,000,000)
Net Capital Gain	$ 14,970
Inclusion Rate	1/2
Net Taxable Capital Gain	$ 7,485
Interest [(4%)($3,000,000)]	120,000
Total	$ 127,485

2020 Results

With the bankruptcy of the developer, no interest will be collected in 2020 and the balance of the loan must be written off as a bad debt, resulting in a capital loss of $1,500,000 [(Nil - ($4,500,000 - $3,000,000)].

Lawrence will include the 2019 reserve of $1,014,970 in income. Since the loan was to be paid off in 2020, there would have been no new reserve to be deducted, regardless of the bankruptcy.

The capital loss can be deducted to the extent of the capital gain of $1,014,970. The remaining allowable capital loss of $242,515 [(1/2)($1,500,000 - $1,014,970)] can only be deducted in 2020 to the extent of taxable capital gains in that year. However, it can be carried back to be applied to the capital gains that were recognized in previous years.

Summary (Not Required)

The results can be summarized as follows:

Year	Interest	Net Taxable Gain (Allowable Loss)
2017	Nil	$737,545
2018	$180,000	507,485
2019	120,000	7,485
2020	Nil	(242,515)
Totals	$300,000	$1,010,000

The amount of the taxable capital gain can be verified as follows:

Initial Capital Gain	$4,520,000
Warranty Payment	(1,000,000)
Bad Debt	(1,500,000)
Capital Gain	$2,020,000
Inclusion Rate	1/2
Taxable Capital Gain	$1,010,000

Self Study Solution Eight - 7

The gains on the two properties can be calculated as follows:

	Country Home	Condominium
Proceeds Of Disposition	$1,200,000	$900,000
Adjusted Cost Base	(850,000)	(625,000)
Real Estate Commissions		
[(5%)($1,200,000)]	(60,000)	
[(5%)($900,000)]		(45,000)
Total Capital Gain	$ 290,000	$230,000

The annual gain was $18,125 ($290,000 ÷ 16) on the country home and $28,750 ($230,000 ÷ 8) on the condominium. This would indicate that the maximum number of years should be allocated to the condominium. However, because of the plus 1 in the reduction formula, one year can be left off.

Based on this analysis, the seven years 2011 through 2017 should allocated to the condominium, with the nine years 2002 through 2010 being allocated to the country home. The required calculations would be as follows:

	Country Home	Condominium
Total Capital Gain	$ 290,000	$230,000
Exemption:		
Country Home		
[$290,000][(9 + 1) ÷ 16]	(181,250)	
Condominium		
[$230,000][(7 + 1) ÷ 8]		(230,000)
Capital Gain	$108,750	Nil
Inclusion Rate	1/2	N/A
Taxable Capital Gain	$ 54,375	Nil

This gives a total taxable capital gain on the two properties of $54,375.

Self Study Solution Eight - 8

Listed personal property consists of these specified items as listed in ITA 54:

(i) print, etching, drawing, painting, sculpture, or other similar work of art,
(ii) jewelry,
(iii) rare folio, rare manuscript, or rare book,
(iv) stamp, or
(v) coin.

The tax consequences of the dispositions can be described as follows:

1. **Oil Painting** She will have a listed personal property capital gain on this disposition of $4,000 ($780,000 - $78,000 - $698,000).

2. **Miniature Vehicles** She will have a personal use property capital gain of $11,000 ($23,000 - $12,000).

3. **Antique Doll House** She will have a personal use property capital gain of $3,050 ($4,500 - $450 - $1,000 Floor).

4. **Sailboat** She will have a personal use property loss on the sailboat of $13,000 ($48,000 - $23,000 - $38,000). As the sailboat is not listed personal use property, the loss cannot be deducted against any source of income

5. **Jewelry Collection** She will have a listed personal property capital loss on this disposition of $18,000 ($43,000 - $61,000). As jewelry is included in the definition of listed personal property, this loss can be deducted to the extent that Rita has gains on listed personal property.

6. **First Edition** She will have a listed personal property capital gain on this disposition of $1,300 ($14,200 - $400 - $12,500).

The overall amount to be included in Net Income For Tax Purposes can be calculated as follows:

Personal Use Property		
Gain On Miniature Vehicles	$11,000	
Gain On Antique Doll House	3,050	
Loss On Sail Boat	Nil	$14,050
Listed Personal Property		
Gain On Oil Painting	$4,000	
Gain On First Edition	1,300	
Total Listed Personal Property Gains	$5,300	
Loss On Jewelry (See Note)	(5,300)	Nil
Net Capital Gains		$14,050
Inclusion Rate		1/2
Addition To Net Income For Tax Purposes		$ 7,025

Note The deduction for the jewelry loss is limited to the amount of gains on listed personal property. This will leave an allowable listed personal property loss carry over of $6,350 [(1/2)($18,000 - $5,300)]. As covered in Chapter 11, this unused amount can be carried back 3 years and forward 7 years to be deducted against gains on listed personal property in those years.

Self Study Solution Eight - 9

The taxable capital gain on the sale of securities would be calculated as follows:

Proceeds Of Disposition [(3,500)(€33.50)($1.49)]	$174,703
Adjusted Cost Base [(3,500)(€30.00)($1.46)]	(153,300)
Capital Gain On Sale Of Securities	$ 21,403
Inclusion Rate	1/2
Taxable Capital Gain	$ 10,702

The taxable capital gain on the foreign exchange conversion would be calculated as follows:

Proceeds Of Conversion [(€117,250)($1.52)]	$178,220
Adjusted Cost Base Of Currency [(€117,250)($1.49)]	(174,703)
Capital Gain On Foreign Exchange	$ 3,517
ITA 39(1.1) Reduction Of Capital Gain	(200)
Net Capital Loss	$ 3,317
Inclusion Rate	1/2
Allowable Capital Loss	$ 1,659

Ms. Laval's minimum Net Income For Tax Purposes inclusion would a total taxable capital gain of $12,361 ($10,702 + $1,659).

Because Ms. Laval is an individual, the ITA 39(1.1) deduction of $200 reduces the capital gain on the foreign exchange conversion.

Self Study Solution Eight - 10

2015 Results

During 2015, 100 percent of the property was used for income producing purposes. The CCA for the year would be calculated as follows:

Capital Cost ($645,000 - $120,000)	$525,000
One-Half Net Additions	(262,500)
CCA Base	$262,500
Maximum CCA [(4%)($262,500)]	(10,500)
One-Half Net Additions	262,500
UCC - January 1, 2016	$514,500

There are no additional tax consequences during this year.

2016 Results

On January 1, 2016, there would be a deemed disposition/acquisition of 25 percent of the depreciable property. The transaction would be measured using the building's fair market value of $460,000 ($560,000 - $100,000). Given this, the maximum CCA on the remaining 75 percent would be calculated as follows:

Opening UCC	$514,500
Deemed Disposition - Lesser Of:	
• Capital Cost [(25%)($525,000)] = $131,250	
• Deemed Proceeds [(25%)($460,000)] = $115,000	(115,000)
CCA Base	$399,500
Maximum CCA [(4%)($399,500)]	(15,980)
UCC - January 1, 2017	$383,520

While the value of the building has declined from $525,000 ($645,000 - $120,000) to $460,000 ($560,000 - $100,000), no loss can be recognized. As there is still an asset in the Class, a terminal loss cannot be recognized. In addition, we would remind you that you cannot have a capital loss on a depreciable asset disposition.

The allowable capital loss on the land of $2,500 [(25%)(1/2)($120,000 - $100,000)] can be deducted against the taxable capital gains on dispositions from her portfolio. Since her income from other sources is so high, she will deduct maximum CCA regardless of how the business is doing.

The cost to Laci of the 25 percent of the property that is being used for personal purposes would be $115,000 [(25%)($460,000)] allocated to the building and $25,000 [(25%)($100,000)] allocated to the land.

2017 Results

On January 1, 2017, there would be a deemed acquisition of 25 percent of the depreciable property. The capital cost of the building acquisition would be $140,000 [(25%)($690,000 - $130,000)]. However, as the change is from personal use to business use and the fair market value of the building is greater than its cost, the UCC will be limited to her cost plus one-half of the difference between fair market value and cost or $127,500 [$115,000 + (1/2)($140,000 - $115,000)].

Maximum CCA for would be calculated as follows:

Opening UCC	$383,520
Deemed Acquisition	
[$115,000 + (1/2)($140,000 - $115,000)]	127,500
Deduct: One-Half Net Additions [(1/2)($127,500)]	(63,750)
CCA Base	$447,270
Maximum CCA [(4%)($447,270)]	(17,891)
Add: One-Half Net Additions	63,750
UCC - January 1, 2018	$493,129

As a result of the deemed disposition, Laci would have a taxable capital gain on both the land and the building. They would be calculated as follows:

	Land	Building
Proceeds Of Disposition		
[(25%)($130,000)]	$32,500	
[(25%)($560,000)]		$140,000
Adjusted Cost Base [(25%)($100,000)]	(25,000)	
Capital Cost [(25%)($460,000)]		(115,000)
Capital Gains	$ 7,500	$ 25,000
Inclusion Rate	1/2	1/2
Taxable Capital Gains	$ 3,750	$ 12,500

Even though Laci has a home other than the apartment, she could eliminate these gains by making use of the +1 year in the principal residence exemption formula. Assuming she did that, she would have to allow for the designated year in the exemption formula when she sells her home.

Self Study Solution Eight - 11

2016 Solution

As the property is being transferred from personal to business use and its fair market value is greater than its cost, ITA 13(7)(b) requires that, for the purposes of calculating CCA, the property be recorded at an amount equal to its cost, plus one-half of the excess of its fair market value over cost. The half-year rule is applicable as the personal residence was not used to produce business or property income. The UCC would be calculated as follows:

Cost Of Building ($528,000 - $249,000)	$279,000
Bump-Up On Transfer -	
{[1/2][($759,000 - $318,000) - ($528,000 - $249,000)]}	81,000
Capital Cost For CCA Purposes Only	$360,000
Rental Share	32%
Opening UCC	$115,200
One-Half Net Additions	(57,600)
CCA Base	$ 57,600
CCA [($57,600)(4%)]	(2,304)
One-Half Net Additions	57,600
January 1, 2017 UCC	$ 112,896

Based on the preceding information, the 2016 net rental income would be calculated as follows:

Rents [(12)($2,550)]	$30,600
Expenses [(32%)($16,800)]	(5,376)
CCA	(2,304)
Net Rental Income	$22,920

There would also be taxable capital gains on the land and the building, calculated as follows:

	Land	Building
Deemed Proceeds Of Disposition		
Land	$318,000	
Building ($759,000 - $318,000)		$441,000
Adjusted Cost Base/Capital Cost		
Land	(249,000)	
Building ($528,000 - $249,000)		(279,000)
Subtotal	$ 69,000	$162,000
Rental Share	32%	32%
Capital Gain	$ 22,080	$ 51,840
Inclusion Rate	1/2	1/2
Taxable Capital Gain	$ 11,040	$ 25,920

Note that the capital cost used for determining the capital gain on the building ($441,000) is not the same value that was used for determining CCA ($360,000). For capital gains purposes, the fair market value is used. As shown in the CCA calculation, the value for CCA and UCC purposes is limited by ITA 13(7)(b) to its cost plus the bump up.

As Mr. Blake does not use the principal residence exemption, the increase in his Net Income For Tax Purposes would total $59,880 ($22,920 + $11,040 + $25,920).

2017 Solution

In this year, the transfer is from business to personal use and, as a consequence, the disposition will result in a deduction from UCC in an amount equal to the lesser of 11 percent of the capital cost for CCA purposes ($120,000) and 11 percent of the fair market value of $168,000 ($278,000 - $110,000). The calculations are as follows:

Opening UCC	$112,896
Plus: Additions (Improvements)	37,050
Less: Dispositions - Lesser Of:	
Cost [(11%)($360,000)] = $39,600	
Deemed Proceeds	
[(11%)($834,000 - $330,000)] = $55,440	(39,600)
One-Half Net Additions	Nil
CCA Base	$110,346
CCA [($110,346)(4%)]	(4,414)
January 1, 2018 UCC	$105,932

Based on the preceding information, the 2017 net rental income would be calculated as follows:

Rents [(6)($2,550) + (6)($2,250)]	$28,800
Expenses {[(32%)($8,700)] + [(21%)($9,600)]}	(4,800)
CCA	(4,414)
Net Rental Income	$19,586

There would also be taxable capital gains on the land and building, calculated as follows:

	Land	Building
Deemed Proceeds Of Disposition		
Land	$330,000	
Building ($834,000 - $330,000)		$504,000
Adjusted Cost Base		
Land	(318,000)	
Building ($759,000 - $318,000)		(441,000)
Subtotal	$ 12,000	$ 63,000
Rental Share	11%	11%
Capital Gain	$ 1,320	$ 6,930
Inclusion Rate	1/2	1/2
Taxable Capital Gain	$ 660	$ 3,465

The increase in Mr. Blake's Net Income For Tax Purposes would total $23,711 ($19,586 + $660 + $3,465).

Self Study Solution Eight - 12

Mr. Lange's taxable capital gain on deemed dispositions resulting from his departure from Canada would be calculated as follows:

Vacant land	N/A
Automobile	N/A
Coin Collection ($11,000 - $5,000)	$ 6,000
Enbridge Shares ($38,000 - $24,000)	14,000
BCE Shares ($35,000 - $42,000)	(7,000)
Royal Bank Shares ($23,000 - $15,000)	8,000
Nal Enterprises Ltd. Shares ($153,000 - $26,000)	127,000
Capital Gain	$148,000
Inclusion Rate	1/2
Taxable Capital Gain On Departure	$ 74,000

The vacant land is exempt from the deemed disposition rules that are applicable to individuals leaving Canada. However, as it is taxable Canadian property, a later sale of this land will attract Canadian income taxes, even though Mr. Lange is no longer a Canadian resident.

The loss on the automobile is not deductible as the vehicle is a personal use property.

Self Study Solution Eight - 13

In both Cases, since the common shares have been held for more than 185 days, the sales are qualifying dispositions. In both Cases, the eligible small business corporation common shares were purchased within 120 days after the end of the year in which the qualifying disposition took place. As a result, they can be designated as replacement shares.

Case A

The capital gain on the disposition is $800,000 ($2,200,000 - $1,400,000). As the cost of the replacement shares is only $1,800,000, the permitted deferral would be $654,545 [($1,800,000 ÷ $2,200,000)($800,000)].

The adjusted cost base of the replacement shares would be $1,145,455 ($1,800,000 - $654,545).

Case B

The capital gain on the disposition is $700,000 ($1,900,000 - $1,200,000). As the cost of the replacement shares is only $1,400,000 ($500,000 + $900,000), the permitted deferral would be $515,789 [($1,400,000 ÷ $1,900,000)($700,000)].

The cost base of the two investments would be calculated as follows:

	A Shares	B Shares
Purchase Price	$500,000	$900,000
Deferral:		
[($515,789)($500,000 ÷ $1,400,000)]	(184,210)	
[($515,789)($900,000 ÷ $1,400,000)]		(331,579)
Adjusted Cost Base	$315,790	$568,421

Self Study Solution Eight - 14

2017 Results

The insurance proceeds would create recaptured CCA, calculated as follows:

Opening UCC Balance		$ 368,000
Disposition - Lesser Of:		
• Cost = $500,000		
• Proceeds Of Disposition = $490,000	(	490,000)
Negative Closing Balance = Recapture	($	122,000)
Recapture		122,000
January 1, 2018 UCC		Nil

The $122,000 in recapture would be taken into 2017 income and added back to the UCC to create a UCC balance of nil.

2018 Results

Using ITA 13(4), Trail Resources Ltd. would file an amended return for the 2017 taxation year. The revised recapture would be calculated as follows:

January 1, 2017 UCC Balance		$368,000
Deduction:		
Lesser Of:		
• Proceeds Of Disposition = $490,000		
• Capital Cost = $500,000	$490,000	
Reduced By The Lesser Of:		
• Normal Recapture = $122,000		
• Replacement Cost = $650,000	(122,000)	(368,000)
Recapture Of 2017 CCA (Amended)		Nil

The new nil figure for the recapture on the disposition of the old building will replace the old figure of $122,000 that was included in the original 2017 return.

The UCC of the new building will be adjusted for this change as follows:

Cost Of New Building	$ 650,000
Reversal Of Recapture - ITA 13(4) Election	(122,000)
UCC	$ 528,000

Given this, the required maximum CCA for 2018 and the January 1, 2019 UCC balance would be calculated as follows:

Opening UCC - Class 1	Nil
Addition Of UCC Of New Building	$528,000
One-Half Net Additions	(264,000)
Base For CCA	$264,000
Maximum CCA [($264,000)(6%)]	(15,840)
Add: One-Half Net Additions	264,000
January 1, 2019 UCC	$512,160

The reasonableness of the CCA base calculation can be verified by noting that the $528,000 is equal to the initial UCC of $368,000, plus the cost of the new building of $650,000, less the insurance proceeds of $490,000. The half-year rule is applied to the addition to Class 1.

Self Study Solution Eight - 15

Part A

The 2017 tax consequences of the voluntary disposition would include both taxable capital gains and recapture. The amounts on the land and building would be calculated as follows:

	Land	Building
Proceeds Of Disposition:	$1,720,000	$1,200,000
Adjusted Cost Base/Capital Cost	(325,000)	(1,100,000)
Capital Gain	$1,395,000	$ 100,000
Inclusion Rate	1/2	1/2
Taxable Capital Gain	$ 697,500	$ 50,000

January 1, 2017 UCC Balance - Building	$ 720,000
Deduct Disposition - Lesser Of:	
• Cost = $1,100,000	
• Proceeds Of Disposition = $1,200,000	(1,100,000)
Negative Closing UCC Balance = Recapture	($ 380,000)
Recapture (Included In Income)	380,000
January 1, 2018 UCC	Nil

The Company would have recapture on its equipment calculated as follows:

January 1, 2017 UCC Balance - Equipment	$240,000
Deduct Disposition - Lesser Of:	
• Capital Cost = $620,000	
• Proceeds Of Disposition = $320,000	(320,000)
Negative Closing UCC Balance = Recapture	($ 80,000)
Recapture (Included In Income)	80,000
UCC - January 1, 2018	Nil

As a result of this voluntary disposition, Voltec will have an addition to 2017 Net Income For Tax Purposes of $1,207,500 ($697,500 + $50,000 + $380,000 + $80,000).

Part B - Land

As the land and building was replaced before the end of the second taxation year following the sale, Voltec can use both ITA 44(1) and ITA 13(4) to modify these results. These changes will be implemented through an amended return.

With respect to the Land, the capital gain resulting from the use of the ITA 44(1) election would be the lesser of:

- $1,395,000 (regular capital gain); and
- $770,000 (the excess of the $1,720,000 proceeds of disposition for the old land over the $950,000 cost of the replacement land).

As you can see, the inability to completely eliminate the capital gain on the land results from the fact that the cost of the replacement land was $770,000 less than the proceeds of disposition from the sale of the old land.

The taxable amount of the capital gain would be $385,000 [(1/2)($770,000)] and this would be included in the revised 2017 Net Income For Tax Purposes instead of $697,500.

Part B - Building

With respect to the building, the capital gain resulting from the use of the ITA 44(1) election would be nil, the lesser of:

- $100,000 (regular capital gain); and
- Nil ($1,200,000 - $1,350,000)

In the case of the building, the entire capital gain can be eliminated, reflecting the fact that the $1,350,000 cost of the replacement building was greater than the $1,200,000 proceeds of disposition from the old building.

Under ITA 13(4), the revised recapture would be calculated as follows:

January 1, 2017 UCC Balance		$720,000
Deduction:		
Lesser Of:		
• Proceeds Of Disposition = $1,200,000		
• Capital Cost = $1,100,000	($1,100,000)	
Reduced By The Lesser Of:		
• Normal Recapture = $380,000		
• Replacement Cost = $1,350,000	380,000	(720,000)
Recapture Of 2017 CCA (Amended)		Nil

Part B - Equipment

As this is a voluntary disposition, the ITA 13(4) and 44(1) elections can only be used on real property (land and buildings). They cannot be used on the equipment and, as a consequence, the $80,000 in recapture will not be altered in the amended return.

Part B - Income Effect of ITA 44(1) and ITA 13(4) Elections

As reported in Part A, the disposition of the land, building, and equipment resulted in an addition of $1,207,500 to the Company's 2017 Net Income For Tax Purposes. After applying the two elections, this was reduced to $465,000 ($385,000 + $80,000) in the amended return for that year. This is a reduction of $742,500 ($1,207,500 - $465,000).

Part C - Land And Building

Assuming Voltec decides to use the elections under ITA 44(1) and ITA 13(4), the deemed cost and UCC of the replacement properties would be as follows:

	Land	Building
Actual Cost Of Replacement Property	$950,000	$1,350,000
Capital Gain Reversed By Election		
Land ($1,395,000 - $770,000)	(625,000)	
Building ($100,000 - Nil)		(100,000)
Deemed Cost Of Replacement Property	$325,000	$1,250,000
Deemed Capital Cost Of Building		$1,250,000
Recaptured CCA Reversed By Election ($380,000 - Nil)		(380,000)
UCC - Replacement Building		$ 870,000

With respect to the economic basis for these amounts, the deemed adjusted cost base of the replacement land is equal to the adjusted cost base of the old land.

The deemed cost of the replacement building is equal to the capital cost of the old building ($1,100,000), plus the additional $150,000 ($1,350,000 - $1,200,000) in funds required for its acquisition.

The UCC for the new building is equal to the UCC of the old building ($720,000), plus the additional $150,000 ($1,350,000 - $1,200,000) in funds required for its acquisition.

Part C - Equipment

As the ITA 13(4) election could not be used, both the capital cost and the UCC of the new equipment will be $475,000.

Part D - Optimal Transfer

The ITA 44(6) election applies when there is a disposition involving a combination of part land and part building. If, for either of the assets, the proceeds of disposition exceed the adjusted cost base, the election allows the transfer of all or part of that excess to the other asset.

As will be demonstrated in this problem, this can provide some relief when ITA 44(1) and ITA 13(4) fail to eliminate all of the capital gains arising on one part of the disposition of the old property. ITA 44(1) fully eliminated the capital gain on the building. However, a $770,000 capital gain remained on the land. This would suggest that it could be advantageous to transfer some of the proceeds of disposition from the land to the building.

The excess of the proceeds of disposition of the old land over the cost of the replacement land was $770,000 ($1,720,000 - $950,000). This is the maximum available transfer from the land to the building. However, the excess of the cost of the replacement building over the old building's proceeds of disposition is only $150,000 ($1,350,000 - $1,200,000). If a transfer in excess of this amount is made, any reduction in the capital gain on the land will be matched by an increased capital gain on the building.

Applying ITA 44(6) in an optimal manner will result in the following adjusted proceeds of disposition:

	Land	Building
Actual Proceeds Of Disposition	$1,720,000	$1,200,000
Optimal Transfer Land To Building	(150,000)	150,000
Adjusted Proceeds Of Disposition	$1,570,000	$1,350,000

Part D - Application To Land

If both the ITA 44(1) and the ITA 44(6) elections are used, the capital gain on the land will be the lesser of:

- $1,245,000 ($1,570,000 - $325,000); and
- $620,000 (the excess of the $1,570,000 adjusted proceeds of disposition for the old land over the $950,000 cost of the replacement land).

This is a reduction of $150,000 ($770,000 - $620,000) from the amount calculated when only ITA 44(1) was applied. Note, however, the adjusted cost base of the replacement land would be unchanged and would still be equal to the adjusted cost base of the old land:

Actual Cost	$950,000
Capital Gain Reversed By The Two Elections	
($1,245,000 - $620,000)	(625,000)
Deemed Adjusted Cost Base Of Replacement Land	$325,000

Part D - Application To Building

With the proceeds of disposition transfer limited to $150,000, the capital gain on the building is still nil. Specifically, the gain will be the lesser of:

- $250,000 (1,350,000 - $1,100,000); and
- Nil ($1,350,000 - $1,350,000)

However, the capital cost and the UCC of the replacement building will be reduced by the application of ITA 44(6):

Actual Cost		$1,350,000
Capital Gain Reversed By The Two Elections		(250,000)
Deemed Capital Cost		$1,100,000
Recapture Reversed By ITA 13(4)		(380,000)
UCC - Replacement Building		$ 720,000

Part D - Comparison

The table which follows compares the results of using only ITA 44(1) and ITA 13(4) with the results that arise when the ITA 44(6) election is also used.

	No ITA 44(6)	With ITA 44(6)	Difference
Capital Gains			
Land	$ 770,000	$620,000	($150,000)
Building	Nil	Nil	Nil
Replacement Property			
Adjusted Cost Base Of Land	$ 325,000	$ 325,000	Nil
Capital Cost Of Building	1,250,000	1,100,000	(150,000)
UCC	870,000	720,000	(150,000)

As you can see in the table, the use of ITA 44(6) has reduced the capital gain on the land by $150,000. However, it has done so at the cost of reducing the capital cost and UCC of the replacement building. There is a tax cost associated with this trade off in that only one-half of the capital gain would have been taxed in the current year, whereas the future CCA that has been lost would be fully deductible.

Self Study Solution Eight - 16

Part A

The proceeds of disposition were greater than the relevant capital costs for all the destroyed and expropriated assets. As a result, with respect to Net Income For Tax Purposes, the 2017 tax effects related to the involuntary dispositions would be as follows:

	Old Land	Old Building	Old Contents
Proceeds Of Disposition	$723,000	$4,800,000	$1,256,000
Adjusted Cost Base/Capital Cost	(256,000)	(3,700,000)	(972,000)
Capital Gains	$467,000	$1,100,000	$ 284,000
Inclusion Rate	1/2	1/2	1/2
Taxable Capital Gains	$233,500	$ 550,000	$ 142,000
Opening UCC		$1,856,000	$ 72,000
Capital Cost (Less Than Proceeds)		(3,700,000)	(972,000)
Closing UCC		($1,844,000)	($900,000)
Recapture Of CCA		1,844,000	900,000
UCC - January 1, 2018		Nil	Nil

The increase in Net Income For Tax Purposes totals $3,669,500 ($233,500 + $550,000 + $142,000 + $1,844,000 + $900,000).

Part B - Land

As the land, building and contents were replaced before the end of the second taxation year following the involuntary dispositions, Fraser can use both ITA 44(1) and ITA 13(4) to modify these results. These changes will be implemented through an amended return.

With respect to the land, the capital gain resulting from the use of the ITA 44(1) election would be the lesser of:

- $467,000 (regular capital gain); and
- $223,000 (the excess of the $723,000 proceeds of disposition for the old land over the $500,000 cost of the new land).

The taxable amount of this capital gain will be $111,500 [(1/2)($223,000)]. The original gain of $467,000 would be eliminated in the revised return.

Part B - Building

With respect to the building, the capital gain resulting from the use of the ITA 44(1) election would be nil, the lesser of:

- $1,100,000 (regular capital gain); and
- Nil (reflecting the fact that there was no excess of the $4,800,000 proceeds of disposition for the old building over the $5,700,000 cost of the replacement building).

Under ITA 13(4), the revised recapture would be calculated as follows:

January 1, 2017 UCC Balance		$1,856,000
Deduction:		
Lesser Of:		
• Proceeds Of Disposition = $4,800,000		
• Capital Cost = $3,700,000	($3,700,000)	
Reduced By The Lesser Of:		
• Normal Recapture = $1,844,000		
• Replacement Cost = $5,700,000	1,844,000	(1,856,000)
Recapture Of 2017 CCA (Amended)		Nil

These new nil figures for the capital gain and recapture on the building disposition will replace the old figures of $1,100,000 and $1,844,000 that were included in the original 2017 return.

Part B - Building Contents

If this was a voluntary disposition, the building contents would not be "former business property" and would not qualify for either the ITA 13(4) election or the ITA 44(1) election. However, as this is an involuntary disposition, both elections are available.

Under ITA 44(1), the revised capital gain would be $23,000, the lesser of:

- $284,000 (regular capital gain); and
- $23,000 (the excess of the $1,256,000 proceeds of disposition for the old building contents over the $1,233,000 cost of the replacement contents)

The taxable amount of the gain will be $11,500 [(1/2)($23,000)].

Under ITA 13(4), the revised recapture would be reduced from $900,000 to nil. The calculation is as follows:

January 1, 2017 UCC Balance		$ 72,000
Deduction:		
Lesser Of:		
• Proceeds Of Disposition = $1,256,000		
• Capital Cost = $972,000	($972,000)	
Reduced By The Lesser Of:		
• Normal Recapture = $900,000		
• Replacement Cost = $1,233,000	900,000	(72,000)
Recapture Of 2017 CCA (Amended)		Nil

These new figures for the capital gain and recapture on the contents disposition will replace the old figures of $284,000 and $900,000 that were included in the original 2017 return.

Comparison - Part A and Part B

As shown in the table which follows, the disposition of the land, building and contents resulted in an increase in 2017 Net Income For Tax Purposes of $3,669,500. When the two elections are used, the amended 2017 return will show a Net Income For Tax Purposes of only $123,000. This is a savings of $3,546,500 ($3,669,500 - $123,000)

	Part A As Reported	Part B With Elections
Land - Taxable Capital Gain	$ 233,500	$111,500
Building - Taxable Capital Gain	550,000	Nil
Contents - Taxable Capital Gain	142,000	11,500
Building - Recaptured CCA	1,844,000	Nil
Contents - Recaptured CCA	900,000	Nil
Total Increase	$3,669,500	$123,000

Part C

Assuming Fraser decides to use the elections under ITA 44(1) and ITA 13(4), the deemed cost and UCC of the replacement properties would be as follows:

	Land	Building	Contents
Actual Cost Of Replacement Property	$500,000	$5,700,000	$1,233,000
Capital Gain Reversed By Election			
Land ($467,000 - $223,000)	(244,000)		
Building ($1,100,000 - Nil)		(1,100,000)	
Contents ($284,000 - $23,000)			(261,000)
Deemed Cost Of Replacement Property	$256,000	$4,600,000	$ 972,000

	Building	Contents
Deemed Capital Cost Of Replacement Property	$4,600,000	$ 972,000
Recaptured CCA Reversed By Election		
Land ($1,844,000 - Nil)	(1,844,000)	
Contents ($900,000 - Nil)		(900,000)
UCC - Replacement Property	$2,756,000	$ 72,000

The deemed adjusted cost base of the replacement land has been reduced to the adjusted cost base of the old land.

The $4,600,000 deemed capital cost of the replacement building is equal to the $3,700,000 capital cost of the old building, plus the additional $900,000 ($5,700,000 - $4,800,000) in funds paid by Fraser in excess of the insurance proceeds.

In a similar fashion, the UCC for the new building is equal to the UCC of the old building ($1,856,000), plus the additional $900,000 ($5,700,000 - $4,800,000) in funds paid by Fraser in excess of the insurance proceeds.

The deemed capital cost of the new Class 8 assets is equal to the $972,000 capital cost of the old assets.

In a similar fashion, the UCC for the new Class 8 assets is equal to the $72,000 UCC of the old Class 8 assets. Since the $1,233,000 cost of the replacement assets is less than the $1,256,000 in insurance proceeds, there is no increase in the UCC.

Part D - Optimal Transfer

The ITA 44(6) election applies when there is a disposition involving a combination of part land and part building. If, for either of the assets, the proceeds of disposition exceed the adjusted cost base, the election allows the transfer of all or part of that excess to the other asset.

As will be demonstrated in this problem, this can provide some relief when ITA 44(1) and ITA 13(4) fail to eliminate all of the capital gains arising on one part of the disposition of the old property. ITA 44(1) fully eliminated the capital gain on the building. However, a $223,000 capital gain remained on the land. This would suggest that it could be advantageous to transfer some of the proceeds of disposition from the land to the building.

The excess of the proceeds of disposition of the old land over the cost of the replacement land was $223,000 ($723,000 - $500,000). This is the maximum transfer needed from the land to the building. Since the excess of the cost of the replacement building over the old building's proceeds of disposition is $900,000 ($5,700,000 - $4,800,000), this transfer can be made with creating a capital gain on the building.

Applying ITA 44(6) will result in the following adjusted proceeds of disposition:

	Land	Building
Actual Proceeds Of Disposition	$723,000	$4,800,000
Transfer Needed - Land To Building	(223,000)	223,000
Adjusted Proceeds Of Disposition	$500,000	$5,023,000

Part D - Application To Land

If both the ITA 44(1) and the ITA 44(6) elections are used, the capital gain on the land will be nil, calculated as follows:

- $244,000 ($500,000 - $256,000); and
- Nil (the excess of the $500,000 adjusted proceeds of disposition for the old land over the $500,000 cost of the new land).

Given this result, the adjusted cost base of the replacement property will be calculated as follows:

Actual Cost	$500,000
Capital Gain Reversed By The Two Elections	(244,000)
Deemed Adjusted Cost Base Of Replacement Land	$256,000

Note that this is equal to the adjusted cost base of the old land.

Part D - Application To The Building

With the proceeds of disposition transfer limited to 223,000, the capital gain on the building is still nil. Specifically, the gain will be the lesser of:

- $1,323,000 ($5,023,000 - $3,700,000); and
- Nil (there is still no excess of the $5,023,000 proceeds of disposition over the replacement cost of $5,700,000).

The deemed capital cost and UCC for the building would be calculated as follows:

Actual Cost	$5,700,000
Capital Gain Reversed By The Two Elections	(1,323,000)
Deemed Capital Cost	$4,377,000
Recapture Reversed By ITA 13(4)	(1,844,000)
UCC - Replacement Building	$2,533,000

Part D - Comparison

The table which follows compares the results of using only ITA 44(1) and ITA 13(4) with the results that arise when the ITA 44(6) election is also used.

	No ITA 44(6)	With ITA 44(6)	Difference
Capital Gains			
Land	$223,000	Nil	($223,000)
Building	Nil	Nil	
Replacement Property			
Adjusted Cost Base Of Land	$ 256,000	$256,000	Nil
Capital Cost Of Building	4,600,000	4,377,000	(223,000)
UCC	2,756,000	2,533,000	(223,000)

Note that this election is not made without a cost. Had the $223,000 been left as a capital gain, tax would have applied on only one-half of the total. While we have eliminated this $111,500 in income, we have given up future CCA for the full amount of the $223,000. In other words, we have given up $223,000 in future deductions in return for eliminating $111,500 of income in 2017.

Self Study Solution Eight - 17

Business Income

The required calculations here would be as follows:

Net Cash Inflow	$53,000
January 1 Accounts Receivable	(10,000)
January 1 Inventories	(22,000)
January 1 Accounts Payable	14,000
June 30 Accounts Receivable	8,000
June 30 Inventories	18,000
June 30 Accounts Payable	(16,000)
Accrual Based Income	$45,000
Recapture On Sale Of Building ($250,000 - $211,000)	39,000
Terminal Loss On Furniture And Fixtures ($12,900 - $9,800)	(3,100)
Terminal Loss On Car ($25,075 - $18,000)	(7,075)
Net Business Income	$73,825

Since the capital cost of the Furniture and Fixtures and the Car was greater than their proceeds of disposition, the proceeds were used to calculate the terminal losses. There is no deduction for CCA as the assets were sold prior to the end of the year.

Employment Income
The required calculations here would be as follows:

Salary	$56,000
Bonus (Note 1)	Nil
RPP Contributions	(2,500)
Automobile Benefit (Note 2)	3,975
Net Employment Income	$57,475

Note 1 The bonus will not be included in 2017 employment income as it will not be paid until 2018.

Note 2 The automobile benefit would be calculated as follows:

Standby Charge [(2%)($62,000)(6)(4,000 ÷ 10,002)]	$2,975
Operating Cost Benefit - Lesser Of:	
• [(1/2)($2,975)] = $1,488	
• [(4,000)($0.25)] = $1,000	1,000
Total Benefit	$3,975

Property Income
The required calculations here would be as follows:

Eligible Dividends	$ 5,600
Gross Up On Eligible Dividends [(38%)($5,600)]	2,128
Interest On GICs	4,275
Income Trust Income Distribution ($6,800 - $2,600)	4,200
Mutual Fund Distribution [(1,000)($0.50)]	500
Fees To Professional Investment Counsellor	(875)
Total Property Income	$15,828

Net Taxable Capital Gains
The required calculations here would be as follows:

Gain On Building ($308,000 - $250,000)	$ 58,000	
Gain On Land ($125,000 - $50,000)	75,000	
Commissions	(17,320)	
Gain On Sale Of Property		$115,680
Gain On Income Trust Units [$63,000 - ($56,000 - $2,600)]		9,600
Loss On New World Equity Units [$9,000 - ($9,650 + $500)]		(1,150)
Net Capital Gains		$124,130
Inclusion Rate		1/2
Net Taxable Capital Gains		$ 62,065

Net Income For Tax Purposes

The required calculations here would be as follows:

Net Business Income	$ 73,825
Net Employment Income	57,475
Property Income	15,828
Net Taxable Capital Gains	62,065
Net Income For Tax Purposes	$209,193

Taxable Income

As there are no Taxable Income deductions available, Ms. Barnes' Taxable Income is equal to her Net Income For Tax Purposes.

Federal Tax Payable

The required calculations here would be as follows:

Tax On First $202,800		$46,966
Tax On Next $6,393 ($209,193 - $202,800) At 33 Percent		2,110
Tax Before Credits		$49,076
Tax Credits:		
Basic Personal Amount	($11,635)	
Common-Law Partner		
($11,635 - $4,600)	(7,035)	
Canada Caregiver - Alicia	(6,883)	
EI	(836)	
CPP	(2,564)	
Canada Employment	(1,178)	
Adoption Expenses (Note 3)	(19,670)	
Medical Expenses (Note 4)	(13,450)	
Transfer Of Tuition (Note 5)	Nil	
Total Credit Base	($63,251)	
Rate	15%	(9,488)
Subtotal		$39,588
Charitable Donations Credit (Note 6)		(492)
Dividend Tax Credit [(6/11)($2,128)]		(1,161)
Federal Tax Payable		$37,935

Note 3 The $15,670 maximum for the adoption expenses credit is applied to each child. Andrew's legal expenses are limited to $15,670, while all of Allison's $4,000 in legal expenses are eligible for the credit. This results in a total of $19,670 ($15,670 + $4,000) that can be claimed.

Note 4 Since Laura paid Alicia's medical expenses, Laura can claim them. The medical expense credit base would be calculated as follows:

Medical Expenses Of Laura, Julia, Allison, And Andrew		$11,400
Lesser Of:		
• [(3%)($209,193)] = $6,276		
• 2017 Threshold Amount = $2,268		(2,268)
Subtotal		$ 9,132
Alicia's Medical Expenses	$4,600	
Reduced By The Lesser Of:		
• $2,268		
• [(3%)($9,400)] = $282	(282)	4,318
Medical Expense Tax Credit Base		$13,450

Note 5 Although Laura paid her mother's tuition fees and her mother is dependent on her, Alicia's tuition credit cannot be transferred to her daughter. The transfers can only be made to a spouse, parent or grandparent. Alicia will carry forward any unused tuition credit.

Note 6   The charitable donations tax credit would be calculated as follows:

15 Percent Of $200	$ 30
33 Percent Of The Lesser Of:	
$1,400 ($1,600 - $200)	
$6,393 ($209,193 - $202,800	462
29 Percent Of Nil ($1,400 - $1,400)	Nil
Total Credit	$492

Self Study Solution Eight - 18

Employment Income
Lorenzo's commission income of $43,000 is large enough not to limit the deduction of his employment related expenses. The required calculations here would be as follows:

Salary	$136,000
Additions	
Commissions	43,000
One-Half Total Bonus (Note 1)	11,000
Expense Allowance [(12)($2,500)]	30,000
Stock Option Benefit [(500)($108 - $92)]	8,000
Deductions	
RPP Contributions	(4,200)
Professional Association Dues	(1,500)
Automobile Costs	
CCA (Note 2)	(6,120)
Operating Costs [(80%)($6,300)]	(5,040)
Hotel Costs	(9,700)
Airline And Other Transportation	(5,400)
Client Meals And Entertainment [(1/2)($9,300)]	(4,650)
Workspace In Home Expenses (Note 3)	(978)
Net Employment Income	$190,412

Note 1   As the bonus is paid more than 180 days after the employer's year end, the employer will not be able to deduct the accrual in 2017. This, however, does not change Lorenzo's tax position. He will not have to include one-half of the bonus in income until it is paid in 2018.

Note 2 The 2017 CCA would be based on a UCC calculated as though 100 percent of the available CCA had been taken in 2016. The 100 percent CCA of the Class 10.1 vehicle for 2016 would be $4,500 [(1/2)(30%)($30,000 maximum)]. Using this figure, the deductible 2017 CCA would be $6,120 [(80%)(30%)($30,000 - $4,500)].

Note 3 As Lorenzo has commission income, he can deduct 12 percent of all of the costs except the mortgage interest. This will provide a deduction of $978 [(12%)($1,250 + $1,300 + $5,600)].

Property Income

The required calculations here would be as follows:

Net Rental Income (Note 4)	$ 8,870
Income Trust Distribution [(500)($2.40)]	1,200
Eligible Dividends	4,200
Gross Up On Eligible Dividends [(38%)($4,200)]	1,596
Total Property Income	$15,866

Note 4 As the change in use is from personal to business, the base for calculating CCA would be as follows:

Cost Of Building ($105,000 - $42,000)		$63,000
Fair Market Value At Change In Use		
($350,000 - $100,000)	$250,000	
Cost	(63,000)	
Increase In Value (Bump Up)	$187,000	
Inclusion Factor	1/2	93,500
Cost For UCC And CCA Purposes		$156,500
One-Half Net Additions		(78,250)
CCA Base		$ 78,250
Rate For Class 1		4%
CCA		$ 3,130

Using this CCA figure, net rental income would be $8,870 ($12,000 - $3,130).

Net Taxable Capital Gains

The required calculations here would be as follows:

Stock Option Shares [(500)($115 - $108)]		$ 3,500
Sculpture (Note 5)		38,000
Change In Use:		
Cottage - Land ($100,000 - $42,000)	$ 58,000	
Cottage - Building ($250,000 - $63,000)	187,000	245,000
Real Property Income Trust (Note 6)		2,161
Land Sale ($180,000 - $78,000)	$102,000	
Reserve For Land Sale (Note 7)	(71,400)	30,600
Net Capital Gains		$319,261
Inclusion Rate		1/2
Net Taxable Capital Gains		$159,631

Note 5   As the actual adjusted cost base of this personal use property is less than $1,000, its deemed adjusted cost base is $1,000 (the floor). This results in a gain of $38,000 ($39,000 - $1,000).

Note 6   The $1,200 income trust distribution was used to acquired 20.51 additional units ($1,200 ÷ $58.50). Using this figure, the capital gain calculation would be:

Proceeds Of Disposition [(520.51)($60.25)]	$31,361
Adjusted Cost Base [(500)($56) + $1,200)]	(29,200)
Capital Gain	$ 2,161

Note 7   The gain on the land would be $102,000 ($180,000 - $78,000). The maximum reserve would be $71,400, the lesser of:

- $71,400 [($102,000)($126,000 ÷ $180,000)]
- $81,600 [($102,000)(20%)(4 - 0)]

Net And Taxable Income

The required calculations here would be as follows:

Net Employment Income	$190,412
Property Income	15,866
Net Taxable Capital Gains	159,631
Net Income For Tax Purposes	$365,909
Stock Option Deduction [(1/2)($8,000)]	(4,000)
Taxable Income	$361,909

Federal Tax Payable

The required calculations here would be as follows:

Tax On First $202,800		$46,966
Tax On Next $159,109 ($361,909 - $202,800) At 33 Percent		52,506
Tax Before Credits		$99,472
Tax Credits:		
Basic Personal Amount	($11,635)	
Spouse ($11,635 - $6,300)	(5,335)	
Canada Caregiver For Child - Anita	(2,150)	
Transfer Of Anita's Disability	(8,113)	
Disability Supplement	(4,733)	
Transfer Of Tuition - Lesser Of:		
• Absolute Limit Of $5,000		
• Actual Tuition Of $9,300	(5,000)	
Medical Expenses (Note 8)	(15,357)	
EI	(836)	
CPP	(2,564)	
Canada Employment	(1,178)	
Total Credit Base	($56,901)	
Rate	15%	(8,535)
Subtotal		$90,937
Charitable Donations Credit (Note 9)		(756)
Dividend Tax Credit [(6/11)($1,596)]		(871)
Federal Tax Payable		$89,310

Note 8 The base for the medical expense tax credit would be calculated as follows:

Total Medical Expenses	$17,625
Lesser Of:	
• [(3%)($365,909))] = $10,977	
• 2017 Threshold Amount = $2,268	(2,268)
Medical Expense Tax Credit Base	$15,357

Note 9 The charitable donations tax credit would be calculated as follows:

15 Percent Of $200	$ 30
33 Percent Of The Lesser Of:	
$2,200 ($2,400 - $200)	
$159,109 ($361,909 - $202,800)	726
29 Percent Of Nil ($2,200 - $2,200)	Nil
Total Credit	$756

Chapter 8 Learning Objectives

After completing Chapter 8, you should be able to:

1. Explain the economic basis for treating capital gains more favourably than other types of income (paragraph [P hereafter] 8-1 to 8-10).
2. Apply the general rules for the determination of gains and losses on the disposition of capital assets (P 8-11 to 8-36).
3. Calculate capital gains and losses on dispositions of identical properties (P 8-37 to 8-38).
4. Determine the tax consequences associated with partial dispositions of capital assets (P 8-39).
5. Calculate capital gains and losses on dispositions of capital assets with warranties attached (P 8-40 to P 8-41).

6. Apply the rules related to capital gains reserves (P 8-42 to 8-61).
7. Determine the tax consequences of a bad debt arising on a debt from the sale of capital assets (P 8-62 and 8-63).
8. Apply the special rule for sales of real property (P 8-64 to 8-71).
9. Apply the basic rules related to the reduction of taxation of capital gains arising from the disposition of a principal residence (P 8-72 to 8-81).
10. Describe the approaches available on the disposition of farm property that is also a principal residence (P 8-82 to 8-86).

11. Determine the tax consequences that result from dispositions of personal use property (P 8-87 to 8-91).
12. Determine the tax consequences that result from dispositions of listed personal property (P 8-92 to 8-94).
13. Determine the tax consequences that result from foreign currency transactions (P 8-95 to 8-106).
14. Determine the tax consequences that result from dispositions of options (P 8-107 to 8-112).
15. Determine the amount of capital gain or loss resulting from a change in the use of a capital asset (P 8-113 to 8-121).

16. Describe the principal residence elections that are available when there is a change in use (P 8-122 to 8-130).
17. Describe how an individual deals with the CCA on automobiles where the amount of employment or business usage changes over time. (8-131).
18. Explain the basic requirements for deemed dispositions on departures from Canada (P 8-132 to 8-133).
19. Apply the deferral provisions for capital gains arising on the disposition of small business investments (P 8-134 to 8-136).
20. Apply the deferral provisions for capital gains arising on voluntary and involuntary dispositions of property that is subsequently replaced (P 8-137 to 8-149).
21. Apply the deferral provisions for recapture arising on voluntary and involuntary dispositions of capital property that is subsequently replaced (P 8-150 to 8-165).
22. Explain the role of capital gains and losses in tax planning (P 8-166 to 8-168).

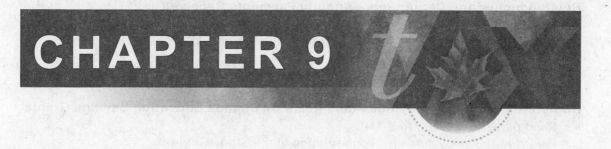

CHAPTER 9

How To Work Through Chapter 9

We recommend the following approach in dealing with the material in this Chapter:

Coverage And Organization Of Chapter 9
- Read paragraph 9-1 to 9-10 (in the textbook).

Inclusions - Pension Benefits, Retiring Allowances, And Death Benefits
- Read paragraph 9-11 to 9-19.

Inclusions - Deferred Income Plans, Scholarships, Social Assistance Payments, Universal Child Care Benefits
- Read paragraph 9-20 to 9-27.

Deductions - CPP Contributions On Self-Employed Earnings
- Read paragraph 9-28 to 9-31.

Deductions - Moving Expenses
- Read paragraph 9-32 to 9-45.
- Do Exercise Nine-1 (in the textbook) and check the solution in this Study Guide.
- Do Self Study Problem Nine-1 which is available on the Companion Website and check the solution in this Study Guide.

Deductions - Child Care Expenses
- Read paragraph 9-46 to 9-57.
- Do Exercise Nine-2 and check the solution in this Study Guide.
- Do Self Study Problems Nine-2 and Nine-3 and check the solutions in this Study Guide.

Deductions - Disability Supports Deduction
- Read paragraph 9-58 to 9-66.
- Do Exercise Nine-3 and check the solution in this Study Guide.

Related Inclusions/Deductions - Employment Insurance Benefits
- Read paragraph 9-67 and 9-68.

Related Inclusions/Deductions - Pension Income Splitting
- Read paragraph 9-69 to 9-77.
- Do Exercise Nine-4 and check the solution in this Study Guide.
- Do Self Study Problems Nine-4 and Nine-5 and check the solutions in this Study Guide.

Related Inclusions/Deductions - Spousal And Child Support
- Read paragraph 9-78 to 9-87.
- Do Exercise Nine-5 and check the solution in this Study Guide.

Related Inclusions/Deductions - Annuity Payments Received
- Read paragraph 9-88 to 9-96.
- Do Exercise Nine-6 and check the solution in this Study Guide.

Tax Free Savings Accounts (TFSAs)
- Read paragraph 9-97 to 9-101.

Registered Education Savings Plans (RESPs), Canada Education Savings Grants
- Read paragraph 9-102 to 9-110.
- Do Exercise Nine-7 and check the solution in this Study Guide.
- Read paragraph 9-111 to 9-129.
- Do Self Study Problem Nine-6 and check the solution in this Study Guide.

Comparison of TFSAs, RRSPs And RESPs
- Read paragraph 9-130 to 9-138.

Registered Disability Savings Plans (RDSPs)
- Read paragraph 9-139 to 9-141.

Non-Arm's Length Transfers Of Property - Inadequate Considerations (ITA 69)
- Read paragraph 9-142 to 9-156.
- Do Exercise Nine-8 and check the solution in this Study Guide.
- Read paragraph 9-157 to 9-159.
- Do Exercise Nine-9 and check the solution in this Study Guide.
- Do Self Study Problem Nine-7 and check the solution in this Study Guide.

Inter Vivos Transfers To A Spouse
- Read paragraph 9-160 to 9-167.
- Do Exercise Nine-10 and check the solution in this Study Guide.

Non-Arm's Length Transfers Of Depreciable Assets
- Read paragraph 9-168 to 9-172.
- Do Exercises Nine-11 and Nine-12 and check the solutions in this Study Guide.
- Do Self Study Problem Nine-8 and check the solution in this Study Guide.

Inter Vivos Transfer Of Farm Or Fishing Property To A Child
- Read paragraph 9-173 to 9-176.
- Do Exercise Nine-13 and check the solution in this Study Guide.

Deemed Dispositions - On Death
- Read paragraph 9-177 to 9-185.
- Do Exercise Nine-14 and check the solution in this Study Guide.
- Read paragraph 9-186.
- Do Self Study Problem Nine-9 and check the solution in this Study Guide.

Income Attribution
- Read paragraph 9-187 to 9-205.
- Do Exercises Nine-15 to Nine-17 and check the solutions in this Study Guide.
- Read paragraph 9-206 to 9-209.
- Do Self Study Problems Nine-10 and Nine-11 and check the solutions in this Study Guide.

Anti-Avoidance Provisions And Tax Planning
- Read paragraph 9-210 to 9-212.
- Do Self Study Problems Nine-12 and Nine-13 and check the solutions in this Study Guide.

To Complete This Chapter

- If you would like more practice in problem solving, do the Supplementary Self Study Problems for the chapter. These are available on the Companion Website.
- Review the Key Terms Used In This Chapter in the textbook at the end of Chapter 9. Consult the Glossary for the meaning of any key terms you do not know.
- Test yourself with the Chapter 9 Glossary Flashcards available on the Companion Website.
- Ensure you have achieved the Chapter 9 Learning Objectives listed in this Study Guide.
- As a review, we recommend you view the PowerPoint presentation for Chapter 9 that is on the Companion Website.

Practice Examination

- Write the Practice Examination for Chapter 9 that is on the Companion Website. Mark your examination using the Practice Examination Solution that is also on the Companion Website.

Solutions to Chapter Nine Exercises

Exercise Nine - 1 Solution

Ms. Chevlak cannot deduct the $1,300 house hunting trip. However, this amount can be reimbursed by her employer without creating a taxable benefit. Given these facts, the employer should reimburse this amount directly, with the balance of $4,700 being paid as a general moving allowance. The amount that can be deducted in 2017 against this general allowance, as well as the amount to be carried forward would be calculated as follows:

Allowance Paid By Employer ($6,000 - $1,300)	$4,700
Moving Costs	(6,400)
Lease Penalty	(1,200)
Available Deduction	($2,900)
Income At New Location = Maximum Deduction	2,000
Carry Forward	($ 900)

The maximum moving expense deduction is limited to $2,000, the income at the new location. The remaining $900 can be carried forward and deducted against income earned at the new location in a subsequent year.

If a $6,000 moving allowance had been paid, the full amount would have been included in employment income with the same deductions of $7,600 ($6,400 + $1,200). After the $2,000 in income, this would have left $400 in income rather than a future deduction of $900. The $1,300 difference is the cost of the house hunting trip.

Exercise Nine - 2 Solution

The deduction will have to be made by the lower income spouse, Mr. Sampras. The deduction will be the least of the following amounts:

- The actual costs of $10,500.
- Annual Child Care Expense Amount of $18,000 [(1)($8,000) + (2)($5,000)].
- 2/3 of Mr. Sampras' earned income, an amount of $13,000 [(2/3)($14,000 + $5,500)].

The least of these three amounts is $10,500.

Exercise Nine - 3 Solution

As Jose is not eligible for the disability tax credit, he will deduct the cost of full time attendant care under ITA 64. When combined with the other disability support costs and the reimbursement, the qualifying costs total $36,000 ($23,000 + $18,000 - $5,000). As this is less than his income from employment, he will be able to deduct the full amount of these costs as his disability supports deduction.

Solutions to Chapter Nine Exercises

Exercise Nine - 4 Solution

In the absence of pension income splitting John would not pay any taxes for 2017. Joanna's Net Income For Tax Purposes before any OAS clawback would be $92,000 ($85,000 + $7,000). There would be an OAS clawback of $2,582 [(15%)($92,000 - $74,788)], leaving Joanna with a Net and Taxable Income of $89,418 ($92,000 - $2,582). Based on this figure, her 2017 Amount Owing would be calculated as follows:

Tax Of First $45,916		$ 6,887
Tax On Next $43,502 ($89,418 - $45,916) At 20.5%		8,918
Total Before Credits		$15,805
Basic Personal	($11,635)	
Credits:		
Spousal ($11,635 - $7,000)	(4,635)	
Age [$7,225 - (15%)($89,418 - $36,430)	Nil	
Pension	(2,000)	
Spouse's Age	(7,225)	
Total	($25,495)	
Rate	15%	(3,824)
Federal Tax Payable		$11,981
OAS Clawback		2,582
Total Amount Owing - Joanna Only		$14,563

If maximum pension splitting is used, it will give both Joanna and John Net and Taxable Income of $49,500 [($85,000)(1/2) + $7,000]. Since this is below the income threshold, there will be no clawback of OAS for Joanna or John. Based on these figures, the Amount Owing for both Joanna and John would be the same and is calculated as follows:

Tax On First $45,916		$6,887
Tax On Next $3,584 ($49,500 - $45,916) At 20.5%		735
Total Before Credits		$7,622
Credits:		
Basic Personal	($11,635)	
Age [$7,225 - (15%)($49,500 - $36,430)	(5,265)	
Pension	(2,000)	
Total	($18,900)	
Rate	15%	(2,835)
Federal Tax Payable		$ 4,787
OAS Clawback		Nil
Total Amount Owing For Each		$ 4,787

With pension income splitting, the total amount owing by Joanna and John would be $9,574 [(2)($4,787)]. This is an improvement of $4,989 over the $14,563 that Joanna would have paid without income splitting. Further savings would be available at the provincial level.

Exercise Nine - 5 Solution

The total required child support is $9,000 [(6 Months)($1,500)] and Sandra's $12,000 [(3)($1,500 + $2,500)] in payments will be allocated to this requirement first. This means that $9,000 of her payment will not be deductible to her or taxable to Jerry. The remaining $3,000 ($12,000 - $9,000) will be considered a payment towards spousal support and will be deductible to Sandra and taxable to Jerry.

Exercise Nine - 6 Solution

A total of $63,492 [(4)($15,873)] in payments will be received from this annuity. The $15,873 will be included in his annual tax return. However, because the annuity was purchased with after tax funds, he is eligible for a deduction equal to:

$$\left[\frac{\$55,000}{\$63,492}\right] [\$15,873] = \$13,750 \text{ Deduction}$$

As a result, Mr. Hollock's Net Income For Tax Purposes will increase by $2,123 ($15,873 - $13,750) each year.

Exercise Nine - 7 Solution

For 2016, the contributions to Jeanine's RESP total $1,700 ($500 + $1,200). This is within the $2,500 limit for contributions eligible for CESGs. This means that the 2016 CESG would be calculated as follows:

First $500 At 40 Percent	$200
Remaining $1,200 ($1,700 - $500) At 20 Percent	240
Total CESG For 2016	$440

For 2017, the contributions to Jeanine's RESP total $3,900 ($1,500 + $2,400). The CESG room is limited to $3,300 [(2)($2,500) - $1,700 from the previous year]. This means that $600 ($3,900 - $3,300) of the total contributions will not be eligible for CESGs. Given this, the 2017 CESG would be calculated as follows:

First $500 At 40 Percent	$200
Remaining $2,800 ($3,300 - $500) At 20 Percent	560
Total CESG For 2017	$760

If it is expected that annual contributions to Jeanine's RESP will be less than $2,500 in the future, this would suggest that Jeanine's father should limit his 2017 contribution to $900 and defer the extra $600 to the following year. In that year, it would be eligible for the CESG.

Exercise Nine - 8 Solution

Mr. Lipky's proceeds of disposition will be the amount received of $95,000, resulting in a capital loss of $5,000 ($95,000 - $100,000). His brother's adjusted cost base will be the fair market value of the land, or $75,000, and he will have no gain or loss on his sale at $75,000. In this case, the application of the ITA 69 rules has resulted in the potential loss of $20,000 ($95,000 - $75,000) not being available to either Carl Lipky or his brother.

Exercise Nine - 9 Solution

Under ITA 69(1.2), the proceeds of disposition in this case will be the greater of the $33,000 actual proceeds and the $211,000 fair market value of the property without considering the lease. The greater amount would be $211,000, resulting in a taxable capital gain for Mr. Bates of $89,000 [(1/2)($211,000 - $33,000)]. The adjusted cost base to the corporation would be the actual transfer price of $33,000. This would lead to double taxation on a subsequent sale of the property on the difference between $211,000 and $33,000.

Exercise Nine - 10 Solution

ITA 73(1) Applies   If Mr. Schwartz does not elect out of ITA 73(1), the results are as follows:

- His deemed proceeds of disposition will be equal to the $225,000 adjusted cost base of the land. Given this, there will be no tax consequences as a result of this transfer.

- The adjusted cost base to his spouse will be deemed to be $225,000, despite the fact that she paid $300,000 for the land.

Elect Out Of ITA 73(1)   If Mr. Schwartz elects out of ITA 73(1):

- The adjusted cost base of the land to his spouse will be $300,000, the amount she paid.

- He will have to include a taxable capital gain in his Net Income For Tax Purposes calculated as follows:

Proceeds Of Disposition	$300,000
Adjusted Cost Base	(225,000)
Capital Gain	$ 75,000
Inclusion Rate	1/2
Taxable Capital Gain	$ 37,500

Exercise Nine - 11 Solution

ITA 73(1) Applies   If Ms. Sharp does not elect out of ITA 73(1), the results will be as follows:

- The deemed proceeds to Ms. Sharp will be the $110,000 UCC value, resulting in no tax consequences for her at the time of transfer.

- For CCA and recapture purposes the spouse will receive the property at $110,000.

- Despite the fact that her spouse paid $225,000, he would retain her $175,000 capital cost, with the difference between $175,000 and the $110,000 UCC balance considered to be deemed CCA.

Elect Out Of ITA 73(1)   If Ms. Sharp elects out of ITA 73(1):

- For capital gains purposes, the capital cost for Ms. Sharp's husband would be $225,000. However, for CCA and recapture purposes, ITA 13(7)(e) would deem his capital cost to be $200,000 [($175,000 + (1/2)($225,000 - $175,000)].

- She will include the following amounts in her Net Income For Tax Purposes:

Proceeds Of Disposition	$225,000
Capital Cost	(175,000)
Capital Gain	$ 50,000
Inclusion Rate	1/2
Taxable Capital Gain	$ 25,000
UCC	$110,000
Deduct Lesser Of:	
Proceeds Of Disposition = $225,000	
Capital Cost = $175,000	(175,000)
Negative Ending Balance = Recapture Of CCA	($ 65,000)

Exercise Nine - 12 Solution

Ms. Lee   The tax consequence for Ms. Lee is as follows:

UCC For Ms. Lee	$37,200
Deduct Lesser Of:	
Proceeds Of Disposition = $40,000	
Capital Cost = $53,000	(40,000)
Negative Ending Balance = Recapture Of CCA	($ 2,800)

Ms. Lee's Father   As this was a non-arm's length transfer at a value below the transferor's capital cost, ITA 13(7)(e) will deem the father's capital cost to be equal to Ms. Lee's capital cost of $53,000. The $13,000 difference between this value and the $40,000 he paid for the asset is treated as deemed CCA, resulting in a UCC value of $40,000. When he later sells the asset for $44,000, the result will be as follows:

UCC For Ms. Lee's Father	$40,000
Deduct Lesser Of:	
Proceeds Of Disposition = $44,000	
Deemed Capital Cost = $53,000	(44,000)
Negative Ending Balance = Recapture Of CCA	($ 4,000)

Exercise Nine - 13 Solution

With respect to the land, the $280,000 paid is between the $250,000 adjusted cost base floor and the $325,000 fair market value ceiling. Therefore, the proceeds of disposition would be $280,000, resulting in a taxable capital gain for Mr. Nobel of $15,000 [(1/2)($280,000 - $250,000)]. The $280,000 would also be the adjusted cost base for his daughter.

With respect to the barn, as there was no consideration given, the transfer would take place at the UCC floor of $85,000. There would be no tax consequences for Mr. Nobel. With respect to his daughter, she would assume a UCC value of $85,000 but would retain the original capital cost of $115,000. The $30,000 difference would be considered deemed CCA.

Exercise Nine - 14 Solution

With respect to truck A, it would be transferred to her husband at its UCC value of $25,500 [(1/2)($51,000)]. No income would be included in Ms. Lardner's final tax return and, while the UCC value for the truck in Michel's hands would be the $25,500 transfer value, it would retain its original capital cost of $42,000 with the difference between the two values being treated as deemed CCA.

Truck B would be transferred to Melinda at its fair market value of $33,000. This means that the proceeds of disposition for the two trucks would be $58,500 ($25,500 + $33,000). This would result in recapture of $7,500 ($51,000 - $58,500) being included in Ms. Lardner's final tax return. The $33,000 transfer price would be the UCC value to Melinda. Since Ms. Lardner's original capital cost exceeds the $33,000 fair market value, Melinda would retain Ms. Lardner's $42,000 capital cost with the difference between the two values being treated as deemed CCA.

Exercise Nine - 15 Solution

NOTE You may find it helpful to review Exercises Nine-10 and Nine-11 before completing this Exercise as many students find the rules related to the ITA 73(1) roll-overs difficult to understand.

ITA 73(1) provides for a tax free rollover of capital property to a spouse. The tax consequences for Mr. and Mrs. Moreau for the two years can be outlined as follows:

- 2016 for Mr. Moreau - none.
- 2016 for Mrs. Moreau - none.
- 2017 for Mr. Moreau - none.
- 2017 for Mrs. Moreau - total income of $12,950. She would have taxable dividends of $3,450 and the taxable capital gain of $9,500 [(1/2)($42,000 - $23,000)] attributed to her.

Exercise Nine - 16 Solution

There is no provision for a tax free transfer of shares to a child. The tax consequences for Norah and Nicki Moreau for the two years can be outlined as follows:

- 2016 for Nicki - none.
- 2016 for Norah - a taxable capital gain of $7,000 [(1/2)($37,000 - $23,000)].
- 2017 for Nicki - a taxable capital gain of $2,500 [(1/2)($42,000 - $37,000)].
- 2017 for Norah - taxable dividends of $3,450 attributed to her.

Exercise Nine - 17 Solution

Since Mr. Bronski does not elect out of ITA 73(1) by including a gain on his tax return at the time of the transfer, the income attribution rules will apply. Even if he did elect out of ITA 73(1), the rules would still apply as the loan does not bear interest at the prescribed rate.

There will be no tax consequences for either Mr. or Mrs. Bronski in 2016. Because the transfer is a tax free rollover, the adjusted cost base of the bonds to Mrs. Bronski will be $115,000. All of the 2017 interest income of $6,100 will be attributed to Mr. Bronski. In addition to the interest of $6,100, there would be a taxable capital gain of $7,000 [(1/2)($129,000 - $115,000)], which would also be attributed to Mr. Bronski. The total addition to Mr. Bronski's income for 2017 is $13,100 ($6,100 + $7,000). There will be no tax consequences for Mrs. Bronski in 2017.

Self Study Solution Nine - 1

Employment Income At New Location

Moving costs can only be deducted against "income earned at the new work location". This raises the question of how the payments made by the employer should be allocated. While this is not specifically covered in the relevant legislation, it would be our opinion that taxable part of the payments made by the Kelowna office should be considered to be from the new work location. However, the $20,000 general moving allowance paid by the Regina office would not be included. Base on this view, the employment income at the new work location would be calculated as follows:

Salary At New Location (One Month)	$12,000
Compensation For Loss On Regina Residence (Note 1)	10,000
Payment For Higher Housing Costs (Note 2)	15,000
General Moving Allowance	N/A
Total Employment Income At New Location	$37,000

Note 1 Under ITA 6(20), one-half of any housing loss reimbursement in excess of $15,000 must be included in income. As the total reimbursement was $35,000, the inclusion would be $10,000 [(1/2)($35,000 - $15,000)].

Note 2 Any amounts paid to compensate an employee for higher housing costs must be included in income in full.

Deductible Moving Cost

Costs for food and lodging at or near an old or new residence are limited to a maximum period of 15 days. On the first trip to Kelowna, only the cost of meals and lodging that were incurred on the 1 day after the acquisition of the new residence would be eligible. The airfare, the cost of car rentals, and the cost of meals and lodging prior to the acquisition of the new residence would not be deductible.

Leonard has a total of 29 eligible days: 1 day on his first trip to Kelowna, the 10 days in Regina and 18 days during which they lived in a hotel on arriving in Kelowna. Note that the 2 days spent travelling to Kelowna are not included in the 15 day total.

As the hotel in Kelowna is the most expensive, he will deduct all 15 days using a $300 per night rate. The deductible moving expenses can be calculated as follows:

House Hunting Trip Hotel And Food		Nil
Real Estate Commission - Regina Home		$14,400
Legal Fees - Regina Home		625
Other Regina Home Costs (Not Deductible)		Nil
Legal Fees - Kelowna Property		895
Land Transfer Tax - Kelowna Property		4,600
Storage And Moving Costs		8,500
Regina Hotel And Food		Nil
Expenses Of Travel To Kelowna:		
Gas (Using Simplified Method)	Nil	
Saskatchewan Vehicle Rate		
[(1,375 @ $0.455)	$626	
Hotel (2 Nights - Total)	475	
Food (2 Days, 4 People At $51 Flat Rate)	408	1,509
Hotel In Kelowna (15 Nights At $300)		4,500
Food - Maximum (15 Days, 4 People At $51 Flat Rate)		3,060
Total Allowable Expenses		$38,089
Employment Income In New Location		(37,000)
Carry Forward Of Moving Costs		$ 1,089

Notes:

1. The vehicle flat rate used is the one for the province from which the move began.

2. The taxes on the old home to the date of sale would not be an allowable moving expense.

3. The storage costs are deductible.

4. The unused moving cost balance of $1,089 can be carried forward and applied against employment income earned at the new location in a subsequent year.

Self Study Solution Nine - 2

Generally, the spouse with the lower income must claim the deduction for child care expenses. However, under certain circumstances, for example if this spouse is hospitalized, the spouse with the higher income can claim the deduction for the period of hospitalization.

The relevant calculations for determining the deductible costs for each individual are as follows:

	Mr. Pleasant	Mrs. Pleasant
Actual Costs (48 weeks at $100)	$ 4,800	$ 4,800
Annual Expense Limit [($5,000)(2) + ($8,000)(1)]	$18,000	$18,000

2/3 Of Earned Income For Child Care Expenses
  [(2/3)($99,000)]
  [(2/3)($18,000)]
	$66,000	$12,000

Periodic Expense Limit [($125)(2)(6 weeks) + ($200)(1)(6 weeks)]	$ 2,700	N/A

There does not appear to be any requirement that actual child care costs claimed by the higher income spouse need to be limited to the specific amounts paid during the six week period of eligibility. This means that the lowest of the preceding figures for Mr. Pleasant would be the Periodic Expense Limit of $2,700. Note that Mr. Pleasant's earned income for child care cost purposes is his gross employment income, before the deduction of employment related expenses.

The lowest figure for Mrs. Pleasant is the actual costs of $4,800. This amount will be reduced by the $2,700 that was deducted by Mr. Pleasant. This results in a $2,100 ($4,800 - $2,700) deduction for Mrs. Pleasant.

Self Study Solution Nine - 3

The deductible actual costs are as follows:

Actual Costs Excluding Camp Costs (48 weeks At $260)	$12,480
Periodic Cost Limit For Camp Weeks	
[($125)(1)(4 weeks) + ($200)(1)(4 weeks) + ($275)(1)(4 weeks)]	2,400
Deductible Actual Costs	$14,880

Generally, the common-law partner with the lower income must claim the deduction for child care expenses. In this case, that would be Sue Brendal. However, under certain circumstances, the common-law partner with the higher income can claim a deduction that is subject to a weekly limitation.

One of these circumstances is when the lower income common-law partner is in attendance on a full time basis at a designated financial institution. This means that for the 5 week period that Sue is attending the accounting course, Maureen can deduct limited child care expenses.

The relevant calculations for determining the deductible costs for each individual are as follows:

	Maureen	Sue
Actual Costs And Limited Camp Costs	$14,880	$14,880
Annual Expense Limit		
[($5,000)(1) + ($8,000)(1) + ($11,000)(1)]	$24,000	$24,000
2/3 Of Earned Income		
[(2/3)($216,000)]	$144,000	
[(2/3)($24,000)]		$16,000
Periodic Expense Limit [($125)(1)(5 weeks)		
+ ($200)(1)(5 weeks) + ($275)(1)(5 weeks)]	$3,000	N/A

The least of these amounts for Maureen is $3,000. You should note that there is no requirement that actual payments be allocated on the basis of the time that Sue was attending the accounting course.

The lowest figure for Sue is $14,880, the actual child care costs. Sue's deduction for the current year of $11,880 ($14,880 - $3,000) has been reduced by the amount claimed by Maureen.

As Maureen is the higher income common-law partner, her 3 week stay in the hospital has no effect on the child care expense calculations.

Self Study Solution Nine - 4

Net And Taxable Income

John's Income	No Split	With Split
Pension Receipt	$ 64,000	$64,000
Net Rental Income	23,000	23,000
Pension Income To Fatima	N/A	(32,000)
Net And Taxable Income	$87,000	$55,000

Fatima's Income	No Split	With Split
Interest Income	$8,400	$ 8,400
Pension Income From John	N/A	32,000
Net And Taxable Income	$8,400	$40,400

Federal Tax Payable With No Pension Income Splitting

Fatima   Fatima's federal Tax Payable with no pension income splitting would be calculated as follows:

Tax Before Credits [(15%)($8,400)]	$1,260
Basic Personal Credit [(15%)($11,635)]	(1,745)
Federal Tax Payable - Fatima	Nil

John   Without pension income splitting, John's Tax Payable would be calculated as follows:

Tax Of First $45,916		$6,887
Tax On Next $41,084 ($87,000 - $45,916) At 20.5%		8,422
Total Before Credits		$15,309
Credits:		
Basic Personal	($11,635)	
Spousal ($11,635 - $8,400)	(3,235)	
Pension	(2,000)	
Total	($16,870)	
Rate	15%	(2,531)
Federal Tax Payable - John		$12,778

Federal Tax Payable With Pension Income Splitting

Fatima   When pension income splitting is used, Fatima's Tax Payable would be as follows:

Tax Before Credits [(15%)($40,400)]		$6,060
Credits:		
Basic Personal	($11,635)	
Pension	(2,000)	
Total	($13,635)	
Rate	15%	(2,045)
Federal Tax Payable - Fatima		$ 4,015

John With pension income splitting, John's Tax Payable would be calculated as follows:

Tax On First $45,916		$6,887
Tax On Next $9,084 ($55,000 - $45,916) At 20.5%		1,862
Tax Before Credits		$8,749
Credits:		
Basic Personal	($11,635)	
Spousal	Nil	
Pension	(2,000)	
Total	($13,635)	
Rate	15%	(2,045)
Federal Tax Payable - John		$6,704

Comparison

Federal Tax Payable Without Income Splitting (John Only)	$12,778
Federal Tax Payable With Income Splitting ($4,015 + $6,704)	(10,719)
Savings With Pension Income Splitting	$ 2,059

Self Study Solution Nine - 5

Net And Taxable Income

Jean's Income	No Split	With Split
Pension Receipt	$168,000	$168,000
OAS	7,000	7,000
Pension Income To Carole	N/A	(84,000)
Net Income Before OAS Clawback	$175,000	$91,000
OAS Clawback (Note 1 and 2)	(7,000)	(2,432)
Net And Taxable Income	$168,000	$88,568

Carole's Income	No Split	With Split
Monthly Annuity [(12)($3,500)]	$42,000	$ 42,000
OAS	7,000	7,000
Pension Income From Jean	N/A	84,000
Net Income Before OAS Clawback	$49,000	$133,000
OAS Clawback (Note 3 and 4)	Nil	(7,000)
Net And Taxable Income	$49,000	$126,000

Note 1 Without pension income splitting, at Jean's income level, all of the $7,000 in OAS payments would be clawed back [(15%)($175,000 - $74,788) = $15,032].

Note 2 With pension income splitting, the OAS clawback would be $2,432 [(15%)($91,000 - $74,788)].

Note 3 Without pension income splitting, at Carole's income level, there would be no OAS clawback.

Note 4 With pension income splitting, all of the OAS received by Carole would be clawed back [(15%)($133,000 - $74,788) = $8,732].

Part A - Amount Owing With No Pension Income Splitting

Without pension income splitting, Jean's Amount Owing would be calculated as follows:

Tax On First $142,353		$29,436
Tax On Next $25,647 ($168,000 - $142,353) At 29%		7,438
Total Before Credits		$36,874
Credits:		
Basic Personal	($11,635)	
Age [$7,225 - (15%)($168,000 - $36,430)]	Nil	
Pension	(2,000)	
Total	($13,635)	
Rate	15%	(2,045)
Federal Tax Payable		$34,829
OAS Clawback		7,000
Total Amount Owing - Jean		$41,829

Without pension income splitting, Carole's Amount Owing would be calculated as follows:

Tax On First $45,916		$6,788
Tax On Next $3,084 ($49,000 - $45,916 At 20.5 Percent		632
Total Before Credits		$7,420
Credits:		
Basic Personal	($11,635)	
Age [$7,225 - (15%)($49,000 - $36,430)	(5,340)	
Disability	(8,113)	
Total	($25,088)	
Rate	15%	(3,763)
Total Amount Owing (No Clawback) - Carole		$3,657

Part B - Amount Owing With Pension Income Splitting

With pension income splitting, Jean's Amount Owing would be calculated as follows:

Tax On First $45,916		$6,788
Tax On Next $42,652 ($88,568 - $45,916) At 20.5 Percent		8,744
Tax Before Credits		$15,532
Credits:		
Basic Personal	$11,635)	
Age [$7,225 - (15%)($88,568 - $36,430)]	Nil	
Pension	(2,000)	
Total	($13,635)	
Rate	15%	(2,045)
Federal Tax Payable		$13,487
OAS Clawback		2,432
Total Amount Owing - Jean		$15,919

With pension income splitting, Carole's amount owing would be calculated as follows:

Tax On First $91,831		$16,300
Tax On Next $34,169 ($126,000 - $91,831) At 26%		8,884
Tax Before Credits		$25,184
Credits:		
Basic Personal	($11,635)	
Age [$7,225 - (15%)($126,000 - $36,430)]	Nil	
Disability	(8,113)	
Pension	(2,000)	
Total	($21,748)	
Rate	15%	(3,262)
Federal Tax Payable		$21,922
OAS Clawback		7,000
Total Amount Owing - Carole		$28,922

Comparison

The total amount owing for Jean and Carole in the absence of pension income splitting and with maximum pension income splitting would be calculated as follows:

	No Split	50:50 Split
Jean	$41,829	$15,919
Carole	3,657	28,922
Total Amount Owing	$45,486	$44,841

This problem illustrates the complexity associated with pension income splitting. Maximum pension income splitting results in an amount owing that is $645 ($45,486 - $44,841) lower. While the income splitting moved Jean's income from the 29 percent bracket to the 20.5 percent bracket and reduced his OAS clawback, the 50:50 split resulted in Carole having all of her OAS payments clawed back and losing all of her age credit.

If pension income splitting was limited to an amount that would leave Carole's Net Income equal to the OAS clawback income threshold, only Jean would have any OAS clawback, rather than both. However, that may not be the best solution. Finding the optimum solution is not an intuitive process, especially if there are other factors such as medical costs, and would require the proper use of tax software.

Self Study Solution Nine - 6

Part A - Net Income For Tax Purposes

The minimum Net Income For Tax Purposes that can be reported by Mr. Masters is calculated as follows:

Wages From Summer Employment		5,400
Moving Costs To Pelican Lake (Note 1)		(350)
Scholarship Received	$3,500	
Exempt Portion Of Scholarship (100%)	(3,500)	Nil
Moving Costs To Winnipeg (Note 1)		Nil
Eligible Dividends Received		2,000
Gross Up Of Dividends (38 Percent)		760
Child Support Received (Note 2)		Nil
Inheritance (Not Taxable)		Nil
TFSA Contributions (Note 3)		Nil
TFSA Withdrawal (Note 3)		Nil
Net Income For Tax Purposes		$7,810

Note 1   The cost of the move to Pelican Lake is deductible against the income that was earned there as it is more than 40 km from Winnipeg. Since there was no addition to his Net Income For Tax Purposes due to his scholarship, he cannot deduct the cost of the move back to Winnipeg.

Note 2   While spousal support is taxable to the recipient and deductible to the payor, child support is not taxable to the recipient or deductible to the payor.

Note 3   TFSA contributions and withdrawals have no tax consequences since the total $20,000 contributed is less than the maximum contribution allowable. There is also no income attribution as a result of the TFSA contribution by Mr. Masters' wife.

Part B - Registered Education Savings Plan

Payments into an RESP are not deductible. However, no tax liability is created by the amounts earned on the assets held in the plan. Rather, the earnings of these assets will be taxed in the hands of the recipient (presumably Mr. Masters' son) when the funds are withdrawn. However, to be eligible to receive these payments, the child must be in full time or part time attendance at an institution that would qualify the child for the education tax credit.

Mr. Masters must obtain information regarding the contribution room available for the Canada Education Savings Grant (CESG). Since his parents have been contributing to the RESP, it is not possible to determine how much CESG his son has available without more information.

Given his wife's profession, it is likely the family income is far too high to qualify for the Canada Learning Bonds program. As a result, that program would have no impact on any advice related to Mr. Masterson's son's RESP.

Self Study Solution Nine - 7

A. Gift To Sally

The result for Bryant would be as follows:

Deemed Proceeds Of Disposition - ITA 69(1)(b)	$400,000
Adjusted Cost Base	(275,000)
Capital Gain	$125,000
Inclusion Rate	1/2
Taxable Capital Gain	$ 62,500

With respect to the subsequent sale by Sally, the results for her would be as follows:

Proceeds Of Disposition (Actual)	$400,000
Adjusted Cost Base - ITA 69(1)(c)	(400,000)
Capital Gain	Nil

B. Sale To Sarah

The result for Bryant would be as follows:

Proceeds Of Disposition (Actual)	$400,000
Adjusted Cost Base	(275,000)
Capital Gain	$125,000
Inclusion Rate	1/2
Taxable Capital Gain	$ 62,500

C. Sale To Bob

The result for Bryant would be as follows:

Deemed Proceeds Of Disposition - ITA 69(1)(b)	$400,000
Adjusted Cost Base	(275,000)
Capital Gain	$125,000
Inclusion Rate	1/2
Taxable Capital Gain	$ 62,500

With respect to the subsequent sale by Bob, the results for him would be as follows:

Proceeds Of Disposition (Actual)	$400,000
Adjusted Cost Base (Actual)	(275,000)
Capital Gain	$125,000
Inclusion Rate	1/2
Taxable Capital Gain	$ 62,500

Despite the fact that Bryant has to record the sale at the fair market value of $400,000, Bob's adjusted cost base would be limited to the $275,000 that he paid for the land. The result would be that Bob would have to include the same $62,500 taxable capital gain that was recorded by Bryant. While Bob would get the benefit of having the $125,000 taxed at a low tax bracket, this will not make up for the fact that the $62,500 taxable capital gain will be subject to double taxation.

D. Sale To Norman

The result for Bryant would be as follows:

Proceeds Of Disposition (Actual)	$500,000
Adjusted Cost Base	(275,000)
Capital Gain	$225,000
Inclusion Rate	1/2
Taxable Capital Gain	$112,500

With respect to the subsequent sale by Norman, the results for him would be as follows:

Proceeds Of Disposition (Actual)	$400,000
Adjusted Cost Base - ITA 69(1)(a)	(400,000)
Capital Gain	Nil

Despite the fact that Bryant had to record the actual proceeds of $500,000, Norman's adjusted cost base will be the fair market value of $400,000. This means that he did not achieve his goal of having a capital loss to offset his realized gain.

Summary

These results can be summarized as follows:

	Taxable Capital Gain To Bryant	ACB To Family Member	Taxable Capital Gain To Family Member
A. Sale To Sally	$62,500	$400,000	$ Nil
B. Sale To Sarah	62,500	400,000	N/A
C. Sale To Bob	62,500	275,000	62,500
D. Sale To Norman	112,500	400,000	Nil

Self Study Solution Nine - 8

Scenario 1 - FMV > Transferor's Capital Cost

The results of the disposition for Martin can be calculated as follows:

UCC Balance	$36,000
Lesser Of:	
Proceeds Of Disposition = $87,000	
Capital Cost = $52,000	(52,000)
Negative Ending UCC Balance = Recapture Of CCA	($16,000)

Proceeds Of Disposition	$87,000
Capital Cost	(52,000)
Capital Gain	$35,000
Inclusion Rate	1/2
Taxable Capital Gain	$17,500

Martin's Net Income For Tax Purposes will increase by $33,500 ($16,000 + $17,500).

For his sister, her capital cost for capital gains purposes will be the transfer price of $87,000. However, because the fair market value of the asset exceeded its original capital cost, ITA 13(7)(e) will limit the value used for CCA and recapture calculations to the following amount:

$$[\$52,000 + (1/2)(\$87,000 - \$52,000)] = \$69,500$$

Scenario 2 - FMV < Transferor's Capital Cost

The results of this disposition for Marion can be calculated as follows:

UCC Balance	$105,000
Lesser Of:	
Proceeds Of Disposition = $142,000	
Capital Cost = $212,000	(142,000)
Negative Ending UCC Balance = Recapture Of CCA	($ 37,000)

Marion's Net Income For Tax Purposes will increase by $37,000.

In this case, where the fair market value of the asset is less than its capital cost, ITA 13(7)(e) deems the transferee's capital cost of the transferred asset to be equal to the transferor's capital cost, an amount of $212,000. This capital cost will be used for purposes of determining any capital gain and/or recapture on a future disposition.

The $70,000 ($212,000 - $142,000) difference between this value and the transfer price will be considered deemed CCA. The resulting UCC balance of $142,000 will be used by Marion's brother for calculating future CCA.

Self Study Solution Nine - 9

> **Note** Part B of this problem requires knowledge of ITA 13(21.1) as there is a capital gain on the land and a terminal loss on the building. This provision is covered in detail in Chapter 8.

Case A(1)

Assuming that the transfer was to Ms. Kneebone's common-law partner, the land would have been transferred at its cost and the building would have been transferred at its UCC. As a consequence, there would have been no tax effects to be included in Ms. Kneebone's final return.

For CCA purposes, the building would have been transferred at Ms. Kneebone's UCC of $234,000. Given this, maximum CCA would be $9,360 [(4%)($234,000)] for 2017 leaving a UCC of $224,640. Since the acquisition of the building is a non-arm's length transaction and its previous use was to produce income, it is exempt from the half-year rules.

Note, however, that after the transfer, Alice would have retained the building's old capital cost of $330,000. Using this figure for the building, the tax effects that would occur at the time of the 2018 sale of the property would be as follows:

	Land	Building
Proceeds Of Disposition	$376,000	$408,000
Adjusted Cost Base/Capital Cost	(122,000)	(330,000)
Capital Gain	$254,000	$ 78,000
Inclusion Rate	1/2	1/2
Taxable Capital Gain	$127,000	$ 39,000
UCC		$224,640
Deduct Disposition - Lesser Of:		
• Capital Cost = $330,000		
• Proceeds Of Disposition = $408,000		(330,000)
Negative Closing UCC Balance = Recaptured CCA		($105,360)

A total of $271,360 ($127,000 + $39,000 + $105,360) would be added to the 2018 Net Income For Tax Purposes of Alice.

Case A(2)

As the transfer was to her son, the deemed proceeds will be recorded at fair market value for the land and building. Based on this, the following calculations show the tax effects that will be included in Ms. Kneebone's final return:

	Land	Building
Deemed Proceeds	$425,000	$451,000
Adjusted Cost Base/Capital Cost	(122,000)	(330,000)
Capital Gain	$303,000	$121,000
Inclusion Rate	1/2	1/2
Taxable Capital Gain	$151,500	$ 60,500
UCC		$234,000
Deduct Disposition - Lesser Of:		
• Capital Cost = $330,000		
• Deemed Proceeds = $451,000		(330,000)
Negative Closing UCC Balance = Recaptured CCA		($ 96,000)

A total of $308,000 ($151,500 + $60,500 + $96,000) would be added to Ms. Kneebone's 2017 Net Income For Tax Purposes.

With respect to her son's tax records, the land will have a tax cost of $425,000 and the building will be a Class 1 asset with a tax cost equal to Mrs. Kneebone's deemed proceeds of $451,000.

Maximum 2017 CCA is $18,040 [($451,000)(4%)], leaving a UCC of $432,960 ($451,000 - $18,040). Since the acquisition of the building is a non-arm's length transaction, it was used and continues to be used to produce income and was owned for more than one year by Ms. Kneebone, the half year rule does not apply to Chester. In addition, ITA 13(7)(e), which requires the calculation of a limited UCC balance, is not applicable to transfers at death.

Since there cannot be a capital loss on depreciable property and the building is the only asset in the class, the 2018 tax effects associated with the sale of the building would be calculated as follows:

	Land	Building
Proceeds Of Disposition	$376,000	$408,000
Adjusted Cost Base	(425,000)	
Lesser Of:		
Capital Cost = $451,000		
Proceeds Of Disposition = $408,000		(408,000)
Capital Gain (Loss)	($ 49,000)	Nil
Inclusion Rate	1/2	N/A
Allowable Capital Loss	($ 24,500)	Nil
UCC		$432,960
Deduct Disposition - Lesser Of:		
• Capital Cost = $451,000		
• Proceeds Of Disposition = $408,000		(408,000)
Positive Closing UCC Balance = Terminal Loss		$ 24,960

A total of $49,460 ($24,500 + $24,960) would be deducted from the 2018 Net Income For Tax Purposes of Chester as the problem indicates that he has sufficient income and taxable capital gains.

Comparison Case A(1) And A(2)

The overall tax consequences in the two cases are as shown in the following table:

	Case A(1) Alice	Case A(2) Ms. Kneebone	Case A(2) Chester
2017	Nil	$308,000	Nil
2017 - CCA Taken	($ 9,360)		($18,040)
2018	271,360		(49,460)
Net Income For Tax Purposes (Loss)	$262,000	$308,000	($67,500)

There is a difference in the Case A(1) and Case A(2) results of $21,500 [$262,000 - ($308,000 -$67,500)]. This reflects the fact that, in Case A(2), a portion of the amount that was taxed as a capital gain (50 percent) in Ms. Kneebone's final return was deducted by Chester as CCA and a terminal loss (100 percent).

This can be shown in the following calculation:

Actual Sale Price Of Building For Chester	$408,000
Fair Market Value (Deemed Proceeds) At Death	(451,000)
Amount Deducted By Chester As CCA And Terminal Loss	($ 43,000)
Portion Taxed As Capital Gain In Final Return [(1/2)($43,000)]	21,500
Difference	($ 21,500)

Part B

If the proceeds of the sale of the property by Chester were allocated $435,000 to the land and $349,000 to the building, the tax effects associated with the sale of the building would be initially calculated as follows:

	Land	Building
Proceeds Of Disposition	$435,000	$349,000
Adjusted Cost Base	(425,000)	
Lesser Of:		
Capital Cost = $451,000		
Proceeds Of Disposition = $349,000		(349,000)
Capital Gain	$ 10,000	Nil
Inclusion Rate	1/2	1/2
Taxable Capital Gain	$ 5,000	Nil
UCC		$432,960
Deduct Disposition - Lesser Of:		
• Capital Cost = $451,000		
• Proceeds Of Disposition= $349,000		(349,000)
Positive Closing UCC Balance = Terminal Loss		$ 83,960

Since there is a capital gain on the land and a terminal loss on the building, ITA 13(21.1)(a) requires the deemed proceeds of disposition for the building to be determined as follows:

The Lesser Of:

- The FMV of the land and building — $784,000
  Reduced By The Lesser Of:
  - The ACB of the land = $425,000
  - The FMV of the land = $435,000 — (425,000) — $359,000

- The Greater Of:
  - The FMV of the building = $349,000
  - The Lesser Of:
    The cost of the building = $451,000
    The UCC of the building = $432,960 — $432,960

The proceeds that would be allocated to the building would be $359,000, leaving $425,000 ($784,000 - $359,000) to be allocated to the land. The net result is that the terminal loss would be reduced by $10,000 (the amount of the potential capital gain) to $73,960 ($359,000 - $432,960) and the capital gain would be nil ($425,000 - $425,000).

Self Study Solution Nine - 10

Case A

With ITA 73(1) in effect, the December 31, 2016 transfer would be a deemed disposition at the adjusted cost base for the securities of $85,000. This means that Mr. Tucker would not record a capital gain at the time of the transfer and the adjusted cost base of the securities to Mrs. Tucker would be $85,000.

In 2017, the $8,970 in taxable dividends would be attributed back to Mr. Tucker and included in his Net Income For Tax Purposes for that year. He would claim the related dividend tax credit ($1,347 at the federal level).

When Mrs. Tucker sells the securities, the 2018 taxable capital gain of $33,000 [(1/2)($151,000 - $85,000)] would also be attributed back to Mr. Tucker.

This transfer would not affect Mrs. Tucker's Net Income For Tax Purposes in any of the three years under consideration.

Case B

With ITA 73(1) in effect, the December 31, 2016 transfer would still take place at the adjusted cost base of $85,000, and the results for both Mr. Tucker and Mrs. Tucker would be identical to Case A.

Case C

When a taxpayer elects out of ITA 73(1) and a transfer is made for consideration that is less than fair market value, the provisions of ITA 69(1) are applicable to the transferor. Under these provisions, if a taxpayer disposes of a property for less than its fair market value, the proceeds of disposition are deemed to be the fair market value amount. This will result in Mr. Tucker recording a 2016 taxable capital gain of $19,000 [(1/2)($123,000 - $85,000)].

As the transfer is for consideration that is less than the fair market value of the securities, the income attribution rules will be applicable, resulting in the 2017 taxable dividends of $8,970 being included in Mr. Tucker's 2017 Net Income For Tax Purposes. He would claim the related dividend tax credit ($1,347 at the federal level).

Under the provisions of ITA 69, Mrs. Tucker's adjusted cost base for the shares will be the $95,000 price that she actually paid. As a consequence, when the shares are sold in 2018, the taxable capital gain would be $28,000 [(1/2)($151,000 - $95,000)]. This amount would be attributed back to Mr. Tucker and included in his 2018 Net Income For Tax Purposes.

This transfer would not affect Mrs. Tucker's Net Income For Tax Purposes in any of the three years under consideration.

> **Note** Mr. Tucker's total taxable capital gain on these shares is $47,000 ($19,000 + $28,000). This is $14,000 more than the $33,000 taxable capital gain in Cases A and B. This $14,000 amount reflects the fact that, under ITA 69, there is double taxation of one-half the difference between the $95,000 price paid by Mrs. Tucker for the securities and their $123,000 fair market value at that time.

Case D

Under ITA 69, a non-arm's length gift is deemed to be a disposition and acquisition to be recorded by both parties at fair market value. This means that Mr. Tucker would have to record a 2016 taxable capital gain of $19,000 [(1/2)($123,000 - $85,000)].

As a gift to a minor was involved, income attribution rules will apply and the 2017 taxable dividends of $8,970 will be included in the 2017 Net Income For Tax Purposes of Mr. Tucker. He would claim the related dividend tax credit ($1,347 at the federal level).

However, the attribution rules do not apply to capital gains when the attribution results from a transfer to someone under 18 years of age. As a consequence, Doreen Tucker will include a taxable capital gain of $14,000 [(1/2)($151,000 - $123,000)] in her 2018 Net Income For Tax Purposes.

The transfer will have no effect on the 2016 and 2017 Net Income For Tax Purposes of Doreen Tucker, or on the 2018 Net Income For Tax Purposes of Mr. Tucker.

Case E

As the transfer is at fair market value, Mr. Tucker will have a taxable capital gain of $19,000 [(1/2)($123,000 - $85,000)] included in his 2016 Net Income For Tax Purposes. Martin's adjusted cost base for the securities will be $123,000, and the transfer will not affect his 2016 Net Income For Tax Purposes.

As Martin is not under 18 years of age, the attribution rules found in ITA 74.1(2) do not apply. As a consequence, the $8,970 in taxable dividends would be included in Martin's 2017 Net Income For Tax Purposes. He would claim the related dividend tax credit ($1,347 at the federal level).

In addition, the taxable capital gain of $14,000 [(1/2)($151,000 - $123,000)] would be included in Martin's 2018 Net Income For Tax Purposes.

The transfer will have no effect on the 2016 Net Income For Tax Purposes of Martin Tucker, or on the 2017 or 2018 Net Income For Tax Purposes of Mr. Tucker.

Summary Results (Not Required)

	Net Income For Tax Purposes		
	2016	2017	2018
Case A (Sum Of Incomes = $41,970)			
Mr. Tucker	Nil	$8,970	$33,000
Mrs. Tucker	Nil	Nil	Nil
Case B (Sum Of Incomes = $41,970)			
Mr. Tucker	Nil	$8,970	$33,000
Mrs. Tucker	Nil	Nil	Nil
Case C (Sum Of Incomes = $55,970)			
Mr. Tucker	$19,000	$8,970	$28,000
Mrs. Tucker	Nil	Nil	Nil
Case D (Sum Of Incomes = $41,970)			
Mr. Tucker	$19,000	$8,970	Nil
Doreen Tucker	Nil	Nil	$14,000
Case E (Sum Of Incomes = $41,970)			
Mr. Tucker	$19,000	Nil	Nil
Martin Tucker	Nil	$8,970	$14,000

Self Study Solution Nine - 11

Note

As the farm would be considered qualified farm property, any capital gains arising from a disposition could be eligible for the lifetime capital gains deduction. If Long Consulting Ltd. is a qualified small business corporation, capital gains on the disposition of these shares could also be eligible for the lifetime capital gains deduction. As this deduction is not discussed until Chapter 11, the problem specifies that these possibilities should be ignored.

Long Consulting Ltd.

1. Gift To Spouse - ITA 73(1) Applies

ITA 73(1) permits transfers of a capital property to a spouse at its tax value (adjusted cost base or UCC). This means that the shares in Long Consulting Ltd. could be gifted to Mr. Long with no immediate tax consequences.

The tax basis for these shares for the spouse would remain at the adjusted cost base of $210,000.

Any dividends paid on the shares would be attributed to Mrs. Long.

If Mr. Long subsequently sell these shares for $525,000 ($50,000 more than the $475,000 fair market value at the time of the gift), the resulting taxable capital gain of $157,500, as calculated in the following table, would also be attributed to Mrs. Long.

Proceeds (Fair Market Value)	$525,000
Adjusted Cost Base	(210,000)
Capital Gain	$315,000
Inclusion Rate	1/2
Taxable Capital Gain	$157,500

2. Gift To Spouse - Elect Out Of ITA 73(1)

As an alternative, Mrs. Long could elect out of the provisions of ITA 73(1). Under ITA 69, the gift would be recorded as a disposition at the $475,000 fair market value. Mrs. Long would have an immediate taxable capital gain of $132,500 [(1/2)($475,000 - $210,000)] and Mr. Long's adjusted cost base would be $475,000. However, since the transfer is a gift, and Mr. Long does not use his own funds to purchase the shares, income attribution would apply to any dividends received by Mr. Long. In addition, if the property was subsequently sold by Mr. Long for $525,000, the resulting taxable capital gain of $25,000 [(1/2)(525,000 - $475,000)] would be attributed back to Mrs. Long.

3 And 4. Gift To Children

Under ITA 69, a gift to a related party is deemed to be a transfer at fair market value. Given this, a taxable capital gain of $132,500 [(1/2)($475,000 - $210,000) would result from a transfer to either child.

The adjusted cost base to the children would be the fair market value of $475,000.

Under the general income attribution rules, the dividend income paid on the shares given to Mary, who is under 18, would be attributed back to Mrs. Long. The problem specifies that the tax on split income should be ignored. However, as is discussed in Chapter 11, this dividend income would be subject to the tax on split income and, because of this, it would be exempt from the general income attribution rules.

As Barry is over 18, the gift would not result in attribution of dividends. We would also note that it would not be subject to the tax on split income.

There is no attribution of capital gains on assets transferred to children, without regard to their age. This means that, if the property was later sold for $525,000, the resulting taxable capital gain of $25,000 would be taxed in the hands of the child who received the gift.

Rental Property

1. Gift To Spouse - ITA 73(1) Applies

Here again, ITA 73(1) would permit a transfer to Mr. Long at tax values with no immediate tax consequences.

The tax cost of the building to Mr. Long would be the UCC of $125,000. However, Mr. Long would retain the capital cost of $190,000. With respect to the land, its adjusted cost base would be $100,000. This was Mrs. Long's tax cost and the current fair market value of the land.

As the transfer is a gift, income attribution rules would apply. This means that any net rental income would be attributed to Mrs. Long.

If Mr. Long were to later sell the building for $325,000 ($50,000 more than its fair market value at the time of the gift), the following amounts would be attributed to Mrs. Long:

Capital Cost	$190,000
UCC	(125,000)
Recaptured CCA	$ 65,000

Proceeds Of Disposition	$325,000
Adjusted Cost Base	(190,000)
Capital Gain	$135,000
Inclusion Rate	1/2
Taxable Capital Gain	$ 67,500

Since we are assuming the value of the land on which the building was situated has not changed, the sale of the land by Mr. Long would have no tax consequences for Mrs. Long. As you are asked to assume that no CCA is taken between the date of the gift and the date the property is sold, there would be no recapture of CCA resulting from the sale.

2. Gift To Spouse - Elect Out Of ITA 73(1)

Mrs. Long could also elect out of the provisions of ITA 73(1) and transfer the rental property at its fair market value. However, if she does, she would immediately be taxed on the recapture of $65,000, as well as the taxable capital gain of $42,500 [(1/2)($275,000 - $190,000)]. There would be no tax consequences related to the land as its tax cost is equal to its fair market value.

In this case, the cost of the building to Mr. Long for capital gains purposes would be $275,000. For CCA and recapture purposes, the value would be limited to $232,500 [$190,000 + (1/2)($275,000 - $190,000)]. His cost for the land would be $100,000.

Electing out of ITA 73(1) would not change the fact that the transfer is a gift to a spouse and, as a consequence, future rental income would be attributed to Mrs. Long.

If Mr. Long subsequently sells the building for $325,000, the additional taxable capital gain of $25,000 [(1/2)($325,000 - $275,000)] would also be attributed back to Mrs. Long. As we are assuming the value of the land remains at $100,000 and that no CCA is taken prior to the sale, there are no tax consequences associated with its sale.

3 And 4. Gift To Children

There is no exemption from the general rules of ITA 69 for transfers of depreciable property to children. As a consequence, Mrs. Long would be subject to taxation based on a disposition of the property at its fair market value of $275,000. This would result in immediate taxation on a $42,500 [(1/2)($275,000 - $190,000)] taxable capital gain, as well as on recapture of $65,000 ($190,000 - $125,000). There would be no tax consequences related to the land as its tax cost is equal to its fair market value.

The cost of the building to either of the children for capital gains purposes would be $275,000. The cost for the land would be $100,000. For CCA and recapture purposes, the value would be limited to $232,500 [$190,000 + (1/2)($275,000 - $190,000)].

If this property was given to Mary, the income attribution rules of ITA 74.1 would apply to any amount of property income subsequently earned. This would mean that until Mary reached 18 years of age, any property income from the rental property would be attributed to Mrs. Long. Alternatively, if the property was gifted to her son, Barry, all subsequent income would be taxed in his hands.

There is no attribution of capital gains on gifts to related children under 18. There would be no attribution of capital gains on a gift to either child. This means that if the property were later sold for $325,000 ($275,000 + $50,000), the $25,000 taxable capital gain would be taxed in the hands of the child who received the gift. As noted in the discussion of the alternative gift recipients, there would be no recapture of CCA resulting from the sale.

Dynamics Inc.

1. Gift To Spouse - ITA 73(1) Applies

As with the other properties, these shares could be given to Mr. Long and, under the provisions of ITA 73(1), no immediate tax consequences would arise.

The tax basis for Mr. Long would be unchanged at $212,000.

Any dividend income on the shares would be attributed to Mrs. Long.

If Mr. Long were to subsequently sell the shares for $434,000 ($50,000 more that their $384,000 fair market value at the time of the gift), the income attribution rules of ITA 74.1 would require that the following taxable capital gain be attributed to the income of Mrs. Long:

Proceeds Of Disposition	$434,000
Adjusted Cost Base	(212,000)
Capital Gain	$222,000
Inclusion Rate	1/2
Taxable Capital Gain	$111,000

2. Gift To Spouse - Elect Out Of ITA 73(1)

Mrs. Long could elect out of ITA 73(1) by recording the $86,000 [(1/2)($384,000 - $212,000)] taxable capital gain at the time of the transfer to her spouse.

In this case the adjusted cost base to Mr. Long would be $384,000.

However, as long as the property was transferred as a gift, attribution would apply to both dividend income received by Mr. Long and to any further capital gains realized on a subsequent sale. If the property was subsequently sold for $434,000, Mr. Long would have a taxable capital gain of $25,000 [(1/2)($434,000 - $384,000)] that would be attributed back to Mrs. Long.

3 And 4. Gift To Children

In the case of a transfer to either of her children, ITA 69 would require that the gift be treated as a deemed disposition with the proceeds at the fair market value of $384,000. This would result in an immediate taxable capital gain of $86,000 [(1/2)($384,000 - $212,000)]

The tax base to the children would be the fair market value of $384,000.

A transfer to Mary would result in the application of the income attribution rules of ITA 74.1. This would mean that subsequent dividend income on these shares would be allocated to Mrs. Long until Mary reaches 18 years of age. If the shares were transferred to Barry, there would be no attribution of dividends. While we are ignoring this possibility, note that dividends on the shares of public companies are not subject to the tax on split income.

There is no attribution of capital gains on assets transferred to children, without regard to their age. This means that, if the property was later sold for $434,000, the resulting taxable capital gain of $25,000 [(1/2)($434,000 - $384,000)] would be taxed in the hands of the child who received the gift.

Farm Land

1. Gift To Spouse - ITA 73(1) Applies

As with all of the other properties, Mrs. Long could make a tax free transfer of the farm land to her husband under ITA 73(1).

The adjusted cost base to Mr. Long would remain unchanged at $80,000.

As farm income is considered to be business income rather than property income, there would be no attribution of any farm income that arises while Mr. Long is holding the property.

In the event of a subsequent sale of the farm land for $225,000 ($50,000 more than the fair market value at the time of transfer), the following taxable capital gain would be attributed to Mrs. Long under ITA 74.1:

Proceeds Of Disposition	$225,000
Adjusted Cost Base	(80,000)
Capital Gain	$145,000
Inclusion Rate	1/2
Taxable Capital Gain	$ 72,500

2. Gift To Spouse - Elect Out Of ITA 73(1)

Alternatively, Mrs. Long could elect out of ITA 73(1) and transfer the property at its fair market value of $175,000. This would result in an immediate taxable capital gain of $47,500 [(1/2)($175,000 - $80,000)].

In this case the adjusted cost base to Mr. Long would be $175,000.

A noted, farm income is business income and this would not be attributed to Mrs. Long

As the transfer was a gift, the income attribution rules would apply to subsequent capital gains on the property. If Mr. Long sells the property for $225,000, the resulting $25,000 [(1/2)($225,000 - $175,000)] taxable capital gain would be attributed back to Mrs. Long.

3 And 4. Gift To Children

ITA 73(3) permits the inter vivos transfer of farm property used by the taxpayer or her family to a child on a tax free basis. The deemed proceeds would be Mrs. Long's adjusted cost base, which means that Mrs. Long would incur no taxation at the time of the gift to either child.

The adjusted cost base to either child would be the same $80,000 that was deemed to be the proceeds of the disposition.

As noted in our discussion of the transfer of this property to Mr. Long, because farm income is business income rather than property income, there will be no attribution of farm income in the case of a transfer to either child.

On most transfers to related minors, there is no attribution of capital gains. This is a reflection of the fact that, unlike the rules for transfers to a spouse, there is no general rollover provision for transfers to related minors on a tax free basis. However, when a transfer is made to a related minor under the provisions of ITA 73(3) and the transfer value is below fair market value, ITA 75.1 requires that any subsequent gain resulting from a disposition by the transferee before they reach age 18 be attributed back to the transferor.
This means that, if the farm property is transferred to Mary and she sells the property for $225,000 before she reaches age 18, a taxable capital gain of $72,500 [(1/2)($225,000 - $80,000)] will be attributed to Mrs. Long. If the transfer was to Barry, this capital gain would not be attributed to Mrs. Long and would be taxed in his hands.

Self Study Solution Nine - 12

Net Employment Income

Carolyn's employment income would be calculated as follows:

Salary [(10 Months)($5,000)]	$50,000
RPP Contributions (Note 1)	(2,600)
Automobile (Note 2)	6,047
Travel Allowance (Note 3)	Nil
Moving Cost Allowance	10,000
Housing Loss Reimbursement (Note 4)	Nil
Housing Cost Allowance (Note 5)	7,500
Net Employment Income	$70,947

Note 1 While Carolyn's RPP contributions can be deducted, the matching contribution by her employer does not create a taxable benefit.

Note 2 The automobile benefit would be calculated as follows:

Standby Charge [(2%)($42,000)(9)(8,000 ÷ 15,003*)]	$4,031
Operating Cost Benefit - Lesser Of:	
• [(1/2)($4,031)] = $2,016	
• [(8,000)($0.25)] = $2,000	2,016
Total Benefit	$6,047

* [(9)(1,667)]

Note 3 As the allowance appears to be reasonable, it does not have to be included in income. Given this, Carolyn cannot deduct her actual costs.

Note 4 As the housing loss reimbursement is less than $15,000, it does not have to be included in income.

Note 5 Assistance with higher housing costs related to a required move must be included in an employee's income.

Property Income

Carolyn's property income is calculated as follows:

Eligible Dividends Received	$ 5,800
Gross Up At 38 Percent	2,204
Recapture On Rental Property (Note 6)	20,000
Total Property Income	$28,004

Note 6 The fair market value of the rental building when it is bequeathed to Carolyn is $270,000 ($320,000 - $50,000). While this would be the UCC value that Carolyn would use to calculate CCA, because the fair market value of the property at the time of transfer is less than its capital cost, Carolyn must use her mother's capital cost of $300,000 ($400,000 - $100,000).

Carolyn's proceeds from the sale of the building is $290,000 ($340,000 - $50,000) and, when she subtracts the lesser of the capital cost ($300,000) and the proceeds ($290,000) from the $270,000 UCC, the result is recapture of $20,000 ($270,000 - $290,000).

Taxable Capital Gains

Carolyn's only capital gains will arise on the sale of the shares that were gifted to her by her father. Note that her adjusted cost base for these shares will be their fair market value at the time of the gift.

Proceeds Of Disposition	$74,000
Adjusted Cost Base	(62,000)
Capital Gain	$12,000
Inclusion Rate	1/2
Taxable Capital Gain	$ 6,000

Other Income And Deductions

Carolyn's other income and other deductions amount is calculated as follows:

Spousal Support (Note 7)	$ 500
Moving Costs (Note 8)	(27,871)
Child Care Cost (Note 9)	(7,300)
Total Other Income And Deductions	($34,671)

Note 7   When the full amount of support is not paid, the first payments are deemed to be for child support. Given the total payments of $12,500 and the required child support of $12,000 [(12)($1,000)], Carolyn will include only $500 in her Net Income For Tax Purposes.

Note 8   Costs for food and lodging at or near an old or new residence are limited to a maximum period of 15 days. Carolyn has a total of 23 eligible days: 14 days in Lethbridge and 9 days in Edmonton. Note that the 2 days spent travelling to Edmonton are not included in the 15 day total. As the hotel in Edmonton is the more expensive, she will deduct all 9 days spent there. Carolyn's deductible moving costs can be calculated as follows:

Selling Cost Of Lethbridge Property	$12,500
Legal Fees - Sale Of Lethbridge Property	600
Legal Fees - Purchase Of Edmonton Property	450
Storage Costs - February 15 Through March 10	1,400
Cost Of Moving Belongings	7,250
Lodging In Lethbridge And Edmonton	
(9 @ $200 + 6 @$175)	2,850
Simplified Meal Cost [(3)($51)(15 + 2 Days)]	2,601
Simplified Milage [($.435)(506)]	220
Total Deductible Moving Costs	$27,871

As this amount is less than her income at her new job, she will be able to deduct the full amount of these expenses.

Note 9   Carolyn's deductible care costs would be the least of three amounts:

Actual Costs Plus Deductible Camp Costs		
Edmonton Cost [(38)(($175)]	$6,650	
Camp [(2)($200 + $125)]	650	$ 7,300
Annual Limit ($8,000 + $5,000)		$13,000
Two-Thirds Earned Income		
[(2/3)($70,947 + $2,600 RPP)]		$49,031

The least of these three amounts is the actual cost of $7,300.

Net Income For Tax Purposes

Carolyn's Net Income For Tax Purposes would be determined as follows:

Net Employment Income	$70,947
Property Income	28,004
Taxable Capital Gains	6,000
Other Income And Deductions	(34,671)
Net Income For Tax Purposes	$70,280

Taxable Income

As Carolyn has no Division C deductions, her Taxable Income would be equal to her Net Income For Tax Purposes.

Tax Payable

Carolyn's Tax Payable would be determined as follows:

Tax On First $45,916		$ 6,887
Tax On Next $24,364 ($70,280 - $45,916) At 20.5 Percent		4,995
Tax Before Credits		$11,882
Tax Credits:		
Basic Personal	($11,635)	
Eligible Dependant	(11,635)	
EI Premiums	(836)	
CPP Contributions	(2,564)	
Canada Employment	(1,178)	
Medical Expenses (Note 10)	(5,492)	
Total Credit Base	($33,340)	
Rate	15%	(5,001)
Dividend Tax Credit [(6/11)($2,204)]		(1,202)
Charitable Donations (Note 11)		
[(15%)($200) + (29%)($600 - $200)]		(146)
Federal Tax Payable		$ 5,533

Note 10 The medical expenses eligible for the credit are as follows:

Total Medical Costs	$7,600
Lesser Of:	
• $2,108 [(3%)($70,280)]	
• 2017 Threshold Amount = $2,268	(2,108)
Medical Expense Tax Credit Base	$5,492

Note 11 As none of her income is taxed at 33 percent, this rate will not be applicable to the calculation of the charitable donations tax credit.

Self Study Solution Nine - 13

Net Employment Income

Chantale's employment income would be calculated as follows:

Salary	$90,000
RPP Contributions (Note 1)	(4,500)
Professional Dues	(1,200)
Automobile Benefit (Note 2)	9,071
Moving Allowance	6,000
Travel Allowance (Note 3)	Nil
Net Employment Income	$99,371

Note 1   The employer's matching contribution to the RPP would not be a taxable benefit.

Note 2   The automobile benefit would be calculated as follows:

Standby Charge [(2%)($28,000)(12)(18,000 ÷ 20,004*)]	$6,047
Operating Cost Benefit - Lesser Of:	
• [(1/2)($6,047)] = $3,024	
• [(18,000)($0.25)] = $4,500	3,024
Total Benefit	$9,071

* [(12)(1,667)]

Note 3   As the allowance appears to be reasonable, it does not have to be included in income. Given this, Chantale cannot deduct her actual costs.

Property Income

As Chantale is divorced from her former husband the income attribution rules are no longer applicable. This means the eligible dividends would be included in her income and will result in an income inclusion calculated as follows:

Dividends Received	$1,500
Gross Up At 38 Percent	570
Taxable Dividends = Total Property Income	$2,070

Taxable Capital Gains

Here again, because income attribution no longer applies, the following capital gain would be included in Chantale's Net Income For Tax Purposes:

Proceeds Of Disposition	$34,400
Adjusted Cost Base	(26,000)
Capital Gain	$ 8,400
Inclusion Rate	1/2
Taxable Capital Gain	$ 4,200

Other Income And Deductions

Chantale's other income and other deductions amount is calculated as follows:

Spousal Support Received (Note 4)	$ 800
Moving Expenses (Note 5)	(12,850)
Child Care Costs (Note 6)	(13,000)
Total Other Income And Deductions	**($25,050)**

Note 4 As the required payments were not made in full, the payments that were made are first applied to child support. The taxable spousal support would be calculated as follows:

Total Payments	$8,000
Required Child Support [(12)($600)]	(7,200)
Taxable Spousal Support Received	**$ 800**

Note 5 As she is moving more than 40 kilometers closer to her work, moving costs are deductible. The deductible amounts are as follows:

Lease Cancellation Penalty	$ 1,200
Cost Of Storing Belongings	1,500
Cost Of Moving Belongings	6,400
Legal Fees On Purchase Of New Home	Nil
Food And Hotel In Ottawa (Limited To 15 Days At $250)	3,750
Deductible Moving Costs	**$12,850**

As this amount is less than her income at her new job location of $30,000 [(4/12)($90,000)], she will be able to deduct the full amount of these expenses. The costs of the house hunting trips are not deductible. In addition, because she did not own a home in Carleton Place, the legal costs of purchasing the new home are not deductible.

Note 6 The child care costs would be $13,000, the least of the following three amounts:

Actual Costs And Deductible Camp Costs		
Carleton Place [(32)(($300)]	$9,600	
Ottawa [(16)($350)]	5,600	
Camp [(4)($200) + (4)($125)]	1,300	$16,500
Annual Limit ($8,000 + $5,000)		$13,000
Two-Thirds Earned Income*		
[(2/3)($99,371 + $4,500 + $1,200)]		$70,047

*The income limit is based on gross employment income, without consideration of the RPP contributions or professional dues.

Net Income For Tax Purposes

Chantale's Net Income For Tax Purposes would be determined as follows:

Net Employment Income	$99,371
Property Income	2,070
Taxable Capital Gains	4,200
Other Income And Deductions	(25,050)
Net Income For Tax Purposes	**$80,591**

Taxable Income

As Chantale has no Division C deductions, her Taxable Income would be equal to her Net Income For Tax Purposes.

Tax Payable

Chantale's Tax Payable would be determined as follows:

Tax On First $45,916		$ 6,887
Tax On Next $34,675 ($80,591 - $45,916) At 20.5 Percent		7,108
Tax Before Credits		$13,995
Tax Credits:		
Basic Personal	($11,635)	
Eligible Dependant	(11,635)	
EI Premiums	(836)	
CPP Contributions	(2,564)	
Canada Employment	(1,178)	
Medical Expenses (Note 7)	(11,282)	
Total Credit Base	($39,130)	
Rate	15%	(5,870)
Dividend Tax Credit [(6/11)($570)]		(311)
Balance Before Charitable Contributions		$ 7,814
Charitable Donations (Note 8)		(7,814)
Federal Tax Payable		Nil

Note 7 The medical expenses eligible for the credit are as follows:

Total Medical Costs		$13,550
Reduced By The Lesser Of:		
• [(3%)($80,591)] = $2,418		
• 2017 Threshold Amount = $2,268		(2,268)
Medical Expense Tax Credit Base		$11,282

Note 8 As none of her income is taxed at 33 percent, this rate will not be applicable to the calculation of the charitable donations tax credit.

While Chantale has available a charitable donation of $200,000, the use of this credit is limited to 75 percent of her Net Income For Tax Purposes. This would be $60,443 [(75%)($80,591)]. However, using this total would create a credit of $17,500 [(15%)($200) + (29%)($60,443 - $200)]. As this is in excess of her Tax Payable, it would make no sense to claim the maximum because unused donations can be carried forward for 5 years.

The best solution would be to use an amount of these contributions that is sufficient to eliminate her federal Tax Payable. This amount would be $27,041. The credit would be $7,814 [(15%)($200) + (29%)($27,041 - $200)].

The required credit base is determined by solving the following simple equation for X:

$$\$7,814 = [(29\%)(X - \$200) + (15\%)(\$200)]$$
$$X = [(\$7,814 + \$58 - \$30) \div 29\%]$$

This would leave a charitable donations carry forward of $172,959 ($200,000 - $27,041).

Chapter 9 Learning Objectives

After completing Chapter 9, you should be able to:

1. Identify the major other sources of income that are listed under Subdivision d of the *Income Tax Act* (paragraph [P hereafter] 9-1 to 9-19).
2. Identify the income inclusions from deferred income plans (P 9-20 and 9-21).
3. Apply the rules related to education assistance payments, social assistance, workers' compensation payments and the universal child care benefit (P 9-22 to 9-27).
4. Determine the deductible amount of CPP contributions on self-employed income (P 9-28 to 9-31).
5. Determine the deductible amount of moving expenses for an individual (P 9-32 to 9-45).

6. Determine the deductible amount of child care expenses (P 9-46 to 9-57).
7. Apply the provisions related to the disability supports deduction (P 9-58 to 9-66).
8. Apply the provisions related to EI benefits and repayments (P 9-67 and 9-68).
9. Explain the general rules for pension income splitting (P 9-69 to 9-77).
10. Explain the tax treatment of child support and spousal support payments and receipts (P 9-78 to 9-87).

11. Determine the taxable portion of annuity payments received (P 9-88 to 9-96).
12. Describe the major features of Tax Free Savings Accounts (P 9-97 to 9-101).
13. Explain the provisions associated with Registered Education Savings Plans, Canada Education Savings Grants and Canada Learning Bonds (P 9-102 to 9-129).
14. Compare the major features of TFSAs, RRSPs and RESPs (P 9-130 to 9-138).
15. Describe the major features of Registered Disability Savings Plans (P 9-139 to 9-141).

16. Determine the tax consequences of non-arm's length transfers of property at values other than fair market value (P 9-142 to 9-159).
17. Describe the special rollover provisions applicable to inter vivos transfers of capital property to a spouse (P 9-160 to 9-167).
18. Determine the tax consequences of non-arm's length transfers of depreciable property (P 9-168 to 9-172).
19. Describe the special rollover provisions applicable to inter vivos transfers of farm or fishing property to a child (P 9-173 to 9-176).
20. Explain the basic requirements for deemed dispositions on death and any rollovers available at that time (P 9-177 to 9-186).

21. Apply the income attribution rules to inter vivos transfers of capital property to a spouse and to related individuals who are under the age of 18 (P 9-187 to 9-205).
22. Describe the income attribution rules applicable to transfers to other related parties (P 9-206 to 9-209).
23. Describe some of the anti-avoidance provisions that relate to the income attribution rules (P 9-210 and 9-211).
24. Describe some of the tax planning techniques that are available to mitigate the income attribution rules (P 9-212).

CHAPTER 10

How To Work Through Chapter 10

We recommend the following approach in dealing with the material in this Chapter:

Planning For Retirement
- Read paragraph 10-1 to 10-19 (in the textbook).

Registered Retirement Savings Plans (RRSPs)
- Read paragraph 10-20 to 10-36.
- Do Exercise Ten-1 (in the textbook) and check the solution in this Study Guide.
- Read paragraph 10-37.

RRSP Deduction Limit
- Read paragraph 10-38 to 10-48.
- Do Exercises Ten-2 and Ten-3 and check the solutions in this Study Guide.

Pension Adjustments (PAs)
- Read paragraph 10-49 to 10-51.
- Do Exercise Ten-4 and check the solution in this Study Guide.
- Read paragraph 10-52 to 10-59.
- Do Exercise Ten-5 and check the solution in this Study Guide.

Past Service Pension Adjustments (PSPAs) And Pension Adjustment Reversals
- Read paragraph 10-60 to 10-71.
- Do Self Study Problem Ten-1 which is available on the Companion Website and check the solution in this Study Guide.

Examples Of RRSP Deduction Calculations
- Read paragraph 10-72.
- Do Exercises Ten-6 and Ten-7 and check the solutions in this Study Guide.

Undeducted And Excess RRSP Contributions, Including Tax Planning For
- Read paragraph 10-73 to 10-78.
- Do Exercise Ten-8 and check the solution in this Study Guide.
- Read paragraph 10-79 to 10-82.
- Do Self Study Problem Ten-2 to Ten-5 and check the solutions in this Study Guide.

RRSP And RRIF Administration Fees
- Read paragraph 10-83.

RRSP Withdrawals, Voluntary Conversions And Involuntary Termination (Age)
- Read paragraph 10-84 to 10-93.

Spousal RRSP
- Read paragraph 10-94 to 10-102.
- Do Exercise Ten-9 and check the solution in this Study Guide.

Home Buyers' Plan (HBP) And Lifelong Learning Plan (LLP)
- Read paragraph 10-103 to 10-113.
- Do Exercise Ten-10 and check the solution in this Study Guide.
- Read paragraph 10-114 to 10-122.
- Do Exercise Ten-11 and check the solution in this Study Guide.

RRSPs - Departure From Canada And Death Of The RRSP Registrant
- Read paragraph 10-123 to 10-138.
- Do Self Study Problem Ten-6 and check the solution in this Study Guide.

Registered Pension Plans (RPPs)
- Read paragraph 10-139 to 10-157.

Pooled Registered Pension Plans, Target Benefit Plans And Expanded CPP
- Read paragraph 10-158 to 10-167.

Registered Retirement Income Funds (RRIFs) - General Rules
- Read paragraph 10-168 to 10-178.
- Do Exercise Ten-12 and check the solution in this Study Guide.

RRIFs - Death Of The RRIF Registrant And Evaluation Of RRIFs
- Read paragraph 10-179 to 10-186.

Deferred Profit Sharing Plans And Profit Sharing Plans
- Read paragraph 10-187 to 10-196.

Transfers Between Plans And Retiring Allowances
- Read paragraph 10-197 to 10-200.
- Do Exercise Ten-13 and check the solution in this Study Guide.
- Do Self Study Problems Ten-7 and Ten-8 and check the solutions in this Study Guide.

Retirement Compensation Arrangements, Salary Deferral Arrangements And Individual Pension Plans
- Read paragraph 10-201 to 10-221.
- Do Self Study Problems Ten-9 and Ten-10 and check the solutions in this Study Guide.

To Complete This Chapter
- If you would like more practice in problem solving, do the Supplementary Self Study Problems for the chapter. These problems and solutions are available on the Companion Website.
- Review the Key Terms Used In This Chapter in the textbook at the end of Chapter 10. Consult the Glossary for the meaning of any key terms you do not know.
- Test yourself with the Chapter 10 Glossary Flashcards available on the Companion Website.
- Ensure you have achieved the Chapter 10 Learning Objectives listed in this Study Guide.
- As a review, we recommend you view the PowerPoint presentation for Chapter 10 that is on the Companion Website.

Practice Examination
- Write the Practice Examination for Chapter 10 that is on the Companion Website. Mark your examination using the Practice Examination Solution that is also on the Companion Website.

Solutions to Chapter Ten Exercises

Exercise Ten - 1 Solution

Invested Inside RRSP

Deductible Contribution	$20,000
Dividends Received [(5)(5%)($20,000)]	5,000
Balance After Five Years	$25,000
Tax On Withdrawal [(40%)($25,000)]	(10,000)
Available For Vacation	$15,000

Invested Inside TFSA

Initial Investment [($20,000)(1 - .40)]	$12,000
Tax Free Dividends [(5)(5%)($12,000)]	3,000
Available For Vacation	$15,000

Invested Outside RRSP And TFSA

Initial Investment [($20,000)(1 - .40)]	$12,000
After Tax Dividends [(5)(5%)($12,000)(1 - .22)]	2,340
Available For Vacation	$14,340

Investing outside the RRSP or TFSA is the worst alternative by $660 ($15,000 - $14,340).

Exercise Ten - 2 Solution

His Earned Income for RRSP purposes would be $70,500 ($56,000 + $2,500 + $12,000).

Exercise Ten - 3 Solution

Her Earned Income for RRSP purposes would be $54,500 ($82,000 + $3,000 - $12,500 - $18,000).

Exercise Ten - 4 Solution

The basic mechanism here is the Pension Adjustment (PA). Individuals who belong to an RPP or a DPSP have their RRSP Deduction Limit reduced by the amount of their PA for the previous year. PAs are designed to reflect the amount of contributions or benefits that have been accumulated in employer sponsored RPPs and DPSPs.

Exercise Ten - 5 Solution

The Pension Adjustment will be $6,400 ($2,300 + $1,800 + $2,300).

Exercise Ten - 6 Solution

The required calculations would be as follows:

Unused Deduction Room - End Of 2016	$4,800
Lesser Of:	
• 2017 RRSP Dollar Limit = $26,010	
• 18% Of 2016 Earned Income Of $38,000 = $6,840	6,840
2017 RRSP Deduction Limit	$11,640
RRSP Deduction Is Least Of:	
• RRSP Deduction Limit = $11,640	
• Available Contributions = $6,000	
• Amount Mr. Haslich Chooses To Deduct = $4,500	(4,500)
Unused RRSP Deduction Room - End Of 2017	$ 7,140

Assuming Mr. Haslich deducted only $4,500, he would have $1,500 ($6,000 - $4,500) in undeducted contributions that can be carried forward and deducted in a subsequent year.

If Mr. Haslich wanted to deduct his maximum RRSP deduction of $11,640, he would have to contribute an additional $5,640 ($11,640 - $6,000).

Exercise Ten - 7 Solution

The required calculations would be as follows:

Unused Deduction Room - End Of 2016	$10,750
Lesser Of:	
• 2017 RRSP Dollar Limit = $26,010	
• 18% Of 2016 Earned Income Of $66,530* = $11,975	11,975
Less 2016 PA	(4,800)
2017 RRSP Deduction Limit	$17,925
RRSP Deduction Is Lesser Of:	
• RRSP Deduction Limit = $17,925	
• Available Contributions = $19,760 ($6,560 + $13,200)	(17,925)
Unused RRSP Deduction Room - End Of 2017	Nil

*Earned Income = $6,530 - $18,000 + $75,600 + $2,400 (RPP)

Mr. Black's maximum RRSP deduction is $17,925. While he has no Unused RRSP Deduction Room, he has $1,835 ($19,760 - $17,925) in undeducted contributions that can be carried forward and deducted in a subsequent year in which there is sufficient RRSP deduction room.

Exercise Ten - 8 Solution

In 2015 and 2016, 18 percent of Ms. Brownell's $160,000 in earned income is more than the RRSP dollar limit for those years. Her 2017 earned income is not relevant in this Exercise as it will not be used until 2018. Given this, the calculation of the excess amount of contributions is as follows:

2016 Contribution (July 1)	$27,350
2016 Addition To Deduction Room = RRSP Dollar Limit	(25,370)
Excess Contributions For 2016 (Less Than $2,000)	$ 1,980
2017 Contribution (May 1)	30,000
2017 Addition To Deduction Room = RRSP Dollar Limit	(26,010)
Permitted $2,000 Cushion	(2,000)
Excess Contributions Subject To Penalty	$ 3,970

As the excess contribution for 2016 was less than $2,000, there is no penalty for that year. There will be a 2017 penalty of $318 [(1%)($3,970)(8 Months)]. The fact that there is no RRSP deduction is not relevant to the penalty.

Exercise Ten - 9 Solution

As a spousal contribution was made in 2016, one of the two years prior to 2017, income attribution will apply. However, it will only apply to the extent of the $5,000 contribution made by Mrs. Garveau. This means that $5,000 of the withdrawal will be taxed in the hands of Mrs. Garveau, with the remaining $4,000 taxed in the hands of Mr. Garveau.

Exercise Ten - 10 Solution

Ms. DeBoo will have to repay $867 [(1/15)($18,000 - $5,000)] during 2017. Note that the voluntary payment that was made during 2016 did not reduce the fraction of the remaining balance that must be paid in 2017.

Exercise Ten - 11 Solution

There are no tax consequences associated with the withdrawal of $5,000. He is not enrolled in a qualifying education program in either 2016 or 2017 and, as a consequence, his repayment period begins in 2017. As he makes the required payments of $500 ($5,000 ÷ 10) within 60 days of the end of each of the years 2017 through 2026, there are no tax consequences associated with his repayments.

Exercise Ten - 12 Solution

He has no required minimum withdrawal for 2017, the year the RRIF is established. His minimum withdrawal for 2018 will be $27,500 [$660,000 ÷ (90 - 66)].

Exercise Ten - 13 Solution

It would appear that Mr. Bartoli began working for his employer in 1976. Given this, he can rollover a total of $59,500 [($2,000)(20 Years Before 1996) + ($1,500)(13 Years Before 1989)] to his RRSP. The remainder of the retiring allowance will be taxed in 2017.

Self Study Solution Ten - 1

Case A

The required 2017 PA would be calculated as follows:

Employer's Contribution To RPP	$2,200
Employer's Contribution To DPSP	1,500
Mrs. Anderson's Contribution To RPP	1,800
PA	$5,500

Case B

The required 2017 PA would be calculated as follows:

$$[(9)(1.75\%)(\$45,000)] = \$7,087.50$$

Note that the contributions made during 2017 have no influence on the PA for a defined benefit RPP.

Case C

Miss Carr's 2017 PSPA would be calculated as follows:

$$[(9)(1.25\%)(\$38,000)(2 \text{ Years})] = \$8,550$$

The 2017 PA will reflect the benefits earned during 2017. It is equal to $4,275 [(9)(1.25%)($38,000)].

Case D

Ms. Dexter's 2017 PSPA is based on the PAs that would have been reported in the relevant years, less the PAs actually reported. The calculation would be as follows:

$$[(9)(1.8\% - 1.6\%)(\$59,000)(2 \text{ Years})] = \$2,124$$

The 2017 PA will reflect the benefits earned during 2017. It is equal to $9,558 [(9)(1.8%)($59,000)].

Self Study Solution Ten - 2

Part A - Maximum RRSP Deduction

Mark's maximum 2017 RRSP deduction would be calculated as follows:

Unused Deduction Room - January 1, 2016	$25,000
2016 Addition (Based On 2015 Earned Income Of Nil)	Nil
2017 Addition (Based On 2016 Earned Income Of Nil)	Nil
Maximum 2017 RRSP Deduction	$25,000

Part B - Excess RRSP Contributions

At the beginning of 2016, Mark's undeducted contributions of $27,000 are equal to his $25,000 unused deduction room, plus the permitted $2,000 cushion. As he withdrew $15,000 and made no further contributions during 2016, there are no excess contributions during the 2016 taxation year.

The excess contributions for 2017 would be calculated as follows:

Undeducted Contributions		
January 1, 2016 Balance	$27,000	
2016 Withdrawal	(15,000)	
2017 Addition	50,000	$62,000
Unused Deduction Room		(25,000)
Permitted Cushion		(2,000)
Excess Contributions Subject To Penalty		$35,000
Penalty Rate		1%
Monthly Penalty		$ 350
Months (March To December)		10
Total Penalty		$ 3,500

Since the $15,000 is withdrawn from the RRSP prior to the end of the year following the year in which an assessment is received for the year in which the contribution is made, an offsetting deduction is available.

Note that the fact that Mark has Earned Income for RRSP purposes in 2017 will not generate an addition to his deduction room until 2018.

Self Study Solution Ten - 3

Mr. Barnes' 2016 Earned Income for RRSP purposes would be calculated as follows:

Salary	$55,000
Taxable Benefits	1,150
Union Dues	(175)
Net Employment Income	$55,975
Business Income	4,150
Rental Loss	(11,875)
Spousal Support Received	2,400
Earned Income	$50,650

Note that CPP and EI contributions do not reduce Earned Income for RRSP purposes.

Since Mr. Barnes has no undeducted RRSP contributions, his maximum deductible RRSP contribution for 2017 is equal to his RRSP Deduction Limit.

This is calculated for Part A (not a member of RPP or DPSP) and Part B (member of RPP) as follows:

	Part A	Part B
Unused Deduction Room - End Of 2016	Nil	Nil
Annual Addition - Lesser Of:		
• 2017 RRSP Dollar Limit = $26,010		
• 18% of 2016 Earned Income Of $50,650 = $9,117	9,117	9,117
Less 2016 PA	N/A	(4,200)
Maximum Deductible RRSP Contribution	$9,117	$4,917

Self Study Solution Ten - 4

Part A

Mr. Beasley's net employment income for 2016 would be $34,700, his gross salary of $36,000, reduced by his RPP contributions of $1,300.

Part B

The annual addition for 2017 would be the lesser of $26,010 and 18 percent of Earned Income for 2016. The latter amount would be calculated as follows:

Net Employment Income (Part A)	$34,700
Add Back RPP Contributions	1,300
Spousal Support	9,000
Net Rental Loss	(5,000)
Earned Income	$40,000
Percent	18%
Annual Addition (Less than $26,010)	$ 7,200

Note that the damage award, royalties on someone else's work, interest, dividends, and gift are not included in Earned Income for RRSP purposes.

Mr. Beasley's maximum deductible RRSP contribution would be calculated as follows:

Opening Unused Deduction Room		Nil
Annual Addition		$ 7,200
Less 2016 PA		(2,600)
Maximum Deductible RRSP Contribution		$ 4,600

Part C

As Mr. Beasley has made no contributions prior to 2017, he has no undeducted contributions. In addition, he has interest income and dividends that are subject to current Tax Payable. Given this, as well as the fact that his damage award and separation gift leave him cash in excess of his needs, he should contribute the maximum deductible amount of $4,600 to his RRSP for 2017.

While he could deduct $4,600 of his total contribution in 2017, it would be advantageous to defer this deduction until 2018 when he expects to be in the maximum tax bracket. At the federal level, the tax savings will be $1,518 [(33%)($4,600)] in 2018, as compared to $690 [(15%)($4,600)] in 2017.

Since he has made no contributions to a TFSA, in 2017 he could make a contribution of $52,000 (4@$5,000 for 2009 to 2012, 4@$5,500 for 2013, 2014, 2016, and 2017 and $10,000 for 2015).

Given his available funds, Mr. Beasley should be advised to consider contributing the maximum allowable amount to a Tax Free Savings Account, as well as over contributing up to $2,000 to his RRSP. Although he would not be able to deduct these contributions, they would enjoy the benefit of having any income earned while in the plan compounded on a tax free basis. An over contribution to his RRSP would be deductible in a future year with sufficient RRSP deduction room.

All of these contributions should be made as soon as possible in order to maximize the tax free earnings that will accrue inside of his RRSP and/or TFSA.

Self Study Solution Ten - 5

Part A

Mr. Detwiller's Net Income For Tax Purposes would be calculated as follows:

Income Under ITA 3(a):		
Net Employment Income	$56,000	
Eligible Dividends	7,800	
Gross Up [(38%)($7,800)]	2,964	$66,764
Income Under ITA 3(b):		
Taxable Capital Gains	$ 5,400	
Allowable Capital Losses	(8,200)	Nil
Balance From ITA 3(a) And (b)		$66,764
Subdivision e Deductions		(2,500)
Balance From ITA 3(c)		$64,264
Deductions Under ITA 3(d):		
Net Rental Loss		(9,000)
Net Income For Tax Purposes		$55,264

Mr. Detwiller's Net Income For Tax Purposes is $55,264 and he has a net capital loss carry over of $2,800 ($5,400 - $8,200).

Part B - Case 1

Mr. Detwiller's 2016 Earned Income would be calculated as follows:

Net Employment Income	$56,000
Add Back RPP Contributions	1,500
Net Rental Loss	(9,000)
Earned Income	$48,500

Given this, his maximum 2017 contribution would be calculated as follows:

Unused Deduction Room - End Of 2016	$10,000
Annual Addition - Lesser Of:	
• 2017 RRSP Dollar Limit = $26,010	
• 18% of 2016 Earned Income Of $48,500 = $8,730	8,730
Less 2016 PA ($1,500 + $3,000 + $1,000)	(5,500)
2017 RRSP Deduction Limit	$13,230
Allowable Excess Amount	2,000
Non-Penalty Contribution Limit	$15,230
Undeducted Contributions From Previous Years	(4,500)
Maximum RRSP Contribution	$10,730

If Mr. Detwiller contributes this amount of $10,730, his deduction will be equal to $13,230 and he will carry forward RRSP contributions of $2,000 ($4,500 + $10,730 - $13,230).

Part B - Case 2

Mr. Detwiller's 2016 Earned Income would be calculated as follows:

Net Employment Income	$56,000
Net Rental Loss	(9,000)
Earned Income	$47,000

Given this, his maximum 2017 contribution would be calculated as follows:

Unused Deduction Room - End Of 2016	$10,000
Annual Addition - Lesser Of:	
• 2017 RRSP Dollar Limit = $26,010	
• 18% of 2016 Earned Income Of $47,000 = $8,460	8,460
Less 2016 PA	(4,500)
2017 RRSP Deduction Limit	$13,960
Allowable Excess Amount	2,000
Non-Penalty Contribution Limit	$15,960
Undeducted Contributions From Previous Years	(4,500)
Maximum RRSP Contribution	$11,460

If Mr. Detwiller contributes this amount of $11,460, his deduction will be equal to $13,960 and he will carry forward RRSP contributions of $2,000 ($4,500 + $11,460 - $13,960).

Part B - Case 3

Mr. Detwiller's 2016 Earned Income would be calculated as follows:

Net Employment Income		$ 56,000
Net Rental Loss		(9,000)
Business Income		220,000
Earned Income		$267,000

Given this, his maximum 2017 contribution would be calculated as follows:

Unused Deduction Room - End of 2016	$10,000
Annual Addition - Lesser Of:	
• 2017 RRSP Dollar Limit = $26,010	
• 18% of 2016 Earned Income Of $267,000 = $48,060	26,010
Less 2016 PA	Nil
2017 RRSP Deduction Limit	$36,010
Allowable Excess Amount	2,000
Non-Penalty Contribution Limit	$38,010
Undeducted Contributions From Previous Years	(4,500)
Maximum RRSP Contribution	$33,510

If Mr. Detwiller contributes this amount of $33,510, his deduction will be equal to $36,010 and he will carry forward RRSP contributions of $2,000 ($4,500 + $33,510 - $36,010).

Self Study Solution Ten - 6

Part A

Mr. Sabatini's minimum net employment income would be calculated as follows:

Salary	$ 58,000
Commissions	74,000
Registered Pension Plan Contributions	(3,500)
Net Disability Benefits (Note 1)	3,950
Life Insurance Premium Taxable Benefit	
[(50%)($3,000)]	1,500
Automobile Benefit (Note 2)	6,461
Stock Option Benefit	
[($23.50 - $12.50)(1,000 Shares)]	11,000
Golf And Country Club Costs (Note 3)	(3,400)
Net Employment Income	$148,011

Note 1 As Mr. Sabatini's employer has made contributions to the sickness and accident plan, the benefit of $4,500 is taxable. This is reduced by the payments of $550 [($100)(12 - 1)/2] that were made by Mr. Sabatini during the year, leaving a net benefit of $3,950.

Note 2 With respect to the standby charge, Mr. Sabatini's employment related usage is over 50 percent of the total and, as a consequence, he can reduce his standby charge to the extent of personal usage that is less than 1,667 kilometers per month. Also note that, as the car was not available during November, his standby charge would be based on 335 days of availability. This would be rounded to 11 months (335/30). Given this, the standby charge would be as follows:

$$[(\$68,000)(11 \text{ Months})(2\%)(7,000/18,337)] = \$5,711$$

As Mr. Sabatini's employment related use was over 50 percent of the total use, he can base his operating cost benefit on one-half of the standby charge. Given this, the benefit would be the lesser of:

- [($0.25)(7,000)] = $1,750; and
- [(1/2)($5,711)] = $2,856

Using the lesser figure of $1,750, the total benefit would be calculated as follows:

Standby Charge	$5,711
Operating Cost Benefit	1,750
Payment To Employer	(1,000)
Total Automobile Benefit	$6,461

Note 3 Only 50 percent of the $6,800 country club entertainment costs can be deducted by Mr. Sabatini. The $5,000 membership fee would not be a taxable benefit and would not be deductible by his employer.

Other Notes

- The travel costs that the corporation reimbursed to Mr. Sabatini have no tax effect.
- The CPP and EI contributions are not deductible. They can be used to create credits against Tax Payable.
- Income taxes withheld are not deductible.
- Donations to a registered charity will create a credit against Tax Payable, but cannot be deducted in the determination of net employment income.
- Parking fees related to Mr. Sabatini's normal employment location are not deductible.
- Although he cannot deduct his share of the life insurance premiums, the life insurance proceeds will not be taxable.
- The use of frequent flyer points earned on employment related travel does not normally create a taxable benefit.
- The discounts on merchandise provided by the employer are not a taxable benefit.

Part B

Mr. Sabatini's 2016 Earned Income and maximum deductible 2017 RRSP contribution would be calculated as follows:

2016 Earned Income From Employment (Given)	$116,000
2016 Business Loss	(12,500)
2016 Rental Income	7,500
2016 Earned Income	$111,000

Unused Deduction Room - End Of 2016	Nil
Annual Addition - Lesser Of:	
• 2017 RRSP Dollar Limit = $26,010	
• 18% of 2016 Earned Income Of $111,000 = $19,980	$19,980
Less 2016 PA	(6,800)
2017 RRSP Deduction Limit	$13,180
RRSP Deduction For 2017	$ 2,600

While Mr. Sabatini has deduction room of $13,180, only the $2,600 contribution to his wife's plan can be deducted. His $10,000 contribution to his own RRSP is not relevant as it was deducted in the previous year.

Part C

Since the RRSP has no beneficiary specified, an amount equal to the fair market value of all the property held in the RRSP at the time of death will have to be reported on Mr. Sabatini's return for 2018, the year of death.

Part D

Since Mr. Sabatini's wife is the sole beneficiary, she can choose to transfer all the assets in the RRSP to an RRSP in her name. If this is done, there will be no tax consequences for either his wife or Mr. Sabatini's final return. This would likely be the most tax advantageous arrangement for dealing with Mr. Sabatini's RRSP.

Note that there are also provisions that allow RRSPs to be transferred to a financially dependent child on a basis that shifts the tax burden to the child. Given Mr. Sabatini is receiving child support for an 8 year son, this approach might also be tax advantageous.

Self Study Solution Ten - 7

Part A

With respect to the retiring allowance, ITA 56(1)(a)(ii) requires that the entire $125,000 must be included in income. Then, to the extent that such amounts are transferred or contributed to an RRSP for which the taxpayer is the registrant, the taxpayer is entitled to a deduction under ITA 60(j.1), equal to $2,000 for each year of service prior to 1996 with the employer, plus an additional $1,500 for each year of service before 1989, for which the employee was not a member of an RPP or a DPSP. This provides for the following maximum deduction under ITA 60(j.1):

19 Years At $2,000 Per Year (1977 Through 1995)	$38,000
12 Years At $1,500 Per Year (1977 Through 1988)	18,000
Allowable Rollover	$56,000

Given this calculation, the maximum RRSP deduction that Mr. Colt would be allowed for 2017 would be calculated as follows:

Opening RRSP Deduction Room	$32,000
Annual Addition - Lesser Of:	
• 2017 RRSP Dollar Limit = $26,010	
• 18% of 2016 Earned Income Of $46,000 = $8,280	8,280
Less 2016 PA	(8,000)
RRSP Deduction Limit For 2017	$32,280
Retiring Allowance Rollover (See Preceding Calculation)	56,000
Maximum Deduction	$88,280

Part B

The $56,000 eligible portion of the retiring allowance can only be deducted if it is contributed to Mr. Colt's RRSP. If Mr. Colt contributes only $50,000 to his RRSP, the remaining $6,000 ($56,000 - $50,000) cannot be deducted if it is contributed to a spousal RRSP. If Mr. White chooses to make a tax free transfer to an RRSP, the transaction does not change his RRSP Deduction Limit for the year. That is, the maximum deductible RRSP contribution for 2017 will be the same, whether or not he transfers part of the retiring allowance into his plan.

Mr. Colt will be able to deduct contributions to the spousal RRSP of $32,280, his RRSP Deduction Limit. If he makes his planned RRSP contributions, he will have the following amount of non-deductible contributions:

Total Contributions	$125,000
Maximum Deduction Under ITA 60(j.1)	(50,000)
Maximum Deductible Spousal Contribution	(32,280)
Non-Deductible Contributions	$ 42,720

To the extent that non-deductible contributions exceed $2,000, they are subject to a heavy penalty of 1 percent per month. Unless Mr. Colt anticipates having Earned Income from another source in the future, overcontributing to his or the spousal RRSP would not be a good idea. Any over contribution would be taxable when it is withdrawn despite the fact that it was never deducted.

As a consequence, Mr. Colt should revise his planned RRSP contributions so that he contributes $56,000 to his RRSP and $32,280 to a spousal RRSP. This will maximize his RRSP deduction.

Mr. Colt will have additional unused funds of $86,720 ($175,000 - $56,000 - $32,280) available. It would be advisable to contribute as much as possible of this amount to TFSAs for himself and his wife.

Self Study Solution Ten - 8

General Tax Planning Goals
The most desirable solution would be to find benefits that would be fully deductible to the Company and free of taxation for Mr. Jones. The only items that fall into this category would be:

- payments for private health care plans;
- payments for disability insurance;
- discounts on company merchandise; and
- annual non-cash gifts with a value of $500 or less.

Discounts on industrial engines are not likely to be of any value to Mr. Jones. However, Mr. Jones should arrange to have the Company provide private health care coverage, including a dental plan. The Company could also pay the premiums on a disability insurance plan without it becoming a taxable benefit to Mr. Jones at the time of payment (benefits received would be taxable). Finally, an annual non-cash gift with a value of $500 or less would be deductible to the company and received tax free by Mr. Jones.

Use Of RPP, DPSP, RRSP And Retiring Allowance
In terms of tax deferral, Mr. Jones should be included in the Company's Registered Pension Plan (RPP). Once he is admitted to the plan, both he and the Company should make the maximum contributions that are permitted under the terms of the plan. The limiting factor here is that these contributions cannot result in a Pension Adjustment that is in excess of the lesser of 18 percent of Mr. Jones' compensation for the year or the money purchase limit for the year under consideration ($26,230 for 2017).

While there is no indication that the Company has such an arrangement, a Deferred Profit Sharing Plan (DPSP) might also be useful. Whether or not Mr. Jones would be able to use such an arrangement would depend on the total employee/employer contributions to the Company's RPP. Contributions to a DPSP are included in the calculation of Mr. Jones' Pension Adjustment and, when combined with the RPP contributions, the total is subject to the limitation described in the preceding paragraph.

It would also be advisable for Mr. Jones to arrange for some of the compensation to be received in the form of a retiring allowance to be paid to a Registered Retirement Savings Plan (RRSP) at the end of the three years. The amount that could be paid on a tax free basis would be $28,000 ($2,000 per year for the 11 years 1985 through 1995, plus $1,500 per year for the 4 years 1985 through 1988).

If the RRSP funds are subsequently withdrawn in the form of an annuity or transferred to a RRIF, the payments will be eligible for the pension income tax credit after Mr. Jones reaches age 65. The payments will also be eligible for the pension income splitting provisions. (See Chapter 9)

Housing Loan

The Company could provide a loan to Mr. Jones to purchase his new residence. As Mr. Jones is moving, he is eligible for a deduction of the benefit associated with a $25,000 interest free "home relocation" loan. Any additional low interest or interest free loan will result in imputed interest being added to Mr. Jones' Taxable Income without an offsetting deduction.

Note, however, that the prescribed rate for this purpose is at the low rate of 1 percent. At this rate, even if the loan is interest free, the fact that the taxable benefit associated with amounts above $25,000 (the relocation deduction maximum) is very small could make a large interest free loan desirable. On the $100,000 he requires to buy a residence, the benefit on an interest free loan would only be $750. This is the $1,000 [(1%)($100,000)] benefit, less the $250 deduction [(1%)($25,000)] related to the relocation deduction.

As there is an intent to compensate, arrangements would have to be made for forgiving the loan after Mr. Jones retires. While such forgiveness would be taxable to Mr. Jones, he expects to be in a lower tax bracket after retiring, resulting in an absolute tax savings.

Company Car

The Company could provide Mr. Jones with an automobile. In this case, Mr. Jones will be assessed for a personal benefit of a standby charge (24 percent per year of the capital cost or two-thirds of the lease payments, if he is not eligible for a reduction) and for operating costs (one-half of the standby charge or $0.25 per kilometer of personal use). Whether or not this will be desirable depends on an analysis of how Mr. Jones would actually use the car. In some cases, especially if the car has a list price of more than $30,000, the taxable benefit may exceed the actual benefit, making this an undesirable form of compensation.

Recreational Facilities

The Company could pay the dues for any recreational facilities that Mr. Jones might wish to use. While these amounts will not be treated as a taxable benefit to Mr. Jones, the payments will not be deductible to the Company. Given that the Company is subject to a marginal tax rate that is lower than Mr. Jones' combined rate, it is unlikely the Company would agree to do this.

Moving Costs

The Company could provide assistance with the costs that will be incurred by Mr. Jones in moving to Hamilton. With respect to costs that Mr. Jones would be permitted to deduct, it makes little difference whether the Company pays the costs, or simply pays an equivalent amount in salary and lets Mr. Jones pay the costs and deduct them. However, certain types of moving costs that would not be deductible by Mr. Jones can be paid by the Company without creating a taxable benefit. An example of this would be compensation for a loss on a personal residence owned by Mr. Jones if a loss exists on his house in Windsor. (See Chapter 9)

Bonus And/Or Stock Options

If Martin Manufacturing has a year end after July 6, it can declare a bonus in the third year, but not pay it until the following calendar year. This will defer Mr. Jones' taxation of the bonus by one year without deferring Martin's deduction.

As an incentive, the Company could grant Mr. Jones options to purchase its stock. This would have no tax cost to the Company. The timing of the tax cost of the options for Mr. Jones could be delayed until after retirement.

Services As A Self-Employed Contractor Or Through A Corporation

Since Mr. Jones has been operating as a consultant, it may be possible to structure the project so that he will be considered an independent contractor rather than an employee. This would considerably increase the amount and type of expenditures that would be deductible by him and also create an opportunity to income split with his wife, if she could assist him in the project in some way. Her assistance would have to have a business purpose (supernatural phenomena expertise would have questionable value) and any payments to her would have to be reasonable in the circumstances.

In considering this alternative it should be kept in mind that, if Mr. Jones is not an employee, some of the possibilities that have been previously discussed would no longer be feasible. For example, unless Mr. Jones is an employee, it would not be possible for him to be a member of the Company's RPP.

Another possibility would be for Mr. Jones to provide his services through a corporation. However, this would probably not be helpful. Given his relationship with Martin Manufacturing Company, any corporation would likely be viewed as a personal services business and taxed at full corporate rates. (Personal services corporations are covered in Chapter 12, Taxable Income And Tax Payable For Corporations.)

Self Study Solution Ten - 9

Part A - RRSP Contribution

In order to calculate the maximum deductible RRSP contribution, net employment income and net rental income must first be calculated.

Net Employment Income

The calculations required for 2016 (to be used in the RRSP earned income calculation) and 2017 would be as follows:

	2016	2017
Gross Salary	$47,000	$53,000
Commissions	6,200	7,800
RPP Contributions	(1,800)	(1,950)
Work Space In Home Costs (Note 1)	(1,001)	(1,073)
Net Employment Income	$50,399	$57,777

Note 1 As an employee, Kerri cannot deduct either the listed mortgage interest or CCA on this office space. Because she has commission income, Kerri can deduct all of the other listed costs. Given this, the 2016 and 2017 deductions are as follows:

	2016	2017
Utilities And Maintenance	$1,850	$2,040
Insurance	625	715
Property Taxes	4,200	4,400
Total	$6,675	$7,155
Percentage Used	15%	15%
Deductible Amount	$1,001	$1,073

Net Rental Income

The calculations required for 2016 and 2017 would be as follows:

	2016	2017
Rents	$ 8,400	$13,800
Expenses Other Than CCA	(10,300)	(11,100)
Income (Loss) Before CCA	($ 1,900)	$ 2,700
CCA (Note 2)	N/A	(2,700)
Net Rental Income	($ 1,900)	Nil

Note 2   As CCA cannot be used to increase or create a rental loss, no deduction can be made in 2016. For 2017, the maximum available CCA deduction is $10,400 [(4%)($340,000 - $80,000)]. However, the actual deduction is limited to the $2,700 of rental income prior to the deduction of CCA. The first year one-half rule is not applicable as this is the second year the property is owned. The fact that no CCA was deducted in the first year is not relevant.

RRSP Calculations

Determining the appropriate amount here requires the calculation of Earned Income for 2016. The calculation is as follows:

2016 Net Employment Income	$50,399
2016 RPP Contributions Deducted	1,800
Spousal Support Received [(12)($500)]	6,000
2016 Net Rental Loss	(1,900)
2016 Earned Income	$56,299

Using this figure, Ms. Sosteric's maximum 2017 deduction, along with the additional contribution required to make this deduction, would be calculated as follows:

Opening Unused Deduction Room	$ 6,200
Annual Addition - Lesser Of:	
• 2017 RRSP Dollar Limit = $26,010	
• 18% Of 2016 Earned Income Of $56,299 = $10,134	10,134
Less 2016 PA (Employee And Employer RPP Contributions)	(3,600)
Maximum RRSP Deduction	$12,734
Undeducted Contributions In Plan	(5,800)
Required Additional Contribution	$ 6,934

Part B - Net Income For Tax Purposes And Taxable Income

Other Required Information

While we can use several of the figures from Part A to calculate Net Income For Tax Purposes, two other items must be calculated before we can complete this figure.

Taxable Capital Gain And Dividends - Employer's Shares

The tax consequences related to buying, holding, and selling her employer's shares are as follows:

Proceeds Of Disposition [(5,000)($14.75)]	$73,750
Adjusted Cost Base [(5,000)($12.00)]	(60,000)
Capital Gain	$13,750
Inclusion Rate	1/2
Taxable Capital Gain	$ 6,875

Eligible Dividends [(5,000)($0.60)]	$3,000

Child Care Costs

Kerri's deductible child care costs are the least of three amounts:

Actual Costs   The actual costs were given as $8,600.

Annual Limit The annual limit is $13,000 ($8,000 for Barry and $5,000 for Kim).

Income Limit For this purpose, Ms. Sosteric's "earned income" is her gross employment income of $60,800 ($53,000 + $7,800). Two-thirds of this amount is $40,533.

The least of these figures is the actual costs of $8,600.

As Ms. Sosteric has no deductions applicable to the determination of Taxable Income, her Taxable Income is equal to her Net Income For Tax Purposes which is as follow:

Net Employment Income (Part A)	$57,777
Net Rental Income (Part A)	Nil
RRSP Deduction (Part A)	(12,734)
Spousal Support Received	6,000
Taxable Capital Gains	6,875
Eligible Dividends [(5,000)($0.60)]	3,000
Gross Up [(38%)($3,000)]	1,140
Child Care Costs	(8,600)
Net Income For Tax Purposes And Taxable Income	$53,458

Part B - Tax Payable

The required calculations for her Tax Payable are as follows:

Tax On First $45,916		$6,887
Tax On Next $7,542 ($53,458 - $45,916) At 20.5 Percent		1,546
Tax Before Credits		$8,433
Tax Credits:		
Basic Personal Amount	($11,635)	
Eligible Dependant - Either Child	(11,635)	
EI Premiums	(836)	
CPP Contributions	(2,564)	
Canada Employment	(1,178)	
Medical Expenses (Note 3)	(1,016)	
Total Credit Base	($28,864)	
Rate	15%	(4,330)
Dividend Tax Credit [(6/11)($1,140)]		(622)
Federal Tax Payable		$3,481

Note 3   The base for Ms. Sosteric's medical expense tax credit would be calculated as follows:

Eligible Expenses	$2,620
Reduced By The Lesser Of:	
• [(3%)($53,458)] = $1,604	
• 2017 Threshold Amount = $2,268	(1,604)
Base For Credit	$1,016

Self Study Solution Ten - 10

Part A - Spousal RRSP Contribution

As noted in the problem, we are to assume that Ahmed's 2016 Earned Income is equal to his 2017 Earned Income. In order to calculate the 2017 Earned Income, we need to calculate both net employment income and net rental income. These are the only components of Mr. Sidi's Earned Income.

Net Employment Income

Even though Ahmed is no longer an employee, he has employment income related to the exercise of his stock option shares. The calculations are as follows:

Exercise Date Value [(5,000)($21)]	$105,000
Option Price [(5,000)($15)]	(75,000)
Employment Income Inclusion	$ 30,000

There will be a deduction in the determination of Taxable Income equal to one-half of this inclusion or $15,000.

Net Rental Income

The required calculations here are as follows:

Revenues ($34,000 + $42,000 + $26,000)	$102,000
Recapture On Property A (Note 1)	138,000
Expenses Other Than CCA	
($29,000 + $37,000 + $23,000)	(89,000)
CCA (Note 1)	(38,240)
Net Rental Income	$112,760

Note 1 CCA on the rental properties would be calculated as follows:

	Property A	Property B	Property C
UCC On January 1	$422,000	$571,000	$385,000
Dispositions - Capital Cost	(560,000)	N/A	N/A
Subtotal	($138,000)	$571,000	$385,000
Recapture	138,000	N/A	N/A
Balance Subject To CCA	Nil	$571,000	$385,000
Rate	N/A	4%	4%
CCA	Nil	$ 22,840	$ 15,400

The total 2017 CCA would be $38,240 ($22,840 + $15,400).

RRSP Deduction

Since we are assuming that Ahmed's 2016 Earned Income is equal to his 2017 Earned Income, the required figure is calculated as follows:

Employment Income	$ 30,000
Net Rental Income	112,760
2016 Earned Income (Assumed To Be Equal To 2017)	$142,760

The maximum deductible spousal RRSP contribution for 2017 would be the lesser of $25,697 [(18%)($142,760)] and the 2017 RRSP Dollar Limit of $26,010. Using the lesser figure, the maximum deductible contribution would be $25,697.

Part B - Net Income For Tax Purposes

While the employment income and rental income figures from Part A are components of Net Income For Tax Purposes, other figures are needed to complete this Part B calculation.

Taxable Capital Gains

There will be a taxable capital gain on the sale of the shares, calculated as follows:

Proceeds Of Disposition [(5,000)($23)]	$115,000
Adjusted Cost Base [(5,000)($21)]	(105,000)
Capital Gain	$ 10,000
Inclusion Rate	1/2
Taxable Capital Gain	$ 5,000

In addition, there will be a capital gain on the sale of Property A, calculated as follows:

	Land	Building
Proceeds Of Disposition	$340,000	$620,000
Adjusted Cost Base/Capital Cost	(100,000)	(560,000)
Capital Gain	$240,000	$ 60,000

The total capital gain is $300,000 ($240,000 + $60,000). However, as the total proceeds were not collected in the year of sale, he can reduce his income inclusion through the use of a reserve.

Total Capital Gain ($240,000 + $60,000)	$300,000
Reserve - Lesser Of:	
• [($300,000)($864,000 ÷ $960,000)] = $270,000	
• [($300,000)(20%)(4 - 0)] = $240,000	(240,000)
Capital Gain	$ 60,000
Inclusion Rate	1/2
Taxable Capital Gain For 2017	$ 30,000

Minimum RRIF Withdrawal

A registrant can irrevocably elect to base the minimum RRIF withdrawal calculation on the age of his spouse rather than his own age. If the spouse is younger, this will minimize the required withdrawal. Adrianna is aged 66, which is 5 years younger than Ahmed.

For individuals under the age of 71, the minimum RRIF withdrawal is calculated by dividing the fair market value of the assets in the plan at the beginning of the year by the number 90, less the registrant's age, or the spouse's age if elected.

The minimum RRIF withdrawal would be $52,083 [$1,250,000 ÷ (90 - 66)].

Pension Income Splitting

The election to split CPP benefits is provided for in the Canada Pension Plan regulations and results in an actual split of the payments. The ITA 60.03 legislation allows certain other types of pension income to be split. Both payments of RPPs and withdrawals from RRIFs qualify for this split which is implemented solely on the tax returns. The total qualifying pension income for Ahmed is $138,083 ($86,000 + $52,083), one-half of which is $69,042.

Net Income For Tax Purposes

Based on the preceding calculations and the Other Information provided in the problem, Ahmed's minimum Net Income For Tax Purposes can be calculated as follows:

Employment Income - Part A	$ 30,000
Net Rental Income - Part A	112,760
Spousal RRSP Deduction - Part A	(25,697)
RPP Receipts (Pension Split)	86,000
CPP Receipts After Election To Split With Wife	5,500
Taxable Capital Gain - Option Shares	5,000
Taxable Capital Gain - Rental Property	30,000
Minimum RRIF Withdrawal (Pension Split)	52,083
Interest From Canadian Sources	18,000
Eligible Dividends Received	2,200
Gross Up [(38%)($2,200)]	836
Foreign Source Interest (100 Percent)	3,000
Net Income For Tax Purposes Before Pension Split	$319,682
Income Allocated To Wife [(1/2)($86,000 + $52,083)]	(69,042)
Net Income For Tax Purposes	$250,640

Part B - Taxable Income

Ahmed's Taxable Income would be calculated as follows:

Net Income For Tax Purposes	$250,640
Stock Option Deduction - Part A	(15,000)
Taxable Income	$235,640

Part B - Tax Payable

As the problem requires the minimum Tax Payable, Ahmed has claimed the credits for his son, the medical expenses and charitable donations. These could have been claimed by Adrianna. The required calculations are as follows:

Tax On First $202,800		$46,966
Tax On Next $32,840 ($235,640 - $202,800) At 33 Percent		10,837
Tax Before Credits		$57,803
Tax Credits:		
Basic Personal Amount	($11,635)	
Spousal (Note 2)	Nil	
Age (Net Income Too High)	Nil	
Canada Caregiver - Son	(6,883)	
Canada Employment (Stock Option Benefit)	(1,178)	
Pension Income	(2,000)	
Transfer Of Disability From Son	(8,113)	
Medical Expenses (Note 3)	(13,132)	
Total Credit Base	($42,941)	
Rate	15%	(6,441)
Charitable Donations (Note 4)		(1,284)
Dividend Tax Credit On Eligible Dividends [(6/11)($836)]		(456)
Foreign Tax Credit (Amount Withheld)		(300)
Federal Tax Payable		$49,322

Note 2   While Adrianna has only $7,000 of OAS and the $5,500 in CPP benefits in her name, the added amounts resulting from the pension income splitting of more than $69,000 will be more than enough to eliminate the spousal tax credit. This additional income will use up all of her other tax credits (age and pension), preventing any transfers to Ahmed.

Note 3   The base for the medical expense tax credit is calculated as follows:

Ahmed And Adrianna ($2,500 + $3,100)		$5,600
Lesser Of:		
• [(3%)($250,640)] = $7,519		
• 2017 Threshold Amount = $2,268		(2,268)
Subtotal		$ 3,332
Son's Medical Expenses	$9,800	
Reduced By The Lesser Of:		
• $2,268		
• [(3%)(Nil)] = Nil	Nil	9,800
Allowable Amount Of Medical Expenses		$13,132

Note 4   Ahmed's charitable donations tax credit would be calculated as follows:

15 Percent Of $200		$ 30
33 Percent Of The Lesser Of:		
($4,000 - $200) = $3,800		
($235,640 - $202,800) = $32,840		1,254
Total Credit		$1,284

Part C - Pension Income Splitting

Given Ahmed's high Taxable Income, even after pension splitting, more than $32,000 is being taxed at the maximum 33 percent federal rate. Despite splitting the maximum amount of pension income, none of Adrianna's income is taxed at higher than 20.5 percent federally.

As a result, maximum pension income splitting appears to be advantageous if only federal tax rates are considered.

What should also be considered is the effect of the pension income splitting on the OAS clawback for Adrianna and the effect of provincial income taxes on both Ahmed and Adrianna. The effect of the OAS clawback and provincial taxes could make it more advantageous to reduce the amount of income splitting so that Adrianna's Net Income For Tax Purposes is below the OAS clawback income threshold.

While the ability to claim more medical expenses could be a factor in some pension income splitting analyses, it would have very little influence in this case given the high levels of Net Income involved.

Chapter 10 Learning Objectives

After completing Chapter 10, you should be able to:

1. Explain the general procedures used to provide tax deferral on retirement saving (paragraph [P hereafter] 10-1 to 10-16).
2. Describe the difference between a defined benefit pension plan and a defined contribution (a.k.a. money purchase) pension plan (P 10-17 to 10-19).
3. Describe the basic operation of RRSPs (P 10-20 to 10-37).
4. Understand the terms: RRSP Deduction Limit, Unused RRSP Deduction Room and RRSP Dollar Limit (P 10-38 to 10-45).
5. Calculate Earned Income for RRSP purposes (P 10-46 to 10-48).

6. Explain the concepts underlying Pension Adjustments (PAs) (P 10-49 to 10-60).
7. Explain the concepts underlying Past Service Pension Adjustments (PSPAs) (P 10-61 to 10-66).
8. Explain the concepts underlying Pension Adjustment Reversals (PARs) (P 10-67 to 10-71).
9. Calculate an individual's maximum RRSP deduction and Unused RRSP Deduction Room (P 10-72).
10. Apply the tax treatment for undeducted RRSP contributions (P 10-73 and 10-74).

11. Determine whether an individual has made "excess" contributions to an RRSP and identify associated tax planning issues including the use of TFSAs (P 10-75 to 10-82).
12. Recall the tax treatment of RRSP and RRIF administration fees (P 10-83).
13. Apply the provisions relating to RRSP withdrawals and voluntary conversions of RRSPs (P 10-84 to 10-91).
14. Apply the provisions relating to RRSP terminations due to the age limitation (P 10-92 to 10-93).
15. Apply the provisions associated with spousal RRSPs and identify associated tax planning issues (P 10-94 to 10-102).

16. Describe and apply the provisions of the Home Buyers' Plan (P 10-103 to 10-113).
17. Describe and apply the provisions of the Lifelong Learning Plan (P 10-114 to 10-122).
18. Apply the RRSP provisions relating to departure from Canada and death of the registrant (P 10-123 to 10-138).
19. Explain the general provisions associated with Registered Pension Plans (RPPs) (P 10-139 to 10-157).
20. Describe, in general terms, Pooled Registered Pension Plans (PRPPs) and Target Benefit Plans (P 10-158 to 10-161).

21. Describe how an expanded CPP program could help the retirement savings problem (P 10-162 to 10-167).
22. Describe the basic operation of RRIFs and the role that RRIFs play in tax planning for retirement (P 10-168 to 10-186).
23. Explain the general rules for Deferred Profit Sharing Plans (P 10-187 to 10-192).
24. Describe, in general terms, Profit Sharing Plans (P 10-193 to 10-196).
25. Describe the tax free transfers that can be made between various types of plans (P 10-197 and 10-198).

26. Apply the special rules associated with RRSP contributions and retiring allowances (P 10-199 and 10-200).
27. Explain the general provisions related to Retirement Compensation Arrangements (P 10-201 to 10-210).
28. Describe Salary Deferral Arrangements (P 10-211 to 10-218).

CHAPTER 11

How To Work Through Chapter 11

We recommend the following approach in dealing with the material in this Chapter:

Taxable Income Introduction And Overview
- Read paragraph 11-1 to 11-7 (in the textbook).

Lump-Sum Payments
- Read paragraph 11-8 to 11-13.

Loss Carry Over Provisions, Listed Personal Property Losses
- Read paragraph 11-14 to 11-35.
- Do Exercise Eleven-1 (in the textbook) and check the solution in this Study Guide.

Non-Capital Losses
- Read paragraph 11-36 to 11-38.
- Do Exercise Eleven-2 and check the solution in this Study Guide.
- Read paragraph 11-39 to 11-40.

Net Capital Losses (Including Special Rules At Death)
- Read paragraph 11-41 to 11-49.
- Do Exercise Eleven-3 and check the solution in this Study Guide.
- Read paragraph 11-50 to 11-54.
- Do Exercise Eleven-4 and check the solution in this Study Guide.

Allowable Business Investment Losses (ABILs)
- Read paragraph 11-55 to 11-62.
- Do Exercise Eleven-5 and check the solution in this Study Guide.
- Do Self Study Problem Eleven-1 which is available on the Companion Website and check the solution in this Study Guide.

Farm Losses
- Read paragraph 11-63 to 11-67.
- Do Exercise Eleven-6 and check the solution in this Study Guide.
- Do Self Study Problem Eleven-2 and check the solution in this Study Guide.

Lifetime Capital Gains Deduction
- Read paragraph 11-68 to 11-85.
- Do Exercise Eleven-7 and check the solution in this Study Guide.
- Read paragraph 11-86 to 11-93.
- Do Exercise Eleven-8 and check the solution in this Study Guide.
- Do Self Study Problem Eleven-3 and check the solution in this Study Guide.

Ordering Of Deductions And Losses

- Read paragraph 11-94 to 11-103.
- Do Exercise Eleven-9 and check the solution in this Study Guide.

Tax Payable Overview And Tax On Split Income (Kiddie Tax)

- Read paragraph 11-104 to 11-120.
- Do Exercise Eleven-10 and check the solution in this Study Guide.

Transfer Of Dividends To A Spouse Or Common-Law Partner

- Read paragraph 11-121.
- Do Exercise Eleven-11 and check the solution in this Study Guide.
- Do Self Study Problems Eleven-4 and Eleven-5 and check the solutions in this Study Guide.

Charitable Donations Credit - Gifts Of Capital Property

- Read paragraph 11-122 to 11-139.
- Do Exercise Eleven-12 and check the solution in this Study Guide.
- Read paragraph 11-140 to 11-142.
- Do Exercise Eleven-13 and check the solution in this Study Guide.
- Read paragraph 11-143 to 11-147.

Foreign Tax Credits Revisited

- Read paragraph 11-148 to 11-159.
- Do Exercise Eleven-14 and check the solution in this Study Guide.

Alternative Minimum Tax (AMT)

- Read paragraph 11-160 to 11-173.
- Do Exercise Eleven-15 and check the solution in this Study Guide.

Comprehensive Tax Payable And Sample Personal Tax Return For Chapter 11

- Read paragraph 11-174.
- Do Self Study Problems Eleven-6 to Eleven-10 and check the solutions in this Study Guide.
- Read the Sample Personal Tax Return For Chapter 11 found in this Chapter of this Study Guide. The complete tax returns are available on the Companion Website in two formats, a T1 ProFile return file and a .PDF file.

Tax Software Self Study Problem

- Do Tax Software Self Study Problem - Chapter 11 using the ProFile T1 Software. The Self Study Case is found in this Chapter of this Study Guide. The complete tax return is available on the Companion Website.

To Complete This Chapter

- If you would like more practice in problem solving, do the Supplementary Self Study Problems for the chapter. These are available on the Companion Website.
- Review the Key Terms Used In This Chapter in the textbook at the end of Chapter 11. Consult the Glossary for the meaning of any key terms you do not know.
- Test yourself with the Chapter 11 Glossary Flashcards on the Companion Website.
- Ensure you have achieved the Chapter 11 Learning Objectives listed in this Study Guide.
- As a review, we recommend you view the PowerPoint presentation for Chapter 11 that is on the Companion Website.

Practice Examination

- Write the Practice Examination for Chapter 11 that is on the Companion Website. Mark your examination using the Practice Examination Solution that is also on the Companion Website.

Sample Personal Tax Return For Chapter 11

The following example contains a T1 individual income tax returns completed using the ProFile T1 Personal Income Tax Program for 2016 tax returns from Intuit Canada. As software for 2017 is not yet available, this example contains 2016 rates and credits.

The updated 2017 filing version of the ProFile software will be available in January, 2018. Non-filing versions will be available prior to that date, but include a number of 2017 draft forms that have not yet been updated. On installation, the program defaults to check for updates, so non-filing versions may be installed automatically. In January, 2018, after the first 2017 filing version is released, the updated 2017 version of this sample return will be available on the Companion website at:

www.pearsoncanada.ca/byrdchen/ctp2018

For comparison purposes, you might find it useful to review the Chapter 4 version of this example. The Chapter 4 version also contains more information on how to view the files.

In the following example, the relevant T1 schedule or ProFile form name is provided in square brackets to make it easier for users to find where the information is input.

Sample Problem Data

DISCLAIMER: All characters appearing in this example are fictitious. Any resemblance to real persons, living or dead, is purely coincidental.

George Pilot (SIN 527-000-145) is a married, semi-retired air force pilot living in Banff, Alberta. His wife, Deborah (SIN 130-692-544) was mauled by a grizzly bear while hiking 3 years ago. The attack left her blind and limited her mobility.

They have been your clients for many years. George was born on February 24, 1965 and Deborah was born on April 10, 1969. They are both Canadian citizens.

After some discussion with George and Deborah, you confirm that they have never owned any foreign property. They both authorize the CRA to provide information to Elections Canada and authorize you to e-file their returns. They are currently living at 69 BBB Street in Banff, Alberta T9Z 0C0. Their home phone number is (403) 111-1111.

George and Deborah have three children:

- Bryan (SIN 527-000-947) was born on March 12, 2009 and had no income during the year.

- Janice (SIN 527-000-269) was born on June 6, 2003 and is in high school. She had income from babysitting totalling $400 during 2016.

- Willa (SIN 527-000-228) was born on January 22, 1997 and is attending university in Edmonton. Willa had Net Income of $3,300 during 2016.

George loves flying and was hired in February to fly fire bombers June 1 to September 30 for the provincial forest service fire control squad located in Banff.

George informs you that on February 12, 2016, he received $2 million from his mother's estate. Using some of these funds, George bought a house in Banff. The remainder of the funds were invested with his stockbroker, $$$$ Inc.

Deborah, a voice teacher, adapted to her blindness quickly and required no outside help to take care of the family last year or for the first eight months of 2016. She decided to move temporarily to Edmonton with Willa to attend the music program at the University of Alberta.

Deborah received Universal Child Care Benefits of $720 during the year. [RC62 on George's return in Part A. Will also be on Deborah's RC62 in Part B.]

During 2016, Deborah made a $50,000 loan to her brother, Andrew, who used the funds to expand his business. On December 15, 2016, Andrew paid her interest of $1,500 and principal of $5,000. Also during 2016, Deborah gave private voice lessons and earned a total of $3,200 in teaching fees. [S2 for Deborah's income in Part A. In Part B, Deborah's income is on S4 and T2125.]

George brings you the following receipts and documents:

1. A T4, T4A and a T5 (included in this example). A statement from his bank stating that he paid $7,382 in interest on the mortgage on his house during 2016. (See Items 18 and 24.)

2. A T2202A "Tuition And Education Amounts Certificate" for himself from Athabasca University. It showed he was a part time student for 6 months and paid $591 in tuition for 2016. [T2202]

3. Two charitable donation receipts. One in George's name for $1,000 from the Canadian Wildlife Federation dated April 10, 2016. He has donated regularly to this registered charity. A second receipt in Deborah's name for $100 from the Canadian National Institute for the Blind (CNIB) dated December 3, 2016. This is her second donation to this registered charity. [Donations]

4. A statement from the Banff Dental Clinic that George paid a total of $1,650 during 2016. This consisted of $850 for himself on November 24, and $200 each for Deborah, Bryan, Willa and Janice on December 15. [Medical]

5. An invoice from the CNIB in Deborah's name for $375 dated December 26, 2016 for computer peripherals designed exclusively for a person who is blind to use a computer. She had obtained a prescription from her doctor specifying her need for this equipment. [Medical]

6. Twelve monthly bus passes that were purchased during 2016 by Janice for $30 per month. [OtherCredits]

7. An agreement of purchase and sale for a house at 69 BBB St. in Banff. The purchase price was $800,000 and the invoice for legal fees totalled $1,200. The deal closed March 31, 2016 and George paid the purchase price of the house in cash. George and his family had been living in a rented townhouse for the last 5 years. Prior to that George had owned a house, but it went to his ex-wife in the divorce settlement. Deborah has never owned a principal residence. [OtherCredits for the Home Buyers' Credit.]

8. George spent $14,700 during 2016 on various permanent modifications to the house. His goal for these changes was to allow Deborah to be more mobile inside and outside the house (ex., outside ramps and railings in the halls and stairways) and to reduce the risk of harm to her (a walk-in bathtub). George has detailed invoices for the renovations. Since Deborah's mobility impairment is not severe, these expenditures do not qualify as allowable medical expenses. [Schedule 12]

9. An instalment statement for 2016 that showed that George had paid the CRA instalments of $1,500 on September 14 and December 14 ($3,000 in total). These were the instalments requested by the CRA for the year due to his self-employed income in the previous year. [OtherCredits]

10. A T2202A "Tuition And Education Amounts Certificate" for Deborah from the University of Alberta. It showed she was a full time student for 4 months and paid $2,600 in tuition for 2016. [S2 in Part A, Deborah's T2202 in Part B.]

11. A T2202A "Tuition And Education Amounts Certificate" for Willa from the University of Alberta. It showed she was a full time student for 8 months and paid $5,200 in tuition for 2016. She had signed the certificate authorizing the transfer of her education related amounts to her father. [Dependant]

12. His 2015 Notice of Assessment that shows that his 2016 RRSP Deduction Limit is $13,979. He has no undeducted RRSP contributions from previous years. [RRSP]

13. A contribution receipt to a spousal RRSP (George contributed to Deborah's RRSP) for $2,000 from $$$$ Inc. dated February 20, 2017. [RRSP]

14. A receipt for $2,000 from George's 40 year old sister, Shirley Burns (SIN 527-000-582) for child care. She took care of Bryan after school during 2016 while Deborah was in Edmonton. [Input on Dependants, flows to T778]

15. A receipt for Janice, an accomplished trombone player, from the Peak Music Camp in Whistler, B.C. The receipt for $1,600 was for two weeks of intensive music instruction at the camp. This fee also included $400 in accommodations and $325 for meals. [Input on Dependants, flows to T778]

16. A receipt for $2,148 from the Mountain Moving Company dated April 1, 2016. The invoice showed that the fee was charged to pack and move George's household effects from 123 CCC Avenue, Calgary to his new house in Banff, a total of 125 kilometers. George's new home is 5 kilometers from the Alberta Fire And Brimstone Control offices. George and his family made the move in his truck. Since George has no travel receipts, he agrees that you should use the simplified method to calculate his moving costs. [T1M]

17. In July, 2016, George asked you how much he could contribute to TFSAs for himself, and Deborah. By accessing their accounts through the CRA's online Represent A Client service, you informed him that he could contribute $25,000 for both himself and Deborah. George brings in TFSA Statements for himself and Deborah that shows he made the maximum contribution to each TFSA on October 20, 2016. It also shows that Deborah withdrew $3,000 from her TFSA on December 15, 2016.

18. George's new stockbroker, Mr. Ace Securities at $$$$ Inc., convinces him to take out a mortgage on his new home in order to invest the funds in various stocks. George assumes a $500,000 mortgage as of June 1, 2016. On that date, the funds from his mortgage are transferred to $$$$ Inc. into a trading (i.e., non-registered) account. The $7,382 mortgage interest on the bank statement relates to this mortgage. The stockbroker assures George that the funds will remain fully invested in the trading account. [S4]

19. George's transaction summary statement from $$$$ Inc. for 2016 lists the details of 33 sales of stock in George's trading account. The net result, after commissions, is a capital gain of $4,072. [S3Details]

20. On January 8, 2016, George sold his 1971 Ford Mustang for $50,000. The car was driven only on sunny Sunday afternoons. Its original price in 2000 was $6,000, and George reconditioned it over the years at a cost of $12,000. [S3Details]

21. At the beginning of 2016, George has a net capital loss carry forward of $2,580 [(1/2)($5,160)] from 2014. [LossNetCap]

22. During 2016, he paid $6,000 in spousal support to his ex-wife, Marilyn (SIN 527-000-103), pursuant to a written agreement. [Support payments]

23. George owns a commercial property at 999 JJJ Avenue, Edmonton, Alberta T9Z 0C0. The property was 10 years old when he purchased it on February 15, 2014 for $600,000 of which $160,000 was allocated to the land. Shortly after George purchased the building, the major tenant went bankrupt and he had rental losses for 2014 and 2015. No capital additions were made since the building's acquisition. The financial information for the property, for the year ended December 31, 2016, is as follows [Rental]:

Rental income	$46,700
Mortgage interest	$19,500
Maintenance and repairs	5,100
Management and administration fees	8,200
Legal fees	1,000
Property taxes	11,750
Total expenses	$45,550
Net Income before amortization	$ 1,150

24. In Calgary in prior years, George gave the occasional private flying lesson and found it very rewarding. After moving to Banff, he began to pursue private pilot training in earnest beginning April 1 through his business, Pilot's Flying School. A portion of his new house is used exclusively for various training activities such as one-to-one ground instruction. He also writes and reviews practice pilot exams. George's fiscal year end for the business is December 31.

   The business area of the house occupies 420 square feet of the 2,100 square foot house. George does not intend to claim any CCA on the house. At your request, he provides the following costs related to the house during the period April 1, 2016 through December 31, 2016 [T2125]:

Utilities	$1,500
Repairs And Maintenance	4,325
Home Insurance	700
Mortgage Interest	7,382
Property Taxes	2,600

25. On April 15, 2016, George purchased a laptop computer and various software that will be used solely for his business activities. The laptop cost $1,900 and the software costs totalled $800. Prior to this, George had not been using a computer for business purposes. [T2125]

26. George provides the following other information for Pilot's Flying School, for the fiscal period ended December 31, 2016:

Lesson and training fees received	$40,200
Plane rental fees	9,600
Business meals with clients	3,250
Licenses and fees	1,650
Office expenses	550
Accounting fees	300

Notes To The Chapter 11 Return - No Pension Splitting
Only George Is Filing A Return

General Notes

- You must open Deborah's return (F5) to claim her disability tax credit on the info page even if she is not filing. If you do not, Deborah's disability tax credit cannot be transferred to George.

- When the Universal Child Care Benefits are input on George's Form RC62, the amounts will be transferred to show on S2 as Deborah's income.

- Inheritances are not taxable.

- Willa's education related credits total more than $5,000. As a result, her transfer to George is limited to the $5,000 maximum. Only Willa can claim the unused credits in the future. Willa should file a return in order to receive the GST credit and to help her keep track of her education related credits carry forward.

- Since Willa is over 17 years of age, her medical expenses are reduced by 3 percent of her Net Income For Tax Purposes.

- George is not eligible for the refundable medical expense supplement or the working income benefit as his income is too high. Given 3 percent of his Net Income is greater than the medical expense threshold, the only allowable medical expenses are those of Willa. In the ProFile tax file there is a memo attached to the line "Total medical expenses - line 330" (green highlight) that says "Net Income too high, do not claim medical expenses except for Willa so carry forward is optimized". Since they were paid in November and December, they could be claimed in the following year if the 12 month limit is used.

- Deborah has UCCB income of $720, interest income of $1,500 and professional fees of $3,200. As a result, the spousal credit base is decreased by this amount on Schedule 2. Note that the principal repayment of $5,000 is not income. Deborah's disability credit has been transferred to George, as well as all of her education related tax credits since they total less than $5,000.

Item Specific Notes

- (Item 3) Since George has donated regularly to a charity and Deborah has previously donated to the CNIB, he will not be eligible for the first-time donor's super credit on Schedule 9. For couples, the CRA's administrative practices permit either spouse to claim some or all of the donations made by the couple. George should claim both donations as combining them is advantageous given the 15 percent rate on the first $200 of donations.

- (Item 5) Both ITA 118.2 and Income Tax Folio S1-F1-C1 clearly state that medical expenses can only be deducted by the individual who paid for them. However, in the T1 Guide, this rule is contradicted for couples. According to this Guide, either spouse can claim the medical expense credit, without regard to who actually paid for the expenses. This administrative position is used in practice. As a result, Deborah's invoice for computer peripherals is added to the medical expenses carried forward.

- (Item 7) The Home Buyers' Tax Credit of $750 [(15%)($5,000)] is available since George had been living in a rented town house for five years and neither he nor Deborah had another principal residence.

- (Item 8) George's receipts for the expenses eligible for the Home Accessibility Credit total more than the $10,000 maximum for the year. As a result, the maximum credit of $1,500 [(15%)($10,000)] is available.

- (Items 14 and 15) Since Deborah was in full time attendance at the University of Alberta, George could have deducted child care costs of up to $4,000 [(2)($125)(16 weeks)]. The $2,000 paid to Shirley Burns is totally deductible. The deduction for child care costs is limited to $125 per week for overnight camp fees. This results in maximum deductible child care costs of $2,250.

- (Item 16) Form T1M, Claim For Moving Expenses should be filled out to calculate the deductible moving expenses. George cannot deduct the legal fees related to the purchase of his new home because he had been living in a rented townhouse in Calgary. On Form T1M, since the "Simplified Method" box is checked, the program calculates the allowable deduction for milage using the 2016 Alberta rate on Line 2.

- (Item 18) The house was purchased for cash and the mortgage was obtained for investment purposes only. As a result, all of the interest is deductible on Schedule 4. In order that all of the interest remains deductible in the future, George should ensure that the $500,000 from the mortgage remain invested and is not used for personal purposes.

- (Item 19) As long as the transaction summary from the bank is available if requested by the CRA, it is not necessary to list separately each stock sale. Only the net capital gain needs to be input on S3Details.

- (Item 21) George has claimed his net capital loss carry forward of $2,580 as his total taxable capital gains were well in excess of this amount.

- (Item 23) Since the rental property has been showing a loss since its acquisition, no CCA could have been taken prior to 2016. As a result, the beginning of the year UCC of the building will be George's original allocation of $440,000 ($600,000 - $160,000 land cost). The CCA for 2016 is limited to $1,150, the amount that reduces his rental income to nil.

T2125 (Items 24 to 26)

- The Industry Code must be chosen from the list near the top right corner of the T2125. The appropriate choice is 611690, "All Other Schools And Instruction".

- The mortgage interest is not included in the workspace in the home costs. The house was purchased for cash and the mortgage was obtained for investment purposes only and is not a cost of maintaining the house. As a result, all of the interest is deductible on Schedule 4. (See Item 18)

- The non-deductible portion of business meals of $1,625 (50% of $3,250) has been excluded.

- The laptop computer has been allocated to CCA Class 50 (55 percent). The software has been allocated to CCA Class 12 (100 percent). Because of the short fiscal year, the CCA has been prorated beginning April 1, the start of the business, not the date of the purchase of the assets.

Tax Planning Points

- If he has sufficient funds, George should contribute the maximum deductible for 2017 of $16,810 [see RRSPLimit form] to a spousal RRSP as soon as possible. Since George is already getting a pension and Deborah appears to have little income, a spousal RRSP would offer more opportunity for future income splitting. Although the pension income splitting legislation allows for some flexibility, the maximum split is 50 percent. With a spousal RRSP, Deborah can be taxed on 100 percent of the funds from her RRSP.

- George should consider opening RESPs for Bryan and Janice if he has not already done so. How much he should contribute will depend on many factors (see the text), but it is probably advisable that he contribute enough to take advantage of the Canada Education Savings Plan each year if he has sufficient funds.

- Deborah has created some RRSP contribution room with her professional income. George should consider whether Deborah should contribute to her own RRSP. Funds for George's RRSP and the RESPs should probably have priority given George's higher tax bracket and the Canada Education Savings Plan, though with his inheritance there should be sufficient funds to contribute to all the plans.

- Since TFSA contributions are not deductible and withdrawals are not taxable, the TFSAs will not have an effect on any of the tax returns. George should try to contribute the maximum to both his and Deborah's TFSA on an ongoing basis if he has sufficient funds. He should replace Deborah's withdrawal as soon as possible as it was withdrawn in the preceding calendar year. As long as there are other funds available where related income would be taxable, it would be advisable not to make withdrawals from the TFSAs in order to take advantage of the tax free earnings.

- George should consider a TFSA for Willa. If her income is earned income for RRSP purposes, he should also consider contributing to an RRSP in Willa's name.

Notes To The Chapter 11 Returns - With Pension Splitting
Both Are Filing Returns With Pension Income Splitting

The notes to the return with no pension income splitting are also relevant in this scenario.

In creating Deborah's tax return, the following forms and schedules were filled in:

- T2202 - Tuition slips
- T2125 - Statement of Business or Professional Activities
- T1032 - Joint Election To Split Income (originated from George's return)
- Schedule 4 - Statement of Investment Income

Neither Deborah nor George should claim the medical expenses, other than George claiming the medical expenses for Willa. Although 3 percent of Deborah's Net Income is less than the threshold, which would enable her to make a claim where George cannot, the tuition fee credit is calculated before consideration of medical expenses, so the claim for medical expenses has no effect on her Tax Payable and does not save her any taxes.

To test this, click Yes that Deborah should claim the medical expenses. What you will find is that her total non-refundable tax credits are greater than her tax payable because her tuition tax credit does not change. This means that the medical expense credit is wasted. Since they were paid in November and December, they could be claimed in the following year if the 12 month limit is used. On the medical expenses list subtotal in both returns is a memo not to claim any of the listed medical expenses, but to carry them forward in case they make a difference in the following year.

Willa's medical expenses could have been claimed by Deborah, but since it will make no difference to her federal tax payable, it is more advantageous to have George claim Willa's medical expenses.

In addition, although we do not cover provincial tax rules in the text, if you examine Deborah's Alberta tax credits [AB428], you will see that she does not utilize all of her non-refundable Alberta tax credits, even if she does not claim any medical expenses. Claiming Willa's medical credit will decrease George's Alberta and federal tax payable.

Since the couple has elected to split the pension income, the withholdings on the pension income must also be split.

The tax savings can be calculated by comparing the Tax Summary for the couple with and without pension income splitting.

Combined Balance Owing - No Pension Splitting	$4,804
Combined Balance Owing - With Pension Splitting	(2,682)
Tax Savings	$2,122

Note the effect of the Family Caregiver Amount. In the no pension income splitting case, when George claims the spousal credit for Deborah, he is eligible for the Family Caregiver Amount due to her blindness.

In the pension splitting scenario, Deborah can only claim the basic personal amount for herself and the Family Caregiver Amount is not available to the family unit.

Completed Tax Returns

There are three sample tax returns available on the Companion Website in two versions, a T1 ProFile return file and a .PDF file.

A. A single return assuming George does not elect to pension income split and Deborah does not file a tax return.
B. A coupled return assuming George elects to split his pension income with Deborah and she files a tax return as well.

Tax Software Self Study Problem - Chapter 11

This Problem is an expansion of the Tax Software Self Study Problem - Chapter 4.

Note The following problem contains 2016 (not 2017) information as software for 2017 is not yet available. If you have an updated 2017 version of ProFile installed on your computer, ensure that when you begin, you open a file for 2016, not 2017 as this data is for 2016. Shortly after the first filing version of the 2017 Intuit ProFile software is available in January, 2018, the updated 2017 version of this problem will be available on the textbook web site at:

www.pearsoncanada.ca/byrdchen/ctp2018

DISCLAIMER: All characters appearing in this problem are fictitious. Any resemblance to real persons, living or dead, is purely coincidental.

Ms. Eleanor Victoria's husband died two years ago. After her husband died, she moved from her house in Prince George, B.C., to a rented house in Victoria, B.C.

Ms. Victoria's widowed mother, Marjorie Vancouver lives with Ms. Victoria and takes care of the house, Ms. Victoria's younger daughter, Amy, and all of the household cooking. In addition to OAS benefits, Marjorie has a very small income from her deceased husband's life insurance policy. She has never filed a tax return and she is not infirm.

Diane Victoria, Eleanor's older daughter, is studying psychology at McGill University in Montreal. Her field is addiction research with a special emphasis on gambling. She does volunteer work at a gambling addiction treatment centre in Montreal in the summers. As Eleanor has paid for her tuition and living costs, Diane has agreed that the maximum education related amount should be transferred to her mother.

Diane has decided not to file a tax return this year as she knows she does not owe any taxes. Her income was earned driving for a client of the addiction treatment centre who had lost his licence after being charged with impaired driving.

Late in December, 2016, Eleanor was notified that she had inherited $500,000 from an aunt. Eleanor loves her work and though she plans to travel more, she has no plans to retire.

Information concerning Ms. Victoria for 2016 is given on the following pages.

Required:

A. With the objective of minimizing Ms. Victoria's Tax Payable, prepare the 2016 income tax return of Eleanor Victoria using the ProFile tax software program. List any assumptions you have made, and any notes and tax planning issues you feel should be discussed with Ms. Victoria. Ignore HST implications in your solution by assuming that Ms. Victoria does not qualify for the GST/HST rebate.

B. Calculate the maximum deductible contribution Ms. Victoria can make to her RRSP for the 2017 taxation year. What advice would you give Ms. Victoria concerning the various deferred savings plans available to her given the funds from her inheritance?

Personal Information

Title	Ms.
First Name	Eleanor
Last Name	Victoria
SIN	527-000-087
Date of birth (Y/M/D)	1969-05-15
Marital Status	Widowed
Canadian citizen?	Yes
Provide information to Elections Canada?	Yes
Own foreign property of more than $100,000 Canadian?	No

Taxpayer's Address

111 VVV Street Victoria, B.C. V4H 3W4
Phone number (250) 111-1111

Dependants

Dependants	Child 1	Child 2	Mother
First Name	Diane	Amy	Marjorie
Last Name	Victoria	Victoria	Vancouver
SIN	527-000-293	None	527-000-483
Date of birth (Y/M/D)	1996-05-14	2004-10-11	1944-05-21
Net income	$2,300	$360	$8,000
UCCB received (RC62)	N/A	$360	N/A

T4

T4	Box	Amount
Issuer - 1750 Canada Inc.		
Employment income	14	60,201.80
Employee's CPP contributions	16	2,544.30
Employee's EI premiums	18	955.04
RPP contributions	20	2,406.16
Pension adjustment	52	7,829.00
Income tax deducted	22	6,408.00
Employment commissions	42	0
Union dues	44	748.59
Charitable donations	46	175.00

Eleanor has a signed T2200 from her employer specifying her work requires her to have an office in the home. She meets the conditions required to deduct work space in the home expenses. Of the 1,800 square feet in the house, her office, waiting area and storage space totals 310 square feet.

During 2016 she paid the following:

Rent for the year (No GST charged)	$30,000
Utilities (hydro and gas) for the year	2,500
Cleaning services (No GST charged)	1,200
Insurance for household effects (No GST charged)	400
Car insurance (No GST charged)	700

T2202A - (Diane)	Box	Amount
Tuition fees - for Diane Victoria (daughter)	A	7,000
Number of months in school - part-time	B	2
Number of months in school - full-time	C	8

Eleanor and her family had the following medical expenses, all of which Eleanor paid for:

Patient	(Y/M/D)	Medical Expenses	Description	Am't
Eleanor	2016-08-15	Grace Hospital	Ambulance charge	392
Eleanor	2016-08-18	Paramed Home Health	Nursing care	1,350
Marjorie	2016-05-20	Dr. Zhang (Optometrist)	Contact lenses	110
Marjorie	2016-07-06	Pharmacy	Prescription	75
Diane	2016-09-01	Dr. Glassman	Physiotherapist	100
Amy	2016-05-11	Walk Right Foot Clinic	Orthotics	450
Amy	2016-01-23	Dr. Tamo	Dental Fees	1,120

Because of donations in previous years, neither Diane nor Eleanor qualify for the first-time donor super credit.

Donor	Charitable Donation Receipts	Am't
Eleanor	Heart and Stroke (annual donation)	375
Eleanor	Terry Fox Foundation (annual donation)	50
Diane	Addiction Research Council of Canada (annual donation)	100

T3	Box	Amount
Issuer - Global Strategy Financial		
Foreign country - United States		
Capital gains (Foreign)	21	982.22
Foreign non-business income	25	310.94

T4A	Box	Amount
Issuer - 3601 Canada Inc. (Survivor benefit from husband)		
Pension	16	22,249.44
Income tax deducted	22	3,510.78

T4A(P)	Box	Amount
Survivor benefit	15	4,823.28
Income tax deducted	22	Nil

T5	Box	Slip 1	Slip 2
Issuer		Scotia Bank	Bank of Montreal
Actual amount of eligible dividends	24		1,603.00
Taxable amount of eligible dividends	25		2,212.14
Interest from Canadian sources	13	509.45	

RRSP information	(Y/M/D)	Amount
Issuer of receipt - Scotia Bank	2017-02-10	2,620.00
Earned income for 2015		38,873.00
Pension adjustment for 2015		4,376.00
Unused deduction room at the end of 2015		1,666.00

Child	Child Care Expenses	No. of weeks	Amount
Amy	Croft Computer Camp (14 days overnight)	2	1,000
Amy	Y Day Camp (July)	3	400

Neither of the camps would issue a receipt that qualified for either the child fitness credit or the children's arts credit.

Eleanor did not sell her house in Prince George when she moved to Victoria as it was her intention to move back into it within three years. It has been rented on a month-to-month lease since November, 2015. She claimed a rental loss of $4,250 in 2015.

Real Estate Rental	Amount
Address - 222 PPP Street, Prince George, B.C. V4H 3W4	
Gross rents (12 months for 2016)	15,600.00
Property taxes	2,190.00
Insurance	1,093.27
Interest on mortgage	5,377.58
Payment on principal	3,688.95
Plumbing repairs	290.94
Snow plow annual contract	300.00
Lawyer's fees for new lease	172.54
Hydro (during vacancy)	288.34
Building purchased October 1, 2013 for $168,900 - UCC beginning of year	168,900.00
Washer/dryer purchased May 9, 2015 for $921 - UCC beginning of year	921.00
Stove and refrigerator purchased August 17, 2016	1,500.00

Solutions to Chapter Eleven Exercises

Exercise Eleven - 1 Solution

Mr. Smothers will have a listed personal property loss carry forward from 2016 of $5,500 [(1/2)($89,000 - $100,000)]. This can only be applied against the 2017 taxable gain on listed personal property of $2,000 [(1/2)($5,000 - $1,000)]. Based on this, his Net and Taxable Income would be calculated as follows:

Income Under ITA 3(a)	$62,000
Income Under ITA 3(b) ($2,000 - $2,000)	Nil
Net Income For Tax Purposes And Taxable Income	$62,000

In this case, the listed personal property loss carry forward of $3,500 ($5,500 - $2,000) can only be applied against taxable capital gains on listed personal property.

If the sale had been of shares, Mr. Smothers would have had a regular net capital loss carry forward of $5,500 from 2016. His Net and Taxable Income would be calculated as follows:

Income Under ITA 3(a)	$62,000
Income Under ITA 3(b)	2,000
Net Income For Tax Purposes ($2,000 Higher)	$64,000
Loss Carry Forward (Limited To Taxable Capital Gains)	(2,000)
Taxable Income (Same)	$62,000

In this case, the $3,500 net capital loss carry forward can be applied against any taxable capital gains.

Exercise Eleven - 2 Solution

The required calculation is as follows:

Amount E ($58,000 + $2,200)	$60,200
Amount F ($35,000 + $13,000)	(48,000)
Amount D	(2,200)
Non-Capital Loss	$10,000

Note that this is the excess of the business loss of $58,000, over the $48,000 in positive sources of income for the year. The additional farm loss of $2,200 would be allocated to a separate loss balance. It is included in the E component and then deducted in the D component. Since it is less than $2,500, the farm loss is fully deductible, without regard to whether it is restricted.

Exercise Eleven - 3 Solution

If Laura makes no effort to minimize the net capital loss carry forward, her Net Income For Tax Purposes and Taxable Income would be calculated as follows:

Net Taxable Capital Gain	$40,000
Rental Loss	(30,000)
Net Income For Tax Purposes	$10,000
Net Capital Loss Carry Forward (Taxable Income To Nil)	(10,000)
Taxable Income	Nil

This approach results in a net capital loss carry forward of $5,000, and a non-capital loss carry over of nil.

Alternatively, if she chooses to completely eliminate the net capital loss carry forward, the non-capital loss would be calculated as follows:

Amount E ($30,000 + $15,000)	$45,000
Amount F - Income Under ITA 3(c)	(40,000)
Non-Capital Loss Carry Over	$ 5,000

While Taxable Income remains unchanged at nil, the net capital loss carry forward has been reduced from $5,000 to nil, with the non-capital loss carry forward increased from nil to $5,000.

Exercise Eleven - 4 Solution

The carry forward must be applied on an adjusted basis to eliminate the 2017 taxable capital gain. To implement this, the $7,500 amount (three-quarter basis) must be adjusted to $5,000 (one-half basis). The $2,000 taxable capital gain will use $2,000 of the adjusted 1990 carry forward, leaving $3,000. This amount must be adjusted back to the 3/4 inclusion rate. The resulting $4,500 [(3/2)($3,000)] can be applied against any other type of income in 2017 or, if there is not sufficient other income in that year, against any other type of income in 2016 (amended return). This can be verified using the 100 percent figures, which give the same $4,500 [(3/4)($10,000 - $4,000)] amount.

Exercise Eleven - 5 Solution

The Allowable Business Investment Loss for the year would be calculated as follows:

Actual Loss On Disposition	$50,000
Disallowed By Lifetime Capital Gains Deduction Use	(26,000)
Business Investment Loss	$24,000
Inclusion Rate	1/2
Allowable Business Investment Loss	$12,000

All of the $12,000 can be deducted against Mr. Latvik's employment income. With respect to the disallowed $26,000, it becomes an ordinary capital loss, of which $18,000 can be deducted against the current year's capital gains on the publicly traded securities. This leaves a net capital loss carry over of $4,000 [(1/2)($26,000 - $18,000)].

Exercise Eleven - 6 Solution

It appears that Ms. Bodkin's farming activities are a subordinate source of income. Given this, the deduction of the 2016 loss would be limited to $17,500 [$2,500 + (1/2)($32,500 - $2,500)]. The remaining $18,500 ($36,000 - $17,500) is a restricted farm loss carry forward.

In 2017, $3,500 of this carry forward can be deducted against the 2017 farm income. This leaves a restricted farm loss carry forward of $15,000 ($18,500 - $3,500). Ms. Bodkin's 2017 Net Income For Tax Purposes is $88,500 ($85,000 + $3,500) and her 2017 Taxable Income is $85,000 ($85,000 + $3,500 - $3,500).

Exercise Eleven - 7 Solution

The annual gains limit is **$26,000** ($42,000 - $16,000). This is calculated using the ITA 110.6 formula of A - B where:

The A component of the formula would be equal to **$42,000**, the lesser of:

- $74,000 ($114,000 + $42,000 - $82,000); and
- $42,000.

The B component would be **$16,000**, the sum of:

- $13,000*; and
- $3,000.

    *The amount by which $45,000, exceeds $32,000 ($114,000 - $82,000 + $42,000 - $42,000).

Note that the net taxable capital gain on non-qualified property was $32,000 ($114,000 - $82,000). The mechanics of the B component of the formula are such that the first $32,000 of the $45,000 net capital loss deduction was charged against these gains and did not erode the annual gains limit. Only the remaining $13,000 ($45,000 - $32,000) served to reduce the annual gains limit.

To make maximum use of her lifetime capital gains deduction, it would be advisable for Ms. Slovena to deduct only $32,000 of the net capital loss carry forward. If she did this, the B component would be $3,000 and her annual gains limit would increase to $39,000 [$42,000 - (Nil + $3,000)]. Although she would have used $13,000 ($39,000 - $26,000) more of her lifetime capital gains deduction, her tax liability for 2017 would not change and she would have a net capital loss carry forward of $13,000 ($45,000 - $32,000) that could be applied against any type of capital gain for an unlimited period of time.

Exercise Eleven - 8 Solution

His maximum lifetime capital gains deduction is $223,500, the least of the following:

Available Deduction   His remaining deduction would be $399,858 ($417,858 - $5,000 - $13,000).

Annual Gains Limit   In the absence of capital gains on non-qualified property in any of the years under consideration, the simplified version of this calculation can be used. Given this, this limit would be calculated as follows:

Qualified Gain [(1/2)($510,000)]	$255,000
Net Capital Loss Deducted [(1/2)($63,000)]	(31,500)
Annual Gains Limit	$223,500

Cumulative Gains Limit   In the absence of capital gains on non-qualified property in 2010 and 2012, the annual gains limits for 2010 and 2012 would simply be the amount of the taxable capital gains on shares in a qualified small business corporation in those years.   Given this, the required calculation would be as follows:

Sum Of Annual Gains Limits	
($5,000 + $13,000 + $223,500)	$241,500
Previous Years' Capital Gains Deduction ($5,000 + $13,000)	(18,000)
Cumulative Net Investment Loss	Nil
Cumulative Gains Limit	$223,500

Exercise Eleven - 9 Solution

Alan's Net Income For Tax Purposes would be calculated as follows:

Income Under ITA 3(a):		
Business Income	$12,000	
Employment Income	56,000	
Farming Income	3,500	$71,500
Income Under ITA 3(b):		
Taxable Capital Gains		9,000
Net Income For Tax Purposes		$80,500

Alan's Taxable Income is as follows:

Net Income For Tax Purposes	$80,500
Loss Carry Forwards:	
Restricted Farm Losses (Limited to farming income)	(3,500)
Net Capital Losses (Limited to taxable capital gains)	(9,000)
Non-Capital Losses (All)	(36,000)
Taxable Income	$32,000

Loss Carry Forwards

• Restricted farm loss carry forward ($8,000 - $3,500)	$ 4,500
• Net capital loss carry forward ($20,000 - $9,000)	$11,000
• Non-capital loss carry forward	Nil

Exercise Eleven - 10 Solution

The regular Tax Payable would be calculated as follows:

Income Sources:	
Taxable Non-Eligible Dividends [(117%)($15,000)]	$17,550
Contract Income	12,200
Taxable Eligible Dividends [(138%)($8,600)]	11,868
Deduction For Split Income - Taxable Non-Eligible Dividends	(17,550)
Net Income For Tax Purposes = Taxable Income	$24,068
Rate	15%
Tax Payable Before Credits	$ 3,610
Basic Personal Credit [(15%)($11,635)]	(1,745)
Dividend Tax Credit - Eligible Dividends [(6/11)(38%)($8,600)]	(1,783)
Regular Tax Payable	$ 82

The Tax Payable on split income would be calculated as follows:

Split Income - Taxable Non-Eligible Dividends	$17,550
Rate	33%
Tax Payable Before Dividend Tax Credit	$ 5,792
Dividend Tax Credit [(21/29)(17%)($15,000)]	(1,847)
Tax Payable On Split Income	$ 3,945

The total Tax Payable would be $4,027 ($82 + $3,945).

Exercise Eleven - 11 Solution

Without the transfer, Mr. Ho's wife would have income of $11,730 [(138%)($8,500)] and, as her income is greater than $11,635, he would have no spousal tax credit. With the transfer, he would be eligible for the full $1,745. Given this, the analysis of his position at the federal level is as follows:

Additional Taxes On Dividends [(33%)(138%)($8,500)]	$3,871
Increase In Spousal Tax Credit	(1,745)
Dividend Tax Credit [(6/11)(38%)($8,500)]	(1,762)
Tax Increase (Decrease)	$ 364

As the result of the transfer is a tax increase, the election would not be desirable. With or without the election Mrs. Ho will have no Tax Payable.

Exercise Eleven - 12 Solution

With the gift being made at $85,000, Ms. Felder will have a taxable capital gain of $11,500 [(1/2)($85,000 - $62,000)], plus recapture of $34,000 ($62,000 - $28,000), for a total Net Income For Tax Purposes of $45,500. Given this, her maximum credit base would be calculated as follows:

75% Of Net Income For Tax Purposes [(75%)($45,500)]	$34,125
25% Of Taxable Capital Gain [(25%)($11,500)]	2,875
25% Of Recaptured CCA [(25%)($34,000)]	8,500
Charitable Donations Credit Base Limit (Equals Income From Donation)	$45,500

Note that, because Ms. Felder's Taxable Income is less than $202,800, the 33 percent tax rate is not relevant in calculating the charitable donations tax credit. This base results in a potential credit of $13,167 [(15%)($200) + (29%)($45,500 - $200)]. While this amount could be used, she does not have sufficient Tax Payable to utilize the whole potential credit. Her federal Tax Payable for the year would be calculated as follows:

Tax Before Credits [(15%)($45,500)]	$6,825
Basic Personal Credit	(1,745)
Federal Tax Payable Before Donations Credit	$5,080

In order to reduce her Tax Payable to nil, Ms. Felder should use a sufficient amount of her charitable donations credit base to produce a tax credit of $5,080. To arrive at the credit base that will result in this tax credit, the following equation must be solved for X:

$$\$5,080 = [(15\%)(\$200)] + [(29\%)(X - \$200)]$$
$$\$5,080 - \$30 + \$58 = [(29\%)(X)]$$

Solving this equation for X provides a value of $17,614 which equals the amount of her donation that produces the $5,080 [(15%)($200) + (29%)($17,614 - $200)] credit that will reduce her federal Tax Payable to nil. This leaves a carry forward of $67,386 ($85,000 - $17,614).

Exercise Eleven - 13 Solution

As a donation of publicly traded shares is involved, there will be no recognized capital gain on the sale. This means that Mr. Radeem's Taxable Income for 2017 will consist of his employment income of $90,000. The limit for the base of Mr. Radeem's charitable donations tax credit would be $67,500 [(75%)($90,000)]. If he were to use this amount, his 2017 charitable donations tax credit would be $19,547 [(15%)($200) + (29%)($67,500 - $200)]. Note that, because Mr. Radeem's Taxable Income is less than $202,800, the 33 percent tax rate is not relevant in calculating the charitable donations tax credit.

As it would exceed his Tax Payable after other tax credits, Mr. Radeem will not want to deduct the maximum available charitable donations tax credit. Given this, he needs to determine the amount of the credit that will reduce his Tax Payable to nil. This is determined as follows:

Tax On First $45,916	$6,887
Tax On Next $44,084 ($90,000 - $45,916) At 20.5 Percent	9,037
Tax Before Credits	$15,924
Tax Credits (Given)	(4,000)
Federal Tax Payable Before Donations Credit	$11,924

In order to reduce his Tax Payable to nil, Mr. Radeem should use a sufficient amount of his charitable donations credit base to produce a tax credit of $11,924. To arrive at the credit base that will result in this tax credit, the following equation must be solved for X:

$$\$11,924 = [(15\%)(\$200)] + [(29\%)(X - \$200)]$$
$$\$11,924 - \$30 + \$58 = [(29\%)(X)]$$

Solving this equation for X provides a value of $41,214 which equals the amount of his donation that will produce the $11,924 [(15%)($200) + (29%)($41,214 - $200)] credit that will reduce his federal Tax Payable to nil. This leaves a carry forward of $68,786 ($110,000 - $41,214).

Exercise Eleven - 14 Solution

Ms. Cheung's Net Income For Tax Purposes and Taxable Income would be calculated as follows:

Net Rental Income	$44,000
Net Taxable Capital Gains	2,500
Foreign Non-Business Income	3,500
Net Income For Tax Purposes	$50,000
Net Capital Loss Carry Forward	(2,500)
Adjusted Division B Income	$47,500
Non-Capital Loss Carry Forward	(4,000)
Taxable Income	$43,500

Ms. Cheung's credit for foreign tax paid would be the lesser of the foreign tax withheld of $385 [(11%)($3,500)] and an amount determined by the following formula:

$$\left[\frac{\text{Foreign Non} - \text{Business Income}}{\text{Adjusted Division B Income}} \right] [\text{Tax Otherwise Payable}]$$

In this formula, the Adjusted Division B Income would be $47,500 (as shown in the preceding table). Note that, because the non-capital loss is not deducted here, this is not the same as her Taxable Income of $43,500.

Ms. Cheung's Tax Otherwise Payable would be calculated as follows (note that the foreign tax credit is not subtracted in this calculation):

Tax Before Credits [(15%)($43,500)]	$6,525
Basic Personal Credit	(1,745)
Tax Otherwise Payable	$4,780

Using this information, the formula amount would be $352 [($3,500 ÷ $47,500)($4,780)]. As this is less than the $385 withheld, this would be the foreign tax credit. Based on this, Ms. Cheung's actual federal Tax Payable would be calculated as follows:

Tax Before Credits [(15%)($43,500)]	$6,525
Basic Personal Credit	(1,745)
Foreign Tax Credit	(352)
Federal Tax Payable	$4,428

Exercise Eleven - 15 Solution

Mr. Blouson's regular Tax Payable would be calculated as follows:

Tax On First $45,916	$ 6,887
Tax On Next $39,084 ($85,000 - $45,916) At 20.5%	8,012
Total	$14,899
Basic Personal Credit	(1,745)
Dividend Tax Credit [(6/11)(38%)($20,000)]	(4,145)
Regular Federal Tax Payable	$ 9,009

For alternative minimum tax purposes, his adjusted taxable income would be calculated as follows:

Regular Taxable Income	$85,000
30 Percent Of Capital Gains [(30%)(2)($22,500)]	13,500
Dividend Gross Up [(38%)($20,000)]	(7,600)
Adjusted Taxable Income	$90,900

Calculation of the alternative minimum tax would be as follows:

Adjusted Taxable Income	$90,900
Basic Exemption	(40,000)
Amount Subject To Tax	$50,900
Rate	15%
Minimum Tax Before Credit	$ 7,635
Basic Personal Credit	(1,745)
Alternative Minimum Tax	$ 5,890

Mr. Blouson would not pay the alternative minimum tax as it is less than the regular Tax Payable. Note that the $50,000 RRSP deduction does not affect the alternative minimum tax calculation.

Self Study Solution Eleven - 1

The calculation of Miss Atwater's Taxable Income for 2016 would be as follows:

Net Rental Income	$34,200
Interest Income	4,000
Net Income For Tax Purposes And Taxable Income	$38,200

The corresponding calculation for 2017 is as follows:

Net Rental Income	$ 35,200	
Interest Income	4,200	$39,400
Allowable Business Investment Loss [(1/2)($170,000)]		(85,000)
Net Income For Tax Purposes And Taxable Income		Nil

There is a deemed disposition of the shares for proceeds of nil due to the bankruptcy of the company. As the capital loss relates to the shares of a small business corporation, it is a Business Investment Loss. This means that, in contrast to other types of capital losses, the allowable portion can be deducted against any source of income. The total Allowable Business Investment Loss (ABIL) that is available for deduction in 2017 is $85,000 [(1/2)($170,000)].

As the ABIL was recognized in 2017, it must first be used to reduce that year's income to nil. Note that, because of this rule, she cannot deduct a smaller amount in order to have sufficient income to absorb her basic personal tax credit. This will use up $39,400 of the $85,000 total and leave a balance of $45,600 to be carried over to other years.

In carrying this amount back to 2016, the optimum solution would leave $11,474 of Taxable Income so that Miss Atwater can take advantage of her basic personal tax credit. Note that the calculation of the optimum carry back uses the basic personal amount of the carry back year, not the current year.

This means that she needs a loss carry back deduction of $26,726 ($38,200 - $11,474) in 2016. This deduction will leave a Taxable Income of $11,474. As planned, the federal taxes on this amount will be eliminated by the basic personal credit.

A carry back of $26,726 to 2016 leaves a carry forward balance of $18,874 ($45,600 - $26,726) to be used in future years.

The undeducted Allowable Business Investment Loss can be deducted against other sources of income in the 10 (not 20) year carry forward period. If it has not been utilized within the 10 years, it then becomes a net capital loss carry forward, deductible for an unlimited number of future periods, but only against net taxable capital gains.

Self Study Solution Eleven - 2

2014 Analysis

Mr. Fox's Net Income For Tax Purposes and Taxable Income would be calculated as follows:

ITA 3(a)		
Employment Income	$18,000	
Business Income	14,500	
Taxable (Grossed Up) Dividends	6,250	$38,750
ITA 3(b)		
Taxable Capital Gains	$ Nil	
Allowable Capital Losses [(1/2)($3,600)]	(1,800)	Nil
ITA 3(c)		$38,750
ITA 3(d)		
Farm Loss (See Note)		(4,250)
Net Income For Tax Purposes And Taxable Income		$34,500

> **Note** Given that Mr. Fox is only a part time farmer, his deductible farm loss would be restricted as follows:
>
> | | | |
> |---|---|---|
> | Total Farm Loss | | $6,000 |
> | Deductible Amount: | | |
> | First $2,500 | ($2,500) | |
> | One-Half Of $3,500 ($6,000 - $2,500) | (1,750) | (4,250) |
> | Restricted Farm Loss Carry Forward | | $1,750 |

As noted in the problem, none of the losses can be carried back before 2014. This would leave the following carry forward balances at the end of 2014:

- Restricted Farm Loss Carry Forward $1,750
- Net Capital Loss Carry Forward [(1/2)($3,600)] $1,800

2015 Analysis

Mr. Fox's Net Income For Tax Purposes and Taxable Income would be calculated as follows:

ITA 3(a)		
Employment Income	$16,000	
Taxable (Grossed Up) Dividends	8,156	$24,156
ITA 3(b)		
Taxable Capital Gains [(1/2)($7,400)]	$ 3,700	
Allowable Capital Losses	Nil	3,700
ITA 3(c)		$27,856
ITA 3(d)		
Business Loss		(39,000)
Net Income For Tax Purposes		Nil
2014 Net Capital Loss Carry Forward (Less Than $3,700)		(1,800)
Taxable Income		Nil

Mr. Fox does not have the option to retain $15,000 in Taxable Income to utilize his tax credits. A non-capital loss carry over is only available after the current year's income is reduced to nil.

Since there are taxable capital gains this year, and the problem states that Mr. Fox would like to deduct the maximum amount of his net capital loss carry forwards, the net capital loss carry forward of $1,800 is added to the balance of the non-capital loss. The non-capital loss for the year would be calculated as follows:

Business Loss	$39,000
2014 Net Capital Loss Deducted	1,800
ITA 3(c) Income	(27,856)
Non-Capital Loss Carry Over For 2015	$12,944

This non-capital loss will be carried back to 2014, resulting in the following amended Taxable Income for that year:

2014 Taxable Income (As Reported)	$34,500
Non-Capital Loss Carry Back From 2015	(12,944)
2014 Amended Taxable Income	$21,556

This carry back leaves Mr. Fox with more than his required $15,000 in Taxable Income. There would be the following carry forward balances at the end of 2015:

- Restricted Farm Loss Carry Forward (unchanged) $1,750

2016 Analysis

Mr. Fox's Net Income For Tax Purposes and Taxable Income would be calculated as follows:

ITA 3(a)		
Employment Income	$19,000	
Business Income	34,000	
Farming Income	8,000	
Taxable (Grossed Up) Dividends	10,000	$71,000
ITA 3(b)		
Taxable Capital Gains [(1/2)($6,300)]	$ 3,150	
Allowable Capital Losses	Nil	3,150
ITA 3(c)		$74,150
ITA 3(d)		Nil
Net Income For Tax Purposes		$74,150
Farm Loss Carry Forward (Less Than $8,000)		(1,750)
Taxable Income		$72,400

Given the deduction of the farm loss carry forward, there are no loss carry overs remaining at the end of 2016.

2017 Analysis

Mr. Fox's Net Income For Tax Purposes and Taxable Income would be calculated as follows:

ITA 3(a)		
Employment Income	$12,000	
Taxable (Grossed Up) Dividends	12,656	$24,656
ITA 3(b)		
Taxable Capital Gains	$ Nil	
Allowable Capital Losses [(1/2)($6,000)]	(3,000)	Nil
ITA 3(c)		$24,656
ITA 3(d)		
Business Loss	($52,000)	
Farm Loss	(2,000)	(54,000)
Net Income For Tax Purposes And Taxable Income		Nil

The non-capital loss carry over for the year would be calculated as follows:

Business Loss	$52,000
ITA 3(c) Income	(24,656)
Non-Capital Loss Carry Over	$27,344
Farm Loss (Unrestricted)	2,000
Total Loss Carry Over For 2017	$29,344

Although technically, the farm loss is accounted for separately from the non-capital loss, since the farm loss is less than $2,500 it is treated as an unrestricted farm loss and can be applied against all types of income. Given the carry over rules are the same, we have treated this farm loss as part of the non-capital loss carry over. The entire loss carry over could be carried back to 2016, but the problem requires that losses be carried back to the earliest possible year. As a result, some of this loss must be carried back to 2014. Since Mr. Fox requires $15,000 in Taxable Income to fully utilize his tax credits, the maximum carry back to 2014 is $6,556, calculated as follows:

2014 Taxable Income (As Amended)	$21,556
Non-Capital Loss Carry Back From 2017	(6,556)
2014 Amended Taxable Income (Minimum)	$15,000

This carry back leaves Mr. Fox with his required $15,000 in Taxable Income. The remaining loss carry over of $22,788 ($29,344 - $6,556) can be carried back to 2016.

There would be a $3,000 net capital loss carry over for 2017. This entire amount can be carried back to 2016, since the carry back is less than the $3,150 taxable capital gains recorded in 2016.

This will result in the following amended Taxable Income for that year:

2016 Taxable Income (As Reported)	$72,400
Non-Capital Loss Carry Back From 2017	(22,788)
Net Capital Loss Carry Back From 2017	(3,000)
2016 Amended Taxable Income	$46,612

There are no loss carry forwards remaining at the end of 2017.

Self Study Solution Eleven - 3

To the extent that there has been use of the lifetime capital gains deduction in previous years, business investment losses (BILs) are disallowed. When they are disallowed, they become ordinary capital losses that must be deducted against the current year's taxable capital gains. Given this, the non-disallowed portion of the BIL would be calculated as follows:

2017 BIL Realized ($59,000 - $186,000 - $500)	$127,500
BIL Disallowed By Previous Use Of ITA 110.6 ($60,000 + $50,000)	(110,000)
Remaining Business Investment Loss	$ 17,500
Inclusion Rate	1/2
Allowable Business Investment Loss	$ 8,750

Using this analysis, Ms. Berger's minimum Net Income For Tax Purposes and Taxable Income would be calculated as follows:

Net Employment Income		$85,000
Net Taxable Capital Gains:		
Taxable Capital Gain		
[(1/2)($290,000 - $142,000 - $1,000)]	$73,500	
Disallowed ABIL [(1/2)($110,000)]	(55,000)	18,500
Allowable Business Investment Loss		(8,750)
Net Income For Tax Purposes		$94,750
Lifetime Capital Gains Deduction (Note 1)		(8,250)
Net Capital Loss Carry Forward Deducted (Note 2)		Nil
Taxable Income		$86,500

Note 1 The lifetime capital gains deduction is the least of:

Amount Available [(1/2)($835,716*)]	$417,858
Amount Used [(1/2)($60,000 + $50,000)]	(55,000)
Amount Available	**$362,858**

*This is the 2017 limit for gains on dispositions of shares of a qualified small business corporation. For gains on qualified farm or fishing property, the 2017 limit would be $1,000,000.

As there are no capital gains during 2017 that do not qualify for the lifetime capital gains deduction, the simplified Annual Gains Limit formula can be used.

Net Taxable Capital Gain On Qualified Property	$18,500
Net Capital Loss Carry Forward Deducted (Note 2)	Nil
ABIL Realized	(8,750)
Annual Gains Limit	**$ 9,750**

Sum Of Annual Gains Limits	
[(1/2)($60,000 + $50,000) + $9,750]	$64,750
Amounts Deducted In Previous Years	
[(1/2)($60,000 + $50,000)]	(55,000)
CNIL	(1,500)
Cumulative Gains Limit	**$ 8,250**

Note 2 As there remains a net taxable capital gain for 2017, a casual look at the situation suggests that the net capital loss carry over of $7,000 could be deducted. However, if we were to do so, any amount deducted would have to be subtracted from the Annual Gains Limit in the lifetime capital gains deduction calculation. In other words, deducting any amount of the net capital loss carry forward would result in a dollar-for-dollar reduction in the lifetime capital gains deduction. This would be in conflict with the goal of maximizing the use of this deduction.

Self Study Solution Eleven - 4

Part A

Mr. and Mrs. Brock's Taxable Income would be calculated as follows:

	Mr. Brock	Mrs. Brock
Registered Pension Plan Receipts	Nil	$62,000
RRIF Withdrawals	Nil	14,000
Interest	$ 600	4,200
Eligible Dividends Received	3,200	Nil
Gross Up On Dividends (38 Percent)	1,216	Nil
Old Age Security Benefits	7,000	7,000
Net Income Before Clawback	$12,016	$87,200
Social Benefits Repayment (Note 1)	Nil	(1,862)
Net Income For Tax Purposes And Taxable Income		
Before Any Transfer Of Dividends	$12,016	$85,338

Note 1 Mr. Brock would not have to repay any of his OAS benefits as his Net Income is well below the threshold income of $74,788. Mrs. Brock's social benefits repayment would be the lesser of:

- $7,000, and
- [(15%)($87,200 - $74,788)] = $1,862.

Mr. Brock's Tax Payable would be calculated as follows:

Federal Tax Before Credits [(15%)($12,016)]		$1,802
Tax Credits		
Basic Personal	$11,635	
Other (Transferred To Mrs. Brock)	Nil	
Total Base	$11,635	
Rate	15%	(1,745)
Dividend Tax Credit [(6/11)($1,216)]		(663)
Federal Tax Payable - Mr. Brock		Nil

The transfer to Mrs. Brock would be calculated as follows:

Credits Available For Transfer:		
Age		$ 7,225
Disability		8,113
Total Available		$15,338
Reduced By Excess Of:		
Mr. Brock's Net Income	($12,016)	
Over Basic Personal Credit Amount	11,635	(381)
Available For Transfer To Mrs. Brock		$14,957

The amount owing for Mrs. Brock would be calculated as follows:

Tax On First $45,916	$ 6,887	
Tax On Next $39,422 ($85,338 - $45,916) At 20.5 Percent	8,082	$14,969
Tax Credits		
Basic Personal	($11,635)	
Spousal Including Extra Infirm Amount		
($11,635 + $2,150 - $12,016)	(1,769)	
Additional Caregiver Amount (Note 2)	(5,114)	
Age {$7,225 - [(15%)($85,338 - $36,430)]}	Nil	
Pension	(2,000)	
Transfer From Spouse (Preceding Calculation)	(14,957)	
Credit Base	($35,475)	
Rate	15%	(5,321)
Charitable Donations		
[(15%)($200) +(29%)($725 + $1,175 - $200)] (Note 3)		(523)
Federal Tax Payable		$ 9,125
OAS Clawback (Note 1)		1,862
Amount Owing - Mrs. Brock		$10,987

Note 2   Mr. Brock's income was below the regular caregiver income threshold of $16,163. In the absence of the spousal credit, the regular caregiver amount would have been $6,883. Given this, the additional caregiver amount would be $5,114 ($6,883 - $1,769).

Note 3   Charitable donations can be claimed by either spouse, as long as the total donations are less than 75 percent of the claiming spouse's Net Income For Tax Purposes. As Mr. Brock has no Tax Payable, Mrs. Brock will claim his charitable donations. It is usually advantageous for one spouse to claim all the charitable donations if they total more than $200, as the low rate of credit is only applied once. Note that as none of Mrs. Brock's Taxable Income is taxed at the 33 percent federal tax rate, that rate is not relevant to the calculation of her charitable donations tax credit.

Part B - Eligibility For Transfer

Mrs. Brock's current base for the spousal credit is $1,769. If Mr. Brock's dividends are transferred, he would be left with Net Income For Tax Purposes of $7,600 ($12,016 - $3,200 - $1,216). This would leave a base for the spousal credit of $6,185 ($13,785 - $7,600). As this is an increase from the previous amount, the transfer is permitted.

Part C

If Mr. Brock's dividends are transferred to Mrs. Brock, their new Taxable Income figures would be calculated as follows:

	Mr. Brock	Mrs. Brock
Net Income Before Clawback As Per Part A	$12,016	$87,200
Dividend Transfer	(3,200)	3,200
Gross Up Transfer	(1,216)	1,216
Net Income After Dividend Transfer Before Clawback	$ 7,600	$91,616
Social Benefits Repayment (Note 4)	Nil	(2,524)
Net Income For Tax Purposes And Taxable Income	$ 7,600	$89,092

Note 4 Mr. Brock would not have to repay any of his OAS benefits as his Net Income is well below the threshold income of $74,788. Mrs. Brock's social benefits repayment would be the lesser of:

- $7,000, and
- $[(15\%)(\$91,616 - \$74,788)] = \underline{\$2,524}$.

As Mr. Brock's revised income figure is below the basic personal credit base of $11,635, his Tax Payable would continue to be nil. The transfer to Mrs. Brock would be calculated as follows:

Credits Available For Transfer:		
Age		$ 7,225
Disability		8,113
Total Available		$15,338
Reduced By Excess Of:		
Mr. Brock's Net Income	($ 7,600)	
Over Basic Personal Credit Amount	11,635	(Nil)
Available For Transfer To Mrs. Brock		$15,338

With respect to Mrs. Brock, her amount owing would be calculated as follows:

Tax On First $45,916	$6,887	
Tax On Next $43,176 ($89,092 - $45,916) At 20.5 Percent	8,851	$15,738

Tax Credits		
Basic Personal	($11,635)	
Spousal Including Extra Infirm Amount		
($11,635 + $2,150 - $7,600)	(6,185)	
Additional Caregiver Amount (Note 5)	(698)	
Age {$7,225 - [(15%)($89,092 - $36,430)]}	Nil	
Pension	(2,000)	
Transfer From Spouse (Preceding Calculation)	(15,338)	
Credit Base	($35,856)	
Rate	15%	(5,378)
Charitable Donations		
[(15%)($200) + (29%)($725 + $1,175 - $200)]		(523)
Dividend Tax Credit [(6/11)($1,216)]		(663)
Federal Tax Payable		$ 9,174
OAS Clawback (Note 4)		2,524
Amount Owing - Mrs. Brock		$11,698

Note 5   As was the case prior to the transfer of dividends, Mr. Brock's income was below the regular caregiver income threshold of $16,163. In the absence of the spousal credit, the regular caregiver amount would have been $6,883. Given this, the additional caregiver amount would be $698 ($6,883 - $6,185).

Conclusion

The use of the ITA 82(3) dividend transfer has increased Mrs. Brock's federal Tax Payable by $49, from $9,125 to $9,174. In addition, it has increased the OAS clawback by $662, from $1,862 to $2,524.

Overall, the net effect is an increase in the total amount owing of $711 ($11,698 - $10,987. As a result, the transfer of dividends should not be done.

Self Study Solution Eleven - 5

Part A

Mr. and Mrs. Dalton's Taxable Income would be calculated as follows:

	Mr. Dalton	Mrs. Dalton
Old Age Security Benefits	$ 7,000	$ 7,000
Registered Pension Plan Receipts	Nil	62,000
RRIF Income	1,640	12,420
Interest On Government Bonds	1,420	2,580
Eligible Dividends Received	3,420	460
Gross Up On Dividends (38 Percent)	1,300	175
Net Income Before Clawback	$14,780	$84,635
Social Benefits Repayment (Note 1)	Nil	(1,477)
Net Income For Tax Purposes And Taxable Income		
Before Any Transfer Of Dividends	$14,780	$83,158

Note 1   Mr. Dalton would not have to repay any of his OAS benefits as his Net Income is well below the threshold income of $74,788. Mrs. Dalton's social benefits repayment would be the lesser of:

- $7,000, and
- [(15%)($84,635 - $74,788)] = $1,477.

Mr. Dalton's Tax Payable would be calculated as follows:

Federal Tax Before Credits [(15%)($14,780)]		$2,217
Tax Credits		
Basic Personal	($11,635)	
Other (Transferred To Mrs. Dalton)	Nil	
Total Base	($11,635)	
Rate	15%	(1,745)
Dividend Tax Credit [(6/11)($1,300)]		(709)
Federal Tax Payable		Nil

The transfer to Mrs. Dalton would be calculated as follows:

Credits Available For Transfer:		
Age		$ 7,225
Pension (Limited To RRIF Receipts)		1,640
Disability		8,113
Total Available		$16,978
Reduced By Excess Of:		
Mr. Dalton's Net Income	($14,780)	
Over Basic Personal Credit Amount	11,635	(3,145)
Available For Transfer To Mrs. Dalton		$13,833

The amount owing for Mrs. Dalton would be calculated as follows:

Tax On First $45,916	$ 6,887	
Tax On Next $37,242 ($83,158 - $45,916) At 20.5 Percent	7,635	$14,522
Tax Credits		
Basic Personal	($11,635)	
Spousal Including Extra Infirm Amount		
($11,635 +$2,150 - $14,780)	Nil	
Additional Caregiver Amount (Note 2)	(6,883)	
Age {$7,225 - [(15%)($83,158 - $36,430)]}	(216)	
Pension	(2,000)	
Transfer From Spouse (Preceding Calculation)	(13,833)	
Credit Base	($34,567)	
Rate	15%	(5,185)
Charitable Donations		
[(15%)($200) +(29%)($350 + $960 - $200)] (Note 3)		(352)
Dividend Tax Credit [(6/11)($175)]		(95)
Federal Tax Payable		$ 8,890
OAS Clawback (Note 1)		1,477
Amount Owing - Mrs. Dalton		$10,367

Note 2   Mr. Dalton's income was below the regular caregiver income threshold of $16,163. In the absence of the spousal credit, the regular caregiver amount would have been $6,883. Given this, the additional caregiver amount would be $6,883 ($6,883 - Nil)

Note 3   Charitable donations can be claimed by either spouse, as long as the total donations are less than 75 percent of the claiming spouse's Net Income For Tax Purposes. As Mr. Dalton has no Tax Payable, Mrs. Dalton will claim his charitable donations. It is usually advantageous for one spouse to claim all the charitable donations if they total more than $200, as the low rate of credit is only applied once. Note that as none of Mrs. Dalton's Taxable Income is taxed at the 33 percent federal tax rate, that rate is not relevant to the calculation of her charitable donations tax credit.

Part B - Eligibility For Transfer

Mrs. Dalton cannot currently take the spousal credit because Mr. Dalton's Net Income is more than the $13,785 ($11,635 + $2,150) base for the credit. However, Mr. Dalton can transfer his dividends under ITA 82(3) as the transfer would leave Mr. Dalton with a Net Income of $10,060 ($14,780 - $3,420 - $1,300). This is below the $13,785 base for the spousal credit and, as a result, the transfer would create a spousal tax credit and is permitted.

Part C

If all of Mr. Dalton's dividends are transferred to Mrs. Dalton, their new Taxable Income figures would be calculated as follows:

	Mr. Dalton	Mrs. Dalton
Net Income Before Clawback As Per Part A	$14,780	$84,635
Dividend Transfer	(3,420)	3,420
Gross Up Transfer	(1,300)	1,300
Net Income After Dividend Transfer Before Clawback	$10,060	$89,355
Social Benefits Repayment (Note 4)	Nil	(2,185)
Net Income For Tax Purposes And Taxable Income	$10,060	$87,170

Note 4   Mr. Dalton would not have to repay any of his OAS benefits as his Net Income is well below the threshold income of $74,788. Mrs. Dalton's social benefits repayment would be the lesser of:

- $7,000, and
- [(15%)($89,355 - $74,788)] = $2,185.

As Mr. Dalton's revised income figure is below the basic personal credit of $11,635, his Tax Payable would continue to be nil. The transfer to Mrs. Dalton would be calculated as follows:

Credits Available For Transfer:		
Age		$ 7,225
Pension (Limited To RRIF Receipts)		1,640
Disability		8,113
Total Available		$16,978
Reduced By Excess Of:		
Mr. Dalton's Net Income	($10,060)	
Over Basic Personal Credit Amount	11,635	(Nil)
Available For Transfer		$16,978

With respect to Mrs. Dalton, her amount owing would be calculated as follows:

Tax On First $45,916	$6,887	
Tax On Next $41,254 ($87,170 - $45,916) At 20.5%	8,457	$15,344
Tax Credits		
Basic Personal	($11,635)	
Spousal Including Extra Infirm Amount		
($11,635 +$2,150 - $10,060)	(3,725)	
Additional Caregiver Amount (Note 5)	(3,158)	
Age {$7,225 - [(15%)($87,170 - $36,430)]}	Nil	
Pension	(2,000)	
Transfer From Spouse (Preceding Calculation)	(16,978)	
Credit Base	($37,496)	
Rate	15%	(5,624)
Charitable Donations [(15%)($200) +		
(29%)($350 + $960 - $200)]		(352)
Dividend Tax Credit [(6/11)($175 + $1,300)]		(805)
Federal Tax Payable		$ 8,563
OAS Clawback (Note 4)		2,185
Amount Owing - Mrs. Dalton		$10,748

Note 5 As was the case before the transfer of dividends, Mr. Dalton's income is below the regular caregiver income threshold of $16,163. In the absence of the spousal credit, the regular caregiver amount would have been $6,883. Given this, the additional caregiver amount would be $3,158 ($6,883 - $3,725)

Conclusion

The use of the ITA 82(3) dividend transfer has decreased Mrs. Dalton's federal Tax Payable by $327 ($8,890 - $8,563). However, it has increased the OAS clawback by $708 ($2,185 - $1,477). Since the net effect is an increase in the amount owing of $381 ($10,748 - $10,367), the dividend transfer should not be done.

Self Study Solution Eleven - 6

Case One

The regular Tax Payable calculation for Tom Barlow would be as follows:

Net Business Income	$50,000
Eligible Dividends Received	55,000
Gross Up [(38%)($55,000)]	20,900
Loss On Tax Shelter Investment	(32,000)
RRSP Deduction	(28,000)
Net And Taxable Income	$65,900
Tax On First $45,916	$ 6,887
Tax On Next $19,984 ($65,900 - $45,916) At 20.5%	4,097
Tax Before Credits [(15%)($20,900)]	$10,984
Basic Personal Credit	(1,745)
Dividend Tax Credit [(6/11)($20,900)]	(11,400)
Regular Federal Tax Payable	Nil

The alternative minimum tax calculations are as follows:

Regular Taxable Income	$65,900
Loss On Tax Shelter Investment	32,000
Dividend Gross Up	(20,900)
Adjusted Taxable Income	$77,000
AMT Exemption	(40,000)
AMT Base	$37,000
Rate	15%
Federal AMT Before Credit	$ 5,550
Basic Personal Credit	(1,745)
Federal AMT	$ 3,805

Since the regular federal Tax Payable is nil, the AMT is larger and must be paid. The excess AMT over regular tax payable for Tom of $3,805 can be carried forward for seven years and applied against any future excess of regular Tax Payable over the alternative minimum tax.

Case Two

The regular Tax Payable calculation for Samantha Loft would be as follows:

Net Taxable Capital Gains	$165,000
Employment Income	21,000
Net Income For Tax Purposes	$186,000
Lifetime Capital Gains Deduction	(162,000)
Taxable Income	$ 24,000
Federal Tax Before Credit [(15%)($24,000)]	$3,600
Basic Personal Credit	(1,745)
Regular Federal Tax Payable	$1,855

The alternative minimum tax calculations are as follows:

Regular Taxable Income	$ 24,000
30 Percent Of Capital Gains [(30%)(2)($165,000)]	99,000
Adjusted Taxable Income	$123,000
AMT Exemptions	(40,000)
AMT Base	$ 83,000
Rate	15%
Federal AMT Before Credit	$ 12,450
Basic Personal Credit	(1,745)
Federal AMT	$ 10,705

Since the MT is larger than the regular federal Tax Payable, it must be paid. The excess AMT over regular tax payable for Samantha of $8,850 ($10,705 - $1,855) can be carried forward for 7 years and applied against any future excess of regular Tax Payable over the alternative minimum tax.

Self Study Solution Eleven - 7

Part A - Net Income For Tax Purposes

Ms. Worthmore's minimum Taxable Income is calculated as follows:

Employment Income		
Gross Salary - Intra Graphics	$73,532	
Gross Salary - Lindworth Inc.	2,500	
RPP Contributions	(1,233)	$74,799
Income From Property		
Eligible Dividend Attribution (Note One)	$ 182	
Gross Up [(38%)($182)]	69	
Non-Eligible Dividends From Lindworth	4,325	
Gross Up [(17%)($4,325)]	735	5,311
Taxable Capital Gains		
Attribution From Husband (Note Two)	$ 1,144	
Transfer To Jayne (Note Three)	122	
Lackmere Shares (Note Four)	394	
Agricultural Land (Note Five)	9,000	10,660
Other Income And Deductions		
Spousal Support Payments [($225)(12)]	($ 2,700)	
RRSP Deduction (Note Six)	(6,849)	(9,549)
Net Income For Tax Purposes		$81,221

Note One There would be income attribution for the $182 [($3.50)(52)] in dividends received by Mr. Dalton on the shares received as a gift.

Note Two In the case of transfers to a spouse, unless an election is made not to have Section 73 apply, the property is transferred at the adjusted cost base of the transferor. There is no recognition of capital gains at the time of transfer. However, when Mr. Dalton sells the shares on August 31, 2017, there would be attribution of taxable capital gains in the amount of $1,144 [($56 - $12)(52)(1/2)].

Note Three In the case of a gift to a minor child, it is treated as a deemed disposition at fair market value. This results in a taxable capital gain at the time of transfer in the amount of $122 [($27 - $18)(27)(1/2)].

Note Four The taxable capital gain on the Lackmere Ltd. shares would be computed using the average value for the shares. The average value would be calculated as follows:

122 Shares At $92	$11,224
178 Shares At $71	12,638
Total Cost	$23,862
Average Cost ($23,862 ÷ 300 Shares)	$ 79.54

Based on this, the gain would be calculated as follows:

Proceeds Of Disposition [(122)($86)]	$10,492	
Adjusted Cost Base [(122)($79.54)]	(9,704)	
Capital Gain	$ 788	
Inclusion Rate	1/2	
Taxable Capital Gain	$ 394	

Note Five   When there is a non-arm's length transfer of property for consideration of less than fair market value, ITA 69 deems that, for the transferor, the transfer takes place at fair market value. Given this, the taxable capital gain would be calculated as follows:

Deemed Proceeds Of Disposition (FMV)	$28,000
Adjusted Cost Base	(10,000)
Capital Gain	$18,000
Inclusion Rate	1/2
Taxable Capital Gain	$ 9,000

Note Six   Ms. Worthmore's 2016 Earned Income (assumed to be equal to the 2017 figure) is as follows:

Gross Salary - Intra	$73,532
Gross Salary - Lindworth	2,500
Spousal Support Paid And Deducted [(12)($225)]	(2,700)
Earned Income	$73,332

Ms. Worthmore's maximum deductible 2017 RRSP contribution is calculated as follows:

Unused Deduction Room - End of 2016	Nil
Lesser Of:	
• 2017 RRSP Dollar Limit = $26,010	
• [(18%)($73,332)] = $13,200	$13,200
Less 2016 PA	(6,351)
Maximum Deductible RRSP Contribution	$ 6,849

This means the excess contribution of $651 ($7,500 - $6,849) can be carried forward and deducted in future years.

Part B - Taxable Income

As Ms. Worthmore has no deductions from her Net Income For Tax Purposes, her 2017 Taxable Income would be $81,221, the same amount as her 2017 Net Income For Tax Purposes

Part C - Tax Payable

Ms. Worthmore's federal Tax Payable can be calculated as follows:

Tax On First $45,916		$ 6,887
Tax On Next $35,305 ($81,221 - $45,916) At 20.5 Percent		7,238
Gross Federal Tax Payable		$14,125
Basic Personal Amount	($11,635)	
Spousal $11,635 - $1,065	(10,570)	
CPP Contribution	(2,564)	
EI Premiums	(836)	
Canada Employment	(1,178)	
Transfer Of Spouse's Tuition Credit - Lesser of:		
• Absolute Limit Of $5,000		
• Tuition Paid Of $2,300	(2,300)	
Medical Expenses (Note Seven)	(10,838)	
Credit Base	($39,921)	
Rate	15%	(5,988)
Eligible Dividend Tax Credit [(6/11)($69)]		(38)
Non-Eligible Dividend Tax Credit [(21/29)($735)]		(532)
Charitable Donations (Note Eight)		
[(15%)($200) + (29%)($342 - $200)]		(71)
Political Contributions [(3/4)($100)]		(75)
Federal Tax Payable		$ 7,421

Note Seven Ms. Worthmore can claim all of the medical expenses of her husband and daughters, Joyce and June without taking into consideration June's income, as she is under 18 years of age. Allowable medical expenses are as follows:

John Dalton, Joyce And June Medical Expenses		
($1,056 + $2,200 + $9,850)		$13,106
Threshold - Lesser Of:		
[(3%)($81,221)] = $2,437		
2017 Limit Of $2,268		(2,268)
Allowable Medical Expenses		$10,838

Note Eight As none of her income is taxed at 33 percent, this rate will not be applicable to the calculation of the charitable donations tax credit.

Self Study Solution Eleven - 8

Taxable Income

Mr. Slater's Net Income For Tax Purposes And Taxable Income would be calculated as follows:

Employment Income - Salary		$ 35,000
Proprietorship Income ($28,300 - $2,300 - Note One)		26,000
Property Income:		
Interest On Savings Account	$ 4,450	
Interest On Loans To Friends	12,000	
Eligible Canadian Dividends	44,000	
Gross Up [($44,000)(38%)]	16,720	
Dividends From U.S. Corporations		
(Before Withholding, No Gross Up)	10,000	87,170
Taxable Capital Gain [(1/2)($111,500 - $23,000)]		44,250
CPP Benefits		5,100
Old Age Security Benefits (Note Three)		7,000
Restricted Farm Loss (Note Two)		(5,750)
Net Income Before OAS Repayment		$198,770
OAS Repayment (Note Three) - Lesser Of:		
• $7,000		
• $18,597 [(15%)($198,770 - $74,788)]		(7,000)
Net Income For Tax Purposes And Taxable Income		$191,770

Note One   The drawings from the proprietorship have no effect on the Taxable Income of Mr. Slater. Funds invested are capital and not deductible. The proprietorship income of $28,300 is reduced by the interest of $2,300 on the proprietorship bank loan.

Note Two   Since Mr. Slater's farming operation is a subordinate source of income, his farm loss would be restricted as follows:

Farm Revenues	$36,000
Farm Expenses	(45,000)
Total Farm Loss	($ 9,000)
Deductible Portion [$2,500 + (1/2)($9,000 - $2,500)]	5,750
Restricted Farm Loss Carry Over	($ 3,250)

The $3,250 restricted farm loss carry over could be carried back to the preceding 3 years and forward for 20 years, to be deducted against farming income.

Note Three   Even though Mr. Slater did not receive the $7,000, it must be included in income and deducted because he has received an information return which includes the amount.

Tax Payable

Mr. Slater's federal Tax Payable would be calculated as follows:

Tax On First $142,353		$29,436
Tax On Next $49,417 ($191,770 - $142,353) At 29 Percent		14,331
Gross Federal Tax		$43,767
Tax Credits:		
Basic Personal Amount	($11,635)	
Spousal, Including Extra Amount For Infirmity		
($11,635 + $2,150)	(13,785)	
Mr. Slater's Age		
{$7,225 - [(15%)($191,770 - $36,430)]}	Nil	
Spouse's Disability	(8,113)	
Canada Employment	(1,178)	
Credit Base	($34,711)	
Rate	15%	(5,207)
Charitable Donations (Note Four)		
[(15%)($200) + (29%)($2,700 - $200)]		(755)
Subtotal = Tax Otherwise Payable For Foreign Tax Credit		$37,805
Dividend Tax Credit [(6/11)($16,720)]		(9,120)
Foreign Tax Credit (Note Five)		(1,500)
Federal Political Contributions Tax Credit (Note Six)		(350)
OAS Clawback		7,000
OAS Withheld		(7,000)
Federal Tax Payable		$26,835

Note Four   As none of his income is taxed at 33 percent, this rate will not be applicable to the calculation of the charitable donations tax credit.

Note Five   The federal foreign tax credit will be the lesser of the foreign tax actually paid of $1,500 and an amount determined by the following formula:

$$\left[\frac{\text{Foreign Non}-\text{Business Income}}{\text{Adjusted Division B Income}}\right][\text{Tax Otherwise Payable}]$$

The Tax Otherwise Payable is equal to federal Tax Payable before the dividend tax credit and political contributions tax credit is deducted (the Subtotal in the preceding table). This amount would be $1,971 [($10,000 ÷ $191,770)($37,805)], leaving the actual taxes of $1,500 as the lesser amount.

Note Six   The political contributions tax credit can be calculated as follows:

3/4 Of First $400	$300
1/2 Of The Next $100	50
Total Credit	$350

Other Notes

- The gambling income would not be taxable as Mr. Slater's activity is not extensive enough to be considered a business given his winnings and funds lost in gambling.
- Inheritances are capital receipts and do not constitute Taxable Income.
- The life insurance premiums are not deductible.
- The mortgage payments on his personal residence are not deductible.

Self Study Solution Eleven - 9

Deemed Dispositions Immediately Before Death
Immediately before the time of Mrs. Steele's death, there is a deemed disposition of all of her capital property. If the beneficiary is a spouse, the deemed proceeds of disposition will, in general, be equal to the tax cost of the property (ACB or UCC). If Andrea's representatives choose to do so, they can elect out of this rollover and record the transfer at fair market value. For the transfers to her daughter, the deemed proceeds of disposition must be equal to fair market value.

Principal Residence To Daughter
The bequest of the family home to her daughter would result in a capital gain of $134,600 ($544,000 - $409,400). As it appears to have been Mrs. Steele's principal residence, the application of the principal residence exemption formula to this amount would result in a deduction of the maximum amount of $134,600.

Other Properties At Death
Under ITA 70(6), property may be transferred at death to a spouse on the basis of adjusted cost base or its UCC. This means that the Rolston Inc. shares, the painting, and the assets of the boutique can be transferred to Mr. Steele with no tax effects in Mrs. Steele's final return. The adjusted cost base and UCC of these properties to Mr. Steele will be the same amounts that applied to Mrs. Steele, prior to her death.

Although the AGF Industries shares would also be eligible for a tax free rollover, it would not be advantageous to do so as there is an unrealized capital loss on these shares. It would be preferable for the legal representative of Mrs. Steele to elect in the final return to have the AGF Industries shares transferred to Mr. Steele at fair market value in order to utilize the capital loss. Electing out of ITA 70(6) is implemented in the final tax return and does not require the filing of a form.

There is no rollover available for the rental property as that is being transferred to her daughter. There is a taxable capital gain for the rental property on both the building and the land and recaptured CCA on the building.

The allowable capital loss resulting from the election on the shares, and the taxable capital gains and recaptured CCA on the deemed disposition of the rental property can be calculated as follows:

	AGF Shares	Land	Building
Fair Market Value	$ 7,900	$164,000	$235,000
Adjusted Cost Base/Capital Cost	(10,600)	(92,000)	(183,000)
Capital Gain (Loss)	($ 2,700)	$ 72,000	$ 52,000
Inclusion Rate	1/2	1/2	1/2
Taxable Capital Gain (Loss)	($ 1,350)	$ 36,000	$ 26,000

	Building
Capital Cost	$183,000
UCC	(144,800)
Recapture Of CCA	$ 38,200

Mortgage Interest - Attribution

With respect to the mortgage interest received by Mr. Steele, it was earned on mortgages given to him by Mrs. Steele and, as a consequence, it would be attributed to her up until her death on June 3, 2017. This means that $886 [(154/365)($2,100)] of the $2,100 would be included in her income. As attribution from a spouse ceases when the transferor spouse dies, the remaining $1,214 ($2,100 - $886) would be included in Mr. Steele's income. When this is combined with his $425 boutique salary, his total income for the year is $1,639. His income for the whole year, not just prior to Mrs. Steele's death, will decrease the spousal credit available on Mrs. Steele's final return.

Net Income For Tax Purposes And Taxable Income

Mrs. Steele's minimum Taxable Income (ignoring CPP) would be calculated as follows:

Business Income		$55,200
Property Income:		
Eligible Dividends Received	$1,090	
Gross Up [(38%)($1,090)]	414	
Interest	2,025	
Mortgage Interest Attributed From Spouse	886	
Rent Revenues	41,200	
Rental Expenses (Note One)	(24,650)	
Recaptured CCA On Rental Property	38,200	59,165
Net Taxable Capital Gains:		
Taxable Capital Gains On Rental Property		
($26,000 + $36,000)	$62,000	
Allowable Capital Loss On AGF Industries Shares	(1,350)	60,650
Net Income		$175,015
Net Capital Loss Carry Forward (Note Two)		(76,500)
Taxable Income		$ 98,515

Note One As there was a deemed disposition of the rental property immediately before the time of Mrs. Steele's death, no CCA can be taken for 2017.

Note Two In the year of death, any capital losses and capital loss carry forwards can be deducted against any type of income, not just capital gains, as long as the lifetime capital gains deduction has not been claimed. As a result, although she has net taxable capital gains of only $60,650, she can deduct her total net capital loss carry forward of $76,500.

Tax Payable

Mrs. Steele's minimum federal Tax Payable would be calculated as follows:

Tax On First $91,831		$16,300
Tax On Remaining $6,684 ($98,515 - $91,831) At 26 Percent		1,738
Gross Federal Tax		$18,038
Basic Personal Amount	($11,635)	
Spousal ($11,635 - $1,639)	(9,996)	
Credit Base	($21,631)	
Rate	15%	(3,245)
Dividend Tax Credit [(6/11)(38%)($1,090)]		(226)
Federal Tax Payable		$14,567

Self Study Solution Eleven - 10

Net Employment Income

Katherine's Net Employment Income would be calculated as follows:

Salary	$85,000
Loan Benefit (Note 1)	1,500
RPP Contribution	(2,875)
Net Employment Income	$83,625

Note 1 The loan benefit is $1,500 [(1%)($150,000)(4/4)]. Note that, because this is a housing loan to an employee, Katherine can calculate the benefit as using the lesser of the prescribed rate at the time the loan is granted (1 percent) and the current rate (2 percent). This privilege is available during the first five years of the loan.

Income From Rental Properties

Katherine's rental income from the two properties would be $8,600 ($2,900 + $5,700), calculated as follows:

	Property A	Property B
2017 Rents	$26,400	$28,800
2017 Expenses Other Than CCA	(23,500)	(23,100)
Income Before CCA	$ 2,900	$ 5,700
CCA	Nil	Nil
Net Rental Income	$ 2,900	$ 5,700

As there is a deemed disposition of these properties immediately before the time of Ms. O'Hara's death, CCA cannot be deducted for 2017.

Dispositions Of Darcy Inc. Shares

Since the problem requires the minimum Net Income For Tax Purposes, Mick (as executor) would not elect out of the ITA 73(1) spousal rollover and the gift of 2,500 shares to Mick would have no immediate tax consequences. However, the gifts to her two children and the sale to her daughter will be recorded at the current fair market value of $14. This will result in a taxable capital gain as follows:

Proceeds Of Disposition [(7,500)($14)]	$105,000
Adjusted Cost Base [(7,500)($120,000 ÷ 10,000)]	(90,000)
Capital Gain	$ 15,000
Inclusion Rate	1/2
Taxable Capital Gain	$ 7,500

Income On Securities

Katherine would include the following amounts in her 2017 Net Income For Tax Purposes:

Darcy Inc. Dividends The dividends on the Darcy Inc. shares that were gifted to Katherine's husband and her minor son, Sean, will be attributed to her. The amount would be $4,500 [(5,000)($0.90)]. The dividends on the shares gifted to Sylvia and purchased by Sylvia would not be subject to income attribution and would be included in Sylvia's 2017 Net Income For Tax Purposes.

Barton Income Trust Distributions Katherine's income inclusion here would be $12,000 [(12,000)($1.50 - $0.50)].

Fidel Mutual Fund Distributions Katherine's income inclusion here would $8,000 [(8,000)($1.00)].

Tax Consequences Of Katherine's Death

There would be a deemed disposition of all of Katherine's capital property immediately before the December 31, 2017 date of her death. The tax consequences would be as follows:

Principal Residence The bequest of the principal residence to Sean would result in a capital gain of $38,000 ($510,000 - $472,000). However, application of the principal residence exemption formula to this amount would result in an exemption of the maximum amount of $38,000.

Barton Income Trust Units As there is no general rollover of capital property to children, the fact that Katherine gave all of these units to Sean and Sylvia will result in a taxable capital gain. The resulting taxable capital gain would be calculated as follows:

Proceeds Of Disposition [($17.50)(12,000)]		$210,000
ACB On January 1, 2017	($180,000)	
Less: 2017 Return Of Capital		
[($0.50)(12,000)]	6,000	(174,000)
Capital Gain		$ 36,000
Inclusion Rate		1/2
Taxable Capital Gain		$ 18,000

Rental Property A Under ITA 70(6), there is a tax free rollover of capital property to a spouse. Since the problem requires the minimum Net Income For Tax Purposes, Mick, as executor for Katherine's estate, would not elect out of ITA 70(6). Given this, there would be no tax consequences resulting from the bequest of rental property A to Mick O'Hara. He would be deemed to have acquired the building with a capital cost of $326,000 and a UCC of $297,000, with the difference being treated as deemed CCA. The land would be deemed to be acquired at its adjusted cost base of $50,000.

Rental Property B The results of this disposition are as follows:

	Land	Building
Fair Market Value	$60,000	$495,000
Capital Cost	(60,000)	(347,000)
Capital Gain	Nil	$148,000
Inclusion Rate	N/A	1/2
Taxable Capital Gain	Nil	$ 74,000

Capital Cost (Building)		$347,000
UCC		(311,000)
Recapture Of CCA		$ 36,000

Fidel Mutual Fund Units With the reinvestment of the 2017 distribution, the adjusted cost base of these units would be $80,000 [$72,000 + (8,000)($1)]. The reinvestment of the distribution would result in the acquisition of 800 new units ($8,000 ÷ $10.00), giving a total holding of 8,800 units. Since the problem requires the minimum Net Income For Tax Purposes, Mick, as executor for Katherine's estate, would elect out of the ITA 70(6) rollover in order to allow her to claim the allowable capital loss. The loss would be calculated as follows:

Fair Market Value [(8,800)($8.30)]	$73,040
Adjusted Cost Base	(80,000)
Capital Loss	($ 6,960)
Inclusion Rate	1/2
Allowable Capital Loss	($ 3,480)

Part A - Net Income For Tax Purposes And Taxable Income

The required calculations here are as follows:

Net Employment Income		$ 83,625
Net Rental Income ($2,900 + $5,700)		8,600
Recapture On Rental Property B		36,000
Net Taxable Capital Gains:		
Darcy Inc. Shares	$ 7,500	
Barton Income Trust Units	18,000	
Rental Property B	74,000	
Fidel Mutual Fund Units	(3,480)	96,020
Attributed Dividends On Darcy Inc. Shares		4,500
Gross Up Of 38 Percent		1,710
Barton Income Trust Distributions		12,000
Fidel Mutual Fund Distribution		8,000
Net Income For Tax Purposes		$250,455
Net Capital Loss Carry Forward		(10,000)
Taxable Income		$240,455

Part A - Tax Payable

The required calculations here would be as follows:

Tax On First $202,800		$46,966
Tax On Next $37,655 ($240,455 - $202,800) At 33 Percent		12,426
Tax Before Credits		$59,392
Tax Credits:		
Basic Personal	($11,635)	
Employment Insurance	(836)	
Canada Pension Plan	(2,564)	
Canada Employment	(1,178)	
Transfer - Sylvia's Tuition Credit (Note 2):	(5,000)	
Medical Expenses (Note 3)	(3,116)	
Total Credit Base	($24,329)	
Rate	15%	(3,649)
Dividend Tax Credit [(6/11)(38%)($4,500)]		(933)
Federal Tax Payable		$54,810

Note 2 Sylvia owned a total of 5,000 shares of Darcy Inc., 2,500 that were gifted to her and 2,500 that she purchased. Sylvia's Net Income from the eligible dividends received from Darcy Inc. totaled $6,210 [(5,000)($.90)(138%)]. This amount would be completely eliminated by her basic personal credit, leaving her with no Tax Payable. Given this, the transfer would be the lesser of:

- the absolute transfer limit of $5,000; and
- the actual tuition paid of $8,150.

Note 3 The base for the medical expense tax credit would be calculated as follows:

Unreimbursed Medical Expenses Of Katherine, Mick, And Sean		
[(50%)($3,700 + $2,420 + $300)]		$3,210
Reduced By The Lesser Of:		
• [(3%)($250,455)] = $7,514		
• 2017 Limit Of $2,268		(2,268)
Subtotal		$ 942
Sylvia's Medical Expenses (No Reimbursement)	$2,360	
Reduced By The Lesser Of:		
• [(3%)($6,210)] = $186		
• $2,268	(186)	2,174
Medical Expense Tax Credit Base		$3,116

Part B - Mike O'Hara's Net Income For Tax Purposes

The results with respect to rental property A would be as follows:

	Land	Building
Proceeds Of Disposition	$75,000	$395,000
Adjusted Cost Base	(50,000)	(326,000)
Capital Gain	$25,000	$ 69,000
Inclusion Rate	1/2	1/2
Taxable Capital Gain	$12,500	$ 34,500
Capital Cost (Building)		$326,000
UCC		(297,000)
Recapture Of CCA		$ 29,000

There would be no capital gain or loss on the Fidel Mutual Fund units as the transfer to Mick occurred at the December 31, 2017 fair market value.

The total increase in Mick's Net Income For Tax Purposes due to the sales would be $76,000 ($12,500 + $34,500 + $29,000).

Solution to Tax Software Self Study Problem - Chapter 11

The complete tax return is available on the Companion Website in two versions, a T1 ProFile return file and a .PDF file. Note that prior to late January, 2018, the returns will be for 2016, not 2017 as the 2017 filing version will not yet be available.

For more information on how to use the ProFile tax program, refer to the Chapter 4 sample tax return in this Study Guide.

Notes to tax return

- Diane transfers the $5,000 maximum education related credits to Eleanor and carries forward the remaining $6,000 [$7,000 + (8)($400) + (8)($65) + (2)($120) + (2)($20) - $5,000]. The carry forward can only be used by Diane.

- Eleanor cannot claim the charitable donation made by Diane, but Diane can carry it forward for up to five years.

- Since Amy is under 18 and wholly dependent, Eleanor claimed the eligible dependant credit for Amy.

- Eleanor elected to include the UCCB in Amy's income as this will reduce her tax liability.

- Eleanor claimed the full caregiver credit for Marjorie as her income is well below the income threshold. Note that, because Marjorie is not infirm, the family caregiver amount is not added to this credit.

- Since Diane and Marjorie are over 17 years of age, their medical expenses are reduced by 3 percent of their Net Income For Tax Purposes. This means that none of Marjorie's medical expenses can be claimed by Eleanor.

- In calculating work space in the home costs, the household insurance is not deductible as the T4 information shows she has no commission income. The car insurance is not relevant as there is no information that Eleanor uses her car for employment related purposes.

- The Croft Computer Camp was an overnight camp which means that the deductible costs are limited to $125 per week, a total of $250 [(2)($125)]. In contrast, there is no limit on the costs of day camps. This provides for the deduction of the entire $400 cost of the Y Day Camp.

- Since Eleanor is currently renting out her house, but plans to move back into it, no CCA is taken on the Class 1 building to preserve her principal residence status. Since she had a rental loss in the previous year, and the cost is equal to the UCC, no CCA has been taken on the building. Her CCA on the Class 8 assets would not affect her principal residence election and should be taken. The payments on principal are not deductible.

  If she chose to take CCA on the building, the maximum potential CCA for the year would be $6,756 [(4%)($168,900)] since the first year one-half rule does not apply to the second year of rental. The maximum deductible CCA on the building would be limited to the net rental income after the CCA on the Class 8 assets of $5,553 ($5,887 - $334). This would reduce her Tax Payable for 2016, but she would no longer be eligible for the principal residence gain reduction on the property. In addition, the CCA would be recaptured on a subsequent sale if the proceeds were greater than the UCC.

  Given her inheritance, she should have more than sufficient funds to pay her income taxes without taking CCA on her rental property. As a result, she should preserve her ability to claim the principal residence gain reduction by not taking CCA on the house.

Tax Planning Points

- Since Marjorie is taking care of Amy and is over 18 years old, Eleanor could pay her for child care costs and deduct them. Given Marjorie's low income, it is probable that Eleanor is already providing some funds to her. The amount should be calculated on a basis that is no more than the going rate per hour for similar services for the time when Amy is home and Eleanor is not. As long as Marjorie's income remains below the basic personal credit plus the age credit, it would not result in any income tax liability for Marjorie or decrease Eleanor's caregiver credit. Since she is over 80 years old, there would be no CPP liability.

- Although she is not required to file, Marjorie should file a tax return, otherwise she will not be eligible for the GST credit. If Eleanor pays her for child care in the future, filing a tax return could also reduce the probability that Eleanor will be asked for proof of payment.

- Although she is not required to file, Diane should file a tax return, otherwise she will not be eligible for the GST credit and she will not benefit from the RRSP deduction room created during the year. Filing a tax return will also make her education related tax credits and charitable donation tax credit easier to keep track of for carry forward purposes.

- With the inflow of funds from the inheritance, Eleanor should review her debt outstanding and pay off any balances that have non-deductible interest, such as credit card balances. Although it is not exactly a tax planning point, Eleanor should compare the after tax cost of the interest she is paying on her rental property mortgage with the after tax yields that she can obtain on her investments to determine whether she should pay off her mortgage.

Part B

The maximum deductible RRSP contribution that Eleanor can make for 2017 is calculated as $5,538 by the program on the form "RRSPLimit". To access the form, press <F4> and type "rrsplimit" in the form box.

Note that if Eleanor chooses to deduct CCA on her rental building and reduce her net rental income to nil, her maximum deductible RRSP contribution will be reduced by $1,000 [(18%)($5,553)]. This is another reason she should not take CCA on the rental building.

Given her inheritance, Eleanor should contribute the maximum deductible RRSP contribution as early in 2017 as possible.

Eleanor should open an RESP for Amy if she has not already done so. How much she should contribute will depend on many factors (see the text), but she should request that her accountant create a contribution schedule that will maximize Canada Education Savings Plan contributions and optimize RESP contributions.

Eleanor should open TFSAs for herself, Diane and possibly Marjorie and determine how much she should contribute to each. This would involve many investment and budgeting factors, as well as her future financial plans. Since the contributions are not deductible and the withdrawals are not taxable, the TFSAs will not have an effect on any of the tax returns.

Given her inheritance she should also consider overcontributing up to $2,000 to her RRSP which would allow her to take advantage of the tax free earnings in the RRSP without penalty. This would only be advantageous as long as she plans to have earned income for RRSP purposes sufficient to deduct the $2,000 in the future.

Chapter 11 Learning Objectives

After completing Chapter 11, you should be able to:

1. Recall the specified deductions from Net Income For Tax Purposes in the calculation of Taxable Income (paragraph [P hereafter] 11-1 to 11-7).
2. Apply the rules related to lump-sum payments (P 11-8 to 11-13).
3. Recall the general rules for the treatment of losses and loss carry overs (P 11-14 to 11-29).
4. Explain the treatment of losses on personal use property (P 11-30).
5. Apply the loss carry over provisions applicable to losses on listed personal property (P 11-31 to 11-35).

6. Apply the loss carry over provisions applicable to non-capital losses (P 11-36 to 11-40).
7. Apply the loss carry over provisions applicable to net capital losses (P 11-41 to 11-44).
8. Apply the rules for the conversion of a net capital loss carry over to a non-capital loss carry over (P 11-45 to 11-49).
9. Explain the special rules for net capital losses that are applicable to deceased taxpayers (P 11-50 to 11-54).
10. Explain the special features associated with Allowable Business Investment Losses (P 11-55 to 11-62).

11. Apply the loss carry over provisions applicable to regular and restricted farm losses (P 11-63 to 11-67).
12. Apply the provisions of the lifetime capital gains deduction (P 11-68 to 11-97).
13. Describe the importance of the ordering of deductions and losses in computing Net Income For Tax Purposes and Taxable Income (P 11-98 to 11-103).
14. Describe Basic Federal Tax Payable (P 11-104 to 11-109).
15. Calculate the amount of federal Tax Payable on split income (P 11-110 to 11-120).

16. Apply the provisions for the transfer of dividends to a spouse or common-law partner (P 11-121).
17. Calculate the charitable donations tax credit for donations of various types of property (P 11-122 to 11-147).
18. Calculate foreign business and non-business income tax credits (P 11-148 to 11-159).
19. Apply the provisions associated with the alternative minimum tax (P 11-160 to 11-173).
20. Review a personal tax return completed using the ProFile T1 tax preparation software program.

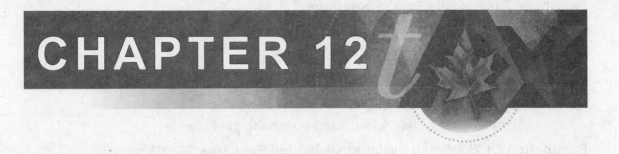

CHAPTER 12

How To Work Through Chapter 12

We recommend the following approach in dealing with the material in this Chapter:

Computation Of Net Income For Corporations
- Read paragraph 12-1 to Figure 12-1 (in the textbook).
- Do Exercise Twelve-1 (in the textbook) and check the solution in this Study Guide. All solutions to Exercises and Self Study Problems can be found in this Study Guide and the page numbers all start with the prefix S-.
- Do Self Study Problem Twelve-1 which is available on the Companion Website and check the solution in this Study Guide.

Deductions Available For Corporations In The Computation Of Taxable Income
- Read paragraph 12-5 to Figure 12-2.

Dividends Received From Other Corporations
- Read paragraph 12-10 to 12-12.
- Do Exercise Twelve-2 and check the solution in this Study Guide.

Dividends Received - Other Situations Including Stop Loss Rules
- Read paragraph 12-13 to 12-22.
- Do Exercise Twelve-3 and check the solution in this Study Guide.
- Read paragraph 12-23.
- Do Self Study Problem Twelve-2 and check the solution in this Study Guide.

Non-Capital Loss Carry Over For A Corporation
- Read paragraph 12-24 to 12-30.
- Do Exercises Twelve-4 and Twelve-5 and check the solutions in this Study Guide.

Ordering Of Taxable Income Deductions
- Read paragraph 12-31 to 12-36.
- Do Self Study Problems Twelve-3 and Twelve-4 and check the solutions in this Study Guide.

Geographical Allocation Of Income To Permanent Establishments
- Read paragraph 12-37 to 12-44.
- Do Self Study Problem Twelve-5 and check the solution in this Study Guide.

Federal Tax Payable For Corporations
- Read paragraph 12-45 to 12-51.
- Do Exercise Twelve-6 and check the solution in this Study Guide.

Provincial Tax Payable For Corporations
- Read paragraph 12-52 to 12-61.

Other Goals Of The Corporate Tax System
- Read paragraph 12-62 to 12-63.

Small Business Deduction - Definitions And Calculation
- Read paragraph 12-64 to 12-98.
- Do Exercise Twelve-7 and check the solution in this Study Guide.

Elimination Of The Small Business Deduction For Large CCPCs
- Read paragraph 12-99 to 12-109.
- Do Exercise Twelve-8 and check the solution in this Study Guide.

Personal Services Corporations, Professional Corporations And Management Companies
- Read paragraph 12-110 to 12-118.

Manufacturing And Processing Profits Deduction
- Read paragraph 12-119 to 12-135.
- Do Exercise Twelve-9 and check the solution in this Study Guide.

General Rate Reduction
- Read paragraph 12-136 to 12-143.
- Do Exercise Twelve-10 and check the solution in this Study Guide.
- Read paragraph 12-144 to 12-149.
- Do Exercise Twelve-11 and check the solution in this Study Guide.
- Do Self Study Problems Twelve-6 to Twelve-9 and check the solutions in this Study Guide.

Foreign Income Tax Credits For Corporations
- Read paragraph 12-150 to 12-162.
- Do Exercise Twelve-12 and check the solution in this Study Guide.
- Do Self Study Problem Twelve-10 and check the solution in this Study Guide.

To Complete This Chapter
- If you would like more practice in problem solving, do the Supplementary Self Study Problems for the chapter. These problems and solutions are available on the Companion Website.
- Review the Key Terms Used In This Chapter in the textbook at the end of Chapter 12. Consult the Glossary for the meaning of any key terms you do not know.
- Test yourself with the Chapter 12 Glossary Flashcards available on the Companion Website.
- Ensure you have achieved the Chapter 12 Learning Objectives listed in this Study Guide.
- As a review, we recommend you view the PowerPoint presentation for Chapter 12 that is on the Companion Website.

Practice Examination
- Write the Practice Examination for Chapter 12 that is on the Companion Website. Mark your examination using the Practice Examination Solution that is on the Companion Website.

Solutions to Chapter Twelve Exercises

Exercise Twelve - 1 Solution

Item 1   You would add the accounting loss of $5,600 ($48,300 - $53,900). You would also add the recapture of CCA of $13,700 ($34,600 - $48,300), for a total addition of $19,300.

Item 2   As goodwill is not amortized for accounting purposes and there was no impairment during the year, no adjustment of the accounting figures is required. However, when the goodwill is added to Class 14.1, it would be subject to the half-year rule and amortization at a rate of 5 percent per year. This means that you would subtract CCA $4,500 [($180,000)(1/2)(5%)].

Item 3   You would add the charitable donations of $15,000.

Item 4   You would deduct the premium amortization of $4,500.

Exercise Twelve - 2 Solution

Net Income For Tax Purposes	$263,000
Dividends Received	(14,200)
Charitable Donations	(8,600)
Non-Capital Loss Carry Forward (All)	(82,000)
Net Capital Loss Carry Forward*	(14,250)
Taxable Income	$143,950

*While there is a net capital loss of $18,000 available, the actual deduction is limited to the current year's taxable capital gains of $14,250. The remaining net capital loss carry forward is $3,750 ($18,000 - $14,250).

Exercise Twelve - 3 Solution

Although Loren has held the shares for more than 365 days, it owns more than 5 percent of the shares. As a result, this transaction would be subject to the stop loss rules. The deductible loss would be calculated as follows:

Proceeds Of Disposition [($21.15)(1,000)]	$21,150
Adjusted Cost Base [($25.30)(1,000)]	(25,300)
Total Loss	($ 4,150)
Disallowed Portion [($2.16)(1,000)]	2,160
Capital Loss	($ 1,990)
Inclusion Rate	1/2
Allowable Capital Loss	($ 995)

Exercise Twelve - 4 Solution

Hacker's Net Income For Tax Purposes would be nil, the business and property income of $63,500, less the allowable business investment loss of $75,750 [(1/2)($151,500)].

The net capital loss carry over balance at the end of the year would be $7,650 [(1/2)($23,100 - $38,400)].

The non-capital loss carry over would be calculated as follows:

Amount E (The ABIL)	$75,750
Amount F - ITA 3(c) Income	(63,500)
Non-Capital Loss At End Of Year	$12,250

Exercise Twelve - 5 Solution

The non-capital loss balance at the end of the year would be calculated as follows:

Amount E:

Net Business Loss		$273,000
ABIL		5,250
Dividends Received And Deducted		48,000
Net Capital Loss Carry Forward Deducted		
(Limited To Net Taxable Capital Gains For The Year)		13,500
Total For Amount E		$339,750
Amount F - ITA 3(c) Income:		
Interest	($27,200)	
Dividends	(48,000)	
Net Taxable Capital Gains		
[(1/2)($111,000 - $84,000)]	(13,500)	(88,700)
Non-Capital Loss At End Of Year		$251,050

Net Capital Loss Carry Forward ($19,000 - $13,500)	$ 5,500

Because the net capital loss carry forward is larger than the net taxable capital gains for the year, the non-capital loss for the year is equal to the net business loss plus the ABIL less the interest income ($273,000 + $5,250 - $27,200).

Exercise Twelve - 6 Solution

The percentage of Taxable Income earned in each province would be calculated as follows:

	Gross Revenues		Wages And Salaries	
	Amount	Percent	Amount	Percent
Ontario	$1,303,000	44.6%	$ 52,000	31.5%
Manitoba	896,000	30.7%	94,000	57.0%
Not Related To A Province	724,000	24.7%	19,000	11.5%
Total	$2,923,000	100.0%	$165,000	100.0%

The average of the two percentages applicable for income not related to a province is 18.1%, leaving an average for income related to a province of 81.9%. Given this, federal Tax Payable can be calculated as follows:

Base Amount Of Part I Tax [(38%)($226,000)]	$85,880
Federal Tax Abatement [(10%)(81.9%)($226,000)]	(18,509)
General Rate Reduction [(13%)($226,000)]	(29,380)
Federal Tax Payable	$37,991

Exercise Twelve - 7 Solution

As a CCPC throughout the year and with no associated companies, Kartoom is eligible for the full amount of the $500,000 annual business limit. The amount eligible for the small business deduction will be the least of:

Active Business Income	**$425,000**
Adjusted Taxable Income (See following calculation)	**$292,857**
Annual Business Limit	**$500,000**

Net Income For Tax Purposes	$570,000
Dividends Received	(85,000)
Non-Capital Loss Carry Forward	(160,000)
Taxable Income	$325,000
100/28 Times Foreign Non-Business Tax Credit [(100/28)(15%)($60,000)]	(32,143)
Adjusted Taxable Income	$292,857

The least of these figures is the adjusted Taxable Income of $292,857.

Exercise Twelve - 8 Solution

The B component of the ITA 125(5.1) reduction formula is $2,925 [(.00225)($11,300,000 - $10,000,000)]. Given this, the required reduction would be calculated as follows:

$$[(\$500,000)(\$2,925 \div \$11,250)] = \underline{\$130,000}\ \textbf{Reduction}$$

This reduction leaves the annual business limit at $370,000 ($500,000 - $130,000).

The foreign non-business income tax credit is equal to $5,400 [(15%)($36,000)]. The small business deduction for Largely Small Inc. is equal to 17.5 percent of the least of:

• Active Business Income ($1,233,000 - $36,000)		$1,197,000
• Taxable Income ($1,233,000 - $914,000)	$319,000	
Less 100/28 Times Non-Business Income FTC		
Of $5,400	(19,286)	$ 299,714
• Reduced Annual Business Limit ($500,000 - $130,000)		$ 370,000

The small business deduction is equal to $52,450 [(17.5%)($299,714)].

Exercise Twelve - 9 Solution

The small business deduction for Marion Manufacturing would be equal to 17.5 percent of the least of:

• Canadian Active Business Income (M&P Profits)		$411,000
• Taxable Income ($462,000 - $310,000)	$152,000	
Less 4 Times Business Income FTC Of $3,150	(12,600)	$139,400
• Annual Business Limit		$500,000

Based on this, the small business deduction would be $24,395 [(17.5%)($139,400)].

The M&P deduction would be equal to 13 percent of the lesser of:

• M&P Profits	$411,000	
Less Amount Eligible For Small Business Deduction	(139,400)	$271,600
• Taxable Income ($462,000 - $310,000)	$152,000	
Less:		
Amount Eligible For Small Business Deduction	(139,400)	
4 Times Business FTC Of $3,150	(12,600)	
Aggregate Investment Income (Taxable Capital Gain)	(30,000)	$ Nil

The M&P profits deduction would be equal to nil.

It would have been possible to increase the small business deduction to the full $411,000 of active business income by increasing Taxable Income to $423,600 ($411,000 + $12,600 FTC adjustment that will be deducted). This could be accomplished by limiting the deduction for charitable donations to $38,400 ($462,000 - $423,600). The remaining unclaimed donations of $271,600 ($310,000 - $38,400) could be carried forward for up to five years.

Although this increases Taxable Income and the total Tax Payable for the year, there could still be an ultimate tax savings with this approach, as the small business deduction cannot be carried forward, while charitable donations can be. As the Exercise states that Marion expects large increases in income in the future, this approach would be advantageous if Marion's expectations turn out to be correct.

Exercise Twelve - 10 Solution

The federal Tax Payable for Marchand Inc. would be calculated as follows:

Base Amount Of Part I Tax [(38%)($320,000)]	$121,600
Federal Tax Abatement [(10%)($320,000)]	(32,000)
M&P Deduction [(13%)($180,000)]	(23,400)
General Rate Reduction [(13%)($320,000 - $180,000)]	(18,200)
Federal Tax Payable	$ 48,000

As you would expect, the overall tax rate is equal to 15 percent ($48,000 ÷ $320,000).

Exercise Twelve - 11 Solution

The federal Tax Payable for Redux Ltd. would be calculated as follows:

Base Amount Of Part I Tax [(38%)($200,000)]	$76,000
Federal Tax Abatement [(10%)($200,000)]	(20,000)
Small Business Deduction (Note One)	(24,500)
M&P Deduction (Note Two)	(650)
General Rate Reduction (Note Three)	(7,150)
Federal Tax Payable	$23,700

Note One   The small business deduction would be equal $24,500, 17.5 percent of $140,000, the least of:

Active Business Income	$200,000
Taxable Income	200,000
Business Limit	140,000

Note Two   The M&P deduction would be equal to $650, 13 percent of $5,000, the lesser of:

• M&P Profits	$145,000	
Amount Eligible For Small Business Deduction	(140,000)	$ 5,000

- Taxable Income $200,000
  Amount Eligible For Small Business Deduction   (140,000) $60,000

Note Three The general rate reduction would be calculated as follows:

Taxable Income	$200,000
Amount Eligible For The SBD	(140,000)
Amount Eligible For The M&P Deduction	(5,000)
Full Rate Taxable Income	$ 55,000
Rate	13%
General Rate Reduction	$ 7,150

Exercise Twelve - 12 Solution

The Taxable Income figure would be calculated as follows:

Net Income For Tax Purposes	$146,000
Dividends Received	(30,000)
Non-Capital Loss Carry Forward	(75,000)
Net Capital Loss Carry Forward	(25,000)
Taxable Income	$ 16,000

Starting with this figure, the required calculation of Part I Tax Payable would be as follows:

Base Amount Of Part I Tax [(38%)($16,000)]	$6,080
Federal Tax Abatement [(88%)(10%)($16,000)]	(1,408)
General Rate Reduction [(13%)($16,000)]	(2,080)
Foreign Business Income Tax Credit (See Note)	(879)
Part I Tax Payable	$1,713

Note The foreign business income tax credit would be $879, the least of:

- The amount withheld $3,000

- $\left[\dfrac{\$20,000}{\$146,000 - \$30,000 - \$25,000} \right]$ [$6,080 - $2,080]$879

- $6,080 - $2,080 $4,000

The unused foreign business tax amount of $2,121 ($3,000 - $879) can be carried back 3 years and forward for 10 years. In calculating the allowable tax credit for such carry overs, these unused amounts will be added to the foreign tax paid factor in the calculation of the foreign business income tax credit.

Self Study Solution Twelve - 1

1. The required adjustments would be:

   - Add: Amortization expense of $254,000.
   - Deduct: CCA of $223,000.

2. The required adjustment would be:

   - Deduct: Premium amortization of $2,000.

3. The capital gain on this sale is $40,000 ($120,000 - $80,000). Because $48,000 ($120,000 - $72,000) of the proceeds are outstanding at the end of the current year, a reserve can be deducted. The reserve will be the lesser of:

   - $16,000 [($40,000)($48,000 ÷ $120,000)]
   - $32,000 [($40,000)(20%)(4 - 0)]

   The deduction of the lesser value of $16,000 will leave a capital gain of $24,000 ($40,000 - $16,000). Based on this, the required adjustments are:

   - Deduct: Accounting gain of $67,000 ($120,000 - $53,000).
   - Add: Taxable capital gain of $12,000 [(1/2)($24,000)].

   There is no recapture on this disposition as the Company still owns Class 44 assets, and there is a positive balance in the class at the end of the year.

4. The required adjustments would be:

   - Add: Membership fees of $8,000.
   - Add: Non-deductible entertainment expenses of $6,000 [(50%)($12,000)].

5. The required adjustment would be:

   - Add: Charitable donations of $11,000.

6. The required adjustments would be:

   - Add: Accounting loss of $16,000 ($23,000 - $39,000).
   - Add: Recapture of $23,000 (Nil - $23,000).

Self Study Solution Twelve - 2

Part A
The adjustments for Part A would be:

- Add amortization expense of $28,000.
- Deduct CCA of $22,500.

Part B
The adjustments for Part B would be:

- Add the $4,800 in estimated warranty costs deducted.
- Deduct the $5,100 in actual warranty costs incurred.

Part C
The adjustment for Part C would be:

- Deduct the $2,400 in premium amortization.

Part D
The adjustments for Part D would be:

- Add the accounting loss of $31,000 ($87,000 - $56,000).
- Deduct the $6,000 terminal loss ($62,000 - $56,000).

Part E
The adjustment for Part E would be:

- Add the $3,700 in charitable donations.

Part F

The adjustment for Part F would be:

- Add the $2,000 accounting loss.
- Do not deduct the allowable capital loss, as there are no taxable capital gains.

Self Study Solution Twelve - 3

The required calculation of Net Income For Tax Purposes and Taxable Income is as follows:

ITA 3(a) Dividends		$ 22,300
ITA 3(b) Taxable Capital Gains	$15,600	
Allowable Capital Losses	(3,450)	12,150
ITA 3(c)		$ 34,450
ITA 3(d) Business Loss		(126,000)
Net Income For Tax Purposes		Nil
Dividends Received		($ 22,300)
Net Capital Loss Carry Forward		
(Limited To Net Taxable Capital Gains)		(12,150)
Charitable Donations		Nil
Taxable Income		Nil

The carry forward balances available at the end of the year are as follows:

Net Capital Loss Carry Forward

Beginning Balance	$42,300
Used During Year	(12,150)
Net Capital Loss Carry Forward	$30,150

Charitable Donations Carry Forward

Beginning Balance	$3,500
Added During Year	2,600
Used During Year	Nil
Unused Charitable Donations	$6,100

Non-Capital Loss

Balance Under E	
Dividends	$ 22,300
Business Loss	126,000
Net Capital Loss Carry Forward Deducted	12,150
Subtotal	$160,450
Balance Under F - Income Under ITA 3(c)	(34,450)
Non-Capital Loss	$126,000

Non-Capital Loss Carry Forward

Balance From Previous Years	$ 33,500
Added During Year	126,000
Used During Year	Nil
Non-Capital Loss Carry Forward	$159,500

As per the policy of the Company, this solution minimizes the net capital loss carry forward. In the absence of this policy, an alternative solution could minimize the non-capital loss balance.

Self Study Solution Twelve - 4

2014 Analysis

Net And Taxable Income

The required calculations for Net Income For Tax Purposes and Taxable Income are as follows:

Accounting Income	$110,000
Accounting Gain On Disposition Of Land	(18,000)
Taxable Capital Gains [(1/2)($18,000)]	9,000
Charitable Donations	3,200
Net Income For Tax Purposes	**$104,200**
Charitable Donations	(3,200)
Dividends	(11,000)
Taxable Income	**$ 90,000**

Carry Forwards

There are no amounts carried forward at the end of 2014.

2015 Analysis

The required calculations for Net Income For Tax Purposes and Taxable Income are as follows:

Accounting Loss	($180,000)
Accounting Loss On Disposition Of Land	9,000
Charitable Donations	5,800
Net Income For Tax Purposes	**Nil**
Dividends	(19,000)
Taxable Income	**Nil**

The 2015 accounting loss of $180,000 includes dividends of $19,000, an accounting loss on the sale of land of $9,000, and a deduction for charitable donations of $5,800. Given this, business income must have been a loss of $184,200 ($180,000 + $19,000 - $9,000 - $5,800). This can be verified by the following schedule:

Business Income (Loss)	($184,200)
Dividends	19,000
Accounting Loss	(9,000)
Charitable Donations	(5,800)
Accounting Income (Loss)	($180,000)

Using this information, the 2015 non-capital loss would be calculated as follows:

Amount E ($184,200 + $19,000)	$203,200
Income Under ITA 3(c) - Dividends	(19,000)
Non-Capital Loss	$184,200

The 2015 net capital loss is equal to $4,500 [(1/2)($9,000)].

Loss Carry Back And 2014 Amended Return

As the Company's policy is to deduct non-capital losses prior to deducting net capital losses, there is a $90,000 carry back of the non-capital loss to 2014. The amended return for 2014 is as follows:

Taxable Income As Reported	$90,000
Non-Capital Loss Carry Back from 2015	(90,000)
Amended 2014 Taxable Income	Nil

2015 Carry Forwards

The following carry forward amounts are available at the end of 2015:

Charitable Donations   All of the charitable donations of $5,800 will have to be carried forward. There is no provision for a carry back of such donations.

Non-Capital Losses   The non-capital loss carry forward, after the carry back, is equal to $94,200 ($184,200 - $90,000).

Net Capital Losses   As the non-capital loss carry back eliminated all of the 2014 Taxable Income, all of the $4,500 net capital loss will have to be carried forward.

2016 Analysis

Net And Taxable Income

The required calculations for Net Income For Tax Purposes and Taxable Income are as follows:

Accounting Income	$85,000
Accounting Gain On Disposition Of Land	(12,000)
Taxable Capital Gain [(1/2)($12,000)]	6,000
Charitable Donations	4,100
Net Income For Tax Purposes	**$83,100**
Charitable Donations	(4,100)
Dividends	(18,000)
Taxable Income Before Carry Forwards	$61,000
Charitable Donations Carry Forward (All)	(5,800)
Non-Capital Loss Carry Forward (Note)	(55,200)
Taxable Income	**Nil**

Note   The amount of the non-capital loss carry forward that was deducted was the amount required to reduce the 2016 Taxable Income to nil.

2016 Carry Forwards

The following carry forward amounts are available at the end of 2016.

Charitable Donations   All of the current and previous years' charitable donations were deducted. There is no carry forward balance.

Non-Capital Loss Carry Forward   The non-capital loss carry forward balance is calculated as follows:

Carry Forward From 2015	$94,200
Used In 2016	(55,200)
Balance At December 31, 2016	$39,000

Net Capital Loss Carry Forward   The $4,500 net capital loss balance from 2015 remains at the end of 2016.

2017 Analysis
Net And Taxable Income
The required calculations for Net Income For Tax Purposes and Taxable Income are as follows:

Accounting Loss	($42,000)
Accounting Gain On Disposition Of Land	(2,000)
Taxable Capital Gain [(1/2)($2,000)]	1,000
Charitable Donations	2,900
Net Income For Tax Purposes	**Nil**
Dividends	(12,000)
Taxable Income	**Nil**

The 2017 accounting loss of $42,000, includes dividends of $12,000, the accounting gain on the sale of land of $2,000, and a deduction for charitable donations of $2,900. Given this, the business loss for 2017 must be $53,100 ($42,000 + $12,000 + $2,000 - $2,900). This can be verified by the following schedule:

Business Income (Loss)	($53,100)
Dividends	12,000
Accounting Gain	2,000
Charitable Donations	(2,900)
Accounting Income (Loss)	($42,000)

Based on this, the 2017 non-capital loss would be calculated as follows:

Amount E ($53,100 + $12,000)	$65,100
Income Under ITA 3(c) [$12,000 + (1/2)($2,000)]	(13,000)
Non-Capital Loss	$52,100

As the 2016 Taxable Income was reduced to nil, none of this 2017 loss can be carried back to that year.

2017 Carry Forwards
The following carry forward amounts are available at the end of 2017.

Charitable Donations   There is a $2,900 carry forward of charitable donations at the end of 2017.

Non-Capital Loss Carry Forward   The non-capital loss carry forward balance is calculated as follows:

Carry Forward From 2016	$39,000
2017 Addition	52,100
Balance At December 31, 2017	$91,100

Net Capital Loss Carry Forward   While there was a capital gain available in 2016, the non-capital loss carry forward eliminated all of that year's income. Given this, the $4,500 net capital loss balance from 2015 remains at the end of 2017.

Self Study Solution Twelve - 5

From the descriptions in the problem, it would appear that each of the provincial offices of Borodin Ltd. would qualify as a permanent establishment. As a consequence, the allocation to each of these provinces would be based on the following calculations:

Province	Salaries And Wages		Gross Revenues	
	Amount	Percent	Amount	Percent
Alberta	$ 928,000	16%	$ 3,338,400	16%
British Columbia	1,160,000	20%	4,798,950	23%
Nova Scotia	754,000	13%	2,921,100	14%
Saskatchewan	464,000	8%	2,503,800	12%
Ontario	2,494,000	43%	7,302,750	35%
Total	$5,800,000	100%	$20,865,000	100%

The province by province average of the two percentages, calculated above, would be used to allocate the total Taxable Income of $2,983,000 as follows:

Province	Wages	Revenues	Average	Taxable Income
Alberta	16%	16%	16.0%	$ 477,280
British Columbia	20%	23%	21.5%	641,345
Nova Scotia	13%	14%	13.5%	402,705
Saskatchewan	8%	12%	10.0%	298,300
Ontario	43%	35%	39.0%	1,163,370
Total	100%	100%	100.0%	$2,983,000

Self Study Solution Twelve - 6

Kannon's Part I tax payable for the year would be calculated as follows:

Base Amount Of Part I Tax [(38%)($473,000)]	$179,740
Federal Tax Abatement [(10%)(88.6%)($473,000)] (Note One)	(41,908)
Small Business Deduction (Note Two)	(43,944)
General Rate Reduction (Note Three)	(28,846)
Part I Tax Payable	$ 65,042

Note One The federal tax abatement must be reduced because of the foreign business income. The percentage would be calculated as follows:

Canadian Wages And Salaries As Percentage Of Total ($560,000 + $642,000) ÷ $1,298,000	92.6%
Canadian Gross Revenues As Percentage Of Total ($1,200,000 + $1,232,000) ÷ $2,879,000	84.5%

Based on these calculations, the percentage of income on which the federal tax abatement would be available is 88.6 percent [(92.6% + 84.5%) ÷ 2].

Note Two   Since Kannon's Taxable Capital Employed In Canada during 2016 was greater than $10 million, its small business deduction is reduced. The B component of the ITA 125(5.1) reduction formula is $5,600 [(.00225)($12,488,890 - $10,000,000)]. Given this, the required reduction would be calculated as follows:

$$[(\$500,000)(\$5,600 \div \$11,250)] = \$248,889 \textbf{ Reduction}$$

The small business deduction is equal to 17.5 percent of the least of:

- Canadian Active Business Income $440,000
- Taxable Income   473,000
- Reduced Annual Business Limit ($500,000 - $248,889)   251,111

The small business deduction would be $43,944 [(17.5%)($251,111)].

Note Three   The general rate reduction would be calculated as follows:

Taxable Income	$473,000
Amount Eligible For Small Business Deduction	(251,111)
Full Rate Taxable Income	$221,889
Rate	13%
General Rate Reduction	$ 28,846

Self Study Solution Twelve - 7

The Taxable Income and Tax Payable for the Serendipity Shop Corp. for the year would be calculated as follows:

Net Income For Tax Purposes		$240,000
Deductions:		
Dividends	($20,000)	
Donations	(48,000)	(68,000)
Taxable Income		$172,000

Base Amount Of Part I Tax [(38%)($172,000)]	$ 65,360
Federal Tax Abatement [(10%)($172,000)]	(17,200)
Small Business Deduction (Note)	(23,625)
General Rate Reduction [(13%)($172,000 - $135,000)]	(4,810)
Part I Federal Tax Payable	$ 19,725

Note   The small business deduction is based on the least of the following:

Active business income	$220,000
Taxable Income	172,000
Allocated annual business limit	135,000

The small business deduction is equal to $23,625 [(17.5%)($135,000)].

Self Study Solution Twelve - 8

Part A - Net Income For Tax Purposes

The minimum Net Income For Tax Purposes for Borscan Inc. would be calculated as follows:

Accounting Income Before Taxes		$1,275,000
Additions:		
Taxable Capital Gain - Building		
[(1/2)($625,000 - $500,000 - $100,000)]	$ 12,500	
Taxable Capital Gain - Land ($100,000 - $100,000)	Nil	
Recaptured CCA ($500,000 - $350,000)	150,000	
Amortization Expense	255,000	
Interest And Penalties - Late Payment	500	
Charitable Donations	13,500	431,500
		$1,706,500
Deductions:		
Capital Cost Allowance	($287,000)	
Gain On Expropriated Building		
(From Income Statement)	(25,000)	(312,000)
Net Income For Tax Purposes		$1,394,500

Part B - Taxable Income

The minimum Taxable Income for Borscan Inc. would be calculated as follows:

Net Income For Tax Purposes	$1,394,500
Dividends Received	(25,000)
Charitable Donations	(13,500)
Net Capital Loss Carry Forward (Note)	(12,500)
Non-Capital Loss Carry Forward	(35,000)
Taxable Income	$1,308,500

Note The net capital loss carry forward can be used only to the extent of the taxable capital gain for the year, resulting in a deduction of $12,500. This leaves a remaining net capital loss carry forward of $17,500 ($30,000 - $12,500).

Part C - Tax Payable

The minimum federal Tax Payable for Borscan Inc. is as follows:

Base Amount Of Part I Tax [(38%)($1,308,500)]	$497,230
Federal Tax Abatement [(10%)($1,308,500)]	(130,850)
General Rate Reduction [(13%)($1,308,500)]	(170,105)
Federal Tax Payable	$196,275

Self Study Solution Twelve - 9

Part A - Net Income

Net Income For Tax Purposes for Industrial Tools Ltd. would be calculated as follows:

Accounting Income Before Taxes		$2,305,000
Additions:		
Taxable Capital Gain On Building (Note)	$ 37,500	
Taxable Capital Gain On Land		
($200,000 - $200,000)	Nil	
Recaptured CCA ($875,000 - $625,000)	250,000	
Charitable Donations	28,000	
Interest And Penalties	2,500	
Warranty Reserve	20,000	
Amortization Expense	478,000	816,000
		$3,121,000
Deductions:		
Accounting Gain On Building (Given)	($225,000)	
CCA	(523,000)	(748,000)
Net Income For Tax Purposes		$2,373,000

Note The taxable capital gain on the building would be calculated as follows:

Proceeds Of Disposition ($1,150,000 - $200,000)	$950,000
Adjusted Cost Base ($1,075,000 - $200,000)	(875,000)
Capital Gain	$ 75,000
Inclusion Rate	1/2
Taxable Capital Gain	$ 37,500

As its value has not changed, there is no capital gain on the land.

Part B - Taxable Income

Taxable Income for Industrial Tools Ltd. would be calculated as follows:

Net Income For Tax Purposes	$2,373,000
Dividends Received	(42,000)
Charitable Donations	(28,000)
Net Capital Loss Carry Forward (Note)	(37,500)
Taxable Income	$2,265,500

Note The net capital loss carry forward can be used only to the extent of the taxable capital gain for the year, resulting in a deduction of $37,500. This leaves a remaining net capital loss carry forward of $52,500 ($90,000 - $37,500).

Part C - Tax Payable

Federal Tax Payable for Industrial Tools Ltd. would be calculated as follows:

Base Amount Of Part I Tax [(38%)($2,265,500)]	$860,890
Federal Tax Abatement [(10%)($2,265,500)]	(226,550)
General Rate Reduction [(13%)($2,265,500)]	(294,515)
Federal Part I Tax Payable	$339,825

Self Study Solution Twelve - 10

Part A - Net Income For Tax Purposes

The minimum Net Income For Tax Purposes would be calculated as follows:

Accounting Income Before Taxes	$530,400
Accounting Gain On Sale Of Shares	(22,900)
Taxable Capital Gain [(1/2)($22,900)]	11,450
Donations To Registered Canadian Charity	18,700
Net Income For Tax Purposes	$537,650

Part B - Taxable Income

The minimum Taxable Income would be calculated as follows:

Net Income For Tax Purposes	$537,650
Donations To Registered Canadian Charity	(18,700)
Dividends From Taxable Canadian Corporations	(9,400)
Non-Capital Loss Carry Forward	(21,950)
Net Capital Loss Carry Forward*	(11,450)
Taxable Income	$476,150

*While there is a net capital loss carry forward of $13,500, the deduction is limited to $11,450, the taxable gain that was recognized during the current year. This leaves a net capital loss carry forward of $2,050.

Part C - Tax Payable

The minimum federal Part I Tax Payable is as follows:

Base Amount Of Part I Tax [(38%)($476,150)]	$180,937
Federal Tax Abatement [(10%)(90%)($476,150)] (Note One)	(42,854)
Small Business Deduction (Note Two)	Nil
M&P Deduction (Note Three)	(51,136)
General Rate Reduction (Note Four)	(10,764)
Foreign Non-Business Tax Credit (Assumed Equal To Withheld)	(4,845)
Foreign Business Tax Credit (Assumed Equal To Withheld)	(20,700)
Part I Tax Payable	$ 50,638

Note One No income would be allocated to Manitoba as there are no permanent establishments in that province. However, the Manitoba sales would be included in the Ontario total, as the Manitoba customers are serviced through that province. Based on this, the allocation would be as follows:

Gross Revenues	Amount	Percent
Ontario And Manitoba	$5,725,000	91.0
New York	565,000	9.0
Total	$6,290,000	100.0

Salaries And Wages	Amount	Percent
Ontario	$3,540,000	89.0
New York	438,000	11.0
Total	$3,978,000	100.0

Average Ontario Percent [(91.0% + 89.0%) ÷ 2]	90.0%
Average New York Percent [(9.0% + 11.0%) ÷ 2]	10.0%
Total	100.0%

Based on the preceding calculations, the federal tax abatement would be $42,854 [(10%)(90%)($476,150)].

Note Two There is no small business deduction in the calculation of Part I tax, as Mercury Manufacturing Company is not Canadian controlled.

Note Three Since Mercury Manufacturing Company is not a Canadian controlled private corporation, aggregate investment income is not relevant to the M&P calculation. The M&P deduction would be equal to $51,136. This amount is 13 percent of $393,350, which is the lesser of:

M & P Profits (Given)		$410,000
Taxable Income	$476,150	
Less 4 Times Foreign Business Tax Credit [(4)($20,700)]	(82,800)	$393,350

Note Four The general rate reduction would be calculated as follows:

Taxable Income	$476,150
Amount Eligible For The M&P Deduction	(393,350)
Full Rate Taxable Income	$ 82,800
Rate	13%
General Rate Reduction	$ 10,764

Part D - Foreign Tax Credits

To calculate the M&P deduction, both the foreign business and non-business tax credits must first be calculated without considering the general rate reduction. This is necessary as otherwise there would be a circular calculation that could not be solved since the general rate reduction calculation requires the income eligible for the M&P deduction and the calculation of the M&P deduction uses the foreign business tax credit.

Although the foreign non-business tax credit is not used directly in the M&P deduction calculation, it is required to calculate the foreign business tax credit which is used.

In Part C of this problem, it is assumed that the credits are equal to the foreign tax withheld so that the alternative calculations were not necessary.

Using the amounts from Part C, the actual foreign tax credits can be calculated as follows:

Foreign Non-Business Tax Credit The Tax Otherwise Payable for this calculation would be calculated as follows:

Base Amount Of Tax [(38%)($476,150)]	$180,937
Federal Tax Abatement (Note One)	(42,854)
General Rate Reduction (Note Four)	(10,764)
Tax Otherwise Payable (Foreign Non-Business Credit)	$127,319

Using this information, the foreign non-business tax credit would be the lesser of:

- The Amount Withheld $4,845

- $\left(\dfrac{\text{Foreign Non - Business Income}}{\text{Adjusted Net Income}}\right)$ (Part I Tax Otherwise Payable)

  $\left(\dfrac{\$32,300}{\$537,650 - \$11,450 - \$9,400}\right)(\$127,319)$ $7,957

The lesser figure would be the actual withholding of $4,845.

Foreign Business Tax Credit   The Tax Otherwise Payable for this calculation would be calculated as follows:

Base Amount Of Tax [(38%)($476,150)]	$180,937
General Rate Reduction (Note Four)	(10,764)
Tax Otherwise Payable (Foreign Business Credit)	$170,173

Using this information, the foreign business tax credit would be the least of:

- The Amount Withheld $20,700

- $\left(\dfrac{\text{Foreign Business Income}}{\text{Adjusted Net Income}}\right)$ (Part I Tax Otherwise Payable)

  $\left(\dfrac{\$64,200}{\$537,650 - \$11,450 - \$9,400}\right)(\$170,173)$ $21,140

- Tax Otherwise Payable, Less The Foreign Non-Business Tax Credit
  [($170,173) - $4,845] $165,328

The least of these three figures would be the U.S. taxes withheld of $20,700.

Chapter 12 Learning Objectives

After completing Chapter 12, you should be able to:

1. Calculate a corporation's Net Income For Tax Purposes (paragraph [P hereafter] 12-1 to 12-4).
2. List the deductions that are available to corporations in calculating Taxable Income (P 12-5 to 12-9).
3. Apply the treatment for different types of dividends received, including the application of the stop loss rules (P 12-10 to 12-23).
4. Calculate the non-capital loss carry over for a corporation (P 12-24 to 12-30).
5. Determine the optimum ordering of the deductions available in calculating corporate Taxable Income (P 12-31 to 12-36).

6. Allocate corporate Taxable Income to specific provinces (P 12-37 to 12-44).
7. Apply the basic corporate tax rate and explain the effect of the federal tax abatement and the general rate reduction (P 12-45 to 12-51).
8. Calculate provincial Tax Payable for a corporation using a supplied schedule of rates and other data (P 12-52 to 12-61).
9. List the important non-revenue raising goals of the corporate tax system (P 12-62 and 12-63).
10. Explain the rules for determining which corporations and what amounts of income are eligible for the small business deduction (P 12-64 to 12-87).

11. Calculate the amount of the small business deduction (P 12-88 to 12-98).
12. Calculate the reduction in the small business deduction that is applicable to large CCPCs (P 12-99 to 12-109).
13. Identify personal services corporations and explain their tax treatment (P 12-110 to 12-116).
14. Identify professional corporations and management companies and explain their tax treatment (P 12-117 and 12-118).
15. Calculate the manufacturing and processing profits deduction for all types of corporations (P 12-119 to 12-135).

16. Calculate the general rate reduction that is available to all corporations and the specific application of the general rate reduction to CCPCs (P 12-136 to 12-149).
17. Calculate the foreign non-business (property) and business income tax credits for corporations and apply the rules that deal with any excess of foreign tax withheld over the foreign tax credit (P 12-150 to 12-162).

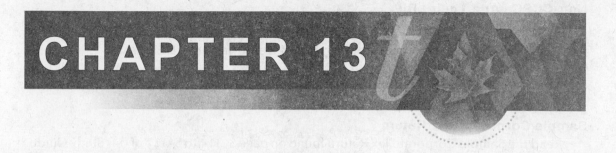

CHAPTER 13

How To Work Through Chapter 13

We recommend the following approach in dealing with the material in this Chapter:

Integration
- Read paragraph 13-1 to 13-24 (in the textbook).
- Do Exercises Thirteen-1 and Thirteen-2 (in the textbook) and check the solutions in this Study Guide.
- Do Self Study Problem Thirteen-1 which is available on the Companion Website and check the solution in this Study Guide.

Refundable Tax On Aggregate Investment Income
- Read paragraph 13-25 to 13-38.

Additional Refundable Tax On Investment Income (ART)
- Read paragraph 13-39 to 13-42.
- Do Exercise Thirteen-3 and check the solution in this Study Guide.
- Read paragraph 13-43 to 13-47.

Refundable Portion Of Part I Tax
- Read paragraph 13-48 to 13-67.
- Do Exercise Thirteen-4 and check the solution in this Study Guide.

Refundable Part IV Tax On Dividends Received
- Read paragraph 13-68 to 13-93.
- Do Exercise Thirteen-5 and check the solution in this Study Guide.
- Read paragraph 13-94 and 13-95.

Refundable Dividend Tax On Hand (RDTOH)
- Read paragraph 13-96 to 13-120.
- Do Exercises Thirteen-6 and Thirteen-7 and check the solutions in this Study Guide.

Working Through Large Corporate Problems
- Read paragraph 13-121 and 13-122.
- Do Self Study Problems Thirteen-2 and Thirteen-3 and check the solutions in this Study Guide.

Designation Of Eligible Dividends
- Read paragraph 13-123 to 13-128.

CCPCs And Their GRIP
- Read paragraph 13-129 to 13-134.
- Do Exercise Thirteen-8 and check the solution in this Study Guide.

Non-CCPCs And Their LRIP
- Read paragraph 13-135 to 13-138.

Part III.1 Tax On Excessive Eligible Dividend Designations (EEDDs)
- Read paragraph 13-139 to 13-147.
- Do Self Study Problems Thirteen-4 to Thirteen-7 and check the solutions in this Study Guide.

Sample Corporate Tax Return
- Read the Sample Corporate Tax Return found on page S-314 to S-317 of this Study Guide. The complete tax return is available on the Companion Website in two formats, a T2 ProFile return file and a .PDF file.

To Complete This Chapter
- If you would like more practice in problem solving, do the Supplementary Self Study Problems for the chapter. These problems and solutions are available on the Companion Website.
- Review the Key Terms Used In This Chapter in the textbook at the end of Chapter 13. Consult the Glossary for the meaning of any key terms you do not know.
- Test yourself with the Chapter 13 Glossary Flashcards available on the Companion Website.
- Ensure you have achieved the Chapter 13 Learning Objectives listed in this Study Guide.
- As a review, we recommend you view the PowerPoint presentation for Chapter 13 that is on the Companion Website.

Practice Examination
- Write the Practice Examination for Chapter 13 that is on the Companion Website. Mark your examination using the Practice Examination Solution that is on the Companion Website.

Sample Corporate Tax Return

The following simplified example contains a T2 corporate income tax return completed using the ProFile T2 corporate tax preparation program from Intuit Canada. It contains 2016 (not 2017) information as the current Profile software release does not support fiscal periods ending after April 30, 2017. Shortly after the first filing version of the 2017 Intuit ProFile software is available in January, 2018, the updated 2017 version of this problem will be available on the Companion website at:

www.pearsoncanada.ca/byrdchen/ctp2018

As this example is designed to illustrate corporate tax return calculations, limited GIFI (General Index of Financial Information) data has been included. The relevant T2 schedule or form name is provided in square brackets to make it easier for users to find where the information is input. Note that capital dividends are covered in detail in Chapter 14.

Sample Files On Companion Website
To View The Tax Return Files
The complete sample tax return is available on the Companion Website in two versions, a T2 ProFile return file and a .PDF file.

To view the ProFile return file (with a .GT2 extension), you must have the ProFile program installed. For information on how to obtain the program for free, see the Companion Website.

To view the .PDF files, you must have the Adobe Reader program installed. This program can be installed for free from the Adobe website (www.adobe.com).

Sample Problem Data

Note: The government's Crown Copyright does not permit us to use fake Business Numbers in software examples. To reduce the number of ProFile's error messages because of this, we have used NR (for not registered) in the Business Number field.

MetroFaux Inc. is a Canadian controlled private corporation based in Saskatoon that manufactures metal and composite office furniture. Its head office is located at 123 ABC Avenue, Saskatoon, SK S7G 1A1, phone number (306)111-1111. The signing officer and contact person is the President of the company, Jack Saskatoon. MetroFaux Inc. was incorporated on August 28, 1977.

Most of its income is earned from active business in Canada. The Company has no associated corporations. Although the company has a sophisticated website, it is only for information purposes. It has no income from a web page or website. [Schedule 88 is not applicable.]

As at December 31, 2015, the following information applied to MetroFaux Inc:

Taxable Capital Employed In Canada [Info]	$1,590,000
RDTOH [T2, line 460]	Nil
Dividends Declared And Paid During 2015	Nil
GRIP Balance [Schedule 53]	276,000

During the taxation year ending December 31, 2016, the condensed before tax Income Statement of MetroFaux Inc. was prepared in accordance with the International Financial Reporting Standards (IFRS). In condensed form it is as follows:

MetroFaux Inc.
Condensed Income Statement
Year Ending December 31, 2016

Sales	$3,980,000	
Gain On Building Sale	160,000	$4,140,000
Amortization Expense	$ 607,000	
Other Expenses Excluding Taxes	1,773,000	2,380,000
Accounting Income Before Taxes		$1,760,000

Preliminary GIFI Procedures

On the ProFile schedule titled "Info", the Filing question "Complete return from GIFI?" is answered Yes by default. Ignore the GIFI requirements except as follows:

- On GIFI Schedule 125 (Income Statement), input the total sales as "Trade sales of goods and services" (Code 8000) and the Gain On Building Sale as "Realized gains / losses on disposal of assets" (Code 8210) from the drop down menu under Revenues. Input the Amortization Expense as "Amortization of tangible assets" (Code 8670) and the Other Expenses as "Other expenses" (Code 9270) from the drop down menu under Operating Expenses.

- On GIFI Schedule 100 (Balance Sheet), input the Net Income figure as "Cash and deposits" (Code 1000) in order to make the total assets equal to the total liabilities and equity.

Although this will not properly complete the GIFI statements, the amounts input will carry forward to the appropriate cells in the tax return.

To prevent audit warnings, S141, "Notes Checklist", has to be completed. Assume there are no notes to the financial statements and answer "No" to any other relevant questions.

Other Information:

1. Expenses include interest and penalties of $2,300 resulting from late income tax installments and a failure to file the 2015 tax return within the prescribed time period. [Schedule 1]

2. Expenses include a deduction for charitable donations to the Cancer Research Society in the amount of $15,000. [Schedule 2]

3. Revenues include eligible dividends of $36,000 from Canadian Tax Save Inc., a taxable Canadian corporation. MetroFaux Inc. has no association with Canadian Tax Save Inc. and considers the dividends portfolio dividends. [Schedule 3. Note that under the GRIP/LRIP double column, "Column F deduction type" = s. 112 and X must be placed in the "Indicate eligible dividends" column.]

4. The Company paid $100,000 in taxable eligible dividends during 2016. [Schedule 3]

5. The Company has available a non-capital loss carry over from the previous year of $56,000 [S4Supp]. The net capital loss carry forward from 2013 is $22,500 (1/2 of $45,000). [Schedule 4 - note 100 percent figures are used for the capital loss]

6. During 2016, the Company earned $97,000 of interest income on bonds purchased in 2015 that mature in 2020. [Schedule 7]

7. Amortization expense on the Income Statement amounts to $607,000 The opening UCC balance was $905,000 for Class 8, $800,000 for Class 10 and $429,000 for Class 53. The only fixed asset acquisition was $100,000 in Class 53 manufacturing equipment. There were no dispositions in Classes 8 or 10. [Schedule 8 flows to Schedule 1]

8. The Gain On Building Sale resulted from the sale of a building for proceeds of $792,000 of which $120,000 was allocated to the land. The building at 456 DEF Street, Regina, Saskatchewan S7G 1A1, was acquired on August 28, 2007 for $764,000, of which $100,000 was allocated to the land. The sales office of the Company had been located in this building and the sales office has subsequently moved to leased space in Saskatoon. As the Company leases all of its other buildings and equipment, the building was the only asset in Class 1. The Undepreciated Capital Cost of this class prior to the disposition of the building was $514,000. [Schedules 1, 6 and 8]

9. Information related to Canadian manufacturing and processing activities for the year is as follows: [Schedule 27]

Cost of capital [(10% of $6,000,000) + ($200,000 in rental costs)]	$ 800,000
Portion of capital used in M&P activities	500,000
Cost of labour	1,000,000
Portion of labour used in M&P activities	760,000

10. All of the common shares of MetroFaux Inc. are held by the president, Jack Saskatoon (SIN 527-000-582). [Schedule 50]

11. The beginning balance in the Company's capital dividend account is nil [CDA]. Note that capital dividends are covered in detail in Chapter 14.

12. The Company paid one federal income tax instalment of $212,000 on September 1, 2016 [TaxPaid].

Notes On Sample Corporate Tax Return

Loss Carry Forwards

The losses of prior taxation years deducted in the calculation of Taxable Income consist of the non-capital loss of $56,000 and a $14,000 net capital loss. As calculated on Schedule 4, the net capital loss carry forward deduction is limited by the $28,000 capital gain for the year and leaves a capital loss carry forward of $17,000. Note Schedule 4 uses the 100 percent amounts. There is no non-capital loss carry forward remaining.

Building Sale

The $160,000 Gain On Building Sale is deducted on Schedule 1 as the tax effects of the disposition are included in Net Income For Tax Purposes. As calculated on Schedule 6, the taxable capital gain on the building sale is $14,000 [(1/2)($792,000 - $764,000)].

As calculated on Schedule 8, the recapture of CCA on the building is equal to $150,000 ($664,000 - $514,000). This is shown as an addition on Schedule 1, separate from the CCA.

Aggregate Investment Income

As calculated on Schedule 7, Part 1, the aggregate investment income of $97,000 consists of:

- the taxable capital gains of $14,000, less
- the $14,000 net capital loss carry forward claimed, plus
- net property income of $133,000 (dividends received of $36,000 plus interest income of $97,000), less
- taxable dividends deductible of $36,000.

This figure is used in calculating the refundable portion of Part I tax.

Active Business Income

As calculated on Schedule 7, Part 5, income from active business carried on in Canada of $1,580,800 is Net Income For Tax Purposes of $1,727,800 less the sum of:

- the taxable capital gains of $14,000, plus
- net property income of $133,000 (dividends received of $36,000 plus interest income of $97,000).

This figure is used in the small business deduction calculation and in Schedule 27 for the M&P deduction.

M&P Labour

As the grossed up M&P Labour of $1,013,333 [(100/75)($760,000)] is greater than the $1,000,000 Cost of Labour, M&P Labour in the Schedule 27, Part 7 calculation is limited to $1,000,000.

As mentioned in the text, although the effect of the federal M&P deduction has been negated by the general rate reduction, there are still provincial M&P tax reductions available. In this example, MetroFaux Inc. is eligible for the Saskatchewan M&P tax reduction. (See Schedule 404.)

Capital Dividend Account

The balance in the Capital Dividend Account is $14,000 [(1/2)($692,000 - $664,000)]. A tax free capital dividend of $14,000 could have been paid if form T2054 had been filed. (See Chapter 14.)

GRIP

As no dividends were declared or paid during 2015, no eligible dividends could have been paid. As a result, Schedule 53 has no amount on line 300, "Eligible dividends paid in the previous tax year".

Solutions to Chapter Thirteen Exercises

Exercise Thirteen - 1 Solution

If she incorporates, the corporation will pay taxes of $15,000 [(15%)($100,000)], leaving $85,000 to be distributed as dividends. Her individual Tax Payable on these non-eligible dividends would be calculated as follows:

Dividends Received	$ 85,000
Gross Up [(17%)($85,000)]	14,450
Grossed Up Dividends	$99,450
Personal Tax Rate	45%
Tax Before Credit	$ 44,753
Dividend Tax Credit [(21/29 + 30%)($14,450)]	(14,799)
Tax Payable On Dividends	$29,954

The net after tax retention would be $55,046 ($85,000 - $29,954). This compares to $55,000 [($100,000)(1 - .45)] retained if a corporation is not used. This result reflects offsetting factors. While the corporate tax rate is above the 14.53 percent required for perfect integration, the provincial dividend tax credit is higher than the 27.6 percent required for perfect integration. The net result is that incorporation would provide a small improvement in after tax retention.

Exercise Thirteen - 2 Solution

If he incorporates, the corporation will pay taxes of $30,000 [(30%)($100,000)], leaving $70,000 to be distributed as dividends. His individual Tax Payable on these eligible dividends would be calculated as follows:

Dividends Received	$70,000
Gross Up [(38%)($70,000)]	26,600
Grossed Up Dividends	$96,600
Personal Tax Rate	42%
Tax Before Credit	$40,572
Dividend Tax Credit [(6/11 + 28%)($26,600)]	(21,957)
Tax Payable On Dividends	$18,615

The net after tax retention would be $51,385 ($70,000 - $18,615). This compares to $58,000 [($100,000)(1 - .42)] retained if a corporation is not used. Clearly the use of a corporation is not desirable in this situation. While the corporate tax rate of 30 percent is greater than the required 27.54 percent, the real problem here is the fact that the provincial dividend tax credit of 28 percent is significantly below the required 45.5 percent.

Exercise Thirteen - 3 Solution

Zircon's Taxable Income would be calculated as follows:

Net Income For Tax Purposes	$281,000
Dividends From Taxable Canadian Corporations	(22,000)
Net Capital Loss Carry Forward	(26,000)
Non-Capital Loss Carry Forward	(23,000)
Taxable Income	$210,000

Zircon's amount eligible for the small business deduction of $198,000 is the least of active business income of $198,000, Taxable Income of $210,000, and the annual business limit of $500,000.

Given these calculations, Zircon's additional refundable tax on investment income would be calculated using the lesser of:

Aggregate Investment Income		
Taxable Capital Gains	$46,000	
Net Capital Loss Deducted	(26,000)	
Interest Income	15,000	$35,000
Taxable Income	$210,000	
Amount Eligible For SBD	(198,000)	$12,000

The additional refundable tax on investment income would be $1,280 [(10-2/3%)($12,000)]. Note that the Taxable Income limit is $23,000 ($35,000 - $12,000) less than the Aggregate Investment Income. This difference is the result of the deduction of the $23,000 non-capital loss carry forward.

Exercise Thirteen - 4 Solution

If Ms. Nicastro receives the income directly, she will retain $49,000 [($100,000)(1 - .51)]. Alternatively, if the investments are transferred to a corporation, the results would be as follows:

Corporate Investment Income	$100,000
Corporate Tax At 52 Percent	(52,000)
After Tax Income	$ 48,000
Dividend Refund [($48,000 ÷ .61667) - $48,000]	29,837
Non-Eligible Dividends Paid To Ms. Nicastro	$ 77,837
Non-Eligible Dividends Received	$ 77,837
Gross Up Of 17 Percent	13,232
Personal Taxable Income	$ 91,069
Personal Tax Rate	51%
Tax Payable Before Dividend Tax Credit	$ 46,445
Dividend Tax Credit [(21/29 + 30%)($13,232)]	(13,551)
Personal Tax Payable With Corporation	$ 32,894
Non-Eligible Dividends Received	$ 77,837
Personal Tax Payable	(32,894)
After Tax Cash Retained With Corporation	$ 44,943

There would be no tax deferral with the corporation as the corporate taxes of $52,000 are $1,000 more than the $51,000 she would pay on direct receipt of the income. In addition, the use of a corporation would reduce the after tax funds retained by $4,057 ($44,943 vs. $49,000). There is clearly a disadvantage resulting from the use of a corporation.

Exercise Thirteen - 5 Solution

The amount of Part IV Tax Payable would be calculated as follows:

Tax On Portfolio Investments [(38-1/3%)($14,000)]	$5,367
Tax On Emerald Inc. Dividends	Nil
Tax On Ruby Inc. Dividends [(30%)($15,000)]	4,500
Part IV Tax Payable	$9,867

Exercise Thirteen - 6 Solution

The refundable amount of Debut Inc.'s Part I tax would be the least of the following three figures:

Foreign Non-Business Income (100 Percent)		$15,000
Taxable Capital Gains [(1/2)($38,250)]		19,125
Net Rental Income		6,500
Interest Income		9,200
Net Capital Loss Carry Forward Deducted		(9,000)
Aggregate Investment Income Under ITA 129(4)		$40,825
Rate		30-2/3%
Amount Before Foreign Income Adjustment		$12,520
Deduct Excess Of:		
Foreign Non-Business Tax Credit	($ 750)	
Over 8 Percent Of Foreign Non-Business		
Income [(8%)($15,000)]	1,200	Nil
Amount Under ITA 129(3)(a)(i)		$12,520
Taxable Income ($121,825 - $22,000 - $9,000)		$90,825
Deduct:		
Amount Eligible For The Small Business Deduction ($8,750 ÷ 17.5%)	(	50,000)
[(100/38-2/3)($750)] Foreign Non-Business Tax Credit	(	1,940)
Adjusted Taxable Income		$38,885
Rate		30-2/3%
Amount Under ITA 129(3)(a)(ii)		$11,925
Amount Under ITA 129(3)(a)(iii) = Part I Tax Payable (Given)		$20,286

The least of these three amounts is $11,925, and this would be the refundable portion of Part I tax for the year.

Exercise Thirteen - 7 Solution

The balance in the RDTOH account of Quan Imports would be as follows:

Opening Balance	$12,500	
Less: Previous Year's Dividend Refund (Given)	(2,300)	$10,200
Part I Refundable Addition [(30-2/3%)($24,000)]	$ 7,360	
Part IV Tax On Portfolio Dividends [(38-1/3%)($6,000)]	2,300	9,660
Closing Balance - RDTOH		$19,860

The dividend refund would be $5,750 [(38-1/3%)($15,000)], the lesser of (38-1/3 percent of the $15,000 dividend paid and the $19,860 balance in the RDTOH account.

Exercise Thirteen - 8 Solution

Since Taxable Income is greater than Aggregate Investment Income (comparison used in D in the following table), the 2017 ending balance in GRIP will be calculated as follows:

C - GRIP Balance At End Of 2016		$365,000
D - Taxable Income	$960,000	
Income Eligible For SBD ($39,375 ÷ 17.5%)	(225,000)	
Aggregate Investment Income		
($65,000 + $23,000 - $14,000)	(74,000)	
Adjusted Taxable Income	$661,000	
Rate	72%	475,920
E - Eligible Dividends Received		85,000
G - Eligible Dividends Designated in 2016		(140,000)
GRIP At End Of 2017		$785,920

The eligible dividends paid during 2017 will be deducted from the GRIP in 2018.

Self Study Solution Thirteen - 1

The required calculations would be as follows:

Corporate Taxes

Income For The Year	$50,000
Corporate Taxes (17%)	(8,500)
Income Available For Dividends	$41,500

Personal Taxes On Dividends

Dividend Income	$41,500
Gross Up (17%)	7,055
Taxable Dividends	$48,555

Tax Payable Before Dividend Tax Credit	
[(33% + 16%)($48,555)]	$23,792
Dividend Tax Credit [(21/29 + 8/29)($7,055)]	(7,055)
Personal Tax Payable	$16,737

Total Taxes On Corporate Flow Through

Corporate Taxes	$ 8,500
Personal Taxes	16,737
Total Taxes	$25,237

Total Taxes On Income Earned Directly

Income For The Year	$50,000
Combined Federal/Provincial Tax Rate (33% + 16%)	49%
Personal Tax Payable	$24,500

While the provincial dividend tax credit is at the rate required for perfect integration, the combined corporate federal/provincial tax rate is above the 14.53 percent that is required to achieve this goal. The result is that taxes on $50,000 of income flowed through a corporation is $737 ($25,237 - $24,500) higher than the taxes on the same $50,000 of income received directly.

Self Study Solution Thirteen - 2

Part A - FOL's Dividend Refund
The ending RDTOH balance for FOL would be as follows:

Refundable Dividend Tax On Hand - End Of Previous Year	$2,000
Refundable Portion Of Part I Tax [(30-2/3%)($7,000)]	2,147
Refundable Dividend Tax On Hand - Ending	$4,147

As FOL has no foreign investment income or deductions for loss carry overs, the calculation of the addition to the RDTOH for the refundable portion of Part I tax is based solely on the interest income.

The dividend refund would be $4,147, the lesser of:

- 38-1/3% Percent Of $75,000 Of Taxable Dividends Paid $28,750
- Refundable Dividend Tax On Hand $ 4,147

Part B - SHI's Part IV Tax Payable
The Part IV tax for SHI would be calculated as follows:

Portfolio Dividends [(38-1/3%)($8,000)]	$3,067
SHI's Share Of FOL's Dividend Refund (100%) - Part A	4,147
Part IV Tax Payable	$7,214

Part C - SHI's Dividend Refund
SHI's aggregate investment income totals $35,625, the sum of $12,000 in interest income and $23,625 [(1/2)($47,250)] in taxable capital gains. This means that the ending RDTOH balance for SHI would be as follows:

Refundable Dividend Tax On Hand - End Of Previous Year	$10,000
Refundable Portion Of Part I Tax [(30-2/3%)($35,625)]	10,925
Part IV Tax Payable (Part B)	7,214
Refundable Dividend Tax On Hand - Ending	$28,139

The dividend refund would be $19,167, the lesser of:

- 38-1/3 Percent Of $50,000 Of Taxable Dividends Paid $19,167
- Refundable Dividend Tax On Hand $28,139

Note that the appropriate calculation of the refundable portion of Part I tax would require selecting the least of the amounts described in ITA 129(3)(a)(i), (ii), and (iii). This problem does not contain sufficient information to calculate ITA 129(3)(a)(ii) or (iii) and as a result, you are asked to assume that the refundable portion of Part I tax is the amount determined under ITA 129(3)(a)(i).

Self Study Solution Thirteen - 3

Part IV Refundable Tax

The Part IV Tax Payable for Insal Ltd. would be calculated as follows:

Dividend Refund Received By Dorne Inc.	$8,400
Insal's Percentage Of Ownership	45%
Part IV Payable On Dorne Inc. Dividends	$3,780
Part IV Tax On Enbridge Dividends [(38-1/3%)($6,200)]	2,377
Part IV Tax Payable	$6,157

Part I Refundable Tax

The refundable portion of the Part I tax would be the least of the following amounts:

Taxable Capital Gain [(1/2)($24,600)]	$12,300
Net Rental Income	4,200
Aggregate Investment Income	$16,500
Rate	30-2/3%
ITA 129(3)(a)(i)	$ 5,060

Taxable Income	$123,400
Amount Eligible For Small Business Deduction (See Note)	(45,000)
Total	$ 78,400
Rate	30-2/3%
ITA 129(3)(a)(ii)	$ 24,043

ITA 129(3)(a)(iii) Part I Tax Payable - Given	$ 23,960

Note The problem states that Insal's $45,000 share of the annual business limit is less than active business income. In addition, it is less than the Company's Taxable Income. These facts establish that the amount eligible for the small business deduction is Insal's share of the annual business limit.

The refundable portion of Part I tax is equal to $5,060, which is the least of the preceding three amounts.

RDTOH

The end of year balance in the Refundable Dividend Tax On Hand account and refundable Part I tax can be calculated as follows:

RDTOH Balance - End Of The Preceding Year	$ 6,450
Dividend Refund For The Preceding Year	(2,300)
Opening Balance	$ 4,150
Part IV Tax Payable	6,157
Refundable Part I Tax	5,060
RDTOH Balance - End Of The Year	$15,367

Dividend Refund

The dividend refund will be $6,996 the lesser of:

- $6,996 (38-1/3% of the $18,250 in dividends paid); and
- the $15,367 balance in the RDTOH.

Self Study Solution Thirteen - 4

Part A - Part I Tax Payable

The required calculations to determine Part I federal Tax Payable are as follows:

Net Income For Tax Purposes	$473,900
Dividends ($108,000 + $56,000)	(164,000)
Taxable Income	**$309,900**

Base Amount Of Part I Tax [(38%)($309,900)]	$117,762
Federal Tax Abatement [(10%)($309,900)]	(30,990)
Small Business Deduction (Note One)	(37,853)
Additional Refundable Tax On Investment Income (Note Two)	9,984
General Rate Reduction (Note Three)	Nil
Part I Federal Tax Payable	**$ 58,903**

Note One The small business deduction is 17.5 percent of the least of the following three amounts:

1. Active Business Income	$216,300
2. Taxable Income (no foreign tax credit adjustment)	$309,900
3. Allocated Annual Business Limit ($500,000 - $200,000)	$300,000

The lowest of these figures is the active business income of $216,300 and this gives a small business deduction of $37,853 [(17.5%)($216,300)].

Note Two The aggregate investment income of $93,600 is calculated as follows:

Interest On Government Bonds	$ 36,300
Taxable Capital Gains	57,300
Aggregate Investment Income	**$ 93,600**

The ITA 123.3 refundable tax (ART) is 10-2/3 percent of the lesser of:

1. Aggregate Investment Income		$93,600
2. Taxable Income	$309,900	
Deduct: Amount Eligible For The SBD	(216,300)	$93,600

The ITA 123.3 tax on aggregate investment income is $9,984 [(10-2/3%)($93,600)].

Note Three The general rate reduction would be calculated as follows:

Taxable Income	$309,900
Amount Eligible For The Small Business Deduction	(216,300)
Aggregate Investment Income (Note Two)	(93,600)
Full Rate Taxable Income	Nil
Rate	13%
General Rate Reduction	**Nil**

Part B - Part IV Tax Payable

The required calculation of the Part IV Tax Payable on the portfolio investment dividends is as follows:

Part IV Tax [($56,000)(38-1/3%)]	$21,467

Part C - RDTOH Balance

The calculation of the ending balance in the Refundable Dividend Tax On Hand account is as follows:

RDTOH, End Of The Preceding Year	Nil
Dividend Refund For The Preceding Year	Nil
Opening Balance	Nil
Refundable Portion Of Part I Tax (Note Four)	$28,704
Part IV Tax (See Part B)	21,467
RDTOH Balance - December 31, 2017	$50,171

Note Four   Using amounts calculated in Part A, the amount of refundable Part I tax is $28,704, the least of three amounts, calculated as follows:

- Amount Under ITA 129(3)(a)(i) [(30-2/3%)($93,600)] $28,704
- Amount Under ITA 129(3)(a)(ii) [(30-2/3%)($309,900 - $216,300)] $28,704
- Amount Under ITA 129(3)(a)(iii) Part I Tax Payable $58,903

Part D - GRIP Balance

Since Taxable Income is greater than Aggregate Investment Income, the December 31, 2017 GRIP balance would be calculated as follows:

GRIP Balance At End Of 2016		$ 59,000
Taxable Income	$309,900	
Income Eligible For SBD	(216,300)	
Aggregate Investment Income	(93,600)	
Adjusted Taxable Income	Nil	
Rate	72%	Nil
Eligible Dividends Received		56,000
Eligible Dividends Designated in 2016		Nil
GRIP At End Of 2017		$115,000

Part E - Dividend Refund

The dividend refund for the year would be $12,420, the lesser of:

- 38-1/3 Percent Of Taxable Dividends Paid [($32,400)(38-1/3%)] = $12,420

- Ending RDTOH Balance (Part C) = $50,171

Part F - Total Federal Tax Payable

The required calculation to determine federal Tax Payable is as follows:

Part I Tax (Part A)	$58,903
Part IV Tax (Part B)	21,467
Dividend Refund (Part E)	(12,420)
Federal Tax Payable	$67,950

Self Study Solution Thirteen - 5

Part A - Part I Tax Payable

The Part I Tax Payable is calculated as follows:

Base Amount Of Part I Tax [(38%)($503,500)]	$191,330
Federal Tax Abatement [(10%)(72.95%)($503,500)]	(36,730)
Small Business Deduction [(17.5%)($200,000 Which Was Given)]	(35,000)
Additional Refundable Tax On Investment Income (Note One)	11,781
General Rate Reduction (Note Three)	(25,097)
Foreign Non-Business Income Tax Credit (Given)	(8,250)
Foreign Business Income Tax Credit (Given)	(34,300)
Part I Tax Payable	$ 63,734

Note One   The aggregate investment income of $110,450 is calculated as follows:

Interest On Loan To Subsidiary	$ 43,250
Foreign Investment Income	55,000
Taxable Capital Gains	24,500
Net Capital Losses Claimed	(12,300)
Aggregate Investment Income (Note Two)	$110,450

The ITA 123.3 refundable tax (ART) is 10-2/3 percent of the lesser of:

1. Aggregate Investment Income		$110,450
2. Taxable Income	$503,500	
Deduct: Amount Eligible For The SBD	(200,000)	$303,500

The ITA 123.3 tax on aggregate investment income is $11,781 [(10-2/3%)($110,450)].

Note Two   The definition contained in ITA 129(4.1) excludes income from property that is incidental to carrying on an active business and, as a consequence, we have left out the $5,050 of term deposit interest. With respect to the interest on the loan to the subsidiary, if the subsidiary had deducted the $43,250 in computing active business income eligible for the small business deduction, ITA 129(6) would have deemed this interest to be active business income rather than investment income. However, the problem notes that the subsidiary was not involved in the production of active business income and, as a consequence, the interest from the subsidiary is included in the above calculation of aggregate investment income.

Note Three   The general rate reduction is based on the amount of Taxable Income that is not subject to other types of favourable tax treatment. The reduction would be calculated as follows:

Taxable Income	$503,500
Amount Eligible For The Small Business Deduction (Given)	(200,000)
Aggregate Investment Income (Note One)	(110,450)
Full Rate Taxable Income	$193,050
Rate	13%
General Rate Reduction	$ 25,097

Part B - Part IV Tax Payable

The Part IV Tax Payable would be calculated as follows:

38-1/3 Percent Of Portfolio Dividends Received [(38-1/3%)($19,600)]	$ 7,513
Share Of Dividend Refund Included In	
Dividends From Subsidiary [(75%)($12,750)]	9,563
Part IV Tax Payable	$17,076

Part C - RDTOH Balance

The refundable portion of Part I tax would be the least of the following three amounts:

Aggregate Investment Income (See Note One)		$110,450
Rate		30-2/3%
Total		$ 33,871
Deduct Excess Of:		
Foreign Non-Business Tax Credit	($8,250)	
Over 8% Of Foreign Non-Business Income		
[(8%)($55,000)]	4,400	(3,850)
Amount Under ITA 129(3)(a)(i)		$ 30,021

Taxable Income	$503,500
Deduct:	
Amount Eligible For The Small Business Deduction	(200,000)
[(100 ÷ 38-2/3)($8,250)] Foreign Non-Business Tax Credit	(21,336)
[(4)($34,300)] Foreign Business Tax Credit	(137,200)
Total	$144,964
Rate	30-2/3%
Amount Under ITA 129(3)(a)(ii)	$ 44,456

Amount Under ITA 129(3)(a)(iii) = Part I Tax Payable	$63,734

The least of these three amounts is $30,021, the amount calculated under ITA 129(3)(a)(i).

The calculation of the ending balance in the Refundable Dividend Tax On Hand account is as follows:

RDTOH Balance - End Of The Preceding Year	$23,500	
Dividend Refund For The Preceding Year	(9,600)	$13,900
Refundable Portion Of Part I Tax	$30,021	
Part IV Tax Payable (Part B)	17,076	47,097
RDTOH Balance - December 31, 2017		$60,997

Part D - Dividend Refund

The dividend refund for the year would be $41,783, the lesser of:

- 38-1/3 percent of taxable dividends paid during the year
  {[38-1/3%][$25,000 + (3)($28,000)]} = $41,783

- RDTOH Balance - December 31, 2017 = $60,997

Note that the dividend refund is calculated on the basis of dividends paid, not dividends declared.

Self Study Solution Thirteen - 6

Part A - Net And Taxable Income

The calculation of Acme Imports' Net Income For Tax Purposes and Taxable Income would be as follows:

Accounting Income Before Taxes		$232,300
Additions:		
Amortization Expense	$20,000	
Charitable Donations	25,000	
Taxable Capital Gain On Sale Of Equipment		
[(1/2)($84,500 - $62,000)]	11,250	
Golf Club Membership	2,800	
50 Percent Of Business Meals And Entertainment	3,360	
Share Issue Costs [(80%)($950)]	760	
Costs Of Supplementary Letters Patent	7,000	
Interest On Mortgage For The Land	12,300	82,470
Deductions:		
CCA (Note One)	($43,550)	
Gain On Sale Of Equipment ($84,500 - $27,500)	(57,000)	(100,550)
Net Income For Tax Purposes		**$214,220**
Charitable Donations		(25,000)
Dividends From Sarco Ltd.		(24,000)
Taxable Income		**$165,220**

Note One   The maximum CCA on the Class 8 equipment would be calculated as follows:

Opening UCC	$256,000	
Disposition - Lesser Of:		
Proceeds Of Disposition = $84,500		
Capital Cost = $62,000		(62,000)
CCA Base		$194,000
Rate		20%
CCA - Class 8		$ 38,800

The customer list, as well as the cost of the supplementary letters patent would be added to Class 14.1. The maximum CCA for this Class would be as follows:

Opening UCC	Nil
Additions ($183,000 + $7,000)	$190,000
One-Half Net Additions [(1/2)($190,000)]	(95,000)
CCA Base	$ 95,000
Rate	5%
CCA - Class 14.1	$ 4,750

Base on this, the maximum total CCA would be $43,550 ($38,800 + $4,750).

Several of the items in this problem need further comment. These are as follows:

- **Item 4**   With respect to the costs of issuing shares, such amounts have to be deducted over at least 5 years at a maximum rate of 20 percent per year.

- **Item 6**   Only 50 percent of the $6,720 in charges at the local golf and country club are deductible.

- **Item 7**   The cars provided to the principal shareholder and to the manager of the Company will result in their being assessed for a substantial taxable benefit. However, the costs are fully deductible to the Company.

- **Item 10**   The fees paid to the site consultant are deductible as indicated in ITA 20(1)(dd). ITA 18(3.1) disallows the deduction of interest on financing related to land during construction. The $12,300 interest on the $244,000 mortgage on the land would be capitalized and is not deductible.

Part B - Active Business Income

The active business income of Acme is as follows:

Net Income For Tax Purposes		$214,220
Dividends		(24,000)
Aggregate Investment Income:		
Interest Revenue	($10,000)	
Taxable Capital Gain	(11,250)	(21,250)
Active Business Income		$168,970

Part C - Federal Tax Payable

The calculation of Acme Ltd.'s federal Tax Payable would be as follows:

Base Amount Of Part I Tax [(38%)($165,220)]	$ 62,784
Federal Tax Abatement [(10%)($165,220)]	(16,522)
Small Business Deduction (Note Two)	(28,914)
Additional Refundable Tax On Investment Income (Note Three)	Nil
General Rate Reduction (Note Four)	Nil
Part I Tax Payable	$ 17,348
Part IV Tax Payable (Note Five)	3,000
Dividend Refund (No Dividends Declared)	Nil
Federal Tax Payable	$ 20,348

Note Two   Since none of the annual business limit has been allocated to Sarco, the small business deduction is 17.5 percent of the least of the following three amounts:

1. Active Business Income (Part B)	$168,970
2. Taxable Income (no foreign tax credit adjustment)	$165,220
3. Annual Business Limit	$500,000

This gives a small business deduction of $28,914 [(17.5%)($165,220)].

Note Three   The ITA 123.3 refundable tax (ART) is 10-2/3 percent of the lesser of:

1. Aggregate Investment Income (Part B)		$21,250
2. Taxable Income	$165,220	
Deduct: Amount Eligible For The SBD	(165,220)	Nil

Since the income eligible for the small business deduction is equal to Taxable Income, there is no ITA 123.3 tax on investment income payable.

Note Four The general rate reduction would be nil, calculated as follows:

Taxable Income	$165,220
Amount Eligible For The Small Business Deduction	(165,220)
Aggregate Investment Income (Part B)	(21,250)
Full Rate Taxable Income	Nil
Rate	13%
General Rate Reduction	Nil

Note Five Acme would have to pay a Part IV tax equal to its share of the dividend refund received from Sarco Ltd. This amount would be $3,000 [(60%)($5,000)].

Part D - RDTOH Balance

The amount of refundable Part I tax will be the least of the following three amounts. In this problem, the calculation of these amounts is greatly simplified by the absence of foreign non-business income. The calculations are as follows:

ITA 129(3)(a)(i) This amount would be $6,517, 30-2/3 percent of aggregate investment income of $21,250 ($10,000 + $11,250).

ITA 129(3)(a)(ii) This amount would be nil, 30-2/3 percent of Taxable Income, reduced by the amount of income that is eligible for the small business deduction [(30-2/3%)($165,220 - $165,220)].

ITA 129(3)(a)(iii) This amount would be Part I Tax Payable of $17,348.

The least of these amounts is nil, so there would be no refundable portion of Part I tax.

The ending balance in this account would be calculated as follows:

RDTOH, End Of The Preceding Year	Nil
Refundable Portion Of Part I Tax	Nil
Part IV Tax Payable (Note Five)	$3,000
RDTOH Balance - December 31	$3,000

Self Study Solution Thirteen - 7

Part A - Net And Taxable Income

Brasco's minimum Net Income For Tax Purposes and Taxable Income would be calculated as follows:

Active Business Income (Given)		$171,000
Net Taxable Capital Gains (Given)		36,000
Canadian Source Interest Income		2,200
Eligible Portfolio Dividends		15,800
Foreign Source Investment Income (Gross Amount)		4,500
Non-Eligible Dividends From Subsidiary		37,800
Net Income For Tax Purposes		**$267,300**
Dividends Received:		
Portfolio	($15,800)	
Subsidiary	(37,800)	(53,600)
Charitable Donations		(11,900)
Non-Capital Loss Carry Forward Deducted		(25,800)
Net Capital Loss Carry Forward Deducted (Note One)		(36,000)
Taxable Income		**$140,000**

Note One   Note that the net capital loss carry forward is limited to the taxable capital gains. This will leave a net capital loss carry forward of $28,500 ($64,500 - $36,000) for subsequent periods.

Part B - Tax Payable (FTC = Amount Withheld)

Assuming the foreign non-business tax credit is equal to the amount withheld, Brasco's Tax Payable would be calculated as follows:

Base Amount Of Part I Tax [(38%)($140,000)]	$53,200
Federal Tax Abatement [(10%)($140,000)]	(14,000)
Small Business Deduction (Note Two)	(21,875)
Additional Refundable Tax On Investment Income (Note Three)	715
General Rate Reduction (Note Four)	(1,079)
Foreign Non-Business Tax Credit (Given As Amount Withheld)	(675)
Part I Tax Payable	$16,286
Part IV Tax Payable (Note Five)	20,547
Total Tax Payable	$36,833
Dividend Refund (Note Eight)	(14,950)
Net Federal Tax Payable	$21,883

Note Two   The small business deduction is 17.5 percent of the least of the following three amounts:

1. Active Business Income (Given)		$171,000
2. Taxable Income	$140,000	
Deduct:		
[(100/28)($675)] Foreign Non-Business Tax Credit (2,411)		$137,589
3. Allocated Annual Business Limit (Given)		$125,000

The lowest of these figures is the allocated annual limit of $125,000 and this gives a small business deduction of $21,875 [(17.5%)($125,000)].

Note Three   The aggregate investment income of $6,700 is calculated as follows:

Taxable Capital Gains	$36,000
Net Capital Loss Carry Forward Deducted	(36,000)
Canadian Interest	2,200
Foreign Investment Income	4,500
Aggregate Investment Income	$ 6,700

The ITA 123.3 refundable tax (ART) is 10-2/3 percent of the lesser of:

1. Aggregate Investment Income		$ 6,700
2. Taxable Income	$140,000	
Deduct: Amount Eligible For The SBD	(125,000)	$15,000

The ITA 123.3 tax on aggregate investment income is $715 [(10-2/3%)($6,700)].

Note Four   The general rate reduction is based on the amount of Taxable Income that is not subject to other types of favourable tax treatment. The reduction would be calculated as follows:

Taxable Income		$140,000
Amount Eligible For The Small Business Deduction (Note Two)		(125,000)
Aggregate Investment Income (Note Three)		(6,700)
Full Rate Taxable Income		$ 8,300
Rate		13%
General Rate Reduction		$ 1,079

Note Five The calculation of Part IV Tax Payable would be as follows:

Part IV Tax Transfer From Masco [(60%)($24,150)]	$14,490
Part IV Tax On Portfolio Dividends [(38-1/3%)($15,800)]	6,057
Part IV Tax Payable	$20,547

Note Six The refundable portion of Part I tax will be the least of the following three amounts:

Aggregate Investment Income (Note Three)		$ 6,700
Rate		30-2/3%
		$ 2,055
Deduct Excess Of:		
Foreign Non-Business Tax Credit	($675)	
Over 8.0% Of Foreign Non-Business Income		
[(8.0%)($4,500)]	360	(315)
Amount Under ITA 129(3)(a)(i)		$ 1,740

Taxable Income	$140,000
Deduct:	
Amount Eligible For The Small Business Deduction	(125,000)
[(100 ÷ 38-2/3)($675)] Foreign Non-Business Tax Credit	(1,746)
Adjusted Taxable Income	$ 13,254
Rate	30-2/3%
Amount Under ITA 129(3)(a)(ii)	$ 4,065

Amount Under ITA 129(3)(a)(iii) = Part I Tax Payable	$ 16,286

The least of these three amounts would be $1,740, the amount calculated under ITA 129(3)(a)(i).

Note Seven The Balance in the RDTOH would be calculated as follows:

RDTOH Balance - End Of The Preceding Year	$ 7,000	
Dividend Refund For The Preceding Year	Nil	$ 7,000
Refundable Portion Of Part I Tax (Note Six)	$ 1,740	
Part IV Tax (Note Five)	20,547	22,287
RDTOH Balance - December 31, 2017		$29,287

Note Eight   The dividend refund would be equal to the lesser of:

- 38-1/3 percent of taxable dividends paid [(38-1/3%)($39,000)] = $14,950
- RDTOH Balance - December 31, 2017 (Note Seven) = $29,287

The lesser of these two figures is $14,950 and that would be the refund for the year.

Part C - GRIP Balance

Since Taxable Income is greater than Aggregate Investment Income, the 2017 ending balance in GRIP will be calculated as follows:

GRIP Balance At End Of 2016		$126,000
Taxable Income	$140,000	
Income Eligible For SBD	(125,000)	
Aggregate Investment Income	(6,700)	
Adjusted Taxable Income	$ 8,300	
Rate	72%	5,976
Eligible Dividends Received		15,800
Eligible Dividends Designated in 2016		Nil
GRIP At End Of 2017		$147,776

The eligible dividends paid during 2017 will be deducted from the GRIP in 2018.

Part D - Foreign Tax Credit

If you cannot assume that the foreign tax credit is equal to the amount withheld, the actual foreign tax credit is a complex calculation in this situation. The use of foreign taxes paid as credits against Canadian Tax Payable is limited by a formula that includes the "tax otherwise payable".   In the case of foreign taxes paid on non-business income, the "tax otherwise payable" in the formula includes the ART that is assessed under ITA 123.3 and the general rate reduction. This creates a problem in that the calculation of the ART and the general rate reduction include the amount eligible for the small business deduction [ITA 123.3(b)].   In turn, the determination of the amount eligible for the small business deduction requires the use of the foreign tax credits for foreign taxes paid on non-business and business income [ITA 125(1)(b)(i) and (ii)].

To solve this circular calculation, for the purpose of calculating the small business deduction, the foreign tax credit for taxes paid on non-business income is calculated using a "tax otherwise payable" figure that does not include the ART under ITA 123.3 or the general rate reduction. This means that in situations where foreign non-business income, the small business deduction, and the ART are involved, the following procedures should be used:

1. Calculate the foreign non-business tax credit using a "tax otherwise payable" that excludes both the ART and the general rate reduction. This initial version of the foreign non-business tax credit will be used only for determining the small business deduction, with the actual credit available calculated after the ART and the general rate reduction have been determined.

2. Calculate the amount eligible for the small business deduction using the number determined in step 1.

3. Calculate the ART and the general rate reduction using the amount eligible for the small business deduction determined in step 2.

4. Calculate the actual foreign non-business tax credit using a "tax otherwise payable" figure that includes the ART and the general rate reduction.

The initial version of the foreign non-business tax credit (Step 1) will be the lesser of the actual tax paid of $675, and an amount determined by the following formula:

$$\left(\frac{\text{Foreign Non - Business Income}}{\text{Adjusted Net Income}}\right)(\text{Part I Tax Otherwise Payable Excluding The ART And GRR})$$

$$= \left(\frac{\$4,500}{\$267,300 - \$53,600 - \$36,000}\right)(\$53,200 - \$14,000)$$

$$= \quad \$993$$

Part I tax otherwise payable in the preceding formula does not include the ART under ITA 123.3 or the general rate reduction. Adjusted Net Income in the formula is Net Income For Tax Purposes minus deductible dividends and the net capital loss carry forward claimed in the current year. In this case, the actual tax paid of $675 will be the credit. This means that the previously calculated small business deduction will be unchanged (Note 2, Step 2) and, in turn, the ART (Note 3, Step 3) and general rate reduction (Note 4, Step 3) will be unchanged.

We can now calculate the actual foreign non-business tax credit which takes into consideration the ART and the general rate reduction (Step 4). It is the lesser of the actual taxes paid of $675 and an amount determined by the following formula:

$$\left(\frac{\text{Foreign Non - Business Income}}{\text{Adjusted Net Income}}\right)(\text{Part I Tax Otherwise Payable Including The ART And GRR})$$

$$= \left(\frac{\$4,500}{\$267,300 - \$53,600 - \$36,000}\right)(\$53,200 - \$14,000 + \$715 - \$1,079)$$

$$= \$983$$

In this calculation, the actual taxes paid of $675 will again be the credit.

Chapter 13 Learning Objectives

After completing Chapter 13, you should be able to:

1. Explain the goal of integration in the design of the Canadian corporate tax system (paragraph [P hereafter] 13-1 to 13-6).
2. Calculate after-tax income retained from eligible and non-eligible dividends received (P 13-7 to 13-14).
3. Demonstrate how the dividend gross up and tax credit procedures work to implement integration with respect to business income (P 13-15 to 13-24).
4. List the components of aggregate investment income as it is defined in ITA 129(4) and describe the basic concept of refundable taxes (P 13-25 to 13-38).
5. Calculate the additional refundable tax (ART) on the investment income of a CCPC (P 13-39 to 13-47).

6. Calculate the Part I refundable tax on the investment income of a CCPC (P 13-48 to 13-67).
7. Apply the provisions related to the Part IV refundable tax on private corporations, including those related to dividends from a connected corporation (P 13-68 to 13-95).
8. Calculate the balance in the Refundable Dividend Tax On Hand (RDTOH) account and the dividend refund (P 13-96 to 13-120).
9. Use a logical approach to deal with comprehensive calculations of corporate Taxable Income and Tax Payable (P 13-121 to 13-122).
10. Explain how the gross up and tax credit procedures for eligible dividends improve integration (P 13-123 to 13-128).

11. Explain and apply the eligible dividend designation calculations relevant to CCPCs and their GRIP (P 13-129 to 13-134).
12. Explain and apply the eligible dividend designation calculations relevant to non-CCPCs and their LRIP (P 13-135 to 13-138).
13. Describe and calculate the Part III.1 tax on excessive eligible dividend designations (EEDD) (P 13-139 to 13-147).
14. Review a simple corporate tax return completed using the ProFile T2 tax preparation software program.

How To Work Through Chapter 14

We recommend the following approach in dealing with the material in this chapter:

Acquisition Of Control Rules, Including Effect On Loss Carry Forwards
- Read paragraph 14-1 to 14-21 (in the textbook).
- Do Exercise Fourteen-1 (in the textbook) and check the solution in this Study Guide.
- Read paragraph 14-22 to 14-24.
- Do Exercise Fourteen-2 and check the solution in this Study Guide.
- Read paragraph 14-25 to 14-34.
- Do Exercise Fourteen-3 and check the solution in this Study Guide.
- Do Self Study Problems Fourteen-1 and Fourteen-2 which are available on the Companion Website and check the solutions in this Study Guide.

Associated Companies
- Read paragraph 14-35 to 14-50.
- Do Exercise Fourteen-4 and check the solution in this Study Guide.
- Do Self Study Problems Fourteen-3 and Fourteen-4 and check the solutions in this Study Guide.

Investment Tax Credits And SR&ED Expenditures By CCPCs
- Read paragraph 14-51 to 14-60.
- Do Exercise Fourteen-5 and check the solution in this Study Guide.
- Read paragraph 14-61 to 14-63.
- Do Exercise Fourteen-6 and check the solution in this Study Guide.

Refundable Investment Tax Credits
- Read paragraph 14-64 to 14-69.
- Do Exercise Fourteen-7 and check the solution in this Study Guide.
- Do Self Study Problem Fourteen-5 and check the solution in this Study Guide.
- Read paragraph 14-70 to 14-73.

Shareholders' Equity Under GAAP
- Read paragraph 14-74 to 14-76.

Paid Up Capital
- Read paragraph 14-77 to 14-80.
- Do Exercise Fourteen-8 and check the solution in this Study Guide.

Tax Basis Retained Earnings
- Read paragraph 14-81 to 14-89.

Capital Dividend Account
- Read paragraph 14-90 to 14-93.
- Do Exercise Fourteen-9 and check the solution in this Study Guide.
- Do Self Study Problem Fourteen-6 and Fourteen-7 and check the solutions in this Study Guide.

Distributions Of Corporate Surplus Through Cash, Stock And In Kind Dividends
- Read paragraph 14-94 to 14-105.
- Do Exercise Fourteen-10 and check the solution in this Study Guide.
- Read paragraph 14-106 to 14-108.
- Do Exercise Fourteen-11 and check the solution in this Study Guide.

Capital Dividends
- Read paragraph 14-109 to 14-113.

ITA 84(1) Deemed Dividends - Increase In PUC
- Read paragraph 14-114 to 14-118.
- Do Exercise Fourteen-12 and check the solution in this Study Guide.
- Read paragraph 14-119.

ITA 84(2) Deemed Dividends - On Winding-Up
- Read paragraph 14-120 to 14-124.
- Do Exercise Fourteen-13 and check the solution in this Study Guide.

ITA 84(3) Deemed Dividends - Redemption, Acquisition, Or Cancellation Of Shares
- Read paragraph 14-125 to 14-128.
- Do Exercise Fourteen-14 and check the solution in this Study Guide.

ITA 84(4) And ITA 84(4.1) Deemed Dividends
- Read paragraph 14-129 to 14-134.
- Do Exercise Fourteen-15 and check the solution in this Study Guide.
- Do Self Study Problem Fourteen-8 and check the solution in this Study Guide.

To Complete This Chapter
- If you would like more practice in problem solving, do the Supplementary Self Study Problems for the chapter. These problems and solutions are available on the Companion Website.
- Review the Key Terms Used In This Chapter in the textbook at the end of Chapter 14. Consult the Glossary for the meaning of any key terms you do not know.
- Test yourself with the Chapter 14 Glossary Flashcards available on the Companion Website.
- Ensure you have achieved the Chapter 14 Learning Objectives listed in this Study Guide.
- As a review, we recommend you view the PowerPoint presentation for Chapter 14 that is on the Companion Website.

Practice Examination
- Write the Practice Examination for Chapter 14 that is on the Companion Website. Mark your examination using the Practice Examination Solution that is on the Companion Website.

Solutions to Chapter Fourteen Exercises

Exercise Fourteen - 1 Solution

No Acquisition Of Control   Net Income For Tax Purposes for 2017 is $289,000 ($42,000 + $247,000) and, if there was no acquisition of control, the total $135,000 non-capital loss carry forward could be deducted. This would result in a 2017 Taxable Income of $154,000 ($289,000 - $135,000).

Acquisition Of Control   If there was an acquisition of the control on January 1, 2017, Net Income For Tax Purposes would still be $289,000. However, in this case, the non-capital loss carry forward could only be used to the extent of the pen business income of $42,000. This means that Taxable Income would be $247,000 ($289,000 - $42,000) with a non-capital loss carry forward of $93,000 ($135,000 - $42,000).

Exercise Fourteen - 2 Solution

The tax consequences of the acquisition of control procedures are as follows:

Land   As the fair market of the land is less than its adjusted cost base, ITA 111(4)(c) will require that it be written down to its fair market value of $215,000. This will result in an allowable capital loss of $39,000 [($293,000 - $215,000) ÷ 2].

Class 8 Assets   As the fair market value of this property is less than its UCC, ITA 111(5.1) requires that it be written down to its fair market value. The $92,000 ($276,000 - $184,000) write-down will be treated as CCA to be deducted in the deemed taxation year. For capital gains purposes, the property will retain its original capital cost of $416,000.

Exercise Fourteen - 3 Solution

It would clearly be desirable to elect to have a deemed disposition of the non-depreciable assets. This could be achieved by electing to have a deemed disposition of the non-depreciable assets for $650,000. This would result in a $75,000 taxable capital gain [(1/2)($650,000 - $500,000)] on the deemed disposition. This will leave $35,000 ($110,000 - $75,000) of the net capital loss carry forward.

This $35,000 could be eliminated by electing to have a deemed disposition of the depreciable property at an elected value of $470,000. This election would produce the required taxable capital gain of $35,000 [(1/2)($470,000 - $400,000)].

The election would also produce recapture of $50,000 ($400,000 - $350,000). As this is $5,000 ($50,000 - $45,000) greater than the operating loss, this would result in Taxable Income and Tax Payable. However, the ability to use the remaining $35,000 net capital loss carry forward is probably worth the cost of the Tax Payable on the extra $5,000 of income. In addition, the election would result in increased future CCA based on a new capital cost, for CCA purposes only, of $435,000 [$400,000 + (1/2)($470,000 - $400,000)].

Exercise Fourteen - 4 Solution

Top And Middle   Top and Middle are associated under ITA 256(1)(a) as Top controls Middle.

Top And Bottom   Top and Bottom are associated under ITA 256(1)(b) as they are both controlled by the same person, Mr. Top. He controls Top directly. In addition, he controls Bottom through a combination of direct ownership, indirect ownership, and deemed ownership. His majority interest would be calculated as follows:

Direct Interest in Bottom	5%
Indirect Interest Through Top Company [(100%)(10%)]	10%
Indirect Interest Through Control Of Middle Company	35%
Deemed Interest Through Son - ITA 256(1.3)	15%
Deemed Interest Through Options - ITA 256(1.4)	10%
Controlling Interest	75%

Middle And Bottom   Middle and Bottom are associated under ITA 256(1)(b) as they are both controlled by the same person, Mr. Top. Mr. Top controls Middle indirectly through Top. He controls Bottom through a combination of direct and indirect control, as described in the discussion of Top and Bottom.

Exercise Fourteen - 5 Solution

With respect to the $125,000 in apprentice salaries, the investment tax credit is available on an annual salary maximum of $20,000 per apprentice. As a result, there will be a $10,000 [(5)(10%)($20,000)] credit against 2017 federal Tax Payable. This $10,000 credit will be added to income in 2018.

With respect to the $3,000,000 in capital expenditures, there will be a 2017 credit against federal Tax Payable of $300,000 [(10%)($3,000,000)]. The $300,000 credit will not influence the calculation of 2017 CCA. This amount will be $750,000 [(50%)(1/2)($3,000,000)].

In 2018, the $300,000 credit will be deducted from the January 1, 2018 UCC, leaving a balance of $1,950,000 ($3,000,000 - $750,000 - $300,000). Given this, 2018 CCA will be $975,000 [(50%)($1,950,000)].

Exercise Fourteen - 6 Solution

For 2017, the annual limit would be $2,250,000, calculated as follows:

[$8 million − (10)($560,000)][($40 million − $2,500,000) ÷ $40 million] = $2,250,000

Exercise Fourteen - 7 Solution

As Sci-Tech has Taxable Income of less than $500,000 in the previous year, and its Taxable Capital Employed in Canada is less than $10 million, the Company's annual expenditure limit is not reduced from the maximum value of $3,000,000.

Given the $3,000,000 annual expenditure limit for the 35 percent rate, the total amount of investment tax credits available can be calculated as follows:

Qualified Property [(10%)($123,000)]	$ 12,300
SR&ED Current Expenditures [(35%)($1,200,000)]	420,000
Total Available Amount	$432,300

The refund available would be as follows:

Qualified Property [(40%)($12,300)]	$ 4,920
SR&ED Current Expenditures [(100%)($420,000)]	420,000
Total Refund Available	$424,920

The non-refunded investment tax credit of $7,380 ($432,300 - $424,920) can be carried forward 20 years to be applied against Tax Payable. There was no Tax Payable in the last three years so it cannot be carried back.

The cost of the qualified property will be reduced in the following year by the refundable investment tax credit of $4,920. The $420,000 tax credit on current SR&ED expenditures will be added to income in the following taxation year.

Exercise Fourteen - 8 Solution

The adjusted cost base of the shares would be determined as follows:

	Number of Shares	Cost/Share	Total Cost
First Purchase	2,400	$1.10	$2,640
Second Purchase	3,850	$1.82	7,007
Totals	6,250		$9,647

The adjusted cost base for all of the investor's shares is $9,647. The adjusted cost base per share would be $1.54 ($9,647 ÷ 6,250).

The PUC for the investor's shares would be calculated as follows:

	Number of Shares	PUC/Share	Total PUC
First Sale	100,000	$1.10	$110,000
Second Sale	50,000	$1.35	67,500
Third Sale	30,000	$1.82	54,600
Total PUC Of Outstanding Shares	180,000		$232,100

Number Of Shares (From First Table)	6,250
PUC Per Share [$232,100 ÷ 180,000 Shares]	$ 1.29
PUC For Investor's Shares	$8,063

Exercise Fourteen - 9 Solution

The balance in the capital dividend account as at December 31, 2017 would be as follows:

2015 Capital Gain On Land [(1/2)($22,000)]	$11,000
2016 Capital Dividend Received	8,200
2017 Sale Of Goodwill [(1/2)($43,000 - Nil)]	21,500
2017 Capital Dividend Paid	(16,000)
Balance - End Of 2017	$24,700

Exercise Fourteen - 10 Solution

The required calculations are as follows:

Fair Market Value Per Share	$25.00
New Shares Received [(5%)(1,000)]	50
Non-Eligible Dividend Received	$1,250.00
Gross Up [(17%)($1,250.00)]	212.50
Taxable Dividend	$1,462.50
Dividend Tax Credit [(21/29)(17%)($1,250)]	$153.88

Jean's Net Income For Tax Purposes would be increased by the taxable dividend of $1,462.50. His federal Tax Payable would be decreased by the dividend tax credit of $153.88.

	Number of Shares	ACB/Share	Total ACB
Pre-Dividend Shares	1,000	$18	$18,000
Stock Dividend Addition	50	$25	1,250
Totals	1,050		$19,250

The per share adjusted cost base of Jean's shares would be $18.33 ($19,250 ÷ 1,050).

Exercise Fourteen - 11 Solution
The required calculations for the corporation are as follows:

Proceeds Of Disposition [($51)(150,000)]	$7,650,000
Adjusted Cost Base [($42)(150,000)]	(6,300,000)
Capital Gain	$1,350,000
Inclusion Rate	1/2
Taxable Capital Gain	$ 675,000

The calculations for Sandrine are as follows:

Dividend Received [(15%)($51)(150,000)]	$1,147,500
Gross Up [(17%)($1,147,500)]	195,075
Taxable Dividend	$1,342,575
Dividend Tax Credit [(21/29)(17%)($1,147,500)]	$ 141,261

Cloutier Ltd.'s Net Income For Tax Purposes would be increased by the $675,000 taxable capital gain. Sandrine's Net Income For Tax Purposes would be increased by the taxable dividend of $1,342,575. Her federal Tax Payable would be decreased by the dividend tax credit of $141,261.

Exercise Fourteen - 12 Solution
This transaction will result in an ITA 84(1) deemed dividend for all shareholders, calculated as follows:

PUC Of New Shares [(40,000)($12.70)]	$508,000
Increase In Net Assets	(450,000)
ITA 84(1) Deemed Dividend	$ 58,000

This would be allocated to all 166,000 (126,000 + 40,000) shares outstanding, on the basis of $0.35 per share. This would be a taxable dividend, subject to either the eligible or non-eligible dividend gross up and tax credit procedures. The $0.35 per share dividend would also be added to the adjusted cost base of all 166,000 shares.

With the addition of $0.35 resulting from the ITA 84(1) deemed dividend to the original issue price of $10.50, the adjusted cost base of these shares is now $10.85 per share. Mr. Uni's sale of 5,000 shares at $13.42 per share would result in a taxable capital gain calculated as follows:

Proceeds Of Disposition [($13.42)(5,000)]	$67,100
Adjusted Cost Base [($10.85)(5,000)]	(54,250)
Capital Gain	$12,850
Inclusion Rate	1/2
Taxable Capital Gain	$ 6,425

Exercise Fourteen - 13 Solution

The analysis of the $2,350,000 distribution would be as follows:

Cash Distributed	$2,350,000
PUC Of Shares	(250,000)
ITA 84(2) Deemed Dividend	$2,100,000
ITA 83(2) Capital Dividend	(340,000)
ITA 88(2)(b) Taxable Dividend	$1,760,000

To the extent the Company has a balance in its GRIP account, some amount of the $1,760,000 dividend could be designated as eligible. Any remainder will be taxed as a non-eligible dividend.

The wind-up results in a disposition of the shares. The tax consequences of this disposition are as follows:

Cash Distributed	$2,350,000
ITA 84(2) Deemed Dividend	(2,100,000)
ITA 54 Proceeds Of Disposition	$ 250,000
Adjusted Cost Base	(250,000)
Capital Gain	Nil

As shown by the preceding calculation, there would be no capital gain on the disposition.

Exercise Fourteen - 14 Solution

The redemption transaction would have no tax consequences for Ms. Tandy. The tax consequences to Jesuiah Tandy resulting from the redemption of his shares would be as follows:

Proceeds Of Redemption [(15,000)($11.75)]	$176,250
PUC [(15,000)($8.25)]	(123,750)
ITA 84(3) Deemed Dividend	$ 52,500
Gross Up Of 17 Percent	8,925
Taxable Dividend	$ 61,425

Dividend Tax Credit [(21/29)(17%)($52,500)]	$ 6,463

Proceeds Of Redemption [(15,000)($11.75)]	$176,250
ITA 84(3) Deemed Dividend	(52,500)
ITA 54 Proceeds Of Disposition	$123,750
Adjusted Cost Base [(15,000)($7.90)]	(118,500)
Capital Gain (PUC - ACB)	$ 5,250
Inclusion Rate	1/2
Taxable Capital Gain	$ 2,625

Both the taxable dividend and the taxable capital gain would increase Jesuiah's Net Income For Tax Purposes by a total of $64,050 ($61,425 + $2,625). The federal dividend tax credit would decrease federal Tax Payable by $6,463.

Exercise Fourteen - 15 Solution

To the extent of the $225,000 PUC reduction, the dividend will be treated as a tax free distribution. The tax consequences will be a reduction in the PUC of these shares to $225,000 ($450,000 - $225,000), as well as an adjusted cost base reduction to $400,000 ($625,000 - $225,000). The $105,000 ($330,000 - $225,000) excess of the distribution over the PUC reduction will be an ITA 84(4) deemed dividend, subject to either the eligible or non-eligible dividend gross up and tax credit procedures. As it will be taxed as a dividend, this part of the distribution will not be subtracted from the adjusted cost base of the shares.

Self Study Solution Fourteen - 1

Part A - Non-Capital And Net Capital Losses

Net Business Loss   The net business loss for the period to March 31, 2017 would be as follows:

Loss As Per March 31, 2017 Income Statement	($23,000)
Required Accounts Receivable Adjustment ($45,000 - $33,000)	(12,000)
Building Election - Recaptured CCA ($285,000 - $270,000)	15,000
Fixtures And Equipment - Deemed CCA ($95,000 - $90,000)	(5,000)
Vehicles Election - Recaptured CCA ($87,000 - $80,000)	7,000
Net Business Loss For Period Ending March 31, 2017	($18,000)

Net And Taxable Income   Net Income For Tax Purposes and Taxable Income for the period ending March 31, 2017, calculated as per the ITA 3 rules, would be as follows:

ITA 3(a) - Non-Capital Income (Positive Amounts Only)		Nil
ITA 3(b) - Net Taxable Capital Gains (Losses):		
Elections Under ITA 111(4)(e):		
Gain On Land [(1/2)($420,000 - $275,000)]	$ 72,500	
Gain On Building [(1/2)($320,000 - $285,000)]	17,500	
Required Write-Down - ITA 111(4)(c) And (d)		
Loss On Temporary Investments		
[(1/2)($53,000 - $23,000)]	(15,000)	75,000
ITA 3(c) - Total		$ 75,000
ITA 3(d) - Business Loss For The Period		(18,000)
Net Income For Tax Purposes		$ 57,000
Net Capital Loss Carry Forward		
(Limited To Amount Included Under ITA 3(b)		(75,000)
Taxable Income		Nil

Lost Net Capital Loss   The net capital loss that would be lost would be calculated as follows:

From 2015 [(1/2)($68,000)]	$34,000
From 2016 [(1/2)($85,000)]	42,500
Net Capital Loss Balance At March 31, 2017	$76,500
Amount Deducted In 2017	(75,000)
Net Capital Loss Lost On Acquisition of Control	$ 1,500

Non-Capital Loss Carry Forward   The non-capital loss carry forward would be calculated as follows:

Net Business Loss For Period	$ 18,000
Net Capital Loss Deducted	75,000
Subtotal	$ 93,000
Income Under ITA 3(c)	(75,000)
Non-Capital Loss For The Period Ending March 31, 2017	$ 18,000
Non-Capital Loss Carry Forward From 2015	63,500
Non-Capital Loss Carry Forward From 2016	78,500
Non-Capital Loss Carry Forward At March 31, 2017	$160,000

Part B - Loss Carry Forward In 2017

The April 1 to December 31, 2017 Net Income For Tax Purposes would be $78,000 ($123,000 - $45,000). Note that there is no restriction against deducting the current year loss on bread operations against other sources of income. However, none of the non-capital loss carry forward of $160,000 can be used as these losses can only be applied against income in the bread operations. This leaves the 2017 Taxable Income equal to the Net Income For Tax Purposes of $78,000. The non-capital loss carry forward at December 31, 2017 is unchanged at $160,000.

Part C - Loss Carry Forward In 2018

The $40,000 loss on the figurines must be deducted from the profits of the bread operations to produce a Net Income For Tax Purposes of $171,000 ($211,000 - $40,000). As this income is entirely from bread operations, all of the $160,000 non-capital loss carry forward can be deducted, leaving a Taxable Income of $11,000. There is no remaining non-capital loss carry forward at December 31, 2018.

Self Study Solution Fourteen - 2

Part A

As a result of the acquisition of control, LF will have a deemed taxation year end on April 30, 2017. This results in a short January 1, 2017 through April 30, 2017 taxation year for LF. The effects of this include:

- An additional year will be counted towards the expiry of the non-capital losses.
- If CCA is to be taken, it will have to be calculated for a short fiscal period.
- All of the usual year end procedures (timing of bonuses, inclusion of reserves, etc.) will have to be carried out.
- For the first year after the acquisition of control, LF can choose a new fiscal year end, on any date up to 53 weeks after the deemed year end.

Other implications are as follows:

- Any net capital loss balance that that remains cannot be used after the deemed year end.
- Any non-capital loss balance that is carried forward can only be used against profits earned in the same or a similar line of business.
- The manufacturing equipment, because its fair market value is less than its UCC, will have to be written down to the $285,000 UCC value. The $90,000 ($375,000 - $285,000) amount of the write down will be treated as deemed CCA.

Part B

The land, Class 1 assets, and Class 8 assets all have fair market values in excess of their tax values. If the deemed disposition election is made and the fair market value of these assets is used as the elected value, the results would be as follows:

Asset	Recapture	Capital Gain
Land ($925,000 - $450,000)	N/A	$475,000
Class 1 ($650,000 - $515,000)	$135,000	Nil
Class 8 ($15,000 - $10,000)	5,000	Nil
Total Income	$140,000	$475,000

Part C

If the Companies believe that they will be able to generate sufficient income to use the non-capital loss carry forward in future periods, they will not want to make elections that will result in any unneeded pre-acquisition income. If the elections are made, the losses will increase the adjusted cost base or UCC balance of the assets the elections are made on. In the case of the land, the increased cost will not be of benefit until the land is sold. In the case of the depreciable assets, the increased UCC will only be deductible at the applicable rates of 4 or 20 percent. Alternatively, a non-capital loss carry forward can be deducted in full, as soon as the Companies have sufficient appropriate income to absorb it.

The situation with net capital losses is different. If such losses are not used during the short fiscal period prior to the acquisition of control, they will be lost forever. Given this, it would be appropriate to make an election that would absorb the $65,000 net capital loss from 2015. This will require a capital gain of $130,000 [(2)($65,000)] which can be created by electing a deemed disposition on the land at a value of $580,000. This election will create a taxable capital gain of $65,000 [(1/2)($580,000 - $450,000)].

Given the required write-down of the manufacturing equipment, the Net Business Loss would be calculated as follows:

Operating Loss To April 30, 2017 (Given)	($ 55,000)
Deemed CCA On Class 53 ($375,000 - $285,000)	(90,000)
Net Business Loss For The Period Ending April 30, 2017	($145,000)

Using this figure, along with the results of the election on the land, Net and Taxable Income would be calculated as follows:

ITA 3(a) Non-Capital Income (Positive Amounts Only)		Nil
ITA 3(b) Net Taxable Capital Gains		
Election Under ITA 111(4)(e) On Land	$ 65,000	
ITA 3(c) Total		$ 65,000
ITA 3(d) Net Business Loss For The Period		(145,000)
Net Income For Tax Purposes		Nil
Net Capital Loss Carry Forward (See Following)		($ 65,000)
Taxable Income		Nil

The non-capital loss carry forward at April 30, 2017 would be calculated as follows:

Net Business Loss For The Period	$145,000
Net Capital Loss Deducted	65,000
Subtotal	$210,000
Income Under ITA 3(c)	(65,000)
Non-Capital Loss For The Period Ending April 30, 2017	$145,000
Carry Forward From 2015	180,000
Carry Forward From 2016	140,000
Non-Capital Loss Carry Forward	$465,000

The net capital loss balance from 2015 would be eliminated by the $65,000 carry forward deduction, leaving a balance of nil to be carried forward.

Part D

If there is uncertainty with respect to the ability of OLC and LF to generate income in the same or similar line of business in amounts sufficient to absorb the non-capital loss carry forward, additional elections should be made to absorb as much of this balance as possible. This would require elections on all of the assets with capital gains or recapture. Under this approach Net Business Income would be calculated as follows:

Operating Loss To April 30, 2017 (Given)	($ 55,000)
Deemed CCA On Class 53 ($375,000 - $285,000)	(90,000)
Class 1 - Recaptured CCA	135,000
Class 8 - Recaptured CCA	5,000
Net Business Loss For The Period Ending April 30, 2017	($ 5,000)

The resulting Net and Taxable Income amounts would be calculated as follows:

ITA 3(a) - Non-Capital Income (Positive Amounts Only)	Nil
ITA 3(b) - Net Taxable Capital Gains (Losses):	
Capital Gain On Land [(1/2)($925,000 - $450,000)]	$237,500
ITA 3(c) - Total	$237,500
ITA 3(d) - Business Loss For The Period	(5,000)
Net Income For Tax Purposes	$232,500
Net Capital Loss Carry Forward (All)	(65,000)
Subtotal	$167,500
Non-Capital Loss Carry Forward	
(Maximum Needed To Reduce Income To Nil)	(167,500)
Taxable Income	Nil

Under this Part D approach, the non-capital loss carry forward at April 30, 2017 would be calculated as follows:

Net Business Loss For The Period	$ 5,000
Net Capital Loss Deducted	65,000
Subtotal	$ 70,000
Income Under ITA 3(c)	(237,500)
Non-Capital Loss For The Period Ending April 30, 2017	Nil

Carry Forward From 2015	$180,000
Carry Forward From 2016	140,000
Non-Capital Loss Carry Forward Deducted	
For The Period Ending April 30, 2017	(167,500)
Non-Capital Loss Carry Forward	$152,500

As in Part C, the net capital loss from 2015 is eliminated by the $65,000 loss carry forward deduction.

Self Study Solution Fourteen - 3

Part A

By virtue of ITA 251(2)(a), John Fleming and Eric Flame are related by the fact that they are married to persons who are connected by a blood relationship (their wives). In addition, under ITA 256(1.5) a person who owns shares in two or more corporations shall be, as a shareholder of one of the corporations, deemed to be related to himself as a shareholder of the other corporation(s).

Given this, Fleming Ltd. and Lartch Inc. are associated under ITA 256(1)(d). John Fleming controls Fleming Ltd., is a member of a related group (John Fleming and Eric Flame) that controls Lartch Inc., and owns more than 25 percent of the voting shares of Lartch Inc.

In a similar fashion, Flame Ltd. is associated with Lartch Inc. under ITA 256(1)(d), as Eric Flame controls Flame Ltd., is a member of a related group (John Fleming and Eric Flame) that controls Lartch Inc., and owns more than 25 percent of Lartch Inc.

Based on these associations, Fleming Ltd. and Flame Ltd. are associated under ITA 256(2), as they are both associated with a third corporation, Lartch Inc. If it was desirable, Lartch Inc. could make the appropriate election under ITA 256(2) to be deemed not to be associated with Fleming Ltd. and Flame Ltd. which would allow Fleming Ltd. and Flame Ltd. to avoid association. However, the annual business limit for Lartch Inc. would be reduced to nil.

Part B

Mr. and Mrs. Cuso are a group with respect to both Male Ltd. and Female Inc. [ITA 256(1.2)(a) - two or more persons holding shares in the same corporation]. As a group, they control both Male Ltd. and Female Inc. Therefore, the two Companies are associated under ITA 256 (1)(b). The fact that Mr. and Mrs. Cuso are related is not relevant.

Part C

Ms. Jones and Miss Lange are a group that controls Alliance Ltd. However, they do not control Breaker Inc., as Mrs. Kelly (not a member of the group that controls Alliance Ltd.) owns 50 percent of the shares. Therefore, Alliance Ltd. and Breaker Inc. are not associated.

Part D

While they are not related, Mr. Martin and Mr. Oakley constitute a group [ITA 256(1.2)(a)] with respect to both Martin Inc. and Oakley Ltd. As both Martin Inc. and Oakley Ltd. are controlled by the same group, the two Companies are associated under ITA 256(1)(b).

Part E

The two Companies are related, but not associated. While Lily and James are related, they are not a group with respect to the two Companies and there is no cross-ownership of shares.

Self Study Solution Fourteen - 4

Case 1

As a group, Mr. Jones and Mr. Twitty control both Jones Ltd. and Twitty Inc. As a consequence, these two Companies would be associated under ITA 256(1)(b).

Case 2

Ms. Wynette controls Wynette Enterprises Ltd., and is related to each member of the group that controls Lynn Inc. In addition, Ms. Wynette has the necessary 25 percent plus cross-ownership in Lynn Inc. As a consequence, Wynette Enterprises Ltd. and Lynn Inc. are associated under ITA 256(1)(d).

Case 3

A group, consisting of Mr. Travis and Mr. Cash, has control of both Cowboys Ltd. and Horses Inc. Therefore, Cowboys Ltd. and Horses Inc. are associated under ITA 256(1)(b).

Case 4

As Randy's Boots Inc. controls Hill Inc., those two companies are associated under ITA 256(1)(a).

As Mr. Nelson owns 80 percent of the shares of Willie's Hits Ltd., he controls that company. This gives him control over the 20 percent of Hill Inc. shares that are owned by Willie's Hits.

However, Mr. Nelson does not control Randy's Boots, and this means that his indirect interest in Hill Inc. through Randy's Boots of 24 percent [(30%)(80%)] is the product of the two ownership percentages.

As a result, his overall interest in Hill Inc. is only 44 percent (20% + 24%), which is not sufficient to give him control over Hill. Therefore, Willie's Hits Ltd. and Hill Inc. are not associated and Willie's Hits Ltd. and Randy's Boots Inc. are not associated.

Case 5

Ms. Parton controls Alpha Company, is related to each member of the group (Ms. Parton and her spouse) that control Beta Company, and has cross-ownership of Beta Company in excess of 25 percent. This means that these two Companies are associated under ITA 256(1)(d).

Her spouse controls Centra Company, is related to each member of the group (the spouse and Ms. Parton) that controls Beta Company, and has the necessary cross-ownership of at least 25 percent of Beta Company shares. This means that these two Companies are also associated under ITA 256(1)(d).

As they are not controlled by the same individual or group, Alpha Company and Centra Company are not associated under ITA 256(1). However, as they are both associated with the same third corporation (Beta Company), Alpha and Centra would be associated under ITA 256(2). Note that ITA 256(2) allows Alpha and Centra to avoid association, provided Beta elects not to be associated with either Company. This will mean, however, that Beta will have a business limit for the period of nil.

Case 6

For the purposes of determining associated companies, Ms. Gale is deemed to own the 30 percent interest in Norton Music Inc. that is held by her minor child [ITA 256(1.3)] and the 20 percent interest in Norton Music Inc. for which she holds an option [ITA 256(1.4)]. When this is combined with her own interest of 10 percent, she would be considered to control Norton Music Inc. As she controls both Kristal Enterprises Ltd. and Norton Music Inc., these Companies are associated under ITA 256(1)(b).

Self Study Solution Fourteen - 5

Case A

Luxor's annual expenditure limit would be $423,500. This amount is calculated as follows:

[$8 million – (10)($756,000*)][($40 million – $1,500,000) ÷ $40 million] = $423,500.

*Greater of $500,000 and the corporation's Taxable Income for the preceding year

Case B

Gargle's annual expenditure limit would be $2,827,500, calculated as follows:

[$8 million – (10)($500,000*)][($40 million – $2,300,000) ÷ $40 million]

*Greater of $500,000 and the corporation's Taxable Income for the preceding year

The amount of SR&ED Expenditure that would be eligible for the 35 percent rate can be calculated as follows:

Total Current SR&ED Expenditures	$3,200,000
Annual Expenditure Limit	(2,827,500)
Limited To 15 Percent Rate	$ 372,500

The total amount of investment tax credits available can be calculated as follows:

Qualified Property [(10%)($86,000)]	$ 8,600
SR&ED Current Expenditures:	
At 35 Percent Rate [(35%)($2,827,500)]	989,625
At 15 Percent Rate [(15%)($372,500)]	55,875
Total Available Amount	$1,054,100

Gargle is a qualifying corporation. The refund available would be as follows:

	Rate	ITC	Refund
Qualified Property	40%	$ 8,600	$ 3,440
SR&ED Current Expenditures	100%	989,625	989,625
SR&ED Current Expenditures	40%	55,875	22,350
Total Available		$1,054,100	$1,015,415

The non-refunded investment tax credit of $38,685 ($1,054,100 - $1,015,415) can be carried forward 20 years to be applied against Tax Payable. There was no Tax Payable in the last three years so it cannot be carried back.

The cost of the qualified property will be reduced in 2018 by the refundable investment tax credit of $3,440. The $1,011,975 ($989,625 + $22,350) refundable tax credit on current SR&ED expenditures will be added to income in 2018.

Case C

With respect to the $250,000 in apprentice salaries, the investment tax credit is available on an annual salary maximum of $20,000 per apprentice. As a result, there will be a $17,500 [(5)(10%)($15,000) + (5)(10%)($20,000 maximum)] credit against 2016 federal Tax Payable. This $17,500 credit will be added to income in 2017.

With respect to the $800,000 in capital expenditures, there will be a 2017 credit against federal Tax Payable of $80,000 [(10%)($800,000)].

The $80,000 credit will not influence the calculation of 2016 CCA. This amount will be $120,000 [(30%)(1/2)($800,000)].

In 2017, the $80,000 credit will be deducted from the January 1, 2017 UCC, leaving a balance of $600,000 ($800,000 - $120,000 - $80,000). Given this, 2017 CCA will be $180,000 [(30%)($600,000)].

Self Study Solution Fourteen - 6

The December 31, 2017 balance in the capital dividend account is calculated as follows:

2006 Capital Gain [(1/2)($343,500 - $225,000)]	$ 59,250
2007 Life Insurance Proceeds	162,000
2009 Capital Loss [(1/2)($150,000 - $220,000)]	(35,000)
2011 Capital Dividend Received	26,000
2015 Net Capital Loss	
{[1/2][($80,000 - $50,000) - ($100,000 - $45,000)]}	(12,500)
Capital Dividends Paid [(3)($45,000)]	(135,000)
Balance December 31, 2017	$ 64,750

Self Study Solution Fourteen - 7

The December 31, 2017 balance in the capital dividend account is calculated as follows:

2006 Life Insurance Proceeds	$186,000
2008 Capital Dividend Received	26,300
2013 Capital Dividend Paid	(45,200)
2014 Capital Gain [(1/2)($226,100 - $184,300)]	20,900
2016 Capital Gain [(1/2)($93,400 - $48,600)]	22,400
2016 Capital Loss [(1/2)($108,300 - $112,600)]	(2,150)
2017 Capital Dividend Paid	(16,400)
Balance December 31, 2017	$191,850

Self Study Solution Fourteen - 8

Case 1

To the extent of the $163,000 PUC reduction, the liquidating dividend will be treated as a tax free distribution to Mr. Farnsworth. However, there will be tax consequences related to this distribution:

- The PUC of Mr. Farnsworth's shares will be reduced to $160,000 ($323,000 - $163,000).
- The ACB of Mr. Farnsworth's shares will be reduced to $299,000 ($462,000 - $163,000).

The $97,000 ($260,000 - $163,000) excess of the distribution over the PUC reduction will be an ITA 84(4) deemed dividend. For inclusion in Taxable Income, it will be grossed up to $113,490 [(117%)($97,000)]. It will generate a federal dividend tax credit of $11,941 [(21/29)(17%)($97,000)]. This deemed dividend part of the distribution will not be subtracted from the adjusted cost base of the shares.

Case 2

The tax consequences to Michelle Chawla resulting from the redemption of her shares would be as follows:

Proceeds Of Redemption [($20.80)(125,000)]	$2,600,000
PUC [($20)(125,000)]	(2,500,000)
ITA 84(3) Deemed Dividend	$ 100,000
Proceeds Of Redemption [($20.80)(125,000)]	$2,600,000
ITA 84(3) Deemed Dividend	(100,000)
ITA 54 Proceeds Of Disposition	$2,500,000
Adjusted Cost Base [($16.80)($125,000)]	(2,100,000)
Capital Gain	$ 400,000
Inclusion Rate	1/2
Taxable Capital Gain	$ 200,000

For purposes of determining Taxable Income, the ITA 84(3) dividend will be grossed up to $117,000 [(117%)($100,000)], resulting in a total increase in Taxable Income of $317,000 ($118,000 + $200,000). A federal dividend tax credit of $12,310 [(21/29)(17%)($100,000)] will result from this transaction.

Case 3

This transaction will result in an ITA 84(1) deemed dividend for all shareholders, calculated as follows:

PUC Of New Shares [(42,000)($24.10)]	$1,012;200
Increase In Net Assets (Liability Eliminated)	(900,000)
ITA 84(1) Deemed Dividend	$ 112,200

This would be allocated to all 275,000 (233,000 + 42,000) shares outstanding, on the basis of $0.408 per share ($112,200 ÷ 275,000).

Sue's share of the dividend would be $9,506 [(23,300)($0.408)]. For inclusion in her Taxable Income, this amount will be grossed up to $11,122 [(117%)($9,506)].

The deemed dividend will be added to the adjusted cost base of Sue's shares, resulting in a value of $22.908 ($22.50 + $0.408)] per share. A federal dividend tax credit of $1,170 [(21/29)(17%)($9,506)] will result from this transaction.

The tax consequences of Sue selling her shares would be as follows:

Proceeds Of Disposition [(23,300)($24.85)]	$579,005
Adjusted Cost Base [(23,300)($22.908)]	(533,756)
Capital Gain	$ 45,249
Inclusion Rate	1/2
Taxable Capital Gain	$ 22,625

This will result in a total increase in Taxable Income of $33,747 ($22,625 + $11,122).

Case 4

The analysis of the $3,175,000 distribution would be as follows:

Cash Distributed	$3,175,000
PUC Of Shares	(400,000)
ITA 84(2) Deemed Dividend	$2,775,000
ITA 83(2) Capital Dividend	(427,000)
ITA 88(2)(b) Wind-Up Dividend	$2,348,000

The capital dividend would be distributed tax free. For inclusion in Taxable Income, the $2,348,000 dividend would be grossed up to $2,747,160 [(117%)($2,348,000)]. It would generate a federal dividend tax credit of $289,047 [(21/29)(17%)($2,348,000)].

The transaction would also result in an allowable capital loss calculated as follows:

Cash Distributed	$3,175,000
ITA 84(2) Deemed Dividend	(2,775,000)
ITA 54 Proceeds Of Disposition	$ 400,000
Adjusted Cost Base	(1,450,000)
Capital Loss	($1,050,000)
Inclusion Rate	1/2
Allowable Capital Loss	($ 525,000)

The allowable capital loss can be used in the current year, only to the extent of taxable capital gains realized in the current year.

Chapter 14 Learning Objectives

After completing Chapter 14, you should be able to:

1. Explain the need for, and the tax implications of, a deemed year end when there has been an acquisition of control (paragraph [P hereafter] 14-1 to 14-13).
2. Apply the provisions related to charitable donations and loss carry forwards when there has been an acquisition of control (P 14-14 to 14-21).
3. Explain the treatment of unrecognized losses at a deemed year end resulting from an acquisition of control (P 14-22 to 14-34).
4. Apply the associated companies rules (P 14-35 to 14-50).
5. Apply the general rules applicable to investment tax credits and SR & ED expenditures by CCPCs (P 14-51 to 14-63).

6. Apply the provisions related to refundable investment tax credits (P 14-64 to 14-68).
7. Apply the carry over rules for investment tax credits, as well as describe the influence of an acquisition of control on their availability (P 14-69 to 14-73).
8. Explain the relationship between tax basis Shareholders' Equity and Shareholders' Equity as presented under GAAP (P 14-74 to 14-76).
9. Explain the concept of, and calculate the amount of, Paid Up Capital (P 14-77 to 14-80).
10. Identify and explain the major components of Tax Basis Retained Earnings (P 14-81 to 14-89).

11. Explain the objectives of, and list the major components of, the capital dividend account (P 14-90 to 14-93).
12. List the various types of dividends used to distribute corporate surplus (P 14-94 to 14-98).
13. Apply the procedures related to the declaration and payment of cash dividends (P 14-99 to 14-102).
14. Apply the procedures related to the declaration and payment of stock dividends (P 14-103 to 14-105).
15. Apply the procedures related to the declaration and payment of dividends in kind (P 14-106 to 14-108).

16. Apply the procedures related to the declaration and payment of capital dividends (P 14-109 to 14-113).
17. Explain and apply the procedures related to ITA 84(1) deemed dividends when there has been an increase in PUC (P 14-114 to 14-119).
18. Explain and apply the procedures related to ITA 84(2) deemed dividends on winding up (P 14-120 to 14-124).
19. Explain and apply the procedures related to ITA 84(3) deemed dividends on redemption, acquisition or cancellation of shares (P 14-125 to 14-128).
20. Explain and apply the procedures related to ITA 84(4) and 84(4.1) deemed dividends (P 14-129 to 14-134).

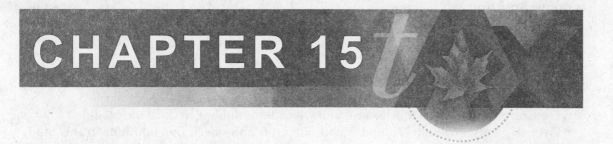

How To Work Through Chapter 15

We recommend the following approach in dealing with the material in this chapter:

The Decision To Incorporate - Tax Considerations
- Read paragraph 15-1 to 15-9 (in the textbook).

Other Advantages And Disadvantages Of Incorporation
- Read paragraph 15-10 to 15-11.
- Do Self Study Problem Fifteen-1 which is available on the Companion Website and check the solution in this Study Guide.

Basic Example Data - Tax Reduction And Deferral
- Read paragraph 15-12 to 15-24.

Public Companies - Tax Reduction And Deferral
- Read paragraph 15-25 to 15-34.
- Do Exercise Fifteen-1 (in the textbook) and check the solution in this Study Guide.

CCPCs - Active Business Income - Tax Reduction And Deferral
- Read paragraph 15-35 to 15-40.
- Do Exercise Fifteen-2 and check the solution in this Study Guide.
- Read paragraph 15-41 to 15-45.

CCPCs - Non-Dividend Investment Income - Tax Reduction And Deferral
- Read paragraph 15-46 to 15-49.
- Do Exercise Fifteen-3 and check the solution in this Study Guide.
- Do Self Study Problem Fifteen-2 and check the solution in this Study Guide.

CCPCs - Dividend Income - Tax Reduction And Deferral
- Read paragraph 15-50 to 15-54.

Conclusions On Tax Reductions And Deferrals
- Read paragraph 15-55 to 15-57.
- Do Exercises Fifteen-4 and Fifteen-5 and check the solutions in this Study Guide.
- Do Self Study Problem Fifteen-3 and check the solution in this Study Guide.

Provincial Taxes And Integration
- Read paragraph 15-58 to 15-76.
- Do Self Study Problem Fifteen-4 and check the solution in this Study Guide.

Tax-Free Dividend Calculations
- Read paragraph 15-77 to 15-88.

Income Splitting
- Read paragraph 15-89 to 15-99.
- Do Self Study Problems Fifteen-5 and Fifteen-6 and check the solution in this Study Guide.

Shareholder Benefits Including Loans
- Read paragraph 15-100 to 15-122.
- Do Exercises Fifteen-6 to Fifteen-8 and check the solutions in this Study Guide.
- Do Self Study Problems Fifteen-7 and Fifteen-8 and check the solutions in this Study Guide.

Management Compensation - General Principles
- Read paragraph 15-123 to 15-129.

Salary Vs. Dividend Decisions For The Owner-Manager
- Read paragraph 15-130 to 15-160.
- Do Exercise Fifteen-9 and check the solution in this Study Guide.

Salary Vs. Dividends - Use Of Tax Credits
- Read paragraph 15-161 to 15-177.
- Do Exercises Fifteen-10 and Fifteen-11 and check the solutions in this Study Guide.

Salary Vs. Dividends - Conclusion
- Read paragraph 15-178 to 15-179.
- Do Self Study Problems Fifteen-9 to Fifteen-11 and check the solutions in this Study Guide.

To Complete This Chapter
- If you would like more practice in problem solving, do the Supplementary Self Study Problems for the chapter. These problems and solutions are available on the Companion Website.
- Review the Key Terms Used In This Chapter in the textbook at the end of Chapter 15. Consult the Glossary for the meaning of any key terms you do not know.
- Test yourself with the Chapter 15 Glossary Flashcards available on the Companion Website.
- Ensure you have achieved the Chapter 15 Learning Objectives listed in this Study Guide.
- As a review, we recommend you view the PowerPoint presentation for Chapter 15 that is on the Companion Website.

Practice Examination
- Write the Practice Examination for Chapter 15 that is on the Companion Website. Mark your examination using the Practice Examination Solution that is on the Companion Website.

Solutions to Chapter Fifteen Exercises

Exercise Fifteen - 1 Solution

As the new corporation would not be allocated any part of the annual business limit, all of the $100,000 would be taxed at full corporate rates:

Corporate Income	$100,000
Corporate Taxes [(26%)($100,000)]	(26,000)
Available For Eligible Dividends	$ 74,000

Eligible Dividends Received By Ms. Ashley	$ 74,000
Gross Up At 38 Percent	28,120
Taxable Dividends	$102,120
Ms. Ashley's Tax Rate	45%
Tax Payable Before Dividend Tax Credit	$ 45,954
Dividend Tax Credit [(6/11 + 43.6%)($28,120)]	(27,599)
Tax Payable	$ 18,355
Dividends Received	$74,000
Tax Payable	(18,355)
After Tax Retention	$55,645

This Exercise uses the highest provincial dividend tax credit and the lowest provincial corporate tax rate, both of which are favourable to the use of a corporation. Even with these very favourable rates, use of a corporation only improves the after tax retention by $645 ($55,645 - $55,000).

Exercise Fifteen - 2 Solution

Mr. Slater's combined tax rate on income earned by the unincorporated business is 49 percent (33% + 16%). If he incorporates, all of the $126,000 will be eligible for the small business deduction. This means it will be taxed at a corporate rate of 14 percent (38% - 10% - 17.5% + 3.5%). Mr. Slater's tax rate on non-eligible dividend income is 40.33 percent [(117%)(49%) - (21/29 + 8/29)(17%)].

Using these tax rates, a comparison of the income retained with and without the use of a corporation is as follows:

	With Corporation	Without Corporation
Business Income	$126,000	$126,000
Tax Rate	14%	49%
Tax Payable	$ 17,640	$ 61,740
Business Income	$126,000	$126,000
Tax Payable	(17,640)	(61,740)
Maximum Non-Eligible Dividend Payable	$108,360	N/A
Personal Tax On Dividends [(40.33%)($108,360)]	(43,702)	N/A
After Tax Income Retained By Mr. Slater	$ 64,658	$ 64,260

There is clearly a significant amount of tax deferral with respect to income left in the corporation. His Tax Payable on direct receipt of the $126,000 of business income would be $61,740, far higher than the $17,640 that would be paid by the corporation. There would also be a tax savings as the $64,658 in income retained using the corporation is $398 greater than the $64,260 in income retained without the use of the corporation.

Exercise Fifteen - 3 Solution

Mr. Slater's combined tax rate on interest income earned outside the corporation is 51 percent (33% + 18%). If he incorporates, the interest income will not be eligible for the small business deduction or the general rate reduction, and it will be subject to the ART. This means that, if the investments are transferred to a corporation, the interest will be taxed at a rate of 50-2/3 percent (38% - 10% + 10-2/3% + 12%). Mr. Slater's tax rate on non-eligible dividends received is 42.67 percent [(117%)(51%) - (21/29 + 8/29)(17%)].

Using these tax rates, a comparison of the income retained with and without the use of a corporation is as follows:

	With Corporation	Without Corporation
Interest Income	$126,000	$126,000
Tax Rate	50-2/3%	51%
Tax Payable	$ 63,840	$ 64,260
Interest Income	$126,000	$126,000
Tax Payable	(63,840)	(64,260)
Net Corporate Income Before Dividend Refund	$ 62,160	N/A
Maximum Dividend Refund (See Note)	38,640	
Maximum Dividend Payable	$100,800	
Personal Tax On Dividends [(42.67%)($100,800)]	(43,011)	
After Tax Income Retained By Mr. Slater	$ 57,789	$ 61,740
RDTOH Balance [(30-2/3%)($126,000)]	$ 38,640	

Note The refund is the lesser of 38-1/3 percent of dividends paid and the balance in the RDTOH account. The available cash of $62,160 would support a dividend of $100,800 ($62,160 ÷ .61667), which includes a potential dividend refund of $38,640 [(38-1/3%)($100,800)]. In this case the two figures are both equal to $38,640.

With Mr. Slater's individual tax rate at 51 percent and the corporate tax rate at 50-2/3 percent, there is a very small amount of deferral. The amount would be $420 ($64,260 - $63,840), not enough to justify the tax cost associated with using a corporation.

The after tax retention results with a corporation are significantly worse than when the income is received directly. After tax retention is reduced from $61,740 to $57,789, a reduction of $3,951. There is clearly a tax cost as a result of transferring the investments to a corporation.

Exercise Fifteen - 4 Solution

Direct Receipt If the income is received directly, the total Tax Payable will be as follows:

Eligible Dividends Received	$46,000	
Gross Up At 38 Percent	17,480	$ 63,480
Non-Eligible Dividends Received	$87,000	
Gross Up At 17 Percent	14,790	101,790
Taxable Dividends		$165,270
Interest Income		32,000
Taxable Income		$197,270
Personal Tax Rate (33% + 18%)		51%
Tax Payable Before Dividend Tax Credit		$100,608
Dividend Tax Credit		
[(6/11 + 5/11)($17,480)]	($17,480)	
[(21/29 + 8/29)($14,790)]	(14,790)	(32,270)
Personal Tax Payable		$ 68,338

The after tax retention can be calculated as follows:

Cash Received ($46,000 + $87,000 + $32,000)	$165,000
Tax Payable	(68,338)
After Tax Retention - Direct Receipt	$ 96,662

Transfer To Corporation   If the investments are transferred to a corporation, the tax rate on the interest income is 50-2/3 percent (38% - 10% + 10-2/3% + 12%). Given this, the corporate taxes will be as follows:

Part IV Tax On Dividends Received [(38-1/3%)($46,000) + $29,000]	$46,633
Tax On Interest Income [(50-2/3%)($32,000)]	16,213
Corporate Tax Payable Before Refund	$62,846

As this Tax Payable is smaller than the Tax Payable that would be paid on the direct receipt of income, the use of a corporation provides significant tax deferral. However, as the client needs all of the income produced by these investments, this advantage will not be used by him.

As this would be a new corporation, it would have no RDTOH balance at the beginning of the year. The RDTOH balance prior to the dividend refund would be calculated as follows:

Part IV Addition	$46,633
Part I Addition [(30-2/3%)($32,000)]	9,813
RDTOH Balance	$56,446

The cash available for paying dividends would be $102,154 ($165,000 - $62,846). This represents 61.667 percent of $165,655. Paying a dividend in this amount would result in a refund of $63,501 [(38-1/3%)($165,655). However, this exceeds the balance in the RDTOH. This means that the refund would be limited to $56,446, with a total dividend of $158,600 ($102,154 + $56,446).

The eligible dividends received by the corporation will be added to the GRIP balance, leaving $46,000 in this account. This means that $46,000 in dividends could be designated as eligible for the enhanced dividend gross up and tax credit procedures. The remainder of the dividends paid of $112,600 ($158,600 - $46,000) would be non-eligible.

This would result in personal taxes as follows:

Eligible Dividends Received	$46,000	
Gross Up At 38 Percent	17,480	$ 63,480
Non-Eligible Dividends Received	$112,600	
Gross Up At 17 Percent	19,142	131,742
Taxable Dividends		$195,222
Personal Tax Rate		51%
Tax Payable Before Dividend Tax Credit		$ 99,563
Dividend Tax Credit		
[(6/11 + 5/11)($17,480)]	($17,480)	
[(21/29 + 8/29)($19,142)]	(19,142)	(36,622)
Personal Tax Payable		$ 62,941
Dividends Received ($46,000 + $112,600)		$158,600
Personal Tax Payable		(62,941)
After Tax Retention - With Corporation		$ 95,659

As this is less than the $96,662 that would be retained on direct receipt of income, there is no tax advantage in going to the trouble and expense of forming a corporation to hold the client's investments.

Exercise Fifteen - 5 Solution

The client's combined tax rate on direct receipt of income is 49 percent (33% + 16%). Based on this, the after tax amount retained on direct receipt of income can be calculated as follows:

Capital Gain	$92,000
Personal Taxes On Taxable Capital Gain [(49%)(1/2)($92,000)]	(22,540)
After Tax Retention - Direct Receipt	$69,460

If the investments are transferred to a CCPC, the aggregate investment income will be $46,000 [(1/2)($92,000)]. The applicable tax rate will be 50-2/3% (38% - 10% + 10-2/3% + 12%). As this rate is higher than the client's personal rate on income received directly, there would be no possible deferral of tax through the use of a corporation. However, even if the rate was more favourable, deferral is not an issue here as the client needs all of the income produced by these investments for her forthcoming bicycle trip.

Based on this corporate tax rate, the maximum distribution that can be made would be calculated as follows:

Available Cash	$92,000
Corporate Tax Payable [(50-2/3%)($46,000)]	(23,307)
Tax Free Capital Dividend [(1/2)($92,000)]	(46,000)
Available For Non-Eligible Dividend	$22,693
Dividend Refund (See Note)	14,107
Non-Eligible Dividend Received	$36,800
RDTOH Balance [(30-2/3%)($46,000)]	$14,107

Note The refund is the lesser of 38-1/3 percent of dividends paid and the balance in the RDTOH account. The available cash of $22,693 would support a dividend of $36,800 ($22,693 ÷ .61667), which includes a potential dividend refund of $14,107 [(38-1/3%)($36,800)]. In this case the two figures are both equal to $14,107.

The client's tax rate on non-eligible dividend income is 40.33 percent [(117%)(49%) - (21/29 + 8/29)(17%)]. Based on this, the net after tax retention when a corporation is used would be as follows:

Tax Free Capital Dividend Received	$46,000
Non-Eligible Dividend Received	36,800
Tax Payable On Non-Eligible Dividend Received	
[(40.33%)($36,800)]	(14,841)
After Tax Retention - With Corporation	$67,959

As this is less than the $69,460 that would be retained on direct receipt of the income, there is no tax advantage in going to the trouble and expense of forming a corporation to hold the client's investments.

Exercise Fifteen - 6 Solution

It is likely that Ms. Rourke will have to include the $50,000 principal amount of the loan in her Net Income For Tax Purposes in 2017. She owns more than 10 percent of the shares, making her a specified employee. This means she does not qualify for the exception under ITA 15(2.4)(a). While she is an employee, it is unlikely that this type of loan would be generally available to all employees and, as a consequence, it is likely that she received the loan because of her position as a shareholder. This means that she does not qualify for the acquisition of an automobile exception under ITA 15(2.4)(d). If the loan is included in income, she will be entitled to a $50,000 deduction under ITA 20(1)(j) when she repays the loan in 2021.

In the unlikely event that the loan is not included in income and ITA 15(2) does not apply, she will have to include imputed interest at the prescribed rate for the period of the loan. Her shareholder benefit for 2017 is $250 [(1%)($50,000)(6/12)]. The imputed interest rate and benefit will vary as the prescribed rate changes. Note, however, if imputed interest is assessed, some portion of the amount may be deductible as it relates to the acquisition of an automobile to be used in employment duties.

Exercise Fifteen - 7 Solution

If the loan is repaid on January 1, 2018, it will not be included in two consecutive Generic Inc. Balance Sheets. As a consequence, the principal amount will not have to be included in Ms. Fisk's income. However, as it is an interest-free loan, she will be assessed with a taxable benefit on the loan. The amount would be $1,890 [($162,000)(2% - Nil)(7/12)].

If the loan is not repaid until December 31, 2018, it will appear in two consecutive Generic Inc. Balance Sheets. This means the $162,000 in principal will have to be included in Ms. Fisk's income for the taxation year ending December 31, 2017. However, there will be no imputed interest benefit based on the loan's low rate of interest. In addition, when the loan is repaid, the payment can be deducted from Net Income For Tax Purposes for the taxation year ending December 31, 2018.

Exercise Fifteen - 8 Solution

Mr. Hasid will repay 25 percent of the loan, or $30,750 on October 31, 2018. This will leave an outstanding balance of $92,250 ($123,000 - $30,750) until October 31, 2019.

If Granted As Employee Provided Mr. Hasid receives the loan in his capacity as an employee of Hasid Ltd., the loan is one of the exceptions listed under ITA 15(2). This means that the principal amount will not have to be included in income. However, as the loan is interest free, a taxable benefit will arise. It will be calculated by applying the prescribed rate of 2 percent to the principal of the loan for all periods that it is outstanding.

The amounts for 2017 would be $410 [($123,000)(2% - Nil)(2/12)] and $2,358 {[($123,000)(2% - Nil)(10/12)] + [($92,250)(2% - Nil)(2/12)]} for 2018. The taxable benefit calculations for 2019 to 2021 would be calculated in a similar fashion.

If Granted As Shareholder If Mr. Hasid cannot claim that he received the loan in his capacity as an employee of Hasid Ltd., $92,250 will be included in his income for 2017. The remaining $30,750 would not be included in income as it will have been repaid before Hasid Ltd.'s second year end. However, this balance will attract an interest benefit of $102.50 [($30,750)(2%)(2/12)] in 2017, and $512.50 [($30,750)(2%)(10/12)] in 2018.

As the remaining balance is repaid in 2019 through 2021, the payments can be deducted under ITA 20(1)(j) in the year they are repaid.

Exercise Fifteen - 9 Solution
(1) Salary Compensation

If the full $550,000 is paid out as salary, it will be deductible and will reduce the Company's Taxable Income to nil. This means that no corporate taxes will be paid. This salary payment will result in Ms. Broad having Taxable Income of $550,000. Given this, her Tax Payable will be calculated as follows:

Tax On First $202,800 (Given)	$ 65,000
Tax On Remaining	
$347,200 ($550,000 - $202,800) At 48%	166,656
Tax Payable Before Credits	$231,656
Personal Tax Credits (Given)	(5,000)
Total Tax Payable	$226,656

Based on the preceding Tax Payable, Ms. Broad's after tax retention would be $323,344 ($550,000 - $226,656), ignoring CPP contributions and the Canada employment credit.

(2) Dividend Compensation

As dividends are not deductible for tax purposes, corporate taxes will have to be paid prior to the payment of any dividends. While the $50,000 of income in excess of the annual business limit of $500,000 would not get the small business deduction, it would be eligible for the general rate reduction of 13 percent. Given this, the corporate rate on this income would be 29% (38% - 10% - 13% + 14%). On income eligible for the small business deduction, the rate would be 15% (38% - 10% - 17.5% + 4.5%). Using these rates, corporate taxes would be calculated as follows:

Income Not Eligible For SBD [(29%)($50,000)]	$14,500
Income Eligible For SBD [(15%)($500,000)]	75,000
Corporate Tax Payable	$89,500

After payment of these taxes, the maximum dividend that could be paid would be $460,500 ($550,000 - $89,500).

The fact that the corporation's Taxable Income was in excess of the annual business limit of $500,000 will create an addition to the GRIP of $36,000 [(72%)($550,000 - $500,000)]. Given this, $36,000 of the dividend can be designated as eligible, leaving a non-eligible dividend of $424,500 ($460,500 - $36,000). The grossed up taxable dividends would be calculated as follows:

Total Eligible And Non-Eligible Dividends Received	$460,500
Gross Up:	
Eligible Dividends [(38%)($36,000)]	13,680
Non-Eligible Dividends [(17%)($424,500)]	72,165
Taxable Dividends	$546,345

Personal taxes on this dividend would be calculated as follows:

Tax On First $202,800 (Given)		$ 65,000
Federal Tax On Remaining		
$343,545 ($546,345 - $202,800) At 48%		164,902
Taxes Payable Before Credits		$229,902
Personal Tax Credits (Given)		(5,000)
Dividend Tax Credit:		
Eligible Dividends [(6/11 + 30%)($13,680)]		(11,566)
Non-Eligible Dividends [(21/29 + 30%)($72,165)]		(73,907)
Personal Tax Payable		$ 139,429

The after tax retention would be equal to $321,071 ($460,500 - $139,429). This is $2,273 less than the after tax retention in the salary option of $323,344.

Exercise Fifteen - 10 Solution

Required Salary   Ms. Mortell's combined tax rate on additional salary is 45 percent (29% + 16%). In order to have $30,000 in after tax funds, she would have to receive salary of $54,545 [$30,000 ÷ (1 - .45)].

Required Dividend   Ms. Mortell's tax rate on non-eligible dividends is 36.1 percent [(117%)(45%) - (21/29 + 25%)(17%)]. In order to have $30,000 in after tax funds, she would have to receive dividends of $46,948 [$30,000 ÷ (1 - .361)].

Tax Cost Of Salary   The net tax cost of paying salary can be calculated as follows:

Personal Tax On Receipt Of Salary [(45%)($54,545)]	$24,545
Tax Savings To Corporation [(14%)($54,545)]	(7,636)
Net Tax Cost Of Salary Alternative	$16,909

Tax Cost Of Dividend   As the dividend payment would not be deductible, its payment would not change corporate taxes. This means that the only tax cost would be the $16,948 [($46,948)(36.1%)] in personal taxes that Ms. Mortell would pay on the dividends received.

Conclusion   As the tax cost associated with the payment of dividend is larger, the salary alternative would be preferable.

Exercise Fifteen - 11 Solution

Salary Alternative - As the available cash is less than Taxable Income, some corporate taxes will have to be paid since there is insufficient cash to pay a salary equivalent to Taxable Income. To determine the maximum salary that can be paid (X), it is necessary to solve the following equation:

$$X = \$18,500 - [(15\%)(\$21,500 - X)]$$

$$X - 0.15X = [\$18,500 - (15\%)(\$21,500)] = \underline{\$17,971}$$

Corporate Cash Before Taxes	$18,500
Corporate Taxes [(15%)($21,500 - $17,971)]	(529)
Corporate Cash Available For Salary	$17,971

Salary Received		$17,971
Personal Tax Payable:		
Personal Tax On Salary [(25%)(17,971)]	($ 4,493)	
Personal Tax Credits (Given)	3,950	(543)
After Tax Cash Retained		$17,428

Dividend Alternative - After tax cash retained with the dividend alternative would be calculated as follows:

Corporate Cash Before Taxes	$18,500
Corporate Taxes [(15%)($21,500)]	(3,225)
Corporate Cash Available For Dividends	$15,275
Non-Eligible Dividend Received	$15,275
Individual Taxes*	Nil
After Tax Cash Retained	$15,275

*No taxes would be paid on this amount of dividends (see Paragraph 15-86 of the text).

Given these calculations, it is clear that the preferred approach is to pay the maximum salary. Note, however, some combination of dividends and salary may provide an even better result.

Self Study Solution Fifteen - 1

Part A - Goal Of Integration

The goal of integration is to ensure that the amount of after tax income that an individual receives from a given income source should be the same regardless of whether that income is earned directly, or whether it is flowed through a corporation.

Part B - Tax Payable Without Corporation

Personal Tax Payable without the corporation would be calculated as follows:

	Business Income	Eligible Dividends
Income	$80,000	$ 96,000
Gross Up (38% Of $96,000)	N/A	36,480
Taxable Income	$80,000	$132,480
Tax Rate (33% + 18%)	51%	51%
Tax Payable Before Dividend Tax Credit	$40,800	$ 67,565
Dividend Tax Credit [(6/11 + 5/11)($36,480)]	N/A	(36,480)
Personal Tax Payable	$40,800	$ 31,085

The personal Tax Payable if the income is received directly totals $71,885 ($40,800 + $31,085).

Part C - Corporate Tax Payable

The portfolio dividends would result in Part IV tax of $36,800 [(38-1/3%)($96,000)]. However, this tax would be refunded on the payment of dividends. As a result, the portfolio dividends received of $96,000 would all be available for distribution.

The after tax corporate income available for distribution would be calculated as follows:

	Business Income	Dividends
Income	$80,000	$96,000
Part I Tax [(28% - 17.5% + 3.5%)($80,000)]	(11,200)	
Part IV Tax [(38-1/3%)($96,000)]		(36,800)
Available For Dividends	$68,800	$59,200
Dividend Refund [($59,200 ÷ .616667) - $59,200]	N/A	36,800
Total Distributable Income	$68,800	$96,000

At this point, Slater Ltd. can pay a dividend of $164,800 ($68,800 + $96,000). Since the eligible dividends received by Slater Ltd. will create an addition to the company's GRIP of $96,000, $96,000 can be designated as eligible dividends. This means that the remaining dividends of $68,800 ($164,800 - $96,000), which is also equal to the business income benefitting from the small business deduction, will not be eligible for the enhanced dividend gross up and tax credit procedures.

Part C - Personal Tax Payable

Keith Slater's personal Tax Payable on receipt of the dividend distribution would be calculated as follows:

	Non-Eligible Dividends	Eligible Dividends
Eligible Dividends	N/A	$ 96,000
Gross Up At 38 Percent	N/A	36,480
After Tax ABI As Non-Eligible Dividends	$68,800	N/A
Gross Up At 17 Percent	11,696	N/A
Taxable Dividends	$80,496	$132,480
Tax Rate (33% + 18%)	51%	51%
Tax Payable Before Dividend Tax Credits	$41,053	$ 67,565
Dividend Tax Credits:		
Eligible Dividends [(6/11 + 5/11)($36,480)]	N/A	(36,480)
Non-Eligible Dividends [(21/29 + 8/29)($11,696)]	(11,696)	N/A
Personal Tax Payable	$29,357	$ 31,085

The corporate and personal Tax Payable if Slater Ltd. is used totals $71,642 ($11,200 + $29,357 + $31,085).

Part D - Comparison Of Results

Comparing the total Tax Payable under the two alternatives provides the following result:

Tax Payable - Without Corporation	$71,885
Tax Payable - With Corporation	(71,642)
Tax Savings With Corporation	$ 243

Flowing the income through Slater Ltd. results in a tax savings of $243. By calculating the tax burden on the active business income separately from the dividends, it is clear that there is perfect integration on the portfolio dividends. The Part IV tax paid at the corporate level is totally refunded and the personal taxes paid on the dividends are the same with or without the corporation.

In this example, the Part I corporate rate of 14 percent on the active business income is lower than the 14.53 percent level that is required for perfect integration. In addition, the combined federal/provincial dividend tax credit is equal to the rate required for perfect integration. As a result, there is a small tax savings of $243 when the income is flowed through the corporation.

Self Study Solution Fifteen - 2

Advantages Of Incorporation

Among the more commonly cited advantages of incorporation would be the following:

Tax Deferral It would appear that, if he incorporates, all of the income earned by the corporation will be eligible for the small business deduction. As the corporate rate on this type of income is given as 13 percent, there would be tax deferral on income left within the corporation. As his marginal tax rate as an individual is in the 45 percent range, the amount of the deferral would be significant.

Tax Reduction For CCPCs earning active business income, the tax rate required for perfect integration is 14.53 percent. As the relevant corporate rate in his province is 13 percent, this suggests that there would be a tax savings on income flowed through a corporation. However, the provincial dividend tax credit must also be considered. The required rate for perfect integration is 27.6 percent of the dividend gross up. If the rate in Gerald's province is below this, the savings resulting from the low corporate rate could be reduced or even eliminated.

Income Splitting With a proper structuring of the ownership of the corporation, income can be channeled into the hands of other members of Mr. Copley's family. This can be in the form of either salary or dividends, and will be subject to what we would assume to be significantly lower rates of taxation.

Lifetime Capital Gains Deduction For 2017, this provision allows for the deduction of up to $835,716 in capital gains. It is available on the disposition of shares in a qualified small business corporation. Properly structured, incorporation could permit all members of his family access to the lifetime capital gains deduction. To qualify, the corporation must be a Canadian controlled private corporation and have at least 90 percent of the fair market value of its assets being used in an active business in Canada. In addition, the shares:

- must not have been owned by anyone other than the taxpayer or a related party for at least 24 months preceding the disposition; and

- throughout this 24 month period, more than 50 percent of the fair market value of the corporation's assets must be used in an active business carried on primarily in Canada.

This deduction could represent a significant advantage of incorporating his business.

Employee Benefits While Mr. Copley's organization may be somewhat small to make this feasible, the corporation can be used to establish various retirement programs, as well as group life and health insurance packages.

Estate Planning A corporation can be useful in estate planning, particularly with respect to freezing the asset values in the estate (see Chapters 17 and 19).

Limited Liability An investor in a corporation is, in general, not liable to the creditors for the debts of the corporation. In the case of large publicly traded corporations this is a very real and important consideration. However, in the case of a small owner-managed business such as Mr. Copley's, it is unlikely that creditors would extend significant sums without getting his personal guarantee for repayment.

However, limited liability could be important if his business is exposed to any type of product liability risk.

Liquidation Losses   If the business is unsuccessful and must be liquidated, the loss on corporate shares would be deductible as an allowable business investment loss. This means that one-half of the total amount could be deducted against any other income. However, it would require further analysis to ensure that this would involve a greater amount of deductions than would be the case if the business were liquidated in its present unincorporated form.

Disadvantages Of Incorporation

A list of the disadvantages associated with incorporation would include the following:

Administrative Costs   There will be higher legal, accounting and other costs associated with meeting the various reporting requirements that are necessary for the startup and maintenance of a corporation.

Losses   The losses of the corporation cannot be offset against other personal income that the shareholders might have. Further, allowable capital losses of corporations can only be deducted against the corporation's taxable capital gains.

Termination   If the corporation is terminated, there is no available rollover for transferring the assets back to Mr. Copley. Taxation will occur at fair market values. There is a further possibility of double taxation in that, while the corporation will be taxed on the disposition of its assets, the shareholder may be taxed on the same amounts when he disposes of his shares.

Higher Taxes   Under advantages we noted that there could be a tax reduction associated with a corporation earning income that is eligible for the small business deduction. On the other hand, if the corporation earns income that is not eligible for the small business deduction, there will be a significant extra payment of combined corporate and personal income tax when such income flows through the corporation in the form of dividends to its shareholders.

Winding Up Procedures   Because of its status as a separate legal entity, the procedures associated with winding up an incorporated business are significantly more complex than those associated with terminating an unincorporated enterprise.

Conclusions On Incorporation

In evaluating the preceding advantages and disadvantages, a recommendation that Mr. Copley incorporate his business seems to be appropriate. He does not appear to need all of the income produced by the business for personal living expenses and, as a consequence, the ability to defer income within the corporation is attractive. Further, his eligibility for the small business deduction could result in a reduction in taxes, even on amounts that are withdrawn from the corporation. Other major advantages related to incorporating Mr. Copley's business are the excellent opportunities that will be available to split income between the various members of his family and for estate planning, especially considering the lifetime capital gains deduction.

Self Study Solution Fifteen - 3

Part A - Direct Personal Investment

Mrs. Martin's marginal tax rate is 46 percent (29% + 17%). If Mrs. Martin invests the $200,000 as an individual, the after tax return can be calculated as follows:

Interest Income (All Taxable)	$14,000

Interest Received	$14,000
Personal Tax Payable At 46 Percent	(6,440)
After Tax Retention - Direct Receipt	$ 7,560

Part B - Investment Through Private Company

If Mrs. Martin invests the $200,000 through her private company, any dividends paid will be non-eligible. The after tax return would be as follows:

Interest Income	$14,000
Corporate Taxes At 52 Percent	(7,280)
Net Corporate Income Before Dividend Refund	$ 6,720
Maximum Dividend Refund (See Note)	4,177
Maximum Non-Eligible Dividend Payable	$10,897
Gross Up At 17 Percent	1,852
Taxable Dividend	$12,749
Personal Tax Rate	46%
Personal Tax Payable Before Dividend Tax Credit	$ 5,865
Dividend Tax Credit [(21/29 + 25%)($1,852)]	(1,804)
Personal Tax Payable	$ 4,061

Dividends Received	$10,897
Personal Tax Payable	(4,061)
After Tax Retention - With Corporation	$ 6,836

Note The available corporate cash would support a dividend of $10,897 ($6,720 ÷ .61667, including a dividend refund of $4,177 [(38-1/3%)($10,897)]. As this is less than the $4,293 [(30-2/3%)($14,000)] balance in the RDTOH, this amount of dividends can be paid. There is additional refundable tax of $116 ($4,293 - $4,177) that is available, but only on the payment of additional dividends.

The difference between the two alternatives is $724 ($7,560 - $6,836) in favour of direct personal investment.

Self Study Solution Fifteen - 4

Part A - Direct Personal Investment

Mr. Martin's marginal tax rate is 46 percent (29% + 17%). If Mr. Martin invests the $200,000 as an individual, the after tax return can be calculated as follows:

Eligible Dividends Received	$14,000
38 Percent Gross Up	5,320
Taxable Dividend	$19,320
Personal Tax Rate	46%
Personal Tax Payable Before Dividend Tax Credit	$ 8,887
Dividend Tax Credit [(6/11 + 25%)($5,320)]	(4,232)
Personal Tax Payable	$ 4,655
Dividends Received	$14,000
Personal Tax Payable	(4,655)
After Tax Retention - Direct Receipt	$ 9,345

Part B - Investment Through Private Company

If Mr. Martin invests the $200,000 through his private company, the eligible dividends received would be classified as portfolio dividends, subject to Part IV tax at 38-1/3 percent. There would also be an addition to the corporation's GRIP account of $14,000 (notice that eligible dividends are not multiplied by 72 percent for the GRIP addition). The after tax retention on the flow through the corporation would be as follows:

Eligible Dividends Received	$14,000
Part IV Tax At 38-1/3 Percent (Portfolio Dividends)	(5,367)
Earnings Retained By Corporation	$ 8,633
Refund When Dividends Paid (See Note)	5,367
Eligible Dividends Paid	$14,000

Note The available cash would support a dividend of $14,000 ($8,633 ÷ .61667), including a refund of $5,367 [(38-1/3%)($14,000)]. This refund is available as it is equal to the $5,367 balance in the RDTOH resulting from the payment of Part IV tax on the receipt of the dividends.

At this point, the corporation has paid no net amount of taxes and will be paying exactly the same amount of eligible dividends that it received. This will result in Mr. Martin paying exactly the same amount of taxes that he would have paid on direct receipt of the dividends. With the use of a corporation, the after tax retention would be identical to the after tax retention resulting from direct receipt of the dividends.

Self Study Solution Fifteen - 5

Approach 1 (Joins Partnership As Individual)

Cora's share of the partnership income would be $70,000 [(10%)($700,000)]. Cora's Tax Payable resulting from this approach would be calculated as follows:

Tax On First $45,916 At 23 Percent (15% + 8%)	$10,561
Tax On Next $24,084 ($70,000 - $45,916)	
At 32.5 Percent (20.5% + 12%)	7,827
Tax Payable Before Credits	$18,388
Personal Tax Credits - Given	(3,342)
Personal Tax Payable	$15,046

Business Income	$70,000
Personal Tax Payable	(15,046)
After Tax Retention - Alternative 1	$54,954

Approach 2 (All Dividends)

The total corporate taxes would be calculated as follows:

First $50,000 At 15 Percent	$ 7,500
Remaining $20,000 At 27 Percent	5,400
Corporate Tax Payable	$12,900

If all of the after tax income is paid out, the resulting dividend will be $57,100 ($70,000 - $12,900).

As $20,000 of the corporation's income was taxed at the general rate, there would be a GRIP balance of $14,400 [(72%)($20,000)]. This means that of the total dividend of $57,100, $14,400 could be designated as eligible, with the remaining $42,700 ($57,100 - $14,400) being non-eligible. Based on this, Cora's Taxable Income would be as follows:

Eligible Dividend	$14,400
Gross Up On Eligible Dividend At 38 Percent	5,472
Non-Eligible Dividend	42,700
Gross Up On Non-Eligible Dividend At 17 Percent	7,259
Total Taxable Income	$69,831

Based on this Taxable Income, her Tax Payable would be as follows:

Tax On First $45,916 At 23 Percent (15% + 8%)	$10,561
Tax On Remaining $23,915 ($69,831 - $45,916)	
At 32.5 Percent (20.5% + 12%)	7,772
Tax Payable Before Credits	$18,333
Personal Tax Credits - Given	(3,342)
Dividend Tax Credit = Gross Up ($5,472 + $7,259)	(12,731)
Personal Tax Payable	$ 2,260

Business Income	$70,000
Corporate Tax Payable	(12,900)
Personal Tax Payable	(2,260)
After Tax Retention - Alternative 2	$54,840

Approach 3 (Salary And Dividends)

With the payment of $20,000 in salaries to reduce corporate income to her $50,000 share of the small business deduction, corporate taxes would be $7,500 [(15%)($50,000)]. This would leave $42,500 ($70,000 - $20,000 - $7,500) for the payment of dividends.

Since no income was taxed at the general rate, the GRIP balance would be nil. This means that the total dividend of $42,500 would be non-eligible. Cora's Taxable Income would be calculated as follows:

Salary	$20,000
Non-Eligible Dividend	42,500
Gross Up On Non-Eligible Dividend At 17 Percent	7,225
Taxable Income	$69,725

Her Tax Payable would be calculated as follows:

Tax On First $45,916 At 23 Percent (15% + 8%)	$10,561
Tax On Next $23,809 ($69,725 - $45,916)	
At 32.5 Percent (20.5% + 12%)	7,738
Tax Payable Before Credits	$18,299
Personal Tax Credits - Given	(3,342)
Dividend Tax Credit = Gross Up	(7,225)
Personal Tax Payable	$ 7,732

Business Income	$70,000
Corporate Tax Payable After Salary [(15%)($70,000 - $20,000)]	(7,500)
Personal Tax Payable	(7,732)
After Tax Retention - Alternative 3	$54,768

Evaluation

The after tax amount retained for each of the three approaches is as follows:

Approach 1 (Joins Partnership As Individual)	$54,954
Approach 2 (All Dividends)	54,840
Approach 3 (Salary And Dividends)	54,768

If only after tax cash flows are considered, Approach 1 provides the highest value and would be the appropriate choice.

Other factors to consider:

- While Approach 1 provides the largest after tax retention, it does not take into consideration CPP contributions. If the effect of CPP was considered, she would pay two times the annual maximum in Approach 1, no CPP in Approach 2 and in Approach 3 both Cora and her corporation would pay less than the annual maximum. Paying CPP contributions would allow her to receive CPP payments in the future, but would incur a liability at the present time. Without going through the required calculations, it is likely that Approach 2 would be best if the required CPP contributions were considered.
- If the Canada employment credit was considered, it would only be applicable in Approach 3.
- If Cora wanted to participate in the Employment Insurance program on a voluntary basis, it would only be available to her in Approach 1 as a self-employed individual.
- If she wanted to contribute to an RRSP or deduct child care costs, she would need earned income. Dividends are not a component of earned income for either purpose. Earned income would be $70,000 in Approach 1 and $20,000 in Approach 3.

- Depending on the province, there could be additional payroll costs that her corporation would have to pay in Approach 3.
- The opportunity for income splitting is much easier with a corporation given that family members could buy shares that entitle them to share in the dividends. Income splitting through the partnership would be much more difficult given that, for the most part, the family members would have to be involved in partnership activity.
- Although an advantage of incorporation is the availability of the lifetime capital gains deduction, given the current situation, it is questionable whether her corporation could be sold for much of a gain given how important her personal services are to its value.

Self Study Solution Fifteen - 6

Part A - Tax Payable With Corporation

The business income of the corporation would be calculated as follows:

Management Fees		$82,900
Expenses:		
Mr. Ashley's Salary	($18,400)	
Office Salaries	(25,400)	
Office Rent	(8,180)	
CCA On Office And Dental Equipment	(5,700)	
Other Business Expenses	(2,170)	(59,850)
Business Income		$23,050
Rate On Active Business Income		14%
Tax Payable On Active Business Income		$ 3,227

Tax Payable on the dividends and investment income would be calculated as follows:

Interest Income	$21,600
Net Rental Income ($34,600 - $27,800)	6,800
Aggregate Investment Income	$28,400
Rate On Investment Income	51-2/3%
Part I Tax On Investment Income	$14,673
Part IV Tax On Dividends Received [(38-1/3%)($13,900)]	5,328
Tax Payable On Property Income	$20,001

Given the preceding taxes on property income, the RDTOH balance is as follows:

Part I Refundable Amount [(30-2/3%)($28,400)]	$ 8,709
Part IV Refundable Amount [(38-1/3%)($13,900)]	5,328
RDTOH Balance	$14,037

The eligible dividends received by the corporation will be added to the GRIP balance, leaving $13,900 in this account (note that the amount received is added, not the amount received multiplied by 72 percent). This means that $13,900 in dividends could be designated as eligible for the enhanced dividend gross up and tax credit procedures.

Given the preceding calculations, the maximum eligible and non-eligible dividend that could be paid is as follows:

Business Income	$23,050
Taxes On Business Income	(3,227)
Interest Income	21,600
Net Rental Income	6,800
Taxes On Property Income	(20,001)
Eligible Dividends	13,900
Balance Before Refund	$42,122
Dividend Refund (See Note)	14,037
Available For Dividends	$56,159
Eligible Dividends (GRIP Balance)	(13,900)
Non-Eligible Dividends (Remainder)	$42,259

Note The available cash of $42,122 would support a dividend of $68,305 ($42,122 - .61667), including a refund of $26,184 ([(38-1/3%)($68,305)]. However, the actual refund is the lesser of this figure and the $14,037 balance in the RDTOH account.

With respect to the eligible dividends, $8,340 [(60%)($13,900)] would go to Mr. Ashley, and $5,560 [(40%)($13,900)] would go to Dr. Ashley. With respect to the non-eligible dividends, $25,355 [(60%)($42,259)] would go to Mr. Ashley, and $16,904 [40%)($42,259)] would go to Dr. Ashley. The resulting Tax Payable would be as follows:

	Dr. Ashley	Mr. Ashley
Salary	Nil	$18,400
Eligible Dividends ($13,900)	$ 5,560	8,340
Gross Up At 38 Percent	2,113	3,169
Non-Eligible Dividends ($42,259)	16,904	25,355
Gross Up At 17 Percent	2,874	4,310
Taxable Income	$27,451	$59,574
Tax Rate	47%	30%
Tax Payable Before Dividend Tax Credit	$12,902	$17,872
Dividend Tax Credits:		
Eligible Dividends [(6/11 + 25%)(Gross Up)]	(1,681)	(2,521)
Non-Eligible Dividends [(21/29 + 25%)(Gross Up)]	(2,800)	(4,199)
Tax Payable	$ 8,421	$ 11,152

This would leave after tax balances available to Dr. and Mr. Ashley as follows:

Ashley Management Services	Nil
Dr. Ashley ($5,560 + $16,904 - $8,421)	$14,043
Mr. Ashley ($18,400 + $8,340 + $25,355 - $11,152)	40,943
After Tax Retention - Dr. And Mr. Ashley	$54,986

Part B - Balances With No Corporation

If Dr. Ashley had received all of the amounts involved directly, her Tax Payable and net retention could be calculated as follows:

Business Income ($23,050 + $18,400 Salary To Husband)	$41,450
Interest Income	21,600
Rental Income (Net)	6,800
Eligible Dividends	13,900
Gross Up At 38 Percent	5,282
Taxable Income	$89,032
Tax Rate	47%
Tax Before Dividend Tax Credit	$41,845
Dividend Tax Credit [(6/11 + 25%)($5,282)]	(4,202)
Tax Payable	$37,643
Income Received ($41,450 + $21,600 + $6,800 + $13,900)	$83,750
Tax Payable	(37,643)
After Tax Retention - Dr. Ashley Only	$46,107

It is clear from these calculations that the use of the management company has had a positive effect on after tax retention of income. Without the corporation, Dr. Ashley would have ended up with only $46,107. This compares to a total of $54,986 for Mr. and Dr. Ashley when the corporation is used, an improvement of $8,879.

You should note, however, that Dr. Ashley could have paid a salary to her husband without using a corporation. This would have significantly improved the results in Part B.

The problem asked you to ignore personal tax credits, the Canada employment tax credit, CPP contributions and GST. Personal tax credits would have made only a small difference, as Dr. Ashley would be able to claim the spousal credit in full if Mr. Ashley had no income.

While it is clear the Canada employment tax credit would favour paying Mr. Ashley salary, the advantage or disadvantage of CPP contributions is less clear cut. Although GST is not covered in detail until Chapter 21, we noted in Chapter 12 that the GST/HST legislation has made management companies for GST exempt services such as dentistry less attractive.

Self Study Solution Fifteen - 7

Dwelling Loan
As such loans are available to all employees, Ms. Lord can claim that she has received the loan in her capacity as an employee. This means that the $200,000 principal does not have to be included in her 2017 Net Income For Tax Purposes. However, as the rate on the loan is below the prescribed rate, there will be a taxable benefit included in Ms. Lord's Net Income For Tax Purposes.

The amount to be accrued for 2017 is $1,000 [($200,000)(2% - 1%)(6/12)]. For 2018, the amount is $1,600 [($200,000 - $40,000)(2% - 1%)(12/12)], and for 2019, the amount is $1,200 [($200,000 - $80,000)(2% - 1%)(12/12)].

Automobile
As there are no bona fide arrangements for repaying the loan, the $25,000 principal amount must be included in Ms. Lord's 2017 Net Income For Tax Purposes. There will be no taxable interest benefit. However, when the loan is repaid, the $25,000 principal amount can be deducted in the determination of Net Income For Tax Purposes.

Other Loans

- **February 1, 2017** As this loan is not repaid prior to August 31, 2018 (the second corporate year end), it has to be included in Ms. Lord's 2017 Net Income For Tax Purposes. In 2019, the year it is repaid, the $35,000 can be deducted from Ms. Lord's Net Income For Tax Purposes. As the loan is included in her income, there will be no benefit associated with the low interest rate. As this result would not be changed if the loan was interest free, paying interest on this loan was not good tax planning.

- **July 1, 2017** As the loan is repaid prior to August 31, 2018 (the second corporate year end), it does not have to be included in Ms. Lord's 2017 Net Income For Tax Purposes. However, as it is interest free, there will be a taxable benefit for imputed interest. For 2017, the amount will be $250 [(2%)($25,000)(6/12)]. For 2018, the benefit will be $333 [(2%)($25,000)(8/12)].

- **December 10, 2017** This loan is repaid prior to its inclusion in a second corporate Balance Sheet. As a consequence, it does not have to be included in income. In addition, as the interest rate of 2 percent on the loan is equal to the prescribed rate, there will be no imputed interest benefit.

Self Study Solution Fifteen - 8

Alternative Treatments

The tax consequences here will depend on whether the loan was given to Mr. Blaine in his capacity as an employee or, alternatively, in his capacity as a shareholder. Note that this loan would not qualify for a home relocation loan deduction as it can be assumed that the property that he is acquiring is not 40 kilometers closer to his work since the house seller is a neighbour and he bicycles to work.

Treatment As Shareholder Loan

If similar loans are not available to the other employees of Blaine Enterprises, it is likely that the CRA will take the view that Mr. Blaine received the loan in his capacity as a shareholder. If this is the case and the loan is included in the Balance Sheet of Blaine Enterprises at two consecutive year ends, the principal amount of the loan will have to be included in Mr. Blaine's Net Income For Tax Purposes in the year of the loan. In this situation, having the company grant the loan has basically the same tax consequences for Mr. Blaine as having the company pay a similar amount of salary. There are, however, several differences:

- When the loan is repaid, the repayment can be deducted under ITA 20(1)(j). In contrast, the receipt of salary cannot be reversed.

- Mr. Blaine's salary of $57,000 does not provide sufficient earned income to allow him to make maximum RRSP contributions. Paying salary would increase his earned income and allow him to make additional RRSP contributions.

- Salary would serve to reduce corporate Tax Payable. While the loan cannot be deducted by Blaine Enterprises in determining Net Income For Tax Purposes, salary payments can be.

Note that since Arthur is receiving a salary of $57,000, he is already eligible for the Canada employment tax credit and paying the maximum CPP contributions so these factors are not relevant.

Treatment As Employee Loan

If similar loans are available to the other employees of Blaine Enterprises, Mr. Blaine can argue that he received the loan in his capacity as an employee. Provided there is a reasonable plan for repayment of the loan, he will not have to include the principal amount of the loan in his

Net Income For Tax Purposes. However, he would be assessed a taxable benefit in the amount of imputed interest on the outstanding loan balance. The interest rate to be used in this calculation would be the prescribed rate (ITR 4301).

Evaluation

If he can claim that he received the loan in his capacity as an employee, the analysis will depend on the relationship between the prescribed rate and the rate that Mr. Blaine would have to pay if he financed his new home with a conventional mortgage. Currently the prescribed rate for the purpose of computing the taxable benefit on employee loans is a very low, well below any current rate for home mortgages. Given this, it would appear that if the loan principal can be kept out of his income, having his company provide the loan would be an effective form of tax planning for Mr. Blaine.

If Mr. Blaine is required to include the loan in income because he has received it as a shareholder, it should be determined whether Blaine Enterprises will require the $125,000 in the future. If the intention is to repay the funds, a loan will allow the deduction of the repayment and there will be no taxable benefit for interest. This analysis requires more information about the corporation to determine whether it is more advantageous to have the $125,000 included in Mr. Blaine's income as a shareholder loan or pay salary when both Mr. Blaine and Blaine Enterprises are considered.

Self Study Solution Fifteen - 9

Tax Reduction

Bonus Down

As salary payments can be deducted by the corporation, the entire $250,000 can be paid as salary since no taxes would be paid by the Company on this amount. Mrs. Litvak's after tax retention would be as follows:

Salary Payment	$250,000
Personal Taxes On Salary [(52%)($250,000)]	(130,000)
After Tax Cash Retained After Bonus Down (2017)	$120,000

No Bonus Down

If Morcan Inc. does not pay the additional $250,000 in salary, an additional $67,500 [(27%)($250,000)] in corporate taxes would have to be paid. There would also be a $180,000 [(72%)($750,000 - $500,000)] addition to Morcan's GRIP account.

The after tax retention of funds in the corporation would be $182,500 ($250,000 - $67,500). If this amount is paid out as dividends in 2021, $180,000 (the balance in the GRIP account) could be designated as eligible, with the remaining $2,500 classified as non-eligible. Given this, the tax consequences of paying out these dividends would be as follows:

Eligible Dividends Received	$180,000
Gross Up At 38 Percent	68,400
Non-Eligible Dividends Received	2,500
Gross Up At 17 Percent	425
Taxable Dividend Paid In 2021	$251,325

Tax At 52 Percent [(52%)($251,325]	$130,689
Dividend Tax Credits:	
Eligible [(6/11 + 5/11)($68,400)] +	
Non-Eligible [(21/29 + 8/29)($425)]	(68,825)
Personal Tax Cost Of Dividends	$ 61,864

Dividends Received ($180,000 + $2,500)	$182,500
Personal Tax Cost	(61,864)
After Tax Cash Retained - No Bonus Down	$120,636

Conclusion

The difference in after tax retention between the two alternatives is only $636 ($120,636 - $120,000). While this is slightly in favor of bonusing down, the difference is not significant.

Tax Deferral

If Morcan Inc. pays the salary, there will be an immediate personal tax cost of $130,000. This is more than the $129,364 ($67,500 + $61,864) in taxes that would be paid if she did not bonus down and instead paid corporate taxes on the $250,000 with the remaining funds paid out as dividends in the future. However, Ms. Litvak has indicated that she does not need the additional income and, as a consequence, the payment of the personal taxes can be deferred until 2021. This means the current tax obligation would be limited to the $67,500 in corporate taxes and would constitute a significant tax deferral.

A potential problem with this is the question of whether the corporation can use the additional funds for business purposes. If not, and the funds were allocated to passive investments, the tax rate on investment income could be higher than the 52 percent rate that is applicable on amounts received directly by Ms. Litvak.

Conclusion

In terms of tax reduction, there is no significant advantage resulting from bonusing down. However, if the retained funds are not paid out as dividends until 2021, there is a significant tax deferral. This would favour not bonusing down. Note that this conclusion is dependent on how the funds will be used within the corporation.

Whether bonusing down will be advantageous will also depend on what use the funds can be put to directly by Mrs. Litvak. If, for example, she has not contributed fully to her RRSP and TFSA and/or her daughter's, bonusing down could be more advantageous.

An added consideration could be how Mrs. Litvak's father might react if she does not take his advice. This could have ramifications for her personally, but should not affect her tax situation.

Self Study Solution Fifteen - 10

Required Salary

Given Miss Morgan's personal tax rate of 51 percent (33% + 18%), a salary of $40,816 [$20,000 ÷ (1 - .51)] would be required to provide an additional $20,000 of after tax funds.

Tax Cost Of Salary Alternative

The net tax cost of this alternative would be calculated as follows:

Personal Taxes On Salary [(51%)($40,816)]	$20,816
Tax Savings To Corporation [(15%)($40,816)]	(6,122)
Net Tax Cost Of Salary Alternative	$14,694

Required Dividend

Miss Morgan's tax rate on non-eligible dividends would be as follows:

[(117%)(51%) - (21/29 + 25%)(17%)] = 43.11%

This gives after tax retention of dividend income in the amount of 56.89 percent (1 - 43.11%). This means a dividend of $35,156 ($20,000 ÷ 56.89%) will be required to provide an additional $20,000 of after tax funds.

Tax Cost Of Dividend Alternative

The personal Tax Payable on the dividend would be calculated as follows:

Non-Eligible Dividends Received	$35,156
Gross Up At 17 Percent	5,976
Taxable Income	$41,132
Tax Rate (33% + 18%)	51%
Tax Payable Before Dividend Tax Credit	$20,977
Dividend Tax Credit [(21/29 + 25%)($5,976)]	(5,821)
Personal Tax Payable On Dividend Alternative	$15,156

Subtracting the Tax Payable of $15,156 from the dividends received of $35,156 gives the required $20,000 in after tax funds.

As the dividend payment would not be deductible, its payment would not change corporate taxes. This means that the only tax cost would be the $15,156 in personal taxes that Miss Morgan would pay on the dividends received.

Conclusion

The salary alternative has a net tax cost that is $462 ($15,156 - $14,694) lower than the additional tax cost of paying dividends. Given this, the salary alternative would have the lower tax cost.

Since Geraldine has already received a salary of $84,000, CPP contributions and the Canada employment credit are not relevant to this analysis as they would have already been accounted for and would not affect the conclusion.

Self Study Solution Fifteen - 11

Part A - Taxes And Salary

The combined federal/provincial tax rate applicable to Speelburg Films Ltd. would be 14% (38% - 10% - 17.5% + 3.5%).

As the corporation's Taxable Income exceeds the amount of cash available, the maximum amount of salary that can be paid (X) must be determined using the following simple equation:

$$X = \$49,000 - [(14\%)(\$123,000 - X)]$$

Solving this equation for X indicates that the maximum salary that can be paid is $36,953. This can be verified by the following calculation:

Corporate Taxable Income Before Salary	$123,000
Maximum Salary	(36,953)
Corporate Taxable Income After Salary	$ 86,047
Corporate Rate	14%
Corporate Tax Payable	$ 12,047

Payment of this amount of taxes will leave $36,953 ($49,000 - $12,047) available for payment of salary.

With this amount of salary, Mr. Lucas would have the following amount of after tax cash:

Salary Payment	$36,953
Rate (15% + 6%)	21%
Tax Before Credits	$7,760
Personal Tax Credits (Given)	(3,900)
Personal Tax Payable	$3,860
Salary Received	$36,953
Personal Tax Payable	(3,860)
After Tax Cash Retained (All Salary)	$33,093

Part B - All Dividends

As dividend payments are not deductible to the Company, taxes of $17,220 [(14%)($123,000)] will have to be paid. This leaves a maximum of $31,780 ($49,000 - $17,220) to be used for the payment of non-eligible dividends. When this is paid, the after tax retention by Mr. Lucas will be as follows:

Non-Eligible Dividends Received	$31,780
Gross Up [(17%)($31,780)]	5,403
Taxable Dividends	$37,183
Personal Tax Rate (15% + 6%)	21%
Tax Payable Before Credits	$ 7,808
Personal Tax Credits (Given)	(3,900)
Dividend Tax Credit [(21/29 + 30%)($5,403)]	(5,533)
Tax Payable	Nil

As there is no Tax Payable, Mr. Lucas will retain all of the $31,780 in dividends.

Part C - Possible Improvement

While the Tax Payable for Mr. Lucas is nil in Part B, subtracting personal and dividend tax credits from the tax balance gives a negative figure of $1,625. This means that the all dividend approach leaves unused tax credits. While not conclusive, this suggests that there may be a better solution than either all salary or all dividends.

Part D - Salary/Dividend Combination

To examine the possibility of an optimum solution using both salary and dividends, consider the result that occurs when $1,000 in salary is paid in lieu of some dividends. Because the deductible salary payment would reduce corporate taxes, dividends would only have to be decreased by $860 [($1,000)(1 - 0.14)]. The tax effects of this switch can be calculated as follows:

Increase In Salary		$1,000.00
Decrease In Dividend [($1,000)(1 - .14)]	(	860.00)
Decrease In Dividend Gross Up [(17%)($860.00)]	(	146.20)
Decrease In Mr. Lucas' Taxable Income	($	6.20)
Personal Tax Rate		21%
Decrease In Tax Payable Before Dividend Tax Credit	($	1.30)
Decrease In Dividend Tax Credit [(21/29 + 30%)($146.20)]		149.73
Net Increase In Personal Tax Payable	$	148.43

The rate on a $1,000 increase in salary is 148.43% ($148.33 ÷ $1,000). Applying this rate to the unused credits of $1,625 (see Part C), gives a required increase in salary of $10,948 ($1,625 ÷ 0.14843).

Payment of this amount of salary would result in corporate Tax Payable as follows:

Corporate Taxable Income Before Salary	$123,000
Salary	(10,948)
Corporate Taxable Income After Salary	$112,052
Corporate Rate	14%
Corporate Tax Payable	$ 15,687

Based on available cash of $49,000, the amount of dividend that could be paid is as follows:

Cash Available	$49,000
Corporate Tax Payable	(15,687)
Salary Payment	(10,948)
Available For Dividends	$22,365

After tax retention at the personal level would be calculated as follows:

Non-Eligible Dividends Received	$22,365
Gross Up [(17%)($22,365)]	3,802
Taxable Dividends	$26,167
Salary	10,948
Mr. Lucas' Taxable Income	$37,115
Personal Tax Rate (15% + 6%)	21%
Tax Payable Before Credits	$ 7,794
Personal Tax Credits (Given)	(3,900)
Dividend Tax Credit [(21/29 + 30%)($3,802)]	(3,894)
Tax Payable	Nil
Amounts Received ($22,365 + $10,948)	$33,313
Personal Tax Payable	Nil
After Tax Cash Retained (Salary And Dividends)	$33,313

The comparative results for the three alternatives are as follows:

All Salary	$33,093
All Dividends	$31,780
Salary/Dividend Combination	$33,313

The combination of salary and dividends will produce the maximum after tax cash retention for Mr. Lucas. It is a $220 ($33,313 - $33,093) improvement over the all salary solution and a $1,533 ($33,313 - $31,780) improvement over the all dividend solution.

Part E - Other Factors

Other factors that might be considered include:

- The Canada employment tax credit was ignored in the calculations as it is not a credit against provincial taxes. However, it would allow the first $1,178 of salary to be received with a nil federal tax cost.
- If the effect of CPP was considered, both Mr. Lucas and Speelburg Films Ltd. would pay CPP contributions if salary was paid. Paying CPP contributions would allow him to receive CPP payments in the future, but would require both a personal and a corporate

cash outflow at the present time.
- If Speelburg Films Ltd. has benefits for employees, such as a private health services plan, this could make being an employee (by taking salary) more advantageous.
- Dividend payments are not Earned Income for purposes of making RRSP contributions or deducting child care costs.
- If Mr. Lucas has a CNIL balance, dividend payments will serve to reduce this constraint on the lifetime capital gains deduction.
- Mr. Lucas should consider declaring a bonus (a form of salary) to be paid after the end of the calendar year if he does not require the cash immediately. This would defer the personal taxes without affecting corporate taxes as long as the bonus was paid within 180 days of December 31.
- Though not relevant in this problem, some provinces have payroll taxes which could be incurred.

Chapter 15 Learning Objectives

After completing Chapter 15, you should be able to:

1. Explain how a corporation can be used to reduce taxes, defer taxes, and facilitate income splitting (paragraph [P hereafter] 15-1 to 15-9).
2. Describe other advantages and disadvantages of incorporation (P 15-10 and 15-11).
3. Use various personal and corporate tax rates in the calculation of after-tax retention of earnings flowed through a corporation (P 15-12 to 15-24).
4. Calculate the amount of tax reduction and tax deferral that is available through the use of a public corporation (P 15-25 to 15-34).
5. Calculate the amount of tax reduction and tax deferral that is available through the use of a CCPC earning active business income (P 15-35 to 15-40).

6. Explain the advantages of bonusing down to the owner of a CCPC eligible for the small business deduction (P 15-41 to 15-45).
7. Calculate the amount of tax reduction and tax deferral that is available through the use of a CCPC earning investment income other than dividends (P 15-46 to 15-49).
8. Calculate the amount of tax reduction and tax deferral that is available through the use of a CCPC earning dividend income (P-50 to 15-54).
9. Summarize the tax reduction and tax deferral that is available through the use of various types of corporations earning different types of income (P 15-55 to 15-57).
10. Identify the effect of provincial taxes on the decision to incorporate (P 15-58 to 15-76).

11. Explain why large amounts of dividends can be received on a tax free basis by individuals with no other source of income (P 15-77 to 15-88).
12. Describe and calculate the benefits that can be achieved by using a corporation to implement income splitting (P 15-89 to 15-99).
13. Determine the tax consequences of various shareholder benefits, including loans (P 15-100 to 15-122).
14. Explain the principles of management compensation in the context of an owner-managed corporation (P 15-123 to 15-129).
15. Describe the basic trade-off between the payment of salary and the payment of dividends for the owner-manager (P 15-130 to 15-136).

16. Calculate the appropriate choice between salary and dividends, taking into consideration factors other than federal tax savings (P 15-137 to 15-160).
17. Optimize the salary/dividend mix when all tax credits are not utilized or there is a limited amount of cash in the corporation (P 15-161 to 15-177).
18. Summarize the various non-tax factors that must be taken into consideration in making salary vs. dividend decisions (P 15-178 and 15-179).

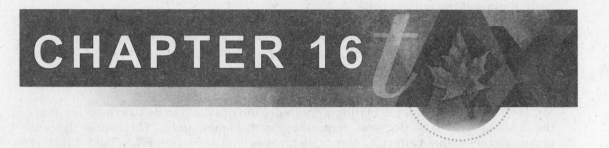

CHAPTER 16

How To Work Through Chapter 16

We recommend the following approach in dealing with the material in this chapter:

Rollovers Under Section 85 - General Rules For The Transfer
- Read paragraph 16-1 to 16-30 (in the textbook).

Transfer Price Rules - Rules Applicable To All Assets
- Read paragraph 16-31 to 16-36.

Transfer Price Rules - Accounts Receivable
- Read paragraph 16-37 to 16-40.

Transfer Price Rules - Inventories And Non-Depreciable Capital Property
- Read paragraph 16-41 to 16-49.
- Do Exercise Sixteen-1 (in the textbook) and check the solution in this Study Guide.

Transfer Price Rules - Non-Depreciable Capital Property
- Read paragraph 16-50 to 16-61.

Transfer Price Rules - Depreciable Property
- Read paragraph 16-62 to 16-69.
- Do Exercise Sixteen-2 and check the solution in this Study Guide.

Transfer Price Rules - Depreciable Property And Disallowed Terminal Losses
- Read paragraph 16-70 to 16-73.

Transfer Price Rules - Eligible Capital Property
- Read paragraph 16-74 to 16-76.
- Do Self Study Problems Sixteen-1 and 2 and check the solutions in this Study Guide.

Allocation Of The Elected Value - Consideration Received By The Transferor
- Read paragraph 16-77 to 16-78.
- Do Exercise Sixteen-3 and check the solution in this Study Guide.

Allocation Of The Elected Value - Assets Acquired By The Corporation
- Read paragraph 16-79 to 16-86.

Paid Up Capital (PUC) Of Shares Issued - General Rules
- Read paragraph 16-87 to 16-89.

Paid Up Capital (PUC) Of Shares Issued - Paid Up Capital Reduction
- Read paragraph 16-90 to 16-94.

Paid Up Capital (PUC) Of Shares Issued - More Than One Class Of Shares
- Read paragraph 16-95 to 16-98.
- Do Exercise Sixteen-4 and check the solution in this Study Guide.
- Do Self Study Problem Sixteen-3 and check the solution in this Study Guide.

Comprehensive Example - Section 85 Rollovers
- Read paragraph 16-99 to 16-114.
- Do Exercise Sixteen-5 and check the solution in this Study Guide.
- Do Self Study Problems Sixteen-4, 5, 6, and 7 and check the solutions in this Study Guide.

Gift To Related Person - Section 85
- Read paragraph 16-115 to 16-129.
- Do Exercise Sixteen-6 and check the solution in this Study Guide.
- Do Self Study Problem Sixteen-8 and check the solution in this Study Guide.

Excess Consideration - Section 85
- Read paragraph 16-130 to 16-133.
- Do Exercise Sixteen-7 and check the solution in this Study Guide.
- Do Self Study Problem Sixteen-9 and check the solution in this Study Guide.

Dividend Stripping - ITA 84.1
- Read paragraph 16-134 to 16-151.
- Do Exercise Sixteen-8 and check the solution in this Study Guide.
- Do Self Study Problem Sixteen-10 and check the solution in this Study Guide.

Capital Gains Stripping - ITA 55(2)
- Read paragraph 16-152 to 16-169.
- Do Exercise Sixteen-9 and check the solution in this Study Guide.
- Do Self Study Problem Sixteen-11 and check the solution in this Study Guide.

To Complete This Chapter
- If you would like more practice in problem solving, do the Supplementary Self Study Problems for the chapter. These problems and solutions are available on the Companion Website.
- Review the Key Terms Used In This Chapter in the textbook at the end of Chapter 16. Consult the Glossary for the meaning of any key terms you do not know.
- Test yourself with the Chapter 16 Glossary Flashcards available on the Companion Website.
- Ensure you have achieved the Chapter 16 Learning Objectives listed in this Study Guide.
- As a review, we recommend you view the PowerPoint presentation for Chapter 16 that is on the Companion Website.

Practice Examination
- Write the Practice Examination for Chapter 16 that is on the Companion Website. Mark your examination using the Practice Examination Solution that is on the Companion Website.

Solutions to Chapter Sixteen Exercises

Exercise Sixteen - 1 Solution
Inventories The $125,000 amount is both the floor and the ceiling, making this the only possible elected value. The transfer would result in a loss of $15,000 ($140,000 - $125,000), an amount that would be fully deductible as a business loss (ITA 23).

Land   The floor would be the boot of $150,000 and the ceiling would be the fair market value of $350,000. Electing the minimum amount would result in a taxable capital gain of $20,000 [($150,000 - $110,000)(1/2)].

Exercise Sixteen - 2 Solution

Class 1 Property   The range would be from a floor of $250,000 (the boot) to a ceiling of $475,000 (fair market value). Election of the $250,000 floor value would result in recapture of $70,000 ($220,000 - $150,000) and a taxable capital gain of $15,000 [($250,000 - $220,000)(1/2)].

Class 10 Asset   The range would be from a floor of $10,000 (the boot) to a ceiling of $12,000 (fair market value). Electing the minimum value of $10,000 would result in recapture of $2,000 ($10,000 - $8,000).

Exercise Sixteen - 3 Solution

The adjusted cost base amounts would be calculated as follows:

Elected Value	$62,000
ACB Of Note (Fair Market Value)	(51,000)
Available For Shares	$11,000
ACB Of Preferred Shares*	(11,000)
ACB Of Common Shares (Residual)	Nil

*Balance available as it is less than the fair market value of $53,000.

Exercise Sixteen - 4 Solution

The adjusted cost base amounts would be calculated as follows:

Elected Value	$114,000
ACB Of Note (Fair Market Value)	(83,000)
Available For Shares	$31,000
ACB Of Preferred Shares*	(31,000)
ACB Of Common Shares (Residual)	Nil

*Balance available as it is less than the fair market value of $97,000.

The total PUC reduction would be calculated as follows:

Increase In Legal Stated Capital ($97,000 + $54,000)		$151,000
Less The Excess Of:		
Total Elected Value	($114,000)	
Over The Total Non-Share Consideration	83,000	(31,000)
PUC Reduction		$120,000

Note that this reduction is equal to the deferred gain on the election ($234,000 - $114,000). The PUC reduction would be allocated on the basis of fair market values as follows:

Preferred Stock [($120,000)($97,000 ÷ $151,000)]	$ 77,086
Common Stock [($120,000)($54,000 ÷ $151,000)]	42,914
Total PUC Reduction	$120,000

Subsequent to applying this reduction, the remaining PUC of the two classes of shares would be as follows:

	Preferred Stock	Common Stock
Legal Stated Capital	$97,000	$54,000
PUC Reduction (From Preceding)	(77,086)	(42,914)
Total PUC	$19,914	$11,086

Note that the sum of these two figures equals $31,000 ($19,914 + $11,086), the total adjusted cost base of the preferred and common shares, as well as the difference between the elected value of $114,000 and the total non-share consideration of $83,000.

Exercise Sixteen - 5 Solution
Part 1 The adjusted cost base of all of the consideration will total the elected value of $275,000. It will be allocated as follows:

Elected Value	$275,000
Non-Share Consideration ($83,000 + $17,000)	(100,000)
Adjusted Cost Base Of All Shares	$175,000
Adjusted Cost Base Of Preferred Shares (FMV)	(125,000)
Adjusted Cost Base Of Common Shares (Residual)	$ 50,000

Part 2 The PUC of the shares issued must be reduced as follows:

Increase In Legal Stated Capital ($125,000 + $925,000)		$1,050,000
Less The Excess Of:		
Elected Value	($275,000)	
Over The Non-Share Consideration	100,000	(175,000)
PUC Reduction		$ 875,000

This PUC reduction would be split between the preferred and common shares on the basis of their fair market values:

Preferred Stock [($125,000/$1,050,000)($875,000)]	$104,167
Common Stock [($925,000/$1,050,000)($875,000)]	770,833
Total PUC Reduction	$875,000

Subsequent to applying this reduction, the remaining PUC of the two classes of shares would be as follows:

	Preferred Stock	Common Stock
Legal Stated Capital	$125,000	$925,000
PUC Reduction (From Preceding)	(104,167)	(770,833)
Total PUC	$ 20,833	$154,167

Part 3 The tax consequences of the preferred stock redemption would be as follows:

Proceeds Of Redemption	$125,000
PUC Of The Preferred Shares	(20,833)
ITA 84(3) Deemed Dividend (Non-Eligible)	$104,167

Proceeds Of Redemption	$125,000
ITA 84(3) Deemed Dividend	(104,167)
ITA 54 Deemed Proceeds Of Disposition	$ 20,833
Adjusted Cost Base	(125,000)
Capital Loss	($104,167)
Inclusion Rate	1/2
Allowable Capital Loss - Disallowed	($ 52,084)

The grossed up non-eligible dividend of $121,875 [(117%)($104,167)] would qualify for a federal dividend tax credit of $12,823 [(21/29)(17%)($104,167)]. The allowable capital loss would be disallowed because the shareholder and the corporation are affiliated.

Exercise Sixteen - 6 Solution

Using the reassessed fair market value of $110,000, the calculation of the gift is as follows:

Fair Market Value Of Property Transferred (Reassessed Value)		$110,000
Less The Greater Of:		
• FMV Of Consideration Received = $65,000		
($50,000 + $15,000)		
• Elected Amount = $50,000		(65,000)
Excess = Gift To Daughter		$ 45,000

Given this gift, the tax consequences of the transfer for Ms. Bellows are as follows:

Deemed Elected Value = Deemed Proceeds Of Disposition	
($50,000 + $45,000 Gift)	$95,000
Adjusted Cost Base	(50,000)
Capital Gain	$45,000
Inclusion Rate	1/2
Taxable Capital Gain	$22,500

The adjusted cost base of her preferred shares would be calculated as follows:

Elected Value (Original)	$50,000
Non-Share Consideration	(50,000)
Adjusted Cost Base Of Preferred Shares	Nil

As shown in the following calculation, there would be no PUC reduction for the preferred shares issued to Ms. Bellows:

Increase In Legal Stated Capital		$15,000
Less Excess, If Any, Of:		
Deemed Elected Value	($95,000)	
Over Non-Share Consideration	50,000	(45,000)
PUC Reduction		Nil
PUC Of Preferred Shares ($15,000 - Nil)		$15,000

The fair market value of the common shares issued to the daughter is $46,000 ($110,000 Reassessed Value + $1,000 - $50,000 - $15,000).

The sale of the shares for their fair market value would result in the following taxable capital gains:

	Preferred	Common
Proceeds (Fair Market Value)	$15,000	$46,000
Adjusted Cost Base	Nil	(1,000)
Capital Gain	$15,000	$45,000
Inclusion Rate	1/2	1/2
Taxable Capital Gain	$ 7,500	$22,500

If the property had simply been sold for its $110,000 post-reassessment fair market value, there would have been a $30,000 [(1/2)($110,000 - $50,000) taxable capital gain. Using ITA 85, Ms. Bellows' total taxable capital gain on the transfer and sale of the preferred shares is also $30,000 ($22,500 + $7,500). However, because the common shares held by the daughter have increased in value by the $45,000 amount of the gift, with their adjusted cost base remaining at $1,000, there is an additional $22,500 taxable capital gain on the sale of her daughter's common shares. This reflects the fact that the $45,000 amount of the gift has been subject to double taxation.

Exercise Sixteen - 7 Solution

The immediate tax consequences of the transfer would be a taxable capital gain on the property and an ITA 15(1) shareholder benefit. These would be calculated as follows:

Elected Value Of Property	$217,000
Adjusted Cost Base	(123,000)
Capital Gain	$ 94,000
Inclusion Rate	1/2
Taxable Capital Gain On Property	$ 47,000

Fair Market Value Of Consideration	
($195,000 + $75,000)	$270,000
Fair Market Value Of Property	(217,000)
ITA 15(1) Shareholder Benefit	$ 53,000

The total effect on Net Income For Tax Purposes is as follows:

Taxable Capital Gain	$ 47,000
Shareholder Benefit	53,000
Total Addition To Net Income For Tax Purposes	$100,000

The ITA 15(1) benefit of $53,000 would be added to the adjusted cost base of the acquired property, resulting in the following ACB for the preferred shares:

Elected Value	$217,000
ACB Of Non-Share Consideration (Fair Market Value)	(195,000)
Available For Shares	$ 22,000
ITA 15(1) Shareholder Benefit	53,000
ACB Of Preferred Shares	$ 75,000

There will be a PUC reduction of $53,000 calculated as follows:

Increase In Legal Stated Capital		$75,000
Less Excess, If Any, Of:		
Total Elected Value	($217,000)	
Over The Non-Share Consideration	195,000	(22,000)
ITA 85(2.1) PUC Reduction		$53,000

This will leave a PUC of $22,000 ($75,000 - $53,000). As this is equal to the $22,000 increase in net assets ($217,000 - $195,000), there is no ITA 84(1) deemed dividend.

Sale Of Shares   If the preferred shares are sold for $75,000, the results would be as follows:

Proceeds Of Disposition	$75,000
Adjusted Cost Base	(75,000)
Capital Gain On Sale	Nil

Redemption Of Shares   If the preferred shares were redeemed for their fair market value of $75,000, the results would be as follows:

Redemption Proceeds	$75,000
PUC	(22,000)
ITA 84(3) Deemed Dividend (Non-Eligible)	$53,000
Proceeds Of Disposition	$75,000
ITA 84(3) Deemed Dividend	(53,000)
Adjusted Proceeds Of Disposition	$22,000
Adjusted Cost Base	(75,000)
Capital Loss	($53,000)
Inclusion Rate	1/2
Allowable Capital Loss - Disallowed	($26,500)

The non-eligible dividend would have a taxable value of $62,010 [(117%)($53,000)] and would qualify for a federal dividend tax credit of $6,524 [(21/29)(17%)($53,000)]. The allowable capital loss would be disallowed because the shareholder and the corporation are affiliated.

Exercise Sixteen - 8 Solution

Miss Cole (an individual) has sold shares of a subject corporation to a purchasing corporation, both corporations do not deal with Miss Cole at arm's length, and the two corporations are connected subsequent to the sale. As a consequence, ITA 84.1 is applicable. Given this, the tax consequences of this transaction to Miss Cole are as follows:

Increase In Legal Stated Capital		$317,000
Less Excess, If Any, Of:		
PUC And ACB Of Subject Shares	($125,000)	
Over The Non-Share Consideration	450,000	Nil
PUC Reduction		$317,000
PUC Of New Shares ($317,000 - $317,000)		Nil

Increase In Legal Stated Capital		$317,000
Non-Share Consideration		450,000
Total		$767,000
Less The Sum Of:		
PUC And ACB Of Subject Shares	($125,000)	
PUC Reduction	(317,000)	(442,000)
ITA 84.1 Deemed Dividend (Non-Eligible)		$325,000

Elected Proceeds Of Disposition For Subject Shares	$767,000
ITA 84.1 Deemed Dividend	(325,000)
Deemed Proceeds For Capital Gains Purposes	$442,000
ACB Of Subject Shares	(125,000)
Capital Gain	$317,000
Inclusion Rate	1/2
Taxable Capital Gain	$158,500

ACB Of New Shares ($767,000 - $450,000)	$317,000

The grossed up non-eligible dividend of $380,250 [(117%)($325,000)] would qualify for a federal dividend tax credit of $40,009 [(21/29)(17%)($325,000)]. In addition, there would be a taxable capital gain of $158,500 that would be eligible for the lifetime capital gains deduction. If Miss Cole claims the deduction, she may need to pay alternative minimum tax.

Economic Analysis Miss Cole is attempting to realize a capital gain of $642,000 ($767,000 - $125,000). However, her non-share consideration was $450,000, $325,000 more than the adjusted cost base of the Cole Inc. shares. ITA 84.1 acts to convert this from a capital gain to a deemed dividend. Note that the remaining $317,000 ($642,000 - $325,000) is allowed to flow through as a capital gain. This reflects the fact that Miss Cole did not attempt to take out the full $767,000 fair market value of the shares in the form of non-share consideration.

Exercise Sixteen - 9 Solution

A deductible dividend has been paid in conjunction with an arm's length sale of shares, and it would appear that the dividend payment served to eliminate the potential capital gain on the transaction. As a consequence, ITA 55 is applicable and the tax consequences of the transaction are as follows:

Dividends Received	$750,000
Dividends Attributable To Safe Income (Tax Free)	(225,000)
Amount Deemed By ITA 55(2)(a) To Not Be A Dividend And By ITA 55(2)(c) To Be A Capital Gain	$525,000
Capital Gain On Sale Of Shares ($90,000 - $75,000)	15,000
Total Capital Gain	$540,000
Inclusion Rate	1/2
Taxable Capital Gain	$270,000

The $225,000 of dividends paid from safe income will retain its status as a dividend and will be deducted in calculating Taxable Income, resulting in no tax cost.

Self Study Solution Sixteen - 1

Part A - No Election

The disposition of a business is a capital transaction and, in the absence of special provisions, any resulting gain or loss must be treated as a capital gain or loss. With respect to the Inventories, a special provision in ITA 23 indicates that, when such assets are sold as part of the disposition of a business, the sale is deemed to be in the ordinary course of carrying on business and any resulting gain or loss is considered business in nature. ITA 23 automatically applies in the disposition of a business and no election is required on the part of the vendor.

ITA 22 provides for a similar treatment of Accounts Receivable. However, a joint election by the vendor and purchaser is required before this business income treatment is applicable. In the absence of this election, losses on Accounts Receivable are treated as capital losses.

If the assets are transferred at fair market values, the Taxable Income resulting from the transfer can be calculated as follows:

Inventories - Business Income ($88,000 - $73,000)	$15,000
Furniture And Fixtures - Recaptured CCA ($45,000 - $38,000)	7,000
Goodwill [(1/2)($150,000)]	75,000
Taxable Income	$97,000

Prior to 2017, the goodwill would have been subtracted from the nil balance that was in the proprietorship's Cumulative Eligible Capital (CEC) account. This would have resulted in business income of $75,000 [(2/3)(1/2 ÷ 3/4)($150,000)]. With the repeal of the CEC legislation, goodwill is a Class 14.1 asset. Following the usual rules for dispositions of capital assets, the result will be a taxable capital gain of $75,000 [(1/2)($150,000)].

There is also an allowable capital loss of $3,000 [(1/2)($51,000 - $45,000)] on the disposition of the Accounts Receivable. However, it is a superficial loss in that the property is re-acquired within 30 days by an affiliated person (the new corporation would be affiliated with Ms. Flack). ITA 40(2)(g) deems such losses to be nil. This loss would be added to the tax cost of the Accounts Receivable on the corporation's books.

Part B - ITA 22 And ITA 85 Elections

The cash is not eligible to be transferred under ITA 85, but can be transferred to the corporation without a rollover. All of the other assets can be transferred at elected values under ITA 85. Under the provisions of this Section, the tax consequences would be as follows:

Accounts Receivable   If the Accounts Receivable are transferred under ITA 85, the maximum value that can be elected is the fair market value of $45,000. This will result in a capital loss of $6,000 (allowable amount of $3,000). However, this loss will be disallowed under ITA 40(2)(g) because the transfer is to a corporation that will be controlled by Ms. Flack.

Inventories   The Inventories can be transferred at an elected value of $73,000, resulting in no Taxable Income on the transfer.

Furniture And Fixtures   The Furniture And Fixtures can be transferred at their UCC of $38,000, resulting in no Taxable Income on the transfer.

Goodwill   The Goodwill can be transferred at a nominal value of $1, resulting in no significant Taxable Income on the transfer.

An alternative with respect to the Accounts Receivable would be to transfer these assets under the provisions of ITA 22. If Ms. Flack and her corporation were to make this joint election, the $6,000 loss resulting from transferring these assets to the corporation would be fully deductible as a business loss. As it is not a capital loss, it would not be disallowed and Ms. Flack would be able to deduct the full $6,000 against any other source of income in the year of transfer. As

ITA 22 is a joint election, the corporation would have to include the $6,000 in income, but could then deduct actual bad debts as they occur. Using the ITA 22 election is the preferable approach to the transfer of these Accounts Receivable.

Self Study Solution Sixteen - 2

Part A - Assets To Be Transferred
Of the assets in the Balance Sheet, Cash is not among the eligible assets listed in ITA 85(1.1). This is of no consequence as the tax value of cash is always equal to its carrying value and can be transferred to the corporation without a rollover.

Accounts Receivable could be transferred under Section 85, but are usually transferred to the corporation under the provisions of ITA 22. ITA 22 is used for two reasons. First, it means that any loss on the transfer will be a fully deductible business loss, rather than a capital loss that will be disallowed on a transfer to a corporation controlled by the transferor under ITA 40(2)(g). In addition, the use of the ITA 22 joint election to make the transfer will permit the transferee corporation to deduct any additional bad debts as business losses, rather than capital losses, only one-half of which would be deductible.

There is a potential terminal loss on the transfer of the equipment as the fair market value of the equipment is less than the UCC of the class. Given this, ITA 13(21.2) indicates that ITA 85 does not apply and the proceeds of disposition are deemed to be the UCC amount thereby disallowing the terminal loss.

Part B - Minimum Transfer Values
The minimum transfer values for the assets to be included in the rollover would be as follows:

Inventories (Cost)	$261,000
Land (Adjusted Cost Base)	196,000
Building (UCC)	103,600
Equipment (UCC)	67,000
Goodwill (Nominal Value)	1

Note The Goodwill has been given a nominal elected value to ensure that it is specifically included in the transfer. A failure to do this could result in the Goodwill being assessed on the basis of a transfer at fair market value.

Part C - Tax Consequences
The tax consequences of the asset transfers with respect to both Ms. Speaks and Speaks Inc. can be described as follows:

Inventories The cost of the Inventories to Speaks Inc. would be the transfer price of $261,000. As this was the cost of the Inventories, there would be no tax consequence to Ms. Speaks.

Land The cost of the Land to Speaks Inc. would be the transfer price of $196,000. As this was the adjusted cost base of the Land, there would be no tax consequence to Ms. Speaks.

Building The capital cost of the Building to Speaks Inc. would be $155,500, and Speaks Inc. would be deemed to have taken CCA in the amount of $51,900. As the net value of the transfer is equal to UCC, there would be no tax consequence to Ms. Speaks.

Equipment The capital cost of the Equipment to Speaks Inc. would be $222,000, and Speaks Inc. would be deemed to have taken CCA in the amount of $155,000. As the net value of the transfer is equal to UCC, there would be no tax consequence to Ms. Speaks.

Goodwill The cost of the Goodwill to Speaks Inc. will be $1. In Ms. Speak's tax records, the proceeds of $1 will be subtracted from Class 14.1, leaving a negative balance in that Class. This amount will be treated as recapture and included in Ms. Speak's income. The

$1 will also be added to Class 14.1, restoring the balance to nil. In the Speaks Inc.'s records, the $1 will be added to Class 14.1.

Self Study Solution Sixteen - 3

Approach 1

Immediate Tax Consequences The $230,000 elected value becomes the proceeds of disposition. As this amount is equal to the adjusted cost base of the land, there are no immediate tax consequences resulting from the transfer.

ACB Of The Land The ACB of the land to the corporation would be equal to the elected value of $230,000.

ACB Of Shares The ACB of the shares issued by the corporation would be calculated as follows:

Elected Value	$230,000
Fair Market Value Of Non-Share Consideration	Nil
ACB Of Shares	$230,000

PUC Of Shares The required PUC reduction and resulting PUC would be calculated as follows:

Legal Stated Capital Of Shares		$660,000
Less Excess, If Any, Of:		
Elected Value	($230,000)	
Over The Non-Share Consideration	Nil	(230,000)
PUC Reduction		$430,000
PUC Of Shares ($660,000 - $430,000)		$230,000

Approach 2

Immediate Tax Consequences The elected value of $500,000 becomes proceeds of disposition. As this value exceeds the $230,000 adjusted cost base of the land, there is a taxable capital gain of $135,000 [(1/2)($500,000 - $230,000).

ACB Of The Land The ACB of the land to the corporation will be equal to the elected value of $500,000.

ACB Of Shares The ACB of the shares issued by the corporation would be calculated as follows:

Elected Value	$500,000
Fair Market Value Of Non-Share Consideration	Nil
ACB Of Shares	$500,000

PUC Of Shares The required PUC reduction and resulting PUC would be calculated as follows:

Legal Stated Capital Of Shares		$660,000
Less Excess, If Any, Of:		
Elected Value	($500,000)	
Over The Non-Share Consideration	Nil	(500,000)
PUC Reduction		$160,000

PUC Of Shares ($660,000 - $160,000)	$500,000

Approach 3

Immediate Tax Consequences   The elected value of $500,000 becomes proceeds of disposition. As this value exceeds the $230,000 adjusted cost base of the land, there is a taxable capital gain of $135,000 [(1/2)($500,000 - $230,000).

ACB Of The Land   The ACB of the land to the corporation will be equal to the elected value of $500,000.

ACB Of Shares   The ACB of the shares issued by the corporation would be calculated as follows:

Elected Value	$500,000
Fair Market Value Of Non-Share Consideration	(500,000)
ACB Of Shares	Nil

PUC Of Shares   The required PUC reduction and resulting PUC would be calculated as follows:

Legal Stated Capital Of Shares		$160.000
Less Excess, If Any, Of:		
Elected Value	($500,000)	
Over The Non-Share Consideration	500,000	Nil
PUC Reduction		$160,000
PUC Of Shares ($160,000 - $160,000)		Nil

Self Study Solution Sixteen - 4

Part A - Adjusted Cost Base Of Consideration

The adjusted cost base for each item of consideration, under the three alternatives, would be calculated as follows:

	Alternative		
	One	Two	Three
Elected Transfer Price	$225,000	$225,000	$225,000
ACB - Boot	(150,000)	(175,000)	(210,000)
Available For Preferred And Common Stock	$75,000	$ 50,000	$ 15,000
ACB - Preferred Stock	(50,000)	(50,000)	N/A
ACB - Common Stock (Residual)	$ 25,000	N/A	$ 15,000

Part B - Legal Stated Capital And PUC

The legal stated capital for the two classes of shares would be as follows:

	Alternative		
	One	Two	Three
Preferred Stock	$ 50,000	$450,000	Nil
Common Stock	425,000	Nil	$415,000
Total Legal Stated Capital	$475,000	$450,000	$415,000

The required PUC reduction would be calculated as follows:

	Alternative		
	One	Two	Three
Increase In Legal Stated Capital - All Shares (A)	$475,000	$450,000	$415,000
Elected Amount	$225,000	$225,000	$225,000
Non-Share Consideration	(150,000)	(175,000)	(210,000)
Elected Amount, Less Boot (B)	$ 75,000	$ 50,000	$ 15,000
Required PUC Reduction (A - B)	$400,000	$400,000	$400,000

Alternative One   In Alternative One, the PUC reduction would have to be split between the two classes of shares on the basis of their relative fair market values. The relevant calculation would be as follows:

Preferred Shares: [($400,000)($50,000 ÷ $475,000)] = $42,105

Common Shares: [($400,000)($425,000 ÷ $475,000)] = $357,895

This would leave a PUC of $7,895 for the preferred shares ($50,000 - $42,105), and a PUC of $67,105 for the common shares ($425,000 - $357,895).

Alternative Two   In Alternative Two, the entire PUC reduction of $400,000 would be allocated to the preferred shares, leaving a PUC of $50,000 ($450,000 - $400,000).

Alternative Three   In Alternative Three, the entire PUC reduction of $400,000 would be allocated to the common stock, leaving a PUC of $15,000 ($415,000 - $400,000).

Self Study Solution Sixteen - 5

Part A - ACB Of The Shares
The adjusted cost base of the shares would be as follows:

Total Elected Value	$467,000
Non-Share Consideration ($122,000 + $128,000)	(250,000)
Adjusted Cost Base Preferred And Common Shares	$217,000
Allocated To Preferred Shares (FMV)	(150,000)
Adjusted Cost Base Of Common Shares (Residual)	$ 67,000

Part B - PUC Of The Shares
The legal stated capital of the preferred and common shares would be their respective fair market values of $150,000 and $326,000. The PUC reduction required under ITA 85(2.1) would be calculated as follows:

Increase In Legal Stated Capital ($150,000 + $326,000)		$476,000
Less Excess Of:		
Total Elected Value	($467,000)	
Over The Total Non-Share Consideration	250,000	(217,000)
Reduction In Paid Up Capital		$259,000

Note that this total reduction is equal to the deferred gain on the election ($726,000 - $467,000). The PUC reduction would be allocated on the basis of fair market values as follows:

Preferred Stock [($259,000)($150,000 ÷ $476,000)]		$ 81,618
Common Stock [($259,000)($326,000 ÷ $476,000)]		177,382
Total PUC Reduction		$259,000

Subsequent to applying this reduction, the remaining PUC of the two classes of shares would be as follows:

	Preferred Shares	Common Shares
Legal Stated Capital	$150,000	$326,000
PUC Reduction	(81,618)	(177,382)
PUC	$ 68,382	$148,618

Note that the combined PUC of the two classes of shares is $217,000 ($68,382 + $148,618). This is the same amount as the combined ACB of the two classes of shares ($150,000 + $67,000).

Part C - Tax Consequences Of Redemption

The tax consequences to Mr. Lardner, if the corporation redeemed both classes of shares at their respective fair market values, would be calculated as follows:

	Preferred Shares	Common Shares
Redemption Proceeds	$150,000	$326,000
PUC (See Preceding Calculations)	(68,382)	(148,618)
ITA 84(3) Deemed Dividend	$ 81,618	$177,382
Redemption Proceeds	$150,000	$326,000
ITA 84(3) Deemed Dividend	(81,618)	(177,382)
Deemed Proceeds Of Disposition	$ 68,382	$148,618
Adjusted Cost Base (Part A)	(150,000)	(67,000)
Capital Gain (Loss)	($ 81,618)	$ 81,618

Mr. Lardner would have a deemed non-eligible dividend of $259,000 ($81,618 + $177,382). The grossed up non-eligible dividend of $303,030 [(117%)($259,000)] would qualify for a federal dividend tax credit of $31,884 [(21/29)(17%)($259,000)]. He has a net capital gain of nil ($81,618 - $81,618).

Self Study Solution Sixteen - 6

Part A - Tax Consequences Of Transfer

With respect to the land, the $250,000 elected value will be both the proceeds of disposition to Mr. Bodin and the adjusted cost base to the corporation. As the elected value is equal to Mr. Bodin's adjusted cost base, there will be no tax consequences resulting from the transfer.

The elected value and proceeds of disposition for the building is $750,000, an amount that is less than its capital cost but more than its UCC. This will result in Mr. Bodin having to report recapture of $116,400 ($750,000 - $633,600). The corporation's tax value will be $750,000. However, the corporation will retain the original capital cost of $1,100,000 ($1,350,000 - $250,000) for recapture and capital gains calculations. The $350,000 difference will be deemed to be CCA taken.

Part B - Adjusted Cost Base Of The Consideration

The adjusted cost base of all consideration received by Mr. Bodin will be the total elected value of $1,000,000 ($250,000 + $750,000). It will be allocated as follow:

Total Elected Value	$1,000,000
Total Non-Share Consideration	
($450,000 Assumed Mortgage + $400,000 New Debt)	(850,000)
Adjusted Cost Base Of Common Shares	$ 150,000

Part C - PUC Of The New Shares

The calculation of PUC would be as follows:

Increase In Legal Stated Capital (Fair Market Value)		$950,000
Less Excess Of:		
Elected Amount	($1,000,000)	
Over The Total Non-Share Consideration	850,000	(150,000)
Reduction In PUC		$800,000

The PUC of the common shares would be reduced to $150,000 ($950,000 - $800,000).

Part D - Sale Of Common Shares

The increase in Net Income For Tax Purposes from a sale of the shares for $950,000 would be as follows:

Proceeds Of Disposition	$950,000
Adjusted Cost Base	(150,000)
Capital Gain	$800,000
Inclusion Rate	1/2
Taxable Capital Gain	$400,000

As Taxable Income consequences are not required, the effect of the lifetime capital gains deduction has not been considered.

Part E - Tax Consequences Of Redemption

The tax consequences of a redemption for $950,000 would be as follows:

Proceeds From Redemption	$950,000
PUC	(150,000)
ITA 84(3) Deemed Dividend (Non-Eligible)	$800,000

There would be no capital gain on this redemption as shown in the following calculation:

Redemption Proceeds	$950,000
ITA 84(3) Deemed Dividend	(800,000)
Deemed Proceeds Of Disposition	$150,000
Adjusted Cost Base	(150,000)
Capital Gain	Nil

The amount to be included in Net Income For Tax Purposes would be $936,000, the $800,000 deemed non-eligible dividend grossed up by 17 percent.

There would also be a federal dividend tax credit of $98,483 [(21/29)(17%)($800,000)]. However, as the problem only asks for the amounts to be included in Net Income For Tax Purposes, this is not a required part of the solution.

Self Study Solution Sixteen - 7

Part A - Use Of ITA 22

Accounts Receivable could be transferred under Section 85, but are usually transferred to the corporation under the provisions of ITA 22. ITA 22 is used for two reasons. First, it means that any loss on the transfer will be a fully deductible business loss, rather than a capital loss that will be disallowed on a transfer to a corporation controlled by the transferor under ITA 40(2)(g). In addition, the use of the ITA 22 joint election to make the transfer will permit the transferee corporation to deduct any additional bad debts as business losses, rather than capital losses.

Using the ITA 22 joint election, the Accounts Receivable are transferred at the $85,000 fair market value. This will result in a fully deductible business loss of $3,000 for Miss Brock. While this does not influence the solution, if Miss Brock had deducted a bad debt reserve in the previous year, it would have to be added back. However, the problem does not indicate that this was the case.

For the transferee corporation, the $3,000 difference between the face value of $88,000 and the transfer value of $85,000 will have to be included in income. However, any amount of the $88,000 face value that cannot be collected will be deductible in full as a business expense.

Part B - Elected Values

The values that should be elected under ITA 85 on the other assets in order to eliminate any current Tax Payable on the transfer, are as follows:

Asset	Tax Value	FMV	Elected
Inventory	$174,000	$208,000	$174,000
Equipment (Cost = $420,000)	234,000	317,000	234,000
Goodwill (See Note)	Nil	350,000	1
Total Assets Transferred	$408,000	$875,000	$408,001

Note It is prudent to add at least a nominal elected value for goodwill. A failure to do so could result in the application of ITA 69, with the transfer assessed to the transferor at fair market value.

Part C - ACB Of Consideration

The total elected value would become the adjusted cost base of the consideration received by Miss Brock. It would be allocated to the individual items as follows:

Total Elected Value	$408,001
Non-Share Consideration ($95,000 + $75,000)	(170,000)
Available For Preferred And Common Stock	$238,001
Adjusted Cost Base - Preferred Stock (Maximum Of Fair Market Value)	(225,000)
Adjusted Cost Base - Common Stock (Residual)	$ 13,001

Part D - PUC Calculations

The calculation of PUC would begin with the legal stated capital associated with the two classes of shares, which is their fair market value. This would be $225,000 for the preferred stock and $480,000 for the common stock, a total of $705,000. ITA 85(2.1) would require a reduction in this total as follows:

Increase In Legal Stated Capital ($225,000 + $480,000)		$705,000
Less Excess Of:		
Total Elected Value	($408,001)	
Over The Total Non-Share Consideration	170,000	(238,001)
Reduction In PUC		$466,999

Note that this reduction is equal to the deferred gain on the election ($875,000 - $408,001 from Part B). The PUC reduction would be allocated on the basis of fair market values as follows:

Preferred Stock [($466,999)($225,000 ÷ $705,000)]	$149,042
Common Stock [($466,999)($480,000 ÷ $705,000)]	317,957
Total PUC Reduction	$466,999

Subsequent to applying this reduction, the remaining PUC of the two classes of shares would be as follows:

	Preferred Stock	**Common Stock**
Legal Stated Capital	$225,000	$480,000
PUC Reduction (From Preceding)	(149,042)	(317,957)
Total PUC	$ 75,958	$162,043

Note that the total PUC of $238,001 ($75,958 + $162,043) is equal to the difference between the total elected value for the assets of $408,001 and the non-share consideration received by Miss Brock of $170,000.

Part E - Tax Consequences Of Redemption

The tax consequences for Miss Brock on the redemption of the preferred and common shares would be calculated as follows:

	Preferred Stock	**Common Stock**
Redemption Proceeds	$225,000	$480,000
Paid Up Capital	(75,958)	(162,043)
ITA 84(3) Deemed Dividend	$149,042	$317,957
Redemption Proceeds	$225,000	$480,000
ITA 84(3) Deemed Dividend	(149,042)	(317,957)
ITA 54 Deemed Proceeds Of Disposition	$ 75,958	$162,043
Adjusted Cost Base	(225,000)	(13,001)
Capital Gain (Loss)	($149,042)	$149,042

Miss Brock would have a deemed non-eligible dividend of $466,999 ($149,042 + $317,957). This is also the amount of the gain that was deferred through the use of Section 85 ($875,000 - $408,001 from Part B).

The grossed up non-eligible dividend of $546,389 [(117%)($466,999)] would qualify for a federal dividend tax credit of $57,489 [(21/29)(17%)($466,999)]. There would be a net capital gain of nil ($149,042 - $149,042).

Self Study Solution Sixteen - 8

Part A

The following table shows that the post-reassessment fair market value of the assets transferred to the corporation exceeds the fair market value of the consideration received:

Fair Market Value Of Assets Transferred	
($1,578,000 + $430,000 - $350,000)	$1,658,000
Less The Greater Of:	
• Fair Market Value Of Consideration Received	
($160,000 + $947,000 + $471,000) = $1,578,000	
• Elected Value = $1,107,000	(1,578,000)
Excess = Gift	$ 80,000

As Sarah Cheng is the only common shareholder of the new corporation, it is clear that Mr. Cheng has made a gift to his daughter. As a consequence, the amount of the gift must be added to the elected value in the rollover to arrive at a deemed proceeds of disposition. As the reassessment was on the non-depreciable capital asset land, the result will be a capital gain. This results in the following tax consequences for Mr. Cheng:

Deemed Elected Value = Deemed Proceeds Of Disposition	
($1,107,000 + $80,000)	$1,187,000
Tax Values Of Assets Transferred	(1,107,000)
Capital Gain	$ 80,000
Inclusion Rate	1/2
Taxable Capital Gain	$ 40,000

The adjusted cost base of the preferred shares received by Mr. Cheng would be calculated as follows:

Elected Value (Original)	$1,107,000
Non-Share Consideration ($160,000 + $947,000)	(1,107,000)
Adjusted Cost Base Of Preferred Shares	Nil

The required PUC reduction and resulting PUC would be calculated as follows:

Increase In Legal Stated Capital		$471,000
Excess, If Any, Of:		
Deemed Elected Value		
($1,107,000 + $80,000)	($1,187,000)	
Over Non-Share Consideration	1,107,000	(80,000)
PUC Reduction		$391,000
PUC Of Preferred Shares ($471,000 - $391,000)		$ 80,000

Part B

The tax consequences to Mr. Cheng of having his shares redeemed would be as follows:

Proceeds Of Redemption	$471,000
PUC Of Shares	(80,000)
ITA 84(3) Deemed Dividend	$391,000

Proceeds Of Disposition	$471,000
ITA 84(3) Deemed Dividend	(391,000)
Adjusted Proceeds Of Disposition	$ 80,000
Adjusted Cost Base Of Shares	Nil
Capital Gain (Loss)	$ 80,000
Inclusion Rate	1/2
Taxable Capital Gain	$ 40,000

This non-eligible deemed dividend would be grossed up to $457,470 [(117%)($391,000)] of Taxable Income and will generate a federal dividend tax credit of $48,133 [(21/29)(17%)($391,000)].

Part C

The tax consequences of Sarah selling her shares would be as follows:

Proceeds Of Disposition	$90,000
Adjusted Cost Base Of Shares	(10,000)
Capital Gain	$80,000
Inclusion Rate	1/2
Taxable Capital Gain	$40,000

Economic Analysis (Not Required)

If Mr. Cheng had simply sold his business assets for their post reassessment fair market value, he would have had income as in the following calculation:

Fair Market Value After Reassessment	
($1,578,000 + $80,000)	$1,658,000
Tax Values Of Assets	(1,107,000)
Income (Capital Gains And Recapture)	$ 551,000

Using the procedures in the problem, the results for Mr. Cheng are as follows:

Capital Gain At Transfer	$ 80,000
ITA 84(3) Deemed Dividend	391,000
Capital Gain On Redemption	80,000
Total	$551,000

While the composition of the income is different, the overall result is the same $551,000 that would have resulted from a simple sale of the listed business assets.

However, there is an impact on Sarah. The $80,000 gift added to the value of her shares with no corresponding increase in the adjusted cost base of the shares. As a result, when she sells the shares, there is a capital gain. In effect, the $80,000 amount of the gift will be subject to double taxation.

Overall, the procedures used in this situation resulted in Mr. Cheng being taxed on the same amount of income as would have been the case without the ITA 85(1) rollover. In addition, Sarah paid taxes on an additional capital gain of $80,000 ($40,000 taxable amount) that would not have occurred if Mr. Cheng had heeded the warnings of his accountant and used a valid fair market value for the land.

Self Study Solution Sixteen - 9

Part A

The immediate tax consequences of the transfer would be a taxable capital gain on the land and an ITA 15(1) shareholder benefit. These would be calculated as follows:

Elected Value Of Land	$105,000
Adjusted Cost Base	(85,000)
Capital Gain	$ 20,000
Inclusion Rate	1/2
Taxable Capital Gain On Land	$ 10,000

Fair Market Value Of Consideration	
($429,000 + $439,000)	$868,000
Fair Market Value Of Transferred Assets	(668,000)
ITA 15(1) Shareholder Benefit	$200,000

The total effect on Taxable Income is as follows:

Taxable Capital Gain	$ 10,000
Shareholder Benefit	200,000
Total Addition To Net Income For Tax Purposes	$210,000
Net Capital Loss Carry Forward	(10,000)
Total Addition To Taxable Income	$200,000

The adjusted cost base of the preferred shares would be calculated as follows:

Elected Value ($48,000 + $105,000 + $276,000)	$429,000
Non-Share Consideration	(429,000)
Available For Shares	Nil
ITA 15(1) Shareholder Benefit	200,000
Adjusted Cost Base Of Shares	$200,000

The PUC of the preferred shares would be calculated as follows:

Increase In Legal Stated Capital		$439,000
Less The Excess, If Any Of:		
Elected Value	($429,000)	
Over The Non-Share Consideration	429,000	Nil
PUC Reduction		$439,000

PUC ($439,000 - $439,000)	Nil

Part B

The tax values for the assets transferred can be described as follows:

Depreciable Assets The tax cost for these assets will be the elected value of $48,000. However, they will retain their original capital cost of $87,000 for recapture and capital gains calculations. The $39,000 difference will be deemed to be CCA taken.

Land The adjusted cost base of the land will be the elected value of $105,000. (Note that the rules in ITA 13(7)(e) to limit the capital cost on non-arm's length transfers do not apply to non-depreciable assets.)

Building The tax cost for this asset will be the elected value of $276,000. However, the building will retain its original capital cost of $378,000 for recapture and capital gains calculations. The $102,000 difference will be deemed to be CCA taken.

Part C-1   Sale Of Shares

If the shares were sold for $439,000, the results would be as follows:

Proceeds Of Disposition	$439,000
Adjusted Cost Base	(200,000)
Capital Gain	$239,000
Inclusion Rate	1/2
Taxable Capital Gain	$119,500

Part C-2   Redemption Of Shares

Alternatively, if the shares were redeemed, the results would be:

Proceeds Of Redemption	$439,000
PUC	Nil
ITA 84(3) Deemed Dividend	$439,000

This non-eligible deemed dividend would be grossed up to $513,630 [(117%)($439,000)]. In addition, there would be federal dividend tax credit of $54,042 [(21/29)(17%)($439,000)].

Proceeds Of Disposition	$439,000
ITA 84(3) Deemed Dividend	(439,000)
Adjusted Proceeds Of Disposition	$ Nil
Adjusted Cost Base	(200,000)
Capital Loss	($200,000)
Inclusion Rate	1/2
Allowable Capital Loss	($100,000)

The allowable capital loss could only be deducted to the extent of Ms. Gilmour's taxable capital gains in the year of sale.

As a further point, notice that the total income of $239,000 resulting from the sale is the same as the total income resulting from the redemption ($439,000 - $200,000). However, because of the higher tax rate on dividends vs. capital gains, as well as the possibility that Ms. Gilmour cannot use any, or all, of her allowable capital loss in the year of sale, the redemption result is much less favourable from a tax point of view.

You should also note that if Ms. Gilmour had simply sold the assets for their fair market value of $668,000, the result would have been income (recapture and capital gains) of $259,000 ($668,000 - $409,000). By trying to remove excess consideration, the total income will be $459,000 ($20,000 + $200,000 + $239,000). In other words, she is paying additional taxes on $200,000 of income. This represents a significant penalty for trying to remove the excess consideration.

Self Study Solution Sixteen - 10

Part A - Tax Consequences Of Proposed Plan

Ms. Chadwick's plan involves the disposition of shares of a corporation resident in Canada to a corporation with which she does not deal at arm's length (Mr. Borque would be considered Ms. Chadwick's common-law partner.). Subsequent to the transaction, the two corporations are connected (Borque Inc. controls Norton Ltd.). Given these facts, the provisions of ITA 84.1 apply to this transaction.

The required calculations begin with the PUC reduction under ITA 84.1(1)(a):

Increase In Legal Stated Capital Of Borque Inc.		$1,590,000
Less The Excess, If Any, Of:		
Greater Of PUC And ACB Of Norton Ltd. Shares	($225,000)	
Over The Fair Market Value Of The Boot	875,000	Nil
PUC Reduction		**$1,590,000**
PUC After Reduction ($1,590,000 - $1,590,000)		Nil

The nil PUC reflects the fact that all of the PUC of the Norton Ltd. shares was taken out as non-share consideration.

The deemed non-eligible dividend under ITA 84.1(1)(b), and federal dividend tax credit, would be calculated as follows:

Increase In Legal Stated Capital Of Borque Inc.		$1,590,000
Fair Market Value Of Boot		875,000
Total		**$2,465,000**
PUC Of Norton Ltd. Shares	($ 225,000)	
PUC Reduction Under ITA 84.1(1)(a)	(1,590,000)	(1,815,000)
Deemed Dividend Under ITA 84.1(1)(b)		**$ 650,000**
Gross Up At 17 Percent		110,500
Taxable Non-Eligible Dividend		**$ 760,500**
Federal Dividend Tax Credit [(21/29)(17%)($650,000)]		$ 80,017

You will note that, because of the application of ITA 84.1, no capital gain eligible for the lifetime capital gains deduction results from this transaction. This can be seen in the following calculation:

Proceeds Before Adjustment Of Norton Shares (Elected Amount)	$875,000
ITA 84.1(1)(b) Deemed Dividend	(650,000)
Adjusted Proceeds Of Disposition (ITA 54)	**$225,000**
Adjusted Cost Base Of Shares	(225,000)
Capital Gain	**Nil**

Part B - An Improved Solution

The approach suggested by Ms. Chadwick will not be successful in producing the required $650,000 capital gain. The reason that this approach cannot be successful is that Ms. Chadwick is trying to take out non-share consideration in excess of the $225,000 PUC and ACB of her Norton Ltd. shares. Fortunately, this situation can be corrected by reducing the amount of non-share consideration to $225,000. In conjunction with this reduction in the amount of non-share consideration, the PUC and fair market value of the retractable preferred shares will have to be increased to $2,240,000, so that the total fair market value of the consideration received by Ms. Chadwick equals $2,465,000, the fair market value of the Norton Ltd. shares given up in the transaction. Using this approach, the required PUC reduction under ITA 84.1(1)(b) would be as follows:

Increase In Legal Stated Capital Of Borque Inc.		$2,240,000
Less The Excess, If Any, Of:		
Greater Of PUC And ACB Of Norton Ltd. Shares	($225,000)	
Over The Fair Market Value Of The Boot	225,000	Nil
PUC Reduction		$2,240,000
PUC After Reduction ($2,240,000 - $2,240,000)		Nil

The deemed non-eligible dividend under ITA 84.1(1)(b) would be calculated as follows:

Increase In Legal Stated Capital Of Borque Inc.		$2,240,000
Fair Market Value Of Boot		225,000
Total		$2,465,000
PUC Of Norton Ltd. Shares	($ 225,000)	
PUC Reduction Under 84.1(1)(b)	(2,240,000)	(2,465,000)
Deemed Dividend Under ITA 84.1(1)(b)		Nil

Given the preceding, the capital gain resulting from this transaction is calculated as follows:

Proceeds Before Adjustment Of Norton Ltd. Shares (Elected Amount)	$875,000
ITA 84.1(1)(b) Deemed Dividend	Nil
Proceeds Of Disposition	$875,000
Adjusted Cost Base Of Norton Ltd. Shares	(225,000)
Capital Gain	$650,000

There would be no tax consequences using this approach, except for the possibility that the alternative minimum tax may be payable. While there would be a $650,000 capital gain, it could be completely eliminated by using Ms. Chadwick's lifetime capital gains deduction.

Part C - Sale Of Shares

As in the other Parts of this question, there is a sale of shares by an individual to a corporation with which the individual is not at arm's length. This means that ITA 84.1 is still applicable.

As no new Borque Inc. shares are issued, no PUC reduction is required.

The ITA 84.1(1)(b) deemed non-eligible dividend would be calculated as follows:

Increase In Legal Stated Capital Of Borque Inc.		Nil
Non-Share Consideration Of Shares Sold		
[(6,530 Shares)($2,465,000 ÷ 22,500)]		$715,398
Total		$715,398
PUC Of Norton Ltd. Shares [(6,530 Shares)($10)]	($65,300)	
PUC Reduction Under ITA 84.1(1)(a)	Nil	(65,300)
Deemed Dividend Under ITA 84.1(1)(b)		$650,098

The taxable non-eligible dividend of $760,615 [(117%)($650,098)] would qualify for a federal dividend tax credit of $80,029 [(21/29)(17%)($650,098)]. Given this deemed dividend, the sale of shares will not result in the desired capital gain. This can be seen in the following calculation:

Unadjusted Proceeds Of Disposition	
[(6,530 Shares)($2,465,000 ÷ 22,500)]	$715,398
Deemed Dividend Under ITA 84.1(1)(b)	(650,098)
Adjusted Proceeds Of Disposition	$ 65,300
Adjusted Cost Base Of Shares [(6,530 Shares)($10)]	(65,300)
Capital Gain	Nil

Self Study Solution Sixteen - 11

Scenario One

In the absence of ITA 55(2), the results for Newcastle would be as follows:

Proceeds Of Redemption	$2,397,000
Paid Up Capital Of Preferred Shares	(479,000)
ITA 84(3) Deemed Dividend	$1,918,000
Proceeds Of Disposition	$2,397,000
Less The ITA 84(3) Dividend	(1,918,000)
Adjusted Proceeds Of Disposition	$ 479,000
Adjusted Cost Base	(479,000)
Capital Gain	Nil

As the ITA 84(3) dividend can be deducted in the determination of Newcastle's Taxable Income, the Company would have succeeded in disposing of the Oldhouse shares without tax consequences.

However, as the redemption was in conjunction with a disposition of the property to an arm's length purchaser, ITA 55(2) alters this result. ITA 55(2)(a) would deem $1,546,000 ($1,918,000, less the Safe Income of $372,000) of the ITA 84(3) dividend to not be a dividend. ITA 55(2)(b) would then deem the $1,546,000 to be proceeds of disposition. The result for Newcastle would be a capital gain determined as follows:

Adjusted Proceeds Of Disposition	$ 479,000
Deemed Proceeds Of Disposition	1,546,000
Total Proceeds Of Disposition	$2,025,000
Adjusted Cost Base	(479,000)
Capital Gain	$1,546,000
Inclusion Rate	1/2
Taxable Capital Gain	$ 773,000

The overall result would be a tax free ITA 84(3) dividend of $372,000, plus a taxable capital gain of $773,000.

Scenario Two

As a dividend has been paid in conjunction with a disposition of property to an arm's length party, ITA 55(2) is applicable. This legislation is designed to prevent capital gains strips. As a result, the following calculation is required for the dividend received by Gaynor:

Dividends Received From Oldhouse	$1,918,000
Dividend Attributable To Safe Income (Tax Free)	(372,000)
Amount Deemed By ITA 55(2)(a) To Not Be A Dividend And By ITA 55(2)(c) To Be A Capital Gain	$1,546,000
Inclusion Rate	1/2
Taxable Capital Gain	$ 773,000

Note that the results here are the same as in Scenario One.

Chapter 16 Learning Objectives

After completing Chapter 16, you should be able to:

1. Describe the type of situation where ITA 85 is applicable (paragraph [P hereafter] 16-1 to 16-4).
2. Explain the general rules that are applicable to the transferor and the transferee under ITA 85 (P 16-5 to 16-11).
3. Describe the types of consideration that can be received by the transferor under ITA 85 (P 16-12 to 16-14).
4. Describe the procedures required for making the ITA 85 election (P 16-15 to 16-17).
5. Calculate the range of values that can be used in a transfer under the provisions of ITA 85 (P 16-18 to 16-30).

6. Apply the general rules applicable to all assets that determine the range of values that can be used in a transfer under the provisions of ITA 85 (P 16-31 to 16-36).
7. Apply the detailed rules for the transfer of accounts receivable, inventories, and non-depreciable capital property under ITA 85 (P 16-37 to 16-49).
8. Describe the rules related to the transfer of non-depreciable capital property, including disallowed capital losses on transfers to affiliated persons and the associated tax planning issues (P 16-50 to 16-61).
9. Apply the detailed rules for the transfer of depreciable assets under ITA 85 (P 16-62 to 16-69).
10. Describe the rules related to the disallowance of terminal losses arising on transfers of depreciable capital property to affiliated persons and associated tax planning issues (P 16-70 to 16-73).

11. Recognize the elimination of the rules related to cumulative eligible capital (P 16-74 to 16-75).
12. Summarize the transfer price rules for all assets under ITA 85 (P 16-76).
13. Calculate the amount of the elected value that will be allocated to each component of the consideration received by the transferor under ITA 85 (P 16-77 and 16-78).
14. Calculate the amount of the elected value that will be allocated to each of the assets acquired by the transferee under ITA 85 (P 16-79 to 16-86).
15. Calculate the Paid Up Capital of the shares received by the transferor in an ITA 85 rollover (P 16-87 to 16-98).

16. Apply the ITA 85 rules to situations involving the incorporation of an unincorporated business (P 16-99 to 16-114).
17. Identify situations where the ITA 85 rules on gifts to related persons are applicable and make the appropriate adjustments that are required by these rules (P 16-115 to 16-129).
18. Identify situations where the ITA 85 rules on benefits to the transferor are applicable and make the appropriate adjustments that are required by these rules (P 16-130 to 16-133).
19. Identify situations where ITA 84.1 (dividend stripping rules) is applicable (P 16-134 to 16-141).
20. Apply the ITA 84.1 rules to situations involving dividend stripping (P 16-142 to 16-151).

21. Identify situations where ITA 55(2) (capital gains stripping rules) is applicable (P 16-152 to 16-158).
22. Apply the ITA 55(2) rules to situations involving capital gains stripping (P 16-159 to 16-169).

How To Work Through Chapter 17

We recommend the following approach in dealing with the material in this chapter:

Introduction
- Read paragraph 17-1 to 17-2 (in the textbook).

Share For Share Exchanges (ITA 85.1)
- Read paragraph 17-3 to 17-11.
- Do Exercise Seventeen-1 (in the textbook) and check the solution in this Study Guide.
- Read paragraph 17-12 to 17-13.
- Do Self Study Problems Seventeen-1 and Seventeen-2 which are available on the Companion Website and check the solutions in this Study Guide.

Exchange Of Shares In A Reorganization (ITA 86)
- Read paragraph 17-14 to 17-29.
- Do Exercises Seventeen-2 to Seventeen-4 and check the solutions in this Study Guide.
- Do Self Study Problem Seventeen-3 and check the solution in this Study Guide.

Gift To Related Party - ITA 86(2) (Benefit Rule)
- Read paragraph 17-30 to 17-40.
- Do Exercise Seventeen-5 and check the solution in this Study Guide.

Using ITA 86 - Practical Considerations And Tax Planning Considerations
- Read paragraph 17-41 to 17-46.
- Do Self Study Problems Seventeen-4 and Seventeen-5 and check the solutions in this Study Guide.

Amalgamations (ITA 87)
- Read paragraph 17-47 to 17-65.
- Do Exercise Seventeen-6 and check the solution in this Study Guide.

Winding-Up Of A 90 Percent Owned Subsidiary
- Read paragraph 17-66 to 17-81.
- Do Exercise Seventeen-7 and check the solution in this Study Guide.
- Read paragraph 17-82 to 17-84.
- Do Exercise Seventeen-8 and check the solution in this Study Guide.
- Read paragraph 17-85 to 17-86.

Tax Planning Considerations - Amalgamation Vs. Winding-Up
- Read paragraph 17-87 to 17-93.
- Do Self Study Problem Seventeen-6 and check the solution in this Study Guide.

Winding-Up Of A Canadian Corporation
- Read paragraph 17-94 to 17-106.
- Do Exercise Seventeen-9 and check the solution in this Study Guide.
- Do Self Study Problem Seventeen-7 and check the solution in this Study Guide.

Convertible Properties
- Read paragraph 17-107 to 17-113.

Sale Of An Incorporated Business - Assets Vs. Shares
- Read paragraph 17-114 to 17-151.
- Do Self Study Problem Seventeen-8 and check the solution in this Study Guide.

To Complete This Chapter
- If you would like more practice in problem solving, do the Supplementary Self Study Problems for the chapter. These problems and solutions are available on the Companion Website.
- Review the Key Terms Used In This Chapter in the textbook at the end of Chapter 17. Consult the Glossary for the meaning of any key terms you do not know.
- Test yourself with the Chapter 17 Glossary Flashcards available on the Companion Website.
- Ensure you have achieved the Chapter 17 Learning Objectives listed in this Study Guide.
- As a review, we recommend you view the PowerPoint presentation for Chapter 17 that is on the Companion Website.

Practice Examination
- Write the Practice Examination for Chapter 17 that is on the Companion Website. Mark your examination using the Practice Examination Solution that is on the Companion Website.

Solutions to Chapter Seventeen Exercises

Exercise Seventeen - 1 Solution
This transaction involves a share for share exchange that meets the conditions of ITA 85.1. Unless Ms. Alee opts out of this rollover provision in her income tax return, the tax consequences of this transaction for Ms. Alee would be as follows:

- Ms. Alee would be deemed to have disposed of her Aayee Ltd. shares at a value equal to their adjusted cost base of $450,000. As a consequence, there would be no capital gain on the disposition.
- Ms. Alee would be deemed to have acquired her Global Outreach Inc. shares at a cost equal to the adjusted cost base of the Aayee Ltd. shares, or $450,000.
- The adjusted cost base of the Aayee Ltd. shares that have been acquired by Global Outreach Inc. would be deemed to be the lesser of their fair market value and their paid up capital. In this case, the $450,000 paid up capital amount is the lower figure.
- The PUC of the Global Outreach Inc. shares that have been issued to Ms. Alee would be $450,000, the PUC of the Aayee Ltd. shares that were given up.

Exercise Seventeen - 2 Solution
The required PUC reduction on the redeemable preferred shares would be calculated as follows:

Increase In Legal Stated Capital		$1,300,000
Less The Excess, If Any, Of:		
PUC Of Common Shares	($1,000,000)	
Over The Non-Share Consideration	1,000,000	Nil
PUC Reduction		$1,300,000

This means that the redeemable preferred shares would have a PUC of nil ($1,300,000 - $1,300,000).

The adjusted cost base of the redeemable preferred shares would be calculated as follows:

Adjusted Cost Base Of Common Shares	$1,000,000
Non-Share Consideration	(1,000,000)
Adjusted Cost Base Of Redeemable Preferred Shares	Nil

Because Sam took back cash equal to his PUC and ACB, there would be no ITA 84(3) deemed dividend and no capital gain or loss. These calculations would be as follows:

PUC Of New Shares	Nil
Plus Non-Share Consideration	$1,000,000
Proceeds Of Redemption Under ITA 84(5)(d)	$1,000,000
PUC Of Old Shares	(1,000,000)
ITA 84(3) Deemed Dividend	Nil

Adjusted Cost Base Of New Shares	Nil
Plus Non-Share Consideration	$1,000,000
Proceeds Of Disposition Under ITA 86(1)(c)	$1,000,000
ITA 84(3) Deemed Dividend	Nil
Adjusted Proceeds	$1,000,000
Adjusted Cost Base Of Old Shares	(1,000,000)
Capital Gain (Loss)	Nil

Exercise Seventeen - 3 Solution

The required PUC reduction on the redeemable preferred shares would be calculated as follows:

Increase In Legal Stated Capital		$1,300,000
Less The Excess, If Any, Of:		
PUC Of Common Shares	($1,000,000)	
Over The Non-Share Consideration	1,000,000	Nil
PUC Reduction		$1,300,000

This means that the redeemable preferred shares would have a PUC of nil ($1,300,000 - $1,300,000).

The adjusted cost base of the redeemable preferred shares would be calculated as follows:

Adjusted Cost Base Of Common Shares	$1,250,000
Non-Share Consideration	(1,000,000)
Adjusted Cost Base Of Redeemable Preferred Shares	$ 250,000

Because Sam took back cash equal to his PUC and less than his ACB, there would be no ITA 84(3) deemed dividend and no capital gain or loss. These calculations would be as follows:

PUC Of New Shares	Nil
Plus Non-Share Consideration	$1,000,000
Proceeds Of Redemption Under ITA 84(5)(d)	$1,000,000
PUC Of Old Shares	(1,000,000)
ITA 84(3) Deemed Dividend	Nil

Adjusted Cost Base Of New Shares	$ 250,000
Plus Non-Share Consideration	1,000,000
Proceeds Of Disposition Under ITA 86(1)(c)	$1,250,000
ITA 84(3) Deemed Dividend	Nil
Adjusted Proceeds	$1,250,000
Adjusted Cost Base Of Old Shares	(1,250,000)
Capital Gain (Loss)	Nil

Exercise Seventeen - 4 Solution

The required PUC reduction on the redeemable preferred shares would be calculated as follows:

Increase In Legal Stated Capital		$1,100,000
Less The Excess, If Any, Of:		
PUC Of Common Shares	($1,000,000)	
Over The Non-Share Consideration	1,200,000	Nil
PUC Reduction		$1,100,000

This means that the redeemable preferred shares would have a PUC of nil ($1,100,000 - $1,100,000).

The adjusted cost base of the redeemable preferred shares would be calculated as follows:

Adjusted Cost Base Of Common Shares	$1,250,000
Non-Share Consideration	(1,200,000)
Adjusted Cost Base Of Redeemable Preferred Shares	$ 50,000

Because the non-share consideration was greater than the PUC of the old shares, the resulting ITA 84(3) deemed dividend and the allowable capital loss would be calculated as follows:

PUC Of New Shares	Nil
Plus Non-Share Consideration	$1,200,000
Proceeds Of Redemption Under ITA 84(5)(d)	$1,200,000
PUC Of Old Shares	(1,000,000)
ITA 84(3) Deemed Dividend (Non-Eligible)	$ 200,000

Adjusted Cost Base Of New Shares	$ 50,000
Plus Non-Share Consideration	1,200,000
Proceeds Of Disposition Under ITA 86(1)(c)	$1,250,000
ITA 84(3) Deemed Dividend	(200,000)
Adjusted Proceeds	$1,050,000
Adjusted Cost Base Of Old Shares	(1,250,000)
Capital Gain (Loss)	($ 200,000)
Inclusion Rate	1/2
Allowable Capital Loss	($ 100,000)

The taxable amount of the non-eligible dividend would be $234,000 [(117%)($200,000)]. It would qualify for a federal dividend tax credit of $24,621 [(21/29)(17%)($200,000)].

Exercise Seventeen - 5 Solution

The amount of the gift can be calculated as follows:

Fair Market Value Of Shares [(80%)($1,600,000)]	$1,280,000
Consideration Received ($300,000 + $800,000)	(1,100,000)
Gift To Daughter	$ 180,000

As a gift is present in this transaction, ITA 86(2) is applicable.

The PUC reduction on the new shares would be calculated as follows:

Increase In Legal Stated Capital		$800,000
Less The Excess, If Any, Of:		
PUC Of Common Shares [(80%)($250,000)]	($200,000)	
Over The Non-Share Consideration	300,000	Nil
PUC Reduction		$800,000

This means that the redeemable preferred shares would have a PUC of nil ($800,000 - $800,000).

Under ITA 86(2)(e), the adjusted cost base of the redeemable preferred shares would be calculated as follows:

Adjusted Cost Base Of Common Shares		$200,000
Deduct:		
Non-Share Consideration	($300,000)	
Gift	(180,000)	(480,000)
Adjusted Cost Base Of Preferred Shares		Nil

Given the $180,000 gift, the ITA 84(3) deemed dividend and the taxable capital gain would be calculated as follows:

PUC Of New Preferred Shares	Nil
Plus Non-Share Consideration	$300,000
Proceeds Of Redemption Under ITA 84(5)(d)	$300,000
PUC Of Shares Given Up	(200,000)
ITA 84(3) Deemed Dividend (Non-Eligible)	$100,000

Proceeds Of Disposition Under ITA 86(2)(c) - Lesser Of:
- Fair Market Value Of Shares Given Up = $1,280,000
- Non-Share Consideration Plus Gift

($300,000 + $180,000) = $480,000	$480,000
Less ITA 84(3) Deemed Dividend	(100,000)
Adjusted Proceeds	$380,000
Adjusted Cost Base Of Shares Given Up	(200,000)
Capital Gain	$180,000
Inclusion Rate	1/2
Taxable Capital Gain	$ 90,000

The taxable amount of the non-eligible dividend would be $117,000 [(117%)($100,000)]. It would qualify for a federal dividend tax credit of $12,310 [(21/29)(17%)($100,000)].

Her total gain is $280,000 ($100,000 + $180,000). In economic terms this reflects the $100,000 excess of the non-share consideration over the PUC and adjusted cost base of the old shares ($300,000 - $200,000), plus the $180,000 gift. Ms. Reviser would also have a deferred gain of $800,000, the excess of the $800,000 fair market value of the preferred shares over their PUC and adjusted cost base of nil.

The combination of the current and deferred gains is $1,080,000 ($800,000 + $280,000). This is the same amount of gain that would have occurred if Ms. Reviser had simply sold her shares for their fair market value of $1,280,000 ($1,280,000 - $200,000 = $1,080,000).

While this transaction has not changed Ms. Reviser's economic position, it has created an additional taxable amount for her daughter. Before this transaction, the fair market value of the daughter's holding was $320,000 [(20%)($1,600,000)]. This holding now has a value of $500,000. This is the $1,600,000 total value of Janrev Inc. prior to the transaction, less the cash of $300,000, less the fair market value of the preferred shares of $800,000. As there is no increase in her adjusted cost base, this extra $180,000 ($500,000 - $320,000) represents a deferred gain that will be taxed if her shares are redeemed or if she chooses to sell them.

Exercise Seventeen - 6 Solution

As Upton Inc. has a clear majority of the shares in Amalgo Inc., it would appear that they have acquired control of Downer Ltd. As the acquisition of control rules would be applicable, there would be a deemed year end for both Companies that coincides with the amalgamated year end. The non-capital loss carry forward of Downer Ltd. will be flowed through to the amalgamated company, Amalgo Inc. However, because of the acquisition of control, the net capital loss carry forward cannot be used. In addition, for the non-capital loss to be used, Amalgo Inc. would have to continue the business in which the loss occurred and the loss carry forward could only be applied against profits in that business.

Exercise Seventeen - 7 Solution

Subsequent to an ITA 88(1) winding-up, the parent company can deduct subsidiary losses in its first taxation year beginning after that date. This would be the year beginning on September 16, 2017.

Side's loss is deemed to occur in Park's taxation year that includes Side's year end. This would be the year ending September 15, 2017. This means that it will expire, after 20 taxation years, at the end of Park's taxation year ending September 15, 2037.

Exercise Seventeen - 8 Solution

Under ITA 88(1), a limited bump-up of non-depreciable capital assets is available. The basic limit would be calculated as follows:

Adjusted Cost Base Of Lorne Inc. Shares	$1,200,000
Tax Values Of Lorne Inc.'s Net Assets	
At Winding-Up ($500,000 - $75,000)	(425,000)
Dividends Paid By Lorne Since Acquisition	Nil
Excess	$ 775,000

However, this basic amount cannot exceed the difference between the fair market value of the non-depreciable capital assets at the time of the share acquisition and their tax cost at that time. This amount would be $130,000 ($270,000 - $140,000). The bump-up in the Land value is limited to that amount, resulting in the following tax values for Lorne's assets at the time of the ITA 88(1) winding-up:

Cash	$120,000
Land ($140,000 + $130,000)	270,000
Depreciable Assets - At UCC	240,000
Total Assets	$630,000

Note that the remaining $645,000 ($775,000 - $130,000) of the excess is lost as a result of this wind up.

Exercise Seventeen - 9 Solution

Given the size of the proceeds, the balance in the RDTOH account will clearly be less than 38-1/3 percent of the dividends to be declared. Given this, the total distribution to shareholders will be $912,000 ($865,000 + $47,000).

The taxable dividend component of the total distribution to the shareholders is calculated as follows:

Total Distribution ($865,000 + $47,000)	$912,000
Paid Up Capital	(88,000)
ITA 84(2) Deemed Dividend On Winding-Up	$824,000
Capital Dividend Account (Election Required)	(26,000)
Non-Eligible Dividend Subject To Tax	$798,000

The non-eligible dividend will be grossed up to $933,660 [(117%)($798,000)]. The shareholders will also have a federal dividend tax credit of $98,237 [(21/29)(17%)($798,000)].

As shown in the following calculation, the shareholders will not have a capital gain on the disposition of their shares:

Total Distribution To Shareholders	$912,000
ITA 84(2) Deemed Dividend	(824,000)
Deemed Proceeds Of Disposition	$ 88,000
Adjusted Cost Base Of Shares	(88,000)
Capital Gain	Nil

Self Study Solution Seventeen - 1

It would appear that this is a share for share exchange that meets the conditions of ITA 85.1. Unless Jenny opts out of this rollover provision in her income tax return, the tax consequences of this transaction for her would be as follows:

- Jenny would be deemed to have disposed of her Jenny's Cupcakes Inc. shares at a value equal to their adjusted cost base of $125,000. As a consequence, there would be no capital gain on the disposition.

- Jenny would be deemed to have acquired her London Speciality Bakeries Ltd. shares at a cost equal to the $125,000 adjusted cost base of the Jenny's Cupcakes Inc. shares.

- The adjusted cost base of the Jenny's Cupcakes Inc. shares that have been acquired by London Speciality Bakeries Ltd. would be deemed to be the lesser of their fair market value ($725,000) and their paid up capital. In this case, the $125,000 paid up capital amount is the lower figure.

- The PUC of the London Speciality Bakeries Ltd. shares that have been issued to Jenny would be $125,000, the PUC of the Jenny's Cupcakes Inc. shares that were given up.

It is important to note that Jenny could opt out of ITA 85.1 by including a taxable capital gain of $300,000 [($725,000 - $125,000)(1/2)] in her income tax return. If Jenny's Cupcakes Inc. is a qualified small business corporation and Jenny still has room to use her lifetime capital gains deduction, this will be a better alternative.

By opting out and recognizing the taxable capital gain, the adjusted cost base of the London Speciality Bakeries shares would be $725,000, resulting in a much lower capital gain on a subsequent sale of these shares.

How much tax this would cost her would depend on how much of her lifetime capital gains deduction she has available. Alternative minimum tax considerations could also be a factor.

Self Study Solution Seventeen - 2

Part A - ITA 85.1 Applies

Sarah elected to transfer her business using ITA 85(1) at a value of $842,000. Given that she took back non-share consideration of $360,000, the adjusted cost base of her Hartman shares would be calculated as follows:

Elected Value	$842,000
Non-Share Consideration	(360,000)
Adjusted Cost Base Of Common Shares	$482,000

The PUC of these shares would be calculated as follows:

Increase in Legal Stated Capital		$1,200,000
Less Excess, If Any, Of:		
Elected Value	($842,000)	
Non-Share Consideration	360,000	(482,000)
PUC Reduction		$ 718,000
PUC Of Common Shares ($1,200,000 - $718,000)		$ 482,000

Using these values for the Hartman shares, if Sarah does not opt out of ITA 85.1, the tax consequences would be as follows:

- Sarah would be deemed to have disposed of her Hartman shares at a value equal to their adjusted cost base of $482,000. Given this, there would be no capital gain on the disposition.

- Sarah would be deemed to have acquired her Grande Ltd. shares at a cost equal to the $482,000 adjusted cost base of her Hartman shares.

- The PUC of the Grande Ltd. shares that have been issued to Sarah would be $482,000, the PUC of the Hartman shares that were given up.

Part A - Opting Out Of ITA 85.1

Sarah can opt out of ITA 85.1 by including a $1,109,000 [(1/2)($2,700,000 - $482,000)] taxable capital gain in her income tax return. This may be desirable in that it will allow her to make use of her $625,000 net capital loss carry forward. However, the disadvantage of opting out of ITA 85.1 is that she will have to pay taxes on the net taxable capital gain of $484,000 ($1,109,000 - $625,000).

Because all of her shares are involved in the exchange, she has no choice as to the amount of the gain to be recognized.

Part B - ACB For Grande Ltd.

The adjusted cost base of the Hartman shares in the hands of Grande would be the lesser of their $2,700,000 fair market value and their PUC. In this case, the PUC amount of $482,000 is lower and will be the adjusted cost base amount.

Part C - Alternative Solutions

There are two possible solutions that would make full use of the $625,000 net capital loss carry forward and minimize the current payment of taxes.

Alternative One Sarah could use ITA 85(1) to exchange the shares at an elected value of $1,732,000. If this value was elected, the resulting taxable capital gain would be equal to the required amount of $625,000 [(1/2)($1,732,000 - $482,000)]. Note that this would leave the adjusted cost base of the acquired shares at the elected value of $1,732,000. If ITA 85.1 were used, this value would be the $482,000 PUC of the shares.

Alternative Two Each share of Hartman Inc. has a fair market value of $450 ($2,700,000 ÷ 6,000) and an adjusted cost base of $80.33 ($482,000 ÷ 6,000). This means that each share that is sold to Grande would generate a taxable capital gain of $184.84 [(1/2)($450 - $80.33)]. Given this, selling 3,382 of these shares to Grande would result in a taxable capital gain of $625,128.88 [(3,382)($184.84)]. This would be largely eliminated by the application of the $625,000 net capital loss carry forward. The remaining 2,618 (6,000 - 3,382) shares of Hartman could then be exchanged for Grande Ltd. shares on a tax free basis under either of ITA 85(1) or ITA 85.1.

Self Study Solution Seventeen - 3

The fair market value of the business is $10,985,000 , which is composed of tangible assets of $12,450,000, plus goodwill of $2,000,000, less the bank loan of $3,465,000.

To implement the ITA 86(1) rollover, the twins should each invest $10,000 in exchange for new common shares of BIL.

At this point, Ms. Boswick can exchange, on a tax free basis, her common shares for new preferred shares with a redemption value of $10,985,000. This would have no immediate tax consequences. The ACB and PUC of the new preferred shares would be calculated as follows:

Adjusted Cost Base Of Shares Given Up	$250,000
Non-Share Consideration	Nil
Adjusted Cost Base Of Preferred Shares	$250,000

Legal Stated Capital - Preferred Shares		$10,985,000
Less Excess, If Any, Of:		
PUC - Shares Given Up	($250,000)	
Non-Share Consideration	Nil	(250,000)
Required PUC Reduction		$10,735,000

| PUC - Preferred Shares ($10,985,000 - $10,735,000) | $250,000 |

Ms. Boswick's preferred shares will not participate in the future growth of the company. This means that all of the future growth in Boswick Industries will accrue to the two children who are holding the common shares.

In order for Ms. Boswick to retain control, the preferred shares should be voting shares.

Subsequent to these transactions, the July 1, 2017 Balance Sheet would be as follows:

Boswick Industries Ltd.
Shareholders' Equity
As At July 1, 2017

| Tangible Assets At Tax Values | |
| ($12,450,000+ $10,000 + $10,000) | $12,470,000 |

Bank Loan	$ 3,465,000
Preferred Shares (Paid Up Capital)	250,000
Common Shares ($10,000 + $10,000)	20,000
Retained Earnings	8,735,000
Total	$12,470,000

Self Study Solution Seventeen - 4

Part A

Gift To Jack   This transaction involves a gift of $320,000 to Mr. Mark's son, Jack, calculated as follows:

Fair Market Value Of Common Shares Given Up	
[(80%)($2,400,000)]	$1,920,000
Fair Market Value Of Preferred Shares Received	(1,600,000)
Gift	$ 320,000

It is fair to assume that this amount is a gift to Jack, as he is the only remaining holder of common shares in Markit Ltd.

PUC Of New Preferred Shares   The PUC reduction required under ITA 86(2.1) would be calculated as follows:

Legal Stated Capital Of New Shares		$8,000
Deduct:		
PUC Of Old Shares	($8,000)	
Non-Share Consideration	Nil	(8,000)
PUC Reduction		Nil

PUC Of Preferred Shares ($8,000 - Nil)	$8,000

As the required PUC reduction is nil, the PUC of the new shares would be equal to the $8,000 PUC of the old shares.

Adjusted Cost Base Of New Preferred Shares   This amount would be calculated as follows:

Adjusted Cost Base Of Old Shares		$ 8,000
Deduct:		
Non-Share Consideration	$ Nil	
Gift	(320,000)	(320,000)
Adjusted Cost Base Of New Shares		Nil

Proceeds Of Redemption For Old Common Shares - ITA 84(5)(d)   For purposes of determining any ITA 84(3) deemed dividend on the redemption of the old shares, the proceeds of redemption would be as follows:

PUC Of New Preferred Shares	$8,000
Non-Share Consideration	Nil
Proceeds Of Redemption	$8,000

As this amount is equal to the old PUC, there is no ITA 84(3) deemed dividend on the transaction.

Proceeds Of Disposition For Old Common Shares - ITA 86(2)(c)   For purposes of determining any capital gain on the redemption of the old common shares, the proceeds of disposition would be the lesser of the $1,920,000 fair market value of the old common shares and the following amount:

Non-Share Consideration	$ Nil
Gift	320,000
Proceeds Of Disposition	$320,000

Using the lesser figure of $320,000, there would be a taxable capital gain on the transaction calculated as follows:

Proceeds Of Disposition	$320,000
ITA 84(3) Deemed Dividend	Nil
Adjusted Proceeds Of Disposition	$320,000
Adjusted Cost Base	(8,000)
Capital Gain	$312,000
Inclusion Rate	1/2
Taxable Capital Gain	$156,000

The total potential gain on Mr. Mark's shares is $1,912,000 ($1,920,000 - $8,000). Because there was a gift to his son, $312,000 of this amount must be recognized at the time of the rollover. The remaining $1,600,000 is deferred until the preferred shares are sold or redeemed. In the absence of the gift, all of this gain could have been deferred.

Part B

This transaction will not alter the total fair market value of the Company and, as a consequence, the value of Jack's common shares will increase by the $320,000 amount of the gift. There will be no corresponding increase in the amount of the tax cost of these shares and, as a consequence, this value will be taxed when Jack sells the common shares. As this value has already been taxed in the hands of Mr. Mark, there will be double taxation on this amount.

Part C

If Mr. Mark's preferred shares were redeemed at their fair market value of $1,600,000, the tax consequences would be as follows:

Redemption Proceeds	$1,600,000
PUC	(8,000)
ITA 84(3) Deemed Dividend (Non-Eligible)	$1,592,000

Redemption Proceeds	$1,600,000
Deemed ITA 84(3) Dividend	(1,592,000)
Adjusted Proceeds Of Disposition	$ 8,000
Adjusted Cost Base	(Nil)
Capital Gain	$ 8,000
Inclusion Rate	1/2
Taxable Capital Gain	$ 4,000

The overall tax consequences of the redemption would be as follows:

Taxable Dividend [($1,592,000)(117%)]	$1,862,640
Taxable Capital Gain	4,000
Income Inclusion	$1,886,640

The deemed non-eligible dividend would qualify for a federal dividend tax credit of $195,981 [(21/29)(17%)($1,592,000)].

Note that Mr. Mark's dividends and capital gains from the rollover total $1,912,000 ($312,000 + $1,592,000 + $8,000). This is equal to the $1,912,000 [(80%)($2,400,000) - $8,000] capital gain that would have resulted from a sale of his shares at fair market value. From his point of view, the redemption result is less favourable in that part of the gain is in the form of more heavily taxed non-eligible dividends. In addition, if his son were to sell his shares, there would be additional income subject to tax of $320,000.

Self Study Solution Seventeen - 5

Approach One - No Gift

Part A

As the fair market value of the cash and preferred shares ($50,000 + $1,300,000) received by Ms. Platt is equal to the fair market value of the common shares she has given up ($1,350,000), no gift is involved.

Part B

The paid up capital of the new shares would be reduced as follows:

Increase In Legal Stated Capital - New Shares		$90,000
Less The Excess, If Any, Of:		
PUC - Old Shares [(75%)($120,000)]	($90,000)	
Over Non-Share Consideration	50,000	(40,000)
Reduction In PUC - New Shares		$50,000

Given this reduction, the PUC of the new preferred shares would be as follows:

Increase In Legal Stated Capital - New Shares	$90,000
Reduction In PUC	(50,000)
PUC - New Shares	$40,000

Part C

The adjusted cost base of the preferred shares would be calculated as follows:

Adjusted Cost Base - Old Shares	$90,000
Non-Share Consideration	(50,000)
Adjusted Cost Base - New Shares	$40,000

Part D

The Proceeds Of Redemption would be calculated as follows:

PUC - New Shares	$40,000
Plus Non-Share Consideration	50,000
Proceeds Of Redemption [ITA 84(5)(d)]	$90,000

The Proceeds Of Disposition would be calculated as follows:

Adjusted Cost Base - New Shares	$40,000
Plus Non-Share Consideration	50,000
Proceeds Of Disposition [ITA 86(1)(c)]	$90,000

Part E   Immediate Tax Consequences

As the ITA 84(5)(d) proceeds of redemption are equal to the PUC of the old shares, there is no ITA 84(3) deemed dividend. As the ITA 86(1)(c) proceeds of disposition are equal to the adjusted cost base of the old shares, there is no capital gain. This means there are no immediate tax consequences.

Part F   Tax Consequences Of Redemption Of New Shares

Redemption Proceeds	$1,300,000
PUC - New Shares	(40,000)
ITA 84(3) Deemed Dividend (Non-Eligible)	$1,260,000
Proceeds Of Disposition	$1,300,000
ITA 84(3) Deemed Dividend	(1,260,000)
Adjusted Proceeds Of Disposition	$ 40,000
Adjusted Cost Base - Preferred Shares	(40,000)
Capital Gain	Nil

The tax consequence would be an income inclusion of $1,474,200 [(117%)($1,260,000)], the grossed up value of the deemed non-eligible dividend. This would qualify for a federal dividend tax credit of $155,110 [(21/29)(17%)($1,260,000)].

Additional Analysis

While not a required part of the problem, you might wish to note that the $1,260,000 deemed dividend is the same amount of unadjusted income that would have been assessed to Ms. Platt if she had simply sold her shares ($1,350,000 - $90,000). However, it would have been more favourably taxed as a capital gain, rather than as a non-eligible dividend.

Approach Two - Gift

Part A

Under this approach, the fair market value of the cash and preferred shares received by Ms. Platt of $1,320,000 ($50,000 + $1,270,000) is less than the fair market value of the common shares she has given up ($1,350,000). As her son is in a residual equity position in PIL, there would appear to be a gift to him in the amount of $30,000 [$1,350,000 - ($50,000 + $1,270,000)]. Given this, ITA 86(2) is applicable.

Part B

The paid up capital of the preferred shares would be reduced under ITA 86(2.1)(a) as follows:

Increase In Legal Stated Capital - New Shares		$1,270,000
Less The Excess, If Any, Of:		
PUC - Old Shares [(75%)($120,000)]	($90,000)	
Over Non-Share Consideration	50,000	(40,000)
Reduction In PUC - New Shares		**$1,230,000**

Increase In Legal Stated Capital - New Shares	$1,270,000
Reduction In PUC	(1,230,000)
PUC - New Shares	**$ 40,000**

Part C

The adjusted cost base of the preferred shares would be calculated as follows:

Adjusted Cost Base - Old Shares		$90,000
Deduct:		
Non-Share Consideration	($50,000)	
Gift	(30,000)	(80,000)
Adjusted Cost Base - New Shares		**$10,000**

Part D

The Proceeds Of Redemption would be calculated as follows:

PUC - New Shares	$40,000
Non-Share Consideration	50,000
Proceeds Of Redemption [ITA 84(5)(d)]	**$90,000**

The Proceeds Of Disposition would be calculated as follows:

Non-Share Consideration	$50,000
Gift	30,000
Proceeds Of Disposition [ITA 86(2)(c)]	**$80,000**

Part E   Immediate Tax Consequences

As the ITA 84(5)(d) proceeds of redemption are equal to the PUC of the old shares, there is no ITA 84(3) deemed dividend. However, the ITA 86(2)(c) proceeds of disposition are less than the adjusted cost base of the old shares, resulting in a capital loss of $10,000 ($80,000 - $90,000). This loss would be disallowed by ITA 86(2)(d).

Part F Tax Consequences Of Redemption

Redemption Proceeds	$1,270,000
PUC - New Shares	(40,000)
ITA 84(3) Deemed Dividend (Non-Eligible)	$1,230,000

Proceeds Of Disposition	$1,270,000
ITA 84(3) Deemed Dividend	(1,230,000)
Adjusted Proceeds Of Disposition	$ 40,000
Adjusted Cost Base - New Shares	(10,000)
Capital Gain	$ 30,000
Inclusion Rate	1/2
Taxable Capital Gain	$ 15,000

The overall tax consequences of the redemption would be as follows:

Taxable Dividend [(117%)($1,230,000)]	$1,439,100
Taxable Capital Gain	15,000
Income Inclusion	$1,454,100

The deemed non-eligible dividend would qualify for a federal dividend tax credit of $151,417 [(21/29)(17%)($1,230,000)].

Additional Analysis

While this analysis is not required by the problem, you might note that the total unadjusted income accruing to Ms. Platt is $1,260,000 ($1,230,000 + $30,000). This is the same total that would have resulted from a sale of her shares [($1,350,000 - $90,000) = $1,260,000]. However, it is received in a less favourable form ($1,230,000 in non-eligible dividends as opposed to all capital gains on a sale of shares). In addition, the market value of her son's shares has increased by the $30,000 amount of the gift. Given that there is no corresponding increase in the adjusted cost base of his shares, this additional amount will be subject to tax if the shares are redeemed or sold.

Self Study Solution Seventeen - 6

Use Of Section 87

If ITA 87 is used, the tax consequences are as follows:

- The land will flow through to the amalgamated corporation at its adjusted cost base of $175,000. No capital gain or loss will be recorded.

- As the subsidiary is 100 percent owned, the ITA 88(1) bump-up provision is available. The bump-up will be the lesser of:

Adjusted Cost Base Of Lynn Shares		$390,000
Deduct:		
Lynn's Tax Value For Land -		
Original Cost	($175,000)	
Dividends Paid By Lynn	Nil	(175,000)
1st Value		$215,000

Value Of Land At Acquisition Of Lynn	$390,000
Adjusted Cost Base Of Land	(175,000)
2nd Value	$215,000

This will leave the adjusted cost base of the land at $390,000 ($175,000 + $215,000).

Use Of Section 88(1)

If ITA 88(1) is used, the tax consequences are as follows:

- Lynn will have proceeds of disposition equal to the adjusted cost base of the land of $175,000. No capital gain or loss will be recorded.

- Ricon Ltd. will have the same bump-up on the land as calculated under the ITA 87 approach. The adjusted cost base of the land will also be the same $390,000 that was calculated in the ITA 87 solution.

Conclusion

Both approaches result in a bump-up of $215,000 and an adjusted cost base for the land of $390,000. It does not appear to make any difference which of the two alternative approaches is used.

Self Study Solution Seventeen - 7

Part A - Funds Available For Distribution

The taxable capital gains and active business income (recapture) at the corporate level can be calculated as follows:

Asset	Taxable Capital Gains	Active Business Income
Inventories	Nil	Nil
Taxable Capital Gains:		
On Land [(1/2)($1,243,000 - $623,000)]	$310,000	Nil
On Building [(1/2)($1,173,000 - $775,000)]	199,000	
Recapture On Building ($775,000 - $586,000)		$189,000
Totals	$509,000	$189,000

As the active business income is less than the $500,000 annual business limit, there will be no addition to the General Rate Income Pool Balance. The taxable capital gains are not eligible for addition to the GRIP balance.

Taxable Income will be $698,000 ($509,000 + $189,000). Tax Payable on this amount will be calculated as follows:

Federal Tax On Business Income [(28% - 17.5%)($189,000)]	$ 19,845
Federal Tax On Investment Income [(28% + 10-2/3%)($509,000)]	196,813
Part I Tax Payable	$216,658
Provincial Tax On Business Income [(3%)($189,000)]	5,670
Provincial Tax On Investment Income [(13%)($509,000)]	66,170
Total Tax Payable	$288,498

The balance in the RDTOH is calculated as follows:

Balance Prior To Asset Dispositions	$ 27,000
Addition - The Least Of:	
• [(30-2/3%)($509,000)] = $156,093	
• [(30-2/3%)($698,000 - $189,000)] = $156,093	
• Part I Federal Tax Payable = $216,658	156,093
Ending RDTOH	$183,093

The amount available for distribution to the shareholders, after the payment of taxes at the corporate level, can be calculated as follows:

Fair Market Values:	
Inventories	$ 35,000
Land	1,243,000
Building	1,173,000
Gross Proceeds	$2,451,000
Tax Payable	(288,498)
Dividend Refund (Note)	183,093
Funds Available For Distribution	$2,345,595

Note Technically, the dividend refund is the lesser of the $183,093 balance in the RDTOH account and 38-1/3 percent of taxable dividends paid. However, given the size of the distribution in this problem, it is clear that $183,093 will be the lower figure.

With respect to the capital dividend account, the final balance is calculated as follows:

Balance Before Dispositions	$215,000
Disposition Of Land	310,000
Disposition Of Building	199,000
Ending Balance	$724,000

Part B - Components Of Distribution

Assuming an election has been made to declare the maximum capital dividend, the taxable dividend component of the total distribution to the shareholders can be calculated as follows:

Distribution To Shareholders	$2,345,595
Paid Up Capital	(447,000)
ITA 84(2) Deemed Dividend	$1,898,595
Capital Dividend (Balance In Account)	(724,000)
Deemed Dividend Subject To Tax (Non-Eligible)	$1,174,595

As Kruger has no GRIP balance, all of this dividend will be non-eligible. The taxable amount will be $1,374,276 [(117%)($1,174,595)]. This dividend will qualify for a federal dividend tax credit of $144,597 [(21/29)(17%)($1,174,595)]

Part B - Capital Gain

With respect to capital gains, ITA 54 indicates that the proceeds of disposition for purposes of determining any capital gain on the disposition of shares does not include any amount paid out as ITA 84(2) dividends. Given the preceding calculation, the capital gain to the shareholders would be calculated as follows:

Actual Distribution To Shareholders	$2,345,595
ITA 84(2) Deemed Dividend	(1,898,595)
Deemed Proceeds Of Disposition	$ 447,000
Adjusted Cost Base For Shares	(447,000)
Capital Gain	Nil

Self Study Solution Seventeen - 8

Sale Of Assets

This calculation requires two steps. First, we must determine the after tax proceeds that will be available at the corporate level subsequent to the sale of the assets. Then, a second stage analysis is required to determine the amount that will be retained by Mr. Brock after he pays all of the taxes that are due on the proceeds that are distributed to him.

Calculation Of Corporate Income On Asset Dispositions

Net Income For Tax Purposes on the disposition of assets would be as follows:

	Active Business Income (Loss)	Taxable Capital Gains
Accounts Receivable	Nil	Nil
Inventory ($109,500 - $105,000)	$ 4,500	Nil
Land [(1/2)($70,000 - $35,000)]	Nil	$ 17,500
Building		
Recapture ($122,500 - $35,000)	87,500	
Capital Gain [(1/2)($136,500 - $122,500)]		7,000
Equipment (Note One)	(21,000)	Nil
Goodwill (Note Two)	Nil	82,250
Taxable Amounts	$ 71,000	$106,750

Note One There is a terminal loss of $21,000 ($63,000 - $42,000).

Note Two The sale of the Goodwill will result in a taxable capital gain of $82,250 [(1/2)($164,500 - Nil)].

Taxable Income And Tax Payable

Taxable Income will total $177,750 ($71,000 + $106,750). The Tax Payable on this amount would be calculated as follows:

Federal Tax On:	
Business Income [(38% - 10% - 17.5%)($71,000)]	$ 7,455
Investment Income [(38% - 10% + 10-2/3%)($106,750)]	41,277
Part I Tax Payable	$48,732
Provincial Tax On Business Income [(4%)($71,000)]	2,840
Provincial Tax On Investment Income [(13%)($106,750)]	13,878
Total Tax Payable	$65,450

RDTOH Balance

There is no opening balance in the RDTOH account. The closing balance, which is the addition for the year, will be the least of:

- 30-2/3 Percent Of Investment Income [(30-2/3%)($106,750)] $32,737
- 30-2/3% Of Taxable Income, Less Income Eligible For The Small
  Business Deduction [(30-2/3%)($177,750 - $71,000)] $32,737
- Part I Federal Tax Payable $48,732

The least of these figures and the balance in the RDTOH account is $32,737.

Funds Available For Distribution

Based on the preceding figures, cash available for distribution would be calculated as follows:

Purchase Price (Given) = Total Fair Market Value Of	
Net Non-Cash Assets ($561,000 - $14,000 - $70,000)	$477,000
Cash Not Purchased	14,000
Funds From Sale Of Assets	$491,000
Tax Payable	(65,450)
Dividend Refund (Note)	32,737
Funds Available For Distribution	$458,287

Note   Technically, the dividend refund is the lesser of the $32,737 balance in the RDTOH account and 38-1/3 percent of taxable dividends paid. However, given the size of the distribution in this problem, it is clear that $32,737 will be the lower figure.

Capital Dividend Account

The balance in the capital dividend account would be calculated as follows:

Balance Before Dispositions	$ 70,000
Non-Taxable One-Half Of Capital Gains	
(From Table Calculating Corporate Income	
On Asset Dispositions)	106,750
Ending Balance	$176,750

GRIP Balance

The GRIP Balance is nil as Brock Enterprises has no Full Rate Taxable Income. As a result, any taxable dividend will be non-eligible.

Taxable Dividend Resulting From Distribution

Assuming an election has been made to declare the maximum capital dividend, the taxable dividend component of the total distribution to Mr. Brock can be calculated as follows:

Funds Available For Distribution	$458,287
Paid Up Capital	(52,500)
ITA 84(2) Deemed Dividend	$405,787
ITA 83(2) Capital Dividend (Balance In Account)	(176,750)
Deemed Dividend Subject To Tax (Non-Eligible)	$229,037

There would be no capital gain on the disposition, as demonstrated in the following calculation:

Funds Distributed	$458,287
ITA 84(2) Deemed Dividend	(405,787)
Deemed Proceeds Of Disposition For Shares	$ 52,500
Adjusted Cost Base	(52,500)
Capital Gain	Nil

Personal Tax Payable

As there is no capital gain and the PUC and the capital dividend are received tax free, the personal Tax Payable on the dividend subject to tax would be calculated as follows:

Deemed Non-Eligible Dividend Subject To Tax	$229,037
Gross Up Of 17 Percent	38,936
Taxable Dividend	$267,973
Personal Tax Rate (Given)	51%
Tax Before Dividend Tax Credit	$136,666
Dividend Tax Credit [(21/29 + 8/29)($38,936)]	(38,936)
Personal Tax Payable	$97,730

Sale Of Shares

The tax payable resulting from a sale of shares would be calculated as follows:

Proceeds Of Disposition	$455,000
Adjusted Cost Base	(52,500)
Capital Gain	$402,500
Inclusion Rate	1/2
Taxable Capital Gain	$201,250
Tax Rate For Mr. Brock	51%
Tax Payable	$102,638

Conclusion

Given the preceding calculations, the after tax, personal cash retention under both alternatives would be as follows:

	Asset Sale	Share Sale
Proceeds From Sale	$458,287	$455,000
Personal Tax Payable	(97,730)	(102,638)
After Tax Retention	$360,557	$352,362

The net proceeds resulting from the sale of shares amounted to $352,362. This compares to $360,557 that would be retained if the assets were sold. The conclusion is clear. The cash retained from the sale of assets and distribution of proceeds is $8,195 ($360,557 - $352,362) larger than the cash retained from selling the shares.

Although the problem asks that you ignore the lifetime capital gains deduction, note that, if Mr. Brock could use his lifetime capital gains deduction to eliminate the capital gain, this result would be altered in favour of selling shares.

Also note that the full $458,287 could be left in the business for further operations as an investment company. Given the current rate of taxation on the investment income of corporations, it is not likely that this would be an attractive alternative, even if the corporation was used to split income with other members of Mr. Brock's family.

Chapter 17 Learning Objectives

After completing Chapter 17, you should be able to:

1. Identify situations where the ITA 85.1 rollover provision is applicable (paragraph [P hereafter] 17-1 to 17-13).
2. Identify situations where the ITA 86 rollover provision is applicable (P 17-14).
3. Apply the ITA 86 rollover procedures to freeze an estate (P 17-15 to 17-16).
4. List the conditions that must be met in order to use the ITA 86 rollover provision (P 17-17 to 17-18).
5. Explain the procedures that are required in implementing an ITA 86 rollover (P 17-19 to 17-29).

6. Identify situations where the ITA 86(2) benefit rule is applicable and apply the required procedures to specific examples (P 17-30 to 17-40).
7. Describe the major tax planning considerations related to the use of ITA 86 (P 17-41 to 17-46).
8. Explain the nature of an ITA 87 amalgamation (P 17-47 to 17-50).
9. Describe the position of the amalgamated company subsequent to an ITA 87 amalgamation (P 17-51 to 17-55).
10. Describe the position of the shareholders of the amalgamated company subsequent to an ITA 87 amalgamation (P 17-56).

11. Identify the specific considerations involved in vertical amalgamations (P 17-57).
12. Explain the "asset bump-up" that is available under both ITA 87 and ITA 88(1) (P 17-58 to 17-61).
13. Explain both the non-tax considerations and tax planning considerations related to ITA 87 amalgamations (P 17-62 to 17-65).
14. Explain the nature of an ITA 88(1) winding-up of a 90 percent owned subsidiary (P 17-66 to 17-73).
15. Apply the procedures for recording the assets acquired by the parent company in an ITA 88(1) winding-up of a 90 percent owned subsidiary (P 17-74 to 17-84).

16. Apply the procedures required for the disposition of shares that occurs in the winding-up of a 90 percent owned subsidiary (P 17-85 and 17-86).
17. Compare the results of applying ITA 87 vs. the results of applying ITA 88(1) and any associated tax planning issues (P 17-87 to 17-93).
18. Apply the procedures required in an ITA 88(2) winding-up of a Canadian corporation (P 17-94 to 17-106).
19. Explain the procedures used under ITA 51 when there is a conversion of a corporation's preferred shares or debt securities (P 17-107 to 17-113).
20. Explain the basic alternatives for the sale of an incorporated business (P 17-114 to 17-115).

21. Explain the provisions relating to restrictive covenants (a.k.a. non-competition agreements) (P 17-116 to 17-119).
22. Describe the procedures used when the individual assets of a business are sold (P 17-120 to 17-122).
23. Describe the procedures used when the assets of a business are sold as a going concern (P 17-123 to 17-132).
24. Describe the procedures used when the shares of a business are sold (P 17-133 to 17-137).
25. Compare an offer to purchase the shares of a business and an offer to purchase its assets and determine the preferable alternative (P 17-138 to 17-151).

How To Work Through Chapter 18

We recommend the following approach in dealing with the material in this chapter:

Introduction To Partnerships
- Read paragraph 18-1 to 18-7 (in the textbook).

Partnerships Defined
- Read paragraph 18-8 to 18-23.
- Do Self Study Problem Eighteen-1 which is available on the Companion Website and check the solution in this Study Guide.

Co-Ownership, Joint Ventures, And Syndicates
- Read paragraph 18-24 to 18-36.
- Do Self Study Problem Eighteen-2 and check the solution in this Study Guide.

Determining Partnership Income, Losses, And Tax Credits
- Read paragraph 18-37 to 18-52.
- Do Exercise Eighteen-1(in the textbook) and check the solution in this Study Guide.
- Read paragraph 18-53 to 18-56.
- Do Exercise Eighteen-2 and check the solution in this Study Guide.
- Read paragraph 18-57 to 18-58.
- Do Exercise Eighteen-3 and check the solution in this Study Guide.

Allocations To Partners And Partner Expenses
- Read paragraph 18-59.
- Do Exercise Eighteen-4 and check the solution in this Study Guide.
- Read paragraph 18-60 to 18-62.
- Do Self Study Problems Eighteen-3 and Eighteen-4 and check the solutions in this Study Guide.

The Partnership Interest
- Read paragraph 18-63 to 18-74.
- Do Exercise Eighteen-5 and check the solution in this Study Guide.

Adjustments To The ACB Of A Partnership Interest
- Read paragraph 18-75 to 18-88.
- Do Exercise Eighteen-6 and check the solution in this Study Guide.
- Read paragraph 18-89 to 18-90.
- Do Self Study Problems Eighteen-5 and Eighteen-6 and check the solutions in this Study Guide.

Limited Partnerships And Limited Partners
- Read paragraph 18-91 to 18-102.
- Do Exercise Eighteen-7 and check the solution in this Study Guide.
- Do Self Study Problem Eighteen-7 and check the solution in this Study Guide.

Transfers Of Property To And From A Partnership - No Rollover
- Read paragraph 18-103 to 18-108.
- Do Exercise Eighteen-8 and check the solution in this Study Guide.
- Read paragraph 18-109.
- Do Exercise Eighteen-9 and check the solution in this Study Guide.

Common Partnership Rollovers
- Read paragraph 18-110 to 18-112.
- Do Exercise Eighteen-10 and check the solution in this Study Guide.
- Read paragraph 18-113 to 18-127.
- Do Self Study Problem Eighteen-8 and check the solution in this Study Guide.

Specified Investment Flow Through Partnerships
- Read paragraph 18-128 to 18-129.

To Complete This Chapter
- If you would like more practice in problem solving, do the Supplementary Self Study Problems for the chapter. These problems and solutions are available on the Companion Website.
- Review the Key Terms Used In This Chapter in the textbook at the end of Chapter 18. Consult the Glossary for the meaning of any key terms you do not know.
- Test yourself with the Chapter 18 Glossary Flashcards available on the Companion Website.
- Ensure you have achieved the Chapter 18 Learning Objectives listed in this Study Guide.
- As a review, we recommend you view the PowerPoint presentation for Chapter 18 that is on the Companion Website.

Practice Examination
- Write the Practice Examination for Chapter 18 that is on the Companion Website. Mark your examination using the Practice Examination Solution that is on the Companion Website.

Solutions to Chapter Eighteen Exercises

Exercise Eighteen - 1 Solution
The following amounts would be added to Mr. Peter's Net Income For Tax Purposes:

Business Income [(50%)($55,000)]	$27,500
Taxable Capital Gains [(50%)(1/2)($40,000)]	10,000
Eligible Dividends [(50%)($10,000)]	5,000
Gross Up [(38%)($5,000)]	1,900
Total Addition	$44,400

In addition, Mr. Peters would be eligible for a federal dividend tax credit of $1,036 [(6/11)($1,900)]. The drawings that he made during the year are not included in his 2017 Net Income For Tax Purposes.

Exercise Eighteen - 2 Solution

The JL Partnership's Net Business Income would be calculated as follows:

Accounting Net Income		$262,000
Add:		
Salary To J	$45,000	
Interest To L	22,000	
Amortization Expense	26,000	
Donations	2,500	95,500
Subtotal		$357,500
Deduct:		
Maximum CCA	($42,000)	
Accounting Gain On Sale Of Land	(24,000)	(66,000)
Net Business Income		$291,500
Priority Allocations For Salary And Interest		(67,000)
Residual To Be Split 60:40		$224,500

The allocation of this Net Business Income to the two partners would be as follows:

	Partner J	Partner L
Priority Allocation For Salary	$ 45,000	N/A
Priority Allocation For Interest	N/A	$22,000
Allocation Of Residual		
[(60%)($224,500)]	134,700	
[(40%)($224,500)]		89,800
Total Business Income Allocation	$179,700	$111,800

While not required, you might note that a taxable capital gain of $12,000 [(1/2)($24,000)] would be allocated to the partners on a 60:40 basis. With respect to the donations, the amount of the charitable donations of $2,500 would allocated on a 60:40 basis, leaving the individual partners to calculate the available credit.

Exercise Eighteen - 3 Solution

The ST Partnership's Net Business Income would be calculated as follows:

Accounting Net Income	$146,000
Amortization Expense = CCA	Nil
Eligible Dividends	(12,000)
Accounting Gain On Sale Of Land	(31,000)
Net Business Income	$103,000

The addition to Net Income For Tax Purposes for each of the two partners would be calculated as follows:

	Partner S	Partner T
Net Business Income [(50%)($103,000)]	$51,500	$51,500
Eligible Dividends [(50%)($12,000)]	6,000	6,000
Gross Up [(38%)($6,000)]	2,280	2,280
Taxable Capital Gain [(50%)(1/2)($31,000)]	7,750	7,750
Net Income For Tax Purposes Addition	$67,530	$67,530

While not required, you might note that each partner would be eligible for a federal dividend tax credit of $1,244 [(6/11)($2,280)].

Exercise Eighteen - 4 Solution

The tax credits that would be allocated to each of the partners would be calculated as follows:

Charitable Donations ($1,750 Each)
[(15%)($200) + (29%)($1,750 - $200)] $ 480

Political Contributions ($600 Each)
[(3/4)($400)] + [(1/2)($200)]   400

Eligible Dividends ($2,100 Each)
[(6/11)(38%)($2,100)]   435

Total Of Credits To Each Partner $1,315

These amounts would serve to reduce the Tax Payable of each of the two partners for the year ending December 31, 2017.

Exercise Eighteen - 5 Solution

After the admission of Caitlan, Alan and Balan will each have a one-third interest in the partnership, down from the previous interest of one-half. They are each, in effect, selling one-third of their partnership interest [(1/2 - 1/3) ÷ 1/2)]. The ACB of their distribution to Caitlan is $16,000 [(1/3)($48,000)], resulting in a capital gain of $24,000 ($40,000 - $16,000). The taxable capital gain is one-half of this amount or $12,000.

The partner capital account transactions and ending balances will be:

	Alan	Balan	Caitlin
Opening Capital Accounts	$48,000	$48,000	Nil
Adjustment For Caitlin's Admission	(16,000)	(16,000)	$32,000
Ending Capital Accounts (Accounting Values)	$32,000	$32,000	$32,000
ACB Of Partnership Interest	$32,000	$32,000	$80,000

Exercise Eighteen - 6 Solution

The ACB of Robert's partnership interest on December 31, 2017 and January 1, 2018 would be determined as follows:

Original Capital Contribution	$12,500
Additional Contribution	7,200
Drawing	(4,000)
ACB - December 31, 2017	$15,700
Adjustment For 2017 Income [(40%)($11,600 + $3,100 + $46,700)]	24,560
ACB - January 1, 2018	$40,260

Robert's inclusion in Net Income For Tax Purposes would be as follows:

Taxable Capital Gain [(40%)(1/2)($11,600)]	$ 2,320
Dividends Received [(40%)($3,100)]	1,240
Gross Up On Dividends [(40%)(38%)($3,100)]	471
Net Business Income [(40%)($46,700)]	18,680
Inclusion In 2017 Net Income For Tax Purposes	$22,711

Note that this $22,711 addition to Robert's Net Income For Tax Purposes is not the same amount as the $24,560 that was added to the ACB of Robert's partnership interest to reflect his share of 2017 partnership income. While not required by the problem, Robert can claim a federal dividend tax credit of $257 [(40%)(6/11)($1,178)].

Exercise Eighteen - 7 Solution

ACB Of Partnership Interest		$200,000
Share Of Partnership Income (Not Loss) For 2017		Nil
Subtotal		$200,000
Amounts Owed To The Partnership	($150,000)	
Other Amounts Intended To Reduce Investment Risk (General Partner Guarantee)	(50,000)	(200,000)
At-Risk Amount - December 31, 2017		Nil

As the at-risk amount is nil, none of the loss can be deducted in 2017. The limited partnership loss at the end of 2017 is 100 percent of the $75,000 loss allocation.

Exercise Eighteen - 8 Solution

Part A Charles is considered to have disposed of the land for $100,000, resulting in a $33,500 [(1/2)($100,000 - $33,000)] taxable capital gain. LIU will be considered to have acquired the land for $100,000. Charles is considered to have made a capital contribution of $100,000 that will be added to the ACB of his partnership interest.

Part B Charles will have the same $33,500 taxable capital gain as in Part A and LIU will be considered to have acquired the land for $100,000. The capital contribution and the addition to the ACB of the partnership interest is equal to $75,000. This is the difference between the fair market value of the land transferred to LIU of $100,000 and the $25,000 in other consideration received by Charles on the property transfer.

Part C Charles will have the same $33,500 taxable capital gain as in Part A and LIU will be considered to have acquired the land for $100,000. No capital contribution is made. As Charles withdrew $12,000 ($112,000 - $100,000) more from LIU than he transferred in, Charles will be considered to have made a net withdrawal. The ACB of his partnership interest will be reduced by $12,000.

Exercise Eighteen - 9 Solution

ITA 98(2) deems DG to have disposed of the share investments for the fair market value of $94,000, resulting in a $55,000 ($94,000 - $39,000) capital gain. One-fifth of the capital gain, or $11,000, will be allocated to Darlene. One-half of this amount, or $5,500, will be a taxable capital gain that she will include in her income for 2017.

Darlene's adjusted cost base for the share investments is $18,800 [(20%)($94,000)].

The adjusted cost base of her partnership interest on December 31, 2017 and on January 1, 2018 is calculated as follows:

Partnership ACB Prior To Distribution	$30,000
Drawings [(20%)($94,000)]	(18,800)
Partnership ACB - December 31, 2017	$11,200
Allocated Capital Gain [(20%)($94,000 - $39,000)]	11,000
Partnership ACB - January 1, 2018	$22,200

Exercise Eighteen - 10 Solution

Using the ITA 85(1) rollover provision, the property would be transferred at the $156,000 ACB of the land. Given this, the transfer would not result in any current income for Samantha. The cost of the land to the partnership would be the $156,000 elected value for the transfer. This same amount would be added to the adjusted cost base of Samantha's partnership interest.

Self Study Solution Eighteen - 1

The determination of the existence of a partnership is a mixed question of fact and law, based upon the intention of the parties that may be expressed clearly through a valid written partnership agreement or inferred from actions. In Canada, the relevant provincial partnership legislation is applicable to answering this question.

In this case, an analysis of the three elements of a partnership is as follows:

1. **Was the business carried on in common by two or more persons?**

   The details of the partnership agreement contain many of the necessary ingredients that the courts will look to in support of this element. Accordingly, it appears that this element has been met.

2. **Was a business carried on by the partnership?**

   A business has a beginning and an end. Ongoing profitable activity within the business may actually only occur between these two extremes, but the activity remains a business throughout the period. In other words, profitability is generally irrelevant to a finding that a business exists. In this case, the selling off of store property will likely occur as part of the wind up process of the two stores. Accordingly, there are arguments that support the carrying on of a business.

3. **Was there a view to profit?**

   This element will be satisfied if there is a potential for profit even though one may never be realized. The facts clearly lead to a conclusion that there is no hope of profit. The additional fact that the partnership will be terminated once the property is sold and that losses are not only expected, but anticipated, speaks for itself. A tax motivation that predominates, such as this, will not invalidate a partnership as long as there is a profit potential and the other elements are met. This is not the case.

Conclusion: A partnership will not be created. As a result, no losses can be allocated to the investors. The losses belong to Wayout Ltd. only.

Self Study Solution Eighteen - 2

Part A - Partnership Results

As the original intention when the land was purchased was to develop and sell lots, the income from the sale of the lots would be reported as business income and not as a capital gain.

Using the provisions of ITA 97(2), Mr. Marrazzo could transfer the land to the partnership at its ACB of $400,000. There would be no effect on his Net Income For Tax Purposes in 2017. His partnership income inclusion for the two years would be calculated as follows:

2017 Addition To Net Income For Tax Purposes	Nil

The total net business income resulting from the 2018 sale of the property would be as follows:

Proceeds From Lot Sales	$4,400,000
Cost Of Land	(400,000)
Site Servicing Costs	(1,200,000)
Net Business Income	$2,800,000

Mr. Marrazzo's 2018 addition to his Net Income For Tax Purposes would be calculated as follows:

Priority Claim Of Accrued Gain ($1,300,000 - $400,000)	$ 900,000
Allocation Of Remaining Business Income [(50%)($2,800,000 - $900,000)]	950,000
2018 Addition To Net Income For Tax Purposes	$1,850,000

Part A - Joint Venture Results

No rollover under ITA 85(1) could take place because land inventory is not an eligible property. As a result, Mr. Marrazzo would recognize a 2017 gain on the transfer to Digger Inc. of $900,000 ($1,300,000 - $400,000). As previously noted, this gain would be treated as business income. His partnership income inclusion for the two years would be calculated as follows:

2017 Addition To Net Income For Tax Purposes	$ 900,000
Proceeds Of Disposition - Digger's Sale Of The Land	$4,400,000
Adjusted Cost Base Of Land	(1,300,000)
Site Servicing Costs	(1,200,000)
Net Business Income	$1,900,000
Mr. Marrazzo's Share	50%
2018 Addition To Net Income For Tax Purposes	$ 950,000

The addition to his Net Income For Tax Purposes over the two years is $1,850,000 ($900,000 + $950,000), the same total as in Part A.

Part A - Comparison

In total, Mr. Marrazzo will report the same increase in Net Income For Tax Purposes regardless of which form of organization is used. However, with the joint venture, he would have to report $900,000 of the income in 2017 and $950,000 in 2018. With the partnership, the entire $1,850,000 in income would be reported in 2018. Given that this approach provides significant tax deferral, the partnership approach appears preferable.

Part B - Adjusted Cost Base

The ACB of Mr. Marrazzo's partnership interest would be calculated as follows:

Capital Contribution - 2017	$ 400,000
Income Allocated To Mr. Marrazzo For 2017	Nil
ACB - December 31, 2018	$ 400,000
Income Allocated To Mr. Marrazzo For 2018 (Part A)	1,850,000
Mr. Marrazzo's ACB - January 1, 2019	$2,250,000

At this point, a winding up of the partnership would have no tax consequences for Mr. Marrazzo.

The ACB of Digger Inc.'s partnership interest would be calculated as follows:

Capital Contribution - 2017	Nil
Income Allocated To Digger For 2017	Nil
Capital Contribution - 2018 = Servicing Costs	$1,200,000
ACB - December 31, 2018	$1,200,000
Income Allocated To Digger For 2018	
[(50%)($2,800,000 - $900,000) - See Part A]	950,000
Digger Inc.'s ACB - January 1, 2019	$2,150,000

Self Study Solution Eighteen - 3

Partnership Net Business Income

The Net Business Income of the partnership is calculated as follows:

Net Income As Per Income Statement		$192,100
Additions:		
Partners' Salaries [(2)($44,000)]	$88,000	
Amortization Deducted	12,500	
Charitable Donations	7,200	
Closing Accounts Receivable (Note One)	56,000	163,700
Deductions:		
Opening Accounts Receivable (Note One)	($27,000)	
Capital Gains On Securities (Note Two)	(14,000)	
Dividends Received (Note Three)	(48,000)	
CCA:		
Class 8 [(20%)($26,000)]	(5,200)	
Class 50 [(55%)(1/2)($8,500)]	(2,338)	(96,538)
Net Business Income		$259,262

Note One   The addition of closing accounts receivable and the deduction of the opening accounts receivable are required to adjust the cash based income figure to an accrual based income figure.

Note Two   The total capital gain is deducted in the calculation of net business income. The taxable one-half of these gains is included on a flow through basis in the income of the individual partners.

Note Three   The dividends received are deducted in the calculation of net business income. They are flowed through as eligible dividends in the income of the individual partners.

Mr. Caldwell's Personal Income

Mr. Caldwell's Net Income For Tax Purposes would be calculated as follows:

Partnership Net Business Income	$259,262	
Mr. Caldwell's Share	50%	$129,631
Automobile Costs:		
CCA [($13,500)(30%)(75%)]		(3,038)
Operating Costs [($4,000)(75%)]		(3,000)
Net Business Income From Professional Practice		$123,593
Other Partnership Income:		
Taxable Capital Gains [(1/2)($14,000)]	$ 7,000	
Eligible Dividends Received	48,000	
Gross Up On Dividends [(38%)($48,000)]	18,240	
Subtotal	$73,240	
Mr. Caldwell's Share	50%	36,620
Net Income For Tax Purposes		$160,213

Mr. Caldwell's $3,600 [(50%)($7,200)] share of the charitable donations can be used as the basis for a credit against his personal Tax Payable. The amount of the credit would be $1,016 [(15%)($200) + (29%)($3,600 - $200)] assuming this is his only charitable donation. Because the partnership makes regular contributions to charities, Mr. Caldwell is not eligible for the first-time donor's super credit.

He is also entitled to a federal dividend tax credit of $4,975 [(50%)(6/11)($18,240)].

Self Study Solution Eighteen - 4

Part A - Income Inclusions

CCC has three sources of income. These are business income, property income (dividends), and taxable capital gains.

The calculation of the partnership's Net Business Income is as follows:

Net Income From Coffee Roasting		$37,200
Add:		
Salaries To Partners [(3)($2,400)]	$7,200	
Interest On Capital Contributions	2,000	
Personal Partner Expenses	1,100	
Charitable Donations	1,000	
Accounting Amortization	1,450	12,750
Deduct:		
CCA		(2,000)
Net Business Income		$47,950

Income inclusions for each partner related to partnership activities would be as follows:

Net Business Income	$47,950
Eligible Dividends Received	3,440
Gross Up [(38%)($3,440)]	1,307
Taxable Capital Gains [(1/2)($6,000)]	3,000
Total To Be Allocated	$55,697
Each Partner's Share	1/3
Addition to Net Income For Tax Purposes	$18,566

Part B - Tax Credits

Charitable Donations   Each partner would be allocated $333 ($1,000 ÷ 3) in charitable donations. This would provide a federal tax credit of $69 [(15%)($200) + (29%)($133)] assuming this is their only charitable donation.

Dividends   Each of the partners would be eligible for a federal dividend tax credit of $238 [(1/3)(6/11)(38%)($3,440)].

Self Study Solution Eighteen - 5

Matt's Federal Tax Payable

The Net Business Income of the partnership would be calculated as follows:

Operating Income		$549,000
Additions:		
Amortization Expense	$12,000	
One-Half Meals And Entertainment	11,500	
Charitable Donations	17,000	40,500
Deductions:		
CCA		(19,000)
Net Business Income		$570,500

Matt's Taxable Income and share of charitable donations for the year ending December 31, 2017 would be calculated as follows:

	Partnership	**Share**	**Taxable Income**
Partnership Business Income	$570,500	1/2	$285,250
Taxable Capital Gain [(1/2)($14,000)]	7,000	1/2	3,500
Partnership Dividends Received	8,000	1/2	4,000
Dividends Received Personally	N/A		34,000
Gross Up On Dividends Received			
[(38%)($4,000 + $34,000)]	N/A		14,440
Taxable Income			$341,190
Charitable Donations	$17,000	1/2	$8,500

Based on the preceding calculations, Matt's 2017 federal Tax Payable would be as follows:

Tax On The First $202,800	$46,966
Tax On Additional $138,390 [($341,190 - $202,800)] At 33%	45,669
Tax Payable Before Credits	$92,635
Basic Personal Credit [(15%)($11,635)]	(1,745)
Dividend Tax Credit [(6/11)($14,440)]	(7,876)
Charitable Donations (See Note)	(2,769)
Federal Tax Payable	$80,245

Note   The charitable donations tax credit would be calculated as follows:

$$[(15\%)(A)] + [(33\%)(B)] + [(29\%)(C)], \text{where}$$

A = $200
B = The Lesser Of:
  • $8,500 - $200 = $8,300
  • $341,190 - $202,800 = $138,390
C = Nil [$8,500 - ($200 + $8,300)]

The charitable donation credit would be equal to $2,769, calculated as [(15%)($200)] + [(33%)($8,300)].

Taxable Capital Gain From Sale Of Partnership Interest

The adjusted cost base of Matt's partnership interest on January 1, 2018 would be calculated as follows:

	Partnership	Share	ACB
Capital Contribution	N/A		$280,000
2016 Partnership Business Income	$180,000	1/2	90,000
2016 Drawings	N/A		(23,000)
2017 Drawings	N/A		(290,000)
December 31, 2017			$ 57,000
2017 Partnership Business Income	$570,500	1/2	285,250
2017 Capital Gain	14,000	1/2	7,000
2017 Partnership Dividends Received	8,000	1/2	4,000
2017 Charitable Donations	(17,000)	1/2	(8,500)
January 1, 2018 Adjusted Cost Base			$344,750

Given this calculation, the taxable capital gain on Matt's sale of the partnership interest would be calculated as follows:

Proceeds Of Disposition	$535,000
Adjusted Cost Base	(344,750)
Capital Gain	$190,250
Inclusion Rate	1/2
Taxable Capital Gain	$ 95,125

Self Study Solution Eighteen - 6

Part A - Adjusted Cost Base

The adjusted cost base of Eric Beam's partnership interest on the date he withdrew from the partnership is calculated as follows:

Initial Capital Contribution	$225,000
Additional Capital Contribution	54,000
Total Capital Contribution	$279,000
Drawings From Partnership	(43,000)
Income Allocations:	
Net Business Income [(1/3)($195,000)]	65,000
Capital Gains [(1/3)($66,000)]	22,000
Charitable Donations [(1/3)($12,000)]	(4,000)
Adjusted Cost Base - January 1, 2018	$319,000

Note Only one-half of the capital gain is included in the partner's income on the flow through of capital gains realized by a partnership. However, the remaining one-half is included in the assets of the partnership and, in the absence of a special provision to deal with this situation, the realization of this amount would be added to any capital gain realized on the disposition of the partnership interest and would result in double taxation. Given this, the full amount of realized capital gains is added to the partnership adjusted cost base.

Part B - Taxable Capital Gain On Disposition

Given the preceding calculation, the gain on the disposition of the partnership interest can be calculated as follows:

Proceeds Of Disposition [(2)($177,500)]		$355,000
Adjusted Cost Base:		
From Preceding Calculation	($319,000)	
Legal And Accounting Fees	(1,800)	(320,800)
Capital Gain		$ 34,200
Inclusion Rate		1/2
Taxable Capital Gain		$ 17,100

This amount would be included in Eric Beam's Net Income For Tax Purposes for 2018 as a taxable capital gain. He would not include any partnership income for the period January 1 to March 1, 2018, as he was not allocated any of this income.

Part C - Effect On Other Partners

Since each partner paid $177,500 to Eric in return for one-half of his interest, both John and Fred Olson would have a $177,500 increase in the adjusted cost base of their partnership interest.

Self Study Solution Eighteen - 7

Timing Of Income Inclusions For At-Risk Amounts vs. ACB

The addition of the share of the partnership income amounts to the at-risk balance as at December 31 is intended to ensure that this amount is taken into consideration in determining the amount that is actually at risk on that date. Notice, however, losses are not deducted at this time in the determination of the at-risk amount.

We would remind you that in calculating the adjusted cost base of the partnership interest, a partner's share of either a loss or a gain is not added until the first day of the following taxation year.

2017 Results

The required amounts would be calculated as follows:

ACB Of Partnership Interest - December 31, 2017	$50,000
Add: Share Of 2017 Partnership Income (Not Loss)	Nil
Subtotal	$50,000
Amounts Owed To The Partnership	(20,000)
At-Risk Amount - December 31, 2017	$30,000
Share of 2017 Loss [(10%)($400,000)]	($40,000)
At-Risk Amount - December 31, 2017	30,000
Limited Partnership Loss - December 31, 2017	($10,000)

Share of 2017 Loss [(10%)($400,000)]	($40,000)
Limited Partnership Loss - December 31, 2017	10,000
Deductible Loss For 2017	($30,000)

There is a limited partnership loss carry forward of $10,000 at the end of 2017.

2018 Results

ACB Of Partnership Interest - December 31, 2017	$50,000
Loss Deducted For 2017	(30,000)
ACB Of Partnership Interest - December 31, 2018	$20,000
Add: Share Of 2018 Partnership Income (Not Loss)	Nil
Subtotal	$20,000
Amounts Owed To The Partnership	Nil
At-Risk Amount - December 31, 2018	$20,000

Share of 2018 Loss [(10%)($70,000)]	($ 7,000)
Limited Partnership Loss Carry Forward	(10,000)
At-Risk Amount - December 31, 2018	20,000
Limited Partnership Loss - December 31, 2018	Nil

Share of 2018 Loss [(10%)($70,000)]	($ 7,000)
Limited Partnership Loss Carry Forward	(10,000)
Limited Partnership Loss - December 31, 2018	Nil
Deductible Loss For 2018	($17,000)

The $10,000 limited partnership loss carry forward from 2017 can be deducted as it is less than $13,000, the December 31, 2018 at-risk amount of $20,000 reduced by the allocated share of the 2018 partnership loss of $7,000. As a result, there is no limited partnership loss carry forward at the end of 2018.

2019 Results

ACB Of Partnership Interest - December 31, 2018	$20,000
Loss Deducted For 2018	(17,000)
ACB Of Partnership Interest - December 31, 2019	$ 3,000
Add: Share Of 2019 Partnership Income	Nil
Subtotal	$ 3,000
Amounts Owed To The Partnership	Nil
At-Risk Amount - December 31, 2019	$ 3,000

There is no limited partnership loss or deductible loss for 2019 and no limited partnership loss carry forward at the end of 2019.

Summary Of Results

The results are summarized in the following table:

	2017	2018	2019
ACB Of The Partnership Interest - December 31	$50,000	$20,000	$ 3,000
At-Risk Amount - December 31	30,000	20,000	3,000
Limited Partnership Loss	10,000	Nil	Nil
Deductible Loss	30,000	17,000	Nil
Limited Partnership Loss Carry Forward - December 31	10,000	Nil	Nil

Self Study Solution Eighteen - 8

Part A - Adjusted Cost Base Of Consideration

Cash   With all non-share consideration, the ACB is equal to its fair market value. In the case of cash, the fair market value is equal to the face value. These amounts would be $78,000 for Porter, $222,000 for Quinn, and $422,000 for Roberts.

Part A - Adjusted Cost Base Of Preferred Shares   With respect to the preferred shares received by each partner, ITA 85(3)(e) indicates that their ACB will be the lesser of:

- Their fair market value, which would be $180,000 for each of the three partners.
- The ACB of each partnership interest, reduced by the amount of non-share consideration received by the partner.

This latter value would be calculated as follows for each of the three partners:

	Porter	Quinn	Roberts
ACB (Equals Total Elected Value Of Corporate Assets Received)	$382,000	$526,000	$726,000
Cash Received	(78,000)	(222,000)	(422,000)
Balance	$304,000	$304,000	$304,000

For each of the three partners, the lower figure would be the fair market value of $180,000 and, as a consequence, this would be the ACB of their preferred shares.

Part A - Adjusted Cost Base Of Common Shares   Under ITA 85(3)(f), the ACB of the common shares received by each partner would be the ACB of their partnership interest, less the sum of the value of the non-share consideration received and the value assigned to the preferred shares received. These amounts would be calculated as follows:

	Porter	Quinn	Roberts
ACB - Partnership Interest	$382,000	$526,000	$726,000
Cash Received	(78,000)	(222,000)	(422,000)
ACB - Preferred Shares	(180,000)	(180,000)	(180,000)
ACB - Common Shares	$124,000	$124,000	$124,000

Part B - Capital Gain Or Loss

As the non-share consideration had a value that was less than the value of the assets transferred, there will be no immediate gain or loss on this rollover. This can be demonstrated with the following calculation:

	Porter	Quinn	Roberts
Proceeds Of Disposition:			
Cash	$ 78,000	$222,000	$422,000
Preferred Shares	180,000	180,000	180,000
Common Shares	124,000	124,000	124,000
Total Proceeds	$382,000	$526,000	$726,000
ACB	(382,000)	(526,000)	(726,000)
Capital Gain (Loss)	Nil	Nil	Nil

From an economic point of view the gain is still present. The partners have simply deferred recording it for tax purposes by placing a value on the common shares of $372,000 [(3)($124,000)]. This is significantly below their current fair market value of $1,080,000. Note that the difference of $708,000 ($1,080,000 - $372,000) is also the difference between the $2,342,000 fair market value of the total consideration given and the $1,634,000 value for the total ACB of the partnership interests.

Chapter 18 Learning Objectives

1. Explain the basic approach of Canadian income tax legislation to the taxation of partnerships (paragraph [P hereafter] 18-1 to 18-7).
2. Define, for income tax purposes, a partnership arrangement (P 18-8 to 18-15).
3. List the various types of partnership arrangements that are used in Canada (P 18-16 to 18-23).
4. Describe the difference between partnership arrangements and such other forms of organization as co-ownership, joint ventures, and syndicates (P 18-24 to 18-36).
5. Explain the basic concepts that are involved in the determination of the partnership income, losses, and tax credits to be allocated to the partners (P 18-37 to 18-52).

6. Calculate the Net Business Income of the partnership (P 18-53 to 18-54).
7. Calculate the amount and type of partnership income other than business income that will be allocated to each partner under the terms of the partnership agreement (P 18-55 to 18-62).
8. Explain the concept of the adjusted cost base of a partnership interest (P 18-63 to 18-66).
9. Apply the procedures required to record the acquisition of a partnership interest (P 18-67 to 18-74).
10. Calculate the amount of the adjusted cost base of a partnership interest (P 18-75 to 18-88).

11. Apply the procedures required to record the disposition of a partnership interest because of a sale or withdrawal (P 18-89 to 18-90).
12. Define limited partner and limited partnership arrangement (P 18-91 to 18-93).
13. Apply the at-risk rules to limited partnership losses (P 18-94 to 18-102).
14. Define a Canadian partnership (P 18-103 to 18-106).
15. Apply the procedures related to transfers between a partnership and its partners when no rollover provision is used (P 18-107 to 18-109).
16. List and apply the common rollover provisions for transfers between a partnership and its partners (P 18-110 to 18-127).

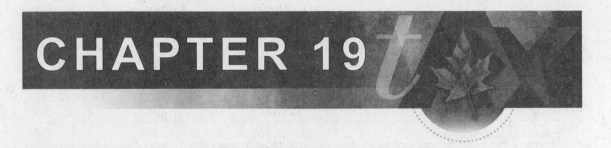

How To Work Through Chapter 19

We recommend the following approach in dealing with the material in this Chapter:

Introduction To Trusts And Estate Planning
- Read the Note at the beginning of the Chapter to 19-7 (in the textbook).

Basic Concepts
- Read paragraph 19-8 to 19-23.

Establishing A Trust
- Read paragraph 19-24 to 19-27.
- Do Exercise Nineteen-1 (in the textbook) and check the solution in this Study Guide.

Returns And Payments - Trusts
- Read paragraph 19-28 to 19-29.

Non-Tax Reasons For Using Trusts
- Read paragraph 19-30 to 19-31.

Classification Of Trusts (Personal, Testamentary And Inter Vivos)
- Read paragraph 19-32 to 19-51.

Taxation Of Trusts - The Basic Model
- Read paragraph 19-52 to 19-55.
- Do Exercise Nineteen-2 and check the solution in this Study Guide.

Rollovers To A Trust
- Read paragraph 19-56 to 19-64.
- Do Exercise Nineteen-3 and check the solution in this Study Guide.
- Read paragraph 19-65 to 19-68.
- Do Exercise Nineteen-4 and check the solution in this Study Guide.

Rollovers To Capital Beneficiaries
- Read paragraph 19-69 to 19-74.
- Do Self Study Problem Nineteen-1 which is available on the Companion Website and check the solution in this Study Guide.

21 Year Deemed Disposition Rule And Other Deemed Dispositions
- Read paragraph 19-75 to 19-78.

Net Income For Tax Purposes And Taxable Income Of A Trust
- Read paragraph 19-79 to 19-92.
- Do Exercise Nineteen-5 and check the solution in this Study Guide.

Income Allocations To Beneficiaries
- Read paragraph 19-93 to 19-109.
- Do Exercise Nineteen-6 and check the solution in this Study Guide.

Allocation Of Business Income, CCA, Recapture of CCA, And Terminal Losses
- Read paragraph 19-110 and 19-111.
- Do Exercise Nineteen-7 and check the solution in this Study Guide.

Principal Residence Exemption
- Read paragraph 19-112.

Tax Payable Of Personal Trusts
- Read paragraph 19-113 to 19-125.
- Do Exercise Nineteen-8 and check the solution in this Study Guide.
- Do Self Study Problems Nineteen-2 to Nineteen-4 and check the solutions in this Study Guide.

Income Attribution - Trusts
- Read paragraph 19-126 to 19-128.
- Do Exercise Nineteen-9 and check the solution in this Study Guide.
- Do Self Study Problems Nineteen-5 and Nineteen-6 and check the solutions in this Study Guide.
- Read paragraph 19-129 to 19-131.

Purchase Or Sale Of An Interest In A Trust
- Read paragraph 19-132 to 19-137.
- Do Exercise Nineteen-10 and check the solution in this Study Guide.

Tax Planning Using Trusts (Family, Spousal And Alter Ego Trusts)
- Read paragraph 19-138 to 19-146.
- Do Exercise Nineteen-11 and check the solution in this Study Guide.
- Read paragraph 19-147 to 19-151.

Estate Planning - Tax And Non-Tax Considerations
- Read paragraph 19-152 to 19-156.

Estate Freeze - Objectives And Techniques, Including ITA 86 Share Exchange
- Read paragraph 19-157 to 19-178.

SIFT Partnerships And Trusts
- Read paragraph 19-179.

To Complete This Chapter
- If you would like more practice in problem solving, do the Supplementary Self Study Problems for the chapter. These problems and solutions are available on the Companion Website.
- Review the Key Terms Used In This Chapter in the textbook at the end of Chapter 19. Consult the Glossary for the meaning of any key terms you do not know.
- Test yourself with the Chapter 19 Glossary Flashcards available on the Companion Website.
- Ensure you have achieved the Chapter 19 Learning Objectives listed in this Study Guide.
- As a review, we recommend you view the PowerPoint presentation for Chapter 19 that is on the Companion Website.

Practice Examination
- Write the Practice Examination for Chapter 19 that is on the Companion Website. Mark your examination using the Practice Exam Solution that is on the Companion Website.

Solutions to Chapter Nineteen Exercises

Exercise Nineteen - 1 Solution

Case A While Mr. Black has transferred property, it is not clear that his intention was to create a trust. No trust would be created by his transfer.

Case B Jane's "friends" cannot be considered to be an identifiable class. As a consequence, there is no certainty as to beneficiaries and no trust would be created by her transfer.

Case C Robert's "children" would be an identifiable class. It would appear that a trust has been created.

Case D While Suzanne has signed the agreement, it does not appear that the property has been transferred. This means that no trust has been created.

Exercise Nineteen - 2 Solution

With respect to Joanne's transfer of her securities to the trust, the transaction would be deemed to take place at fair market value. This would result in a taxable capital gain to Joanne of $10,000 [(1/2)($220,000 - $200,000)]. There would be no tax consequences to Jocelyn or the trust as a result of this transfer.

As the trust distributed all of its income during the year, none of the interest would be taxed in the trust. All of the interest would be included in Jocelyn's income and, because she is an adult, there would be no income attribution to Joanne.

Under ITA 107(2), the transfer from the trust to Jocelyn on January 1, 2018 would take place at the trust's tax cost of $220,000. There would be no tax consequences for Joanne, Jocelyn, or the trust as a result of this transfer. However, as Jocelyn's adjusted cost base is $220,000, the sale at the fair market value of $230,000 would result in a taxable capital gain of $5,000 [(1/2)($230,000 - $220,000)].

Exercise Nineteen - 3 Solution

As there is a rollover available on transfers to a qualifying spousal trust, the accrued $30,000 gain ($90,000 - $60,000) will not be recognized until her husband or the spousal trust eventually disposes of the stocks. The spousal trust acquires the stocks (a non-depreciable capital asset) at Louise's adjusted cost base of $60,000, which will be her husband's adjusted cost base if the trust transfers the stocks to him personally rather than selling them.

Exercise Nineteen - 4 Solution

In Scenarios 1, 2 and 3, the settlor has a taxable capital gain of $300 [(1/2)($1,600 - $1,000)] and the adjusted cost base to the trust is the fair market value of $1,600. In Scenarios 4 to 7, there is a tax free rollover. The results can be summarized as follows:

Scenario	Taxable Capital Gain (Settlor)	Adjusted Cost Base (Trust)
1. Inter vivos trust for adult child	$300	$1,600
2. Inter vivos trust for minor child	300	1,600
3. Testamentary trust for friend	300	1,600
4. Inter vivos qualifying spousal trust	Nil	1,000
5. Testamentary qualifying spousal trust	Nil	1,000
6. Joint spousal trust	Nil	1,000
7. Alter ego trust	Nil	1,000

Exercise Nineteen - 5 Solution

The required calculations are as follows:

Business Income	$220,000
Preferred Beneficiary Election	(50,000)
Distributions To Other Beneficiaries	(170,000)
Designation Under ITA 104(13.1)	
Amounts Deemed Not Paid	35,000
Net Income For Tax Purposes	$ 35,000
Business Loss Carry Forward	(35,000)
Taxable Income	Nil

The preferred beneficiary election would mean that the $50,000 would be taxed in the hands of the disabled beneficiary even though the funds are retained in the trust. Since this is an inter vivos trust, without the election, the $50,000 would be taxed at the maximum rate in the trust. As the disabled beneficiary has no other source of income, the $50,000 would be subject to tax at lower rates than would be the case if it was taxed in the trust.

By designating $35,000 as amounts not paid, the trust can absorb the loss carry forward. As a result, the beneficiaries will not pay tax on this amount even though it has been distributed to them.

Exercise Nineteen - 6 Solution

The income allocation would be as follows:

	Received By Trust	Paid To Bryan	Retained By Trust
Eligible Dividends	$100,000	$ 60,000	$40,000
Non-Eligible Dividends From CCPC	30,000	30,000	Nil
Capital Gain	20,000	20,000	Nil
Totals	$150,000	$110,000	$40,000

The Net Income For Tax Purposes of the trust would be calculated as follows:

Eligible Dividends	$ 40,000
Gross Up Of Eligible Dividends At 38 Percent	15,200
Net Income For Tax Purposes - Trust	$ 55,200

The corresponding calculation for Bryan would be as follows:

Eligible Dividends	$ 60,000
Gross Up Of Eligible Dividends At 38 Percent	22,800
Non-Eligible Dividends From CCPC	30,000
Gross Up Of Non-Eligible Dividends At 17 Percent	5,100
Taxable Capital Gains [(1/2)($20,000)]	10,000
Net Income For Tax Purposes - Bryan	$127,900

Note that the non-taxable one-half of the capital gain would be received by Bryan on a tax free basis. Both the trust and Bryan will be able to deduct a federal dividend tax credit against federal Tax Payable. The tax on split income is not applicable as Bryan is over 18 years of age.

Exercise Nineteen - 7 Solution

If the property is sold in December, 2017, no CCA can be deducted. This means that the total amount of property income to be distributed to Martin and taxed in his hands is $97,000

($32,000 of rental income, plus $65,000 of recapture). Given this distribution, the trust's Net Income For Tax Purposes will be nil.

Alternatively, if the rental property is not sold and all of the income is distributed to Martin, he will include $6,000 ($32,000 - $26,000) in his 2017 Net Income For Tax Purposes. The trust's 2017 Net Income For Tax Purposes will be nil.

Exercise Nineteen - 8 Solution

The Taxable Income in Parts A, B and C is the same and would be calculated as follows:

Eligible Dividends Received	$100,000
Gross Up At 38 Percent	38,000
Taxable Income	$138,000

Part A As all of its 2017 income has been distributed, there would be no Taxable Income or Tax Payable for the trust. This conclusion would not be changed if the trust was an inter vivos trust, rather than a testamentary trust. The beneficiary's federal Tax Payable on the Taxable Income of $138,000 is calculated in the following table.

Part B As none of the dividends are distributed by the trust to the beneficiary, there would be no Taxable Income or Tax Payable for the beneficiary. The trust's federal Tax Payable on the Taxable Income of $138,000 is calculated in the table which follows.

The federal Tax Payable for Parts A and B would be calculated as follows:

	Part A	Part B
Tax On First $91,831	$16,300	$16,300
Tax On Next $46,169 ($138,000 - $91,831) At 26 Percent	12,004	12,004
Total Tax Before Credits	$28,304	$28,304
Personal Tax Credit [(15%)($11,635)]	(1,745)	N/A
Federal Dividend Tax Credit [(6/11)($38,000)]	(20,727)	(20,727)
Federal Tax Payable	$ 5,832	$ 7,577

Notice that the difference between the Tax Payable in Part A and Part B is $1,745 ($7,577 - $5,832). This amount is equal to the basic personal tax credit.

Part C Once again, with no distributions to the beneficiary, the trust's Taxable Income would be $138,000. There would be no Taxable Income or Tax Payable for the beneficiary. Based on this, the Tax Payable for the inter vivos trust would be calculated as follows:

Tax On $138,000 At 33 Percent	$45,540
Federal Dividend Tax Credit [(6/11)($38,000)]	(20,727)
Federal Tax Payable	$24,813

Comparison As a comparison of these examples makes clear, if a trust has beneficiaries with no other sources of income, overall tax payments will be reduced by distributing eligible dividends to beneficiaries (Part A). While these examples do not illustrate this possibility, the conclusion would be the same if non-eligible dividends were involved. Note that the results in Part C would be the same for a testamentary trust that was not designated a graduated rate estate. In Parts B and C where the trust has paid the tax, the dividends would be distributed to the beneficiary on a tax free basis. However, in Part C, if the beneficiaries have a marginal federal tax rate that is less than 33 percent, there will be a tax cost in having the trust pay the tax.

Exercise Nineteen - 9 Solution

Income on the bonds is subject to the attribution rules to the extent that the income is allocated to Trevor's spouse, Carmen, and to their minor son, Mitch. This means that two-thirds of the interest will be attributed back to Trevor. With respect to the capital gain, the attribution rules do not apply on transfers to minors. This means that only Carmen's share of the gain will be attributed back to Trevor. The increase in Taxable Income for Trevor and the trust's beneficiaries are calculated as follows:

	Carmen	Mitch	Rhonda	Attributed To Trevor
Interest Income ($27,000 ÷ 3)	$9,000	$9,000	$ 9,000	
Interest Attribution To Trevor	(9,000)	(9,000)	Nil	$18,000
Taxable Capital Gain [(1/2)($6,000) ÷ 3]	1,000	1,000	1,000	
Capital Gain Attribution To Trevor	(1,000)	Nil	Nil	1,000
Increase In Taxable Income	Nil	$1,000	$10,000	$19,000

If Trevor had died on January 1 of the current year, there would be no income attribution for the year. Each of the beneficiaries would have Taxable Income of $10,000.

Exercise Nineteen - 10 Solution

With respect to Sam, he has acquired a capital interest for consideration of $190,000. This will be the adjusted cost base of the interest he has acquired.

With respect to Mehrdad, he has disposed of a capital asset for proceeds of disposition of $190,000. Since he did not purchase the interest in the trust, his adjusted cost base as usually determined would be nil. However, for this disposition, the adjusted cost base of the capital interest is the greater of nil and the cost amount as determined under ITA 108(1). The cost amount would be $125,000, one-half of the $250,000 tax cost of the assets in the trust. The result would be a taxable capital gain of $32,500 [(1/2)($190,000 - $125,000)].

The original cost of the securities of $120,000 is not relevant in these calculations as the father was taxed on the $130,000 ($250,000 - $120,000) capital gain in the year the securities were transferred.

Exercise Nineteen - 11 Solution

As Sarah's other income places her in the maximum federal tax bracket of 33 percent, her federal tax savings resulting from transferring the assets to the family trust would be $36,300 [($110,000)(33%)]. The federal tax that would be payable on the additional $55,000 received by Jerri is as follows:

Tax On First $45,916	$6,887
Tax On Additional $9,084 ($55,000 - $45,916) At 20.5 Percent	1,862
Tax Before Credit	$8,749
Personal Credit	(1,745)
Tax Payable - Jerri	$7,004

The alternative minimum tax is not relevant for Jerri because the income is in the form of interest, not dividends. As Mark would be in a position to use all of his tax credits prior to receiving the additional $55,000 in income, they are not relevant to the determination of his marginal increase in taxes. The federal tax that would be payable on the additional $55,000 received by Mark is as follows:

Tax At 20.5 Percent ($91,831 - $48,000 = $43,831 @ 20.5%)	$ 8,985
Tax At 26 Percent ($55,000 + $48,000 - $91,831 = $11,169 @ 26%)	2,904
Additional Tax Payable - Mark	$11,889

The total tax paid by the two children would be $18,893 ($7,004 + $11,889). This is $17,407 ($36,300 - $18,893) per year less than the amount that would be paid by Sarah without the trust. When combined with a reduction in provincial taxes, the total tax savings could be significantly larger. This should be more than enough to cover the costs of establishing and maintaining this trust.

One tax planning consideration would be to have the trust pay Mark's wife rather than Mark. Since she has no income, her federal tax payable would be the same as in Jerri's calculation. Although Mark would lose the spousal credit in this case, his wife would claim the basic personal credit herself. Despite the fact that having Mark's wife as the beneficiary would result in less taxes being paid, whether this would be advantageous for Mark (and his mother) would also depend on non-tax considerations such as the state of the marriage.

Self Study Solution Nineteen - 1

Case A

1. The settlor has deemed proceeds of disposition of the fair market value of $1,500. The settlor will be subject to tax on a taxable capital gain of $250 [(1/2)($1,500 - $1,000)].

2. The trust will record the property at a deemed cost equal to the fair market value of $1,500.

Case B

1. The settlor has deemed proceeds of disposition of the fair market value of $1,100, and will record a taxable capital gain of $50 [(1/2)($1,100 - $1,000)]. In addition, there will be recapture of CCA of $250 ($1,000 - $750).

2. The trust acquires the property at a deemed capital cost of $1,100. However, for purposes of calculating CCA and recapture, the ITA 13(7)(e) rules for non-arm's length transactions apply and the value will be $1,050 [$1,000 + (1/2)($1,100 - $1,000)].

Case C

1. The settlor has deemed proceeds of disposition of the fair market value of $1,500. This would result in the settlor having a taxable capital gain of $150 [(1/2)($1,500 - $1,200)].

2. The asset would be recorded in the trust records at the fair market value of $1,500.

3. When the asset is transferred to the capital beneficiary, the deemed proceeds to the trust will be the carrying value of $1,500, resulting in no gain or loss on the transfer. The beneficiary will be deemed to have acquired the property at a cost of $1,500.

Case D

1. The settlor has deemed proceeds of disposition of the fair market value of $1,100. This would result in the settlor having recapture of $300 ($1,100 - $800).

2. The asset would be recorded in the trust records at the settlor's cost of $1,300, with deemed CCA of $200, resulting in a UCC of $1,100.

3. When the asset is transferred to the capital beneficiary, the deemed proceeds to the trust will be the UCC at the date of distribution of $900, resulting in no gain or loss on the transfer. The beneficiary will be deemed to have acquired the property for the UCC amount of $900. However, the beneficiary will have a capital cost of $1,300 for subsequent recapture and capital gains calculation purposes.

Case E

1. The deemed proceeds for the settlor would be the tax cost of $800, resulting in no gain or loss on the transfer.

2. The trust acquires the property at a deemed cost of $800.

Case F

1. Under the general ITA 70(6) rollover provision, the deemed proceeds to the decedent would be the property's cost of $1,000, resulting in no gain or loss on the transfer. As the deceased has net capital loss carry forwards, a better alternative would be to elect out of ITA 70(6) and transfer the property at its fair market value of $4,500. The loss carry forwards could then be used to eliminate the tax on the resulting taxable capital gain of $1,750 [(1/2)($4,500 - $1,000)].

    Note that in the year of death, net capital loss carry forwards can be deducted against any type of income. If the decedent has other income against which the net capital loss carry forward can be deducted, it may not be advantageous to elect out of the rollover. More information on the spouse's current and future taxable income would be needed to optimize the use of the net capital loss carry forward.

2. Under the general ITA 70(6) rollover provision, the trust would record the property at the decedent's cost of $1,000. If the fair market value election is made, the spousal trust will have acquired the property at a deemed cost of $4,500. This higher value will serve to reduce any future gain on the property when it is sold.

Self Study Solution Nineteen - 2

Part A - Taxable Income For The GRE And Its Beneficiaries

The payments made by the GRE administrator will result in the following amounts of Taxable Income for the GRE and the two children:

	Daughter (30%)	Son (50%)	GRE (20%)
Eligible Dividends Received	$26,100	$43,500	$17,400
Gross Up Of 38 Percent	9,918	16,530	6,612
British Interest (Gross Amount Of $110,000)	33,000	55,000	22,000
Net Rental Income ($21,000)	6,300	10,500	4,200
Net And Taxable Income	$75,318	$125,530	$50,212
British Taxes Paid* ($16,500)	$ 4,950	$ 8,250	$ 3,300

*The net interest receipt of $93,500 equals 85 percent of $110,000 ($93,500 ÷ 85%). This means that the taxes withheld totaled $16,500 [(15%)($110,000)].

Part B - Federal Tax Payable For The GRE

Income that remains in a GRE is taxed using the same rates as would be applicable to an individual. However, the GRE would not be able to claim personal tax credits under ITA 118 to reduce the amount of Tax Payable.

The after tax income of the GRE can be distributed tax free to the beneficiaries of the GRE.

Federal Tax Payable for the GRE would be calculated as follows:

Federal Tax Payable:

On First $45,916	$6,887
On Remaining $4,296 ($50,212 - $45,916) At 20.5 Percent	881
Federal Tax Payable Before Credits	$7,768
Federal Dividend Tax Credit [(6/11)($6,612)]	(3,607)
Foreign Tax Credit (See Note)	(3,300)
Federal Tax Payable	$ 861

Note The amount that can be deducted for the foreign tax credit is the lesser of the amount of foreign taxes withheld and an amount determined by the following formula:

[(Foreign Non-Business Income ÷ Adjusted Net Income)(Tax Payable Before Credits)]

= [($22,000 ÷ $50,212)($7,768)]

= $3,403

As this amount is more than the actual foreign taxes of $3,300 allocated to the GRE, the actual foreign taxes paid would be the lesser amount, and would be the foreign tax credit.

Note that, if the foreign taxes withheld had exceeded 15 percent of the gross amount of foreign income, the excess would have been deductible under ITA 20(11), rather than added to the amount of foreign tax withheld in the formula.

Self Study Solution Nineteen - 3

Parts A And B - Alternative One

The following tables assume that one-half of the dividend income will remain in the GRE. They provide the required information on Taxable Income and Tax Payable for the relevant taxation years:

Income Allocation	GRE	Rowena	Roger
Business Income	$ Nil	$12,000	$ 8,000
Interest	Nil	1,800	1,200
Non-Eligible Dividends Received	25,000	15,000	10,000
Dividend Gross Up (17%)	4,250	2,550	1,700
Net Rental Income (Note)	Nil	2,400	1,600
Net Income And Taxable Income	$29,250	$33,750	$22,500
Federal Income Tax At 15 Percent	$4,388	$5,063	$3,375
Basic Personal Credit	N/A	(1,745)	(1,745)
Federal Dividend Tax Credit [(21/29)(Gross Up)]	(3,078)	(1,847)	(1,231)
Federal Tax Payable (Total = $3,180)	$1,310	$1,471	$ 399

Note The $4,000 net rental income is calculated as the rent receipts of $12,000, less the operating expenses of $6,000 and CCA of $2,000. The CCA is claimed at the GRE level.

Parts A And B - Alternative Two

The following income allocation assumes that all of the GRE's income will be allocated to Rowena and Roger. This means that the Taxable Income and federal Tax Payable of the GRE will be nil. The calculations for Rowena and Roger for the year ending December 31, 2017 are as follows:

Income Allocation	Rowena	Roger
Business Income	$12,000	$ 8,000
Interest	1,800	1,200
Non-Eligible Dividends Received	30,000	20,000
Dividend Gross Up (17%)	5,100	3,400
Net Rental Income	2,400	1,600
Net And Taxable Income	**$51,300**	**$34,200**

Federal Income Tax:		
Roger: [(15%)($34,200)]		$5,130
Rowena: On First $45,916 At 15 Percent	$6,887	
Rowena: On Remaining $5,384		
($51,300 - $45,916) At 20.5 Percent	1,104	
Basic Personal Credit	(1,745)	(1,745)
Federal Dividend Tax Credit [(21/29)(Gross Up)]	(3,693)	(2,462)
Federal Tax Payable (Total = $3,476)	**$2,553**	**$ 923**

Part C - Comparison

The total federal Tax Payable in Alternative Two is $296 ($3,476 - $3,180) higher than the total in Alternative One. This difference reflects the fact that in Alternative Two, $5,384 of the total income was taxed at 20.5 percent, while in Alternative One, all of the income was taxed at 15 percent [(20.5% - 15%)($5,384) = $296].

Self Study Solution Nineteen - 4

Part A - Calculation Of Taxable Income

All amounts are allocated 30 percent to Malcolm, 50 percent to Maisy, and 20 percent to the trust. The Taxable Income of the two beneficiaries and the trust would be calculated as follows:

	Malcolm (30%)	Maisy (50%)	Trust (20%)
Interest On Government Bonds	$ 19,500	$ 32,500	$ 13,000
Eligible Dividends Received	75,000	125,000	50,000
Gross Up Of 38 Percent	28,500	47,500	19,000
Taxable Capital Gain On Land			
[(1/2)($2,300,000 - $1,430,000)]	130,500	217,500	87,000
Taxable Capital Gain On Building			
[(1/2)($4,560,000 - $3,840,000)]	108,000	180,000	72,000
Net Rental Income (Note)	183,000	305,000	122,000
Net And Taxable Income	**$544,500**	**$907,500**	**$363,000**

Note The net rental income, including the recapture of CCA, can be calculated as follows:

Revenues From Rental Property		$492,000
Cash Expenses On Rental Property		(342,000)
Recapture Of CCA:		
Capital Cost Of The Building	$3,840,000	
UCC	(3,380,000)	460,000
Net Rental Income, Including Recapture		**$610,000**

Part B - Tax Payable For The Trust

The federal Tax Payable for the trust is as follows:

Federal Tax Before Credits [(33%)($363,000)]	$119,790
Federal Dividend Tax Credit [(6/11)($19,000)]	(10,364
Federal Tax Payable	$ 109,426

As this trust is an inter vivos trust, all of its income is subject to federal tax at 33 percent [ITA 122(1)].

Part C - Dealing With The 21 Year Deemed Disposition Rule

The 21 year deemed disposition rule will have no effect on the trust or beneficiaries for the current year. It will necessitate a deemed disposition of any capital properties still held by the trust in 11 years. To defer the recognition of capital gains, assets with significant accrued gains should be transferred to the children before the trust has been in existence for 21 years.

Self Study Solution Nineteen - 5

A. It is an inter vivos trust. In less technical terms, it could also be described as a family trust in that all of the beneficiaries are family members. In addition, it could be referred to as partially discretionary in that the trustee determines the timing of the income payments.

B. As the trust is an inter vivos trust, the year end will have to be December 31 of each year.

C. All of the income that is allocated to Mr. Dion will be subject to the income attribution rules. As a consequence, it will be included in the Net Income For Tax Purposes of Mrs. Dion. This includes interest, dividends, and capital gains earned by the trust.

As the twins are over the age of 17, the attribution rules will not apply to their share of the trust's income. This means that the income that is allocated to them will be reported as a part of their Net Income For Tax Purposes.

As all of the trust's income is either attributed back to Mrs. Dion or allocated to beneficiaries, the trust's Net Income For Tax Purposes will be nil.

D. The answer here will depend on the terms of the loan to the trust as the rules for non-arm's length loans apply. If it is an interest free loan, the results will be the same as in Part C. That is, the income allocated to Mr. Dion will be attributed back to Mrs. Dion, while the income allocated to the twins will be included in their Net Income For Tax Purposes. This would also be the result if the interest rate on the loan was less than the prescribed rate.

Alternatively, if the loan paid interest at the prescribed rate or higher, the income attribution rules would not apply and the trust income allocated to Mr. Dion would be taxed in his hands. Note that the loan would have to have bona fide repayment terms and the interest would have to be paid within 30 days of the end of each calendar year.

E. ITA 74.5(3) indicates that the income attribution rules do not apply to any income or loss from property that relates to the period throughout which the individuals are living separate and apart because of a breakdown of their marriage or common-law partnership. The attribution rules do not apply to income that accrues subsequent to a separation.

Self Study Solution Nineteen - 6

Part A - Trust For Daughter

The first trust created is a testamentary trust for the benefit of Mrs. Turner's daughter, Melanie. When there is a transfer of assets at death to any taxpayer other than a spouse or a spousal trust, there is a deemed disposition with proceeds equal to fair market value. Capital gains on all of the assets transferred would need to be realized along with recapture of CCA on the warehouse building.

The principal residence exemption could be used to eliminate the $165,000 [($120,000 - $20,000) + ($145,000 - $80,000)] capital gain on the principal residence. Melanie will not have a taxable benefit from use of the residence. However, since the trust pays for the upkeep and maintenance of the residence, the trust can deduct the costs and they are taxable as income to Melanie.

The capital gain and recapture on the disposition of the warehouse building would be included in Mrs. Turner's final tax return. The taxable capital gain on the warehouse land is $10,000 [(1/2)($75,000 - $55,000)]. As the fair market value of the warehouse is equal to its capital cost, there is no capital gain on the warehouse building. However, there would be $40,000 ($85,000 - $45,000) of recaptured CCA. This amount would be included in Mrs. Turner's final tax return.

The trust will be deemed to acquire all of the assets at their fair market values. In the case of the warehouse land, the adjusted cost base will be the fair market value of $75,000. In the case of the warehouse building, the capital cost and the new UCC will be the fair market value of $85,000 which is equal to its original cost.

Part A - Trust For Husband

The second trust appears to be a qualifying spousal trust. Where there is a transfer at death to a qualifying spousal trust, the transfer is deemed to be a disposition with proceeds equal to the deceased taxpayer's tax cost. This would be the capital cost of the cottage and stock portfolio and, as a consequence of using this value, the transfer of assets to the trust will have no tax consequences for Mrs. Turner's final tax return.

The trust will be deemed to have acquired all of the assets at the same capital cost values that were used as proceeds of disposition by Mrs. Turner.

Part B - Death Of Husband

Unless Mr. West has remarried with great haste and can pass these assets on to a new spouse or qualifying spousal trust, his death will result in a deemed disposition of the trust's assets for proceeds equal to fair market value. In the case of the cottage, there is a capital gain of $170,000 [($200,000 - $40,000) + ($122,000 - $112,000)], one-half, or $85,000 of which is taxable. On the stock market portfolio there will be a taxable capital gain of $30,000 [(1/2)($280,000 - $220,000)].

Mr. West's death would have no effect on Mrs. Turner's final return or tax effect on Melanie. Of course if Melanie is a beneficiary in Mr. West's will, his death will result in additional income and income tax for Melanie in the future, but this information is not in the problem.

Part C - Graduated Rate Estate

The principal advantage of a Graduated Rate Estate is that any income that is not distributed is taxed at graduated rates, rather than at the maximum federal rate of 33 percent. As the problem does not state the marginal tax rates for either Mr. Turner or Melanie, we cannot determine whether or not this would be advantageous. If either of their marginal rates are above the minimum 15 percent rate, GRE status for the income producing properties could be advantageous.

Given Mr. West's short remaining life, any benefits from the GRE would be quite limited in his case.

Chapter 19 Learning Objectives

After completing Chapter 19, you should be able to:

1. Explain the basic concepts of trusts (paragraph [P hereafter] 19-1 to 19-16).
2. Explain the difference between a trust and an estate, including the concept of a GRE (P 19-17 to 19-23).
3. Describe the procedures required to establish a trust (P 19-24 to 19-27).
4. Describe the procedures applicable to the filing of trust tax and information returns (P 19-28 to 19-29).
5. List the major non-tax reasons for using trusts (P 19-30 and 19-31).

---

6. Describe the different classifications of trusts (P 19-32 to 19-51).
7. Explain the basic model for the taxation of trusts (P 19-52 and 19-55).
8. Describe the rollovers available for contributions to a trust (P 19-56 to 19-68).
9. Describe the rollovers available to transfer assets to the capital beneficiaries of a trust (P 19-69 to 19-74).
10. Apply the deemed disposition rules after a trust has existed for 21 years and on the death of a settlor of an alter ego trust or survivor spouse of a qualifying spousal trust (P 19-75 to 19-78).

---

11. Calculate the Net Income For Tax Purposes and Taxable Income of a trust (P 19-79 to 19-92).
12. Describe the provisions relating to income allocations to beneficiaries (P 19-93 to 19-112).
13. Calculate the Tax Payable for testamentary and inter vivos trusts (P 19-113 to 19-125).
14. Explain how the income attribution rules may be applicable to trusts and describe any related tax planning considerations (P 19-126 to 19-131).
15. Explain the tax treatment of the purchase and sale of an interest in a trust (P 19-132 to 19-137).

---

16. Describe the major tax planning factors that should be considered when evaluating various types of trusts such as family, spousal and alter ego (P 19-138 to 19-151).
17. List the non-tax and tax considerations that should be considered in estate planning (P 19-152 to 19-156).
18. Explain the objectives of an estate freeze (P 19-157 and 19-158).
19. Describe the estate freeze techniques that do not involve rollovers (P 19-159 to 19-166).
20. Describe the application of an ITA 86(1) share exchange to implement an estate freeze (P 19-167 to 19-175).
21. List the major considerations involved in choosing between a Section 85 and Section 86 rollover when implementing an estate freeze (P 19-176 to 19-178).

CHAPTER 20

How To Work Through Chapter 20

We recommend the following approach in dealing with the material in this Chapter:

Subjects Covered In Chapter
- Read paragraph 20-1 to 20-5 (in the textbook).

Part I Tax On Non-Residents - Introduction
- Read paragraph 20-6 to 20-14.

Non-Residents Carrying On Business In Canada - Part I Tax
- Read paragraph 20-15 to 20-20.
- Do Exercise Twenty-1 and check the solution in this Study Guide.

Non-Residents Earning Employment Income In Canada - Part I Tax
- Read paragraph 20-21 to 20-25.
- Do Exercises Twenty-2 and Twenty-3 and check the solutions in this Study Guide.

Non-Residents Disposing Of Taxable Canadian Property - Part I Tax
- Read paragraph 20-26 to 20-30.
- Do Exercise Twenty-4 and check the solution in this Study Guide.
- Do Self Study Problem Twenty-1 and check the solution in this Study Guide.

Part XIII Tax On Non-Residents - Introduction And Applicability
- Read paragraph 20-31 to 20-37.

Interest Income Earned By Non-Residents - Part XIII Tax
- Read paragraph 20-38 to 20-41.
- Do Exercise Twenty-5 and check the solution in this Study Guide.

Dividend, Royalty And Rental Income Earned By Non-Residents - Part XIII Tax
- Read paragraph 20-42 to 20-52.
- Do Exercise Twenty-6 and check the solution in this Study Guide.

Pension And Other Benefits Earned By Non-Residents - Part XIII Tax
- Read paragraph 20-53 to 20-62.
- Do Self Study Problem Twenty-2 and check the solution in this Study Guide.

Entering Canada - Immigration
- Read paragraph 20-63 to 20-65.

Departing From Canada - Emigration

- Read paragraph 20-66.
- Do Exercises Twenty-7 and Twenty-8 and check the solutions in this Study Guide.
- Read paragraph 20-67 to 20-74.
- Do Exercise Twenty-9 and check the solution in this Study Guide.
- Read paragraph 20-75 to 20-79.
- Do Self Study Problem Twenty-3 and check the solution in this Study Guide.
- Read paragraph 20-80 to 20-87.
- Do Exercise Twenty-10 and check the solution in this Study Guide.

Foreign Source Income Of Canadian Residents - Introduction

- Read paragraph 20-88 to 20-90.

Foreign Source Income Of Canadian Residents - Reporting Requirements (T1135)

- Read paragraph 20-91 to 20-98.
- Do Exercise Twenty-11 and check the solution in this Study Guide.
- Do Self Study Problem Twenty-4 and check the solution in this Study Guide.

Foreign Source Employment Income Of Canadian Residents

- Read paragraph 20-99 to 20-100.
- Do Self Study Problem Twenty-5 and check the solution in this Study Guide.

Foreign Source Unincorporated Business Income Of Canadian Residents

- Read paragraph 20-101 to 20-103.
- Do Exercise Twenty-12 and check the solution in this Study Guide.

Foreign Source Interest Income Of Canadian Residents

- Read paragraph 20-104 and 20-105.

Foreign Source Capital Gains Of Canadian Residents

- Read paragraph 20-106 and 20-107.

Foreign Source Dividend Income Of Canadian Residents - Including From Foreign Affiliates And FAPI

- Read paragraph 20-108 to 20-120.
- Do Self Study Problem Twenty-6 and check the solution in this Study Guide.
- Read paragraph 20-121 to 20-125.
- Do Exercise Twenty-13 and check the solution in this Study Guide.
- Read paragraph 20-126 to 20-151.
- Do Exercise Twenty-14 and check the solution in this Study Guide.
- Read paragraph 20-152 and 20-153.
- Do Exercise Twenty-15 and check the solution in this Study Guide.
- Do Self Study Problem Twenty-7 and check the solution in this Study Guide.

To Complete This Chapter

- If you would like more practice in problem solving, do the Supplementary Self Study Problems for the chapter. These problems and solutions are available on the Companion Website.
- Review the Key Terms Used In This Chapter in the textbook at the end of Chapter 20. Consult the Glossary for the meaning of any key terms you do not know.
- Test yourself with the Chapter 20 Glossary Flashcards available on the Companion Website.
- Ensure you have achieved the Chapter 20 Learning Objectives listed in this Study Guide.
- As a review, we recommend you view the PowerPoint presentation for Chapter 20 that is on the Companion Website.

Practice Examination

- Write the Practice Examination for Chapter 20 that is on the Companion Website. Mark your examination using the Practice Examination Solution that is on the Companion Website.

Solutions to Chapter Twenty Exercises

Exercise Twenty - 1 Solution

Case 1 Jazzco is not carrying on business in Canada and would not be subject to Canadian taxes.

Case 2 Jazzco is carrying on business in Canada in a permanent establishment located in Toronto. Therefore, Jazzco is taxable in Canada under ITA 2(3) on the profits attributable to the Canadian factory.

Case 3 The tax treaty allows Canada to tax business income only if such income is attributable to a permanent establishment in Canada. The warehouse constitutes a fixed place of business regardless of whether it is owned or leased. However, since it appears to be used exclusively to maintain an inventory for delivery, under the Canada/U.S. tax treaty, it would be an excluded facility and would not be considered to be a permanent establishment. Jazzco would not be taxable under ITA 2(3) on its Canadian profits. The fact that the employee acts on behalf of the non-resident employer would not alter the conclusion since the employee does not have the authority to conclude contracts.

Case 4 In this Case, because the employee has authority to conclude contracts on behalf of a non-resident enterprise, the employee is deemed to be a permanent establishment. This means that Jazzco is taxable in Canada under ITA 2(3) on its business profits attributable to the permanent establishment (i.e., the employee).

Case 5 Since the warehouse is not used exclusively for maintaining an inventory, the permanent establishment exception in the tax treaty would not apply with the result that profits attributable to that warehouse would be taxable in Canada.

Exercise Twenty - 2 Solution

Dawn is an individual who has become a resident of another country, but continues to receive remuneration from a resident Canadian taxpayer. Given that the tax treaty exempts her salary from taxation in Egypt, ITA 115(2) deems her to be employed in Canada and, as a consequence, she would be subject to Canadian taxes on her salary.

Exercise Twenty - 3 Solution

Case 1 The employment income is taxable in Canada. The Canada/U.S. tax treaty allows Canada to tax employment income earned in Canada unless either of two exceptions is applicable. The first exception is the $10,000 rule. This exception however does not apply since David earned $11,200 Canadian in 2017 [($2,800)(4 months)]. The second exception is the 183 day rule. Although David was in Canada for only 122 days during 2017 and therefore met the first part of the test, he failed the remaining part of the test since the employer was a Canadian resident and could deduct the payments.

Case 2 The employment income is not taxable in Canada. The 183 day rule exempts the income from Canadian taxation because the employer was not resident in Canada, did not have a permanent establishment in Canada, and could not deduct the payments for Canadian tax purposes.

Case 3 The employment income is taxable in Canada. The Canada/U.S. tax treaty would exempt the income from Canadian tax if the amount was less than $10,000 Canadian, or if Sandra spent less than 183 days in Canada in any 12 month period beginning or ending in 2017. As she earned $50,000 Canadian and spent 238 days at her job in Canada, neither of these exceptions are applicable.

Solutions to Chapter Twenty Exercises

Exercise Twenty - 4 Solution

Case 1 Nancy is not taxable on the gain. As a non-resident, Nancy is only taxable in Canada on the disposition of taxable Canadian property. Shares of a resident public company are only taxable Canadian property if Nancy had owned more than 25 percent of the issued shares of any class of the company in the 60 months preceding the disposition.

Case 2 Joe is taxable on the gain. The condo is taxable Canadian property since it is real property (e.g. land and buildings) situated in Canada. The Canada/U.S. tax treaty gives Canada the right to tax such gains. The property is not exempt from Canadian tax as a principal residence since Joe did not acquire the condo for his own habitation.

Case 3 Joe would be taxable on the gain on the shares. Shares of an unlisted corporation are taxable Canadian property if at any time within the preceding 60 months more than 50 percent of the fair market value of the company is derived from Canadian real property. In addition, the Canada/U.S. tax treaty allows Canada to tax the gain on the disposition of shares if the corporation is resident in Canada and the value of the shares is derived principally from real property situated in Canada.

Case 4 Joe would not be taxable on the gain on the shares. The shares are taxable Canadian property because they represent shares of an unlisted non-resident corporation that, at some time in the 60 months preceding the disposition, derived more than 50 percent of their value from taxable Canadian property. However, the Canada/U.S. tax treaty does not list this as one of the items where Canada is allowed to tax U.S. residents.

Exercise Twenty - 5 Solution

Case 1 As Jason is at arm's length from the bank and the interest is not participating debt interest, he would not be subject to Part XIII tax.

Case 2 As Janice is at arm's length with the Canadian government and the interest is not participating debt interest, the interest would not be subject to Part XIII tax. Note that interest on Canada Savings Bonds is fully exempt interest, but this fact does not affect the result in this case.

Case 3 As Julian is at arm's length from the bank and the interest is not participating debt interest, he would not have to withhold Part XIII tax.

Case 4 The Canada/U.S. tax treaty exempts U.S. residents from Part XIII tax. This means that Jasmine does not have to withhold Part XIII tax despite the fact that her brother is a non-arm's length party.

Exercise Twenty - 6 Solution

Case 1 Rentco appears to be carrying on business in Canada through a permanent establishment. As a result, no Part XIII tax is payable. However, Rentco would be subject to Part I tax on its income attributable to the permanent establishment in Saskatchewan.

Case 2 Jack would be subject to Part XIII tax of $10,500 [(25%)($42,000)]. This represents an effective tax rate of 37.5 percent on his net rental income of $28,000. Alternatively, Jack could elect under ITA 216 to be taxed under Part I on the net rental income of $28,000 ($42,000 - $14,000). Whether this is would be a good alternative depends on Jack's marginal tax rate. The break-even rate would be 37.5 percent ($10,500 ÷ $28,000). If his marginal rate is below this, taxation under Part I would be the better alternative. If his marginal rate exceeds 37.5 percent, taxation under Part XIII would be preferable.

Case 3 Jack would be subject to Part XIII tax on the gross rents received for the boats unless he would be considered to be carrying on a business. However, the Canada/U.S. tax treaty reduces the withholding tax to 10 percent of the gross rents received, or $800. Note that Jack would not be eligible to elect under ITA 216 to be taxed under Part I on the boat rents, since this election is generally restricted to real property.

Exercise Twenty - 7 Solution

There would be a deemed disposition on her departure, leaving her liable for the taxes on a $10,500 [(1/2)($49,000 - $28,000)] taxable capital gain.

Exercise Twenty - 8 Solution

As real property is exempt from the deemed disposition provision contained in ITA 128.1(4)(b), there would be no tax consequences with respect to the rental property at the time of Mr. Chrysler's departure. However, real property is Taxable Canadian Property and, as a consequence, he would be liable for Canadian taxes on both recapture and capital gains resulting from a subsequent sale of the property, even though he will be a non-resident.

Exercise Twenty - 9 Solution

With respect to the shares of the Canadian private company, there would be a required deemed disposition, resulting in a taxable capital gain of $57,500 [(1/2)($235,000 - $120,000)]. In the absence of an election on the rental property, this would be the only tax consequence resulting from her departure.

However, if Ms. Lopez elects under ITA 128.1(4)(d) to have a deemed disposition on her rental property, the results will be as follows:

Deemed Proceeds Of Disposition For Land	$30,000
Adjusted Cost Base	(60,000)
Capital Gain (Loss) On Land	($30,000)

UCC Of Building	$142,000
Lesser Of:	
Capital Cost = $160,000	
Deemed Proceeds Of Disposition = $100,000	(100,000)
Terminal Loss	$42,000

The net result would be as follows:

Taxable Capital Gain On Shares	$57,500
Allowable Capital Loss On Land [(1/2)($30,000)]	(15,000)
Terminal Loss On Building	(42,000)
Net Income Inclusion	$ 500

Exercise Twenty - 10 Solution

In the absence of ITA 128.1(4)(b)(iv), there would be a deemed disposition of both the U.K. shares and the Canadian shares at the time of Mr. Brookings' departure from Canada. As it appears that he has been in Canada for less than 60 months in the last 10 years, there will be no deemed disposition of the U.K. shares that he owned prior to his arrival in Canada. There will, however, be a deemed disposition of the Canadian shares acquired during his stay in Canada. This will result in a taxable capital gain of $8,500 [(1/2)($92,000 - $75,000)].

There will be no deemed disposition of the vacant Canadian land because real property is exempt from the deemed disposition requirement of ITA 128.1(4)(b). Note, however, that vacant land is Taxable Canadian Property. This means that any gain resulting from its disposition will be subject to Canadian taxes, without regard to whether the vendor is a Canadian resident.

Exercise Twenty - 11 Solution

The cost of Simon's foreign investments total £197,000 (£52,000 + £145,000) which put him over the $100,000 Canadian reporting limit [(£197,000)($1.70) = $334,900] for filing Form T1135 and over the $250,000 limit for the simplified method. He is required to report the following information on the T1135:

Funds Held Outside Canada
- The name of the bank that holds the funds - Bank of Scotland
- The country code for the country of residence of the bank (Scotland) - GBR (Available from the CRA website)
- The maximum amount of funds held during the year - $88,400 [(£52,000)($1.70)]
- The funds held at year end - $69,700 [(£41,000)($1.70)]
- Income from the property - $1,700 [(£1,000)($1.70)]

Indebtedness Owed By A Non-Resident
- A description of the indebtedness - Interest free loan to brother-in-law
- The country code for the non-resident issuer's country of residence (Scotland) - GBR (Available from the CRA website)
- The maximum cost amount during the year - $246,500 [(£145,000)($1.70)]
- The year end cost amount - $246,500 [(£145,000)($1.70)]
- The income or loss - Nil
- The gain or loss on disposition - N/A

Exercise Twenty - 12 Solution

The gross amount of the U.S. business income will be subject to tax in Canada. Jason's foreign business income tax credit is $1,800, the lesser of the $1,800 foreign tax withheld and $3,780 [($18,000 ÷ $100,000)($21,000)].

The required solution would be as follows:

Gross Foreign Business Income	$18,000
Canadian Tax Rate	44%
Canadian Tax Payable	$ 7,920
Foreign Tax Credit = Foreign Tax Withheld	(1,800)
Net Canadian Tax Payable	$ 6,120
Foreign Tax Withheld	1,800
Total Taxes Payable	$ 7,920

Based on these figures, his after tax retention and overall tax rate on his foreign source income would be as follows:

After Tax Retention ($18,000 - $7,920)	$10,080
Overall Tax Rate ($7,920 ÷ $18,000)	44%

Exercise Twenty - 13 Solution

Forco 1 Canvest has the required 1 percent investment and, with its related subsidiary, has the required 10 percent investment. Forco 1 is a foreign affiliate.

Forco 2 Canvest has the required 1 percent investment. However, as it is not related to any of the other shareholders, the 10 percent test is not met. This means that Forco 2 is not a foreign affiliate.

Forco 3 Canvest has the required 1 percent investment and, with the controlling shareholder's spouse (a related person), has the required 10 percent investment. Forco 3 is a foreign affiliate.

Exercise Twenty - 14 Solution

Since Forco is a controlled foreign affiliate of Canco, Canco must accrue its proportionate share (100%) of Forco's investment income. The required calculations are as follows:

FAPI [ITA 91(1)]	$100,000
Deduct Lesser Of:	
• FAPI = $100,000	
• ITA 91(4) Deduction [(4)(18%)($100,000)]	(72,000)
Net Addition To Net Income For Tax Purposes	$ 28,000

Exercise Twenty - 15 Solution

Foreign Source Dividend – ITA 90(1)	$82,000
Deduct Lesser Of:	
• Previous FAPI After ITA 91(4) Deduction = $28,000	
• Dividend Received = $82,000	(28,000)
Net Addition To Net Income For Tax Purposes	$54,000

Note that the additions to Net Income For Tax Purposes for the two years total $82,000 ($28,000 + $54,000). This is equal to the $100,000, less the $18,000 in taxes paid in the foreign jurisdiction. Had there been any withholding taxes on the dividend, they would not have been eligible for a foreign tax credit.

While this is not a required part of the problem, you should note that Taxable Income and Tax Payable would be nil in this example. There would be a deduction under ITA 113(1)(b) equal to $54,000 [($18,000)(4 - 1). The resulting Taxable Income of nil reflects the fact that on Forco's income of $100,000, taxes at the usual Canadian rate of 25 percent have already been paid. This $25,000 [(25%)($100,000)] is made up of the $18,000 [(18%)($100,000)] paid by Forco in the foreign jurisdiction, plus the $7,000 [(25%)($28,000)] of Canadian taxes on Canco's 2017 addition to Net Income For Tax Purposes.

Self Study Solution Twenty - 1

Case A

Marion would be generally taxable under ITA 2(3). As her stay in Canada was less than 183 days, there is the possibility that she would be exempted from this taxation under the Canada/U.S. tax treaty. However, her employment income exceeds $10,000 and it would be deductible to her Canadian employer. Therefore, she is not exempted under the treaty and Part I tax would be applicable.

Case B

Marion would be generally taxable under ITA 2(3). However, she would be exempt under the Canada/U.S. tax treaty. She is in Canada for less than 183 days and, while her income exceeds the $10,000 threshold, it is not being deducted by a Canadian employer. This means that Part I tax would not be applicable.

Case C

The warehouse is a fixed place of business that could be viewed as a permanent establishment. However, it is used exclusively for holding inventories and, given this, it is specifically excluded from being considered a permanent establishment by the Canada/U.S. tax treaty. This means that Delcar is not carrying on business in Canada and would not be subject to Part I tax.

Case D

The warehouse is a fixed place of business that would be viewed as a permanent establishment. This would suggest the Company is earning business income in Canada and would be subject, under ITA 2(3), to Part I tax. As it is used as an office as well as a facility for holding inventories, it would not be an excluded facility under the Canada/U.S. tax treaty. Therefore, Part I tax would be applicable.

Case E

Shares of unlisted Canadian companies are viewed as Taxable Canadian Property if, within the preceding 60 months, more than 50 percent of their value is derived from Canadian real property. This means that Michael's shares would be Taxable Canadian Property and the gain would be taxable under ITA 2(3). Further, under the Canada/U.S. tax treaty, this is one of the specific types of property where gains accruing to U.S. residents are subject to Canadian tax. Therefore, Part I tax would be applicable.

Case F

Shares of unlisted companies are viewed as Taxable Canadian Property if, within the preceding 60 months, more than 50 percent of their value is derived from Canadian real property. This means that Michael's shares would be Taxable Canadian Property and the gain would generally be taxable under ITA 2(3). However, because it is not a "Canadian" corporation, it is not on the Canada/U.S. tax treaty list of Taxable Canadian Property where gains accruing to U.S. residents are subject to Canadian tax. Therefore, Michael's gain on the shares would not be taxable under ITA 2(3) and Part I tax would not be applicable.

Self Study Solution Twenty - 2

Case A

The interest she has received is not from holding participating debt and she is at arm's length with the bank. The interest would not be subject to Part XIII tax.

Case B

As the amount of interest is calculated on the basis of the corporation's revenues, it would appear that Mark is receiving interest on a participating debt security. The interest would be subject to Part XIII tax.

Case C

Because the interest is from participating debt, it would normally be subject to Part XIII tax. However, the Canada/U.S. tax treaty exempts U.S. residents from all Canadian taxation on interest income. The interest would not be subject to Part XIII tax.

Case D

As she is not a resident of a country with which Canada has a tax treaty, Darlene would be subject to Part XIII tax at a rate of 25 percent. Depending on whether she uses the available election to be taxed under Part I, the Tax Payable would be as follows:

Without Election - Part XIII [(25%)($35,000)]	$8,750

With Election - Part I [(15%)(148%*)($35,000 - $27,000)]	$1,776

*The 148% reflects the additional federal tax on individual income that is not earned in a province.

The use of the election is clearly desirable in this Case.

Case E

The Canada/U.S. tax treaty reduces the Part XIII rate on rental properties that are not real property from 25 to 10 percent. As Darlene is renting out real property, the 25 percent rate is applicable and the results are the same as Case D. Here again, the use of the election is clearly desirable.

Case F

Dividends from Canadian companies that are received by non-residents are subject to Part XIII tax. Under the Canada/U.S. tax treaty the statutory 25 percent rate is reduced to either 5 percent or 15 percent. Although Brian owns more than 10 percent of the voting shares of the Canadian corporation, he is an individual, not a corporation, so the applicable rate is 15 percent, not 5 percent. Brian's Part XIII tax payable would be $3,300 [(15%)($22,000)].

Self Study Solution Twenty - 3

Immediate Tax Consequences

If Debbie's husband defers his move for six months, the deemed date of non-residence for Debbie will be when he moves to Hong Kong. As discussed later under Planning Points, this may not be advantageous. The following calculation assumes that Debbie becomes a non-resident on her departure on November 1, 2017.

Debbie will have a deemed disposition of all property except Canadian real estate and RRSPs. The deemed dispositions would result in the following minimum tax payable:

Tax On Deemed Dispositions Of Capital Assets

Description	ACB	FMV	Gain (Loss)
Shares in CCPC Inc.	$ 90,000	$140,000	$ 50,000
Shares in Sorrento Co.	180,000	110,000	(70,000)
Sports car (Note 1)	18,000	15,000	Nil
Paintings	50,000	175,000	125,000
Net Capital Gains			$105,000
Inclusion Rate			1/2
Taxable Capital Gains			$ 52,500
Maximum Deemed Security Under ITA 220(4.51)			(50,000)
Balance			$ 2,500
Personal Tax Rate			45%
Personal Tax Payable (Note 2)			$ 1,125

Note 1   Losses on personal use property are not deductible.

Note 2   At her departure, $1,125 is the maximum amount of tax that would be paid. Further, if some form of security is provided, even this amount of tax could be deferred until the assets are sold.

Planning Points

Non-Resident Date   If Debbie's husband defers his move for six months, Debbie's date of non-residence will be when he moves to Hong Kong. This may be undesirable for Debbie, as the Hong Kong tax rates are less than Canadian rates. Until Debbie is officially a non-resident, all of her income will have to be reported in Canada, and will be subject to the higher Canadian tax rates. In addition, the fair market values used in the deemed disposition calculation would likely be different.

As Debbie's husband will be commuting anyway, it could be more advantageous for him to work from his Hong Kong base, and to wind up his Canadian client affairs. In this way, the non-resident date could be advanced and a tax savings would be realized, as well as eliminating uncertainty with regards to the tax on the deemed dispositions.

Canadian Real Property   Since she is not planning to sell her house and chalet at this point, there would be no immediate tax consequences. However, there would be a deferred gain calculated as follows:

Description	ACB	FMV	Deferred Gain
House	$300,000	$450,000	$150,000
Whistler ski chalet	125,000	185,000	60,000

Under ITA 128.1(4)(d), taxpayers can elect to have a deemed disposition on certain assets, such as real property, where a deemed disposition is not automatic. The ITA 128.1(4)(d) election could be used to trigger a deemed disposition on the principal residence and/or the cottage. Debbie should elect to have a deemed disposition on both properties.

As the $20,000 ($60,000/3) annual gain on the Whistler ski chalet is greater than the $15,000 ($150,000/10) annual gain on the house, Debbie should designate the ski chalet as the family's principal residence for 2016 and 2017 thereby eliminating the entire gain on this property (because of the plus one year rule for principal residences, only two years need to be designated to eliminate all three years of the gain). The house can then be designated as the principal residence from 2008 to 2015. This results in only one year of the gain on the house being taxable (again, due to the plus one year rule for principal residences, designating eight years will eliminate nine years of the gain).

If Debbie did not become a non-resident until 2018, the numbers in the calculation would have to be revised.

Moving Expenses   In order for moving costs to be deductible for Canadian tax purposes, the taxpayer's residence must be in Canada both before and after the move (see Chapter 9). As Debbie is moving to Hong Kong, none of her moving costs would be deductible for Canadian tax purposes.

Since the $50,000 allowance would be foreign employment income, it may be taxable in Canada, depending on the date it is paid and the date she ceases to be a resident. If the allowance is paid while Debbie is still considered a Canadian resident (for example paid while her husband is living in Vancouver), it would be part of her worldwide income and subject to Canadian income tax.

If the allowance is paid after Debbie becomes a non-resident, it would then be foreign employment income earned by a non-resident which would have no Canadian tax implications.

RRSP   Debbie will have relatively high income in 2017, so she should not collapse her RRSP while resident in Canada in 2017. If she becomes a non-resident in 2018, she could collapse some of the RRSP early that year, to be taxed at the low Canadian personal tax rates. This assumes that Debbie has no other Canadian income in 2018. It may be more advantageous for Debbie to collapse the RRSP after becoming a non-resident. At that time, a 25 percent Part XIII tax would apply in Canada, and there would likely not be any applicable Hong Kong income tax. Alternatively, Debbie can leave the RRSP invested in Canada and receive withdrawals, after withholding taxes are applied, in later years.

Rental Income   If the house and ski chalet are rented, a 25 percent Part XIII tax will apply to the gross rents received. Debbie can also elect to have the rental income taxed under Part I of the *Income Tax Act*. This may be preferable in that she can deduct expenses against the gross rents if she makes this election.

Self Study Solution Twenty - 4

A. No foreign investment reporting is required as the total amount is less than $100,000.

B. Foreign investment reporting is not required. Since the cottage is personal use property, the fact that the cost is greater than $100,000 is not relevant. The fair market value is also not relevant.

C. Foreign investment reporting is not required. The cost of the one-half of the shares in the trading account is less than $100,000 [(1/2)($112,000) = $56,000]. The current fair market price is not relevant. Specified foreign property held in an RRSP is excluded from form T1135 reporting requirements.

D. No foreign investment reporting is required as the assets are used in an active business.

Self Study Solution Twenty - 5

A. Because he is a resident of Canada, the hockey player will have all US$14,000 of hockey school income subject to tax in Canada. With respect to U.S. taxation, he would not have a tax obligation in that country because his total earnings are only $7,000. The Canada/U.S. tax treaty exempts non-residents from U.S. taxation when their earnings in that country are less than $10,000.

B. Because the expert is a resident of Canada, the full $150,000 of income would be subject to tax in Canada. He would not be taxed in the U.S. because the provisions of the Canada/U.S. tax treaty exempt Canadian residents from U.S. taxation provided they are in the U.S. less than 183 days, their employer does not have a permanent establishment in the U.S., and their employer does not deduct the compensation in computing U.S. taxes. The expert was in the U.S. for only 180 days [(3)(60)], and his compensation is paid by a Canadian company.

Self Study Solution Twenty - 6

The Hispanic Ltd. tax withholding equals 25 percent ($5,750 ÷ $23,000) of the dividend paid. The Deutsch Inc. tax withholding equals 10 percent ($1,400 ÷ $14,000) of the dividend paid. As the foreign non-business tax credit is limited to 15 percent, the additional 10 percent ($2,300) withheld by Foreign Country 1 will have to be deducted in the determination of Mona's Net Income For Tax Purposes.

Net Employment Income	$ 87,000
Hispanic Ltd. Gross Dividends (No Gross Up)	23,000
Deutsch Inc. Gross Dividends (No Gross Up)	14,000
Excess Withholding [(25% - 15%)($23,000)]	(2,300)
Net Income For Tax Purposes And Taxable Income	$121,700

Using this result, her federal Tax Payable would be calculated as follows:

Tax On First $91,831		$16,300
Tax On Next $29,869 ($121,700 - $91,831 At 26%)		7,766
Tax Payable Before Credits		$24,066
Basic Personal Credit	($11,635)	
EI	(836)	
CPP	(2,564)	
Canada Employment	(1,178)	
Total Credit Amount	($16,213)	
Applicable Rate	15%	(2,432)
Tax Otherwise Payable		$21,634
Foreign Tax Credits (See Note)		
Hispanic Ltd.		(3,450)
Deutsch Inc.		(1,400)
Federal Tax Payable		$16,784

Note The foreign non-business tax credits are calculated on a country by country basis (see Chapter 11).

The tax credit on the Hispanic Ltd. shares would be the lesser of:

- Amount Withheld (Limited To 15%) = [(15%)($23,000)] = $3,450

- $\left[\dfrac{\text{Foreign Non - Business Income}}{\text{Adjusted Division B Income}}\right]\left(\text{Tax Otherwise Payable}\right)$

$$= \left[\dfrac{\$23,000}{\$121,700}\right]\left(\$21,634\right) = \$4,089$$

The tax credit on the Deutsch Inc. shares would be the lesser of:

- Amount Withheld (Less Than 15%) = $1,400

- $\left[\dfrac{\text{Foreign Non - Business Income}}{\text{Adjusted Division B Income}}\right]\left(\text{Tax Otherwise Payable}\right)$

$$= \left[\dfrac{\$14,000}{\$121,700}\right]\left(\$21,634\right) = \$2,489$$

Self Study Solution Twenty - 7

Alta Inc. Dividends

As BK Inc. owns more than 10 percent of the Alta Inc. shares, Alta Inc. is a foreign affiliate of BK Inc. Alta Inc. is operating in a country with which Canada has a tax treaty. In addition, all of its income is from active business activities. Given this, all of the dividend is being paid from Exempt Surplus. This means that, while the pre-withholding amount of the dividend will be included in Net Income For Tax Purposes, this amount can be deducted in full under ITA 113(1)(a).

Bolt Ltd. Dividends

While Bolt Ltd. earns all of its income through active business activities, it is not located in a country which has a tax treaty or a TIEA with Canada. Given this, the dividend will be paid from Taxable Surplus. It will be included in Net Income For Tax Purposes and not deductible under ITA 113(1)(a). However, it will be eligible for a deduction under ITA 113(1)(b) for taxes paid by Bolt Ltd. in the foreign jurisdiction, as well as a deduction under ITA 113(1)(c) for taxes withheld on the distribution to BK Inc.

Taxable Income And Tax Payable Calculation

The required calculations for Taxable Income and Tax Payable would be as follows:

Alta Inc. Dividends (Before Withholding)	$ 34,000
Bolt Ltd. Dividends (Before Withholding)	76,000
Addition To Net Income For Tax Purposes	$110,000
Deductions:	
ITA 113(1)(a) Alta Dividends	(34,000)
ITA 113(1)(b) - Note 1	(12,000)
ITA 113(1)(c) - Note 2	(45,600)
Taxable Income	$ 18,400
Rate	25%
Canadian Tax Payable	$ 4,600

Note 1 Given Bolt's local tax rate of 5 percent, the pre-tax income that formed the base for the dividend to BK Inc. was $80,000 [$76,000 ÷ (1 - 5%)]. This means that the local taxes paid by Bolt were $4,000 [(5%)($80,000)] and that the ITA 113(1)(b) deduction would be $12,000 [($4,000)(3)]. See the text for an explanation of the relevant factor of 3.

Note 2 Taxes withheld were $11,400. Given this, the ITA 113(1)(c) deduction is equal to $45,600 [($11,400)(4)]. See the text for an explanation of the relevant factor of 4.

Verification

As indicated in the text, the goal here is to have foreign affiliate dividends paid from Taxable Surplus subject to total Canadian and foreign taxes at a rate of 25 percent. The preceding calculation has achieved this goal as supported by the following calculations:

Bolt's Pre-Tax Income [$76,000 ÷ (1 - 5%)]	$80,000
Rate	25%
Total Tax At 25% Rate	$20,000
Foreign Tax Paid On Bolt's Income [(5%)($80,000)]	$ 4,000
Taxes Withheld From Dividend	11,400
Canadian Tax Payable	4,600
Total Tax Paid	$20,000

Chapter 20 Learning Objectives

After completing Chapter 20, you should be able to:

1. Describe the role of international tax treaties (paragraph [P hereafter] P 20-1 to 20-5).
2. Describe the liability for Part I tax of non-residents earning Canadian source income from business, employment and the disposition of taxable Canadian property (P 20-6 to 20-30).
3. Describe the liability for Part XIII tax of non-residents earning Canadian source property income including income from interest, dividends, royalties, rents and pensions (P 20-31 to 20-62).
4. Describe the deemed disposition/reacquisition provisions related to immigration to Canada (P 20-63 to 20-65).
5. Describe the tax provisions related to emigration from Canada, including those related to elective dispositions and security for departure tax (P 20-66 to 20-79).

6. Describe the provisions available for unwinding a deemed disposition on departure from Canada (P 20-80 to 20-84).
7. Explain the rules applicable to short-term residents of Canada (P 20-85 to 20-87).
8. Describe the foreign investment reporting requirements of form T1135 (P 20-88 to 20-98).
9. Apply the appropriate tax treatment for Canadian residents of foreign source employment income, business income and capital gains (P 20-99 to 20-107).
10. Describe the basic concepts behind the taxation of foreign source dividends received by resident individuals (P 20-108 to 20-120).

11. Describe the taxation of dividends received by resident corporations from non-affiliated corporations (P 20-121).
12. Identify foreign affiliates (P 20-122 to 20-125).
13. Describe the tax treatment of dividends received from non-controlled foreign affiliates, including identification of their various types of surplus balances (P 20-126 to 20-139).
14. Explain the concept of a controlled foreign affiliate (P 20-140 to 20-143).
15. Apply the rules associated with, and the appropriate tax treatment of, foreign property accrual income (FAPI) (P 20-144 to 20-151).
16. Describe the tax treatment of dividends paid from FAPI (P 20-152 to 20-153).

CHAPTER 21

How To Work Through Chapter 21

We recommend the following approach in dealing with the material in this chapter:

Introduction To The GST/HST
- Read paragraph 21-1 to 21-7 (in the textbook).

The Current Situation And How We Will Deal With The Complexity
- Read paragraph 21-8 to 21-16.

Transaction Tax Concepts, Including VATs
- Read paragraph 21-17 to 21-41.
- Do Exercise Twenty-One-1 (in the textbook) and check the solution in this Study Guide.
- Do Self Study Problem Twenty-One-1 which is available on the Companion Website and check the solution in this Study Guide.

Liability For GST/HST And The Concept Of Supply
- Read paragraph 21-42 to 21-46.

Supply Categories (Fully Taxable, Zero-Rated And Exempt)
- Read from the Note before paragraph 21-47 to 21-60.

Applying the GST/HST Rate Using the Place Of Supply Rules
- Read paragraph 21-61 to 21-69.

Responsibility For Collection And Remittance Of GST/HST
- Read paragraph 21-70 to 21-73.

Registration - Including The Small Supplier Exemption
- Read paragraph 21-74 to 21-88.
- Do Exercise Twenty-One-2 and check the solution in this Study Guide.
- Read paragraph 21-89 to 21-92.
- Do Self Study Problem Twenty-One-2 and check the solution in this Study Guide.

Input Tax Credits
- Read paragraph 21-93 to 21-112.
- Do Exercises Twenty-One-3 to Twenty-One-5 and check the solutions in this Study Guide.
- Do Self Study Problems Twenty-One-3 and Twenty-One-4 and check the solutions in this Study Guide.

Relief For Small Businesses (Quick Method And Streamlined ITC Method)

- Read paragraph 21-113 to 21-124.
- Do Exercises Twenty-One-6 and Twenty-One-7 and check the solutions in this Study Guide.
- Do Self Study Problems Twenty-One-5 and Twenty-One-6 and check the solutions in this Study Guide.
- Read paragraph 21-125 to 21-130.
- Do Exercise Twenty-One-8 and check the solution in this Study Guide.

GST/HST Procedures And Administration, Including GST/HST Returns And Payments

- Read paragraph 21-131 to 21-157.

Employee And Partner GST/HST Rebate

- Read paragraph 21-158 to 21-166.
- Do Self Study Problem Twenty-One-7 and check the solution in this Study Guide.

Residential Property And New Housing Rebate

- Read paragraph 21-167 to 21-173.
- Do Self Study Problems Twenty-One-8 and Twenty-One-9 and check the solutions in this Study Guide.

Sale Of A Business

- Read paragraph 21-174 to 21-187.

Specific Applications Including Charities, Not-For-Profits And MUSH

- Read paragraph 21-188 and 21-189.

Partnerships And GST/HST

- Read paragraph 21-190 to 21-198.

Trusts And GST/HST

- Read paragraph 21-199 to 21-201.

To Complete This Chapter

- If you would like more practice in problem solving, do the Supplementary Self Study Problems for the chapter. These problems and solutions are available on the Companion Website.
- Review the Key Terms Used In This Chapter in the textbook at the end of Chapter 21. Consult the Glossary for the meaning of any key terms you do not know.
- Test yourself with the Chapter 21 Glossary Flashcards available on the Companion Website.
- Ensure you have achieved the Chapter 21 Learning Objectives listed in this Study Guide.
- As a review, we recommend you view the PowerPoint presentation for Chapter 21 that is on the Companion Website.

Practice Examination

- Write the Practice Examination for Chapter 21 that is on the Companion Website. Mark your examination using the Practice Examination Solution that is on the Companion Website.

Solutions to Chapter Twenty-One Exercises

Exercise Twenty-One - 1 Solution
Account-Based System   Under an account-based system, the 5 percent would be applied to the value added, resulting in a tax of $7,600 [(5%)($416,000 - $264,000)].

Invoice-Credit System   Alternatively, under an invoice-credit system, $20,800 [(5%)($416,000)] would be owing on sales, but would be offset by an input tax credit of $11,650 [(5%)($233,000)] on purchases. The net tax owing in this case would be $9,150, $1,550 larger than the $7,600 tax using the account based system. Note that this $1,550 is equal to 5 percent of $31,000, the difference between the $233,000 in purchases and the $264,000 cost of the merchandise sold.

Exercise Twenty-One - 2 Solution
As Ms. Salome's sales **exceed** $30,000 in the October to December, 2017 quarter, she will be required to begin collecting GST on the first sale in that quarter that causes her to exceed the $30,000 threshold. This means she will have to begin collecting GST sometime between October 1 and December 31. She will be required to register within 29 days of that date.

As Mr. Laughton's sales **accumulate** to more than $30,000 ($8,000 + $13,000 + $4,000 + $17,000 = $42,000) by the end of the January to March, 2018 quarter, he is required to start collecting GST on the first sale on or after May 1, 2018, one month after the quarter in which the $30,000 threshold is reached. Registration is required within 29 days of the first sale on which GST is collected.

Exercise Twenty-One - 3 Solution
The HST payable would be calculated as follows:

HST On Sales [(13%)($1,223,000)]	$158,990
Input Tax Credits:	
Purchases [(13%)($843,000 + $126,000)]	(125,970)
Salaries	Nil
Interest	Nil
Amortization	Nil
HST Payable For The Quarter	$ 33,020

Exercise Twenty-One - 4 Solution
The HST payable would be calculated as follows:

HST On Sales [(15%)($224,000)]	$33,600
Input Tax Credits:	
Rent [(15%)($25,800)]	(3,870)
Assistant's Salary	Nil
Capital Expenditures [(15%)($36,000 + $20,000)]	(8,400)
HST Payable For The Year	$ 21,330

Exercise Twenty-One - 5 Solution
The pro rata input tax credit for the land and building acquisition would be $24,000 [(5%)(40%)($1,200,000)]. There would be no input tax credit for the office equipment as it is used less than 50 percent for taxable supplies.

Exercise Twenty-One - 6 Solution

The purchases made do not affect the Quick Method calculation since they are non-capital. The GST payable under the Quick Method would be calculated as follows:

Basic Tax [(1.8%)(105%)($42,500)]	$803.25
Credit On First $30,000 [(1%)($30,000)]	(300.00)
GST Payable For The Quarter	$503.25

Exercise Twenty-One - 7 Solution

If the Quick Method is not used, the HST payable (refund) would be calculated as follows:

HST On Sales [(13%)($56,100)]	$7,293.00
Input Tax Credits:	
Current Expenditures [(13%)($23,400)]	(3,042.00)
Capital Expenditures [(13%)($42,000)]	(5,460.00)
HST Payable (Refund) For The Quarter - Regular Method	($1,209.00)

Alternatively, under the Quick Method, the calculation would be as follows:

Basic Tax [(4.4%)(113%)($56,100)]	$2,789.29
Credit On First $30,000 [(1%)($30,000)]	(300.00)
Subtotal	$2,489.29
Input Tax Credits:	
Current Expenditures	Nil
Capital Expenditures [(13%)($42,000)]	(5,460.00)
HST Payable (Refund) For The Quarter - Quick Method	($2,970.71)

As the Quick Method produces a larger refund, it would be the preferable method. Note that input tax credits on capital expenditures are available, even when the Quick Method is used.

Exercise Twenty-One - 8 Solution

To apply the streamlined method, we need to know the tax inclusive amounts of current expenditures (given in the problem), as well as the tax inclusive amounts of capital personal property expenditures. This latter figure is $52,500 [(105%)($50,000)]. Using the streamlined method, the GST payable (refund) would be calculated as follows:

GST Sales [(5%)($315,000 ÷ 1.05)]	$15,000
Input Tax Credits On Purchases And Capital Personal Property	
[(5/105)($189,000 + $52,500)]	(11,500)
Input Tax Credits On Capital Real Property [(5%)($150,000)]	(7,500)
GST Payable (Refund) For The Year	($ 4,000)

Self Study Solution Twenty-One - 1

GST Calculation

Under the normal GST system, a 5 percent tax is applied on the selling price at each stage and the business gets an input tax credit for the tax paid on purchased inputs. The net result is that all payments of GST by vendors are refunded as input tax credits, so there is no net out-of-pocket cost (other than administration) to vendors from the GST.

Vendor	Cost	Selling Price	GST Charged	ITC Claimed
Raw Materials Supplier		$ 100	$ 5.00	Nil
Manufacturer	$100	150	7.50	$ 5.00
Wholesaler	150	225	11.25	7.50
Distributor	225	338	16.90	11.25
Retailer	338	507	25.35	16.90
Totals		$1,320	$66.00	$40.65

The net GST charged for all stages is $25.35 ($66.00 - $40.65). The consumer bears the full cost of the tax by paying GST of $25.35 [(5%)($507)] with no opportunity to get an input tax credit.

Turnover Tax Calculation

The turnover tax is similar to the GST, as it applies to revenue. However, the turnover tax is significantly different as there is no input tax credit for tax paid at each stage on purchased goods (inputs). The tax is passed on to the purchasers in the chain, resulting in pyramiding of the tax. Because of the multiple times goods get taxed, to raise the same amount of tax revenue, the turnover tax rate of 1.92 percent (as shown in the following calculation) is much lower than the 5 percent GST rate.

$$[(\$100)(X\%)] + [(\$150)(X\%)] + [(\$225)(X\%)] + [(\$338)(X\%)] + [(\$507)(X\%)] = \$25.35$$
$$[(\$100 + \$150 + \$225 + \$338 + \$507)(X\%)] = \$25.35$$
$$[(\$1,320)(X\%)] = \$25.35$$
$$X\% = \$25.35 \div \$1,320$$
$$X\% = 1.92\%$$

As verification, the total of the selling price in the above table is $1,320. If the rate of 1.92 percent is applied to this total (the equivalent of each stage charging a turnover tax), the total tax collected would be equivalent to $25.34 (rounding error of $0.01).

Self Study Solution Twenty-One - 2

Case 1

A. Quarterhorse Inc.'s sales are all of fully taxable supplies. Sales during the April through June quarter total $37,000, $7,000 in excess of the $30,000 threshold that is used in the "calendar quarter" (single quarter) test. Given this, the business will be required to start collecting GST in June, 2017, beginning with the sale that causes the limit to be exceeded, even if Quarterhorse is not yet registered. Registration would be required within 29 days of the first sale on which GST is collected.

B. Whether Quarterhorse Inc. should register voluntarily before beginning operations, or delay GST registration until required (a maximum of 4 months delay) depends on a number of factors. If Quarterhorse's clients are primarily GST registrants, they would be able to claim any GST paid as input tax credits so should be indifferent as to whether Quarterhorse is registered or not. As a result, it would be advantageous for Quarterhorse to register as of the beginning of operations in order to claim all input tax credits.

If Quarterhorse's clients are primarily consumers, they cannot claim any GST paid as input tax credits so they would benefit as long as Quarterhorse is not registered. However, with the level of sales, the non-registration period is quite short and non-registration could even cause client dissatisfaction if GST is charged to a repeat client if it was not previously charged.

My recommendation is that Quarterhorse register for GST as of the beginning of operations.

Case 2

A. Quarterhorse Inc.'s sales are all exports which are zero-rated taxable supplies. The rules for registration apply to taxable supplies, so the required registration date is as explained for Case 1. No GST is collected on exports.

B. Although registration could be delayed until July, as explained for Case 1, there is no advantage to clients for a delay. Since GST is not charged on exports, the only effect of registration would be to allow Quarterhorse to claim input tax credits.

My recommendation is that Quarterhorse register for GST as of the beginning of operations.

Case 3

A. Quarterhorse Inc.'s sales are financial services which are exempt supplies, an excluded activity. Registration for GST is not permitted if a person is involved solely with providing exempt supplies. No GST is collected on exempt supplies.

B. Quarterhorse cannot register for GST. No recommendation can be given.

Self Study Solution Twenty-One - 3

The HST refund for Norton's Variety for the current period would be calculated as follows:

HST Collected [(13%)($250,000)]	$32,500
Input Tax Credits - Current Expenditures:	
Purchases Of Fully Taxable Goods	
[(13%)($175,000 + $10,000)]	(24,050)
Purchases Of Zero-Rated Goods (Note 1)	Nil
Amortization Expense (Note 2)	Nil
Salaries And Wages (Note 3)	Nil
Interest Expense (Note 3)	Nil
Other Operating Expenses [(13%)(100%)($10,000)] (Note 4)	(1,300)
Input Tax Credits - Capital Expenditures:	
Building [(13%)(40%)($480,000)] (Note 5)	(24,960)
Equipment (Note 6)	Nil
HST Payable (Refund)	($17,810)

Note 1 HST is not paid on purchases of zero-rated goods. As a consequence, there are no input tax credits to be claimed on these purchases.

Note 2 Amortization expense does not affect the HST calculation.

Note 3 No HST is paid on salaries and wages, or interest. As a result, no input tax credits are available.

Note 4 As more than 90 percent of the Other Expenses related to the provision of taxable supplies, the company is eligible for a 100 percent input tax credit.

Note 5 Input tax credits on real property are available based on a pro rata portion of their usage in providing taxable supplies.

Note 6 No input tax credits are available on capital expenditures other than real property if less than 50 percent of their usage is to provide fully taxable and zero-rated supplies.

Self Study Solution Twenty-One - 4

For Part A and Part B, the HST refund for the year would be calculated as follows:

	Part A	Part B
HST Collected [(13%)($1,955,000)]	$254,150	$254,150
Input Tax Credits:		
Purchases [(13%)($1,356,000 - $212,000)]	(148,720)	(148,720)
Amortization Expense	Nil	Nil
Salaries And Wages	Nil	Nil
Interest Expense	Nil	Nil
Other Expenses [(13%)($162,000 - $5,000)]	(20,410)	(20,410)
Equipment [(13%)($725,000)]	(94,250)	Nil
Building [(13%)(($1,450,000)]	(188,500)	
[(13%)(73%)($1,450,000)]		(137,605)
HST Payable (Refund)	($197,730)	($ 52,585)

In both Part A and Part B, no input tax credit is allowed for HST paid on membership fees or dues in any club whose main purpose is to provide dining, recreational, or sporting facilities.

In Part A, input tax credits are available on both the equipment and the building because 100 percent of their usage is for taxable supplies (fully taxable and zero-rated).

In Part B, there is no input tax credit available on the equipment as it is used less than 50 percent to provide taxable supplies. The building's input tax credit is limited to 73 percent of the HST paid.

Self Study Solution Twenty-One - 5

The following recommendations are based solely on the minimization of the GST payment. No consideration is given to the reduction in accounting costs available through the use of the Quick Method.

Claire - Service Business
The Quick Method would be preferable in this case.

Regular Method

[($150,000 - $35,000) ÷ 1.05][5%]	$5,476

Quick Method

Basic Tax [($150,000)(3.6%)]	$5,400
Credit On First $30,000 [(1%)($30,000)].	(300)
Net GST	$5,100

Barbara - Retailer

The Regular Method is preferable in this case.

Regular Method

[($150,000 - $100,000) ÷ 1.05][5%]	$2,381

Quick Method

Basic Tax [($150,000)(1.8%)]	$2,700
Credit On First $30,000 [(1%)($30,000)]	(300)
Net GST	$2,400

Nicole - Service Business

The Quick Method would be preferable in this case.

Regular Method

[($120,000 - $35,000) ÷ 1.05][5%]	$4,048

Quick Method

Basic Tax [($120,000)(3.6%)]	$4,320
Credit On First $30,000 [(1%)($30,000)]	(300)
Net GST	$4,020

Elizabeth - Retailer

The Quick Method would be preferable in this case.

Regular Method

[($120,000 - $75,000) ÷ 1.05][5%]	$2,143

Quick Method

Basic Tax [($120,000)(1.8%)]	$2,160
Credit On First $30,000 [(1%)($30,000)]	(300)
Net GST	$1,860

Self Study Solution Twenty-One - 6

Part A

As Midvale's GST included taxable sales of $149,100 [(105%)($142,000)] is less than $400,000 and it is not engaged in an ineligible business such as accounting, Midvale can use the Quick Method.

In order to determine the Quick Method remittance rate, the following amounts from the preceding year are required:

Prior Year GST Inclusive Purchases Of Goods For Resale [($93,000)(105%)] $ 97,650

Prior Year GST Inclusive Sales Of Taxable Supplies [($142,000)(105%)] $149,100

Since $97,650 ÷ $149,100 equals 65.5 percent and this is more than 40 percent, Midvale can use the reseller's remittance rate of 1.8 percent.

Part B

The GST refund for the year would be calculated as follows using the regular method:

GST On Sales [(5%)($175,000 - $25,000 - $23,000)]	$6,350
Input Tax Credits:	
Purchases [(5%)($104,000 + $6,000)]	(5,500)
Amortization Expense	Nil
Salaries And Wages	Nil
Interest Expense	Nil
Other Operating Expenses [(5%)($8,000)]	(400)
Equipment	Nil
Building [(5%)(60% + 18%)($150,000)]	(5,850)
GST Payable (Refund)	($5,400)

There is no input tax credit available on the equipment as it is used less than 50 percent to provide taxable supplies.

Part C

Using the Quick Method, the GST refund for the year would be calculated as follows:

Base Tax [(1.8%)(105%)($175,000 - $25,000 - $23,000)]	$2,400
Credit On First $30,000 [(1%)($30,000)]	(300)
Subtotal	$2,100
Input Tax Credits On Capital Expenditures:	
Equipment	Nil
Building [(5%)(60% + 18%)($150,000)]	(5,850)
GST Payable (Refund)	($3,750)

There is no input tax credit available on the equipment as it is used less than 50 percent to provide taxable supplies.

In this case, the regular GST calculation is preferable as it produces a larger refund.

Self Study Solution Twenty-One - 7

The maximum CCA that George can claim is as follows:

Opening UCC ($27,750 - $4,163)	$23,587
GST Rebate Claimed On Car CCA In Preceding Year	(198)
Adjusted UCC	$23,389
Class 10 Rate	30%
Maximum CCA	$ 7,017

The employee GST rebate for George would be calculated as follows:

Total Expenses Other Than CCA	$28,000	
GST Exempt Purchases:		
Interest	(2,600)	
Insurance	(1,200)	
Eligible Expenses Other Than CCA	$24,200	
Rate	5/105	$1,152
Eligible CCA	$7,017	
Rate	5/105	334
Employee GST Rebate		$1,486

Self Study Solution Twenty-One - 8

The calculation of the new housing GST rebate is as follows:

$$[A][(\$450,000 - B) \div \$100,000],\text{ where}$$

A = The lesser of 36 percent of the GST paid and $6,300; and
B = The greater of $350,000 and the cost of the home.

The GST and total cost of each purchase would be as follows.

Property A

As the renovations involve more than 90 percent of the interior, they will be considered substantial. Since the renovations would be done by the vendor prior to the sale, the purchase would be deemed to be that of a "new" home. As a result, the total purchase price would be subject to GST and a new housing rebate could be claimed on the total, as follows:

GST Payable [($370,000)(5%)]	$ 18,500
Less New Housing Rebate, where	
A = the lesser of [(36%)($18,500)] = $6,660 and $6,300	
B = the greater of $350,000 and $370,000	
[$6,300][($450,000 - $370,000) ÷ $100,000]	(5,040)
Net GST Payable	$ 13,460
Purchase Price	370,000
Total Cost	$383,460

Property B

As this property is a used residential unit, no GST will be payable. This means that the total cost will be $387,000.

Property C

GST will be paid on the purchase price of $323,000, plus all of the improvements. However, the new housing rebate is only available on the $10,000 cost of the improvements done by the builder in addition to the purchase price. It is not available on the additional $12,000 of costs incurred by Martin.

GST Payable [($323,000 + $10,000 + $12,000)(5%)]	$ 17,250
Less New Housing Rebate, where	
A = the lesser of [(36%)(5%)($323,000 + $10,000)] = $5,994	
and $6,300	
B = the greater of $350,000 and $345,000	
[$5,994][($450,000 - $350,000) ÷ $100,000]	(5,994)
Net GST Payable	$ 11,256
Purchase Price ($323,000 + $10,000 + $12,000)	345,000
Total Cost	$356,256

Self Study Solution Twenty-One - 9

GST Consequences

As used residential properties are not subject to GST, the renovator would not have paid any tax on the $85,000 purchase.

With respect to the sale, the GST treatment will depend on whether the upgrading was a substantial or non-substantial renovation. Given that 100 percent of the interior was replaced, it would be considered a substantial renovation. As a result, the sale would be treated as a taxable supply of a new home and would be subject to GST. This, in turn, means that GST paid on the costs of renovations can be claimed as input tax credits.

These credits can be claimed when the expenses are incurred, without regard to when the house is sold. The renovator could also claim input tax credits on GST that would be paid on commissions and transfer fees.

Cost Of House And Net Profit

For the purchaser, the usual 5 percent rate applied to the sales price of $200,000 would result in a basic GST figure of $10,000. However, as the house has a purchase price below $350,000, the purchaser would be eligible for a rebate equal to 36 percent of the GST paid. This rebate would be $3,600 [(36%)($10,000)], leaving a net GST payable of $6,400 ($10,000 - $3,600). The net cost of the house to the purchaser would then be $206,400.

The net profit on the transaction for the renovator, calculated net of GST payment and input tax credits, would be calculated as follows:

Selling Price		$200,000
Less Costs:		
Purchase Price	($85,000)	
Subcontractors - No GST Included	(10,700)	
Subcontractors (Net Of $1,000 GST)	(20,000)	
Materials (Net Of $1,500 GST)	(30,000)	
Employee Wages - No GST Included	(6,000)	(151,700)
Net Profit		$ 48,300

GST Remittance

The contractor will have a liability for GST as follows:

GST Charged (Net Of Rebate)		$ 6,400
Less Input Tax Credits:		
Subcontractors [($21,000 ÷ 105%)(5%)]	($1,000)	
Materials [($31,500 ÷ 105%)(5%)]	(1,500)	(2,500)
GST Remittance		$ 3,900

This solution assumes the purchaser assigns the rebate to the builder on closing. If this is not the case, the purchaser would apply personally for the $3,600 GST rebate, and the renovator's GST remittance would be $3,600 larger.

Chapter 21 Learning Objectives

After completing Chapter 21, you should be able to:

1. Describe, in general terms, the current transaction tax situation (GST/HST) in all of the provinces (paragraph [P hereafter] 21-1 to 21-16).
2. Describe the different ways in which transaction taxes can be assessed and the approach the GST/HST uses (P 21-17 to 21-41).
3. Explain the basic charging provision for GST/HST and the concept of supply (P 21-42 to 21-46).
4. Outline the difference between fully taxable supplies, zero-rated supplies, and exempt supplies (P 21-47 to 21-60).
5. Explain the place of supply rules and how the GST/HST is applied to tangible goods, real property and services (P 21-61 to 21-69).

6. Explain who is responsible for collecting and remitting the GST/HST (P 21-70 to 21-73).
7. Determine whether an entity is required to register for GST and if so, at what point in time registration is required (P 21-74 to 21-92).
8. Apply the rules for calculating input tax credits on current and capital expenditures (P 21-93 to 21-99).
9. Explain some of the basic restrictions on claiming input tax credits (P 21-100 to 21-102).
10. Discuss input tax credits as they relate to vendors of exempt supplies (P 21-103).

11. Describe the relationship between amounts determined for accounting, income tax and GST/HST purposes (P 21-104 to 21-108).
12. Calculate the GST/HST payable or refund when fully taxable, zero-rated and exempt supplies are provided (P 21-109 to 21-112).
13. Apply the quick method of accounting for GST/HST (P 21-113 to 21-124).
14. Apply the simplified method of accounting for input tax credits (P 21-125 to 21-130).
15. Outline the basic procedures and administration of the GST/HST (P 21-131 to 21-157).

16. Calculate the employee and partner GST/HST rebate (P 21-158 to 21-166).
17. Calculate the effects of GST/HST on the acquisition and disposition of residential property, including new homes (P 21-167 to 21-173).
18. Describe the possible GST/HST implications resulting from the sale of a business (P 21-174 to 21-187).
19. Briefly describe how the GST/HST applies to certain types of organizations such as those included in MUSH (P 21-188 and 21-189).
20. Describe the GST/HST implications related to partner expenses, dispositions of partnership interests, transfers between a partnership and its partners and the reorganization of partnerships (P 21-190 to 21-198).
21. Explain the applicability of GST/HST legislation to trusts (P 21-199 to 21-201).

GLOSSARY

A

Accrual Basis   A method of accounting for Income based on recording assets when the right to receive them is established and liabilities when the obligation to pay them arises.

Acquisition Of Control   Acquisition of sufficient voting shares of a corporation, by a Person, or Group Of Persons, that they have the right to elect a majority of the board of directors of the Corporation.

Active Business   A business carried on by a Taxpayer, other than a Specified Investment Business or a Personal Services Business.

Active Business Income   Income earned by an Active Business.

Additional Refundable Tax On Investment Income (ART)   A 10-2/3% tax on the Aggregate Investment Income of a CCPC.

Adjusted Active Business Income   A term used in calculating the M&P Deduction, defined as the excess of a Corporation's Income from Active Business, less a Corporation's losses from Active Business. It does not appear to be a different concept than Active Business Income of a Corporation.

Adjusted Cost Base   For depreciable capital property it is the cost of the property to the Taxpayer. For non-depreciable capital property it is the cost of the property to the Taxpayer, subject to ITA 53 adjustments (e.g., deduction of government grants on land purchase).

Adjusted Taxable Income   Regular Taxable Income, adjusted to remove certain tax preferences. Used to calculate the Alternative Minimum Tax.

Adoption Expenses Tax Credit
A credit against Tax Payable that is available to individuals with eligible adoption expenses.

Advance Tax Ruling   Interpretations provided, at the request of a taxpayer, by the Income Tax Rulings Directorate as to how a particular transaction will be treated for tax purposes. Such interpretations are not binding on the CRA.

Affiliated Group Of Persons
A Group Of Persons each member of which is affiliated with every other member.

Affiliated Person [ITA 251.1(1)]
For an Individual, an Affiliated Person is that individual's Spouse or Common-Law Partner. For a Corporation, an Affiliated Person is a Person or an Affiliated Group Of Persons who Controls the Corporation, or the Spouse or Common-Law Partner of either the Person who Controls, or a member of the group that Controls. More complex rules apply to determine affiliation between two Corporations.

Age Tax Credit   A credit against Tax Payable that is available to Individuals who are 65 years of age or older.

Aggregate Investment Income   As defined in ITA 129(4), this concept of investment income includes net Taxable Capital Gains for the year reduced by any Net Capital Loss carry overs deducted in the year, Interest Income, rents, and royalties.

Alimony   A term that was used at an earlier point in time to refer to both Spousal Support and Child Support.

Allowable Business Investment Loss
The deductible portion (currently one-half) of a Business Investment Loss.

Allowable Capital Loss   The deductible portion (currently one-half) of a Capital Loss.

Allowance   An amount paid by an employer to an Employee to provide for certain types of costs incurred by the Employee, usually travel costs or automobile costs.

Alter Ego Trust   An Inter Vivos Trust established by an Individual aged 65 years or more, subject to the conditions that the Individual must be entitled to all of the Trust's Income during his/her lifetime, and the Individual must be the only Person who can access the capital of the Trust during his/her lifetime.

Alternative Minimum Tax (AMT) A tax, calculated at the minimum federal rate on Adjusted Taxable Income, less a basic $40,000 exemption.

Amalgamation A Rollover provision which allows two Taxable Canadian Corporations to be combined into a single Taxable Canadian Corporation, without tax consequences.

Annual Business Limit The maximum amount of Active Business Income that is eligible for the Small Business Deduction in a particular taxation year (currently $500,000).

Annual Child Care Expense Amount The annual per child limit for deductible Child Care Expense. The amount is $5,000, $8,000, or $11,000, depending on the age and health of the child.

Annual Gains Limit Taxable Capital Gains for the current year on qualified assets, less the sum of Allowable Capital Losses and Net Capital Loss Carry Overs deducted during the current year, plus Allowable Business Investment Losses realized during the current year. Used to determine the Lifetime Capital Gains Deduction for the current year.

Annuitant This term is used to describe a Person who is receiving an Annuity. However, in tax publications this term is often (and incorrectly) used to refer to the Beneficiary of an RRSP or RPP.

Annuity A series of periodic payments that continues for a specified period of time, or until the occurrence of some event (e.g., the death of the Annuitant).

Anti-Avoidance Provision A provision in the *Income Tax Act* that is designed to prevent a Taxpayer from taking some action that would allow him to avoid taxes.

Apprenticeship Job Creation Tax Credit An Investment Tax Credit that is available to eligible employers (individuals and corporations) for salaries and wages paid to qualifying apprentices.

Arm's Length ITA 251(1) indicates that Related Persons (see definition) do not deal with each other at arm's length. Also, a taxpayer and a personal trust do not deal with each other at arm's length. In other cases, it is a question of fact as to whether an arm's length relation exists.

ART An acronym for "additional refundable tax on investment income".

Assessment A formal determination of taxes to be paid or refunded. A Reassessment is a form of Assessment.

Associated Corporations Two or more Corporations that have an ownership/control arrangement that falls into one of the categories described in ITA 256(1) (e.g., two Corporations controlled by the same Person).

At-Risk Amount A defined measure that limits the amount of deductions that can be flowed through to a Limited Partner.

At-Risk Rules A set of rules, directed largely at Limited Partners, designed to prevent an investment from creating tax deductions that exceed the amount invested (the At-Risk Amount).

B

Basic Federal Tax Payable An amount of individual Tax Payable that has been reduced by some, but not all of the Tax Credits available to individuals. Used in the calculation of Tax Payable of Canadian Residents who do not live in a province.

Beneficiary The Person who will receive the benefits from a Trust.

Billed Basis A method of determining Net Business Income based on recording inclusions when the relevant amounts are billed. Can only be used by certain specified types of professionals (e.g., accountants).

Bonus Arrangement As used in this material, a tax planning arrangement for Employees. A Corporation declares and deducts a bonus near the end of its fiscal year. It is usually designed to be paid to the Employee early in the following calendar year. As Employment Income is taxed on a Cash Basis, the bonus will not be taxed in the employee's hands until that year.

Bonusing Down A process of paying deductible salary to the owner-manager of a CCPC, or related parties, in order to eliminate corporate Taxable Income that is not eligible for the Small Business Deduction.

Boot A colloquial term used by tax practitioners to refer to Non-Share Consideration.

Business A business is a self-sustaining integrated set of activities and assets conducted and managed for the purpose of providing a return to investors. A business consists of (a) inputs, (b) processes applied to those inputs, and (c) resulting outputs that are used to generate revenues.

Business Combination A transaction in which an enterprise acquires net assets that constitute a business, or acquires an equity interest in a Corporation that gives the enterprise Control over the operating, financing, and investing decisions of that Corporation.

Business Income   Income that is earned through Active Business activity. This would include amounts earned by producing goods, selling goods or services, or delivering services. While usage is not always consistent, this term usually refers to a net amount (i.e., inclusions less deductions, or revenues less expenses).

Business Investment Loss   A loss resulting from the Disposition of shares or debt of a Small Business Corporation.

C

Canada Caregiver Amount For Child   A credit against tax payable that is available to an individual who provides care and/or support for a child under 18 years of age who has a mental or physical infirmity.

Canada Caregiver Tax Credit   A credit against tax payable that is available to an individual who provides care and/or support for certain specified dependants who have a mental or physical infirmity.

Canada Child Benefit   A monthly payment that is available to Individuals with children. The non-taxable payments may be reduced or eliminated if Income is in excess of a threshold amount.

Canada Disability Savings Bonds   A system of grants under which the federal government makes contributions to an Individual's RDSP based on family net income.

Canada Disability Savings Grants   A system of grants under which the federal government makes contributions to an Individual's RDSP based on a percentage of the contributions to that Individual's RDSP that have been made by others.

Canada Education Savings Grants
A system of grants under which the federal government makes contributions to an Individual's RESP based on a percentage of the contributions to that Individual's RESP that have been made by others.

Canada Employment Credit   A credit against Tax Payable that is available to individuals with employment income.

Canada Learning Bonds   A system of grants under which the federal government makes contributions to an Individual's RESP based on the number of years in which the Individual's family is eligible for the National Child Benefit supplement.

Canada Pension Plan (CPP)   A pension plan sponsored by the federal government. Individuals with Employment or Business Income must make contributions based on their income and, in return, receive benefits in future years.

Canada Pension Plan Tax Credit   A credit against Tax Payable that is available to Individuals making contributions to the Canada Pension Plan.

Canadian Controlled Private Corporation
A Corporation that is controlled by Persons Resident in Canada and that does not have any of its shares listed on a designated stock exchange.

Canadian Corporation   A Corporation that is resident in Canada.

Canadian Partnership   A Partnership, all of the members of which are Residents of Canada at the time the term is relevant.

Capital Asset   An asset that is held for the purpose of producing Income.

Capital Cost   The amount paid to acquire a depreciable asset. The tax equivalent of acquisition cost in accounting.

Capital Cost Allowance (CCA)   A deduction in the determination of Business or Property Income based on the capital cost of capital assets. The tax equivalent of accounting amortization.

Capital Dividend   A Dividend paid out of a Private Corporation's Capital Dividend Account. It is received on a tax free basis.

Capital Dividend Account   An account that tracks a group of items, defined in ITA 89(1), that can be distributed by Private Corporations to shareholders as a tax free Capital Dividend (e.g., the non-taxable portion of realized Capital Gains).

Capital Gain   The excess of proceeds resulting from the Disposition of a capital asset, over the sum of the Adjusted Cost Base of the asset plus any costs of disposition.

Capital Gains Reserve   A Reserve that is deductible against Capital Gains. It is available when some part of the Proceeds Of Disposition is not collected in the period of disposition.

Capital Gains Stripping   Procedures designed to allow a Corporation to convert a taxable capital gain resulting from the Disposition of investment shares to an arm's length party, into a tax free intercorporate Dividend.

Capital Interest (In A Trust)   All rights of the Taxpayer as a Beneficiary under the trust, other than those that are an Income Interest in the Trust.

Capital Loss   The excess of the sum of the Adjusted Cost Base of a capital asset plus any costs of disposition, over the proceeds resulting from the Disposition of the asset.

Capital Personal Property   For GST purposes, any capital property other than Real Property.

Capital Tax   A tax assessed on the capital of a Corporation, without regard to its Income.

Carry Over   As used in tax work, the ability to apply current year losses against Income in earlier or later years.

Cash Basis   A method of accounting for Income based on cash receipts and cash disbursements.

Cash Damming   Situations in which a separate bank account is established to receive all deposits of borrowed funds. Expenditures from this account are then limited to those which qualify for interest deductibility. This procedure facilitates linking the borrowed money to income producing investments.

CCPC   An acronym for "Canadian controlled private corporation".

Charitable Donations Tax Credit   A credit against Tax Payable that is available to Individuals making donations to qualifying charitable organizations.

Charitable Gifts   Donations to a registered charity, a registered Canadian amateur athletic association, a housing corporation resident in Canada that is exempt from tax under ITA 149(1)(i), a Canadian municipality, the United Nations or an agency thereof, a university outside of Canada which normally enrolls Canadian students, and a charitable organization outside of Canada to which Her Majesty in right of Canada has made a gift in the year or in the immediately preceding year.

Child Care Expenses   Costs associated with caring for an Eligible Child.

Child Support   A Support Amount that is not identified as being for the benefit of a Spouse or Common-Law Partner, or a former Spouse or Common-Law Partner.

Class   As used in tax work, a defined group of depreciable assets for which the *Income Tax Regulations* specify the CCA rate to be applied, as well as the method to be used in applying the rate.

Clawback   An income tested taxing back, or reduction, in the payment of Old Age Security benefits and Employment Insurance benefits. .

Commercial Activity   This is a GST term which refers to any business or trade carried on by a Person, or any supply of real property made by a Person. Commercial Activity does not include any activity involved with making an exempt supply or any activity engaged in by an Individual without a Reasonable Expectation Of Profit.

Commodity Tax   A type of Transaction Tax that is applied to the sale of certain types of commodities (e.g., taxes on the sale of tobacco products).

Common Shares   Corporate shares that normally have all of the rights which are provided for under the relevant corporate enabling legislation. While there may be variations in the rights of such shares, at a minimum, voting rights would have to be present for the shares to be considered Common Shares.

Common-Law Partner   A Person who cohabits in a conjugal relationship with the Taxpayer and (a) has so cohabited with the Taxpayer for a continuous period of at least one year, or (b) is a parent of a child of whom the Taxpayer is also a parent.

Comparable Uncontrolled Price   A Transfer Pricing method that bases transfer prices on the prices used in comparable transactions between arm's length buyers and sellers, operating in the same market and under the same terms and conditions.

Competent Authority   An authorized representative of a country's tax organization that helps resolve taxpayer disputes by negotiating with the other country on matters not adequately addressed by the tax treaty.

Connected Corporation   Corporation A is connected with Corporation B if Corporation B Controls Corporation A, or if Corporation B owns more than 10% of the voting shares of Corporation A and more than 10% of the fair market value of all issued shares of Corporation A.

Consent Form   A form that is used when a taxpayer wishes to have a different person represent him in dealing with the CRA. This form (T1013) authorizes the CRA to disclose information to, and deal with, a specified representative.

Consumption Tax   A tax levied on the consumption of some product or service. This type of tax is also called a sales tax.

Contributed Capital   In accounting usage, the amount of a Corporation's Shareholders' Equity that was received in return for issuing the shares that are currently outstanding.

Control [ITA 256(1.2)(c)]   A Corporation, Person or Group Of Persons has Control of a Corporation if that Corporation, Person or Group Of Persons owns either more than 50% of the Common Shares of that Corporation or, alternatively, owns shares (common and/or preferred) with a fair market value that exceeds 50% of the fair market value of all of the outstanding shares of that Corporation.

Control (IAS 27)   Control is the power to govern the financial and operating policies of an entity so as to obtain benefits from its activities.

Controlled [ITA 251.1(3)]   Under ITA 251.1(3), Controlled means controlled, directly or indirectly in any manner whatever. [The reference here is to de facto control, which does not necessarily require majority ownership of shares.]

Controlled Foreign Affiliate   A Foreign Affiliate of the Taxpayer that was controlled by (a) the Taxpayer, (b) the Taxpayer and not more than four other Persons Resident in Canada, (c) not more than four Persons Resident in Canada, other than the Taxpayer, (d) a Person or Persons with whom the Taxpayer does not deal at arm's length, or (e) the Taxpayer and a Person or Persons with whom the Taxpayer does not deal at arm's length.

Convertible Property   A debt or equity financial instrument of a Corporation that can be exchanged for an equity financial instrument of the same Corporation, without the payment of additional consideration.

Co-Ownership   Ownership of a single real or personal property by two or more Persons.

Corporation   An artificial legal entity created through either federal or provincial legislation.

Cost Of Capital (M&P)   For purposes of calculating the M&P Deduction, this amount is 10% of the Gross Cost of Capital Assets used by the corporation, plus 100% of rents paid for Capital Assets used by the Corporation.

Cost Of Labour (M&P)   For purposes of calculating the M&P Deduction, this is the total cost of salaries and wages, plus non-salary amounts paid for employee-like services.

Crowdfunding   Funding a project, venture or business by raising funds from a large number of people, usually in small amounts and usually via the internet.

Crown Gifts   Gifts made to Her Majesty in right of Canada or to Her Majesty in right of a province.

Cultural Gifts   Gifts of objects that the Canadian Cultural Property Export Review Board has determined meet the criteria of the *Cultural Property And Import Act*.

Cumulative Eligible Capital (CEC)   This term is used to refer to the amortized balance of Eligible Capital Expenditures. The amortization of this amount that is deducted under ITA 20(1)(b) is usually referred to as the cumulative eligible capital amount. No longer available after 2016.

Cumulative Gains Limit   Taxable Capital Gains on qualified assets that have been realized since 1984, less the sum of Allowable Capital Losses and Net Capital Loss Carry Overs deducted after 1984, plus Allowable Business Investment Losses realized after 1984, capital gains deductions claimed in previous taxation years, and the Cumulative Net Investment Loss at the end of the year. Used to determine the Lifetime Capital Gains Deduction for the current year.

Cumulative Net Investment Loss (CNIL)   The amount by which the aggregate of investment expenses for the current year and prior years ending after 1987, exceeds the aggregate of investment income for that period.

Customs Duties   A tax imposed on the importation or exportation of certain goods or services.

D

Death Benefit   All amounts in excess of $10,000 that are received by a Taxpayer in a taxation year, on or after the death of an Employee, in recognition of the Employee's service in an office or employment.

Declining Balance Method   A method of calculating CCA in which a specified rate is applied to the ending UCC balance in a depreciable asset Class in order to determine the CCA for the period.

Deemed Disposition   A requirement to assume that a Disposition has taken place when, in fact, a disposition transaction has not occurred (e.g., a change in use is deemed to be a Disposition).

Deemed Dividends   A group of capital transactions and distributions, as specified in ITA 84(1), that are deemed to be Dividend payments.

Deemed Resident   An Individual who is considered a Resident of Canada because of some factor other than physical presence in Canada (e.g., members of the Canadian armed forces are deemed to be Canadian Residents under ITA 250 without regard to where they are physically located).

Deemed Year End   A requirement to have a taxation year end at a specified date, or as the result of a specified event.

Deeming Rules   Rules that are used to require that an item or event be given a treatment for tax purposes that is not consistent with the actual nature of the item or event (e.g., members of the Canadian armed forces are deemed to be Canadian Residents even if they are not present in Canada at any time during the year).

Deferred Income Plans   A group of plans that allow Individuals to receive Income on a tax deferred basis. These include Registered Pension Plans, Deferred Profit Sharing Plans, Registered Retirement Savings Plans, and Registered Retirement Income Funds.

Deferred Profit Sharing Plan (DPSP)
A trusteed plan to which employers can make deductible contributions, the amount of which is related to the profits of the enterprise, and which do not create a Taxable Benefit for the recipient employees. Earnings accumulate tax free within the plan. Withdrawals from the plan are subject to tax.

Defined Benefit Plan   A retirement savings plan in which the plan sponsor (usually an employer) promises a known or determinable retirement benefit and assumes financial responsibility for providing that benefit.

Defined Contribution Plan (a.k.a., Money Purchase Plan)   A retirement savings plan in which the plan sponsor (employer or individual) makes known or determinable contributions. The retirement benefit is based on the accumulated contributions and earnings on investments within the plan.

Dependant   As defined in ITA 118(6), an Individual who, at any time during the year, is dependent on the taxpayer for support and is the child or grandchild of the Individual or of the individual's Spouse or Common-Law Partner, the parent, grandparent, brother, sister, uncle, aunt, niece, or nephew, if resident in Canada at any time in the year, of the Individual or of the individual's Spouse or Common-Law Partner.

Depreciable Capital Property   Capital property, such as equipment or furniture and fixtures, that is subject to depreciation or amortization.

Designated Stock Exchange
A stock exchange that has been designated as such by the Minister of Finance. Replaces the term "prescribed stock exchange".

Disability Supports Deduction   A deduction available to individuals for attendant care and other disability support expenses, incurred to allow the disabled individual to work or to attend a designated educational institution.

Disability Tax Credit   A credit against Tax Payable that is available to Individuals with a doctor certified severe mental or physical disability. Can be transferred to a supporting Individual.

Disability Tax Credit Supplement   A supplement to the Disability Tax Credit available to individuals who are under 18 years of age at the end of the year.

Disappearing Source Rules   Rules designed to provide relief to investors who have borrowed money to make an investment and subsequently sold the investment for less than the related borrowings. These rules provide that any amount of debt that remains after the proceeds of the sale are used to pay off a portion of the total balance is deemed to be debt that is used to produce income.

Discretionary Trust   A Trust for which the Settlor has given the Trustee discretion to decide the amounts of income or capital to be allocated to each Beneficiary.

Disposition   The disposal of an asset through sale, gift, physical destruction, conversion, expropriation, or other means.

Dividend Gross Up   An amount that is based on a percentage of the Dividends from Taxable Canadian Corporations that have been received by an Individual or Trust. This amount must be included in the Net Income For Tax Purposes of the Individual or Trust.

Dividend Stripping   Procedures designed to allow an Individual to remove accumulated Income from a Corporation in the form of tax-free capital gains, while still retaining Control of the Corporation.

Dividend Tax Credit   A credit against the Tax Payable of an Individual or Trust. The amount is based on a fraction of the Dividend Gross Up that has been included in Net Income For Tax Purposes.

Dividends   Amounts declared and paid, at the discretion of management, as a return on equity investments.

Dividends In Kind   Dividends, other than Stock Dividends, paid in corporate assets other than cash.

Division B Income   An alternative name for Net Income For Tax Purposes.

Double Taxation   A reference to situations in which the same stream of Income is subject to tax a second time.

Dual Resident   A taxpayer who is considered to be a Resident of two countries.

E

Earned Capital (a.k.a. Retained Earnings)
In accounting usage, the amount of a Corporation's Shareholders' Equity that resulted from the retention of earnings in the corporation.

Earned Income (Child Care Expenses)   For purposes of determining the deductible amount of Child Care Expenses, Earned Income is defined as Employment Income (gross), Business Income (not losses), and Income from scholarships, training allowances, and research grants.

Earned Income (RRSP Deduction Limit)
The sum of Employment Income (without the RPP deduction), Business Income (losses), royalties (if the taxpayer is the author, inventor, or composer), taxable (deductible) support payments, supplementary unemployment benefits, income (loss) as an active partner,

net rental income (loss), research grants (net of certain expenses), and CPP disability benefits.

Earned Surplus   An archaic accounting description of what now is called Retained Earnings. However, the term continues to be found in the *Income Tax Act*.

Ecological Gifts   Gifts of land certified by the Minister of the Environment to be ecologically sensitive land, the conservation and protection of which is important to the preservation of Canada's environmental heritage.

Election   A choice that is available to a Taxpayer with respect to a particular tax outcome (e.g., a Taxpayer can elect to have the spousal Rollover provision not be applicable).

Eligible Capital Expenditure   An amount expended to acquire an intangible asset that is not eligible for either write-off through CCA deductions or as a deduction in the period in which it is incurred.

Eligible Capital Property   An intangible asset that results from making an Eligible Capital Expenditure.

Eligible Child   With respect to the deductibility of Child Care Expenses, a child of the Taxpayer, his Spouse, or a child who is dependent on the Taxpayer or his Spouse, and whose Income does not exceed the basic personal tax credit base amount. An Eligible Child must either be under 16 years of age at some time during the year, or dependent on the Taxpayer or his Spouse by reason of physical or mental infirmity.

Eligible Dependant Tax Credit
A credit against Tax Payable that is available to a single Individual supporting a Dependant in a self-contained domestic establishment.

Eligible Dividends   Dividends that have been designated by the payor as eligible for the enhanced gross up and tax credit procedure.

Emigration   Leaving a country, usually in order to establish permanent residency in another country.

Employee   An Individual who has an employment relationship with an entity that provides remuneration. Whether or not an Individual is working as an Employee or a Self-Employed Individual is dependent on factors such as control, ownership of tools, chance of profit or risk of loss, and the ability to subcontract or hire an assistant.

Employee and Partner GST Rebate   A provision that allows employees and partners to recover the GST paid on their employment or partnership related expenses.

Employer/ Employee Relationship
A written, verbal, or tacit agreement in which an Employee agrees to work on a full-time or part-time basis for an employer for a specified or indeterminate period of time, in return for Salary or wages. The employer has the right to decide where, when, and how the work will be done. In this type of relationship, a contract of services exists.

Employment Income   The Salary, wages, and other remuneration, including gratuities, received by an Employee in the year (see Employer/Employee Relationship).

Employment Insurance (EI)   A federal insurance plan designed to provide benefits to unemployed Individuals. In order to receive benefits, Employees must make contributions when they are employed.

Employment Insurance Tax Credit   A credit against Tax Payable that is available to Employees making payments to the federal Employment Insurance plan.

Estate   As the term is used in the *Income Tax Act*, the property of a deceased Individual.

Estate Freeze   Procedures undertaken by an Individual in order to fix a tax value for all or part of the Individual's property, and to Transfer future growth in the value of this property to other Individuals.

Estate Planning   Tax planning directed towards the distribution of an Individual's property at death.

Excessive Eligible Dividend Designation (EEDD)   A balance, subject to Part III.1 tax, which reflects an inappropriate designation of an amount of dividends paid as an Eligible Dividend.

Exchange Of Shares In A Reorganization (ITA 86)   A Rollover provision that allows one class of shares in a Corporation to be exchanged for a different class of shares, without tax consequences.

Executor   A Person appointed by an Individual in their Will to oversee the administration of the Estate on their death in accordance with the terms of that Will.

Exempt Goods And Services   Goods and services that are not subject to the GST. Registrants who sell Exempt Goods And Services are not eligible for Input Tax Credits for GST paid. Examples include sales of used residential housing, most medical services, and most financial services.

Exempt Surplus   A surplus account that tracks certain sources of income of a Foreign Affiliate.

F

Fairness Package   Replaced by the Taxpayer Relief Provisions.

Family Trust   An Inter Vivos Trust, established by an Individual, with family members as Beneficiaries.

Farm Property   Farm Property includes real estate and property that is used in farming activities, a share of a Corporation that is carrying on a farming business, or an interest in a Partnership that is carrying on a farming business.

Federal Tax Abatement   A 10 percentage point reduction in the federal tax rate on Corporations, applicable to Income earned in a province.

Final Tax Return   A term used to describe the tax return filed for an Individual for the year of their death.

First Time Home Buyer's Tax Credit
A credit against Tax Payable equal to 15% of $5,000 of the cost of an individual's first Principal Residence.

First Time Donor's Super Tax Credit
A temporary addition to the charitable donations tax credit. The amount is equal to 25 percent of the first $1,000 of qualifying donations. It is available if neither the individual nor the individual's spouse or common-law partner has claimed a charitable donations tax credit since 2007.

First Year Rules   See Half-Year Rules.

Fiscal Period   A taxation year that does not exceed 53 weeks.

Fishing Property   Fishing Property includes real estate and property that is used in fishing activities, a share of a Corporation that is carrying on a fishing business, or an interest in a Partnership that is carrying on a fishing business.

Fixed Term Annuity   An Annuity that is paid for a specified number of periods.

Flat Tax System   A tax on Income that is applied at the same rate to all Taxpayers, without regard to the level of their Income.

Foreign Accrual Property Income (FAPI)
Income of a Controlled Foreign Affiliate from property (interest, Dividends, rents, royalties), Income from inactive businesses, Taxable Capital Gains from properties not used in an Active Business, and Income from an investment business, defined as a business the principal purpose of which is to earn Property Income.

Foreign Affiliate   A non-resident Corporation in which a Canadian Taxpayer has an equity percentage of at least 1 percent. As well, the aggregate equity percentages of the Taxpayer and each Person related to the Taxpayer must be at least 10 percent.

Foreign Taxes Paid Credit   A credit against Tax Payable based on taxes withheld by a foreign taxing authority on foreign source income.

Former Business Property   Real property that is used in the operation of a business.

Fringe Benefits   Non-cash benefits provided to Employees by an employer (e.g., contributions to an Employee's Registered Pension Plan).

Full Rate Taxable Income   For purposes of calculating the General Rate Reduction, Taxable Income reduced by amounts which have received preferential treatment under some other provision (e.g., the Small Business Deduction).

Fully Taxable Goods And Services   Goods and services that are taxable at the full 5% GST rate. Registrants who sell Fully Taxable Goods And Services are entitled to Input Tax Credits for GST paid. Examples include clothing, furniture, legal fees, hydro services, building materials, and restaurant meals.

G

GAAP   An acronym for "generally accepted accounting principles".

GAAR   An acronym for "general anti-avoidance rule". This ITA 245 provision attempts, in a very generalized manner, to limit the ability of Taxpayers to avoid tax through certain types of transactions that have no bona fide purpose other than to obtain a tax benefit.

General Partner   A Partner whose personal liability for the debts and obligations of the partnership are not limited.

General Partnership   A Partnership, all of the members of which are General Partners.

General Rate Income Pool (GRIP)
A notional account that tracks amounts of a CCPC's income that can be used for the payment of Eligible Dividends.

General Rate Reduction   A percentage point deduction in the calculation of corporate Tax Payable that is designed to reduce the general corporate tax rate of 38 percent.

Gift   A voluntary Transfer of goods or services without remuneration.

Goods And Services Tax (GST)   A type of Transaction Tax that is assessed on the sale of goods and services. As it is assessed at all stages of the production/distribution chain, the tax that an enterprise must collect and pay to the government is offset by Input Tax Credits for the tax paid on the various inputs required to produce or distribute the goods and services.

Goodwill   The excess, if any, of the total fair value of a business enterprise, over the sum of the fair values of its identifiable tangible and intangible assets.

Graduated Rate Estate   A testamentary trust that is designated as a graduated rate estate. Its special features include the ability to use graduated tax rates and a non-calendar fiscal period for the 36 month period following an individual's death.

Gross Cost   For purposes of calculating Capital Cost in the determination of the M&P Deduction, this is the cost of Capital Assets, without the deduction of government grants or Investment Tax Credits.

Group Of Persons   For purposes of determining Control of a Corporation, a Group Of Persons is any two or more Persons, each of whom owns shares in the Corporation.

GST   An acronym for the "goods and services tax".

GST Tax Credit   A Refundable Tax Credit that is available to all Resident Individuals aged 19 or older who file a T1 tax return. May be reduced or eliminated by a deduction of Income in excess of a threshold amount.

H

Half-Year Rules (a.k.a. First Year Rules)   A group of rules which require, for most CCA Classes, the subtraction of one-half of the year's net additions (additions, less the amount subtracted from the class because of disposals) from the Class, prior to calculating the CCA for the year.

Harmonized Sales Tax (HST)   A combined federal/provincial sales tax that is generally assessed on the same basis as the federal Goods And Services Tax (GST). The combined rate varies across the provinces and is notionally a combination of the 5% GST plus a provincial sales tax ranging from 7% to 10%.

Head Tax   A tax levied on the Individuals that are included in a specified classification.

Hobby Farmer   A part-time farmer who does not have a Reasonable Expectation Of Profit.

Home Accessibility Tax Credit   A tax credit that is available on expenditures made for renovations that will allow seniors and disabled individuals to gain access to, or be more mobile within a dwelling.

Home Buyers' Plan (HBP)   A provision that allows Individuals to make a temporary, non-taxable withdrawal from their RRSP for purposes of acquiring a residence.

Home Relocation Loan   A loan provided by an employer to an Employee to assist that Employee in acquiring a home at a new work location.

I

Identical Property Rules   Rules which require that, for a group of identical Capital Assets (e.g., Common Shares) acquired at different prices, the Adjusted Cost Base used to determine the gain or loss will be the average cost of the group. The rules are used when there is a partial Disposition of the group.

Immigration   Entering a new country, usually for purposes of establishing permanent residence.

Imputed Interest   Interest on outstanding debt calculated at a specified interest rate without regard to the actual interest rate being paid. This concept is used to determine the Taxable Benefit on loans to Employees and Shareholders.

Inadequate Consideration   A term used to refer to a situation where a non-arm's length transfer of property has been made and the Proceeds Of Disposition are not equal to the fair market value.

Income   A measure of either how much an entity has earned during a period or, alternatively, how much its net worth has increased during a period. As the term is used in accounting and tax, it is a rules-based calculation. In the case of accounting, the rules are referred to as generally accepted accounting principles (GAAP), while in tax the rules are found in the *Income Tax Act* and other sources.

Income Attribution   The allocation of some types of Income, on assets that have been transferred to a Spouse or related minors, back to the Transferor for inclusion in the Transferor's Net Income For Tax Purposes.

Income Interest (In A Trust)   A right of the Taxpayer as a Beneficiary under a Personal Trust to receive all or any part of the Income of the Trust.

Income Splitting   A group of Tax Planning techniques designed to divide a given stream of Income among family members or other related parties. The value of these techniques is based on progressive tax rates which means that, if a stream of Income can be divided into a group of smaller streams, a larger portion of it will be taxed at lower rates, resulting in aggregate tax savings.

Income Tax   A tax on the Income of certain defined entities.

Income Tax Application Rules   A set of rules designed to deal with transitional problems associated with the introduction of Capital Gains taxation in 1972. While these rules were very important in the years immediately after 1971, they are of declining importance at this point in time.

Income Tax Folios   A CRA publication providing their interpretation of various technical issues related to income taxes. These will gradually replace the CRA's Interpretation Bulletins.

Income Tax Regulations   A set of rules concerning administration and enforcement of the *Income Tax Act*. One of the major issues covered here is Capital Cost Allowance rates and procedures.

Income Tax Technical News   An irregularly published newsletter prepared by the Income Tax Rulings Directorate.

Income Trust   A Trust that has sold its beneficial interest units to the public in order to raise funds to acquire a business operation. All cash flows from the business are distributed to the unit holders.

Indexation   The process of adjusting tax brackets and some Tax Credits to reflect changes in the consumer price index.

Individual   A single human being.

Individual Pension Plan   A defined benefit pension plan established for one individual.

Information Circulars   A group of separate publications that provides information regarding procedural matters that relate to both the *Income Tax Act* and the provisions of the Canada Pension Plan.

Information Return   ITA 221(1)(d) gives the CRA the right to require any class of Taxpayer to file a return providing any class of information that it would like to have. A common example of an Information Return would be the T4 which employers are required to file in order to provide information on their Employees' earnings and withholdings.

Input Tax Credit (ITC)   An amount, claimable by a registrant, for GST paid or payable on goods or services that were acquired or imported for consumption, use, or supply in the course of the Registrant's Commercial Activity.

Instalment Threshold   An amount, currently $3,000 of net tax owing for Individuals or taxes payable for Corporations that is used to determine the need to make Instalment payments (i.e., Individuals are required to make Instalment payments if their Net Tax Owing in the current year and one of the two preceding years exceeds the Instalment Threshold of $3,000).

Instalments   Payments made during a taxation year by both Individuals and Corporations. They are designed to accumulate to an amount sufficient to cover the tax liability for the year. Individuals and Small CCPCs make quarterly Instalments. Corporations that are not Small CCPCs are required to remit monthly.

Integration   An approach to the taxation of Corporations that attempts to ensure that amounts of Income that are flowed through a Corporation to its Individual shareholders, are subject to the same amount of tax as would be the case if the Individuals had received the Income directly from its source.

Inter Vivos Transfer   A Transfer made by a living Individual, as opposed to a Transfer made subsequent to that Individual's death.

Inter Vivos Trust   A Trust that is not a Testamentary Trust.

Interest Income   An amount that represents compensation for the use of money, is calculated with reference to a principal sum, and that accrues on a continuous basis.

International Tax Treaty (a.k.a., International Tax Convention)   A bilateral agreement between two countries which establishes rules for dealing with cross-jurisdictional tax issues.

International Taxation   Income and other types of taxation related to transactions and events that take place in multiple jurisdictions.

Interpretation Bulletins   A group of over 500 individual publications which provides the CRA's interpretation of the various laws that they administer. Gradually being replaced by Income Tax Folios.

In-The-Money   A term that is used to describe stock options in situations where the fair market value of the stock exceeds the option price.

Inventory   Property, the cost or value of which is relevant in computing a taxpayer's income from a business for a taxation year. The property is being held for resale, as opposed to being held to produce income.

Investment Tax Credit   A credit against Tax Payable, calculated as a percentage of some specified type of expenditure made by the Taxpayer.

Involuntary Disposition   A Disposition of a capital property resulting from theft, destruction through natural causes, or expropriation by a statutory authority.

J

Joint Spousal Or Common-Law Partner Trust   An Inter Vivos Trust established by an Individual aged 65 years or more, subject to the conditions that the Individual and his/her Spouse or Common-Law Partner must be entitled to all of the Trust's Income during their lifetimes, and the Individual and his Spouse or Common-Law Partner must be the only Individuals who can access the capital of the Trust during his/her lifetime.

Joint Tenancy   A holding of property, either real or personal, by two or more Persons with each sharing the undivided interest that cannot be sold without the consent of all joint tenants.

Joint Venture   An arrangement in which two or more Persons work together in a limited and defined business undertaking, which does not constitute a Partnership, a Trust, or a Corporation, the expenses and revenues of which will be distributed in mutually agreed portions.

L

Labour Sponsored Funds Tax Credit
A credit against Tax Payable that is available to Individuals making investments in prescribed labour sponsored venture capital corporations.

Legal Stated Capital   An amount that is specified in corporate enabling legislation. In general, it is equal to the amount of consideration received for the issuance of shares.

Life Annuity   An Annuity that continues until the death of the Annuitant.

Lifelong Learning Plan (LLP)   A provision that allows Individuals to make temporary, non-taxable withdrawals from their RRSP when they are enrolled in a qualifying education program at a qualifying educational institution.

Lifetime Capital Gains Deduction   A deduction in the calculation of the Taxable Income of an Individual. It permits the deduction of a cumulative lifetime amount of Capital Gains resulting from the Disposition of Qualified Small Business Corporation shares or Qualified Farm or Fishing Property.

Limited Liability   A reference to the fact that the liability of investors in equity shares of a Corporation is limited to the amount of their invested capital.

Limited Liability Partnerships   A Partnership, all of the members of which are legislatively specified professionals. The members of such Partnerships are relieved of any personal liability arising from the wrongful or negligent action of their professional Partners, as well as Employees, agents, or representatives of the Partnership who conduct partnership business.

Limited Partner   As defined in most provincial legislation, a Partner whose liabilities for partnership debts is limited to the amount of his contribution to the Partnership, and who is not permitted to participate in the management of the Partnership.

Limited Partnership   A Partnership composed of at least one General Partner and at least one Limited Partner. To be considered a Limited Partnership, the Partnership has to be registered as such under the appropriate provincial registry.

Limited Partnership Loss   The excess of losses allocated to a Limited Partner (other than farming or capital losses), over his At-Risk Amount.

Liquidating Dividend   A Dividend that represents a return of invested capital, as opposed to a distribution from earnings.

Listed Personal Property   A defined subset of Personal Use Property. The included items are works of art, jewelry, rare books, stamps, and coins.

Loss Carry Back   The application of a loss incurred in the current taxation year against the Income reported in a previous taxation year, resulting in a refund of taxes paid in that previous year.

Loss Carry Forward   The application of a loss incurred in the current taxation year against Income reported in a subsequent taxation year, resulting in a reduction of Tax Payable in that subsequent year.

Low Rate Income Pool (LRIP)   A notional account that tracks amounts of a non-CCPC's income that cannot be used for the payment of Eligible Dividends.

Lump-Sum Payments   Retroactive payments for Spousal or Child Support, pension benefits, EI benefits, and Employment Income (including payments for termination), that relate to prior years. Qualifying amounts of such payments are eligible for an alternative Tax Payable calculation.

M

M&P   An acronym for "manufacturing and processing" usually used in connection with the calculation of the Manufacturing And Processing Profits Deduction.

M&P Capital   100/85 of the Cost Of Capital related to Qualified Activities for M&P.

M&P Labour   100/75 of the Cost Of Labour related to Qualified Activities for M&P.

M&P Profits   A concept of Income based on M&P Capital and M&P Labour, applied in a formula contained in ITR 5200.

Manufacturing And Processing Profits Deduction (M&P Deduction)   A deduction in the calculation of corporate Tax Payable. It is equal to the General Rate Reduction rate applied to M&P Profits.

Median Rule   A rule applicable to Capital Assets acquired before 1972.   For purposes of calculating Capital Gains on Dispositions of these assets, the Adjusted Cost Base is equal to the median of the cost of the asset, the Valuation Day value of the asset, and the Proceeds Of Disposition.

Medical Expense Tax Credit   A credit against Tax Payable that is available to Individuals with qualifying medical expenses.

Merger   A combination of two or more business enterprises. While widely used in the *Income Tax Act*, this term does not have a formal definition in that legislation.

Money Purchase Limit   An amount, specified in tax legislation that represents the maximum amount of Employee and employer contributions that can be added, for the benefit of a given Employee, to an RPP in the specified taxation year.

Money Purchase Plan (a.k.a., Defined Contribution Plan)   A retirement savings plan in which the plan sponsor (employer or Individual) makes known or determinable contributions. The retirement benefit is based on the accumulated contributions and earnings on investments within the plan.

Moving Expenses   Costs, as described in ITA 62(3), that can be deducted when an Individual is moving; to a new work location, to commence full-time attendance at a post-secondary institution, to a new work location after ceasing to be a full-time student at a post-secondary institution, or to a new location to take up employment, if unemployed prior to the move.

MUSH   An acronym for "municipalities, universities, schools, and hospitals". It is used in GST work to refer to the special rules applicable to these organizations.

Mutual Fund   A taxable entity, either a Trust or a Corporation, that manages a portfolio of investments on behalf of its unitholders or shareholders.

N

"Negative" Adjusted Cost Base   A term used to refer to situations where negative adjustments to the Adjusted Cost Base of a Capital Asset exceed its original cost plus positive adjustments. While, in general, such amounts must be taken into Income, an exception is made for Partnership Interests, for which such amounts can be carried forward.

Net Assets   Assets minus the liabilities of a business enterprise.

Net Business Income   As used in this text, the net of inclusions less deductions, related to Business Income, with all amounts determined as per Division B, Subdivision b, of the *Income Tax Act*.

Net Capital Loss   The excess of Allowable Capital Losses over Taxable Capital Gains for the current year.

Net Income   As used in this text, the net of revenues plus gains, less expenses plus losses, with all amounts determined through the application of GAAP.

Net Income For Tax Purposes   The sum of Employment Income, Business and Property Income, net Taxable Capital Gains, other sources of income, and other deductions from income, determined using income tax procedures and concepts. These amounts are combined as per the rules in ITA 3. This amount is also referred to as Division B Income or simply Net Income. However, we tend to use the full Net Income For Tax Purposes title in order to avoid confusion with Net Income as determined by accounting rules.

Net Property Income   As used in this text, the net of inclusions less deductions, related to Property Income, with all amounts determined as per Division B, Subdivision b, of the *Income Tax Act*.

Net Tax Owing   A term, applicable to Taxpayers who are Individuals, used to describe the sum of federal and provincial taxes owing for the year, less amounts withheld for the year.

NETFILE   An electronic filing system that requires the use of an approved software program. An Individual uses the Internet to transmit their return directly to the CRA, without the use of a third party.

New Housing GST Rebate   A provision that allows an individual to recover a portion of the GST paid on the acquisition of a new residence.

Non-Arm's Length   ITA 251(1) indicates that Related Persons (see definition) do not deal with each other at arm's length. Also, a taxpayer and a personal trust do not deal with each other at arm's length. In other cases, it is a question of fact as to whether an arm's length relation exists.

Non-Capital Loss   The sum of employment losses (for Individuals), business losses, property losses, Net Capital Losses deducted, and deductible Dividends received (for Corporations), less Income as calculated under ITA 3(c).

Non-Depreciable Capital Property   Capital property, such as land or holdings of securities, that is not subject to depreciation or amortization.

Non-Discretionary Trust   A Trust for which the Trust documents have specified the amounts of Income and capital to be allocated to each Beneficiary.

Non-Eligible Dividends   Dividends that have not been designated by the payor as eligible for the enhanced gross up and tax credit procedure.

Non-Portfolio Property (Definition relevant only to SIFT entities) These properties are made up of (1) securities of a subject entity (corporation, trust, or partnership) where the securities held have a value that is greater than 10% of the equity value of the subject entity or, the securities held, along with securities of entities affiliated with the subject entity, have a fair market value that is greater than 50% of the equity value of the trust or partnership, (2) real estate and resource properties where such properties total more than 50% of the equity value of the trust or partnership, and (3) property used in the course of carrying on a business in Canada.

Non-Refundable Tax Credit A Tax Credit that can only be used against the Tax Payable of an Individual. It will not be "refunded" to Individuals without sufficient Tax Payable to make use of it.

Non-Resident A Corporation, Trust, or any other type of entity that exists, was formed or organized, or was last continued under the laws of a country, or a political subdivision of a country, other than Canada.

Non-Share Consideration Consideration received by a Taxpayer from a Corporation that is in the form of assets other than shares of the Corporation.

Northern Residents Deductions Deductions from the Taxable Income of residents of prescribed areas in northern Canada, designed to compensate them for the higher costs of living in these regions.

Notice Of Assessment A form that the CRA sends to all Taxpayers after they process their returns. It tells Taxpayers whether there were any changes made to the returns and, if so, what they are. It also informs Taxpayers of the amount of their additional tax payable or their refund.

Notice Of Objection A statement made to the CRA which provides a statement of facts and reasons, detailing why a Taxpayer or GST Registrant disagrees with an Assessment. The notice can be filed using Form T400A or by simply writing a letter to the CRA.

O

OAS Clawback A taxing back, or reduction, in the payment of Old Age Security benefits. The federal government taxes back, or retains, an amount of these payments equal to 15% of the Individual's Income in excess of an indexed threshold amount.

Old Age Security Benefits (OAS) A monthly payment to Residents of Canada who are 65 years of age or older (see also OAS Clawback).

Operating Cost Benefit A Taxable Benefit assessed to Employees whose employers pay the operating costs of an automobile provided to the Employee. It is designed to reflect, on a notional basis, the value of these operating costs.

Ordering Rule Rules which establish the sequence or order in which a group of deductions must be made.

Over Integration An application of integration procedures (e.g., gross up and dividend tax credit rates) that results in a situation where income flowed through a corporation is subject to less tax payable than the same income received directly by an individual.

P

Paid Up Capital (PUC) A balance that is, in general, equal to Legal Stated Capital as determined under the legislation governing the particular Corporation. The equivalent of Contributed Capital in accounting usage.

Parent Company A Corporation that Controls one or more Subsidiaries.

Part IV Tax A refundable tax, applicable to Private Corporations and Subject Corporations, and assessed on Portfolio Dividends received as well as some Dividends received from Connected Corporations.

Part Year Resident An Individual who either enters Canada during the year and becomes a Resident or, alternatively, an Individual who departs from Canada during the year and gives up their Resident status. In either case, the Individual will be taxed on their worldwide income for the part of the year that they were considered to be a Resident of Canada.

Partner A Person who is a member of a Partnership.

Partner and Employee GST Rebate A provision that allows partners and employees to recover the GST paid on their partnership or employment related expenses.

Partnership Two or more Persons who combine forces to carry on a business together for the purpose of making a profit by contributing their skills, knowledge, labour, experience, time, or capital.

Partnership Interest A Non-Depreciable Capital Property that reflects the Partner's original cost, adjusted for earnings, withdrawals, and other factors.

Past Service Cost The cost of starting a pension plan and extending the benefits/contributions to years of service prior to the inception of the plan or, alternatively, amending the benefit/contribution formula of an existing plan and extending the change retroactively to years of service prior to the amendment.

Past Service Pension Adjustment (PSPA)
An adjustment to reflect the past service benefits/contributions allocated to an Employee for years of service prior to the current year.

Penalties   Amounts taxpayers or GST registrants must pay if they fail to file returns or remit or pay amounts owing on time, or if they try to evade paying or remitting tax by not filing returns. Penalties must also be paid by people who knowingly, or under circumstances amounting to gross negligence, participate in or make false statements or omissions in their returns, and by those who do not provide the information required on a prescribed form.

Pension Adjustment (PA)   An adjustment reported by employers which reflects, for an individual Employee, the Employee and employer contributions to RPPs and DPSPs for the previous year (in the case of Defined Benefit RPPs, benefits are converted to an equivalent amount of contributions).

Pension Adjustment Reversal (PAR)
An adjustment for amounts of benefits/contributions that were included in previously issued Pension Adjustments, but have subsequently been lost to the Individual (e.g., benefits earned during a pre-vesting period that did not ultimately vest).

Pension Income Tax Credit   A credit against Tax Payable that is available to Individuals with qualifying pension income.

Periodic Child Care Expense Amount
A weekly limit on deductible child care costs, defined as 1/40 of the Annual Child Care Expense Amount.

Permanent Establishment   A fixed place of business of a Corporation, including an office, a branch, a mine, an oil well, a farm, a timberland, a factory, a workshop, or a warehouse.

Person   A term used in the *Income Tax Act* to refer to taxable entities. For income tax purposes, the three taxable entities are Individuals, Corporations, and Trusts.

Personal Services Business   A Corporation that provides the services of a Specified Shareholder [ITA 248(1)] who could reasonably be regarded as an officer or Employee of the business, and that does not have five or more other full time Employees throughout the year.

Personal Tax Credits   A group of credits against Tax Payable that are specified in ITA 118(1). They include credits for Individuals, Spouses, Common-Law Partners and various Dependants, as well as credits for types of income such as pension or employment.

Personal Trust   A Testamentary or Inter Vivos Trust in which no beneficial interest was acquired for consideration paid to the Trust or to a Person who contributed property to the Trust.

Personal Use Property   Any property that is owned by the Taxpayer and used primarily for his enjoyment, or for the enjoyment of one or more Individuals Related to the Taxpayer.

Phased Retirement   A term used to refer to situations where an individual over 55 years of age continues to earn partial pension benefits, despite the fact that he or she has started to receive pension benefits from that employer.

Political Contributions Tax Credit   A credit against Tax Payable that is available to Individuals who have made contributions to a registered federal political party or to a candidate at the time of a federal election.

Pooled Registered Pension Plan   A registered pension plan established by a financial institution. Eligible registrants would be employees and other individuals who are not members of a registered pension plan established by an employer.

Portfolio Dividend   A Dividend received from a Corporation to which the recipient is not connected (see Connected Corporation). Usually applicable if 10% or less of the voting shares are owned.

Post-1971 Undistributed Surplus   Amounts earned by a Corporation after 1971 and retained in the Corporation.

Pre-1972 Capital Surplus On Hand   Capital Gains accrued before 1972 that have been realized as the result of a Disposition after 1971, less Capital Losses that accrued before 1972 that have been realized as the result of a Disposition after 1971.

Pre-1972 Undistributed Surplus   Amounts earned by a Corporation prior to 1972 and retained in the Corporation.

Preferred Beneficiary   An Individual who is a Beneficiary of a Trust and who is either eligible for the Disability Tax Credit or, alternatively, 18 years of age or older and can be claimed by another Individual for purposes of the dependant tax credit for Individuals who are dependant because of mental or physical infirmity.

Preferred Beneficiary Election   An Election which allows trust income to be allocated to a Preferred Beneficiary without being distributed to that Beneficiary by the Trust.

Preferred Shares   Shares that do not have all the rights which are provided for under the relevant corporate enabling legislation. While there are many variations in the rights that such securities have, Preferred Shares would normally have a fixed or determinable Dividend and would not have voting rights.

Prescribed Debt Obligations   A group of non-standard debt contracts that are defined in ITR 7001 (e.g., a debt contract with no interest stipulated as payable).

Prescribed Proxy Amount   An alternative basis for calculating Scientific Research And Experimental Development overhead costs. Instead of calculating actual overhead costs, a Prescribed Proxy Amount, based on 65% of the Salaries and wages of Employees involved in Scientific Research And Experimental Development activities, can be used.

Prescribed Rate   An interest rate which, as described in ITR 4301, changes quarterly and is based on the average interest rate paid on 90 day Treasury Bills during the first month of the preceding quarter. The basic rate is used for a variety of purposes (e.g., calculation of the Taxable Benefits on interest free loans to Employees). The basic rate, plus 2 percentage points, is used to calculate interest owing from the government to Taxpayers (e.g., interest on late payment of a tax refund). The basic rate, plus 4 percentage points, is used to calculate interest owed by Taxpayers to the government (e.g., interest on late Instalments).

Prescribed Stock Exchange   This term has been replaced by "designated stock exchange".

Principal Residence   Any accommodation owned by the Taxpayer that was ordinarily inhabited in the year by the Taxpayer, his Spouse, a former Spouse, or a dependent child, and is designated by the Taxpayer as a Principal Residence.

Private Corporation   A Corporation that is a resident of Canada, but is not a Public Corporation.

Proceeds Of Disposition   Amounts received as the result of a Disposition. Usually related to a capital property Disposition.

Profit Sharing Plan   A trusteed plan to which employers can make deductible contributions, the amount of which is related to the profits of the enterprise. Both the contributions and the earnings resulting from their investment are taxed in the hands of the Employees as they occur. Payments from the plan are received by the Employees on a tax free basis.

Progressive Tax System   A tax system that applies higher effective rates for Individuals with higher Incomes and lower effective rates for Individuals with lower Incomes (e.g., personal income taxes).

Property Income   Income that is earned through the passive ownership of property. It would include rents, interest, Dividends, and some royalties (i.e., royalties paid on assets that have been purchased). While usage is not always consistent, this term usually refers to a net amount (i.e., inclusions less deductions, or revenues less expenses).

Property Tax   A tax on the ownership of some particular set of goods.

Public Corporation   A Corporation that has at least one class of its shares listed on a designated stock exchange in Canada.

Public Transit Pass Tax Credit   A credit against Tax Payable that is available to individuals who purchase monthly or longer public transit passes.

PUC   An acronym for "paid up capital".

Purification Of A Small Business Corporation   A process of disposing of corporate assets that are not being used to produce Active Business Income, so that the Corporation meets the 90% of assets test required to qualify as a Small Business Corporation.

Q

Qualified Activities   Types of activity, as defined in ITR 5202, that are considered to be manufacturing and processing activities.

Qualified Farm Property   A Qualified Farm Property is a Farm Property that, prior to its Disposition was owned by the Taxpayer, his Spouse, or his Common-Law Partner, or their children for a period of 24 months or more.

Qualified Fishing Property
A Qualified Fishing Property is a Fishing Property that, prior to its Disposition was owned by the Taxpayer, his Spouse, or his Common-Law Partner, or their children for a period of 24 months or more.

Qualified Property   Certain specified types of property that, when acquired, qualify the Taxpayer for an Investment Tax Credit.

Qualified Scientific Research And Experimental Development Expenditures
Scientific Research And Experimental Development expenditures that qualify the Taxpayer for Investment Tax Credits.

Qualified Small Business Corporation
A Small Business Corporation that, at the time of its Disposition, has been owned by no one other than the Taxpayer or a related party during the preceding 24 months, and during that 24 month period, more than 50% of the fair market value of its assets were used in an Active Business carried on primarily in Canada.

Qualifying Corporation   A CCPC throughout the year with Taxable Income in the immediately preceding year of no more than $500,000 and previous year Taxable Capital Employed In Canada of $10 million or less, thereby qualifying for the additional 15% tax credit on the first $3,000,000 of Qualified Scientific Research And Development Expenditures.

Qualifying Spousal Or Common-Law Partner Trust   A Spousal Or Common-Law Partner Trust that qualifies for the Rollover of assets into the Trust under ITA 73(1.01) for Inter Vivos Trusts or ITA 70(6) for Testamentary Trusts.

Qualitative Characteristics   This term is used in our text to refer to non-quantitative characteristics of a tax system that are considered to be desirable (e.g., fairness).

Quick Method   A method of determining GST amounts payable or receivable that is available to Registrants with annual GST taxable sales, including those of associated businesses, of $400,000 or less.   Specified percentages are applied to the GST inclusive sales figures to determine the GST payable or the refund. Accounting for Input Tax Credits on non-capital expenditures is not required.   Input Tax Credits on capital expenditures are tracked separately.

R

RDTOH   An acronym for "refundable dividend tax on hand".

Real Property   Land and all appurtenances to it, including buildings, crops, and mineral rights, a.k.a., real estate.

Reasonable Expectation Of Profit (REOP)
A test that involves the determination of whether a business or an investment is likely to have a profit. The CRA has tried to use this test to limit the ability of Taxpayers to deduct losses resulting from businesses and investments that fail their REOP test.

Reassessment   A revision of an original Assessment (see Assessment and Notice Of Assessment).

Recapture Of CCA   An inclusion in Business and Property Income that arises when deductions from a CCA Class, engendered by disposals, leave a negative balance in that Class at the end of the taxation year.

Redemption Of Shares   A transaction in which a Corporation purchases some of its own outstanding shares, either in the open market, or through a direct purchase from shareholders.

Refundable Dividend Tax On Hand (RDTOH)   A balance made up of refundable taxes paid, less refunds received as the result of paying Dividends.

Refundable Investment Tax Credit
An Investment Tax Credit that will be paid to the Taxpayer, even if the amount resulting from the Investment Tax Credit exceeds the Taxpayer's Tax Payable.

Refundable Medical Expense Supplement
A refundable credit against Tax Payable that increases the amount available to certain low income individuals for their eligible medical expenses.

Refundable Part I Tax   The portion of Part I tax that is applicable to a notional amount of Aggregate Investment Income earned by a CCPC.

Refundable Part XI.3 Tax   A 50% tax that is assessed on contributions to a Retirement Compensation Arrangement and on the earnings of amounts invested in the plan.   It is fully refundable when amounts are distributed from the arrangement and taxed in the hands of the recipient Employees.

Refundable Tax Credit   An amount, based on a Tax Credit calculation, that will be paid to an Individual even if the amount resulting from the Tax Credit calculation exceeds the Individual's Tax Payable.

Registered Disability Savings Plan (RDSP)
A trusteed arrangement that allows Individuals to make non-deductible contributions that will be invested on a tax-free basis, with the accumulated funds being used to make distributions to an individual who qualifies for the disability tax credit.

Registered Education Savings Plan (RESP)
A trusteed arrangement that allows Individuals to make non-deductible contributions that will be invested on a tax-free basis, with the accumulated funds being used to provide for the post-secondary education of a child.

Registered Pension Plan (RPP)   A retirement savings plan sponsored by an employer, to which the employer will make contributions which are not taxable to the Employee, and the Employee may make contributions which are deductible. Earnings accumulate tax free within the plan. Withdrawals from the plan are subject to tax.

Registered Retirement Income Fund (RRIF)
A trusteed plan to which a Resident Individual can transfer balances from retirement savings plans on a tax free basis. Earnings accumulate tax free within the plan. Withdrawals from the plan are subject to tax. Unlike RRSPs, a minimum withdrawal is required each year.

Registered Retirement Savings Plan (RRSP)   A trusteed plan to which a Resident Individual can make deductible contributions. Earnings accumulate tax free within the plan. Withdrawals from the plan are generally subject to tax.

Registrant   An entity who is registered to collect and remit the GST.

Regressive Tax System   A tax system that applies higher effective rates for Individuals with lower Incomes and lower effective rates for Individuals with higher Incomes (e.g., most sales taxes).

Related Persons   ITA 251(2)(a) indicates that two Individuals are related if they are connected by blood relationship, marriage or common-law partnership, or adoption. ITA 251(2)(b) describes various situations in which a Corporation would be related to other Persons (e.g., a Corporation is related to the Person who Controls it). ITA 251(2)(c) describes various situations in which two Corporations would be related to each other (e.g., the two Corporations are controlled by the same Person).

Reorganization Of Capital (ITA 86)   A Rollover provision that allows one class of shares in a Corporation to be exchanged for a different class of shares, without tax consequences.

Replacement Property Rules   A set of rules which provide for the deferral of both Recapture and Capital Gains on Involuntary Dispositions and some voluntary Dispositions of capital property. Deferral is conditional on replacing the property within a specified period after the Proceeds Of Disposition are received.

Resale Price Method   A Transfer Pricing method generally used where fair market value comparables are unavailable because of the uniqueness of the products. It also applies to situations where the purchaser adds little or no value and effectively acts as a distributor or sales agent.

Reserve   A deduction in the calculation of net Business Income or net Taxable Capital Gains.

Resident   A Person who is located in a place. This is the basis on which Canadian income taxes are assessed. That is, Canadian Resident Persons are liable for the payment of Canadian income tax, without regard to their citizenship or the source of their Income. While not defined in the *Income Tax Act*, ITF S5-F1-C1 provides guidance on the determination of residency for Individuals and IT-447 provides similar guidance for Trusts.

Residential Ties   Factors that will be considered in determining whether or not an Individual is a Resident of Canada. While there are many such ties, ITF S5-F1-C1 indicates that the most commonly used would be the maintenance of a dwelling in Canada, having one's Spouse or Common-Law Partner remain in Canada, and having one's Dependants remain in Canada.

Restricted Farm Loss   A farmer whose chief source of Income is not farming or a combination of farming and some other source of Income, but who has a reasonable expectation of long-run profitability, can only deduct losses to the extent of the first $2,500, plus one-half of the next $12,500. Losses in excess of this deductible amount are referred to as Restricted Farm Losses.

Restrictive Covenant   An agreement entered into, an undertaking made, or a waiver of an advantage or right by the Taxpayer. This would include, but would not be limited to, non-competition agreements.

Retained Earnings (a.k.a. Earned Capital)   In accounting usage, the amount of a Corporation's Shareholders' Equity that resulted from the retention of earnings in the Corporation.

Retirement Compensation Arrangement   An unregistered plan to which employers make deductible contributions to provide Employees with benefits subsequent to their retirement. Both contributions and earnings are subject to a Refundable Part XI.3 Tax.

Retiring Allowance   Amounts received at retirement as recognition for long service, or as the result of loss of employment.

Revenue Jurisdiction Approach   An international taxation approach under which a country taxes all Income earned by its Residents, without regard to the country in which that Income is earned.

Reversionary Trust   A trust agreement under which the property held by the Trustee can revert to the Settlor.

Rights Or Things   With respect to a deceased Taxpayer, these are amounts that are due, but have not been received (e.g., wages to the end of a pay period prior to death, but not yet received).

Rollover   As this term is used in tax work, it refers to a tax free Transfer of assets under circumstances that, in the absence of a special Rollover provision, would be considered a taxable Transfer.

RRSP Deduction Limit   The amount that is the sum of the Unused RRSP Deduction Room at the end of the preceding year, plus the amount by which the lesser of the RRSP Dollar Limit and 18% of Earned Income for the preceding year exceeds the Pension Adjustment for the preceding year. This sum is adjusted for any Past Service Pension Adjustment or Pension Adjustment Reversal. In simplified terms, it represents the maximum amount of contributions that have been made to an RRSP that can be deducted for a year.

RRSP Deduction Room   The excess of the RRSP Deduction Limit, over the amount of RRSP contributions that have been deducted.

RRSP Dollar Limit   Generally, the Money Purchase Limit for the preceding year.

S

Safe Income   For purposes of applying ITA 55(2) to Capital Gains Stripping, Safe Income is made up of amounts earned by a Corporation after 1971, or if the investment shares in that Corporation were acquired after that date, amounts earned after the acquisition.

Salary   The amount an employer pays an Employee for work done. An employer records this type of Employment Income on a T4. A common component of Employment Income.

Salary Deferral Arrangement   An arrangement, whether funded or not, under which an Individual who has the right to receive compensation postpones the receipt of that compensation, and it is reasonable to assume that one of the main purposes of this postponement was to defer the payment of taxes.

Scientific Research And Experimental Development (SR&ED)   Activities related to basic or applied research, and for the development of new products and processes.

Self-Employed Individual   An Individual who has a business relationship with an entity. Whether or not an Individual is working as an Employee or a Self-Employed Individual is dependent on factors such as control, ownership of tools, chance of profit or risk of loss, and the ability to subcontract or hire an assistant.

Separate Class Rules   Rules that require certain types of assets that would, in the absence of these special rules, be included in a single Class, be allocated to a separate balance for that Class (e.g., each rental property with a cost greater than $50,000 must be placed in a different Class 1).

Settlor   The Individual who creates a Trust by contributing property to be managed and administered by a Trustee for the Beneficiaries.

Share For Share Exchange (ITA 85.1)
A Rollover provision that allows one Corporation to acquire shares in another Corporation by issuing its own shares, without tax consequences to either of the Corporations or their shareholders.

Shared Use Capital Equipment
Capital Assets that are used more than 50 percent, but less than 90 percent, in Scientific Research And Experimental Development activities.

Shareholders' Equity   The residual interest of the shareholders of a Corporation in the Net Assets of the Corporation.

Short Fiscal Year   A taxation year that is less than 12 months in duration. Can occur in the first and last years of operation, as well as certain other situations.

SIFT Partnership   To be a Specified Investment Flow-Through (SIFT) partnership, (1) the partnership must be a Canadian resident partnership; (2) investments in the partnership must be publicly traded; and (3) the partnership must hold one or more non-portfolio properties.

SIFT Trust   To be a Specified Investment Flow-Through (SIFT) trust, (1) the trust must be resident in Canada; (2) investments in the trust must be publicly traded; and (3) the trust must hold one or more non-portfolio properties.

Simplified ITC Accounting   An alternative designation for "Streamlined ITC Accounting".

Small Business Corporation   A Corporation that is a Canadian Controlled Private Corporation that uses all or substantially all (90% or more) of the fair market value of its assets in an Active Business that is carried on primarily (more than 50 percent) in Canada.

Small Business Deduction   A deduction in the calculation of corporate Tax Payable equal to 17.5 percentage points on the first $500,000 of Active Business Income earned by a CCPC.

Small CCPC   A Canadian Controlled Private Corporation that has (1) Taxable Income in the current or previous year of $500,000 or less, (2) has Taxable Capital Employed In Canada in the current or previous year of $10 million or less, (3) is able to claim some amount of the Small Business Deduction in the current or previous year, and (4) has a perfect payment compliance record for the last 12 months.

Small Suppliers Exemption   An exemption from the requirement to register for the collection and remittance of GST for those entities with less than $30,000 in taxable supplies.

Social Benefits Repayment (a.k.a., Clawback) An income tested taxing back, or reduction, in the payment of Old Age Security Benefits and Employment Insurance Benefits.

Soft Costs Costs, such as interest and property tax, on land and buildings that are incurred prior to the capital asset being used for business or income producing purposes.

Sojourner An Individual who is deemed under ITA 250 to be a Canadian Resident for the full taxation year as the result of having sojourned (i.e., been temporarily present) in Canada for 183 days or more.

Source Deductions Amounts that are withheld by an employer from the Income of Employees. The withholdings for income taxes, Canada Pension Plan contributions, and Employment Insurance premiums must be remitted to the government.

Source Jurisdiction Approach An international taxation approach under which a country taxes all Income earned within its borders, without regard to whether it is earned by Residents or Non-Residents.

Specified Class [ITA 256(1.1)] A class of shares that has certain specified terms and conditions, including a fixed or determinable Dividend and an absence of voting rights. Would generally be referred to as Preferred Shares.

Specified Employee An Employee who owns 10% or more of the shares of the Corporation, or who does not deal at arm's length with the Corporation.

Specified Individual An Individual who has not attained the age of 17 before the beginning of the year and who has a parent who is Resident in Canada.

Specified Investment Business A Corporation that does not have five or more full time Employees throughout the year, whose principal purpose is to derive Income from property.

Specified Non-Resident Shareholder A specified shareholder who is a non-resident Person or non-resident investment company.

Specified Shareholder [(ITA 18(5)] A shareholder of a Corporation who owns, either alone or together with other related persons, more than 25% of the voting shares of a corporation or, alternatively, shares that have more than 25% of the market value of all of the corporation's shares.

Specified Shareholder [ITA 248(1)] A shareholder of a Corporation who owns, directly or indirectly, at any time in the year, not less than 10% of the issued shares of any class of the capital stock of the Corporation, or of any other Corporation that is related to the Corporation.

Split Income Certain types of Income received by a Specified Individual from non-arm's length sources that will be taxed at the maximum federal rate of 29 percent.

Spousal Or Common-Law Partner Trust An Inter Vivos or Testamentary Trust that has an individual's Spouse or Common-Law Partner as a Beneficiary (see also Qualifying Spousal Or Common-Law Partner Trust).

Spousal RRSP An RRSP to which the Spouse or Common-Law Partner of the Annuitant (i.e., Beneficiary of the RRSP) has made contributions that the Spouse or Common-Law Partner can deduct in calculating Net Income For Tax Purposes.

Spousal Support A Support Amount that is for the benefit of a Spouse or Common-Law Partner, or a former Spouse or Common-Law Partner.

Spousal Tax Credit A credit against Tax Payable that is available to individuals who have a Spouse or Common-Law Partner.

Spouse An Individual to whom a Taxpayer is legally married.

Standby Charge A Taxable Benefit assessed to Employees who have been provided with an automobile by their employer. It is designed to reflect, on a notional basis, the value of having the car available on a standby basis for personal usage.

Stock Dividend A pro rata distribution of corporation shares to existing shareholders of the corporation.

Stock Option A contractual arrangement which gives the holder the right to purchase a specified number of shares for a specified period of time at a specified acquisition price.

Stop Loss Rules A group of rules which, under specified conditions, prevent the deduction of a loss.

Straight-Line Method A method of calculating CCA in which a specified or determinable rate is applied to the Capital Cost of acquired assets in order to determine the CCA for the period.

Streamlined ITC Accounting A method of determining Input Tax Credits available to small businesses, charities, not-for-profit organizations, and certain public service bodies. The organization must have annual GST taxable sales, including those of associated businesses, of $1,000,000 or less and annual GST taxable purchases of $4,000,000 or less. Input Tax Credits are determined by multiplying all GST inclusive purchases, except real property purchases, by 5/105 rather than using the actual GST paid. Input Tax Credits on real property are tracked separately.

Student Loan Interest Tax Credit A credit against Tax Payable that is based on the amount of interest on a loan under the *Canada Student Loans Act*, or the *Canada Student Financial Assistance Act*.

Subject Corporation For purposes of the Part IV Tax, a Public Corporation that is controlled by, or for the benefit of, an Individual or a related group of Individuals. Also used in the determination of Dividend Stripping (ITA 84.1) and share sales to non-residents (ITA 212.1) to describe a Corporation, the shares of which have been sold.

Subsidiary An enterprise that is controlled by another enterprise (the Parent Company). The Parent Company has the right and ability to obtain future economic benefits from the resources of the Subsidiary and is exposed to the related risks.

Superficial Loss (ITA 54) A loss on the Disposition of property that is disallowed for tax purposes because the Taxpayer has acquired an identical property, either 30 days before the Disposition or, alternatively, 30 days after the Disposition.

Supply A broad range of transactions between Persons. To "make a supply of property or a service" means to provide it in any way, including sale, transfer, barter, exchange, licence, rental, lease, gift, or Disposition.

Support Amount Amounts paid as the result of the separation or divorce of two Individuals who were Spouses or Common-Law Partners. Can be divided into Spousal Support and Child Support.

Surtax An additional or extra tax on something already taxed.

Syndicates A group of Persons combined or making a joint effort to undertake some specific project or to carry out a specific transaction.

T

Target Benefit Plan A hybrid pension plan that is based on defined contributions combined with a target or proposed benefit for retirees. However, unlike defined benefit plans, these plans also allow the benefit to be reduced if funding is not adequate to produce the target benefit.

Tariffs A tax imposed on the importation or exportation of certain goods or services.

Tax Avoidance The undertaking of transactions or arrangements with a view to avoiding or minimizing the payment of taxes. As the term is generally used, it refers to legitimate procedures that could also be described as Tax Planning.

Tax Base The income source, class of transaction, type of property, or other factor on which tax is assessed (e.g., sales tax is assessed on sales).

Tax Court Of Canada A court that hears appeals about income tax and GST/HST assessments. In addition, the Court has jurisdiction to hear appeals under the Canada Pension Plan Act, Employment Insurance Act, and several other Acts. The Tax Court maintains four offices (Vancouver, Ottawa, Toronto, and Montreal) and regularly conducts hearings in major centres across Canada.

Tax Credit A credit against Tax Payable.

Tax Deferral An important type of Tax Planning. The basic idea here is to find procedures that will put off the payment of taxes until a later taxation year. The value of these procedures reflects the time value of money. That is, there is a value associated with making a payment later, rather than sooner.

Tax Evasion This typically involves deliberately ignoring a specific part of the law or willfully refusing to comply with legislated reporting requirements. Tax evasion, unlike tax avoidance, has criminal consequences.

Tax Expenditures Foregone tax revenues due to special exemptions, rate reductions, rebates, and credits that reduce the amount of tax that would otherwise be payable. Often designed to encourage certain kinds of activities or to serve other objectives, such as providing assistance to lower-income Canadians.

Tax Free Savings Accounts (TFSAs) A trusteed arrangement that allows Individuals to make non-deductible contributions that will be invested in qualified assets. Earnings accumulate on a tax free basis within the plan and can be distributed to the Individual who established the plan on a tax free basis.

Tax Haven A foreign country used to avoid or reduce income taxes, especially by investors from another country.

Tax Incidence The Person who ultimately pays a tax, regardless of the legal basis of assessment (e.g., taxes paid by Corporations may be passed on to either Employees or customers).

Tax Planning The undertaking of legitimate transactions or arrangements with a view to avoiding or minimizing the payment of taxes. Some or all of such efforts could also be referred to as Tax Avoidance.

Tax Shelter (ITA 237.1) The acquisition of a property, in respect of which it is represented that the acquisition of the property, or the donation or contribution of the property under a gifting arrangement, would generate any combination of tax credits or deductions that in total would equal or exceed the cost of acquiring the property.

Tax Shelter (Other Meanings)   An investment that shelters Income from other sources (e.g., Employment Income) by producing tax losses, or an investment with a positive cash flow that is sheltered by sufficient non-cash deductions (e.g., CCA) to produce a nil Taxable Income.

Taxable Allowance   An allowance provided by an employer to an Employee that must be included in the Employee's Employment Income. The amount is included on the Employee's T4.

Taxable Benefit   An amount of money, or the value of goods or services, that an employer pays or provides in addition to Salary.

Taxable Canadian Corporation   A Canadian Corporation that is not exempt from Canadian income tax by way of a statutory provision.

Taxable Canadian Property   A group of assets that are listed under the definition of Taxable Canadian Property in ITA 248(1). These assets are distinguished by the fact that gains on their Disposition are taxable without regard to the residence of the selling Taxpayer. For example, if a U.S. Resident sells Canadian real estate, Canadian income tax will be assessed on any gain resulting from the sale.

Taxable Capital Employed In Canada
This amount is the GAAP-determined capital of the Corporation, less the allowance for investments in other Corporations, multiplied by the percentage of the Corporation's activity at Permanent Establishments in Canada as determined under ITR 402. It is used in a number of calculations, including the determination of a small CCPC and the calculation of the reduction of the Small Business Deduction.

Taxable Capital Gain   The taxable portion (currently one-half) of a Capital Gain.

Taxable Entity   A defined organization or Individual that is subject to tax (e.g., Corporations are taxable entities for income tax purposes).

Taxable Income   Net Income For Tax Purposes, less certain deductions that are largely specified in Division C of Part I of the *Income Tax Act*. These deductions include loss carry overs, the Lifetime Capital Gains Deduction, and for Corporations, Dividends and Charitable Gifts.

Taxable Surplus   A surplus account that tracks certain sources of Income of a Foreign Affiliate.

Taxation Year   The period that is covered by a Taxpayer's return. As defined in ITA 249, it is equal to a calendar year for Individuals and Inter Vivos Trusts, and a Fiscal Period for Corporations and Testamentary Trusts.

Taxpayer   An entity that is required to file a tax return and pay taxes. For income tax purposes, a Taxpayer is an Individual, a Corporation, or a Trust.

Taxpayer Relief Provisions   Information Circular 07-01 contains guidelines on the discretionary authority the Minister has to grant relief based on a Taxpayer's situation. An example would be a waiver of late filing interest and penalties because the Individual suffered a serious illness. It replaces the fairness provisions.

Teacher And Early Childhood Educator School Supply Tax Credit   A refundable tax credit available to eligible educators for up to $1,000 of eligible expenditures.

Tenancy In Common   A holding of property, either real or personal, by two or more Persons, with each having a divisible interest that can be sold.

Term Preferred Shares   Preferred Shares which have a provision which allows them to be redeemed by the issuer or redeemed at the request of the holder.

Terminal Loss   A deduction in the calculation of Business and Property Income which arises when the last asset in a CCA Class is retired and a positive balance is left in the Class.

Testamentary Trust   A Trust that arises on, and as a consequence of, the death of an Individual.

Textbook Tax Credit   A credit against Tax Payable that is available to Individuals who qualify for the Education Tax Credit.

Thin Capitalization   A reference to situations where a non-resident Specified Shareholder is receiving interest on an amount of debt that exceeds two times the sum of his share of contributed capital plus 100% of Retained Earnings.

Tie-Breaker Rules   Provisions in International Tax Treaties that are designed to prevent the Double Taxation of Dual Residents.

Transaction Tax   A tax that is assessed on specified types of transactions. Such taxes are most commonly applied to transactions involving the sale of goods or services.

Transfer   To convey or move from one Taxpayer to a different Taxpayer.

Transfer Pricing   An expression used to describe the price at which services, tangible property, and intangible property are traded across international borders between related or non-arm's length parties.

Transfer Tax   A tax on the Transfer of property from one owner to another.

Transferee A Taxpayer to whom a Transfer is made.

Transferor A Taxpayer who makes a Transfer.

Trust A relationship in which one Person holds the title to property for the benefit of another Person.

Trustee An Individual or trust institution that holds legal title to property in trust for the benefit of the Trust Beneficiaries.

Tuition Fees Tax Credit A credit against Tax Payable that is available to Individuals making qualifying tuition payments. The base includes specified ancillary fees and fees and ancillary costs associated with writing university examinations and required examinations in professional programs.

Twenty-One (21) Year Deemed Disposition Rule A requirement, applicable to some types of Personal Trusts, that requires a deemed disposition of the Trust's capital property at the end of every twenty-one years.

U

Undepreciated Capital Cost (UCC) The Capital Cost of a depreciable asset class, less the cumulative CCA that has been taken to date. The tax equivalent of net book value in accounting.

Under Integration An application of integration procedures (e.g., gross up and dividend tax credit rates) that results in a situation where income flowed through a corporation is subject to more tax payable than the same income received directly by an individual.

Unused RRSP Deduction Room The cumulative total of all RRSP Deduction Limits, less amounts deducted in those years. The end of the preceding year balance is used when calculating the RRSP Deduction Limit.

V

Valuation Day (V-Day) December 22, 1971 for publicly traded assets and December 31, 1971 for other assets.

Value Added Tax (VAT) A tax based on the value added to a product at each stage of production or distribution by a particular entity. It is generally based on some accounting measurement of Income.

Vertical Amalgamation An Amalgamation of a Parent Company and one or more of its Subsidiaries.

Vested Benefit A benefit is vested if the beneficiary has an irrevocable right to receive it.

Vested Contribution A contribution is vested if the Individual making the contribution has an irrevocable right to either the amount of the contribution or a benefit of equivalent value.

Volunteer Firefighters Tax Credit A credit against Tax Payable that is available to volunteer firefighters who perform at least 200 hours of volunteer firefighting services during a taxation year.

Volunteer Search And Rescue Workers Tax Credit A credit against Tax Payable that is available to volunteer search and rescue workers who perform at least 200 hours of volunteer search and rescue services during a taxation year.

W - Z

Wholly Dependent Person A Dependant who lives with the Taxpayer (this requirement is not applicable if the Dependant is the Taxpayer's child) in a self-contained domestic establishment and is eligible for the Eligible Dependant Tax Credit.

Will A document that is a legal declaration of an Individual's wishes as to the Disposition of his or her property after death.

Winding-Up Of A 90% Owned Subsidiary A Rollover provision that allows the asset of a 90% or more owned Subsidiary to be combined with the assets of its Parent Company, without tax consequences.

Winding-Up Of A Canadian Corporation A series of transactions that result in substantially all of the assets of a Canadian Corporation being distributed to the shareholders of that Corporation.

Working Income Tax Benefit A refundable credit available to low income individuals who are earning employment and business income.

Zero-Rated Goods And Services Goods and services that are taxable at a zero GST rate. The fact that they are designated as "taxable" means that Registrants who sell such goods and services are eligible for Input Tax Credits for the GST that they pay. Examples include basic groceries (e.g., milk, bread, and vegetables), prescription drugs, and exports.

NOTES

Notes

Notes

Notes

Notes

Notes

Notes